THE DISSENTERS

I

THE DISSENTERS

by

Michael R. Watts

*

FROM THE REFORMATION
TO THE FRENCH REVOLUTION

1478
1978

CLARENDON PRESS · OXFORD

Oxford University Press, Walton Street, Oxford OX26 DP

OXFORD LONDON GLASGOW NEW YORK
TORONTO MELBOURNE WELLINGTON CAPE TOWN
IBADAN NAIROBI DAR ES SALAAM LUSAKA
KUALA LUMPUR SINGAPORE JAKARTA HONG KONG TOKYO
DELHI BOMBAY CALCUTTA MADRAS KARACHI

© *Michael R. Watts, 1978*

British Library Cataloguing in Publication Data
Watts, Michael R.
The Dissenters.
Vol. 1: From the Reformation to the French
Revolution.
1. Dissenters, Religious – England – History
I. Title
301.45'28   BX5203.2   77–30144

ISBN 0–19–822460–5

*Printed in Great Britain by
Cox & Wyman Ltd,
London, Fakenham and Reading*

For

SYLVIA

PREFACE

THIS book constitutes the first volume of what will be, when completed, the first substantial history of English and Welsh Dissent to appear for more than sixty years. A number of brief surveys, of which Dr. Ernest Payne's *Free Church Tradition in the Life of England* is by far the best, have been published over the last half-century, but no full-scale treatment of the subject has been attempted since H. W. Clark's two-volume *History of English Nonconformity* was published between 1911 and 1913. Clark's work made no claim to original scholarship, its usefulness was marred by the author's obscurities of style, and the book was no improvement on the *History of the Free Churches of England* of which the first part had been published by Herbert Skeats as long ago as 1868, and the whole completed by Charles Miall in 1891.

There is thus an obvious need for a new study of the whole subject. Since the publication of the works of Clark and of Skeats and Miall a vast amount of historical research has been devoted to the history of Dissent, the several denominational historical societies have flourished and have encouraged and published work by both amateur and professional historians, and in recent years university theses on various aspects of Dissenting history have proliferated. Above all, historical perspectives have changed. In the twenty years between the publication of the completed works of Skeats and Miall and of H. W. Clark's first volume the Nonconformist churches in England and Wales attained what would prove to be the highest membership figures in their entire history, and with the Liberal landslide election victory in 1906 they reached what would prove to be the height of their political power. When Charles Miall finished his book in 1891 he believed that the Free Churches were making 'progress in every direction'; twenty years later H. W. Clark concluded that, 'if Nonconformity has not reached home . . . it is on the way', whatever he meant by that. But since the first decade of the present century the history of both the spiritual and political influence of Nonconformity

has been one of uninterrupted decline, and the second volume
of this work will necessarily be much concerned with analyzing
the causes of that decline. What is more, in the last half-century
the historian's monopoly of explanation of the behaviour of
past generations has been disputed by psychologists and sociologists; it has been impossible to ignore the question of the
relationship between religious belief and economic activity
since Weber; and the historian writing in the later twentieth
century can no longer ignore, as did so many of his predecessors, the considerable amount of statistical evidence about
religious practice in England and Wales over the last three
centuries. Most important of all, anyone who essays to study the
history of Dissent from the vantage-point of the 1970s must be
concerned not only with those questions of church and state
which determined the legal standing of Nonconformists, must
be concerned not only with the pronouncements of ministers of
religion and the resolutions of denominational assemblies, but
must attempt to recover what can be recovered about the lives,
beliefs, and religious practice of the ordinary lay men and
women who constituted the overwhelming majority of English
and Welsh Dissenters.

This book thus attempts to view the history of Dissent from
the changed perspective of the 1970s, to synthesize and examine
critically the work done by other scholars in the field over the
last half-century, and to add the results of the author's own researches. The first volume deals with the formative period of
Dissenting history: with the first English Anabaptists and the
emergence of the Separatists in the sixteenth century; with the
crystallization of the Baptist, Independent, Quaker, and
Presbyterian denominations in the seventeenth century; and
with the advent of Methodism in the eighteenth century. The
second volume will deal with Dissent at the apogee of its religious, social, and political influence in the nineteenth and early
twentieth centuries, and with its subsequent decline. In a work
which, it is hoped, will cover more than four centuries the
framework is necessarily chronological, but the chronological
bounds of the chapters have sometimes been breached in the
interests of economy of space and the development of themes.
Thus there is no detailed discussion of the geographic distribution, economic and social status, and worship and discipline of

Dissent in the second half of the seventeenth century until Chapter IV is reached, when these topics are dealt with in the light of the more plentiful material available for the early eighteenth century. Similarly Chapter V, though it goes well into the nineteenth century with the discussion of the impact of the Evangelical revival on the Quakers, contains no consideration of the life of Dissent or of Methodism at chapel level in the later eighteenth century as such matters will be discussed in conjunction with early-nineteenth-century material in the second volume.

Historians are ever aware of their dependence on the work of others, and a historian who rashly seeks to deal with over 400 crowded years is particularly conscious of his debt to other scholars. It is hoped that, as far as published works and unpublished theses are concerned, adequate acknowledgement has been made in the footnotes. For personal assistance in the research for this book I have to thank the library staffs of the Nottingham University library, Dr. Williams's Library, the British Library, the Friends House library, and Baptist Church House, and the archivists of the Guildhall library, London, and of the Greater London, Lincolnshire, and Leicestershire County Record Offices. I must also thank the many university librarians who have allowed me to read unpublished theses in their custody; the trustees of Dr. Williams's Library for allowing me access to the manuscripts in their care; Mr. R. E. Eccleston and the deacons of the Castle Gate United Reformed (formerly Congregational) church, Nottingham, for permitting me to see their church records; and Dr. Arthur Warne for lending me the results of his researches into Bishop Claggett's visitation returns for the diocese of Exeter. Four librarians in particular deserve mention for their unfailing courtesy and kindness in dealing with what might well have been considered as unreasonable demands on their time: Mrs. Janet Barnes of Dr. Williams's Library, the speed of whose service has enabled me to make the most of the limited amount of time I have been able to spend in London; Miss Glynis Pickering and Mr. Robert Fleetwood of Nottingham University, for the efficiency with which they have operated their end of the inter-library loan service on my behalf; and Edward Milligan of the Friends House library, who not only guided my way through the

Quaker registers of births, marriages, and deaths in his custody, and allowed me to make use of his splendid 'Index to Meetings for Church Affairs', but also read through an early draft of this book and eliminated some of the un-Quakerly expressions I had used to describe the activities of Friends.

Of my colleagues in the University of Nottingham Dr. Stanley Chapman, Professor A. W. Coats, Dr. Alan Rogers, and Professor Robin Storey have all given me the benefit of their knowledge on periods and topics on which their expertise is greater than mine, and I am particularly indebted to Professor W. R. Fryer for his constant encouragement of, and interest in, this project, and for reading through the manuscript at a time when he was heavily committed in other directions. I have been especially fortunate in receiving the help of the three leading authorities on Dissenting history: Dr. R. Tudur Jones, Dr. Ernest Payne, and Dr. Geoffrey Nuttall. All three have been generous in the time and care they have bestowed on the manuscript, and the book contains fewer errors than it would have done without the benefit of their kindly scrutiny.

Finally, I have to thank my wife Sylvia and my children, Rosemary and Richard, for giving me peace and, for most of the time, quiet, while I have been writing this book. I have disrupted their home life and their social life on more occasions, and for longer periods of time, than I have any right to expect, and for their patience and love I am deeply grateful.

University of Nottingham   MICHAEL WATTS

CONTENTS

V. 'THE WAY TO HEAVEN': THE REVIVAL OF DISSENT, 1730–1791

xiv   *Contents*

LIST OF TABLES

LIST OF ILLUSTRATIONS

FIGURE

MAPS

LIST OF ABBREVIATIONS

Braithwaite, *BQ*	W. C. Braithwaite, *The Beginnings of Quakerism* (2nd edn., Cambridge, 1955)
Braithwaite, *SPQ*	W. C. Braithwaite, *The Second Period of Quakerism* (2nd edn., Cambridge, 1961)
Burrage, *EED*	C. Burrage, *Early English Dissenters* (Cambridge, 1912, 2 vols.)
CSPD	*Calendar of State Papers, Domestic*
DNB	*Dictionary of National Biography* (1921–2)
DWL	Dr. Williams's Library, London
JEH	*Journal of Ecclesiastical History*
JFHS	*Journal of the Friends Historical Society*
Jones, *LPQ*	R. M. Jones, *The Later Periods of Quakerism* (1921)
PRO	Public Record Office
TBHS	*Transactions of the Baptist Historical Society*
TCHS	*Transactions of the Congregational Historical Society*
TUHS	*Transactions of the Unitarian Historical Society*
VCH	*Victoria County History*

All works referred to in the footnotes were published in London, unless otherwise stated. Spelling and punctuation have been modernized, except in the titles of books. Dates before 1752 are given in the Old Style, except that the year is taken as beginning with 1 January and not 25 March.

INTRODUCTION

OVER the last four and a half centuries those English and Welsh Protestant Christians who have chosen to worship outside the established Church of England have been known variously by the name 'Anabaptist', 'Brownist', 'Separatist', 'sectary', 'Dissenter', 'Nonconformist', and 'Free Churchman'. The name has varied with the situation and with the nature of Dissent. The term 'Anabaptist' was applied to men and women in Tudor England who, while not necessarily practising believers' baptism, inherited the more radical attitudes of the Lollards and embraced heterodox opinions emanating from the Netherlands. The epithets 'Brownist' and 'Separatist' were used of small groups of extreme Protestants who, impatient of Puritan hopes of reforming the Church of England from within, repudiated the ordinances and discipline of the established church and met in secret conventicles in the reigns of Elizabeth I and the early Stuarts. During the Civil War and Interregnum the term 'sectary' was applied to those religious radicals who would not conform even to the Church of England as it was reformed by the Long Parliament and purified by Cromwell's Triers and Ejectors. After the return of Charles II the name 'Dissenter' was used both of erstwhile sectaries and of the more numerous body of men and women who, though they had worshipped in their parish churches during the Interregnum, under the leadership of some two thousand ejected clergymen refused to submit to the restored episcopal church.

Initially the term 'Nonconformist' indicated neither Separatist nor Dissenter. It was used in the reign of Elizabeth of Puritans who were in communion with the Church of England but who declined to conform to certain practices prescribed by the Prayer Book of 1559. Only after 1662, when the state required of its clergy their 'unfeigned assent and consent' to everything in that Prayer Book did the word Nonconformist come to mean separation from the Church of England. And it was not until the second half of the nineteenth century that 'Nonconformist' came to replace 'Dissenter' as the usual designation of those

Protestants who worshipped outside the established church, the term popularized by Edward Miall's newspaper, *The Nonconformist*, founded in 1841.

The names 'Separatist', 'Dissenter', and 'Nonconformist' were all negative terms, emphasizing deviation from the accepted norm and carrying with them implications of inferiority and second-class citizenship. Not so the title 'Free Churchman'. This appellation was appropriated by Dissenters to themselves during the most aggressive period of their history, the later nineteenth and early twentieth centuries. It was used not only of the Old Dissenters, whose forefathers had rejected the Prayer Book of 1559, it was used of the newer Methodists, some of whom still used that Prayer Book in their worship. It implies not merely rejection of the national church, it proposes a constructive alternative. The Free Churchman does not, like the ejected clergyman of 1662, reluctantly dissent from the established church; he proclaims what he believes to be a higher form of churchmanship.[1]

The terms 'Separatist', 'Dissenter', 'Nonconformist', 'Free Churchman', suggest not only an evolving attitude towards the established church, they imply a changing relationship with the state. The Anabaptists of the sixteenth century, the Separatists of the early seventeenth century, the Dissenters of the late seventeenth and eighteenth centuries, asked chiefly to be left alone to worship God in their own way. Only once, in the course of the Barebone's Parliament of 1653, did men who rejected the principle of a national church appear to come near to controlling the destinies of the nation, and even then the appearance was deceptive. The Toleration Act of 1689 was the most enduring political achievement of the Dissenters whose history is recorded in the first volume of this book, and it left them in a position of social inferiority. But the Nonconformists of the nineteenth century were economically and politically more powerful than their forefathers and were able to wrest not only religious liberty but also civil equality from the state, while the Free Churchmen of the early twentieth century occupied,

---

[1] My interpretation of the terms 'Puritan', 'Dissent', and 'Nonconformity' is the reverse of that put forward by E. P. Thompson in *The Making of the English Working Class* (2nd edn. 1968), p. 385.

if only for a few years, nearly a third of the seats in the House of Commons. A consistent thread none the less links the Tudor Anabaptists with the twentieth-century Free Churchman, a refusal to accept the dictates of the state in matters of conscience. The refusal to render to Caesar the things that are God's is of the very essence of Dissent.

The Dissenters have always been a minority in English society—though they were a predominant influence in nineteenth-century Wales—and they have rarely been at the centre of the nation's affairs. In the early eighteenth century men, women, and children who were in any way associated with a Dissenting meeting-house constituted only about 6 per cent of the total population of England and Wales; and even in the mid-nineteenth century when the Nonconformist variety of Christianity has its greatest appeal in England and Wales, not more than one person in five worshipped in a chapel, and only one adult in fifteen was a member of a Dissenting or Methodist church, though again the proportions were much higher in Wales. At no time in the 200 years between the fall of Barebone's Parliament in December 1653 and the dissolution of Victoria's third Parliament in July 1852 is it likely that there were sitting in the House of Commons more than thirty M.P.s who can properly be termed Dissenters. No Dissenter sat in a British Cabinet until John Bright became President of the Board of Trade in Gladstone's first government in 1868. And by the time it was conceivable that the product of a Dissenting home might occupy Number 10 Downing Street, in the person of H. H. Asquith, Dissent could no longer retain its hold over its own sons.

But though Dissent has rarely occupied the centre of the national stage, it has played a most important supporting role in the development of the English, and still more of the Welsh, nations. The Elizabethan Separatists claimed the liberty to serve God as they thought he required of them; the General Baptists of the early seventeenth century demanded such liberty for other men as well as for themselves; and the sectaries of the mid-seventeenth century fought for, and for a time secured, that liberty. The twin Separatist conceptions of a free community bound together by voluntary agreement to a covenant, and of a mutual contract between rulers and the

ruled, inspired both the Levellers' *Agreement of the People* and the
political theory of John Locke, and, transmitted to America in
the *Mayflower*, were enshrined in the constitutions of the New
England colonies and served ultimately to justify revolution.
Meanwhile, in old England, the tenacity with which first
Separatists and Baptists, later Quakers, and finally Congregationalists and Presbyterians refused to bow before a persecuting
state church guaranteed that Englishmen would develop,
centuries earlier than other major European nations, a pluralist
society in which men would learn to live in peace with others
with whom they disagreed without resort to the scaffold or the
firing squad.

Dissenters were, admittedly, excluded from the universities
and from the government of eighteenth-century England, but
their very exclusion from established centres of influence and
power encouraged them to make a distinctive contribution to
the nation's educational, scientific, industrial, and commercial
progress. The twin forces of industrial revolution and population explosion in their turn provided opportunity for the rapid
expansion of English and Welsh Dissent, and the presence in
England of a substantial minority of Christians with a tradition
of political radicalism meant that the popular forces unleashed
in the late eighteenth and early nineteenth centuries did not, as
on the continent, necessarily taken an anti-Christian form.
Whereas in nineteenth-century Europe liberalism and socialism
were often synonymous with irreligion, in England and Wales
religious Dissent and political radicalism often went hand in
hand. And if it is too much to claim that this phenomenon saved
England from revolution, there can be little doubt that it
contributed to the stability of English society. Nor was the
influence of nineteenth-century Dissent confined by the English
Channel and the North Sea: English Nonconformists played a
crucial role in the process whereby Protestant Christianity was
taken to America, Asia, Africa, and Polynesia, and the fact that
there are in the world today some 33 million Baptists and nearly
19 million Methodists is in no small measure due to the activities of English Free Churchmen. The origins of two of the
world's largest Protestant denominations are among the themes
of this book.

The religious and moral character of generations of a significant minority of Englishmen, and of a substantial proportion of Welshmen, has been determined by the influence of Dissenting homes and Nonconformist chapels. Dissent taught the value of devotion, discipline, personal probity, and responsibility, values which are today discounted as restrictive and 'puritanical', but which helped to make Englishmen and Welshmen not perhaps what they are, but what they were until the middle of the twentieth century. The Dissenters had their faults. Devotion could turn into sterile religiosity; discipline become censorious fault-finding; personal responsibility degenerate into crippling over-scrupulosity. Their beliefs were too frequently expressed in narrow and exclusive Calvinist creeds; their preachers too often fond of dwelling on the eternal fires of hell; their churches too frequently rent by unseemly quarrels and trivial disputes. But it is of the nature of historical records— and of historians—to emphasize the dramatic at the expense of the normal, the contentious in place of the peaceful, and for most periods of their history their meeting-house or chapel was a place of heart-felt worship, devoted prayer, and warm fellowship. There were no doubt some Dissenters who were hypocrites, making a show of piety to impress their fellow men or to advance their material interests, but such persons appear more frequently in fiction than in fact, on the theatrical stage than in the reality of life. At his best the Dissenter was a man both of rugged individualism and yet of deep humility. Independent of man yet dependent on God, 'he prostrated himself in the dust before his Maker', wrote Macaulay, 'but he set his foot on the neck of his king'.[1]

[1] T. B. Macaulay, *Critical and Historical Essays*, i (1907), 187.

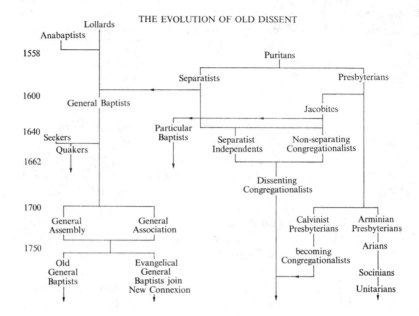

THE EVOLUTION OF OLD DISSENT

I

'THE LORD'S PEOPLE IS OF THE WILLING SORT': THE GENESIS OF DISSENT, 1532–1640

I. THE RADICAL ORIGINS OF DISSENT: LOLLARDS AND ANABAPTISTS

English Dissent springs from two different theological sources and for much of its history flows in two distinct currents, the one radical, the other Calvinist. The second of these two Dissenting streams is a tributary of the wider river of English Puritanism, its doctrine Calvinist, emphasizing the sovereignty of God and the predestination of man either to salvation or to reprobation. The origin of the earlier, radical, stream is less easy to discover: it is likely that it can be traced back to fifteenth-century Lollardy, and that it was subsequently fed from the turbulent waters of continental Anabaptism in the first half of the sixteenth century. But then the stream flows largely underground, to re-emerge with the General Baptists of the seventeenth century. This tradition places great emphasis on a literal interpretation of the Bible, believes that Christ died for all mankind, and repudiates the Calvinist claim that some men are predestined to damnation. Rebaptism was not, initially, an essential element in the tradition, and we do not know that any of the Englishmen accused of 'Anabaptism' in the first fifty years of the sixteenth century had undergone a second baptism.[1] But a common desire to judge the rite by Biblical and rational standards marks the evolution from the Lollard belief that the baptism of the children of Christian parents is unnecessary[2] to the frequent Anabaptist denial of original sin and to the General Baptist insistence on believers' baptism.

The course of this first, radical stream is so elusive that its existence has not always been acknowledged by historians of

[1] I. B. Horst, *The Radical Brethren* (Nieuwkoop, 1972), p. 148.
[2] J. A. F. Thompson, *The Later Lollards* (Oxford, 1965), pp. 76, 106, 245.

sixteenth-century Dissent: both Champlin Burrage and B. R. White have denied that there is any evidence that continental Anabaptism influenced English Dissent before the early seventeenth century, and Lonnie Kliever has argued that it made little impact even then.[1] But while concrete literary evidence may be lacking, there is a good deal of circumstantial evidence to suggest a link between Lollardy, Anabaptism, and the General Baptists of the seventeenth century. Irvin Horst has drawn attention to the existence of an Anabaptist group in London in the 1530s, and while his contention that they were but 'old Lollards' cannot be regarded as proven, he does show that Anabaptist opinions were held and disseminated in England in the reign of Henry VIII not only by immigrants from the Low Countries, but also by native Englishmen. In 1532 three Englishmen and one Scotsman were arrested in London for importing and distributing 'books of [the] Anabaptists' Confession', and four others, two Englishmen and two Flemings, were listed as having escaped detection. The accusation levelled against one of the Englishmen, Paul Broughton, that he held 'strange opinions' 'touching the humanity of Christ', suggests that the group had been influenced by the views of the German Anabaptist Melchior Hofmann, who taught that Christ's body was not of the same substance as Mary's, but had passed through her 'as water through a pipe'.[2]

Melchior Hofmann had joined the Anabaptists in 1530 in Strasburg, where he had proclaimed himself as the second Elijah and prophesied that the city would become the new Jerusalem, for which the ungrateful city council had sentenced him to life imprisonment.[3] But before his incarceration he had made frequent forays into the Netherlands where his eschatological views found a ready hearing among a people threatened by 'plague, flood, and famine'. The apocalyptic expectations which he aroused led his wilder followers, in 1534–5, to walk naked through the streets of Amsterdam and to attempt to storm the town hall, and in Münster to establish a theocratic

---

[1] Burrage, *EED* i. 68. B. R. White, *The English Separatist Tradition* (Oxford, 1971), pp. xii, 162. L. D. Kliever, 'General Baptist Origins', *Mennonite Quarterly Review*, xxxvi (1962), 316–17.

[2] Horst, *Radical Brethren*, pp. 49–53, 183–4. G. H. Williams, *The Radical Reformation* (1962), p. 329.

[3] Williams, *Radical Reformation*, pp. 259–65, 292–3.

state in which property was held in common, adultery made punishable by death, and polygamy encouraged.[1] The fall of Münster to the bishop's besieging army in June 1535 was followed by an orgy of revenge in which thousands perished, and Anabaptism, for more than a century, was branded with the marks of fanaticism and anarchy.

The slaughter of Anabaptists in the Netherlands led some of their number to seek refuge in England where, all too often, they met with similar fate. Fourteen Dutch Anabaptists were burned at the stake in various English towns in 1535, three more in 1538, and three or four men, possibly Anabaptists, were burned at Southwark in 1540 for denying transubstantiation.[2] Of the latter one, 'a crazed man of the name of Collins', was an Englishman. Another Englishman, who is known only from his Christian name of Henry, financed a conference of Anabaptist leaders at Bocholt in Westphalia in June 1536 in an attempt to unite their divided forces after the scandal and the horror of Münster.[3] And a third, Robert Cooche, the keeper of the royal wine-cellar, maintained 'that children have no original sin, and that they ought not to be baptised' in debate with Dr. William Turner, dean-elect of Wells, in 1550.[4] But the most celebrated English Anabaptist was Joan Boucher, known also as Joan of Kent, and it is she who provides the best evidence to support Horst's contention that 'new Anabaptist' was but 'old Lollard'.

Joan Boucher first appears in the records in 1528 as a widow and member of a group of Lollards led by Richard Fox, the curate of Steeple Bumpstead in Essex, who taught his flock that 'the sacrament of the altar is not the body of Christ, but done for a remembrance of Christ's passion'.[5] Joan was said to have subsequently abjured the sacramentarian heresy at Colchester, but in 1541 she turned up at Canterbury, having married again, where she continued to propagate heretical views and

[1] Ibid., pp. 355–9, 368–72.

[2] Horst, *Radical Brethren*, pp. 60–1, 87–8, 93–4.

[3] Ibid., pp. 78–80.

[4] Ibid., p. 115, J. Strype, *Ecclesiastical Memorials* (Oxford, 1822), vol. ii, part i, p. 111.

[5] *Letters and Papers, Foreign and Domestic, of the Reign of Henry VIII*, ed. J. S. Brewer, vol. iv, part ii, p. 1875. J. F. Davis, 'Heresy and Reformation in the South-East of England, 1520–59', Oxford D. Phil. thesis, 1968, p. 412.

broke fast on Easter day morning by eating a calf's head. She was arrested and spent two years in prison until released in 1543.[1] Nothing is known of her activities for the next six years, but during the tolerant protectorship of the Duke of Somerset (1547–9) England once again became a refuge for persecuted Anabaptists from the Netherlands. In April 1549 the Privy Council was disturbed by reports that Dutch Anabaptists were making converts in England, a commission was appointed to search them out, and several supposed Anabaptists were arrested and abjured the heresies with which they were charged.[2] Of those arrested only Joan Boucher did not recant. The chief cause of her offence was her adherence to the Melchiorite doctrine that Christ did not 'take flesh of the virgin'. Entreaties by Archbishop Cranmer failed to move her to renounce the heresy, and in May 1550 she was burned at Smithfield.

Joan claimed at her trial to have a thousand followers in London, and while this was no doubt an exaggeration the existence of Anabaptist influence in Kent and Essex is attested from other sources. In 1550 John Hooper, the future Bishop of Gloucester, wrote that the two counties were 'troubled with the frenzy of Anabaptists more than any other part of the kingdom', and two years later Archbishop Cranmer was sent 'on an embassy to Kent to preach at and convince the Anabaptists, which sect is beginning to swarm'.[3] Something is known of the membership and opinions of two groups of these radicals which met in the Maidstone and Ashford district of Kent and at Bocking in northern Essex. Their existence came to light at Christmas 1550 when some of the Kentish group visited the Bocking group, and they gave themselves away when sixty people tried to crowd into the house of (Thomas ?) Upchard 'for talk of Scriptures'. Upchard himself was arrested, and orders were sent out for the detention of other ringleaders who were arrested and questioned by the Privy Council.[4] Both the Bocking and the Kentish conventiclers probably had Lollard antecedents, for Bocking is only 11 miles from Steeple Bumpstead, once

---

[1] *Letters and Papers of the Reign of Henry VIII*, vol. xviii, part ii, pp. 312–14, 331.
[2] G. Burnet, *History of the Reformation* (1850), i. 371.
[3] Horst, *Radical Brethren*, pp. 109–11, 102–3.
[4] Burrage, *EED* ii. 1–6.

the home of Joan Boucher and a centre of Lollard activity in the 1520s, and the frequently expressed belief of the Kentish group, that 'they ought not to salute a sinner or a man whom they know not', is an echo of the Lollard idea of 'known men'. [1] The conventiclers are not described as Anabaptists and one of their number, Nicholas Sheterden, rejected Hofmann's views on the incarnation of Christ,[2] but the Kentish group, like many of the Anabaptists, repudiated both original sin and pre-destination. 'There is no man so chosen or predestinate but that he may condemn himself', argued Henry Hart, 'neither is there any so reprobate but that he may if he will keep the commandments and be saved.' 'The doctrine of predestination', claimed (Robert ?) Cole of Faversham, 'was meeter for devils than for Christian men.' Champlin Burrage has argued that the evidence is not sufficient to support the conclusion that the two groups of conventiclers had separated from the established church, but men from both groups admitted that they had absented themselves from their parish communion for two years, and one of them, Nicholas Young, stated bluntly that they 'would not communicate with sinners'.[3]

One of the Kentish conventiclers, a schoolmaster named Thomas Cole from Maidstone, denied that he held the views attributed to him in the deposition and two years later preached before Archbishop Cranmer 'against divers errors of the Anabaptists'.[4] But other members of the group —Robert Cole, Henry Hart, John Ledley, Humphrey Middleton, and Nicholas Sheterden—continued to hold and propagate their views in the reign of Mary. The Protestant martyr John Bradford made strenuous attempts, from his cell in the King's Bench prison, to convert them to his own predestinarian views.[5] At least three of the Kentish conventiclers, Nicholas Sheterden, Humphrey Middleton, and George Brodbridge, were burned at Canterbury in 1555, and a possible fourth, Dunstan Chittenden, died

---

[1] Ibid. ii. 3. J. E. Oxley, *The Reformation in Essex* (Manchester, 1965), p. 4 n.

[2] J. Foxe, *The Acts and Monuments of the English Martyrs*, ed. J. Pratt (1870), vii. 307.

[3] Burrage, *EED* ii. 1–6.

[4] Horst, *Radical Brethren*, pp. 123–4.

[5] Foxe, *Acts and Monuments*, viii. 384. *The Writings of John Bradford*, ed. A. Townsend (Parker Society, 1853), ii. 128–35, 164–7, 194.

from starvation in Canterbury gaol.[1] John Simpson, a husbandman from Wigborough in Essex, who was burned at Rochford in 1555, was probably one of the Bocking conventiclers, and he in his turn was associated with the martyrs John Ardley, also a Wigborough husbandman, John Denley, a gentleman, and John Newman, a pewterer.[2] Denley and Newman both came from Maidstone and, like the Kentish conventiclers five years earlier, were discovered in Essex, 'going to visit . . . their godly friends as then they had in the county'.[3] It is also possible that the celebrated tailor-evangelist of Mary's reign, George Eagles, nicknamed 'Trudgeover', was related to one of the Bocking group, 'John Eglise, clothier', or even, given the carelessness with which Christian names were often recorded in sixteenth-century documents, that they were one and the same person. Trudgeover was captured at Colchester in July 1557, found guilty of treason, and executed by hanging, drawing, and quartering.[4] If Trudgeover was associated with the Bocking conventiclers, then his convert, John Johnson of Thorpe-le-Soken, is the tenth name which can be added to the list of Marian martyrs whose ecclesiastical and theological position was radical rather than Anglican.[5] And one can be sure that there were other radicals who suffered under Mary, men and women whose views were suppressed by Foxe in the interests of propaganda and Protestant unity.

Apart from Upchard, who seems to have fled to Frankfurt and to have returned after the accession of Elizabeth to become first a clergyman and then a Nonconformist,[6] all the leaders of the Kent and Essex radicals were killed or silenced by the

---

[1] Foxe, *Acts and Monuments*, vii. 312, 383, viii. 254.

[2] The identification of the Simpson who was arrested at Bocking in 1551 with John Simpson of Wigborough is much more likely than Burrage's and Horst's identification of him with Cuthbert Simpson, the deacon of the Protestant church in London in Mary's reign. A John Simpson is known to have witnessed the will of Robert Cooke, another of the Bocking conventiclers. D. Witard, *Bibles in Barrels, A History of Essex Baptists* (Southend-on-Sea, 1962), p. 21.

[3] Foxe, *Acts and Monuments*, vii. 86–90, 328–35.

[4] Ibid. vii. 393–6. *Acts of the Privy Council*, ed. J. R. Dasent, 1556–8, p. 129.

[5] Foxe, *Acts and Monuments*, viii. 389.

[6] The Upchard in whose house the Bocking conventiclers met in 1550 was probably the 'Thomas Upcher', a weaver of Bocking, who was in Frankfurt in 1557 and later in Aarau and who, in the reign of Elizabeth, was successively rector of Fordham and of St. Leonard's, Colchester, until his resignation in 1582. C. H. Garrett, *The Marian Exiles* (Cambridge, 1938), pp. 316–17.

Marian persecution, and for more than half a century we have no knowledge of any similar native group in England. But a handful of individual Englishmen are known to have held Anabaptist views between the accession of Elizabeth and the establishment of the first General Baptist church in England in 1612, and they are unlikely to have been alone. On Easter day 1575 some twenty-five or so Dutch Anabaptists were arrested 'in a house without the bars of Aldgate at London', and after refusing to recant two were burned at Smithfield. They made at least one English convert, a man known only from his initials 'S.B.' who was involved in controversy with the Puritan William White when both were imprisoned in Newgate. 'S.B.' was a carpenter, an uneducated man who said he 'had not been at university to study Aristotle's divinity'. He defended the Anabaptist views that the Christian should not take up arms, swear on oath, or go to law.[1] Some twenty years later several members of Francis Johnson's Calvinist Separatist church in exile in the Netherlands were excommunicated for having fallen 'into the heresies of the Anabaptists'; one of them appears to have baptized himself and another, probably Thomas Mitchell, returned to England to make converts; and in 1611 Edward Wightman, a draper from Burton-on-Trent, was charged with a long list of heresies, some of which suggest Anabaptist influence. Among the heterodox opinions of which he was accused were 'that there is not the Trinity of persons in the unity of the deity', that Christ 'took not human flesh of the substance of the virgin Mary', that the soul sleeps after the death of the body, and that baptism, which when applied to infants is 'an abominable custom', should be administered 'only to converts of sufficient age of understanding converted from infidelity to the faith'. Wightman was burned at Lichfield in April 1612, the last person in England to be sent to the stake 'solely on account of his religious beliefs'.[2]

The strongest evidence to support the thesis of a continuing radical tradition linking the Lollards and Anabaptists of the early sixteenth century with the General Baptists of the seventeenth is geographic[3]. One of the first General Baptist

---

[1] A Peel, 'A Conscientious Objector of 1575', *TBHS* vii (1920–1), 71–128.
[2] Burrage, *EED* i. 156, 217–20, 222–5.
[3] See below, pp. 283–4.

churches in England, founded before 1626, was established in the old Lollard centre of Coventry; in the 1640s and 1650s General Baptist ideas made rapid headway in the former Lollard strongholds in the Weald of Kent and the Chilterns of Buckinghamshire; and General Baptists also became fairly numerous in the clothing towns of northern Essex, suggesting a link with the Bocking conventiclers of the mid-sixteenth century.[1] B. R. White has maintained that the absence of Melchiorite views on the incarnation among English Separatists is an argument against Anabaptist influence in England,[2] but while such views were repudiated by the General Baptists of Buckinghamshire in 1679 they did win support among the General Baptists of Sussex and Kent and helped to divide the denomination for more than half a century. This strongly suggests that while the General Baptists of Buckinghamshire inherited the radical tradition of the Lollards, uninfluenced by Anabaptist ideas, in Kent and Sussex that tradition received added stimulus from the proximity of south-east England to the centres of continental Anabaptism.[3]

2. THE CALVINIST ORIGINS OF DISSENT: FROM PURITANISM TO SEPARATISM

It was not, though, from Lollardy or Anabaptism, but from Elizabethan Calvinistic Puritanism that the mainstream of English Separatism had its source. While the English General Baptists, whatever the origins of their inspiration, had undoubted affinities with the continental Anabaptists, the affinities of the English Puritans were with the Calvinists of Geneva, Scotland, and the Netherlands, and with the Huguenots of France. But the situations in which the English Puritans and continental Calvinists found themselves in the thirty critical years between the accession of Elizabeth and the defeat of the

---

[1] Witard, *Bibles in Barrels*, p. 15.

[2] White, *Separatist Tradition*, p. 163.

[3] Similar points were made by W. T. Whitley in his introduction to the *Minutes of the General Assembly of the General Baptist Churches in England*, i (1909), p. ix, and by A. H. J. Baines in his article on 'The signatories of the Baptist Confession of 1679', *Baptist Quarterly*, xvii (1957), 35. However, by the time he came to write his *History of British Baptists* in 1923 Whitley had fallen under the influence of Burrage. He made no mention of Lollard influence and wrote that the origin of the General Baptists was 'independent of the Anabaptists' (p. 17).

Spanish Armada were essentially different: whereas in France and the Netherlands, as also in Scotland, the chief opposition to the reform of the national church on the Genevan model came from the Roman Catholic Church and from monarchs loyal to Catholicism, in England the chief opposition to reform came from a monarch who was governor of a church which was neither Protestant nor Catholic, but something in between. As a result, the attitude of the English Puritans towards their country's national church was ambivalent, love for the church being balanced by hatred of its continuing abuses. It was this ambivalence which helped to destroy, in the middle of the seventeenth century, the Elizabethan ideal of a comprehensive national church, and which thereby facilitated the survival and growth of those radical religious sects which on the continent were persecuted and all but annihilated by Catholic and Protestant alike.

Historians have agonized over the meaning of the term 'Puritan' but there is really little need. A brief but comprehensive description was given in the seventeenth century by the Presbyterian minister John Geree in his pamphlet entitled *The Character of an old English Puritane, or Non-Conformist*:

The Old English Puritan was such an one that honoured God above all, and under God gave every one his due. His first care was to serve God, and therein he did not what was good in his own, but in God's sight, making the word of God his rule in worship. He highly esteemed order in the House of God: but would not under colour of that submit to superstititious rites, which are superfluous, and perish in their use. He reverenced authority within its sphere: but durst not under pretence of this subjection to the higher powers, worship God after the traditions of men. . . . He was much in prayer; with it he began and closed the day. In it he was exercised in his closet, family, and public assembly. He esteemed that manner of prayer best, where by the gift of God, expressions were varied according to present wants and occasions; yet did he not account set forms unlawful. . . . He was a man of good spiritual appetite, and could not be content with one meal a day. An afternoon sermon did relish as well to him as one in the morning. . . . The Lord's day he esteemed a divine ordinance, and . . . was very conscientious in the observance of that day as the mart day of the soul. . . . He endeavoured to have the scandalous cast out of communion . . . [but] right discipline he judged pertaining not to the being, but

well-being of a church. . . . Perfection in churches he thought a thing
rather to be desired, than hoped for. And so he expected not a church
state without all defects. . . . Just laws and commands he willingly
obeyed . . . but such as were unjust he refused to observe, choosing
rather to obey God than man: yet his refusal was modest and with
submission to penalties, unless he could procure indulgence from
authority.[1]

Geree hits exactly the right note: in a few sentences we have
that combination of piety and realism, of humility and self-
assertion, of deference and rebellion, which was characteristic
of Puritanism. As a coherent ecclesiastical position Puritanism
was a *media via* which lasted barely a hundred years, ultimately
dissolved by its inner contradictions. The Puritan desired liberty
for self-expression in matters of religion, but not to the point
where it would disrupt the decent order of the church; he challenged the rulings of the magistrate in ecclesiastical affairs, but
not to the point of denying his authority; he scorned many of
the rites of the established church, but not to the point of repudiating the church itself. 'The corruptions that were in
churches he thought his duty to bewail, with endeavours of
amendment,' wrote Geree, 'yet he would not separate.'

Puritanism, as defined by this seventeenth-century Presbyterian, was not Separatism, and I propose to follow Geree in
distinguishing protest within from secession without the established church. But it is with the knowledge that the relationship between the two movements was often close and that,
initially, the difference between them was not clearly defined:
for much of Elizabeth's reign the term 'Puritan' was applied
to those who separated from the established church and was
repudiated by those to whom historians now give the title.
Puritanism and mainstream Separatism shared the same Calvinist theology and issued from a common source: from the

---

[1] J. Geree, *The Character of an old English Puritane, or Non-Conformist* (1646), pp.
1–4. Geree's statement that Puritans did not expect churches to be 'without all
defects' destroys J. F. H. New's contention that the distinguishing feature of Puritan
churchmanship was 'a dogmatic annulment of the distinction between the visible
and the invisible church' (J. F. H. New, *Anglican and Puritan*, 1964, p. 33). The only
Puritan whom New cites in support of his contention is John Cotton, but, as
Edmund Morgan points out, Cotton was far from being a typical Puritan, and the
requirements for church membership adopted by the New England churches
under Cotton's leadership in the 1630s were as exclusive, if not more exclusive, as
those of the Separatists (E. S. Morgan, *Visible Saints*, New York 1963, pp. 88–105).

disillusionment suffered by 'the hotter sort of Protestants' with the Church of England as it was restored in 1559, after Mary's short-lived attempt to reunite England and Rome.

For three years England's frustrated and neurotic Catholic queen had attempted to terrorize English men and women into submission to the Church of Rome: nearly 300 Protestant and radical martyrs had perished, mainly at the stake, another 800 or so had fled abroad, and a lasting hatred of Catholicism had been burned into the Englishman's soul. When, in November 1558, the daughter of Catherine of Aragon mercifully died, to be succeeded by the daughter of Anne Boleyn, bonfires were lit in the streets of London and Protestants emerged from hiding and from exile expecting a total reversal of the religious policy of the previous reign. The Marian exiles, though, were by no means united over the sort of religious settlement they wanted in its stead. At Frankfurt-am-Main they had split into two factions: the moderate supporters of Dr. Richard Cox who remained loyal to the Edwardian Prayer Book of 1552, and the more radical followers of John Knox who, under the influence of Calvin's Geneva, remodelled the Prayer Book to omit the use of the surplice, the litany, and oral responses. In Geneva itself at least 230 English exiles were associated with a church organized on Calvin's model with its own ministers, 'seniores' or elders, and deacons.[1]

These divisions among the Protestant exiles continued into the new reign. Elizabeth's own innermost views on religion have remained a mystery and her opinions on church government a matter of contention. The international situation at her accession, England's war with France and dependence of Spain, necessitated caution, and when she told the Spanish ambassador that she was 'resolved to restore religion as her father left it' she may or may not have meant what she said. But in order to repudiate the authority of the pope and to counter the influence of the Catholic bishops appointed by her sister she needed the assistance both of the Protestant gentry and of the more moderate divines returning from the continent. The resulting settlement was thus a compromise between her own conservative views and the moderate position of Richard Cox:

---

[1] S. J. Knox, 'A Study of the English Geneva Exiles', Trinity College, Dublin, B. Litt. thesis, 1953, pp. 120–55.

the Act of Uniformity prescribed the use of the Edwardian Prayer Book of 1552, revised in a conservative direction to compel the wearing of the vestments in use in the second year of Edward VI. Clergymen who attempted to conduct services other than those authorized by the new Prayer Book were liable to six months' imprisonment for a first offence, a year's imprisonment for a second offence, and life imprisonment for a third.

Radical Protestants were scandalized by the Prayer Book of 1559. It prescribed ceremonies and postures which they regarded as popish and unscriptural: confirmation, bowing at the name of Jesus, kneeling to receive communion, making the sign of the cross at baptism, the use of the ring in marriage. Its services were too long, leaving little or no time for preaching; its prayers were too worldly, seeking material blessings; its discipline was too lax, admitting men and women to communion without examining their lives.[1] Worst of all it compelled ministers to wear the badges of the priestly office, the surplice and the square cap. If, to the twentieth-century reader, conscientious Protestant objections to clerical vestments seem trivial, one should try to imagine the feelings of a German Jew, returning to Germany after the defeat of the Nazis only to find the police dressed in the uniforms of the S.S. 'Have you forgotten those cruel and popish butchers which not long ago burned so many Christian martyrs', asked one opponent of vestments, men 'which had on their heads such woollen horns?'[2]

None the less radical Protestants accepted benefices in the Church of England, only to violate the provisions of the Prayer Book once they were installed, and in January 1565 Elizabeth commanded Archbishop Parker to investigate the 'varieties, novelties, and diversities' which she feared were disturbing the ordered ceremonial of the church. The results of Parker's inquiry confirmed the queen's suspicions, and in March 1566 the archbishop issued 'Advertisements' forbidding ministers to preach without licence from their bishop, requiring parish clergymen to wear the surplice when they administered communion, and insisting that the people kneel to receive the sacrament. Thirty-seven London ministers were suspended for

---

[1] H. Davies, *Worship and Theology in England* (Princeton, 1970), i. 261–8.
[2] P. Collinson, *The Elizabethan Puritan Movement* (1967), p. 95.

refusing to accede to Parker's demands, and although at least half soon conformed rather than lose their livelihoods, a handful held out and were deprived of their livings.

Those Protestants who persisted in their opposition to their ministers dressing themselves up in the 'conjuring garments of popery' were thus obliged to meet in secret, consciously following the example of the underground church which had met in London during the Marian persecution. Initially they met in private houses, but by June 1567 one group had grown so numerous that they hired the Plumbers' Hall for a meeting of a hundred people, claiming, when they were disturbed by the sheriffs, that they were celebrating a wedding. Seventeen or eighteen were arrested, sent to the Counter prison, and questioned by the lord mayor and Bishop Grindal of London, himself a Marian exile. The only account we have of the interrogation, written by one of the prisoners, shows that they were treated with kindness. The lord mayor apologized that they had been troubled, the bishop assured them that he himself would rather do without the cope and surplice when he ministered in St. Paul's, but that he wore them 'for order's sake and obedience to the prince'. The prisoners were not convinced. Popish apparel, they argued, covered popish hearts. 'I know one that in Queen Mary's time did persecute God's saints', said John Roper, 'and brought them forth to Bishop Bonner, and now he is minister allowed of you, and never made recantation.'[1]

Champlin Burrage has argued that the Plumbers' Hall congregation was Puritan and not Separatist, Albert Peel that it was Separatist but not Congregational.[2] The replies of the prisoners to Grindal's questions show that while their intentions were Puritan their actions were Separatist, that they stood at the parting of the Puritan and Separatist ways. In the eyes of John Smith, whom Grindal questioned as the oldest of what was probably a young and headstrong group, the decision to meet in private houses had been forced on them by the ecclesiastical authorities, when 'all our preachers were displaced by your law, that would not subscribe to your apparel'. Their intention

---

[1] *The Remains of Edmund Grindal*, ed. W. Nicholson (Parker Society, 1853), pp. 201–16.

[2] Burrage, *EED* i. 82–3. A. Peel, *The First Congregational Churches* (1920), p. 13.

was not to disrupt the Church of England but to reform it on the Genevan model. 'We will be tried by the best reformed churches,' said William White in characteristic Puritan manner: 'The Church of Scotland hath the word truly preached, the sacraments truly ministered, and discipline according to the word of God.' Yet at the same time they did not deny Grindal's contention that they had absented themselves from their parish churches and administered the sacraments among themselves—actions from which the later Puritans always shrank with horror.

The contemporary confusion over nomenclature can be seen in the account of the antiquary John Stowe, who wrote that early in 1568 there 'were many congregations of the Anabaptists in London, who called themselves Puritans or unspotted lambs of the Lord'. They met 'in the Minories without Aldgate', 'afterwards in a lighter in St. Katherine's Pool', 'then in a chopper's house, nigh Wool Quay in Thames Street' where a preacher named Browne was arrested, then in 'Pudding Lane in a minister's house', then at Mountjoy Place, in Westminster, in a goldsmith's house near the Savoy, in the home of the Bishop of London's servant in Hoxton, and 'in a carpenter's house in Aldermanbury'.[1] The goldsmith's name was James Tynne, and at his house on 4 March seventy-seven men and women were arrested, including six of the leaders of the Plumbers' Hall group. How many were imprisoned we do not know, but at least eight of them were among twenty-four men and seven unnamed women who were released from Bridewell thirteen months later.[2]

Bishop Grindal, sympathizing with their motives if not their actions, was at a loss to know what to do with them. In February 1568 the constables had informed him of the meeting in Mountjoy Place and Grindal had told them to leave the conventiclers alone.[3] In March the bishop hit on the idea of sending the ringleaders to Scotland, apparently in the hope that they would settle in the country whose church they so admired. But the conventiclers found that the Church of Scotland was

---

[1] J. Stowe, *Three Fifteenth Century Chronicles*, ed. J. Gardiner (Camden Society, 1880), new series, xxviii. 143.

[2] Peel, *First Congregational Churches*, p. 10. Burrage, *EED* ii. 12–13.

[3] Stowe, *Fifteenth Century Chronicles*, p. 143.

not as pure as they had been led to believe and by May they were back in England.

Contact with Scotland did, though, begin the process of distinguishing the Puritan from the Separatist elements among the conventiclers. One of the goldsmith's house congregation, John Evans of Holborn, was so disgusted by what he saw at Dunbar on Good Friday, people going 'bare-footed and bare-legged to the church, to creep to the cross', that he made his peace with the Church of England and was excommunicated by his fellow conventiclers.[1] But others returned, as Grindal reported to Cecil, to 'their old practices and assemblies', and their action in excommunicating one of their number is convincing evidence of their Separatist character. Grindal was both kindly disposed towards the conventiclers and well informed about their views, and when he wrote to the Zurich reformer Henry Bullinger in June he had no doubt that they were Separatist. 'Some London citizens of the lowest order,' wrote the bishop, 'together with four or five ministers, remarkable neither for their judgement nor learning, have openly separated from us.' They numbered 'about two hundred, but consisting of more women than men', and met 'sometimes in private houses, sometimes in the fields, and occasionally even in ships', where they had 'ordained ministers, elders, and deacons', 'administered the sacraments', and 'excommunicated some who had seceded from their church'. Because the Puritan ministers Laurence Humphrey, Thomas Sampson, and Thomas Lever would not join them, Grindal claimed, they regarded them as 'semi-papists', and would 'not allow their followers to attend their preaching'.[2] This attitude was strongly deprecated by John Knox, in a letter which one of the conventiclers brought back from Scotland for his companions who had remained in prison, and the conventiclers in their reply denied the accusation.[3] But Knox's criticism of the conventiclers, wishing that their 'consciences had a better ground', further emphasized the differences between the reformers and the Separatists.

Grindal, in his letter to Bullinger, referred to 'four or five

[1] Peel, *First Congregational Churches*, pp. 15–16, 26.

[2] *The Zurich Letters*, ed. H. Robinson (Cambridge, 1842), i. 201–2.

[3] Peel, *First Congregational Churches*, p. 18, quoting J. Lorimer, *John Knox and the Church of England*, pp. 298–300.

ministers' who were associated with the conventiclers, and we know the names of four of them: 'Master Pattenson', who though suspended from preaching told Grindal in September 1567 that he ministered to a private congregation; John Browne, a Marian exile and protégé of the Duchess of Suffolk, who was arrested at the 'chopper's house' early in 1568; and William Bonham and Nicholas Crane, whose names are first connected with the conventiclers in 1569. All four ministers were, in the late 1560s, associated with the Puritan stronghold of the church of the Holy Trinity in the Minories, a parish which claimed 'exemption from episcopal jurisdiction and . . . independence in the appointment of its ministers'.[1]

In April 1569 Grindal obtained the release of thirty-one prisoners from Bridewell, including at least eight of those arrested at the goldsmith's house thirteen months before, 'without condition . . . saving only an earnest admonition to live in good order hereafter'. At the same time he appointed Bonham and Crane to lectureships in the Minories on the understanding that they would not attend private conventicles. The bishop apparently hoped that the released prisoners would attend their public ministrations and that 'taste of liberty' would 'in time work good obedience'. Instead the whole trans-action gave rise to misunderstanding and recrimination. The freed prisoners believed, or claimed to believe, that Grindal had freed them from the obligation to attend their parish churches, 'that we might hear such preachers whom we liked best of in the city', and that he had given them permission to use the Genevan service book. But when Bonham married a couple and baptized a child 'by the order of the said book' he was arrested and 'kept close prisoner', while Crane was 'ordered not to preach'. The conventiclers replied by petitioning the Privy Council that Grindal had broken his word, and the harassed bishop's patience now snapped. 'The heads of this unhappy faction should be with all expediency severely punished,' he wrote to the Privy Council in January 1570. It was doubtless to his great relief that four months later he was translated to the see of York.[2]

[1] H. Gareth Owen, 'A Nursery of Elizabethan Nonconformity', JEH xvii (1966), 65–76.

[2] J. Strype, The History of the Life and Acts of Archbishop Grindal (1821), pp. 226–31.

The Privy Council appears to have acted on Grindal's advice, and there followed the most determined attempt yet under Elizabeth to suppress the Separatist movement and deprive it of its leaders. Some time in 1571 twenty-seven humble men and women—eighteen of whom could not even sign their names—petitioned the queen to 'cast down all high places of idolatry within her land, with the popish canon law and all the superstition and commandments of men'. The demand was one which any group of Puritans might have made, but the rest of the petition reveals that it came not from a company of Puritans but from an organized Separatist church. The petitioners described themselves as 'a poor congregation whom God hath separated from the churches of England and from the mingled and false worshipping therein'; they rejected not only popish ceremonies but even parish churches, the 'temples and chapels which the papists and infidels have builded to the service of their gods'; they themselves served 'the Lord every Sabbath day in houses', and on Wednesdays they met together to pray and to 'exercise discipline on them which do deserve it'. Though they claimed to be but 'humble and obedient subjects' of the queen, they recorded pathetically that their minister Richard Fitz, the church's deacon Thomas Bowland, and two other members, Giles Fowler and Randall Partridge, had all died of 'long imprisonment'.[1] The petition met with no response: other members of the church were soon to die in prison, and ten years later London Separatists arrested in 1570 were still in gaol.[2]

Seven of the men and women who are known to have been associated with Fitz's church were among the seventy-seven arrested at the goldsmith's house in 1568 and one, Thomas Bowland, was also among the leaders of the Plumbers' Hall conventiclers questioned by Grindal in 1567. Champlin Burrage suggested that the members of Fitz's church were excommunicated members of the Plumber's Hall congregation, but his hypothesis is based on the unjustified assumption that the Plumbers' Hall group had in no way separated from the established church.[3] It is possible that in the evolution from the

---

[1] Burrage, *EED* ii. 15–18.
[2] A. Peel, ed., *The Seconde Parte of a Register* (Cambridge, 1915), i. 149.
[3] Burrage, *EED* i. 87–8.

mixed Puritan and Separatist elements among the Plumbers' Hall conventiclers to the outspoken Separatism of Richard Fitz's church we have the development of the views of essentially the same fellowship, their ranks thinned and their opinions sharpened in the fires of persecution.

The failure of Grindal's well-intentioned efforts to contain the conventiclers within the established church, and the subsequent intensification of persecution, certainly seem to have marked a further step in the process of separating the Puritan sheep from the Separatist goats. John Bolton, an elder of Fitz's church, recanted in the face of persecution, was excommunicated by his church, and subsequently hanged himself.[1] William White, a baker, had been arrested both at Plumbers' Hall and at the goldsmith's house, but his answers to Bishop Grindal's questions show that his motives were Puritan rather than Separatist, and by 1575 he was chiding the Anabaptist 'S.B.' for joining a 'sect of heretics' and for 'condemning all public exercises used in Christ his church in England'.[2] Of the four clergymen associated with the conventiclers of 1567–9 one, Pattenson, died in gaol in the 1570s,[3] but the other three, John Browne, William Bonham, and Nicholas Crane, appear to have shrunk from final separation from the Church of England in the 1570s and to have parted company from their more militant lay associates. What little is known of John Browne suggests that he occupied a position analogous to that of the followers of Henry Jacob early in the next century, that he tried to combine membership of 'a Christian congregation gathered together according to [God's] word' with worship at his parish church. He reprimanded a group which broke away from him for 'private assembling of yourselves together', and argued that the Separatists were weakening the Puritan cause by forming four or five different churches 'divided one from another'.[4] William Bonham and Nicholas Crane were both associated in the 1570s with a group of Puritan ministers in London who met twice a week to study the Bible, a meeting which Patrick Collinson sees as bearing 'an embryonic relationship to the *classis* described in the handbooks of Presbyterian

---

[1] Peel, *First Congregational Churches*, pp. 34–5.
[2] Peel, 'A Conscientious Objector of 1575', *TBHS* vii (1920–1), 87.
[3] Peel, *Seconde Parte*, i. 149.   [4] Ibid. i. 59–61.

polity'.[1] Crane subsequently renewed his Separatist contacts and died in prison as a Separatist in 1588, but in the 1570s the associations of all three men were not with the Separatists but with the Presbyterian movement launched by Thomas Cartwright's lectures on the Acts of the Apostles in Cambridge in the spring of 1570. The implications of Cartwright's lectures, that the offices of bishop and archbishop should be abolished in favour of the parity of ministers, and that ministers should be chosen by their congregations within the established church, had greater appeal for radical clergymen than the views of the Separatist conventiclers which had grown more extreme as persecution had intensified. John Browne, who in 1568 had been arrested at a conventicle, was five years later accused before Star Chamber of supporting Cartwright's views.[2]

By 1570 the initial protest against Parker's attempt to force clergymen to wear the pope's 'idolatrous gear' had thus developed into the much more serious matter of criticism of the government of the established church. On the one hand there was Cartwright's Presbyterian movement, seeking to complete the reformation within the Church of England; on the other those conventiclers who persisted in separating from the established church were groping their way to an alternative conception of churchmanship. An anonymous Separatist writer of the early 1570s both repudiated the authority of the queen in matters of conscience and indicated that he had subscribed to a church covenant. 'The queen's highness', he wrote, 'hath not authority to compel any man to believe anything contrary to God's word, neither may the subject give her grace the obedience, in case he do his soul is lost for ever without repentance. Our bodies, goods, and lives be at her commandment. . . . But the soul of man for religion is bound to none but unto God and his holy word.' The covenant which he had signed began with the statement that 'I have now joined myself to the church of Christ wherein I have yielded myself subject to the discipline of God's word as I promised at my baptism.' While it is anachronistic to call the church or churches which used this covenant 'the first Congregational churches', we do have here one of the

---

[1] Ibid. i. 133–6, ii. 69–70. Collinson, *Elizabethan Puritan Movement*, p. 134.
[2] Ibid., p. 148.

essential ingredients of the Congregationalism of the following century. A copy of the covenant was preserved among the papers of Archbishop Parker: 'To this protestation', noted the archbishop, 'the congregation singularly did swear, and after took the communion for ratification of their assent.'[1]

3. REFORMATION 'WITHOUT TARRYING FOR ANY': ROBERT BROWNE AND THE NORWICH SEPARATISTS

Archbishop Parker died in 1575, and the subsequent translation of Grindal from York to Canterbury offered to Puritans the brief hope that the Church of England would be purged of its popish ceremonies and provided with a godly clergy. His episcopate would justify the actions of those Marian exiles who had accepted bishoprics under Elizabeth, of men who, as Grindal had written to Henry Bullinger in 1566, had decided 'not to desert our churches for the sake of a few ceremonies . . . since the pure doctrine of the Gospel remained in all its integrity and freedom'.[2] But Grindal's experiences as Archbishop of Canterbury showed that Elizabeth had no more intention of allowing the freedom of the Gospel than she had of permitting liberties in ceremonial. The 1560s and early 1570s had witnessed the growing popularity of meetings known as 'prophesyings'— periodic gatherings in market towns of the clergy of the surrounding countryside for the study and exposition of the Scriptures. These deliberations were often open to the public and proved a fruitful means both of providing what Collinson calls 'extra-mural education' for the clergy and of stimulating theological debate among the laity. Such proceedings were far removed from Elizabeth's conception of the functions of a national church: free expression among the clergy and theological debate among the laity could alike in her eyes lead to sedition. She ordered Grindal to suppress the prophesyings and to reduce the number of licensed preachers to three or four per

---

[1] Peel, *First Congregational Churches*, pp. 22–3, 37–8. Peel, *Seconde Parte*, i. 55–9. J. Strype, *The Life and Acts of Matthew Parker* (1821), ii. 283–5. Champlin Burrage claimed that one version of this declaration was the covenant of Richard Fitz's church (*EED* ii. 13), but there appears to be no positive evidence to link the covenant with Fitz's congregation apart from the fact that a printed copy follows the church's petition in the state papers in the PRO. State Papers, Domestic, Elizabeth, S.P. 15, Addenda vol. xx, 107.

[2] *Zurich Letters*, i. 169.

county, and when the archbishop refused he was suspended from office and confined to his palace. But other Elizabethan bishops were only too anxious to show obedience to the royal will and Edmund Freke of Norwich began the systematic silencing of Puritan preachers. It was in the light of these proceedings that some of the inhabitants of the city of Norwich proved receptive to the views of Robert Browne and Robert Harrison when, in 1581, they tried to repeat Richard Fitz's experiment of forming a Separatist church.

Robert Browne was the son of Anthony Browne of Tolethorpe Hall, Little Casterton, Rutland, 'a man of some countenance' and a kinsman of Lord Burghley, Elizabeth's Lord Treasurer. Both Browne and Harrison were undergraduates at Cambridge in 1570 when Cartwright was electrifying the university with his lectures on the Acts of the Apostles and Browne 'suffered . . . some trouble' for embracing Puritan views. After graduating from Corpus Christi in 1572 Browne taught at a school in an unnamed town, 'having a special care to teach religion with other learning', but he soon became convinced that the 'woeful and lammentable state of the church' was hampering him in his task, and his outspokenness on this point resulted in his dismissal. Browne, though, had friends at Cambridge and when his old college took over St. Bene't's church in 1578 he was invited to preach there with a view to a permanent appointment. But once in the pulpit he seized the opportunity to challenge the authority of the bishops and to denounce them as 'ravenous and wicked persons' who sought rather 'their own advantage, or glory, or mischievous purpose, than the welfare and benefit of the church'. Since the church could not choose its bishops, he argued, 'nor those hirelings whom the bishops thrust upon them', the bishops aspired to 'be greater than the church'. 'With whom then', he asked, 'do they compare themselves in degree, but with Christ? and so make themselves antichrists.' They had no right, Browne maintained, to license preachers, and when his brother obtained two preaching licences for him 'he lost one and burned another'.[1]

At this juncture Browne came across Robert Harrison, whom

[1] *The Writings of Robert Harrison and Robert Browne*, ed. A. Peel and L. H. Carlson (1953), pp. 397–404.

he had known in his undergraduate days when both were at Corpus Christi. Like Browne, Harrison was an erstwhile school teacher, for he had lost his post at Aylsham grammar school in 1574 when he had objected to the use of the sign of the cross at the baptism of his godchild, and he had subsequently secured appointment as master of St. Giles's hospital in Norwich. When Harrison revisited Cambridge around 1580 Browne was anxious to renew his acquaintance since he had heard that there were people in Norfolk who 'were very forward' in matters of religion, and when Harrison returned to Norwich Browne followed him and was accepted as a paying guest in his house.[1]

Hitherto Browne and Harrison were Puritans, not Separatists. In 1580 or 1581 they joined with 173 other Norfolk Puritans in signing a petition to the queen, urging her to sweep away 'the government of Antichrist . . . with all his archprelates'. Ministers, they proposed, should be chosen not by 'corrupt patrons' but in Presbyterian manner by 'the flock whose souls pertain to the ministers' charge, so that the judgement of the said flock in their choice be examined by a synod of lawful ministers'.[2] And B. R. White has discovered an anonymous Puritan work which can almost certainly be attributed to Browne and which dates from the early part of 1581, in which the writer defines 'the church' in Matthew 18: 17, not as a company of believers but as 'the ministers and elders that are chosen out of the congregation to watch over the rest of the flock'.[3]

But in the course of 1581 Browne developed his rejection of episcopal authority to the point of repudiating the established church itself. The bishops, he came to believe, had so polluted the church that a new beginning had to be made. 'Whereas God commandeth to plant and build his church by gathering the worthy and refusing the unworthy', the bishops forced 'the wretched to their worshippings and service, as if dogs might be thrust upon God for sweet sacrifice.' He came to the conclusion that reformation could not be achieved within the parochial system and declined an invitation to minister to St. Bene't's church. 'He saw the parishes in such spiritual bondage that

---

[1] Ibid., pp. 405–7.
[2] Peel, *Seconde Parte*, i. 157–60.
[3] B. R. White, 'A Puritan Work by Robert Browne', *Baptist Quarterly*, xviii (1959–60), 109–17.

whosoever would take charge of them must also come into bondage with them . . . he judged that the kingdom of God was not to be begun by whole parishes, but rather of the worthiest, were they never so few.' He abandoned the Puritan interpretation of Matthew 18: 17, and arrived at the view that authority in the church should rest, under Christ, with the company of believing Christians. 'The voice of the whole people,' he wrote, 'guided by the elders and forwardest, is said to be the voice of God.'[1]

Browne thus decided to set in train his own reformation, 'without tarrying for any'. He persuaded Robert Harrison to join him, though not without difficulty, for Harrison, unlike Browne, still thought that 'much good' could be done by Puritan ministers who continued to conform to the established church. None the less Browne convinced himself that Harrison had 'wholly yielded to the truth' and they and a few sympathizers 'gave their consent to join themselves to the Lord in one covenant and fellowship together'.[2] Browne attempted to propagate his new views in Bury St. Edmunds where, according to Bishop Freke, he preached at conventicles of a hundred people. He was arrested and twice imprisoned and finally decided, with Harrison and others of his congregation, to leave England to breathe the freer air of the Netherlands.[3]

Nearly fifty years earlier when Anabaptists were being put to the sword by the Habsburg authorities, Dutchmen had fled to England in the vain hope of finding safety. But now, and for the next half-century, with the successful revolt of the Dutch Calvinists against their Spanish rulers, the tide of refugees was to flow in the opposite direction. Browne and his followers settled in Middelburg in Zeeland, liberated from the Spaniards eight years earlier, where the strains of exile acted on their sensitive and scrupulous spirits to produce what was to be the common experience of English exiles in the Netherlands: dissension, divisions, and sometimes disillusionment. Their womenfolk exercised a disruptive influence: Browne, as pastor of the church, got into trouble for censuring Harrison's 'sister Allen', and there was also 'much ado' over Browne's own wife. They

[1] Ibid. 111. *Writings of Harrison and Browne*, pp. 399, 402, 404.
[2] Ibid., pp. 407–8, 422.
[3] D. C. Smith, 'Robert Browne, Independent', *Church History*, vi. 299, 302.

could not agree on whether the children of believing parents should or should not be regarded as members of the church, with Browne taking the stricter, Harrison the more lenient, view. And probably most serious of all, the issue over which Browne and Harrison had argued at Norwich was still unresolved: the attitude they should take to those who conformed to the Church of England.[1]

Browne's views were set out in a series of books he published in 1582.[2] For him the church was by definition 'planted or gathered', 'a company or number of Christians or believers which by a willing covenant made with their God are under the government of God and Christ'. Every member of the church should be a 'king, a priest, and a prophet under Christ': a king because he joined in pronouncing the church's censures, a priest because he shared in its ministry of prayer, a prophet because he should help to 'exhort, move, and stir up to the keeping' of Christ's laws. Just as the foundation of the church was a covenant relationship between Christians and God, so the proper relationship between church members and their pastors and elders was one based on mutual agreement: so that 'governors have right use of the submission and service of inferiors, and the inferiors also have the right use of their authority and guiding'. The officers of the church are 'persons receiving their authority and office of God', but they 'are called thereto by due consent and agreement of the church', 'according to the number of the most which agree'.[3]

We cannot be sure of the origin of Browne's notion of a mutual contract between governors and governed: contract theories of government had been widely held in the middle ages; the Biblical concept of a covenant between God and man had been emphasized, for theological rather than ecclesiastical purposes, by William Tyndale in England and by Oecolampadius, Zwingli, Capito, and other Rhineland and Swiss reformers; the Scottish Calvinists had drawn up a covenant to 'establish the most blessed word of God' in 1557; and, as we have seen, an English Separatist congregation had subscribed to a

[1] *Writings of Harrison and Browne*, pp. 425–8.

[2] *A Treatise of Reformation without tarrying for anie, A Treatise upon the 23 of Matthew,* and *A Book which sheweth the life and manner of all true Christians.*

[3] *Writings of Harrison and Browne*, pp. 253, 276, 334–41.

church covenant in the early 1570s.[1] But a proximate influence may have been the *Vindiciae contra Tyrannos*, published by a French Huguenot in 1579 to justify resistance to rulers who contravened God's will. As Browne was in effect to do, the author of the *Vindiciae* postulated a double covenant: 'the first between God, the king, and the people, that the people might be the people of God', and 'the second between the king and the people, that the people shall obey faithfully and the king command justly'.[2] Browne's chief concern was, of course, to use this concept of a double covenant in the ecclesiastical rather than in the political sphere, but he too was prepared to apply it to 'the civil state'. 'Civil magistrates', wrote Browne in words reminiscent of the *Vindiciae*, 'are persons authorised of God', but they are 'received and called by consent and agreement of the people.'[3]

Wherever sixteenth-century Calvinists found themselves in positions of political power they used the authority of the state to further reformation and to enforce godliness. Only in places such as France where they were on the defensive did they protest against the prince's authority 'to enforce the consciences, which appertains chiefly to Jesus Christ'.[4] Robert Browne, whose prospect of furthering reformation in his native land was far more remote than that of any French Huguenot, adopted an equivocal position on the relationship of church and state. In the hope that the English government might yet tolerate his views he protested his loyalty to Elizabeth and, safely out of her reach in the Netherlands, agreed that she had the right to 'put to death all that deserve it by law, either of the church or commonwealth'. He was conscious of the need to justify the overthrow of the Roman Catholic Church in England by royal authority, and argued that just as Moses had reformed the religion of Israel 'so may our magistrates reform the church and command things expedient for the same'. But whatever

---

[1] L. J. Trinterud, 'The Origins of Puritanism', *Church History* xx (1951), 39, 41. White, *Separatist Tradition*, pp. 55–6. C. Burrage, *The Church Covenant Idea* (Philadelphia, 1904), pp. 28–9.

[2] H. J. Laski, ed., *A Defence of Liberty against Tyrants* (Gloucester, Mass, 1963), p. 71.

[3] *Writings of Harrison and Browne*, pp. 335, 339. Cf. *A Defence of Liberty*, pp. 118, 143.

[4] *Defence of Liberty*, p. 66.

justification state intervention in ecclesiastical affairs may have had in the past, Browne was anxious to limit its authority over his own gathered church. The civil magistrates, he wrote, have no authority over the church as 'prophets, priests, or spiritual kings', but only in so far as the church forms part of the commonwealth. 'To compel religion, to plant churches by power, and to force a submission to ecclesiastical government by laws and penalties belongeth not to them . . . neither yet to the church.' 'For it is the conscience and not the power of man that will drive us to seek the Lord's kingdom.' 'The Lord's people is of the willing sort.'[1]

Browne had been 'a means to bring the truth to light in many points concerning the true government of the church', Robert Harrison acknowledged, but in his eyes Browne's *Treatise of Reformation* contained 'manifold heresy'.[2] Harrison agreed with Browne that the Church of England was not the true church of Christ, that its ministers were for the most part 'blind guides and dumb dogs, destroyers and murderers of souls', that they failed in their duty of 'separating good from the bad'.[3] None the less, as in his Norwich days, Harrison continued to believe that there were many 'true worshippers' in the established church. While Browne was anxious to restrict the authority of the state in ecclesiastical matters, Harrison looked hopefully to the civil power to complete the Reformation. Whereas Browne had argued that Christians should not 'tarry for the magistrates' in setting right the church,[4] Harrison was anxious to dispel any suspicion that he was seeking to take the authority to reform the church 'out of Caesar's hand'. And while Browne had protested vigorously against coercion in religion, Harrison was ready to concede to the civil magistrates the right 'to strike with their sword everyone which, being of the church, shall openly transgress against the Lord's commandments'.[5]

Clashes over principles became intertwined with conflicts of personalities. Harrison accused Browne of 'antichristian pride and bitterness', Browne complained that his congregation forsook him, took away his servant, sold his books, charged him with debts he did not owe, and threatened to turn him and

---

[1] *Writings of Harrison and Browne*, pp. 152, 164, 162.
[2] Ibid., pp. 93, 149.   [3] Ibid., pp. 34–6.   [4] Ibid., p. 164.
[5] Ibid., pp. 119–20.

his wife out of their lodgings.[1] Finally Browne left Middelburg for Scotland, only to find the Presbyterian kirk even less tolerant than the English bishops,[2] and, disillusioned by his experiences, in 1584 he returned to England.

In the summer of the previous year, 1583, Elizabeth had issued a proclamation against the 'seditious, schismatical, and erroneous printed books' of Harrison and Browne, and two men who had circulated their writings in East Anglia, John Copping and Elias Thacker, had been hanged.[3] Browne himself was arrested in 1585 and saved from possible similar fate by the intervention of his kinsman Lord Burghley. Browne was persuaded to make submission to the established church and was freed from prison, henceforward to be denigrated by conformists as a coward and by Separatists as an apostate to their cause.[4] In 1586 he was appointed master of St. Olave's school in Southwark and five years later, again through Burghley's influence, was instituted as rector of the Northamptonshire village of Achurch. But something of the old cantankerousness, if not the courage, remained: in 1588 it was alleged that he was still disseminating Separatist views and neglecting to take the sacrament at his parish church, and George Knifton, later to become an elder in the London Separatist church, claimed that it was 'Browne who persuaded him not to receive the communion'.[5] After a quarter of a century of apparent peace as rector of Achurch in 1617 he again fell foul of ecclesiastical authority for failing to conform to the ceremonies prescribed by the Prayer Book. He was suspended from his duties, excommunicated in 1631, and finally died in his eighties in Northampton gaol in 1633, to which he had been committed for striking a village constable.[6] Harrison was not blessed, or perhaps cursed, by such longevity: he died in Middelburg around 1585, faithful to the end to his separation from the Church of England. Yet it was Browne, not Harrison, who gave his name

[1] Ibid., pp. 93, 428–9.   [2] Ibid., p. 519.

[3] R. W. Dale, in his *History of English Congregationalism* (1907), pp. 141–2, is wrong in stating that William Dennis of Norfolk was also hanged in 1583. The execution of Dennis appears to have taken place some ten years later. W. Walker, *Creeds and Platforms of Congregationalism* (Boston, Mass., 1960), p. 52.

[4] Smith, 'Robert Browne', pp. 315–18.

[5] Ibid., p. 324. Burrage, *EED* i. 120.

[6] Smith, 'Robert Browne', pp. 338, 344–6.

to Separatism and who was the true progenitor of modern
Dissent. Whatever his faults, and they were no doubt many,
before his spirit became embittered by disappointment he saw
more clearly than his one-time friend that religion is a matter
of private conscience rather than public order, that the church
is a fellowship of believers rather than an army of pressed men.
The kingdom of God, he wrote, cannot come through Parliament or the bishops' decrees: 'the kingdom of God should be
within you'.[1]

4. 'IMPRISONMENTS, JUDGEMENT, YEA, DEATH ITSELF':
GREENWOOD, BARROW, PENRY, AND THE LONDON
SEPARATISTS

The death of Harrison and the recantation of Browne impeded
but did not halt the advance of the Separatist tide. Just as
Archbishop Parker's 'Advertisements' had given rise to the
Separatist conventicles of the late 1560s and Bishop Freke's
suspension of Puritan preachers had set the scene for the activities of Browne and Harrison in Norwich in 1581, so the death of
Archbishop Grindal and the translation of John Whitgift from
Worcester to Canterbury in 1583 provoked further separation
from the established church. Whitgift had once entertained
Puritan sympathies, but he was not the man to let scruples
about the wearing of the surplice stand in the way of his
advancement and as vice-chancellor of Cambridge University
in the early 1570s he had led the opposition to Cartwright's
Presbyterian views.[2] Whitgift was by nature a strict discipli-
narian: as Archbishop of Canterbury he sought to impose on
the English church the same uniformity which, as master of
Trinity College, he had imposed on his undergraduates, and
he began his archiepiscopate by demanding that his clergy
subscribe to the Prayer Book as containing 'nothing contrary
to the word of God'.[3] Among the few ministers who, rather than
subscribe, resigned or were deprived of their livings was a
Norfolk clergyman named John Greenwood. Greenwood made

---

[1] *Writings of Harrison and Browne*, p. 157.
[2] Collinson, *Elizabethan Puritan Movement*, pp. 123–4.
[3] H. C. Porter, *Reformation and Reaction in Tudor Cambridge* (Cambridge 1958),
pp. 170–1.

his way to London and there joined up with a small group of Separatists who sought 'the fellowship and communion' of God's servants, 'and together with them' entered into 'covenant with the Lord'.[1]

These London Separatists were the remnant of earlier Separatist churches. In October 1587 Greenwood and twenty others were arrested while he was 'reading a portion of Scripture' at a conventicle in the house of Henry Martin in the parish of St. Andrew's in the Wardrobe, near to St. Paul's.[2] Among those taken prisoner were Edith Bury, who had been arrested at the goldsmith's house nearly twenty years before and had signed the petition of Richard Fitz's church in 1571; Nicholas Crane, the Puritan minister who had been associated with the London Separatists in the Minories in 1569; and John Chandler, who had been a member of Robert Browne's church at Middelburg.[3] The company was probably betrayed by an informer for a certain Clement Gamble, a servant of one of the congregation, was at the conventicle but was allowed to go free and later gave evidence against them.[4] Greenwood was committed to the Clink, and his imprisonment led in turn to that of a man who was to become one of the most effective of the early Separatist propagandists, Henry Barrow.

Barrow, a graduate of Clare College, Cambridge, and a former member of Gray's Inn, was apparently well connected for he had attended Elizabeth's court and was 'a vain and libertine youth' until a sermon by some unknown preacher convinced him of the error of his ways.[5] Not only was Barrow 'turned Puritan' but he befriended the Separatist Greenwood, and while visiting his friend in prison in November 1587 was arrested on Whitgift's orders. Your crimes, the archbishop told him, are 'that you come not to church, are disobedient to her majesty, and say that there is not a true church in England'.[6] Whitgift, exploded the hot-tempered Barrow at a subsequent

---

[1] *The Writings of Henry Barrow, 1587–90*, ed. L. Carlson (1962), pp. 81, 84. Burrage, *EED* i. 122.

[2] Burrage, *EED* ii. 19–20. *The Writings of John Greenwood*, ed. L. *Carlson* (1962), p. 312.

[3] Burrage, *EED* i. 122–3, 108–9, ii. 11, 18, 20.

[4] *Writings of Greenwood*, pp. 292, 294.

[5] F. J. Powicke, *Henry Barrow and the Exiled Church of Amsterdam* (1900), pp. 1–8.

[6] *Writings of Barrow, 1587–90*, p. 96.

interrogation, 'is a monster, a miserable compound . . . neither ecclesiastical nor civil, even that second beast spoken of in the Revelation'.[1] That outburst, before the Privy Council, may well have sealed his fate.[2]

Though deprived of their leaders, the Separatists continued to meet. In summer, revealed the informer Gamble, they gathered 'in the fields a mile or so about London' where 'they sit down upon a bank and divers of them expound out of the Bible'. In winter 'they assemble themselves by five of the clock in the morning to that house where they make their conventicle for that Sabbath day . . . they continue in their kind of prayer and exposition of Scripture all that day'. They did not use the Lord's Prayer, nor any type of set prayer, for 'they teach that all stinted prayers and read service is but babbling in the Lord's sight'; they permitted laymen to speak in their meetings, since 'every man in his own calling was to preach the gospel'; and they excommunicated offenders by giving them 'over to the hands of Satan'. After their religious exercises they dined together and then made 'collection to pay for their diet, and what money is left some of them carrieth it to the prisons where any of their sect is committed'.[3] That duty was one which they were increasingly called upon to discharge.

Though the Separatists changed their place of meeting frequently they were never safe from Whitgift's pursuivants. On one occasion more than fifty were arrested during a service in Islington woods, 'the very place where the persecuted church and martyrs were enforced to use like exercise in Queen Mary's days'.[4] By March 1593, complained a Separatist petition, there were some 'threescore and twelve persons, men and women, young and old, lying in cold, hunger, dungeons, and irons', denied meat, fire, and drink. Seventeen or eighteen had died 'in the same noisome gaols within these six years', among them the aged Nicholas Crane and John Chandler, leaving a widow and eight children.[5] The coffin of one, Roger Rippon, was sent to the house of the judge who had sentenced him, 'the last of sixteen or seventeen', so the inscription on the lid read, 'which that great enemy of God, the Archbishop of Canterbury, with

[1] Ibid., p. 188.   [2] Ibid., p. 177.
[3] *Writings of Greenwood*, pp. 294–5.   [4] Powicke, *Barrow*, p. 64.
[5] Burrage, *EED* ii. 110.

his high commissioners, have murdered in Newgate within these five years, manifestly for the testimony of Jesus Christ'.[1] 'Is not this a Christian bishop?' was Barrow's own bitter comment on Whitgift.[2]

Prison did not weaken their resolution. Though Barrow complained that 'ink and paper were kept from him' and that his writings were rifled,[3] he, and to a lesser extent Greenwood, kept up a formidable flow of propaganda during their years in prison. By means of letter, tract, and book, smuggled out of prison sheet by sheet, they hammered at their fourfold thesis that the 'disordered assemblies' of the Church of England worshipped 'God after a false manner', received 'the profane ungodly multitudes' into 'the bosom of the church', maintained 'a false and unchristian ministry', and were ruled by 'an antichristian and ungodly government'.[4] To Greenwood and Barrow Robert Browne was an apostate with whom 'we never had anything to do',[5] but their views were very similar and B. R. White has suggested that all three drew on the common tradition of the London Separatists of the late 1560s.[6] Unhappily, though, Barrow retreated from the voluntaryist principle enunciated by Browne in his finest passages. It was the duty of princes, wrote Barrow, to compel the profane 'to the hearing of the word', 'to advance and establish . . . the true worship and ministry of God', and 'to suppress and root out all contrary'.[7] Whitgift agreed: in March 1593 Barrow and Greenwood were convicted of devising 'seditious books' and on 6 April they were hanged at Tyburn.[8]

Those books, however, had already done their work. Too dangerous to be published in England, they were printed in the Netherlands where, in 1591, the English ambassador tried to suppress them. He sought the assistance of Francis Johnson, minister to the English Merchant Adventurers at Middelburg. Johnson, once a Fellow of Christ's College, Cambridge, had suffered imprisonment and lost his fellowship in 1589 for his advocacy of a Presbyterian system of church government. But

---

[1] W. Pierce, *John Penry* (1920), p. 374. [2] *Writings of Barrow, 1587–90*, p. 64.
[3] Powicke, *Barrow*, p. 33. [4] *Writings of Barrow, 1587–90*, p. 120.
[5] *Writings of Greenwood*, p. 240.
[6] *Writings of Barrow, 1587–90*, pp. 64, 207. White, *Separatist Tradition*, pp. 72–3.
[7] *Writings of Barrow, 1587–90*, pp. 156, 228.
[8] Powicke, *Barrow*, pp. 75–9.

though a Puritan, Johnson was no friend of Separatism and he eagerly complied with the ambassador's request. With the consent of the Dutch authorities the printing was seized and the books were burnt. Johnson's curiosity, though, got the better of him and he saved two from the flames 'that he might see their errors'. But instead of discovering their errors he was impressed by their argument, so impressed that he travelled to London to confer with Barrow and Greenwood in prison, 'after which conference he was so satisfied and confirmed in the truth' that he did not return to Middelburg but joined the Separatist church in London and in September 1592 was elected its pastor.[1]

About the same time the Separatists received another distinguished accession. John Penry was a graduate of Peterhouse, Cambridge, and of St. Alban's Hall, Oxford, but he was also a native of Breconshire, and while in England the spiritual desolation of his homeland weighed heavily on his soul. The religious destitution of Wales was well attested both by the bishops and by their critics. In 1560 Bishop Meyrick of Bangor had inquired of the clergy of his diocese whether they had ever preached and whether they kept concubines, and the inquiry seems to have yielded more concubines than preachers.[2] Twenty years later Bishop Middleton of St. David's found only fourteen preachers in his diocese, the Gospel hindered, he wrote, through 'ignorant pastors' and the people perishing 'for want of food'.[3] And although an Act of Parliament of 1563 had provided for the translation of the Scriptures into Welsh, it was not until twenty-five years later that the first Welsh Bible appeared.[4]

Penry attempted to awaken Parliament to what he considered to be its religious responsibilities towards Wales. In 1587, in his *Aequity of an Humble Supplication,* he called for the provision of Welsh-speaking preachers in Welsh-speaking areas, for the removal of Welsh-speaking clergymen from England to Wales, for the use of lay preachers to make good the dearth of ordained men, for an end to pluralism and clerical absenteeism. As a result Penry was hauled before Whitgift and his High Commis-

---

[1] W. H. Burgess, *John Smith, the Se-Baptist, Thomas Helwys and the First Baptist Church in England* (1911), pp. 29–34.

[2] T. Rees, *History of Protestant Nonconformity in Wales* (2nd edn. 1883), p. 4. Pierce, *John Penry,* p. 120.

[3] Pierce, *John Penry,* p.127.   [4] Ibid., pp. 110, 117.

sion and imprisoned in the Gatehouse for a month, an experience which turned him into a determined opponent of episcopacy. He played an important part in the printing of the Marprelate tracts, with their penetrating satirization of 'petty pope' Whitgift and the rest of the 'covetous popish bishops', and on the arrest of the tracts' printer, John Hodgkins, he escaped to Scotland. As in the case of Robert Browne five years earlier, Penry's stay in Scotland did not endear him to Presbyterianism, but while Browne had thus been led to return to the Anglican fold Penry's experiences in Scotland led him to Separatism. He returned to London around September 1592, still hoping 'to employ my small talent in my poor country of Wales', and joined the Separatist church of which Francis Johnson had just been chosen pastor.[1]

Johnson and Penry were not to remain free for long. In December Johnson was arrested at the home of Edward Boyes, a haberdasher in Fleet Street, and in March 1593 Penry was caught in Stepney. Johnson was kept in prison for four years, Penry was less fortunate. The young Welshman, by assisting in the printing of the Marprelate tracts, had, like Henry Barrow, committed the unforgivable crime of insulting the arrogant Whitgift. On 29 May 1593, six weeks after the execution of Barrow and Greenwood, Penry shared their fate. 'Imprisonments, judgement, yea, death itself,' he had told his accusers, 'are not meet weapons to convince men's consciences, grounded on the word of God.'[2]

Whitgift perhaps suspected as much. If not even threat of the scaffold could put an end to Separatism, perhaps the Separatists themselves could be persuaded to make a more civilized exit. In April 1593 there was passed *An Act for Retaining the Queen's Subjects in their due Obedience*. Anyone over the age of sixteen who refused to attend church for a month, or who attempted to persuade others not to attend church, or who attended unauthorized religious meetings, was to be committed to prison. If the offender did not conform within three months he was to be given the alternative of exile or death. Most Separatists chose exile rather than risk execution and Johnson's church, with their leader still in prison, left for the

---

[1] Ibid., pp. 169–70, 174–7, 303–5, 356.
[2] Ibid., pp. 366, 385.

Netherlands. After some wanderings and much hardship they settled in Amsterdam, assisted by a legacy which Barrow had bequeathed to them and by gifts from a church of English merchants on the Barbary coast.[1] Four years after the passing of the Act Francis Johnson and his brother George were released from gaol on the understanding that they would join an expedition of Merchant Adventurers to the Gulf of St. Lawrence and there settle. But the captains of the two ships in which they sailed were more concerned with immediate prospects of privateering than with the slower rewards of settlement, and after losing one ship to the French but capturing another they returned to Southampton and in September 1597 Johnson was able to rejoin his church at Amsterdam.[2]

The history of the reunited church, though, was far from happy. George Johnson claimed that his brother was appropriating too much authority to himself, and as in the case of Browne's church at Middelburg there was trouble over the pastor's wife. Edward Boyes, the haberdasher at whose house Francis Johnson had been arrested in 1592, had died soon afterwards and in 1594 Johnson married his widow. When she arrived in Amsterdam Mrs. Johnson continued to dress in the manner to which she had been accustomed as the wife of a prosperous trader. This aroused the anger of her tactless and censorious brother-in-law. George Johnson objected to her use of lace, ruffs, and musk, to the number of rings on her fingers, to the whalebones in her petticoats which he claimed hindered the conceiving or procreating of children, and to her 'wearing of the long white breast after the fashion of young dames, and so low she wore it, as the world calls them cod-piece breasts'. To add to her faults she flaunted herself in shop doors, quaffed her wine greedily, and stayed in bed on Sundays until nine o'clock. The sympathies of the church, however, were with their pastor and his wife. George Johnson was excommunicated, returned to England, and died in Durham gaol, giving out 'very heavy and great exclamations about his sins'.[3]

[1] Powicke, *Barrow*, p. 224.   [2] Burgess, *John Smith*, pp. 37–41.
[3] Burrage, *EED* i. 160–2.

5. 'GOD WOULD HAVE ALL MEN SAVED':
JOHN SMYTH, THOMAS HELWYS, AND THE GENERAL
BAPTISTS

Francis Johnson's troubles did not end with the departure of his brother, for in 1608 an even more disturbing character appeared on the Amsterdam scene. John Smyth had been a student of Johnson's at Christ's College and was indebted to him for his Puritan views.[1] Like his tutor Smyth had been elected to a fellowship and subsequently, in 1600, was appointed lecturer by the corporation of Lincoln, entrusted with the tasks of acting as chaplain to the mayor and preaching twice a week. But Smyth's vigorous, outspoken sermons were not to the taste of all his paymasters. They objected both to his 'erroneous doctrines' and to his 'personal preaching at men in this city' and in October 1602 he was dismissed from his post.[2] Smyth was awarded financial compensation for the loss of his lectureship, but he was further humiliated in the following year when his preaching licence was withdrawn; and when he was subsequently prosecuted in 1606 for reading public prayers in the Gainsborough parish church, on a day when the officiating minister had failed to turn up, his loyalty to the established church was finally undermined.[3]

Five months after Smyth had been deprived of his lectureship at Lincoln, in March 1603, James VI of Presbyterian Scotland had succeeded to the English throne, and the optimism aroused in Puritan circles by this event turned to disillusionment as it was realized that James's experience of Presbyterianism had simply convinced him of the virtues of episcopacy. The publication of the canons of 1604, excommunicating those who maintained that either the Prayer Book or episcopal government was contrary to the word of God, provided a further stimulus to Dissent. Some two years later a group of Puritans living in the lower Trent valley, at the point at which the boundaries of Lincolnshire, Nottinghamshire, and Yorkshire converge, seceded from the established church and

[1] Burgess, *John Smith*, p. 235.
[2] Ibid., pp. 51–2. W. T. Whitley, ed., *The Works of John Smyth* (Cambridge, 1915), vol. i, p. xl.
[3] Burrage, *EED* i. 229. White, *Separatist Tradition*, pp. 118–21.

'as the Lord's free people joined themselves (by a covenant of the Lord) into a church estate'.[1] Their number included William Brewster, the postmaster of Scrooby and bailiff of the Archbishop of York, who had got into trouble in 1598 for his Puritan habit of repeating sermons in the parish church;[2] Richard Clifton, who had been deprived of his living as rector of Babworth in 1605; Hugh Bromhead, curate of North Wheatley; Thomas Helwys, a landed gentleman of Broxtowe Hall near Nottingham; and William Bradford, the seventeen-year-old son of an Austerfield farmer and the future Governor of the Plymouth colony in New England. They were led by John Robinson, a former Fellow of Corpus Christi College, Cambridge, who had been deprived of his living in Norwich in 1604 for refusing to conform to the canons and had returned to his native Sturton-le-Steeple in Nottinghamshire; and by John Smyth.

Governor Bradford, in his subsequent recollections, stated that the Separatists 'became two distinct bodies or churches' on account of the distance between those living in the Gainsborough area and those living near Scrooby, but the reliability of his memory has been questioned both by H. M. Dexter and by W. T. Whitley, who suggest that the division did not take place until after persecution had driven them to the Netherlands in 1608.[3] John Robinson's own memoirs, though, suggest that the division did take place in England, but that the reason was theological rather than geographic, for Robinson could not agree with Smyth in rejecting private fellowship as well as public communion with Puritans who remained within the established church.[4] But, whatever the initial cause, by 1608 the Separatists from the lower Trent valley had divided into two groups. The first, based on Gainsborough, including Helwys and Bromhead, chose Smyth as their pastor while still in England and accompanied him to Amsterdam in 1608. The second, including Brewster and Bradford, also emigrated to the

---

[1] W. Bradford, *Of Plymouth Plantation*, ed. S. E. Morison (New York, 1952), p. 9.

[2] R. A. Marchant, *The Puritans and the Church Courts in the Diocese of York* (1960), pp. 141–2.

[3] Bradford, *Plymouth Plantation*, p. 9. H. M. and M. Dexter, *The England and Holland of the Pilgrims* (1906), p. 384. *Works of John Smyth*, vol. i, pp. lxviii–lxix.

[4] *The Works of John Robinson*, ed. R. Ashton (1851), ii. 102–3.

Netherlands in 1608, but either in England or in exile elected Robinson as their leader. Already they were worried by the lengths to which Smyth was taking his repudiation of conventional religion.

John Smyth was a man of original mind, an enthusiast for new ideas who once having seized a notion would pursue it ruthlessly to its logical conclusion. For Smyth the consistency which indicated a closed mind was no virtue. 'The latter thoughts', he wrote in 1608, 'oft times are better than the former: and I do profess this . . . that I will every day as my errors shall be discovered confess them and renounce them.'[1] When he arrived in Amsterdam the strict Separatist position he had now reached led him into controversy even with the 'ancient' Separatist church of Francis Johnson. The first dispute concerned the use of the Scriptures in public worship. Puritans had always objected to the reading of homilies in the place of the preaching of sermons, but now Smyth took the scruple a stage further, objecting even to the reading of translations of the Bible. The Scriptures, he maintained, were inspired only in their original tongue. It was permissible for the church's officers to bring with them 'the originals of Hebrew and Greek, and out of them translate by voice', but to read them in translation was to introduce an element of formalism into worship and to impede the working of the Holy Spirit. On this ground Smyth's followers broke off communion with Johnson's church and denominated themselves 'the brethren of the Separation of the second English church at Amsterdam'.[2]

The second dispute between the two fellowships concerned church government. The dissensions which had racked Johnson's church since his arrival in Amsterdam had forcibly reminded him of the virtues of Presbyterianism, of which he had once been an advocate, and in order to restrain the petty quarrels fomented by the disciplining of members in full church meeting Johnson attempted to keep the discipline and government of the church in the hands of himself and the church's elders.[3] Henry Ainsworth, the teacher in Johnson's church, defended his pastor's practice. Christ, he wrote, had 'ordained a presbytery or eldership' to which all members should submit.

---

[1] *Works of John Smyth*, i. 271.   [2] Burgess, *John Smith*, pp. 122–30.
[3] Powicke, *Barrow*, p. 269.

He could not approve of popular government for 'Christian liberty (which all have) is one thing, the reins of government (which some have) is another thing'.[1]

Smyth replied with the clearest of all Separatist expositions of democracy in the church. While the pastors and elders, he conceded, had 'a leading, directing, and overseeing power . . . the last definitive determining sentence is in the body of the church whereto the eldership is bound to yield'. Though 'the church may do any lawful act without the elders . . . the elders can do nothing without the approbation of the body or contrary to the body'.[2] It is rare in a confrontation of this nature for one proponent to convince the other, but now it happened. Ainsworth saw the force of Smyth's argument and in 1610 he and others of like mind seceded from Johnson's church. Johnson himself died seven years later. Some of his church joined up again with Ainsworth, the rest left for Virginia, only to die aboard an over-crowded and disease-infested ship.[3]

The most important of all Smyth's new departures was his rejection of infant baptism. The question of baptism had long been a source of embarrassment to the Separatists. They maintained that the Church of England was not a true church yet they did not repudiate their baptism at the hands of that church. Henry Barrow had become utterly confused in his attempt to justify his position, yet he shrank from the logical conclusion of a second baptism, for Anabaptism was ever associated in the sixteenth-century mind with the events which had taken place at Münster in 1534–5 and with the rejection of the contemporary social and political order.[4] But Smyth did not shrink from logic. Not only the baptism of the Church of England, but the baptism of any infant, he now rejected as false. And his justification sprang, as did his objection to the reading of the Scriptures in worship, from his exalted conception of the role of the Holy Spirit. For baptism, he wrote, is not just 'washing with water', 'it is baptism of the Spirit, the confession of the mouth, and the washing with water'. How, he asked, can an infant be washed with the Spirit when it has no knowledge of sin, cannot repent, and cannot confess its repentance by

---

[1] H. Ainsworth, *Counterpoyson* (1608), pp. 176–7.
[2] Burgess, *John Smith*, pp. 137–8. *Works of John Smyth*, ii. 440.
[3] Powicke, *Barrow*, pp. 254–8.   [4] Ibid., p. 112–14.

mouth?[1] Smyth persuaded his company of the validity of his argument and in 1609 his church was reconstituted on the basis of believers' baptism. Smyth baptized first himself, then Thomas Helwys, then the rest of the company by the pouring of water over the face.

Smyth's action in re-baptizing both himself and his followers aroused fierce controversy. He defended himself with characteristic vigour by reference to the teachings of Scripture and the practice of the early church, but on one point his critics made their mark. Richard Clifton, the deprived rector of Babworth, 'a grave and fatherly old man' with 'a great white beard', had been converted to Separatism by Smyth and had followed him to Amsterdam.[2] But Clifton could not countenance Smyth's latest departure: he attached himself to Johnson's church and the case which he now presented against Smyth's action in baptizing himself could not easily be refuted. If Smyth could baptize himself, said Clifton, then any man could do likewise and churches could be established of solitary men, which would be absurd.[3] Smyth's defence was that 'there was no church to whom we could join with a good conscience to have baptism from them', but, as another critic pointed out, this was not true.[4] There existed in Amsterdam a church of Dutch people known as Waterlanders who practised believers' baptism and traced their spiritual descent through Menno Simons to the Anabaptists of the early sixteenth century. Smyth resolved to meet his critics by applying to the Waterlanders for membership and, if necessary, a third baptism.

In making his application Smyth drew up twenty articles of faith explaining his beliefs. The document shows that not only did Smyth agree with the Mennonites in the practice of believers' baptism but that he also concurred in their rejection of the Calvinist doctrines of original sin and predestined election and reprobation. Lonnie Kliever has argued that 'no Anabaptist influence need be considered significant' in Smyth's repudiation of Calvinism and has suggested possible alternative sources: the criticisms which were being levelled against Calvinism by Peter Baro at Cambridge in the 1590s while Smyth was a Fellow of

---

[1] *Works of John Smyth*, ii. 567–8.
[2] W. H. Burgess, *John Robinson, Pastor of the Pilgrim Fathers* (1920), p. 189.
[3] Burgess, *John Smith*, p. 154.   [4] *Works of John Smyth*, ii. 157; i, p. xcvi.

Christ's College; the views of the Dutch theologian Jacob Arminius who died at Leyden in 1609 and whose name was to become synonymous with the rejection of predestination; or Smyth's own independent study of the Bible.[1] But it is the timing of Smyth's conversion which suggests that it was Mennonite influence which was the decisive factor in his break with Calvinism. Had Smyth reached this position by 1608 it would have been evident from his dispute with the 'ancient' Separatist church in Amsterdam. It was, though, some two years later, after he had made contact with the Waterlanders, and not before, that Smyth confessed his belief that God 'has ordained all men (no one being reprobated) to life'. 'There is no original sin,' Smyth announced, 'but all sin is actual and voluntary.' 'God imposes no necessity of sinning on any one; but man freely, by Satanic instigation, departs from God.' The grace of God is not restricted to the supposedly elect, but is 'offered to all without distinction', and as men are able 'to repent, to believe, to turn to God, and to attain to eternal life', so 'they are able themselves to resist the Holy Spirit, to depart from God, and to perish for ever'.[2]

Smyth's action in seeking to join the Waterlanders divided his own church. Though Smyth might have doubts about the validity of his second baptism Thomas Helwys had no doubts about his own, and to Helwys Smyth's desire to seek baptism anew at the hands of an existing church looked suspiciously like a quest after apostolic succession.[3] Helwys and seven or eight others seceded from Smyth's church, leaving him but thirty-two members.[4] The Waterlanders for their part were wary of admitting the English Baptists into membership, and although Smyth and his companions attended their services, the question-mark hanging over the validity of their baptism prevented their immediate acceptance by the Dutch.[5]

[1] L. D. Kliever, 'General Baptist Origins', Mennonite Quarterly Review, xxxvi (1962), 316–17.

[2] W. L. Lumpkin, ed., Baptist Confessions of Faith (Philadelphia, 1959), p. 100. That one of Smyth's followers, Richard Overton, went even further in rejecting Calvinism by repudiating the doctrine of the immortality of the soul in favour of the widely held Anabaptist view that the soul dies with the body, also suggests Mennonite influence on the English exiles.

[3] Burrage, EED ii. 185–6.

[4] Works of John Smyth, i, p. cviii. Burgess, John Smith, pp. 182–4.

[5] Ibid., pp. 192–7.

The controversies and dissensions in which Smyth was involved were not without their compensations. Life was not easy, and to the pain caused by the parting from old friends was added economic hardship. A pathetic note by Smyth in one of his writings raises the question of whether, if the price of 'bread and wine be very great as it falleth out in some countries and some years, and the officers and poor want maintenance, the Lord's Supper may not be deferred, and not be administered every Lord's day'.[1] Smyth earned his living by practising medicine, which he did in a Christian spirit, taking no fees from the poor and giving his cloak to 'one slenderly apparelled'.[2] Yet the years in Amsterdam mellowed his spirit. The rapidity with which he changed his views, the privileges accorded the English exiles by their Dutch hosts, above all his contacts with the Mennonites and his rejection of predestination, persuaded him of the virtues of toleration. Hitherto the Separatists had developed no consistent theory of the separation of church and state: their primary objection was not to the principle of a state-enforced religion, but to the form of religion that was to be enforced. Robert Browne had groped his way confusedly towards the concept of a voluntary church in a free state, only to abandon this position by making submission to the established church; Henry Barrow had seen nothing wrong in the state enforcing outward conformity in religion, provided that it was the religion approved by Henry Barrow; and Francis Johnson's exiled church had in 1596 acknowledged the duty of princes 'to suppress and root out by their authority all false ministers, voluntary religions, and counterfeit worship of God'.[3] Henry Ainsworth, torn between his observation that compulsion in matters of religion produces hypocrites and his knowledge that the kings of Judah used their authority to suppress idolatry, denied the right of a prince to compel his subjects to join a church, but maintained the duty of Christian rulers to 'abolish all idolatry within their dominions' and to procure the conversion of their subjects 'by the word'.[4] John Robinson argued that while it was no part of a king's prerogative 'to compel an apparent profane person' to join or

---

[1] *Works of John Smyth*, i. 320. [2] Burgess, *John Smith*, p. 266.
[3] Walker, *The Creeds and Platforms of Congregationalism*, p. 71.
[4] Ainsworth, *Counterpoyson*, pp. 134, 224, 230.

remain in the church, godly magistrates might 'by some penalty or other provoke their subjects universally unto hearing for their instruction and conversion', and might even punish them 'if after due teaching, they offer not themselves unto the church'.[1] And John Smyth himself had written in 1607 that 'the erecting of visible churches appertaineth to princes' who 'must command all their subjects to enter into them'.[2] But five years later we have from his pen the first unequivocal plea for religious freedom for all Christians ever to come from an Englishman. 'The magistrate,' wrote Smyth, 'is not by virtue of his office to meddle with religion, or matters of conscience, to force and compel men to this or that form of religion or doctrine: but to leave Christian religion free, to every man's conscience, and to handle only civil transgressions, injuries, and wrongs of men against men.'[3]

Smyth came to learn the virtues not only of toleration, but of tolerance also. In 1612 he wrote a remarkable work *Called the Retractation of His Errours and the Confirmation of the Truth* in which he affirmed the beliefs for which he had suffered exile and dissension, yet withdrew the harsh words with which he had so often engaged in controversy. He regretted, he said, his 'former course of censuring other persons, and especially for all those hard phrases, wherewith I have in any of my writings, inveighed against either England or the Separation', for he now admitted that there were zealous Christians who misguidedly conformed to the established church, and that the words he had addressed to other Separatists had all too often been 'stout and mingled with gall'. He now desired 'to end controversies among Christians rather than to make or maintain them, especially in matters of the outward church and ceremonies', and differences of opinion about the outward church would not cause him 'to refuse the brotherhood of any penitent and faithful Christian whatsoever'.[4] These were the words of a dying man. In August 1612 Smyth succumbed to consumption, and three years later the remnant of his following was at last admitted to membership by the Waterlanders and was absorbed by them.[5]

---

[1] *Works of Robinson*, ii. 314–16.   [2] *Works of John Smyth*, i. 267.
[3] Ibid. ii. 748.   [4] Ibid. ii. 753–5.
[5] Burgess, *John Smith*, pp. 272–5.

Smyth had, though, made a lasting contribution to the religious life of his native land, for his views were taken back to England in moderated form by Thomas Helwys and the other secessionists. A *Declaration of Faith* published by Helwys and his followers in 1611 indicated that they could not follow Smyth in all his endeavours at union with the Mennonites. They affirmed their belief in original sin, asserted that God 'had predestinated that all that believe in him shall be saved', and repudiated the Mennonite contention that Christians should not take oaths or hold office as magistrates. At the same time though they retained Smyth's faith in believers' baptism, and while they held that believers were predestined to salvation they followed Smyth in rejecting the Calvinist notion that sinners were predestined to damnation. 'God would have all men saved', wrote Helwys; grace was God-given for men to receive or to reject.[1]

In 1612 Helwys and his small band, having come to the conclusion that it was better to 'lay down their lives in their own country for Christ' than to flee from persecution, returned to England.[2] Since they held to Smyth's belief that God's grace extended to all men, the church they founded at Spitalfields is rightly regarded as the first General Baptist church on English soil. Helwys continued to cherish and even to extend Smyth's views on religious liberty. In 1612 he addressed to James I an appeal for toleration, 'for men's religion . . . is betwixt God and themselves', and the king cannot judge 'between God and man'. Whereas Smyth had appealed for liberty for all Christians, Helwys pleaded for the toleration of all men. 'Let them be heretics, Turks, Jews, or whatsoever, it appertains not to the earthly power to punish them.'[3]

James was not convinced. One of Helwys's companions, John Murton, was in prison in 1613; it is possible that Helwys suffered likewise, certain that by 1616 he was dead.[4] It was

---

[1] Lumpkin, *Baptist Confessions of Faith*, pp. 117–23. Kliever, 'General Baptist Origins', pp. 311–13. Kliever's contention that the views of the English General Baptists owed nothing to the Waterlanders stands or falls on the assumption that Smyth did not derive his anti-Calvinist views from the Mennonites. As I have argued on p. 46 this is an improbable thesis.

[2] T. Helwys, *Mistery of Iniquity* (1935 facsimile of 1612 edition), p. 212. Burgess, *John Smith*, pp. 276–7.

[3] Helwys, *Mistery of Iniquity*, p. 69.

[4] Burrage, *EED* i. 256.

probably Murton who in 1620 addressed from Newgate prison *A Most Humble Supplication* to king and Parliament, written, it was said, in milk on paper brought to him 'as the stopples of his milk bottle', and which, on being smuggled out again, remained invisible until scorched by flame. The Baptists had suffered 'long and lingering imprisonments for many years in divers counties of England', complained Murton, 'in which many have died and left behind them widows and many small children'.[1] Yet despite this persecution the views of Helwys and Murton gained ground, welcomed, it may be conjectured, among people who cherished Lollard traditions and had some sympathy with Anabaptist beliefs. That such were not lacking in England in the reign of James I is shown by the trial and martyrdom of Edward Wightman in 1612. Fourteen years later contact between the English General Baptists and the Dutch Anabaptists was renewed when the former entered into negotiations for union with the Waterlanders of Amsterdam. Though nothing came of the negotiations, mainly because the English would not accept the Mennonite prohibition on the taking of oaths, their denial that a Christian might serve as a magistrate, and their repudiation of the use of arms, the correspondence does show that by 1626 there were some 150 General Baptists in England, gathered in churches in London, Coventry, Lincoln, Salisbury, and Tiverton.[2]

6. THE SEARCH FOR A MIDDLE WAY: HENRY JACOB AND THE 'RIGIDEST SORT' OF PURITANS

The theological innovations of Smyth and Helwys were repudiated by those Separatists from the lower Trent valley who chose Robinson as their pastor. This second group had also arrived in Amsterdam in 1608, but the dissensions in Johnson's church and the radicalism of Smyth's combined with the attractions of a university city to determine them to leave Amsterdam for Leyden in 1609.[3] Robinson's church soon attracted a growing number of English exiles until the original Nottinghamshire and Lincolnshire group was outnumbered by immigrants from Norfolk, Essex, London, and Kent and the

---

[1] Burgess, *John Smith*, pp. 306–9.
[2] Ibid., pp. 333–4. *TBHS* iv (1914–15), 252–4.
[3] Bradford, *Plymouth Plantation*, pp. 16–17.

church membership totalled 300.[1] Robinson had neither the originality of mind of Smyth nor the reckless bravery of Helwys, but he excelled as a pastor. It is a tribute to his moderation and to the love he evoked from his followers that as long as he lived, alone of the Separatist churches in exile, the Leyden church was neither troubled by internal strife nor rent by secession. When a section of his church, led by William Brewster, left Leyden in 1620 and sailed by way of Southampton and Plymouth to the New World, to come down in history as the Pilgrim Fathers, they remained in communion with the Leyden church and it was to their sorrow that Robinson, who died in 1625, was never able to join them.

Robinson and Johnson had both regarded the spread of Anabaptist ideas among the English exiles with horror, and what Robinson described as Smyth's 'instability and wantonness of wit'[2] produced a conservative reaction among the other English Separatists. In order to repudiate the need for a second baptism Johnson maintained that the Church of England and even the Church of Rome, though 'a notorious harlot and idolatress', were churches of God 'and under his covenant',[3] while Robinson himself lent a sympathetic ear to the singular opinions of Henry Jacob.

Jacob, an Oxford graduate and former precentor of Corpus Christi College, was a Puritan who in 1603 had played a major part in organizing the so-called Millenary Petition, the abortive attempt to persuade James I to abolish offensive ceremonies. Jacob had a Puritan's horror of Separatism: in 1596 he had visited Francis Johnson in prison to try to convince him of his 'great ignorance and errors' in separating from the established church, and he had subsequently published his case against Johnson in *A Defence of the Churches and Ministry of England*.[4] But some of Johnson's arguments left their mark on him and the position Jacob finally arrived at was midway between that of the Separatists and of the traditional Puritans. In 1604 Jacob published a work entitled *Reasons taken out of God's Word . . . proving a necessitie for reforming our Church in England,* for which he

---

[1] *Works of John Smyth*, i, p. lxxxiii. Dale, *English Congregationalism*, p. 204.

[2] Burgess, *Robinson*, p. 120.

[3] F. Johnson, *A Christian Plea Concerning three Treatises* (1617), pp. 120–1.

[4] H. Jacob, *A Defence of the Churches and Ministry of England* (Middelburg, 1599), p. 5.

was imprisoned for eight months, in which he made clear that
he had come to agree with Johnson that a universal, national,
provincial, or diocesan church did not constitute a true church.
'Only a particular ordinary constant congregation of Christians in Christ's testament', wrote Jacob, 'is appointed and
reckoned a visible church.' He also came to agree with the
Separatists that such a church should be 'constituted and
gathered . . . by a free mutual consent of believers joining and
covenanting to live as members of a holy society'. But what was
distinctive about Jacob's views was his belief that a gathered
church need not renounce communion with the parish churches
of England. For 'every particular ordinary congregation of
faithful people in England is a true and proper visible church',
argued Jacob, and 'every pastor of each particular church in
England is truly and properly a pastor of the same church
whereof he is'.[1]

Jacob's views were a compromise between what men had
hitherto regarded as irreconcilable positions, and, not surprisingly, historians have disagreed on the place which he
occupies in the ecclesiastical spectrum of his time. Nineteenth-
century historians of Congregationalism for the most part regarded Jacob as a Separatist, and it was one of Champlin
Burrage's many services to the study of early Dissent to draw
attention to Jacob's own repudiation of Separatism. Burrage
called Jacob an 'Independent Puritan', and Perry Miller,
following Burrage, used the term 'non-separatist Congregationalism' to describe Jacob's position. Geoffrey Nuttall, however, prefers to call Jacob a 'semi-Separatist', while Slayden
Yarbrough argues that Jacob was a 'moderate Separatist' on
the ground that he made a distinction between 'churches of
England' which were true churches and with which he was
prepared to communicate, and the Church of England whose
hierarchy he rejected.[2] All these terms, though, are open to

[1] H. Jacob, *Reasons taken out of God's Word* (1604), sig. A 2, pp. 5, 22, 35. Burrage,
EED ii. 157.

[2] Burrage, *EED* i. 287. P. Miller, *Orthodoxy in Massachusetts* (Gloucester, Mass.,
1965), pp. 73–6. G. F. Nuttall, *Visible Saints* (Oxford, 1957), p. 10. S. A. Yarbrough,
'Henry Jacob, A Moderate Separatist, and his Influence on Early English Congre-
gationalism', Baylor Univ. Ph.D. thesis, 1972, pp. 52–4, 93–5. W. R. Goehring,
'The Life and Death of Henry Jacob', *Hartford Quarterly*, vii (1966), 35–50, supports
Burrage. A balanced assessment is provided by R. S. Paul, 'Henry Jacob and
Seventeenth Century Puritanism', *Hartford Quarterly*, vii (1967), 92–113.

objection. Terms such as 'Independent Puritan' or 'non-separating Congregationalist', while accurate when used to describe Jacob's spiritual heirs, are anachronistic when applied to the early seventeenth century, and the term 'semi-Separatist' would have been vigorously repudiated by Jacob himself. In organizing a congregation outside the established church while continuing to communicate with those who remained within, Jacob was practising a form of occasional conformity which would not have deprived him of the title of Dissenter in the later seventeenth or eighteenth centuries, but at the time he lived his position was one which neither himself nor those who were indisputably Separatists would recognize as one of separation. The most appropriate term to use of Jacob's views on church government is the one which contemporaries themselves used, the eponymous term 'Jacobite'. For Henry Jacob gave his name to a group of like-minded Puritans who were to exercise considerable influence over the history of both old and New England in the first four decades of the seventeenth century.

Prominent among these early 'Jacobites' were William Bradshaw, deprived of his lectureship at Chatham in 1602, Paul Baynes, suspended from his lectureship at St. Andrew's, Cambridge, in 1604, Robert Parker, vicar of Stanton St. Bernard in Wiltshire, and William Ames, Fellow of Christ's College, Cambridge, who, after he fled to the Netherlands in 1610, became the leading theologian of the group.[1] How they arrived at their views on church government is not known, but it seems likely that a catalytic factor was James I's uncompromising rejection of Presbyterianism at the Hampton Court conference in 1604. If, as James said, Presbyterianism 'agreeth as well with a monarchy as God and the devil', then Puritans who hoped to see the early reformation of the Church of England had to espouse a form of ecclesiastical organization which would be less objectionable to the new king. William Bradshaw in his *English Puritanisme*, published in 1605, both repudiated the

[1] For Ames see K. L. Sprunger, *The Learned Doctor William Ames* (Urbana, Illinois, 1972). Robert Parker initially held that 'the use of synods was for counsel and advice only', but he subsequently came to the conclusion that synods had 'authority over particular churches' and became a member of the Dutch Presbyterian classis in Amsterdam. Nuttall, *Visible Saints*, p. 10. M. Finlayson, 'Independency in Old and New England', Univ. of Toronto Ph.D. thesis, 1968, pp. 153–4.

Presbyterian subjection of particular churches to the 'superior ecclesiastical jurisdiction' of synods and assemblies, and argued that his own concept of church government gave greater authority to the monarch than did episcopacy. It was not, he wrote, the equality of churches and of ministers, advocated by the 'rigidest sort' of Puritans, which was repugnant to monarchy, but the 'inequality of churches and church-officers' which had 'advanced Antichrist [i.e. the pope] unto his throne, and brought the kings and princes of the earth to such usage . . . that the civil authority and glory of secular princes and states hath ever decayed'.[1] In the same year the Jacobites petitioned James I for permission to organize a 'visible church' and to meet publicly for worship, provided that they took the oath of supremacy, paid 'all payments and duties both ecclesiastical and civil', and 'kept brotherly communion with the rest of our English churches' as did the churches of French and Dutch immigrants in England.[2]

Permission was not granted. In a further petition of 1609 Jacob and his followers assured the king that in their view 'ruling synods and united presbyteries', in so far as they sought the 'authority of imposing laws', usurped 'the supremacy of the civil magistrate'. But James merely noted that their 'Scottish brethren are endued with a contrary light', and could not understand why, if the Jacobites did not intend to challenge his authority in religious matters, they did 'not obey the king's laws that are already made'. In response to their *Supplication for Toleration* James commented that 'the too great toleration of you in Queen Elizabeth's time hath made you now to be prickles in our sides',[3] and Jacob, Parker, and Ames followed the Separatists to the Netherlands.

All three settled for a time in Leyden, and it is probable that it was the conversations which they had there with John Robinson which led the pastor of the Pilgrim Fathers to modify his Separatist views. It is not true, as Champlin Burrage and

---

[1] W. Bradshaw, *English Puritanisme* (1641 edn.), pp. 4, 6–7. Since *English Puritanisme* was first published anonymously and subsequently published in Latin translation by William Ames in 1610, the work is sometimes wrongly attributed to Ames.

[2] Burrage, *EED* ii. 163–4.

[3] H. Jacob, *A Supplication for Toleration addressed to King James I* (1609), reprinted with the king's notes by S. R. Maitland (1859), pp. 13, 32.

Horton Davies have maintained, that Robinson abandoned Separatism:[1] in the writing which is supposed to prove his change of heart he still maintained that he could not communicate with the Church of England 'without being condemned of mine own heart, and therein provoking God . . . to condemn me much more'.[2] But he did moderate his views to the extent that his final position was not unlike that which Robert Harrison had adopted in his controversies with Robert Browne. It seems that before he left England Robinson had disagreed with John Smyth's contention that Separatists should have no fellowship with Puritans who remained in the established church, and although he subsequently adopted the stricter view when he came into contact with other Separatist leaders in the Netherlands, in 1614 he reverted to his earlier opinion that those 'who profess a separation' from the Church of England might none the less 'lawfully communicate in private prayer . . . with the godly amongst them'.[3] Ten years later he went even further and wrote a treatise maintaining that it was lawful for members of separated, visible churches to hear sermons preached by godly ministers of the Church of England.[4] When the Pilgrim Fathers prepared to take leave of their pastor in 1620 Robinson is said to have urged them, in the New World, 'to endeavour to close with the godly party of the kingdom of England'.[5]

While the Jacobites moderated the Separatist views of John Robinson, they were themselves influenced by the Separatists.[6] In 1616 Henry Jacob returned to England and in Southwark he and a few followers 'covenanted together to walk in all God's ways as he had revealed or should make known to them'.[7] The wording of the covenant, as B. R. White points out, was very like that used by the Separatists and by Robinson's own church.[8] Jacob, like the Separatists, believed that it was lawful for any member of the church, except women, to engage in prophesying, and, like the Separatists, denied that the imposition of a compulsory tithe was a legitimate means of supporting

---

[1] Burrage, *EED* i. 293. Davies, *Worship and Theology*, i. 326–7.
[2] *Works of Robinson*, iii. 378.   [3] Ibid. iii. 103, 105.
[4] Ibid. iii. 342–78.   [5] Burgess, *Robinson*, p. 240.
[6] John Cotton admitted this in *The Way of the Congregational Churches cleared* (1648), p. 8.
[7] Burrage, *EED* i. 314.
[8] White, *Separatist Tradition*, p. 166. *Works of Robinson*, ii. 132.

ministers.[1] His church both recognized the Separatists as 'brethren in the common faith' and admitted them to communion.[2] But Jacob none the less still denied that he was guilty of separation or of 'undutifulness to the magistrate'. We do not refuse, he insisted, 'on occasion to communicate with the ordinary public congregations assembled for the exercise of religion in England'.[3]

Jacob's *media via* was scorned by both extremes. The London Separatists denounced his followers as 'idolators' for attending their parish churches, the authorities persecuted them as they would the frequenters of any other conventicle.[4] Trouble attended his church from 'within and without', and in the early 1620s Jacob emigrated to Virginia where he died in 1624.[5] None the less, in the 1620s and 1630s Jacob's attempt to reconcile the concept of a gathered church with conformity to the Church of England met with increasing favour among the more radical Puritans: when the Puritans who took control of the Massachusetts Bay Company in 1629 talked of 'the planting of the Gospel' in New England, it was the Gospel organized according to the ideas of Henry Jacob of which they spoke.[6]

The key to an understanding of the appeal which the views of Jacob, Ames, and Bradshaw had for the Puritans of the reigns of James I and Charles I lies in the near extinction of English Presbyterianism between 1590 and 1640. In the 1580s an incipient Presbyterian organization can be traced in the periodic conferences of Puritan ministers in London and the eastern counties, and it was in order to give this conference movement formal shape that in 1586 the Presbyterian leaders drew up a detailed blueprint for the organization of a Reformed Church of England, the Book of Discipline.[7] Frustrated by the repeated failure of Parliament to secure the further reformation of the established church, the Presbyterian leaders urged Puritan ministers to put the provisions of the Book of Discipline into

---

[1] H. Jacob, *A Confession and Protestation of the Faith of Certain Christians in England* (1616), sigs. C2, C7.

[2] Burrage, *EED* i. 317–18.   [3] Jacob, *A Confession*, sig. A2.

[4] *Works of Robinson*, iii. 382. Burrage, *EED* i. pp. 321–4.

[5] Burrage, *EED* i. 319. Goehring, 'Life and Death of Henry Jacob', p. 43.

[6] Miller, *Orthodoxy in Massachusetts*, p. 104.

[7] The Book of Discipline was published in 1644 as *A Directory of Church-Government* (facsimile edn. 1872), sig. C4.

immediate operation, in 'so far as it may be lawful' so to do.[1] It was a Presbyterian attempt to by-pass Parliament and to advance the Reformation, as Robert Browne would have said, 'without tarrying for any'.

The Presbyterians, like the Separatists, claimed to find the basis for their ecclesiastical organization in the New Testament, but in two vital respects, the nature of the church and authority within the church, Presbyterians and Separatists drew divergent conclusions from what they read in their Bibles. Whereas the Separatists confronted the Church of England with an alternative conception of the church—the gathered church to which only confessing believers could be admitted as members—the chief concern of the Presbyterians was with discipline within the existing established church. The Book of Discipline laid down that only those who have 'made confession of their faith, and submitted themselves to the Discipline' should be admitted to communion, but this sprang from a desire to purify existing parish congregations, not from any intention to construct the church anew. The Presbyterians, complained Henry Barrow, 'still would have the whole land to be the church, and every parish therein a particular congregation'.[2]

The question of authority within the church was the second main issue which divided Presbyterians from Separatists. Admittedly the Book of Discipline, like the works of Browne, Barrow, and Smyth, in theory accorded considerable powers to the congregation: in all the great affairs of the church, wrote the Elizabethan Presbyterians, 'as in excommunicating of any, and in choosing and deposing of church officers, nothing may be concluded without the knowledge and consent of the church'.[3] But this tendency towards democracy in the church was to be severely checked in two directions: by the eldership within the church, and by a hierarchy of conferences (or classes), synods, and assemblies without.

Both the Separatists and the Presbyterians distinguished four male officers in the church: pastors, who were responsible for preaching, teachers who had the task of instructing members in doctrine, elders who had oversight of the behaviour of members,

---

[1] Collinson, *Elizabethan Puritan Movement*, p. 317.

[2] *Writings of Barrow, 1587–90*, p. 558.

[3] *Directory of Church-Government*, sig. A3.

and deacons who were responsible for the care of the poor. To these the Separatists added a fifth officer, that of widow, a woman of sixty years or more who would be 'compassionate and helpful' to church members in adversity.[1] The Book of Discipline, however, provided the chief officers of the church, the pastor, teachers, and elders, with a formal organization, 'a presbytery, which is a consistory . . . as it were a senate of elders' to govern the church and to suspend, though not to excommunicate, communicants from the Lord's Supper.[2] Few Separatists were willing to yield to their officers so much authority. Robert Browne had spoken of the eldership as a meeting of 'the forwardest or wisest . . . for redressing and deciding of matters in particular churches', but it was the 'voice of the whole people', not the voice of the elders, which he equated with the voice of God.[3] Francis Johnson gave more power to the elders than did even the Book of Discipline, denying that 'the people are to have voices in excommunications',[4] but he was opposed by John Smyth and disowned by his own colleague Henry Ainsworth. And though John Robinson, in his more conservative phase, denied that the government of his church was democratic, maintaining that it was 'plainly aristocratical . . . administered by some certain choice men', he was using the term 'democratic' in its classical, not its modern sense. The constitution of a gathered church, as distinct from its government, was, acknowledged Robinson, 'after a sort popular and democratical', with the people freely voting 'in elections and judgements of the church'.[5] The Presbyterians were less equivocal. Their discipline, in the words of John Geree, was 'aristocratical by elders, not monarchical by bishops, nor democratical by the people'.[6]

The authority of the eldership as laid down in the Book of Discipline derived not only from its power to direct 'all things . . . that belong to the state' of the church, but also from the arrangement whereby it would be linked with the eldership of other churches through a system of conferences, synods, and

---

[1] *Writings of Harrison and Browne*, p. 275. *Writings of Barrow, 1587–90*, pp. 218–19.
[2] *Directory of Church-Government*, sig. A2.
[3] *Writings of Harrison and Browne*, pp. 271, 399.
[4] Johnson, *A Christian Plea*, p. 314.
[5] *Writings of Robinson*, iii. 42–3.
[6] Geree, *Character of an old English Puritane*, p. 4.

assemblies. Robert Browne had written vaguely of a synod as the joining 'of many churches . . . for redress and deciding of matters which cannot well be otherwise taken up', and Francis Johnson's church had recommended in 1596 that particular congregations should 'have the counsel and help one of another in all needful affairs of the church', but neither had given a synod power over individual churches.[1] By contrast the Book of Discipline laid down precise regulations to govern the relationship between particular congregations and higher church assemblies. The elderships of approximately twelve churches were each to choose one minister and one lay elder to represent them at a six-weekly conference or classis; twenty-four conferences were each to choose two ministers and two lay elders to represent them at a half-yearly provincial synod; and each provincial synod was to choose three ministers and three lay elders to represent it at the national assembly. Each conference, synod, or assembly would have authority over its constituent parts, and there was to be a right of appeal from a lower to a higher meeting. Ministers and elders who were to attend such conferences, synods, and assemblies were to be instructed to take care that the things agreed at such meetings 'be diligently observed by the churches'.[2]

To a Separatist like Henry Barrow all this was 'a new adulterate forged government'. Half a century before Milton prophesied that new presbyter would be 'but old priest writ large' Barrow conjectured that while the names of Presbyterian elders and synods might be unfamiliar, people acquainted with ecclesiastical courts and High Commission would 'not find the jurisdiction half so strange as it seems'. 'The ordering of all things', he warned, would 'be in the pastor's hands only, especially in some chief men who shall be these presidents and rulers of synods and councils, and so the people be kept as far as from the knowledge and performance of their duties as ever they were.'[3]

It is obvious that if the elaborate ecclesiastical structure proposed in the Book of Discipline were ever to function it would have to have the tolerance, if not the approval, of the state.

---

[1] *Writings of Harrison and Browne*, p. 271. Walker, *Creeds and Platforms*, p. 71.
[2] *Directory of Church-Government*, sigs. A3, C2–3.
[3] *Writings of Barrow, 1587–90*, p. 561.

Unlike the Separatists, who boycotted their parish churches and
met in secret or in exile, the Presbyterians needed not only to
be able to work within at least some of the parishes of the
established church, but to be able to move between churches,
classes, and synods throughout the country. Such conditions
did not exist in England between 1590 and 1640. In the autumn
of 1589 Archbishop Whitgift's pursuivants, searching the
Midlands for the author and printer of the Marprelate tracts,
came across evidence which showed that Presbyterian synods
had met in Cambridge in 1587 and in Warwickshire in 1588,
and discovered a copy of the Book of Discipline itself. The
archbishop responded with the imprisonment and prosecution
of nine Presbyterian leaders, including Cartwright, and managed to extract from them, in 1592, a promise to abstain from
all such secret meetings and assemblies in the future.[1] Whitgift
thereby dealt English Presbyterianism a blow from which it
did not recover for half a century. When the Puritans confronted James I at the Hampton Court conference in 1604 they
made no demand for any change in the government of the
church, and the king for his part made it clear that he would
never tolerate in England the Presbyterian system which had
caused him so much trouble in Scotland. Preaching exercises
continued among the Puritan ministers of remote Lancashire,
linking the Presbyterian movement of Cartwright with that of
the Civil War,[2] but neither in Lancashire nor anywhere else
was there any formal Presbyterian organization, not even, it
would appear, much discussion of distinctive Presbyterian ideas.
For the first forty years of the seventeenth century English
Presbyterianism survived only among the congregations of
English Puritans in the Netherlands, and in particular in the
Amsterdam church of which John Paget was pastor for thirty
years from 1607.[3]

What did survive Whitgift's suppression of Presbyterianism

[1] Collinson, *Elizabethan Puritan Movement*, pp. 403–5, 427–9.
[2] R. C. Richardson, *Puritanism in North-West England* (Manchester, 1972), p. 67.
[3] A. C. Carter, *The English Reformed Church in Amsterdam in the Seventeenth Century*
(Amsterdam, 1964), *passim*. Paget's isolation is illustrated by the difficulty his
church had in finding a co-pastor for him after the death of the original co-pastor,
Thomas Potts, in 1631. Thomas Hooker and John Davenport were both rejected
because of their Jacobite tendencies and it was not until 1635 that a suitable candidate was found, and he was a German. Carter, p. 84.

in the 1590s were informal Puritan meetings for the repetition of sermons, the study of the Bible, and for prayer. Although the hope of reforming the Church of England on the Presbyterian model had gone, Puritan ministers retained their hold of parishes in which the vicar was chosen by the parishioners and of lectureships in the gift of town corporations.[1] In such circumstances, as Collinson has argued, Henry Jacob's belief that the concept of the gathered church could be reconciled with communion with the established church had a natural appeal.[2] John Davenport, for example, arrived at such a position after his experience as vicar of St. Stephen's, Coleman Street (1624–33), a parish where the vestry had purchased the right to elect its own minister.[3] The arguments used to justify what Perry Miller calls the 'non-separating Congregationalism' of the early seventeenth century were in some respects not unlike those adduced in favour of what Thomas Fuller called the 'presbytery in episcopacy' of the 1580s. The Presbyterians Thomas Sperin and Cooper had maintained against Barrow and Greenwood in 1590 that their call to the ministry was derived not 'from the bishop but from a congregation . . . of ministers'; the Jacobite William Ames argued against John Robinson in 1614 that a man who was called to the pastorate of a congregation and subsequently obtained 'the bishop's and patron's admission' owed his calling not to the bishop but to 'the people's choice'.[4] Presbyterians and Jacobites alike justified ordination at the hands of a bishop as a merely civil procedure.[5] But though the Jacobites and Presbyterians had this much in common, the polity favoured by the Jacobites had one immeasurable advantage in the years following Whitgift's suppression of Presbyterianism and its repudiation by James I at Hampton Court: while the reformation of the Church of England on a national scale was now out of the question, the reform of the church at parochial level was still conceivable. John Cotton, while still vicar of Boston in Lincolnshire,

---

[1] C. Hill, *Economic Problems of the Church* (Oxford, 1968), pp. 296–7.

[2] Collinson, *Elizabethan Puritan Movement*, p. 380.

[3] D. A. Kirby, 'The Parish of St. Stephen's, Coleman Street', Oxford B.Litt. thesis, 1968, pp. 7–8, 27.

[4] *Writings of Greenwood*, p. 249. W. Ames, *A Manuduction for Mr. Robinson* (1614), sig. Q1.

[5] Ames, *Manuduction*, sig. Q2. Collinson, *Elizabethan Puritan Movement*, p. 344.

together with 'some scores of godly persons . . . entered into a covenant with the Lord, and one with another, to follow after the Lord in the purity of his worship'.[1]

7. THE PURITAN DIASPORA: THE NETHERLANDS AND NEW ENGLAND

In so far as English Puritans held distinctive views on church government in the first forty years of the seventeenth century —and the majority of them did not—those views were Jacobite and not Presbyterian. This was particularly true of those ministers who were forced out of their livings by William Laud and his fellow bishops in the late 1620s and 1630s and who sought refuge in the Netherlands and New England. Laud's insistence that his clergy conform to the Prayer Book, wear the surplice, raise their communion tables up like altars at the east end of the chancel, rail them off from the laity, and compel their people to kneel at the rails to receive the sacrament, drove scores of ministers out of the country. And once in exile the Puritan ministers' past experience of reforming their parishes at home combined with the present needs of their situation abroad to impress upon them the virtue of organizing churches which were self-governing but not separatist. In the Netherlands exiled Puritan ministers were welcomed as pastors by congregations of English merchants and soldiers who found difficulty in attracting conscientious conformist clergymen to serve them, and although such congregations received official sanction and financial support from the Dutch authorities it proved possible for their Puritan ministers to reorganize them as gathered churches. In 1623 the English church at Middelburg chose as its pastor John Drake on the recommendation of the Jacobite theologian William Ames, who himself had recently accepted a post as professor at the University of Franeker in Friesland. When Drake became minister of the church a covenant was drawn up 'betwixt it and God, betwixt God and the pastor, elders, deacons, and all the church members, and their successors'.[2] Four years later Hugh Peter, deprived of his lectureship at St. Sepulchre's, Farringdon, London, for praying that Charles I's Catholic queen would forsake idolatry, fled to

---

[1] J. Cotton, *The Way of the Congregational Churches Cleared* (1648), p. 20.
[2] Sprunger, *William Ames*, pp. 200, 228.

the Netherlands where he, too, was taken under the protection of William Ames. In 1629 Peter became minister of the English congregation at Rotterdam, hitherto organized on Presbyterian lines, and four years later reorganized it as a gathered church, excluding from communion those who would not accept its covenant. Ames joined Hugh Peter as co-pastor in the latter part of 1633, though he died soon afterwards.[1]

Attempts were even made to secure the appointment of followers of Jacob and Ames as co-pastor to John Paget, the rigidly Presbyterian minister of the English Reformed church at Amsterdam. Thomas Hooker, a lecturer at Chelmsford, fled to the Netherlands in 1630 on being summoned to appear before the court of High Commission. In the following year he was invited to preach to the Amsterdam church with a view to becoming Paget's co-pastor, but because Hooker declined to baptize the children of parents who were not members of the church, and because he would not accept the Presbyterian view that a classis had authority over its constituent churches, Paget used his influence with the Dutch classis to prevent his appointment.[2] Hooker consequently moved from Amsterdam to become assistant to John Forbes, the Scottish minister to the English Merchant Adventurers' church at Delft.[3] A similar experience befell John Davenport, vicar of St. Stephen's, Coleman Street, and one of the feoffees for the purchase of lay impropriations. Davenport went into hiding on Laud's translation to the see of Canterbury in 1633 and he, too, was invited to Amsterdam by Paget's church. But Davenport shared Hooker's views on church government and his objections to indiscriminate baptism and once again the Dutch classis vetoed the appointment.[4]

By 1633 both Archbishop Laud and the Dutch authorities had become alarmed at the way in which Puritan ministers in the Netherlands were leading their churches without reference

---

[1] R. P. Stearns, *The Strenuous Puritan, Hugh Peter* (Urbana, 1954), pp. 36–77. C. B. Jewson, 'The English Church at Rotterdam and its Norfolk Connections', *Original Papers of the Norfolk and Norwich Archaeological Society*, xxx (1952), 324–31.

[2] Carter, *English Reformed Church at Amsterdam*, p. 78.

[3] R. P. Stearns, *Congregationalism in the Dutch Netherlands* (Chicago, 1940), pp. 46–7.

[4] Ibid., pp. 65–6.

either to the Prayer Book or to the rules of the Dutch Reformed Church. Laud forced John Forbes to retire from his pastorate at Delft by insisting that the Merchant Adventurers employ only conformist ministers approved by the king, and Laud's agents helped to secure the unfavourable decision of the Dutch classis against John Davenport by depicting him as a fugitive from justice.[1] In the aftermath of the Davenport affair, in March 1634, the Dutch Council of State warned that pastors who ministered to state-supported English congregations in the Netherlands must conform either to the Church of England or to the Dutch Reformed Church. Thus deprived of their livelihood in the Netherlands the more extreme Puritans turned their eyes to New England as the last place of refuge. Thomas Hooker sailed there in 1633 and persuaded John Cotton to accompany him.[2] John Lathrop, who had succeeded Henry Jacob as pastor of his Southwark church, arrived in Massachusetts in 1634, and in the following year Hugh Peter resigned his Rotterdam pastorate and also made for the colony. Peter was succeeded at Rotterdam by John Davenport, hitherto his assistant, but in 1637 he too sailed to New England with some of his former Coleman Street parishioners and in 1638 founded the colony of New Haven. By the end of the decade New England was in its turn influencing the old country: when William Wroth, the venerable and popular Puritan rector of Llanfaches in Monmouthshire, was deprived of his living he founded, in 1639, a gathered church 'according to the new England pattern'.[3]

Meanwhile a second wave of Puritan exiles had arrived in the Netherlands. William Bridge, rector of St. Peter Hungate, Norwich, was silenced and excommunicated around 1636 and sailed to the Netherlands where he succeeded John Davenport as minister to the English church at Rotterdam. He was followed to Rotterdam by Jeremiah Burroughes, who had been suspended from his rectory at Tivetshall in Norfolk in 1636, and by Sidrach Simpson, once curate of St. Margaret's, Fish Street, London. John Archer, who had been silenced as a lecturer at All Hallows, Lombard Street, in 1629, and Thomas Goodwin, formerly vicar of Trinity church, Cambridge, simi-

---

[1] Ibid., pp. 46–7. H. Trevor-Roper, *Archbishop Laud* (1965), pp. 249–51.
[2] L. Ziff, *The Career of John Cotton* (Princeton, 1962), p. 69.
[3] R. Tudur Jones, *Congregationalism in England* (1962), p. 24.

larly fled to the Netherlands in the late 1630s, joining the church at Arnhem of which another English exile, Philip Nye, had been pastor since 1633. Of these men five, Bridge, Burroughes, Simpson, Goodwin, and Nye, all returned to England between 1640 and 1642 and, as signatories of the *Apologeticall Narration* of 1644, were to constitute the core of the Independent party in the Westminster Assembly. The sixth, John Archer, died in the Netherlands around 1642, but his posthumously famous work, *The Personall Reigne of Christ upon Earth*, was to make an important contribution to the wave of millenarian expectation which swept England in the 1640s.

The non-separatist gathered churches of the Netherlands and New England always contained within them the seeds of more radical tendencies. In Rotterdam Sidrach Simpson tried to persuade William Bridge's church to follow the Separatists in allowing members to prophesy and to question the minister after the sermon, and when Bridge resisted the demand Simpson and a handful of followers seceded to form a rival church.[1] In New England John Cotton was disturbed by the extent to which the practice of the Puritan church at Salem approximated to that of the Pilgrim Fathers' Separatist church at Plymouth.[2] And in Southwark some members of the original Jacobite church under the pastorate of John Lathrop were prompted by the Laudian persecution to reject the church's non-separatist position and in 1630 seceded under John Duppa to form a Separatist church. Further secessions followed in 1633 and some of the secessionists went on to renounce infant baptism. One of their number, a button-maker named Samuel Eaton, underwent a second baptism, supposedly at the hands of a cobbler named John Spilsbury, and then baptized others. Eaton was much imprisoned and died in Newgate in 1639, his funeral attended by some two hundred 'Brownists and Ana-baptists', but Spilsbury survived as pastor of a Separatist church.[3] Spilsbury and his followers, unlike the adherents of Smyth and Helwys, remained orthodox Calvinists, and since they held that salvation was for the elect alone they became

---

[1] T. Edwards, *Antapologia* (1644), pp. 142–3.

[2] Ziff, *John Cotton*, pp. 59–60, 76.

[3] Burrage, *EED* i. 321–9, ii. 299–302. *CSPD*, 1639, p. 466. B. R. White, 'Samuel Eaton, Particular Baptist Pioneer', *Baptist Quarterly*, xxiv (1971), 10–21.

known as Particular Baptists, to distinguish them from the older General Baptists. Though theologically conservative, in one respect the Particular Baptists were innovators. Hitherto all English Baptists, while rejecting infant baptism, had retained the mode of baptism by sprinkling. But in 1640 a Particular Baptist by name of Richard Blunt became convinced that baptism 'ought to be by dipping the body into the water, resembling burial and rising again'. Since a sect of Dutch Mennonites called the Collegiants was known to practise immersion Blunt was sent to the Netherlands to find out how it was done, and after his return immersion quickly became the accepted mode of baptism among both the Particular and the General Baptists.[1]

8. 'COME OUT OF HER MY PEOPLE': THE CONSEQUENCES OF ARCHBISHOP LAUD

By 1640 Laud's attempts to enforce religious uniformity in England had given a final, important, pre-Civil War stimulus to Dissent. The experiences of Parker and Whitgift before him could have taught Laud, had he been the man to learn, that efforts to bludgeon Puritans into conformity drove the more extreme into irreconcilable opposition not merely to episcopal authority but to the established church itself. 'The great thing which is amiss' in his own diocese of Canterbury, Laud confessed to the king in 1639, 'and beyond my power to remedy, is the stiffness of diverse Anabaptists and Separatists from the Church of England.'[2] Of the four celebrated victims of Laud's repression in the late 1630s—the long-winded lawyer William Prynne, the witty physician John Bastwick, the visionary clergyman Henry Burton, and the rebellious clothier's apprentice John Lilburne—the two latter were driven by Laud's policy from Puritanism to Separatism.

Henry Burton, ten years old when the Spanish Armada sailed, was throughout his life tormented by fear of Roman Catholicism, intent, as he believed it was, on subjugating England to 'papal thraldom and to . . . Spanish cruelty'.[3] Educated

---

[1] Burrage, *EED* i. 330–5.
[2] *Works of William Laud* (1853), vol. v, part ii, p. 361.
[3] R. T. Hughes, 'Henry Burton: A Study in Religion and Politics in Seventeenth Century England', Univ. of Iowa D. Phil. thesis, 1972, p. 7 and *passim*.

at St. John's College, Cambridge, he was clerk of the closet successively to Prince Henry and to Prince Charles until, on Charles's accession to the throne, he was dismissed for warning the new king against the 'popishly affected' Laud.[1] Burton subsequently obtained a living as rector of St. Matthew's, Friday Street, and in a stream of pamphlets tried to defend both the Church of England and Charles from the innovations of popish prelates in the hope that the king might 'become the royal standard bearer of Christ against antichrist, utterly to demolish that kingdom of the beast'.[2] Burton was summoned before High Commission in 1626, the Privy Council in 1627, temporarily suspended in 1629, and finally sentenced by Star Chamber in 1637, along with Bastwick and Prynne, to stand in the pillory, to have his ears lopped off, to pay a fine of £5,000, and to suffer perpetual imprisonment. The sufferings of the three men aroused public indignation against Charles's government and turned Burton from a self-appointed guardian to a bitter opponent of the Church of England. In his island prison in Guernsey Castle Burton was denied ink, pen, and paper, but he 'had an art to make ink, and for pens had goose wings, which were to sweep the dust off [his] window', and was thus able to continue his campaign against the influence of the Laudians.[3] His prison writings, smuggled back to England for publication, show that by 1639 he had come to agree with the Separatists that the Church of England was antichristian: its 'church-government and discipline . . . such as the apostles never approved, but expressly reproved and condemned, and practised the contrary'.[4]

Henry Burton was a fifty-nine-year-old seasoned campaigner against popery when he was arrested in 1637, John Lilburne a raw apprentice of twenty-two years. Lilburne, apprehended in December, was accused of importing 'scandalous' books from the Netherlands, in particular the imprisoned John Bastwick's satire on episcopal pomp, the *Letany*, and in February 1638 was

---

[1] H. Burton, *A Narration of the Life of Mr. Henry Burton* (1643), p. 3.

[2] H. Burton, *The Seven Vials* (1628), p. 102. P. K. Christianson, 'English Protestant Apocalyptic Visions, c. 1536–1642', Univ. of Minnesota Ph.D. thesis, 1971, pp. 247–8.

[3] *Life of Burton*, p. 2.

[4] H. Burton, *A Replie to a Relation of a Conference between William Laude and Mr. Fisher the Jesuit* (1640), p. 55.

sentenced to a fine of £500, to be whipped at a cart's tail from
the Fleet prison to Westminster, to stand in the pillory, and to
remain in the Fleet until he conformed. Far from conforming,
Lilburne, like Burton, was propelled from Puritanism to
Separatism. The day of his scourging and pillorying was a day
of profound religious experience: 'for I was mightily filled with
the sweet presence of God's Spirit, which caused me notwithstanding the pains of my suffering to go along the streets with a
joyful countenance not showing the least discontentedness, as
if I had been going to take possession of some great treasures'.[1]
In the tract in which he described his sufferings, *A Worke of
the Beast*, Lilburne called upon those who loved their 'own souls
and looke[d] for that immortal crown of happiness in the world
to come' to withdraw from the 'Antichristian power and slavery' of the Church of England, and in August, 'lying day and
night in fetters of iron, both hands and legs', he expanded this
theme in a pamphlet entitled *Come out of her my People*.[2] The
bishops, he argued, are the limbs of the Beast spoken of in
Revelation 13:2, and whoever listens to sermons preached by
ministers appointed by the bishops listens to the pope, and thus
to the devil. The apostle Paul was lucky to have fallen into the
hands of the pagans rather than on the tender mercies of
Archbishop Laud. But Lilburne did not resent his own captivity, for in prison 'God's holy ones grow in grace and godliness,
like tall cedars as in Lebanon, and get great and large experience of God's goodness, faithfulness, and kindness'.[3] Henry
Burton's prison experience was similar: 'Far from accounting all
this suffering as any the least affliction to me,' wrote the prisoner
of Guernsey, 'I held and valued and enjoyed it as my chief joy,
my glory, and my crown, and the greatest happiness that ever
God vouchsafed to me in all my life.'[4]

John Lilburne's prison writings were smuggled out of the
Fleet across to Amsterdam where they were printed on the
press belonging to John Canne, pastor of the 'ancient' Separatist church of Francis Johnson and Henry Ainsworth. For thirty

[1] J. Lilburne, *A Worke of the Beast* (1638), reprinted in W. Haller, *Tracts on
Liberty in the Puritan Revolution* (New York, 1965), ii. 26.

[2] Ibid., p. 20. P. Gregg, *Free-born John* (1961), p. 69.

[3] J. Lilburne, *Come out of her my People* (1639, facsimile reprint, Exeter, 1971),
pp. 3, 8, 24, 31.

[4] *Life of Burton*, p. 20.

years Canne occupied an important if shadowy position among English religious radicals.[1] His origins are obscure, but he is known to have been a troublesome lecturer at Pilton near Barnstaple in the late 1620s when he caused a decline in attendance at early morning services by persuading parishioners not to attend 'stinted morning prayer'.[2] He was excommunicated in 1629 and appears to have gone to London where he was elected pastor of a Separatist church founded by a Mr. Hubbard eight years earlier.[3] By 1632 Canne was in Amsterdam where he not only became pastor of the 'ancient' Separatist church but, to the disgust of the Presbyterian John Paget, kept a brandy shop, an alchemist's laboratory, and the printing-press which turned out tracts by himself, Lilburne, and other Separatists.[4] Nor did he neglect theology, for in 1634 he published a lengthy work designed to prove the *Necessitie of Separation from the Church of England* from the Puritans' own principles, and in 1642 earned distinction as the first man to produce an English Bible with marginal references and 'profitable annotations upon all the hard places'.[5]

Canne was succeeded as pastor of his London church by Samuel How, a man who had once been a member of Lathrop's Jacobite church but later became a convinced Separatist. How claimed to have 'served the king both by sea and land', but he later earned notoriety as a preaching cobbler, a member of that class of 'artisans in sedentary trades in which conversation is a natural accompaniment to work', to quote Lawrence Stone, men who were 'peculiarly susceptible to radical religious influences'.[6] On one occasion How was said to have attracted an audience of 'above an hundred persons in the Nag's Head tavern near Coleman Street' to hear him preach a sermon which was published, in 1640, as a famous and oft-reprinted tract, *The Sufficiencie of the Spirits Teaching, without Humane Learning*.[7] The burden of the cobbler's message was that only 'such as are

---

[1] J. Wilson, 'Another Look at John Canne', *Church History*, xxxiii (1964), 34–47.

[2] I. W. Gower, 'Puritanism in the County of Devon between 1570 and 1641', Exeter M.A. thesis, 1970, p. 131.

[3] Burrage, *EED* i. 201.

[4] J. Paget, *A Defence of Church-Government, exercised in Presbyteriall, Classicall, and Synodall Assemblies* (1640), p. 160.

[5] J. Canne, *The Bible* (Amsterdam, 1642).

[6] Burrage, *EED* ii. 317. L. Stone, *The Causes of the English Revolution* (1972), p. 99.

[7] Burrage, *EED* ii. 328.

taught by the Spirit, destitute of human learning, are the learned ones who truly understand the Scriptures', for human learning 'is but fleshly and carnal'. How did not deny the value of human learning, it was useful for 'the repairing of that decay which came upon man for sin', and so was necessary to fit men to be 'statesmen, physicians, lawyers, and gentlemen'. But if human learning was used to try to understand 'the mind of God in the holy Scriptures . . . there it is detestable filth, dross, and dung', 'the means of bringing in all those abominable errors that the earth hath drunk in, both in doctrine and practice, and so have occasioned those noisome lusts that drown men in perdition'.[1]

Samuel How died in September 1640 and was succeeded as pastor of the church by its deacon Stephen More who, unlike How, was 'a citizen of good worth, and possessed of some estate'.[2] By 1640 there may have been at least a dozen similar Separatist congregations in England, besides John Canne's church at Amsterdam. In addition to More's church London harboured John Duppa's paedobaptist and John Spilsbury's Particular Baptist congregations, and it is likely that the General Baptist church which met in the capital in 1626 maintained its existence in the 1630s, though no definite evidence survives. As early as 1631 Bishop Joseph Hall had reported to Laud that he had heard that there were eleven congregations of Separatists in London 'who meet together in brewhouses every Sunday', though not too much credence can be given to rumours of this nature.[3] What little information there is concerning Separatism in the rest of the country suggests that it was confined largely to the eastern counties, with a few isolated congregations in the West Country. A Separatist church is known to have existed in Norwich in 1603, perhaps tracing its history back to a company left behind by Browne and Harrison when they fled to Middelburg; there were congregations at Boston and Colchester in the 1610s, and another in the Maidstone and Ashford district of Kent in the 1620s and 1630s which gave Archbishop Laud continuous trouble.[4]

---

[1] S. How, *The Sufficiencie of the Spirits Teaching, without Humane Learning* (1640), sigs. B2, C2, D.

[2] Burrage, *EED* ii. 306–8.   [3] *CSPD*, 1631–3, p. 74.

[4] Burrage, *EED* i. 187–98, 202–3. *Works of William Laud*, vol. v, part ii, pp. 336, 347, 355, 361

Separatists attending conventicles at Great Yarmouth were arrested in 1624 and again in 1630; the Bishop of Hereford complained in 1639 that Brownists were preaching dangerous errors 'in that part of the diocese adjoining to Wales'; a mason was accused of gathering conventicles at Dover in the same year; and, the greatest effrontery of all, in 1632 a conventicle was discovered at Newington Woods in Surrey 'in the very brake where the king's stag should have been lodged for his hunting the next morning'.[1] To these presumably paedobaptist gatherings must be added the congregations of General Baptists which met in Lincoln, Coventry, Salisbury, and Tiverton in 1626 and which are known to have continued into the 1630s, small groups of 'Anabaptists' which were appearing in Lincolnshire villages in the later 1630s, and a probable General Baptist congregation in Colchester.[2] In 1639 John Fort, a clothier of Tiverton, was fined £500 'for Anabaptism', though the fine was later repaid, and in 1640 Thomas Lamb of Colchester, subsequently pastor of the General Baptist church in London's Bell Alley, was committed to the Fleet, his gaoler ordered to restrain him 'from company, keeping of conventicles, and private exercises of religion'.[3] And though the spiritual heirs of Henry Jacob denied that they were Separatists, they were regarded as such by the authorities and they, too, had to meet furtively. By 1640 the original London Jacobite church had 'grown so numerous that they could not well meet together in one place, without being discovered', and in May they divided into two congregations, one under the care of Henry Jessey, the deprived vicar of Aughton in Yorkshire, the other ministered to by a prosperous Fleet Street leather dresser, 'Mr. Praise God Barebone'.[4]

---

[1] J. Browne, *History of Congregationalism in Norfolk and Suffolk* (1877), pp. 74–7. W. T. Pennar Davies, 'Episodes in the History of Brecknockshire Dissent', *Brycheiniog*, iii (1957), 19. *CSPD* 1639–40, p. 80. 1631–3, p. ix. Edward Terrill, in a frequently quoted passage from his *Records of a Church of Christ, meeting in Broadmead, Bristol, 1640–88* (ed. N. Haycroft, 1865), p. 15, claimed that five people came together in Bristol in 1640 'to separate from the worship of the world' and 'to worship the Lord more purely'. But the accuracy of Terrill's account of the early years of Bristol Dissent is open to considerable doubt. Cf. Wilson, 'Another Look at John Canne', pp. 36–7.

[2] Burrage, *EED* i. 275. *TBHS* iii (1912–13), 2, 4. T. Richards, *The Puritan Movement in Wales* (1920), p. 209. J. Plumb, 'Early Nonconformity in Lincolnshire', Univ. of Sheffield M.A. thesis 1940, ii. 23–4.

[3] *CSPD* 1640, pp. 391, 399.   [4] Burrage, *EED* i. 325.

9. 'THE LIBERTY OF THE BRETHREN IN PROPHECIES':
THE MOTIVATION OF DISSENT

Who were the men and women who thus braved prison, exile, and even death to worship God as they believed he commanded them? The rise of sectarianism is sometimes attributed to economic and social frustration,[1] yet so simple a thesis is hardly adequate to explain the rise of English Dissent. The Separatist leadership was provided very largely by the University of Cambridge. Browne, Harrison, Greenwood, Barrow, Penry, Johnson, Ainsworth, Smyth, Robinson, and Burton were all its graduates, and Johnson, Smyth, and Robinson had been Fellows of their colleges. University men, though, are not free from economic frustration, and Mark Curtis has suggested that the universities contributed to the instability of early Stuart England by 'providing too many men for too few places'.[2] Greenwood, Smyth, Robinson, Clifton, Canne, and Burton all took the final step from Puritanism to Separatism after they had been deprived of their livings or lectureships within the established church, and it is possible that the diminishing chances of employment available for troublesome graduates influenced the decision of some of them to renounce communion with the Church of England. But both the available evidence and psychological probability suggest that their frustration was much more religious than economic. In so far as religious zeal was tempered by economic considerations, such considerations pulled in the direction of conformity, not of Dissent. If Robert Browne's actions were ever dictated by worldly motives, it was when he accepted the living of Achurch in Northamptonshire, not when he rejected the call to St. Bene't's church in Cambridge. Had economic security been the prime concern of the future Separatist leaders, then Robert Harrison would have stayed as master of St. Giles's hospital in Norwich, Francis Johnson would not have renounced his £200 a year post at Middelburg, and Thomas Helwys would not have forfeited the comforts of Broxtowe Hall and the company of his wife and

---

[1] R. H. Niebuhr, *The Social Sources of Denominationalism* (Cleveland, 1963), p. 19.
[2] M. H. Curtis, 'The Alienated Intellectuals of Early Stuart England' *Past and Present*, xxiii (November 1962), 27.

seven children. True, John Smyth lost a stipend of £40 a year when he was dismissed as lecturer at Lincoln, and the opponents of Henry Burton claimed that his bitterness against the Laudians was due to his dismissal from court. But Smyth professed to be satisfied with the compensation subsequently paid to him by the Lincoln corporation and Burton claimed to be content with his lot as rector of a City church.[1] Both men, had they acted in accordance with the dictates of economic prudence, would thereafter have conformed to the established church, not carried their rebellion further. For Smyth and Burton, as for the majority of Separatists, religious protest was not a response to economic hardship, it was a cause.

In only one case is there evidence to suggest that there may have been some connection between economic frustration and secession from the established church. Gervase Neville, of Ragnall in Nottinghamshire, had in 1606 to defend his title to land he held against a claim that it was part of the royal demesne. He subsequently became a member of the Gainsborough Separatist church, spent some time in gaol in York Castle, and on his release joined Smyth's church in Amsterdam. But if irritation with the challenge to his right to his land was a factor in Neville's break with the established church, it was one which led to no permanent change of conviction, for by 1611 he had returned to the Church of England, if not to the Church of Rome.[2]

Gervase Neville was one of the very few members of landed families to throw in their lot with the Separatists. Henry Barrow, Thomas Helwys, John Lilburne, and Thomas Brewer, who financed a printing-press which William Brewster set up at Leyden in 1616, are the only other examples, and of those Barrow and Brewer probably, and Lilburne certainly, were younger sons with no title to land. This absence of land-owners among the Separatists is in marked contrast to the support given to the Puritan movement by a section of the gentry, and it helps to illuminate the chief economic characteristic of early Dissent: its actual or potential mobility. While the Separatist

[1] Burgess, *John Smith*, p. 53. *Works of John Smyth*, i. 69. Hughes, 'Henry Burton', pp. 150–1.
[2] Burgess, *Robinson*, pp. 72–9.

leaders were for the most part university men, the rank and file were in the main craftsmen, economically independent but not over-endowed with this world's riches. The occupations of the imprisoned members of the London Separatist church who were examined in March and April 1593 were typical. They included, besides Henry Barrow who described himself as a gentleman, John Greenwood, Francis Johnson and two other former clergymen, five shipwrights, five tailors, three fish-mongers, three haberdashers, two purse-makers, two school-teachers, two scriveners, two shoemakers, and two weavers. There was also an apothecary, a carpenter, a cloth-worker, a copper-smith, a feltmaker, a glover, a goldsmith, a husbandman from Norfolk, a joiner, a servant, a 'scholar', a turner, a trunk-maker, a 'worker of caps', and John Penry, whose literary activities for which he was soon to be martyred were described as those of a 'clerk'.[1] Neither the university graduates on the one hand nor the artisans on the other were tied to the land and both groups had occupations which brought them into contact with men who travelled widely, either in goods or in ideas. Above all they both had skills, and perhaps a little money, with which they could earn their living should they be compelled to flee to a foreign land.

The possession of transferable skills may have provided the opportunity, but it did not provide the motivation for Dissent. The early Separatists were impelled by an intense desire to realize what they saw as the New Testament pattern of church life in their own age. Why else should the followers of John Smyth have spent their Sundays in Amsterdam in the manner described by Hugh Bromhead and his wife? Their 'morning exercise' began at eight o'clock with prayer and the reading of one or two chapters of the Bible, which Smyth insisted was pre-paratory to worship rather than an act of worship itself. Smyth's conception of worship, derived from I Corinthians 14: 30–1, was the spontaneous out-pouring of the Holy Spirit through prophesying, and so the Bible was laid aside and a speaker rose to propound 'some text out of Scripture, and prophesieth out of the same, by the space of one hour or three-quarters of an hour'. Then a second speaker stood up 'and prophesieth out of the said text the like time and space', and after him a third, a

---

[1] Burrage, *EED* i. 146–8. *Writings of Barrow and Greenwood, 1591–3*, pp. 293–4.

fourth, and a fifth 'as the time will give leave'. The service ended at twelve o'clock with prayer and a collection for the poor, and in the afternoon a similar exercise was held from two until five or six o'clock when, 'last of all, the execution of the government of the church is handled'.[1] The little that is known about the worship of the Separatists who remained in England suggests that they placed similar emphasis on spontaneous prophesying and extemporary prayer. They had to be more cautious than their brethren in the Netherlands: according to a hostile witness of a Separatist congregation in London in 1641 they came and went in twos and threes lest their number should arouse suspicion and appointed a door-keeper to give warning of possible disturbance. Their leader prayed 'about the space of half an hour' and then preached for an hour, followed by another who stood 'up to make the text more plain'. They prayed 'that those which come thither to scoff and laugh, God would be pleased to turn their hearts, by which means they think to escape undiscovered'.[2]

By 1640 the Separatists, though persecuted and few in number, had already made a contribution to English religious life which was pregnant with promise, or menace, for the future. They had proclaimed their belief that religion is a matter of personal faith rather than public ceremony, and the wisest of them had concluded that faith cannot be wrought at the point of a sword. They had asserted the democratic duty of every Christian to take part in the government of his church, and some among them, John Penry and Henry Jacob no less than Robert Browne,[3] had applied their covenant theories also to the state. Democracy, it is true, had led to dissension: free churches had displayed fissiparous tendencies, and the pursuit of purity had conflicted with Christian charity. Yet the Separatists had their defence. 'Ignorant persons and peoples', wrote John Robinson, 'are for the most part easily ruled, as being content to trust other men with their faith and religion.' Only those 'who enjoy liberty know how hard a thing it is to use it aright'. When men in England wondered at their dissensions, he thought he saw 'two prisoners, being them-

---

[1] Burrage, *EED* i. 236.
[2] *The Brownists Synagogue* (1641), reprinted in *TCHS* iv (1909–10), 300–4.
[3] Burrage, *EED* ii. 157.

selves fast chained and manacled together by feet and hands, wondering to see that other men, at liberty, walk not closer together than they do'. 'As ignorance begot, so tyranny maintained the greatest peace and unity when popish iniquity most prevailed.'[1]

[1] *Works of Robinson* iii. 99–100.

II

'WHEN WOMEN PREACH AND COBBLERS PRAY': THE LIBERATION OF DISSENT, 1641–1662

1. 'A SWARME OF SECTARIES AND SCHISMATIQUES': THE TESTIMONY OF JOHN TAYLOR

The Civil War was the English counterpart of the continental wars of religion and of the Thirty Years War, provoked by the fear that Charles I and his supporters were agents of the Counter Reformation, intent on transferring to English soil the absolutist tendencies that were taking shape in Europe.[1] The Protestant religion was not the only part of the Englishman's inheritance which appeared to be threatened by the king's policies— the liberties of Parliament and the property of holders of secularized church lands also seemed in jeopardy—but religion was an essential ingredient in the mixture of ambition and fear which brought about the Civil War. It was Charles I's foolhardy attempt to impose a version of the English Prayer Book on the Scots that led to Scottish military resistance and to the summoning of the English Parliament in 1640 after a lapse of eleven years. And it was the need to raise a force to subdue the Catholic rebellion in Ireland which precipitated the struggle between king and Parliament for the control of the armed forces which issued, in August 1642, in war.

The Separatists were numerically too insignificant and politically too impotent to make any direct contribution to the events which led to the outbreak of war, but the accompanying breakdown of royal and episcopal authority inspired them with confidence in the present and hope for the future. Their hatred of Laudianism combined with a depression in the cloth trade to contribute to the disorders which periodically erupted in London on the eve of the Civil War; the imprisonment and subsequent impeachment of Laud encouraged them to hope that the persecution they and their forefathers had endured for a century

[1] C. Russell, ed., *The Origins of the English Civil War* (1973), *passim*.

might soon be brought to an end; and the destruction of
episcopacy in Scotland and the threat to the bishops' power in
England aroused among them apocalyptic expectations of the
fall of Antichrist. The coincidence of economic distress and religious radicalism was seen in June 1639 when an appeal from
the imprisoned Lilburne to his fellow apprentices in the cloth
trade provoked a march on Lambeth Palace which issued in a
riot.[1] The sense of apocalyptic expectation was expressed by
Henry Burton who, shut up in his prison on the island of
Guernsey, pondered on *The Soundings of the Two Last Trumpets*
of the Book of Revelation, coming to the conclusion that the
sounding of the seventh trumpet referred 'to the now approaching time' when 'all the kingdoms of the world shall consent to
the rooting out of Antichrist' and his hierarchy of bishops.[2]
And hopes that Parliament would be more tolerant than the
bishops towards those who dissented from the established
church appeared to be given substance by the unwillingness of
the House of Lords, in January 1641, to take punitive action
against Separatists.

On Sunday 9 January over sixty people, possibly members of
the church of which Samuel How had been pastor until his
death in the previous September, were discovered by constables
at a conventicle in a house in Deadman's Place, Southwark.
Six of the conventiclers were arrested and, on being examined
by Sir John Lenthal, marshal of the King's Bench, told him
that they refused to go to their parish churches for 'those
churches were not true churches', declined to recognize the
Act for Retaining the Queen's Subjects in their Due Obedience since
this 'was not a true law, for . . . it was made by bishops', and
refused to obey the king except 'in civil things'. The matter was
referred by Charles I to the House of Lords and on the following
Sunday three or four peers attended the Southwark conventicle
to judge for themselves the nature of the proceedings. The peers,
so the Separatists claimed, sat through 'two sermons, and the
liberty of the brethren in prophecies and breaking of bread',
and at the end contributed liberally towards the collection for
the poor. It is probable that they reported their favourable impressions back to their fellow peers, for on the following day, 18

---

[1] Gregg, *Free-born John*, pp. 77–8.
[2] H. Burton, *The Soundings of the Two Last Trumpets* (1641), pp. 1, 88.

January, the Upper House resolved to take no action against the conventiclers beyond admonishing them henceforward to 'repair to their several parish churches to hear divine service', and let them go free. Thus encouraged, another group of Separatists, who claimed that their meeting in Whitechapel had been broken up by constables with 'swords, halberts, and clubs' and without 'showing them any warrant for so doing', petitioned the Lords against their detention and were also released.[1]

The reluctance of the peers to enforce the law against dissent from the established church, coupled with the prospect of the imminent collapse of episcopacy, led to the proliferation of conventicles in London, a phenomenon recorded in a spate of anti-Separatist pamphlets which issued from the presses in the summer and autumn of 1641, warning sober citizens of the subversive activities of tub orators and mechanic preachers. The most prolific writer of such pamphlets was John Taylor, the self-styled 'water-poet'. Taylor, a one time waterman who for more than twenty years had earned his living with his doggerel rhymes and accounts of his travels, was a fanatical royalist who combined a not uncommon lower-rank admiration for the traditional rulers of society with contempt for tradesmen, merchants, and Puritans. It was his proud boast that he had once held the infant Prince Rupert in his arms, and for his service to the royal cause in lampooning the parliamentarians Charles I made him a yeoman of the guard.[2] Taylor and his fellow pamphleteers cannot be regarded as reliable observers of the events they purport to describe, but the impression they convey, of a society in which traditional restraints are breaking down and customary relationships are questioned, is well attested by other sources.

The Separatists, warned one pamphleteer, once no more than 'a handful, and then crept in corners', are now like 'the Egyptian locust covering the land'.[3] In June John Taylor claimed to have discovered *A Swarme of Sectaries, and Schismatiques*, men who

[1] *Journal of the House of Lords*, iv. 133–8. W. T. Whitley, 'The Hubbard-How-More Church', *TBHS* ii (1910), 41–2. The doubt concerning whether the six arrested were members of the How-More church arises from the fact that none of them signed the church's covenant when it was renewed in 1648. However, by that date three of the six are known to have become Baptists.

[2] For Taylor see *DNB* and W. Notestein, *Four Worthies* (1956), pp. 169–208.

[3] *Lucifers Lacky* (1641), sig. A3.

earned their living as 'cobblers, tinkers, pedlars, weavers, sow-gelders, and chimney-sweepers'.

> These kind of vermin swarm like caterpillars
> And hold conventicles in barns and cellars,
> Some preach (or prate) in woods, in fields, in stables,
> In hollow trees, in tubs, on tops of tables.[1]

In July another pamphleteer complained that these 'Brownists' had committed 'violent outrages and sacrilegious disorders' in a London church, 'even in the time of divine service . . . by laying violent hands upon the minister, rending his Master of Arts hood from his neck, and tearing the surplice [from] his back', and then 'rending the rails before the communion table, and then chopping them in pieces, and burning them in the church-yard'.[2] In October the writer of a tract called *The Brownists Synagogue* gave the names of seventeen Separatist preachers in London, of whom the chief were Green, a felt-maker, Marler, a button-maker, Spence, a coachman, and Richard Rogers, a glover;[3] in November the author of *Religions Enemies* complained that too many places in England were 'too much Amsterdamni-fied by several opinions', that religion had 'become the common discourse and table-talk in every tavern and ale-house';[4] and in December Bishop Hall told the House of Lords that there were 'in London and the suburbs and liberties no fewer than four-score congregations of several sectaries, instructed by guides fit for them, cobblers, tailors, felt-makers, and such like trash'.[5] On Sunday 12 December 'a great assembly of these Brownists' was said to have 'gathered about St. George's church in South-wark, and one of their preachers, a cobbler by profession, violently went up into the pulpit, and made a sermon above an hour long'.[6] Violent acts were perpetrated against, as well as by, religious radicals, and both the churches formed by the division of the original London Jacobite church in 1640 fell victim. In August Henry Jessey's congregation was raided by the lord mayor, Sir John Wright, who 'came violently on them, beat,

---

[1] J. Taylor, *A Swarms of Sectaries and Schismatiques* (1641), p. 7.
[2] *The Brownists Conventicle* (1641), p. 3.   [3] *The Brownists Synagogue* (1641).
[4] *Religions Enemies* (1641), p. 6.
[5] *Cobbett's Parliamentary History of England* (1807), ii. 990.
[6] *A relation of the disorders, mutinous assemblies, uprores, and distractions committed by the many schismaticall people* (1641), sig. A3.

thrust, pinched, and kicked such men or women as fled not his handling', among them a pregnant woman named Mrs. Berry who, as a result of her ill treatment at the hands of the constables, lost both her child and her own life.[1] On 19 December Praise-God Barebone's congregation, meeting in his Fleet Street premises, the Lock and Key, was attacked by a royalist mob. For more than two hours the mob smashed the windows and tried to break down the door of Barebone's shop until a constable arrived and committed some of the conventiclers to Bridewell and the Counter, while others 'crawled over the tiles and houses, escaping some one way, and some another'.[2]

It is clear that behind the hatred of religious diversity expressed by the anti-Separatist pamphleteers of 1641 lay the fear that society, as they knew it, was on the point of dissolution. This can be seen in their constant satirization of mechanic preachers and their continual harping on the breakdown of family life and sexual morality which, they asserted, was accompanying the spread of Separatism. In August 1641 one pamphleteer claimed to have made *A Discoverie of Six Women Preachers*, including one Joan Bauford of Faversham who taught that husbands who 'crossed their wives' wills might lawfully be forsaken'.[3] In October a certain Edward Harris published what purported to be *A True Relation of a Company of Brownists, Separatists, and Non-Conformists in Monmouthshire*, who had 'drawn divers honest men's wives in the night times to frequent their assemblies' and had caused 'many chaste virgins to become harlots and the mothers of bastards'.[4] And other royalist scribblers claimed to know of the existence of sects such as the Adamites, who would 'not hear the Word preached, nor have the sacraments administered unto them', unless they were naked, and the Family of Love, which was said to 'have no bishops nor governors in the church, but all things in common, as wife,

---

[1] Burrage, *EED* ii. 301.

[2] *The Discovery of a Swarme of Separatists* (1641), sigs. A2, A3. H. A. Glass, in his study of *The Barbone Parliament* (1899), p. 135, argues that the real name of the man from which that assembly took its name was 'Praise Barbon', but I have used the name by which he has been remembered for 300 years. There is no evidence to support the oft-repeated assertion that Barebone was a Baptist, or that he ever retracted the defence of infant baptism which he published in 1642.

[3] *A Discoverie of Six Women Preachers* (1641), p. 4.

[4] E. Harris, A *True Relation of a Company of Brownists, Separatists, and Non-Conformists, in Monmouthshire, in Wales* (1641), sig. A2.

children, goods, etc.'.[1] John Taylor convinced himself that the Separatists were hypocrites. In a passage which presages the Restoration stereotype of the Puritan as a fawning humbug Taylor contrasted the outward religiosity with what he supposed was the secret licentiousness of the Separatists: 'though they are superciliously rigid and censorious, yet they seem very charitable, for rather than their sisters shall want food, they will fill their bellies, and rather than they shall be naked, they will cover their bodies'.[2]

Taylor, though, reserved his most bitter satire for the mechanic preachers. In *A Swarme of Sectaries* he expressed in rhyme his belief that by arrogating to themselves the preaching of the Gospel they were upsetting the division of function within society:

> A preacher's work is not to geld a sow,
> Unseemly 'tis a judge should milk a cow,
> A cobbler to a pulpit should not mount,
> Nor can an ass cast up a true account.

Taylor went on to satirize Samuel How's celebrated sermon on *The Sufficiencie of the Spirits Teaching, without Humane Learning,* delivered, so Taylor claimed, in the Nag's Head tavern in Coleman Street:

> A long three quarters prayer being said
> (The good man knowing scarce for what he prayed) . . .
> A worthy brother gave the text, and then
> The cobbler (How) his preachment straight began
> Extemp'ry without any meditation,
> But only by the Spirit's revelation.[3]

How had been dead nine months when Taylor chose to ridicule him, but the cobbler's message, that it is the Holy Spirit, not a university education, which fits a man to interpret the Scriptures, lived on. The author of *The Brownists Synagogue* shows that by October 1641 other mechanic preachers were taking up the theme that 'no man ought to teach but whom the Spirit moves', that human learning is to be distrusted since 'some of Christ's

---

[1] *The Brownists Conventicle,* p. 2. *Religions Lotterie* (1642).
[2] [J. Taylor], *The Anatomy of the Separatists, alias Brownists* (1642), p. 2.
[3] Taylor, *A Swarme of Sectaries,* pp. 2, 8–10.

apostles were fishermen'.[1] The densely populated parish of St. Stephen's Coleman Street, with its crowded alleyways inhabited by artisans and labourers, had been a centre of Lollard influence in London in the 1520s, and was once again to be the focus of radical religion in the capital in the 1640s and 1650s.[2] 'When women preach and cobblers pray,' warned an anonymous rhymster in 1641, 'the fiends in hell make holiday.'[3]

2. SEPARATION OR REFORMATION?: HENRY BURTON VERSUS THOMAS EDWARDS

The fears expressed by John Taylor and his fellow pamphleteers were not confined to the royalist side in the developing quarrel between king and Parliament. Although the House of Commons approved, in May 1641, the second reading of a bill 'for the utter abolishing and taking away of all archbishops, bishops', deans, archdeacons, and canons, it was not with the intention of undermining the established church or of encouraging the growth of Separatist congregations. Indeed Sir Symonds d'Ewes, who moved the second reading, suggested that any 'distractions' which might occur before a new system of church government could be set up could be guarded against by a short bill 'for the severe punishing of tradesmen and other ignorant persons who shall presume to preach'.[4] And when, in November, Parliament stated its case against the king in the Grand Remonstrance it repudiated any intention of letting 'loose the golden reins of discipline and government in the church,' and of leaving 'private persons or particular congregations to take up what form of divine service they please'. It was emphatic 'that there should be throughout the whole realm a conformity to that order which the laws enjoin according to the word of God', and for the drafting of such laws it proposed the calling of 'a general synod of the most grave, pious, learned and judicious divines of this island'.[5] Charles vetoed the proposal when it was

---

[1] *The Brownists Synagogue*, p. 4.

[2] D. A. Kirby, 'The Parish of St Stephen's, Coleman Street', Oxford B. Litt. thesis, 1968, pp. 1–2.

[3] *Lucifers Lacky*, sig. A3.

[4] W. Shaw, *A History of the English Church during the Civil Wars and under the Commonwealth* (1910), i. 78–83.

[5] J. Rushworth, *Historical Collections* (1721), iv. 450.

embodied in a bill in May 1642, but the opening of the Civil
War in August removed the necessity for his assent, and on 1
July 1643 the Westminster Assembly met to complete the re-
formation of the Church of England.

But was the Church of England capable of reform? It was not
only cobblers and mechanic preachers who had doubts on the
question. One of the first acts of the Long Parliament, when it
met in November 1640, had been to order the release of Henry
Burton from his island prison, and he returned to England to a
hero's welcome. When he and Prynne landed at Southampton
'they were received and entertained with extraordinary demon-
stration of affection and esteem, attended by a marvellous con-
flux of company'; as they approached London 'multitudes of
people of several conditions, some on horseback, others on foot,
met them some miles from town'; and from Charing Cross they
were 'carried into the city by above ten thousand persons, with
boughs and flowers in their hands, the common people strewing
flowers and herbs in the ways as they passed'.[1] Parliament voted
to restore Burton to 'his former liberty of preaching' and to
grant him £6,000 by way of compensation for his sufferings.[2]
But neither the warmth of his reception nor the generosity of
Parliament was sufficient to erase from Burton's mind the lessons
he had learned in prison or to reconcile him to the established
church.

On 3 May 1641 Parliament drew up a 'Protestation' to be
taken by the members of both Houses and by all office-holders
in church and state, abjuring popery and promising to maintain
the 'true reformed Protestant religion expressed in the doctrine
of the Church of England'. To Burton this attempt to equate the
'true reformed Protestant religion' with the established church
involved an inherent contradiction, and he rushed out an
anonymous pamphlet, *The Protestation Protested*, in which he
developed the conviction he had arrived at on Guernsey, that
the Church of England was essentially antichristian. 'Most clear
it is by the Scripture', wrote Burton, 'that the liturgy, discipline, government, rites, and ceremonies of the Church of England are all of them so many branches of popery.' Its liturgy

[1] Edward, Earl of Clarendon, *History of the Rebellion and Civil Wars in England*
(Oxford, 1958), i. 269.
[2] *Journal of the House of Commons*, ii. 102, 171.

was derived from 'the Romish Latin liturgy', its preaching was 'generally corrupted' since 'Evangelical truth' was 'restrained and prohibited by orders and edicts', its government was by archbishops, bishops, and archdeacons, none of which 'rabble is found to be in the Scripture'. Burton complained, as Browne and Harrison had complained sixty years before, that the sacraments were administered in parish churches 'pell-mell . . . to ignorant and profane persons'. Like the Separatist pioneers he insisted that 'a particular church or congregation rightly collected and constituted, consists of none but such as are visible living members of Christ the head'. The Church of England, wrote Burton, 'hath been so universally overspread with profaneness and darkness, so long beslaved under the yoke of prelatical tyranny' that it would 'be very difficult, if not rather impossible, to reconstitute it . . . as is agreeable in all points to a true and visible congregation of Christ'. Instead reformation should begin by 'the new forming of a church', by gathering all believers 'into several congregations, who are fitted and who desire to draw near unto Christ in a holy communion with him'. Godly parish ministers might 'reform their own congregations . . . separate the precious from the vile . . . and set up Christ's government in their congregations', but the 'pastors of such Independent congregations' should not accept tithes or any form of public support and should rely solely on the voluntary contributions of the members of their churches.[1]

Burton prayed that God would direct Parliament in its task of reforming the national church, but he professed to be indifferent as to the result, whether its government be 'by a presbytery or otherwise'. All that he asked was that 'a due respect he had to those congregations and churches which desire an exemption and liberty of enjoying Christ's ordinances in such a purity as a national church is not possibly capable of'.[2] Burton's conviction that the Church of England was antichristian did not, though, prevent his returning to his old parish as lecturer in 1642, after his former parishioners had petitioned Parliament on his behalf. The incumbent of St. Matthew's, Friday Street, exasperated by Burton's return, subsequently

---

[1] [H. Burton], *The Protestation Protested* (1641), sigs. A3, B, B3.
[2] Ibid., sig. C2.

fled to the royalists, leaving Burton free to reorganize the congregation as a gathered church. 'It was not in the power of malice to desire . . . a weekly spectacle so hurtful to the royal cause', wrote John Marsden, as Henry Burton preaching in his pulpit without his ears.[1]

The royalists were not alone in being embarrassed by Burton, for his *Protestation Protested* was a cause of concern to many Puritans currently engaged in the struggle with episcopacy. Hitherto most Puritans had only vague ideas on church government, and though they wished to modify or abolish episcopacy for the most part they had no very clear idea of what to put in its place.[2] But, as the Grand Remonstrance made clear, they assumed that the reformed Church of England would still be a national church, closely tied to the state and exercising discipline and authority over all its citizens. Burton's denial of the possibility of perfecting the reformation of the Church of England and his plea for the toleration of Separatist congregations threatened to cast a blight over the Puritan promised land even before the episcopalian wilderness had been left behind.

One Puritan minister, John Geree of Tewkesbury, found that 'many of the more intelligent Christians' and 'even some of reputation in a higher rank' were influenced by Burton's pamphlet.[3] Robert Greville, Lord Brooke, was already suspected of sympathy with Separatism,[4] and in November 1641 he was to publish *A Discourse opening the Nature of . . . Episcopacie* in which he defended the Separatist contention that only he that 'professeth the truth, and to all appearance . . . practiseth as he professeth' should be 'a member of Christ's church'.[5] Alarmed by such indications of heresy in high places Geree put out a reply to *The Protestation Protested*. He argued that the history of the Jews was sufficient precedent for the identity of church and state; cited Paul's letters to the early church to show that there was no guarantee 'that the members in a particular church' would 'be of better metal than the members of a

---

[1] *DNB* iii. 457–9.

[2] Shaw, *English Church*, i. 5–7.

[3] J. Geree, *Judah's Joy at the Oath*, appendix, *Vindiciae Voti* (1641), sig. A2.

[4] D. Laing, ed., *The Letters and Journals of Robert Baillie* (Edinburgh, 1841), i. 275.

[5] R. Geville, Lord Brooke, *A Discourse opening the Nature of that Episcopacie, which is exercised in England* (1641), p. 99, reprinted in Haller, *Tracts on Liberty*, ii. 143.

national church'; and argued from the parable of the wheat and
the tares 'that a general separation is not to be attempted till
the end of the world'.[1]

The most significant reply to Burton, though, was Thomas
Edwards's *Reasons against the Independant Government of Particular
Congregations*, published in August 1641. Edwards was a Puritan
minister whose marriage to a wealthy lady had freed him from
the ties of a parish living and released his energies for preaching
and pamphleteering.[2] Though he had been silenced by Laud
and prosecuted in the Court of High Commission, Edwards was
no more sympathetic towards religious diversity than were his
persecutors. He shared the royalist John Taylor's horror of the
possible religious and social consequences of the growth of
Separatist congregations, although, so far as can be judged, he
was a much more reliable witness than the water-poet. From
1641 Edwards was the fiercest, shrillest, most intolerant of all
the advocates of a Puritan national church, but the very lack of
inhibition and restraint with which he laid bare his own fears,
and what he saw as the errors of his opponents, gives his writings
value as a historical source.

Edwards feared that the growth and toleration of Independent churches would encourage libertinism, profaneness, and
errors; breed Socinians, Arminians, Anabaptists, and Separatists; and 'by some removes bring many men to be of no religion
at all'. He feared that toleration would 'disturb the peace and
quiet of churches and towns' by setting different families 'one
against another' and by causing disunity within families, 'even
between the nearest relations of husbands and wives, fathers
and children'. And he feared that toleration, by creating such
'insolencies and mischiefs' would not be confined to the ecclesiastical sphere: the effect it would have on the civil state he left
'such who are experienced men in matters of government to
foresee and judge of'.[3]

Edwards was particularly fearful of the effect that the
toleration and multiplication of Independent churches would
have on the status of the clergy. He denied that 'well-meaning'
but ignorant lay Christians were competent to form churches

---

[1] Geree, *Judah's Joy*, appendix, sig. D3.   [2] *DNB* vi. 545–6.
[3] T. Edwards, *Reasons against the Independent Government of Particular Congregations*
(1641), epistle dedicatory, pp. 26, 31.

and to 'examine and try the learning, gifts, soundness of men for the ministry'. He denied that such churches were competent to ordain ministers, 'because the less is blessed by the greater, and they who lay hands on and make ministers should be greater in place and authority and not less, as the common people be'. And he denied that good order could be maintained in such churches without 'synods and councils to supply the defects of each particular by the conjunction of the whole'. If toleration were granted, warned Edwards, 'the most eminent ministers in this kingdom' could have little guarantee of keeping their congregations, for the people would desert their ministers 'upon any discontent taken, or any light occasion of demanding dues, or preaching against anything they like not'. As for the many parish clergy who had 'no great popular gifts for preaching', they would be forsaken in 'swarms' for 'more powerful, practical, and zealous preaching'.[1]

The Puritan clergy were fighting to free themselves from the control of bishops and had no wish to enslave themselves to congregations of uneducated laymen. But to the Separatists who were seeking to establish the visible church of Christ on earth, a synod of clergy was no more the true church than was a bench of bishops. The point was made forcibly by Mrs. Katherine Chidley in her *Justification of the Independant Churches of Christ,* published in October 1641. Mrs. Chidley was a London Separatist, probably the widow of Daniel Chidley who had taken part in John Duppa's secession from John Lathrop's Jacobite church in 1630, and she and her son Samuel were to assist in the formation of a gathered church at Bury St. Edmunds in 1646.[2] Mrs. Chidley lacked both the education and the polemical skill of Henry Burton and her pamphlet is both long and laboured, but when roused by Edwards's claims to clerical and male exclusiveness she made telling points. She questioned the validity of his ordination, whether it had any justification 'but that which he hath successively from Rome'. She denied that an unbelieving husband had authority 'over the conscience of his believing wife'. Above all, she defended the right of lay Christians to form churches and choose ministers, for 'who hath a

---

[1] Ibid., pp. 1, 4, 6, 28–9.
[2] Burrage, *EED* i. 321. Bury St. Edmunds Church Book, DWL Harmer MSS. 76.4, pp. 1–2.

greater measure of the Spirit than believers? and who hath more skill than he that hath been trained up in the school of Christ? . . . and who hath greater authority upon earth than they that are visible saints?' Whereas Edwards had maintained 'that all the ministers are greater than one', Mrs. Chidley countered 'that the church of Christ is greater than all the ministers'.[1] Mrs. Chidley, commented the unchivalrous Edwards, is a 'brazen-faced, audacious old woman'.[2]

3. 'THE NEAREST CONJUNCTION' WITH THE CHURCH OF SCOTLAND: THE REVIVAL OF ENGLISH PRESBYTERIANISM

The issues which divided Henry Burton and Katherine Chidley on the one hand from Thomas Edwards and John Geree on the other assumed increasing significance as the Civil War progressed, shattered the Puritan dream of religious uniformity, and in the end fatally divided the parliamentary cause. Edwards and Geree represented a revived English Presbyterianism, for forty years a lost cause, kept alive virtually single-handed by John Paget, pastor of the English Reformed church in Amsterdam. But now, with Parliament contemplating the abolition of episcopacy 'root and branch', and with Separatist congregations proliferating in the metropolis, Presbyterianism caught on a new relevance and appeal: to Puritan clergy it offered a means of repudiating the superior jurisdiction of bishops and of asserting the equality of ministers, while at the same time preserving the established Church of England and the distinction between clergy and laity as necessary defences against religious disorder. The first statement of this revived Presbyterianism came in February 1641 when five Puritan clergymen, Stephen Marshall, Edmund Calamy, Thomas Young, Matthew Newcomen, and William Spurstowe published a reply to Bishop Joseph Hall's *An Humble Remonstrance* in defence of 'the divine right of episcopacy'. From Scripture and the writings of the church Fathers the five Puritans sought to show that in the early church 'bishops and presbyters were originally the same', that there 'was not

[1] K. Chidley, *The Justification of the Independant Churches of Christ* (1641), preface, pp. 26, 7, 15.
[2] T. Edwards, *Gangraena* (3rd edn. 1646), part iii, p. 170.

one chief bishop or president, but the presidency was in many', that there was parity among them. In the New Testament, they argued, 'bishops and presbyters are the same in name, in office, in edifying the church, in power of ordination and jurisdiction'.[1]

The Unitarian historian Alexander Gordon used to argue that English Presbyterianism was distinguished from Scottish Presbyterianism by the use of the term presbytery to denote 'the governing body of a particular church' rather than 'a meeting of delegates from different congregations', and by the greater authority which the English Presbyterians consequently gave to the local church.[2] Cartwright's Presbyterianism, wrote Gordon over half a century ago, was characterized by 'a strict autonomy of "particular churches" associated only for mutual consent and advice', and in our own day Jeremy Goring has revived the argument.[3] Gordon based his case partly on the Book of Discipline, which the Elizabethan Puritans had drawn up, with Cartwright's approval, in 1586, and which the Westminster Assembly was to publish in 1644 as *A Directory of Church-Government*; partly on William Bradshaw's *English Puritanisme*, published in 1605; and partly on the distinction made in 1645 by the English Presbyterian John Bastwick between 'Presbyterian government dependent' and 'Presbyterian government independent'. The former, argued Gordon, characterized Scottish Presbyterianism, the latter was the native English tradition.

The Book of Discipline and the writings of Bradshaw and Bastwick, though, hardly bear the interpretation which Gordon placed upon them. The Book of Discipline stated categorically that particular churches 'ought to obey the opinion of more churches with whom they communicate', and that superior assemblies had authority over lower ones in the Presbyterian hierarchy.[4] It was one of the purposes of Bradshaw's *English Puritanisme* to repudiate such authority, and his book was written

[1] J. Hall, *An Humble Remonstrance to the High Court of Parliament* (1640), p. 25. 'Smectymnuus' (the initials of Stephen Marshall *et al.*), *An Answer to a Booke Entitled an Humble Remonstrance* (1641), pp. 21, 26.

[2] A. Gordon, 'English Presbyterianism', *Christian Life*, 15 Dec. 1888, p. 597.

[3] A. Gordon, *Freedom after Ejection* (1917), p. 151. J. Goring in G. Bolam *et al.*, *The English Presbyterians* (1968), pp. 20, 43.

[4] *Directory of Church-Government*, sigs. A3^r, C2^v.

on behalf not of the Presbyterians but of 'the rigidest sort of those that are called Puritans'—the men who shared the views of Henry Jacob. And when Bastwick spoke of 'Presbyterian government independent' it is quite clear that he meant not Presbyterianism at all, but what most of his contemporaries understood by the term 'Independent'. The whole burden of the argument of this English Presbyterian was to show that 'Presbyterian government independent'—Gordon's 'English Presbyterianism'—was 'not God's ordinance'.[1]

The term 'Presbyterian government independent' can perhaps be used to describe the polity of the English churches in the Netherlands which John Forbes united in a classis from 1621 to 1634, but Forbes's classis was condemned by both the Amsterdam classis and North Holland synod of the Dutch Reformed Church for its Brownist opinions and Jacobite practices, and most of its surviving members, among them Thomas Hooker, John Davenport, and Hugh Peter, subsequently became Congregationalists, not Presbyterians.[2] John Paget, as a member of the Dutch Amsterdam classis, refused to join Forbes's English classis and it was he, not Forbes's associates, who helped to turn the thoughts of English Puritans towards Presbyterianism in the early 1640s. When Paget wrote his *Defence of Church-Government, exercised in Presbyteriall, Classicall, and Synodall Assemblies,* which was published posthumously in 1641, it was to insist that such government should conform, not to some native tradition, but to 'the practice of the Reformed churches'.[3] He did indeed refer to Cartwright, but only to refute the contention of the Jacobite John Davenport that the Elizabethan Puritan sought to restrict 'all jurisdiction unto a particular church'. Cartwright, argued Paget, recommended the example of the Reformed churches, and it was undeniable that those churches 'allow the use of classes and synods, not only for counsel or admonition, but also for the exercise of ecclesiastical authority and jurisdiction'.[4] This, too, was the opinion of Stephen Marshall and his fellow contributors to the *Answer* to Bishop Hall's *Humble Remonstrance.* They cited St. Jerome to support their contention that the early

---

[1] J. Bastwick, *Independency not Gods Ordinance* (1645), esp. pp. 7–8.
[2] Stearns, *Congregationalism in the Dutch Netherlands, passim.* Burrage, *EED* ii. 271.
[3] Paget, *Defence of Church-Government,* title-page.
[4] Ibid., p. 83.

church was governed, not merely advised, 'by the council of the presbyters in common'.[1]

That Presbyterianism became the dominant religious influence on the parliamentary side in the early years of the Civil War, despite the eclipse it had suffered ever since the days of Whitgift, was due to two factors: to the fear of the Puritan clergy and the propertied laity of the anarchy that would follow any relaxation of ecclesiastical discipline, and to the necessity imposed on Parliament, by the plight of its arms, of seeking an alliance with the Scots. When the abolition of episcopacy had been debated in the Commons in the summer of 1641 no M.P. appears to have advocated its replacement with a Presbyterian system of church government, and the House had resolved that the functions of the bishops be transferred to a body of lay commissioners appointed by Parliament. In November 1641 Sir Edward Dering had stated that he had never heard a fellow M.P. advocate either Independency or Presbyterianism 'within these walls'.[2] But the succession of defeats suffered by parliamentary armies in May and June 1643, in the West Country at the hands of Sir Ralph Hopton and at Adwalton Moor in Yorkshire at the hands of the Marquis of Newcastle, forced Parliament to face the problem of the country's ecclesiastical government. Five days after the defeat at Adwalton Moor, on 5 July, the Commons resolved to request Scottish help against the king.[3]

In August six English commissioners arrived in Scotland to negotiate the terms of an alliance. They included Sir Henry Vane, Treasurer of the Navy and M.P. for Hull, who in 1636–7 had served as Governor of Massachusetts, and Philip Nye, who had been pastor of the Jacobite church at Arnhem from 1633 until his return to England in 1640. Both Vane and Nye were thus opponents of Presbyterianism and tried to modify the terms of the religious covenant which the Scots sought to impose on the English Parliament as the price of a political and military alliance. The Scots insisted that the English should agree to bring the Church of England 'to the nearest conjunction and uniformity in religion, confessing of faith, form of church-government, [and] directory for worship' with the Church of

---

[1] 'Smectymnuus', *An Answer*, p. 29.
[2] Shaw, *English Church*, i. 95–101.   [3] Ibid. i. 140.

Scotland.[1] But Vane and Nye succeeded in freeing Parliament, in their eyes, from an unequivocal commitment to a Presbyterian form of church government by inserting the provision that the reformation of the Church of England should also be 'according to the word of God'. It was an amendment which the Scots could hardly oppose, but which gave the English infinite scope for debate and dissension. With that significant alteration the Scottish terms, embodied in the Solemn League and Covenant, were approved by the English Parliament in September and eight commissioners were appointed by the General Assembly of the Church of Scotland 'to treat with the English Parliament or Assembly for the union of England and Scotland in one form of kirk government'.[2]

Initially, it seemed, the Scottish commissioners would not have a difficult task. Parliament had entrusted the task of drawing up proposals for the reform of the Church of England to the Westminster Assembly, consisting of ninety divines, ten peers, and twenty commoners, nominated by both Houses.[3] Of these 120 there were, according to Clarendon, some twenty who were favourable to episcopacy, but most of these never appeared in the Assembly.[4] Another ten favoured, ideally, the reform of the Church of England according to the 'New England way'. But the most important element in the Assembly consisted of some two dozen or so divines who had conformed to the established church before the war, but who now wanted to institute a Presbyterian Church of England on the Scottish model.[5] With the Assembly for the most part ill attended, and with those divines who had no very fixed views on matters of ecclesiastical polity anxious above all for order to be restored in the church, it was possible for the minority with strong Presbyterian convictions to dominate the proceedings.[6] The Scottish commissioners complained of the Assembly's ultimate

---

[1] J. Rushworth, *Historical Collections* (1721), v. 478–9.

[2] Shaw, *English Church*, i. 149–50.

[3] R. D. Bradley, '"Jacob and Esau Struggling in the Wombe": a Study of Presbyterian and Independent Religious Conflicts, 1640–48', Univ. of Kent Ph.D. thesis, 1975, pp. 73–4.

[4] Clarendon, *History of the Rebellion*, ii. 73.

[5] Bradley lists twenty-six 'leading divines who accepted the advisability of the Scottish system', 'Presbyterian and Independent conflicts', p. 78.

[6] Ibid., pp. 74–6.

dependence on Parliament and despaired of the long-winded-
ness of the English divines and their interminable debates, but
as long as Parliament needed the assistance of the Scottish army
to defeat the king they could be reasonably optimistic of the
outcome.

4. SEPARATIST OR CONGREGATIONALIST?: THE PROBLEM OF THE INDEPENDENTS

The opponents, on the parliamentary side, of the reformation
of the Church of England on Presbyterian lines came to be
known by the name that Henry Burton had coined in 1641,
that of 'Independent'. The question of who precisely can be
denominated by the epithet 'Independent', and the associated
problems of the relationship between the Independents and the
Separatists who had preceded them, and between the Independents and the Congregationalists who emerged in the
1640s, have long been matters of controversy. In the 1640s those
Puritans who were in effect the successors of Henry Jacob, men
such as John Cotton, not only dissociated themselves from
Separatism but repudiated the term 'Independency' and
appropriated the word 'Congregational' to distinguish themselves from the Presbyterians.[1] 'Neither in whole nor in part do
we partake' of Browne's schism, insisted Cotton. 'He separated
from churches and from saints: we only from the world, and
that which is of the world.'[2] On the other hand Robert Baillie,
one of the Scottish commissioners in England, denied Cotton's
distinction between separation from churches and separation
from the world, and argued that if Cotton and his co-religionists
disliked the term Independent, they could not object if 'in
place of it, the title of Brownists and Separatists [were] fastened
upon them'. Indeed, argued Baillie, 'the grounds of the Brownists were a great deal more reasonable than that of the Independents', for 'the Brownists did build their separation on the
tyranny of bishops, on the superstition of the ceremonies and
service-book' whereas the Independents of the 1640s had 'no

---

[1] G. F. Nuttall suggests that the earliest printed use of the term 'Congregational
way' was by the future Particular Baptist William Kiffin in the epistle to the
reader in *A Glimpse of Sions Glory* (1641). Nuttall, *Visible Saints* (Oxford, 1957), p. 8,
n. 4.

[2] J. Cotton, *The Way of Congregational Churches Cleared* (1648), pp. 9–11.

such stumbling blocks in their way, bishops and books being abolished'.[1]

The controversy has continued to the present day. English Congregational historians, themselves for the most part advocates of the separation of church and state, have not been ashamed to own the Elizabethan and early-seventeenth-century Separatists as their spiritual forbears. R. W. Dale regarded the church of Richard Fitz as 'the first regularly constituted English Congregational church'; Albert Peel wrote of the early Elizabethan Separatist churches as the 'first Congregational churches'; F. J. Powicke believed that Robert Browne's was the first 'Congregational church regularly planted in England'; and Geoffrey Nuttall acknowledges the Brownists to have an 'honoured place in Congregationalism's origins'.[2] By contrast American scholars, more conscious of the need to explain the phenomenon of state-supported Congregational churches in seventeenth-century Massachusetts, have tended to dissociate Congregationalism from any connection with the turncoat Browne or the martyred Barrow, Greenwood, and Penry. Champlin Burrage contended that 'the beginnings of Independency or Congregationalism' are to be traced not 'to the Brownists or Barrowists, but to the Congregational Puritanism of Henry Jacob'; Douglas Horton, unlike Burrage, recognizes that the terms Independent and Congregational were not synonymous in the mid-seventeenth century, but he agrees with Burrage that 'if any single person is to be named the father of Congregationalism, it is Henry Jacob'; and Verne Morey has called for 'the complete removal of Robert Browne and Brownism from the genetic tree of Congregationalism'.[3] George Yule similarly denies that the Elizabethan Separatists were 'the ancestors of the Independents'.[4]

In attempting to decide who should or should not be designated as 'Independent' it is essential to examine contemporary

[1] R. Baillie, *A Dissuasive from the Errours of the Times* (1645), p. 103.

[2] Dale, *English Congregationalism*, p. 95. Peel, *The First Congregational Churches, passim.* F. J. Powicke, 'English Congregationalism in its Greatness and Decline', in *Essays Congregational and Catholic*, ed. A. Peel (1931), p. 283. Nuttall, *Visible Saints*, p. 7.

[3] Burrage, *EED* i. 33. D. Horton. *Congregationalism, a Study in Church Polity* (1952), p. 58. V. D. Morey, 'History corrects itself; Robert Browne and Congregational Beginnings', *Bulletin of the American Congregational Association*, v (1964), 19.

[4] G. Yule, *The Independents in the English Civil War* (Cambridge, 1958), p. 8.

usage. The word 'Independent' came into common use in 1641 as a result of the pamphlet war between Henry Burton and Thomas Edwards. Until that year, wrote Richard Baxter, when 'Mr. Ball wrote for the liturgy . . . and Mr. Burton published his *Protestation Protested*, I never thought what Presbytery or Independency was, nor ever spake with a man who seemed to know it'.[1] However John Ball's *Friendly Triall of the Grounds Tending to Separation*, which sought 'to raze the foundation of Separation' by proving 'the lawfulness of a stinted liturgy', set forms of prayer, and 'communion in mixed multitudes', did not use the term 'Independent'. Henry Burton appears to have been the first writer to have used the terms 'Independent congregations', 'Independent churches', and 'the church-way of Independency' consistently to describe a form of ecclesiastical polity, while Thomas Edwards gave the word wider currency in his *Reasons against the Independant Government of Particular Congregations*.

Edwards attempted to make a distinction between the Brownists and the Independents and to apply the latter appellation only to the Jacobite 'semi-Separatists' and to the churches of New England.[2] Similarly Edwards's fellow Presbyterian Francis Cheynell distinguished the Independents from the Brownists on the ground that the former were prepared to 'communicate even in a parish-assembly where the ministers and people' were in favour of further reformation.[3] And the Separatist David Brown, a Scottish writing-master and member of the church formed by John Duppa's secession from John Lathrop's Jacobite church in 1630, likewise made a clear distinction between the terms 'Independent' and 'Separatist'. In 1645 a meeting took place between three Separatists – Brown, John Duppa, and Katherine Chidley's son Samuel—and the leaders of Henry Burton's Independent church, to discover whether their respective congregations might have fellowship with each other. Their 'professions and covenants' appeared to be alike, one of Burton's elders pointed out that the royalists regarded their church as Separatist, and Burton himself emphasized that 'he had renounced his ministry and orders which he had of

---

[1] B. Hanbury, *Historical Memorials relating to the Independents* (1841), ii. 69.

[2] Edwards, *Reasons against Independant Government*, pp. 32–3. Edwards, *Antapologia* (1644), p. 204.

[3] F. Cheynell, *The Rise, Growth and Danger of Socinianism* (1643), pp. 65–6.

the Church of England'. But this was not enough for Brown, who objected to the fact that Burton continued to preach, and his members to worship, in parish churches, 'whereas they should have no spiritual fellowship at all with the unfruitful works of darkness'. In the eyes of David Brown and his fellow rigid Separatists Burton's church was 'still in Babel', unequally yoked 'with those of the parish assemblies'.[1]

On the other hand there is a great deal of evidence to show that the term 'Independent' was widely used in the 1640s to embrace not only Jacobite 'semi-Separatists' and 'non-separating Congregationalists' but also men and women who stood in the traditions of Robert Browne and Henry Barrow. Though Thomas Edwards tried to distinguish between Independents and Separatists, he did not always adhere to that distinction strictly; he defined Anabaptism as 'the highest form of Independency' and Brownism as 'the middle form of Independency'; and he numbered among the advocates of Independency the Separatist John Robinson and the Separatist author of *Syons Prerogative Royal*.[2] The Presbyterian John Geree wrote of 'Independent Separate churches' as though the terms were synonymous; another Presbyterian, Charles Herle, who in 1643 sought to prove *The Independency on Scriptures of the Independency of Churches*, included in his own list of Independents the Separatists Henry Ainsworth, John Robinson, John Canne, and Katherine Chidley; and William Prynne argued that 'Separatism or Brownism' was the 'ancient proper title of Independency'.[3]

All this might be dismissed as a Presbyterian plot to tar Congregationalists with the sectarian brush, but it was not only among Presbyterians that the term 'Independent' was used to include Separatists as well as followers of the 'New England way'. Though David Brown declined to recognize Henry Burton as a fellow Separatist in 1645, four years earlier the man who had introduced the word 'Independent' to describe his

---

[1] D. Brown, *Two Conferences between some of those that are called Separatists and Independents* (1650), pp. 1–4.

[2] Edwards, *Antapologia*, pp. 201, 204, 294. *Reasons against Independant Government*, p. 4.

[3] J. Geree, *Vindiciae Voti*, sig. D2. C. Herle, *The Independency on Scriptures of the Independency of Churches* (1643), p. 4. W. Prynne, *A Full Reply to Certaine Briefe Observations and Anti-Queries* (1644), p. 11.

views on church polity at the same time acknowledged them to be those of a Separatist. 'God's people', wrote Burton, 'must be Separatists from the world and from false churches,' of which the Church of England, in his view, unquestionably was one.[1] The Separatist Mrs. Chidley accepted the term 'Independent' as applying to her own views on church government; John Canne used the word to cover 'sectaries, Brownists, and Anabaptists'; and John Rogers, pastor of an Independent church at Dublin in the early 1650s, acknowledged the Separatist Henry Ainsworth as a fellow Independent.[2] The future Leveller William Walwyn distinguished Independents from Brownists in 1644, but in 1645 wrote of 'all sorts of Independents, whether Anabaptists or Brownists or Antinomians'; the future Fifth Monarchist Christopher Feake, successively vicar of All Saints, Hertford, and lecturer at St. Anne's, Blackfriars, London, used the term 'separated congregations' to describe the type of gathered church of which he was a pastor.[3] Even John Winthrop, the Governor of Massachusetts, acknowledged that in England not only the 'godly and orthodox . . . Mr. Goodwin, Mr. Nye, and Mr. Burroughes', but even Anabaptists, Antinomians, and Seekers 'went under the name of Independents'.[4] The clearest contemporary elucidation of the relationship between the Separatists and the Independents came from the pen of an anonymous critic of Walwyn in 1649 who wrote that while 'all sectaries are Independents . . . all Independents be not properly sectaries'.[5]

It is thus legitimate to use the term 'Independent' to embrace both Separatists and Congregationalists in the 1640s, the spiritual heirs of Robert Browne and of Henry Jacob alike. The usage can be justified both by contemporary practice and in logic, for Separatists and Congregationalists, no matter how much they might disagree in their attitude to the established church, agreed in asserting the independence of the local

---

[1] Burton, *Protestation Protested*, sig. B3.

[2] J. Canne, *The Improvement of Mercy* (1649), p. 22. J. Rogers, *Ohel or Beth-Shemesh. A Tabernacle for the Sun* (1653), p. 45.

[3] W. Walwyn, *The Compassionate Samaritane* (1644), pp. 75–6; Walwyn, *A Help to a Right Understanding of a Discourse concerning Independency* (1645), p. 6; both reprinted in Haller, *Tracts on Liberty*, iii. 102, 198. C. Feake, *A Beam of Light* (1659), p. 37.

[4] Miller, *Orthodoxy in Massachusetts*, p. 301, quoting J. Winthrop, *Journal*, ii. 279.

[5] Anon., *Church-Levellers* (1649), p. 1.

congregation from any higher ecclesiastical authority. It is probable that it was from the Separatist Francis Johnson that Henry Jacob had derived his views on the visible church and, as Robert Baillie pointed out, the Separatist and Congregational conceptions of ecclesiastical polity were essentially the same. Brownists and Jacobites agreed in putting 'the power of gathering churches, and joining together by covenant in a church way, in the hands of private Christians alone, without . . . the authority of any magistrate'; they both maintained that as few as 'seven persons make a full ministerial and completely organised church'; and they both gave unto those 'seven covenanted persons the whole ecclesiastical power, and that independently upon any person under heaven'. They were at one, Baillie complained, in denying the sacraments to the vast majority of Christians, for they would administer baptism only to those children 'whose immediate parents are members of their congregation', and in determining who should be admitted to communion the Jacobites were 'as strict as any of the Brownists'.[1] In the 1640s and 1650s the Separatists and Congregationalists formed two distinct but collateral branches of the larger tree of Independency.

5. GODLY UNITY OR LIBERTY FOR
TENDER CONSCIENCES?:
THE DILEMMA OF THE CONGREGATIONALISTS

Far from having an exclusive right to the name 'Independent', the ten or so Congregational ministers who made up the minority party in the Westminster Assembly were at first far more reluctant to accept the description than were the self-confessed Separatists Henry Burton and Katherine Chidley. They disowned, they said, 'that proud and insolent title of Independency', conveying as it did 'to all men's apprehensions . . . a trumpet of defiance' against both spiritual and civil power.[2] The leaders of this group were the five men who put their names to the *Apologeticall Narration*, early in 1644: William Bridge, Jeremiah Burroughes, Thomas Goodwin, Philip Nye,

---

[1] Baillie, *Dissuasive from the Errours*, pp. 107–9, 119–20.
[2] T. Goodwin, *et al.*, *An Apologeticall Narration* (1643 old style), pp. 15, 23, reprinted in Haller, *Tracts on Liberty*, ii. 306–39.

and Sidrach Simpson.[1] All five had emigrated to the Netherlands in the 1630s rather than conform to the Laudian innovations, and all returned to England after the summoning of the
Long Parliament, Bridge becoming pastor of a gathered church
at Norwich and Yarmouth, Burroughes securing appointment
as lecturer to congregations in Stepney and Cripplegate, Goodwin setting up a gathered church in London, Nye securing
livings successively as vicar of Kimbolton in Huntingdonshire
and as rector of Acton in Middlesex, and Simpson returning to
St. Margaret's, Fish Street, as lecturer.

That men such as Nye were able to accept benefices within
the established church, while at the same time upholding the
concept of the gathered church, is evidence of the gulf that
divided the Jacobites from the Separatists, the conservative
Congregationalists from the radical Independents. In the early
months of the Westminster Assembly the Congregationalist
minority seemingly hoped that the divines might sanction the
setting-up of gathered churches within the state system, as had
happened in New England. To that end they were initially
prepared to co-operate with the Presbyterians both in presenting a united front against the royalists and in opposing the
formation of Separatist congregations. When, in November
1643, Puritan clergy in the city of London presented a petition
to the Westminster Assembly complaining of 'the lamentable
confusion of their church under the present anarchy, the increase of Anabaptists, Antinomians, and sectaries, [and] the
boldness of some in the city, and about it, in gathering separate
congregations', the Congregationalists in the Assembly were as
willing as the Presbyterians to respond to the petition and to
discourage such activities.[2] In December seven Congregationalists, including the five Apologists, joined with fourteen other
members of the Assembly in publishing *Certaine Considerations
to Dis-swade Men from Further Gathering of Churches*. Congrega-

---

[1] R. D. Bradley points out that it is inaccurate to describe the five authors of the
Apologeticall Narration as the 'Dissenting Brethren'. The term 'Dissenting Brethren'
was used originally of the seven Congregationalists who dissented from the majority
recommendations of the Westminster Assembly in November 1644. The 'Dissenting
Brethren' thus constituted the five Apologists plus William Carter and William
Greenhill. Bradley, 'Presbyterian and Independent conflicts', p. 316.

[2] L. Kaplan, 'Presbyterians and Independents in 1643', *English Historical Review*,
lxxxiv (April 1969), 254.

tionalist and Presbyterian alike declared it to be 'an undoubted maxim, that it belongs to Christian magistrates in an essential manner to be authorisers of . . . reformation', and urged ministers and people 'to forbear for a convenient time the joining of themselves into church-societies' until they could see what form of church government the Assembly would recommend.[1]

When, a fortnight later, Bridge, Burroughes, Goodwin, Nye, and Simpson submitted to Parliament their *Apologeticall Narration*, they sought to minimize the extent to which they differed from the Presbyterians. They had delayed publishing their opinions, they wrote, for fear of 'dividing the godly Protestant party in this kingdom'; they now ventured to put their views before Parliament only because they had been provoked by the 'common misunderstandings and misrepresentations of our opinions and practices'; all that they desired was liberty to enjoy 'the ordinances of Christ . . . with the allowance of a latitude of some lesser differences'. They affirmed that they were as orthodox in doctrine as the Presbyterians; they recognized that 'multitudes of the assemblies and parochial congregations' of the established church were true churches; they claimed that they had remained in communion with the Church of England even when they had been in exile. They assured Parliament that throughout their sojourn in the Netherlands they had given 'the right hand of fellowship' to, and received it from, the Dutch Reformed Church; that they had been allowed to ring a public bell to summon members to their meetings; that some of their number had been allowed 'a full and liberal maintenance' from the Dutch state. Above all, they repudiated 'the odious name of Brownism'. What they professed, they wrote, 'was a middle way betwixt that which is falsely charged on us, Brownism, and that which is the contention of the times, the authoritative Presbyterial government'.[2]

In thus proclaiming their common cause with the Presbyterians, while differing from them, in calling for each congregation to have 'complete power of jurisdiction', yet emphasizing their dependence on the magistrate, in pleading for toleration for

---

[1] *Certaine Considerations to Dis-swade Men from Further Gathering of Churches* (1643), pp. 2–3.

[2] Goodwin, *Apologeticall Narration*, pp. 6–8, 23–5, 28, 31. Thomas Edwards recorded, probably truthfully, that Philip Nye stated that Henry Burton's *Protestation Protested* contained 'gross Brownism'. *Gangraena*, part iii, p. 243.

themselves, yet not for all men, the Apologists were on the horns of a perplexing dilemma. As always, there were men on both left and right ready to expose the illogicalities of the Jacobite middle way. The Presbyterians resented their appeal from the Assembly to the civil power, asked how they could claim to be in communion with the Church of England when they would not admit all members of that church to the sacrament, and argued that if toleration were granted to the Congregationalists it could not 'well be denied to other sects'.[1] The Apologists might not be Brownists, quipped the indefatigable Thomas Edwards, but their's was the way of 'Browne's younger brother'.[2] In the Westminster Assembly the Presbyterians outvoted the Congregationalists on all questions of importance. The attempts by the Congregationalists to secure for each congregation control over its own discipline, their defence of the right of a congregation to ordain its own minister, their opposition to the subordination of the congregation to 'classical, provincial, and national assemblies' were alike defeated.[3] When the Assembly reported its decisions to Parliament in November 1644 only seven members—the 'Dissenting Brethren'—demurred. When it finalized its recommendations on church government in April 1645 these were, wrote Baillie, 'according to the doctrine and practice of the Church of Scotland, in everything material'.[4] And when, in August, Parliament approved the ordinance for the election of elders in the London province, it took the first step towards the creation of a national Presbyterian church.[5]

The victory of the Presbyterians in the Assembly emphasized the dilemma facing the Apologists in their attempt to reconcile their ideal of Congregational church government with their repudiation of separation from the national church. The day after the Westminster Assembly presented the completed draft of its recommendations on church government to Parliament in July, Robert Baillie wrote that the Presbyterians hoped 'to get the Independents put to it to declare themselves either to be for the rest of the sectaries, or against them'. 'If they declare

[1] A [dam] S[teuart], *Some Observations and Annotations upon the Apologeticall Narration* (1644), pp. 4–5, 7, 61.

[2] Edwards, *Antapologia*, p. 296.   [3] Shaw, *English Church*, i. 168, 174, 178.

[4] Bradley, 'Presbyterian and Independent conflicts', pp. 315–16, *Letters of Baillie*, ii. 266.

[5] Shaw, *English Church*, i. 190–7.

against them,' he predicted, 'they will be but a small inconsiderable company; if for them, all honest men will cry upon them for separating from all the Reformed churches, to join with Anabaptists and libertines.'[1]

The danger of the second of these courses had been emphasized by the arrival in England in September 1643 of Roger Williams, founder of the colony of Rhode Island, who had returned to his native land to seek a charter for his settlement. Williams's presence in England was an embarrassment to the Congregationalists in the Westminster Assembly. In the *Apologeticall Narration* they had admitted the influence of their fellow countrymen who had transported 'themselves many thousand miles distance, and that by sea, into a wilderness, merely to worship God more purely'.[2] But, as their Presbyterian critics never tired of pointing out, the Congregationalists of New England did not practise towards others the toleration which the Congregationalists of old England desired for themselves. The Massachusetts Congregationalists had maintained as vigorously as the English and Scottish Presbyterians that religious toleration would disrupt the churches and disturb the state, and to guard against these evils the franchise had been restricted to members of the Congregational churches. Yet all the inhabitants of the colony were compelled to attend Congregational worship, contribute to the financial support of the Congregational churches, and to abstain from heresy, blasphemy, and the creation of other churches by order of the civil magistrate.[3]

Roger Williams had had experience of Massachusetts intolerance. Born in 1603 the son of a London merchant and educated at Pembroke Hall, Cambridge, he had arrived in Boston in 1631 and was invited to become teacher of its Jacobite church. But Williams was already entertaining Separatist views and declined to minister to a congregation which made a virtue of its refusal to separate from the Church of England. He did, though, accept an invitation to preach to the church at Salem two years later, and so encouraged those Separatist tendencies which had already alarmed John Cotton that in 1635 the Massachusetts magistrates banished him from the

---

[1] *Letters of Baillie*, ii. 299.   [2] Goodwin, *Apologeticall Narration*, p. 5.
[3] Miller, *Orthodoxy in Massachusetts*, pp. 243, 252–7.

colony. Driven from 'house and land and wife and children in the midst of a New England winter', he settled on unclaimed land to the north of Narragansett Bay and here at Providence established the first community 'in the modern western world to be founded explicitly on separation of the civil and ecclesiastical powers'.[1]

His settlement soon attracted other refugees from Massachusetts, including Mrs. Anne Hutchinson and a number of Baptists, and Williams was himself baptized by affusion. His association with the Baptists was, however, brief. He soon began to have doubts about the validity of his second baptism, and though he believed that the practice of the Baptists came 'nearer the first practice of our great founder Christ Jesus, than other practices of religion do', he could not follow the example of those Baptists who underwent a third baptism by immersion.[2] The position which Williams finally arrived at was one which contemporaries described as that of a Seeker.[3] Williams, said John Cotton, 'fell off from his ministry, and then from all church fellowship, and then from his baptism . . . and then from the Lord's Supper and from all ordinances of Christ dispensed in any church way, till God shall stir up . . . some . . . new apostles, to recover and restore all the ordinances and churches of Christ out of the ruins of anti-Christian apostasy'.[4] Williams, though, would never admit to the name of Seeker, nor to the membership of any other sect.[5] He became what the opponents of Separatism had always prophesied would be its *reductio ad absurdum*, the one-man church.

Though he repudiated his church membership Williams remained on friendly terms with the Baptists and became a celebrated exponent of their views of religious liberty. While in London in 1643–4 not only did he obtain a charter for his colony, and thus thwart Hugh Peter's attempts to claim Providence for Massachusetts, he made his own contribution to the debate then raging over England's religious future. He published three pamphlets, *Queries of Highest Consideration*, a reply to John *Cottons Letter Lately Printed,* and *The Bloudy Tenent of Persecution.* In the first, addressed both to the five Apologists

---

[1] J. Garrett, *Roger Williams* (1970), p. 19.   [2] Burrage, *EED* i. 365.
[3] Garrett, *Roger Williams*, pp. 147, 152.   [4] Ibid., p. 153.
[5] Ibid., p. 29.

and the Scottish commissioners, he ridiculed the consequences of state control of religion, the violent fluctuations in England's ecclesiastical history whereby 'the fathers made the children heretics, and the children the fathers'. In the second he exposed the illogicalities of non-separating Congregationalism. And in the third he defended a Baptist plea for toleration, the *Most Humble Supplication* which the imprisoned John Murton had penned in milk in 1620. 'In vain', he wrote, 'have English Parliaments permitted English Bibles in the poorest English houses, and the simplest man or woman to search the Scriptures, if yet against their soul's persuasion from the Scripture, they should be forced (as if they lived in Spain or Rome itself, without the sight of a Bible) to believe as the church believes.'[1]

A generation earlier Smyth, Helwys, and Murton had advocated such views, and they had died in exile, prison, and obscurity. Now, on 9 August 1644, Parliament voted that Williams's books be publicly burned. Yet only five weeks later the House of Commons ordered a committee of both Houses, the Westminster Assembly, and the Scottish commissioners to attempt to reconcile the differences of opinion within the Assembly and, failing that, 'to endeavour the finding out some ways how far tender consciences, who cannot in all things submit to the common rule which shall be established, may be borne with, according to the Word'.[2] In demanding toleration of the things wherein they differed from their Presbyterian brethren, the Congregationalists of England opened the door for the toleration of sects and schisms which the Congregationalists of New England sought to proscribe. And once opened, that door would prove none too easy to close. For behind the pen of Roger Williams there threatened the swords of the army that Parliament itself had raised.

6. 'THE SOUL OF THE ARMY':
CROMWELL AND THE INDEPENDENTS

For the first year of the war the parliamentary army was a volunteer force which attracted to its ranks both poor people inspired by the prospect of pay and plunder and men for whom

---

[1] P. Miller, *Roger Williams* (New York, 1962), pp. 83, 94–8, 111.

[2] W. Haller, *Liberty and Reformation in the Puritan Revolution* (New York, 1955), pp. 130, 133.

the war was a religious crusade. While it was concern for 'public safety and liberty' which chiefly motivated 'the nobility and gentry who adhered to Parliament', wrote Richard Baxter, it was 'principally the differences about religious matters that filled up the Parliament's armies and put the resolution and valour into their soldiers'.[1] These soldiers did not share the enthusiasm of the divines of the Westminster Assembly for a clerically controlled Presbyterian establishment and were anxious to use their new-found freedom from episcopacy to search the Scriptures for themselves and to draw their own conclusions on the proper doctrine, worship, and polity of the church. They were aided by the failure of the more orthodox Puritan clergy to appreciate the significance of these developments until it was too late. Though at the beginning of the war each regiment in the parliamentary army had been accompanied by an orthodox minister, at the time of the battle of Edgehill in October 1642 'almost all of them went home', preferring their comfortable parish livings to the rigours and dangers of army life.[2] The soldiers were thus left largely to their own devices and the army became a training ground for lay preachers whose activities Parliament laboured in vain to suppress.[3] Though Parliament resorted to impressment in August 1643, thus adding to the original volunteers conscripts whose devotion to radical religion was more open to question, this did not change the distinctive religious character of the army. Half the infantry in the reorganized New Model army of 1645 were pressed men, but the majority were ill-educated persons who could not even sign their names,[4] and they were pliable tools in the hands of the minority of religious enthusiasts. Thomas Edwards believed that only one in six of the officers and soldiers of the army were sectaries or Independents, and Richard Baxter put the figure at less than one in twenty. But they were, admitted Baxter, 'the soul of the army'.[5]

Clerical critics of the growth of religious radicalism in the

---

[1] M. Sylvester, ed., *Reliquiae Baxterianae, or Richard Baxter's Narratives of the Most Memorable Passages of his Life and Times* (1696), part i, p. 31.

[2] Ibid., part i, p. 51.

[3] L. F. Solt, *Saints in Arms* (Stanford, 1959), pp. 9–10.

[4] C. H. Firth, *Cromwell's Army* (1962), pp. 36, 40.

[5] Edwards, *Gangraena*, part i, § i, pp. 13–14. *Reliquiae Baxterianae*, part i, p. 50.

army put much of the blame on Cromwell. A member of the younger branch of a Huntingdonshire landed family whose fortunes had been founded on the dissolution of the monasteries, Cromwell had spent his early manhood in 'good fellowship and gaming', but at the age of about thirty he had a conversion experience which henceforward committed him to the Puritan cause. He was elected to represent Huntingdon in the Parliament of 1628 and to represent Cambridge in both the Short and Long Parliaments of 1640, and soon after the outbreak of war he was given responsibility for the defence of the eastern counties. His victories at Grantham and Gainsborough in 1643 relieved an otherwise gloomy year for the parliamentary forces and laid the foundation for his subsequent rapid rise. In 1644 he was appointed lieutenant-general to the Earl of Manchester, the commander of the Eastern Association.

Despite the many volumes which have been devoted to the life of Cromwell, his views on church polity remain something of a mystery. He was never a Separatist, and his theology was that of a Calvinist whose experiences convinced him that he was a chosen instrument of God. Baxter recalled that in the early days of the war, when the threats of a royalist mob had obliged him to leave his living in Kidderminster and seek refuge in Coventry, he had received an invitation to be pastor to Cromwell's troop of cavalry, which 'his officers purposed to make . . . a gathered church'.[1] But Baxter declined the invitation and denounced the scheme, and the incident is hardly sufficient, as Robert Paul claims, to resolve the problem of Cromwell's churchmanship.[2] There is no evidence that this intention to constitute Cromwell's troop as a gathered church was in fact ever carried out, nor is there any evidence, apart from Baxter's solitary and inconclusive reference, that Cromwell himself ever joined a gathered church. Had an event of such importance in the life of Cromwell ever occurred, one would have expected some more substantial evidence to have survived. What gives Cromwell his importance in the history of Dissent is not his views on church polity, but his hatred of religious intolerance. Cromwell was one of the several deeply religious men of his

---

[1] *Reliquiae Baxterianae*, part i, p. 51.

[2] R. S. Paul, *The Lord Protector* (1955), pp. 66–7. For another criticism of Paul's thesis see G. F. Nuttall, *The Puritan Spirit* (1967), pp. 137–9.

generation, of whom Roger Williams and John Milton are other examples, who sympathized with the radical sects, but who were unwilling or unable to decide between their conflicting claims and give wholehearted adherence to one or the other. When, in April 1644, Robert Baillie referred to Cromwell as 'the great Independent' he was indicating where his sympathies lay, but he was not describing his churchmanship.[1]

Though the practice of using the term 'Independent' to denote a political as distinct from a religious party can be justified by reference to contemporary polemic, it has led to seemingly endless confusion among historians and should be abandoned.[2] George Yule has suggested that there is a 'strong connexion' between 'the parliamentary Independent party and religious Independency', but his own carefully researched list of 'political Independents' hardly supports his case. For only twelve of the M.P.s who sat in the Long Parliament before Pride's Purge does Yule provide concrete evidence that they were ever religious Independents or Baptists, and of these twelve Sir Henry Vane's Congregational church membership does not appear to have survived his return from Massachusetts, while in the case of two more the evidence for their religious affiliation dates from well after the Restoration.[3] Stephen Foster's attempt to discern a nascent 'Independent party' in the thirty-nine signatories of an appeal sent to Massachusetts in 1642, asking John Cotton, Thomas Hooker, and John Davenport to return to England to participate in the forthcoming Westminster Assembly, is similarly unconvincing.[4] Foster's

[1] *Letters of Baillie*, ii. 153.

[2] See e.g., J. H. Hexter, 'The Problem of the Presbyterian Independents', *American Historical Review*, xliv (1938); G. Yule, *The Independents in the English Civil War*; the articles by D. Underdown and Yule in *Journal of British Studies*, iii (May 1964), vii (May 1968), viii (Nov. 1968); the article by V. Pearl in *Trans. Royal Historical Society*, 5th series, xviii (1968); the article by S. Foster in *Past and Present*, xliv (Aug. 1969); and the articles by B. Worden, Pearl, Underdown, Yule, Hexter, and Foster in *Past and Present*, xlvii (May 1970). Underdown comes closest to jettisoning the 'political Independents' when he writes 'that the term "Independent" is worthless as a party name except in 1646–8, and then only the strictest definition will do'. *Journal of British Studies*, iii (May 1964), 80.

[3] The twelve are J. Bingham (1672), J. Carew, M. Corbet, J. Dixwell, E. Dunch (1669), T. Harrison, H. Lawrence, I. Pennington, W. Sydenham, Sir H. Vane, B. Whitelocke, and R. Wilson. Yule, *Independents in the English Civil War*, pp. 84–128.

[4] S. Foster, 'The Presbyterian Independents Exorcized', *Past and Present*, xliv (1969), 68–9.

case is undermined by the presence among his list of signatories of such conservative Puritans as the Earl of Warwick and the Earl of Manchester: men who may have sympathized with the New England way at a distance, but whose sympathy was to turn to hostility when it became clear that Congregationalism was not going to play in old England the conservative role it had performed in Massachusetts. Of the thirty-nine signatories of the appeal to New England only Isaac Pennington, Miles Corbet, and perhaps Lord Brooke can be identified as religious Independents. A person can be properly described as an Independent only if he is known to have been a member of a gathered church, and this cannot be said of most of the supposedly 'political Independents', least of all of Cromwell. When Baxter joined the New Model army as chaplain in 1645 he found that Cromwell headed an alliance of people he described as 'Anabaptists, Antinomians, Seekers, or Separatists at best', an alliance bound together by their common interest in liberty of conscience. But Cromwell, wrote Baxter, did not 'openly profess what opinion he was of himself'.[1]

Because Cromwell chose his officers for their strength of character and depth of religious conviction rather than for their social position, because he dared even to justify his appointment of Baptists, he was accused by Presbyterians and conservative Puritans of packing the army with wild sectaries. The Earl of Manchester himself protested that Cromwell 'desired to have none in my army but such as were of the Independent judgement'.[2] But the parliamentary victory at Marston Moor in July 1644 added to Cromwell's prestige, notwithstanding the important part played in the battle by the Scottish army, and when in September the House of Commons voted its order for the accommodation of tender consciences, Baillie attributed it to Cromwell, whose 'great shot' it was 'to have a liberty for all religions'.[3]

In the latter half of 1644 the war aims of the more conservative Parliamentarians and of their radical critics began openly to diverge. Cromwell accused Manchester of dilatoriness in

[1] *Reliquiae Baxterianae*, part i, p. 57. Lady Antonia Fraser's conclusions on the question of Cromwell's churchmanship are similar to my own, *Cromwell, Our Chief of Men* (1974), pp. 404–5.
[2] Firth, *Cromwell's Army*, p. 315.
[3] *Letters of Baillie*, ii. 226, 230.

action, of not wanting to end the war by the sword, of maintaining 'that if we were to beat the king ninety-nine times he would be king still'.[1] The quarrel was resolved by dismissing Manchester and by creating the New Model army, a national army which was not dependent on the county committees, with Fairfax as Lord General and Cromwell as his second-in-command. When Baxter visited the New Model two days after its first and greatest victory at Naseby in June 1645 he was appalled at what he found. He heard soldiers plotting 'their intention to subvert both church and state'. 'Independency and Anabaptistry were most prevalent: Antinomianism and Arminianism were equally distributed.'[2] It was in order to counter these anarchic and heretical tendencies that Baxter accepted an invitation to become chaplain to the regiment of the orthodox Colonel Whalley, and set himself 'to find out the corruptions of the soldiers, and to discourse and dispute them out of their mistakes'. They were being influenced, he found, by 'men that had been in London, hatched up among the old Separatists'. They contended 'sometimes for state democracy, and sometimes for church democracy, sometimes against set forms of prayer, and sometimes against infant baptism . . . sometimes about free-grace and free-will, and all the points of Antinomianism and Arminianism'. 'But their most frequent and vehement disputes were for liberty of conscience . . . that the civil magistrate had nothing to do to determine of anything in matters of religion . . . but every man might not only hold, but preach and do in matters of religion what he pleased.'[3]

In attempting to disabuse the soldiers of such notions Baxter was fighting a lone and losing battle, and Whalley 'grew odious among the sectarian commanders at the headquarters for my sake'.[4] The conservative Baxter, who would not even own the name Presbyterian and always insisted that he was but a moderate Episcopalian, arrived too late to counter the influence of radical chaplains like William Dell and John Saltmarsh, whom their opponents accused of Antinomianism, of William Erbery, who was moving away from an Independent position to that of a Seeker, and of the returned exile Hugh Peter.[5]

---

[1] Paul, *The Lord Protector*, pp. 87–8.   [2] *Reliquiae Baxterianae*, part i, p. 50.
[3] Ibid., part i, p. 53.   [4] Ibid., part i, p. 55.
[5] For Baxter's repudiation of the name Presbyterian see *Reliquiae Baxterianae*,

Hugh Peter had come to England in 1641 as the agent of Massachusetts to obtain money and supplies for the colony, and stayed to advocate religious toleration as passionately as he had supported the enforcement of Congregational ortho-doxy in New England.[1] He was employed by Parliament to win the uncertain loyalties of the people of Kent and Sussex to the parliamentary cause, to obtain loans from the Dutch and undo the work of Laud among the English merchants in the Nether-lands, and to accompany the Earl of Essex on his ill-fated attempt to capture Devon and Cornwall for Parliament in the summer of 1644. Hugh Peter was noted for his sense of humour, but he was in deadly earnest when, on Salisbury plain in July 1645, he tried to persuade Fairfax to delay his march to the relief of Taunton to enable the army to demolish 'the monu-ments of heathenism' at Stonehenge.[2]

7. 'THE GANGRENE OF HERESY AND ERROR': THE FAILURE OF THE PRESBYTERIANS

For orthodox Puritans such as Baxter and Thomas Edwards one of the most alarming aspects of the growth of heretical views in the army was the way in which these in their turn were infecting the civilian population. In February 1646 Edwards published the first part of his most famous book, *Gangraena, or a Catalogue and Discovery of many of the Errors, Heresies, Blasphemies and pernicious practices of the Sectaries of this time*. Two further parts followed, in May and December, giving in all 700 pages in which Edwards listed sixteen sorts of sectaries, catalogued 271 different errors, and kept up his high-pitched tone of outraged indignation to the very end.

'Every taking of a town or city' by the parliamentary army, he bewailed, 'is a further spreading over this kingdom the gan-grene of heresy and error, where the errors were never known nor heard of before.'[3] Parliament's orders for the silencing of unordained preachers and for the restriction of unlicensed printing were violated, so that 'sects and schisms increase and

part i, pp. 55–6, part ii, p. 373. The fullest accounts of Dell and Saltmarsh are in Solt, *Saints in Arms*, and of Erbery in J. I. Morgan, 'The Life and Work of William Erbery', Oxford B. Litt. thesis, 1968.

[1] Stearns, *The Strenuous Puritan*, pp. 125, 154.
[2] Ibid., pp. 215, 218–19, 226–31, 251.
[3] Edwards, *Gangraena*, part i, § ii, p. 80.

grow daily', the country swarmed with 'all sorts of illiterate mechanic preachers, yea of women and boy preachers', and meetings of sectaries flourished especially in the city of London, 'eleven at least in one parish'.[1] Edwards supported his case with a wealth of evidence, much of it gathered from correspondence with distracted Presbyterian ministers throughout the country. He complained of the activities of Hugh Peter, who travelled 'here and there, in this country and that country, in the army and at London', disseminating Independent propaganda and attempting to secure the return of like-minded men to vacant seats in Parliament.[2] He reported the growing influence in the army of Dell and Saltmarsh, who preached 'free grace' and argued that if men had 'Christ in their heart, though they do not read and pray, and trade in duties', they would be judged 'according to their heart'.[3] He drew attention to the missionary endeavours of the General Baptist Thomas Lamb, chandler and soap-boiler and pastor of a church which met in Bell Alley, off Coleman Street, and of his associate Samuel Oates, a weaver. They 'preached universal grace, the Arminian tenets', and travelled through Surrey, Hampshire, and Essex 'to preach their corrupt doctrines and to dip'.[4] To these he added the exploits of another member of Lamb's church, Henry Denne, whom he described as both 'a great Arminian' and 'a desperate Antinomian', who had got possession of the parish church at Eltisley in Cambridgeshire through the influence of the lord of the manor. Before the war Denne had been 'a great time-server, an high-altar man', but now maintained that 'ministers must work with their hands', became a carter, preached 'much against tithes', and carried on missionary work in Cambridgeshire, Huntingdonshire, Bedfordshire, Lincolnshire, and Kent.[5] Nor did Edwards ignore the activities of Particular Baptists like William Kiffin, 'who went his progress in Kent, and did a great deal of hurt'; Thomas Collier, 'an illiterate carter and husbandman', 'the first that sowed the seeds of Anabaptism' in the West Country; and Hanserd Knollys, a former clergyman who had been banished from New England and 'went into the army

---

[1] Ibid., part i, epistle dedicatory, sig. B.   [2] Ibid., part i, § i, p. 61; § ii, p. 40.
[3] Ibid., part iii, p. 45.   [4] Ibid., part i, § ii, p. 35.
[5] Ibid., part i, § ii, pp. 22, 106, part iii, pp. 86–7. E. B. Underhill, ed., *Records of the Churches of Christ, gathered at Fenstanton, Warboys, and Hexham* (1854), p. x.

which was under the command of the Earl of Manchester, where he did a great deal of mischief'.[1] England, wrote Edwards 'is become already in many places a chaos, a Babel, another Amsterdam . . . and in the high way to Münster'.[2]

Edwards had a full stock of tales to tell of the misdeeds of the sectaries. Thomas Lamb's church in Bell Alley, he claimed, was notorious for its 'disputes and wranglings'. It was frequented by many people, 'especially young youths and wenches', so that they filled the house in which the church met and spilled over into the yard. The meetings were marked by 'confusion and noise, as if it were at a play'. It was usual for 'the company to stand up and object against the doctrine delivered when the exerciser of his gifts hath made an end', or even to interrupt him in the middle of his discourse, so that sometimes the 'standing up and objecting' continued 'for almost an hour'.[3] Not content with holding their own disorderly meetings, the sectaries frequently disturbed services in parish churches and on occasion dragged ministers from their pulpits and installed themselves in their stead.[4] They resisted the payment of tithes, and in Northamptonshire a 'Captain Reformado' threatened that 'their swords shall never [be] out of their hands as long as one priest continued in England'. 'They call them fools that pay tithes, and thieves that receive them.'[5]

Many of the sectaries, according to Edwards, rejected the Puritans' moral code. They 'play at cards and tables, are very loose on the Sabbath days, go to bowls and other sports on days of public thanksgiving', and 'wear strange long hair'.[6] They were often guilty, so he alleged, of sexual licence: there was a man who deprived a girl of her virginity on the ground that 'marriage was but an idle ceremony' and then deserted her and her child; and a woman preacher, a Mrs. Attaway, who because she was married to an 'unsanctified' man regarded this as justification for running off with another woman's husband[7].

---

[1] Edwards, *Gangraena*, part i, § ii, pp. 36, 39, part iii, p. 41. Edwards's correspondent was in error in claiming that Collier was an Arminian. See B. R. White, 'Thomas Collier and Gangraena Edwards', *Baptist Quarterly*, xxiv (1971), 101–2.

[2] Edwards, *Gangraena*, part i, § ii, p. 57.

[3] Ibid., part i, § ii, pp. 35–6.   [4] Ibid., part iii, pp. 250–2.

[5] Ibid., part iii, p. 21.   [6] Ibid., part i, § i, p. 63.

[7] Ibid., part ii, p. 9, part i, § ii, p. 113.

A prominent Independent who made advances to his maid defended his actions on Antinomian grounds: 'that God saw no sin in his children, that these were but sins in the flesh, which Christ had satisfied for'.[1]

The rejection of infant baptism and the adoption of immersion by the Baptists were a particular cause of scandal in Edwards's eyes. The Baptists had 'dressed up a cat like a child to be baptized, inviting many people . . . as to baptizing of a child, and then when neighbours were come, having one to preach against baptizing of children'. They had 'baptized many ancient women naked in rivers, whereupon some [had] sickened and died', and had 'baptized young maids . . . about one or two o'clock in the morning, tempting them out of their fathers' houses'.[2] After Samuel Oates had been baptizing in Essex 'some young women who having been married divers years, and never were with child, now since their dipping are proved with child', and when one of the women baptized by Oates 'in a very cold season' subsequently died, the General Baptist preacher was imprisoned at Colchester.[3] At Yaxley in Huntingdonshire, in order to stop an infant baptism, a troop of parliamentary soldiers barred the way to the church, and 'some of the soldiers got into the church, pissed in the font, and went to a gentleman's stable in the town and took out a horse, and brought it into the church, and there baptized it'.[4]

But what disturbed Edwards most of all was that in the wake of the familiar errors of Anabaptism, Arminianism, and Antinomianism, there followed even more dreadful heresies. A certain Paul Best maintained the 'most horrid blasphemies of the Trinity . . . calling the doctrine of the Trinity a mystery of iniquity'.[5] A young man named Thomas Webb went about London, Suffolk, and Essex preaching not only Antinomianism but speaking against 'all baptism by water', maintaining that 'for him to say he was equal to Christ was no robbery', arguing against the Trinity, and claiming that the Scriptures were but 'a human tradition'.[6] A certain Marshall, a bricklayer, 'maintained that there was no hell, but all men should be saved',

[1] Ibid., part ii, p. 120.   [2] Ibid., part i, § i, p. 58.
[3] Ibid., part iii, p. 189, part ii, pp. 121–2.
[4] Ibid., part iii, p. 17.   [5] Ibid., part i, § i, p. 33.
[6] Ibid., part i, § ii, pp. 21–2.

'that the Scriptures are full of contradictions', and that 'Christ was no more God' than he was.[1] Edwards quoted the opinion of the Independent Philip Nye that 'the denying of the divinity of Christ was a growing opinion', and revealed the existence of sectarian meetings in Coleman Street and Red Cross Street at which the divinity of Christ was repudiated.[2] But the sum of Edwards's fears was represented in the career of Clement Wrighter, once 'a professor of religion' who had fallen 'off from the communion of our churches to Independency and Brownism . . . from that he fell to Anabaptism and Arminianism, and to Mortalism, holding the soul mortal'; and 'after that he fell to be a Seeker, and is now an Anti-scripturist, a Questionist, and a Sceptic, and I fear an Atheist'.[3] Wrighter's declension from Independency to atheism, Edwards feared, would be the experience of his generation.

Edwards offered various solutions to the problem: Parliament should proclaim a public fast, renew the Covenant, order the burning of all heretical books, punish the sectarian missionaries as 'vagrants and rogues', and he cited with evident approval the decree of the senate of Zurich 'that whosoever rebaptised any that had been formerly baptised, he should be cast into the water and drowned'.[4] Parliament initially proceeded more cautiously. It proscribed unordained preachers, rejected liberty of worship, and compelled attendance at church every Sunday.[5] But though the majority of M.P.s shared Edwards's antipathy towards sectarian religion and were equally fearful of its social consequences, they were just as anxious that the reformed Church of England should remain firmly under parliamentary control. The victories of the New Model army had reduced Parliament's dependence on the Scots, and with it Parliament's enthusiasm for the establishment of a Presbyterian church on the Scottish model. Although Parliament had approved the legislation for the setting up of a Presbyterian organization in London in August 1645, its implementation was delayed until July 1646, the month after the surrender of Oxford brought the First Civil War to a close.[6] For twelve months Parliament and

---

[1] Ibid., part i, § ii, p. 26.   [2] Ibid., part iii, p. 93.
[3] Ibid., part i, § ii, p. 27.   [4] Ibid., part ii, pp. 97–8.
[5] W. K. Jordan, *Development of Religious Toleration in England* (1938), iii. 93–6, 103.
[6] Shaw, *English Church*, i. 199.

the Westminster Assembly had been at deadlock over the question of exclusion from communion, and the issue was resolved only when the Assembly yielded to Parliament's demand that it specify the offences for which exclusion was warranted and agreed to the setting up of a parliamentary committee to act as a court of appeal.[1] Elections for elders took place in most London parishes in July and August 1646, and an ordinance for the setting up of classical presbyteries in Lancashire followed in December.[2] But in the rest of the country the establishment of Presbyterianism proceeded slowly and imperfectly, and in only fourteen of the forty English counties is there any evidence that Presbyterian classes ever functioned.[3] As for Wales, there appears to have been no Presbyterian organization outside the English-speaking areas of Flint, and even there Presbyterianism operated only as part of the fourth Shropshire classis.[4] The prestige of Presbyterianism was fatally undermined by the alliance between Charles I and the Scots which ushered in the Second Civil War in May 1648, and the defeat of the Scots at Preston in August ensured that, though the legislation establishing Presbyterianism would remain on the statute book until 1660, it would never be fully implemented. In the absence of effective compulsion from the state, there were never enough Presbyterians to make possible the creation of a national Presbyterian Church of England.

The Second Civil War left the parliamentary army a company of angry and bitter men: angry at the failure of Parliament to safeguard the liberties for which they had fought, bitter that Charles through his incorrigible duplicity had plunged the country again into war, yet still refused to accept the consequences of his defeat. On 1 May 1648, the day after the Second Civil War had begun with a royalist insurrection in Pembrokeshire, the Commons had approved a Blasphemy Act imposing the death penalty for denying the existence of God, the divinity of Christ, the doctrine of the Trinity, or that the Scriptures are the word of God. At the same time imprisonment was prescribed for Arminians, Antinomians, and Anabaptists, and any

[1] Ibid. i. 259, 297, ii. 1–2. [2] Ibid. ii. 3, 11.
[3] Ibid. ii. 29–33. C. E. Surman, 'Classical Presbyteries in England, 1643–1660', Manchester M.A. thesis, 1949, pp. 35–59.
[4] T. Richards, *Religious Developments in Wales, 1654–1662* (1923), p. 163.

who disputed the lawfulness of Presbyterian government. This second provision, wrote R. W. Dale, 'would have imprisoned half or a third of both the officers and the private soldiers in the army'.[1] It was not enforced. On 6 December Colonel Pride refused entry into the Palace of Westminster to some 110 M.P.s with the intention of excluding those who on the previous day had voted in favour of further negotiations with the king. On 25 December the Council of Officers, urged on by Hugh Peter, decided that Charles I should be brought to trial for treason. And on 30 January the king, convinced to the last that England could not be ruled without him, was taken to the block. England was henceforth a Commonwealth, governed by a Council of State with Cromwell as its first temporary president.

8. 'LIVING PEACEABLY WITHOUT MOLESTATION': THE RISE AND FALL OF THE LEVELLERS

Though Cromwell and his fellow officers refused to enforce Presbyterianism, this did not mean that they believed that the state should abrogate its responsibilities in religion. It was this issue which, in December 1648, brought Cromwell and his son-in-law Henry Ireton into conflict with the men on whom they bestowed the name of 'Leveller'. The Levellers, who consistently repudiated the title with its implication of seeking to reduce all men to a common plane, constituted the left wing of the parliamentary forces in the Civil War. They represented artisans and small masters whose economic position was threatened by the growth of monopolies, soldiers who were increasingly sceptical of Parliament's willingness to make up their arrears of pay and grant them indemnity for acts performed during the war, and sectaries apprehensive of Parliament's attempts to curtail religious liberty after the freedom of the Civil War. Among their demands were an extension of the franchise, at very least to all men who were not servants, wage-earners, or in receipt of poor relief; a more equitable division of parliamentary constituencies; the removal from Parliament's jurisdiction of power to compel men's religion or to impress them to serve in the armed forces; the replacement of the excise by a proportionate tax on property; the abolition of tithes and

---

[1] Dale, *English Congregationalism*, pp. 310–11.

monopolies; and the end of imprisonment for debt and of capital punishment for any crime except murder.[1] Some of these demands had a Separatist heritage: Robert Browne had argued from the church member's right to choose his officers to the citizen's right to elect his rulers, John Smyth and the early Baptists had denied the authority of the state to bludgeon men into religious conformity, and all Separatists had argued that ministers of religion should be supported financially, if at all, by voluntary contributions alone. The very title of the successive Leveller manifestos, *The Agreement of the People*, was a secular echo of the covenant of the gathered churches.

Some of the Leveller leaders and many of their followers were Separatists. Of the three leading Leveller propagandists two, John Lilburne and Richard Overton, were at some time members of Separatist churches, and the third, William Walwyn, was an eloquent advocate of toleration for Separatists. Lilburne had contributed to John Canne's armoury of Separatist publications from his cell in the Fleet prison in 1638, and after his release at the behest of the Long Parliament in November 1640 he had joined a Separatist congregation ministered to by a certain Edmund Rosier.[2] On the outbreak of war he had enlisted as captain in the regiment commanded by the Separatist sympathizer Lord Brooke, but left the army in April 1645 rather than subscribe to the Covenant. The next ten years Lilburne spent campaigning for what he considered to be his own and his country's liberties, and for his pains was imprisoned by Parliament, Commonwealth, and Protectorate in turn. Handsome, attractive, yet contentious and quarrelsome, he was, wrote Thomas Edwards, 'a darling of the sectaries'.[3]

Lilburne's Leveller confederate, the printer Richard Overton, was also a Separatist, a General Baptist who had been in exile in the Netherlands. He had joined the Waterlanders' church with the followers of John Smyth in 1615, but thirty

---

[1] *The Second Agreement of the People* (1648), reprinted in A. S. P. Woodhouse, *Puritanism and Liberty* (1966), pp. 355–67.

[2] Little is known of Rosier. Lilburne had known him since 1636, and it was Rosier who had introduced him to Bastwick, but Lilburne's reference to Rosier as his 'pastor and teacher' belongs quite clearly to the period after 1640. Lilburne, *The Legall Fundamental Liberties of the People of England* (1649), pp. 19, 24, reprinted by W. Haller and G. Davies, *The Leveller Tracts* (New York, 1944), pp. 401, 408.

[3] Edwards, *Gangraena*, part i, § ii, p. 38.

years later he was back in England, taking part in the debates in Thomas Lamb's church in Bell Alley.[1] Whereas Lilburne was, for most of his life, an orthodox Calvinist, Overton's religious views, influenced no doubt by his sojourn on the continent, became increasingly heretical. In 1644 he published a notorious tract, *Mans Mortalitie*, wherein he sought to prove 'both theologically and philosophically, that whole man (as a rational creature) is a compound wholly mortal, contrary to that common distinction of soul and body: and that the present going of the soul into heaven or hell is a mere fiction: and that at the resurrection is the beginning of our immortality, and then actual condemnation, and salvation, and not before'.[2] Overton's treatise provided the heresy hunters of the 1640s with further evidence of the need to restrain liberty of speculation in matters of religion, but it is wrong to regard his work, as some writers have done, as presaging modern scientific materialism.[3] The belief that the soul goes to sleep at the death of the body to await eventual resurrection was held by both Martin Luther and William Tyndale; it was widespread among the sixteenth-century Anabaptists, together with the more radical view that the soul dies temporarily with the body; and both the English Anabaptists who seceded from Francis Johnson's Separatist church in the 1590s and the martyred Edward Wightman were accused of holding that 'souls do sleep in the grave with the bodies until the resurrection'.[4] Overton himself argued that the doctrine of the immortality of the soul was a heathen invention, 'reported to be Plato's', while for the apostle Paul 'hope of future life was grounded upon the Resurrection'.[5]

[1] Burrage, *EED* i. 250. B. Evans, *The Early English Baptists* (1862), i. 254–6. Edwards, *Gangraena*, part ii, p. 14.

[2] The first two editions of *Mans Mortalitie* stated on the title-page that they were printed by John Canne at Amsterdam, but there is good reason to suspect that the attribution is fictitious. P. Zagorin, 'The Authorship of *Mans Mortalitie*', *The Library*, 5th series, v (1951), 179–83.

[3] A. S. P. Woodhouse, *Puritanism and Liberty*, p. [55]. See also the discussions in W. Schenk, *The Concern for Social Justice in the Puritan Revolution* (1948), p. 170, and in N. T. Burns, *Christian Mortalism from Tyndale to Milton* (Cambridge, Mass., 1972), *passim*. and especially pp. 158–63. Burns, on pp. 192–4, provides evidence of the widespread support for mortalist views among leading twentieth-century theologians.

[4] Burns, *Christian Mortalism*, pp. 28, 100, 120. Williams, *The Radical Reformation*, *assim*. Burrage, *EED* i. p. 219.

[5] R. Overton, *Mans Mortalitie*, ed. H. Fisch (Liverpool, 1968), pp. 13, 19.

The third member of the Leveller triumvirate, the prosperous cloth merchant William Walwyn, also had connections with a radical religious group. Though he remained loyal to his parish church, Walwyn was for a time on friendly terms with the members of the Independent church which met in Coleman Street under the pastorate of John Goodwin.[1] Goodwin, once a Fellow of Queens' College, Cambridge, had been elected in 1633 by the vestry of St. Stephen's, Coleman Street, to succeed the exiled John Davenport as vicar of this radical parish. Goodwin, however, was as much a rebel as his predecessor and not only came to adopt Davenport's Congregational views on church government but, unusually in an Independent, modified his Calvinist theology in the direction of Arminianism. In 1645 Goodwin was deprived of his living by the Presbyterian Committee for Plundered Ministers on the ground that he refused to administer baptism and communion indiscriminately to all his parishioners, and he and his followers withdrew from the parish church to form an Independent church which met in a rented building in Coleman Street.[2] Walwyn listened to Goodwin's sermons, conversed with members of his church, and defended Goodwin as a 'faithful servant of God and sincere lover of his country' against the attacks of the Erastian William Prynne.[3] In return Goodwin's church donated 50s. in May 1646 towards the printing of Walwyn's pamphlet *A Word in Season*, in which he appealed for unity among the supporters of the parliamentary cause, and the congregation also supplied Lilburne with provisions during his imprisonment in the Tower in 1646–7 for contempt of the House of Lords.[4]

It was probably Walwyn who wrote the anonymous tract entitled *The Compassionate Samaritane*, published in June 1644, in which the author, though no Separatist himself, appealed to the House of Commons 'to put an end to the sufferings of the

---

[1] W. Walwyn, *A Whisper in the Eare of Mr. Thomas Edwards* (1646), p. 5, in Haller, *Tracts on Liberty*, iii. 325. *Walwyns Just Defence*, p. 30, in Haller and Davies, *Leveller Tracts*, pp. 391–2.

[2] The fullest account of this controversy is in D. A. Kirby, 'The Parish of St Stephen's, Coleman Street', Oxford B.Litt. thesis, 1968, pp. 67–70.

[3] W. Walwyn, *A Helpe to the Right Understanding of a Discourse concerning Independency* (1645), p. 5, in *Tracts on Liberty*, iii. 197.

[4] *Walwyns Just Defence*, p. 31, in *Leveller Tracts*, p. 393. J. Lilburne, *Jonahs Cry out of the Whales Belly* (1647), p. 5.

Separatists'. The Brownists and Anabaptists, he argued, deserved the thanks of all reformers for having furthered the Reformation and endured 'the hate and brunt of persecution' when Presbyterians conformed and Congregationalists fled abroad, 'in the times of the bishops domineering'. Walwyn criticized the authors of the *Apologeticall Narration* for dissociating themselves from the Brownists and for grounding their claim to toleration on 'the nearness between them and the Presbyterians', and sought to place the case for toleration on a firmer foundation. Knowledge, he argued, is uncertain in this life: 'no man, nor no sort of men can presume of an unerring spirit: 'tis known that the Fathers, General Councils, National Assemblies, Synods, and Parliaments in their times have been most grossly mistaken'.[1]

It was in defending religious liberty against the assaults of William Prynne that Lilburne, Walwyn, and Overton first co-operated in 1645, and their passionate concern for toleration helped them to recruit other Separatists and religious radicals to their cause.[2] Samuel Chidley, son of the indomitable Katherine and like her an Independent and Separatist, was an important figure among the second tier of Leveller leaders. A prosperous stocking-seller with a social conscience, Chidley was imprisoned in 1647 for presenting a Leveller petition to the Commons, acted as treasurer of the Leveller organization in 1648, and in the early 1650s campaigned to secure the abolition of the death penalty for theft and to obtain justice for soldiers who had been given debentures in lieu of arrears of pay.[3] His mother also had Leveller sympathies and as late as 1653 was to lead a deputation of twelve women to the Commons to present a petition, signed it was claimed by 6,000 women, asking for Lilburne's release from Newgate.[4] Another Independent who assisted the Levellers was Christopher Feake, who obtained the vicarage of All Saints, Hertford, in 1646 and early in 1647 helped in the collection of signatures for a petition pleading for

---

[1] [W. Walwyn], *The Compassionate Samaritane* (1644), sigs. A3, A5, pp. 1–2, 10–11, 75, in *Tracts on Liberty*, iii, 62–5, 69–70, 102. Haller gives his reasons for attributing this tract to Walwyn in *Tracts on Liberty*, i. 123.

[2] J. Frank, *The Levellers* (New York, 1969), pp. 45–52. *Walwyns Just Defence*, p. 2, in *Leveller Tracts*, p. 352.

[3] Schenk, *Concern for Social Justice*, pp. 74–7.

[4] Gregg, *Free-born John*, p. 326.

the release of Lilburne and Overton from prison.[1] In December the Antinomian army chaplain John Saltmarsh, two days before his death, rode from his home at Ilford to Windsor to plead with Fairfax and Cromwell on behalf of Leveller soldiers imprisoned for mutiny.[2] Among the Baptists who supported the Levellers were Thomas Lamb, at whose meeting a Leveller petition was seized by an informer in March 1647, Samuel Highland, the army agitator William Allen, and the unreliable Edmund Chillenden who, having once betrayed Lilburne before the Star Chamber in 1638, betrayed the Levellers again when some of their number mutinied at Corkbush Field near Ware in November 1647.[3] Finally, it is probable that the 'Mr. Stasmore' who petitioned the Commons on behalf of the Levellers in 1647 was the Sabine Staresmore who had been a founder member of Henry Jacob's non-separating church in London in 1616 and subsequently emigrated to the Netherlands where he occasioned much controversy by seeking admission to the 'ancient' Separatist church in Amsterdam.[4] The political and economic demands of the Levellers, their denunciations of monopoly capitalists on the one hand and their apparent willingness to exclude paupers and wage-earners from the franchise on the other, are indicative of the extent to which Leveller support was derived from independent craftsmen and small traders, groups which ever since the 1590s had formed the backbone of the Separatist rank and file, at least in London, and from whose ranks the 'mechanic preachers' so abhorred by Thomas Edwards were recruited.

It was, though, only a minority of sectaries who gave their active support to the Levellers, and while the more conserva-

---

[1] Lilburne, *Jonahs Cry*, p. 5.

[2] Schenk, *Social Justice*, pp. 88–9.

[3] Gregg, *Free-born John*, pp. 154–5. *Walwyns Just Defence*, p. 4, in *Leveller Tracts*, p. 356. H. N. Brailsford, *The Levellers and the English Revolution* (1961), pp. 182–3, 225. Some confusion has been caused by the fact that two men by the name of Thomas Lamb(e) flourished in the Coleman Street area in the 1640s and both are mentioned in *Walwyns Just Defence*. However, it is clear from the context that one, the General Baptist pastor and soap-boiler, 'Thomas Lamb of the Spittle', was sympathetic to the Levellers, while the other, a 'linen draper in Cornhill' and a member of Goodwin's church, was regarded by Walwyn as an opponent (*Leveller Tracts*, pp. 355–6, 374, 391–2). That 'Thomas Lamb of the Spittle' was the General Baptist pastor and not the Independent draper is confirmed by Edwards, *Gangraena*, part ii, p. 14.

[4] *Walwyns Just Defence*, p. 4, in *Leveller Tracts*, p. 356. Burrage, *EED* i. 171–8.

tive non-separating Congregationalists regarded the Levellers with suspicion from the start, Leveller support among the separatist Independents and Baptists dwindled as their views became increasingly radical. Five factors contributed to a gradual worsening of relations between the Levellers and the gathered churches from 1647 to 1649: growing concern on the part of the churches with the doctrinal heresies of some of the Leveller leaders, the refusal of the more conservative Independents to support the Leveller demand for complete religious liberty, the unwillingness of the Leveller leaders to approve the political regime of the Commonwealth, the opposition of the Levellers to Cromwell's expedition to Ireland, and the emerging conviction, on the part of at least some Independents and Baptists, that Leveller plans for a more democratic political system conflicted with their own dreams of an approaching theocratic millennium.

Though all the gathered churches advocated a degree of religious toleration and were accused by Thomas Edwards of fostering the growth of heresy, they did have bounds beyond which they would not tolerate unorthodox views, not only in their own communions but also among those with whom they associated. That Richard Overton was the author of *Mans Mortalitie* was one obstacle to closer Leveller–sectarian co-operation, and suspicions of William Walwyn's unorthodoxy proved to be another. Walwyn's relations with John Goodwin's Independent church were marred in 1646 by the accusation levelled by 'one Master Husbands, a linen draper in Cornhill', that Walwyn was 'an atheist and denier of Scriptures, a loose and vicious man' who associated with 'a lewd woman'. And although Husbands subsequently withdrew the accusation, it led 'some leading people of Master John Goodwin's' to set themselves up as a committee to investigate Walwyn's beliefs.[1] Walwyn, for his part, had embraced the doctrine 'called then Antinomian, of free justification by Christ alone', and as a result became increasingly critical of Goodwin's sermons.[2] By February 1647 Lilburne was complaining that some members of Goodwin's church were obstructing the collection of signatures for a petition pleading for his release from the Tower,

---

[1] *Walwyns Just Defence*, pp. 2–3, in *Leveller Tracts*, p. 353.
[2] *Walwyns Just Defence*, p. 8, 29, in *Leveller Tracts*, pp. 361, 391.

and Walwyn noted a split developing in the attitude of the
gathered churches to the Levellers—the sympathy of Baptists
like Thomas Lamb contrasting with the growing hostility of
'the uppermost Independents'.[1]

This division was crystallized by the debates which took place
at Whitehall in December 1648 and January 1649. At the end
of the Second Civil War in the autumn of 1648 Cromwell and
his fellow officers had been faced with the prospect of an
alliance between the king and the now conservative majority
in Parliament and, anxious to widen their support by winning
allies to the left, Cromwell suggested a meeting between representatives of the army and Levellers in an attempt to resolve
their differences. Lilburne insisted that the basis for co-operation must be the acceptance of a written constitution, an
Agreement of the People, and the most contentious part of the
Leveller proposals proved to be their demand that the state
should not have 'any compulsive and restrictive powers in
matters of religion'. Thirty-odd years earlier John Smyth
and Thomas Helwys had taken a radical new stand on this
issue: while other Separatists had yielded to the ruler the power
to suppress idolatry and the duty to influence their subjects'
behaviour in a godly direction, the first Baptists had denied to
the magistrate any right whatsoever to meddle in matters of
conscience. This same division now reappeared when the
Leveller proposals were debated in the Council of Officers at
Whitehall. Henry Ireton, in opposing the Leveller view, based
his argument, as Henry Ainsworth had done forty years before,
on the authority which the Old Testament gave to the magistrate in questions of religion. While he was prepared to agree
that the state should have no power to punish 'men that are
members and servants of Jesus Christ', he could not concede
that liberty should be given to men 'to practise idolatry, to
practise atheism, and anything that is against the light of
God'.[2] Ireton was supported by the conservative Independent
Philip Nye who, as rector of Acton, was firmly wedded to the
state church and who maintained that the magistrate might
exercise power in matters of religion as 'it was once exercised

---

[1] Lilburne, *Jonahs Cry*, pp. 5–6. *Walwyns Just Defence*, p. 4, in *Leveller Tracts*,
p. 356.
[2] Woodhouse, *Puritanism and Liberty*, pp. 146, 155, 143.

under the Jewish commonwealth'.¹ The Leveller case was
supported by the Baptist Thomas Collier and, after initial
hesitation, by the radical Independent John Goodwin. Collier
held that 'those laws or commands and that judicial law, given
under the time of the Law, have no reference to us under the
Gospel', while Goodwin countered Nye by arguing that the
authority over religion entrusted to the magistrate in the Old
Testament was transferred to the churches of Christ in the
New.² But the proposal to deny the state coercive power in the
realm of religion was too novel and, it was believed, too subversive of social order to gain the approval of the Council of
Officers. The officers rejected the Leveller view by thirty-seven
votes to twelve, and when the *Agreement of the People*, shorn of
this crucial clause, was presented to the Rump of the Long
Parliament in January 1649, the Commons declined to do more
than listen to its preamble.³

It seems likely that it was Philip Nye's opposition to the
Leveller proposal on religious toleration which stung an
anonymous Leveller, probably William Walwyn, to publish
early in 1649 an attack on the Independents under the title
The Vanitie of the Present Churches. The Independents, argued the
author of the tract, had won the support of friends of religious
liberty when they had 'condemned the persecuting practices
of the new raised presbyters', but now that they had 'obtained
much countenance from authority' they in their turn manifested 'a most destructive and persecuting disposition' to those
whom they judged heretical. The Independent and other
gathered churches claimed to be true churches, but how could
they possess the spirit of God when they did not agree amongst
themselves in their interpretation of Scripture? Some were 'for
the baptizing of infants', others 'for the baptizing of believers
only', yet others 'for no baptism at all, for want of a true ministry'. There were 'some that for many years have preached up
election and reprobation, and afterwards have as much
preached it down, and cried up general redemption, and that
man hath free will'. The Independents were 'no more infallibly
certain of the truth they raise from the Scriptures than any of

¹ Ibid., p. 60.   ² Ibid., pp. 157–8, 164.
³ Jordan, *Religious Toleration*, iii. 128. B. Worden, *The Rump Parliament* (Cambridge, 1974), p. 76.

those whom they so much condemn; they, as the rest, pray, preach, and do all for money'.[1]

The Vanitie of the Present Churches, recorded Lilburne, made 'some of the Congregational preachers . . . very mad', and set the scene for the final rupture between the Levellers and the gathered churches which took place in 1649.[2] As long as the Independents and Baptists had felt threatened either by the royalists or by the Presbyterians they had been prepared to give the Levellers a measure of support, but once Pride's Purge had removed the one threat, and the execution of the king had eliminated the other, the gathered churches came to regard the continuing political activity of the Levellers as an embarrassment. The army's victory in the Second Civil War and the forcible expulsion of the more conservative M.P.s from Westminster held out the promise that Independent and Baptist congregations would be legally free to worship in their own way for the first time in English history, and in August and September 1650 Parliament was to sweep away the worst features of the Blasphemy Act of 1648 and all statutes imposing penalties for failure to attend the services of the established church.[3] Independents and Baptists who had hitherto been sympathetic to the Levellers were consequently increasingly irritated by Lilburne's warnings that Cromwell and Ireton were replacing the tyranny of king and Parliament with the tyranny of officers.

In February and March 1649 Lilburne published two new manifestos with the title *Englands New Chains Discovered* in which he claimed that the Council of Officers had removed the king, abolished the House of Lords, and purged the Commons merely to concentrate power in their own hands and so oppress the people with the old injustices.[4] For publishing the second of these two manifestos Lilburne, Overton, Walwyn, and Thomas Prince were committed to the Tower, and when it was read in Baptist meetings on 25 March, as earlier Leveller peti-

---

[1] *The Vanitie of the Present Churches* (1649), pp. 1–11, in *Leveller Tracts*, pp. 253–7.

[2] J. Lilburne, *Picture of the Council of State* (1649), p. 24, in *Leveller Tracts*, p. 213.

[3] Jordan, *Religious Toleration*, iii. 134–5, 137–8. Blair Worden has argued that the government press played down the Act repealing the statutes prescribing compulsory church attendance, but this may have been due to the fact that the Act was merely legalising what by Semptember 1650 had become established practice. Worden, *The Rump Parliament*, pp. 238–9.

[4] J. Lilburne, *The Second Part of Englands New Chaines Discovered* (1649), pp. 12–13, in *Leveller Tracts*, p. 183.

tions had been publicized, at least seven Particular Baptist ministers, claiming to represent their churches, dissociated themselves from the document. The spokesman for these Baptist ministers was William Kiffin, who had known Lilburne ever since they had both been apprentices in London in the late 1630s. Kiffin was described by Lilburne as his 'quondam servant', he had written an introductory commendation to one of Lilburne's early works,[1] and he was to remain a friend of the Leveller leader despite their political differences. But whereas Lilburne had never outgrown the mental attitudes of the radical apprentice of the previous decade, Kiffin was already laying the foundation of the career that was to make him one of the wealthiest merchants in England, and for Kiffin by 1649 the revolution had gone far enough. On 2 April he appeared at the bar of the House of Commons to assure the House that the Particular Baptist churches of London did not support the *Second Part of Englands New-Chaines Discovered*, and to express their thanks to God 'in affording to us the mercy of living peaceably without molestation, in the profession of godliness and honesty, under your authority and jurisdiction'.[2]

Some of the members of the Baptist churches were apparently more sympathetic to the Leveller cause than were their pastors, for Lilburne claimed that 'most, if not all, their congregations' disapproved of the ministers' disavowal of the Leveller manifesto.[3] The Independent churches in London were certainly divided in their attitude to the Levellers, for when a petition was circulated among their female members on behalf of Lilburne and his fellow prisoners on 22 April, 'in some places many signed it, in other places none at all, and in some places it was disputed'.[4] But whatever may have been the misgivings of some of his members—and Lilburne no doubt exaggerated them—Kiffin pursued his opposition to the Levellers. At the end of April, Kiffin, Edmund Rosier, Lilburne's old Separatist pastor, and five other Independents signed a commendatory epistle to an attack on William Walwyn, probably written by John Price, a member of John Goodwin's church. The author

---

[1] J. Lilburne, *The Christian Mans Triall* (1641).

[2] *The Humble Petition and Representation of Several Churches of God in London, commonly (though falsely) called Anabaptists* (1649), pp. 3–5.

[3] Lilburne, *Picture of the Councel of State*, p. 24, in *Leveller Tracts*, p. 213.

[4] *Perfect Occurrences*, No. 121, 26 Apr. 1649, p. 990.

of *Walwins Wiles* revived the old accusation of heresy against the Leveller merchant—that he questioned whether the Bible is the word of God and asserted that hell is but a bad conscience—and added the new complaint that the Levellers characterized the proposal to send the English army to Ireland as a 'cruel and bloody work to go to destroy the Irish natives for their consciences'.[1] It was the proposal to send part of the army to Ireland which occasioned mutiny in the army at Salisbury and Banbury in May, and Cromwell's defeat of the mutineers at Burford can only have increased Leveller disgust with the gathered churches. For prominent among the mutineers was the General Baptist preacher Henry Denne, who escaped sentence of death by doing penance in a white sheet and publishing a repudiation of his comrades, *The Levellers Design Discovered*.[2]

The defeat at Burford marked the virtual eclipse of the Leveller party as an effective political force and, deprived of its support both in the army and among the gathered churches, the movement disintegrated. In Lilburne's eyes the sectarian *coup de grâce* was administered by his old publisher and patriarch of the Separatist cause, John Canne, lately returned from Amsterdam and now in government employ. Canne was credited with part responsibility for the authorship of two anonymous tracts which appeared in June and July, the first and second parts of *The Discoverer*, tracts which claimed to expose the 'destructive design' of the Levellers to 'deprive the nations of their religion, rights, liberties, properties, laws, government, etc., and to bring a total and universal ruin upon the land'.[3] Lilburne, languishing in the Tower a bitter and

---

[1] J. Price, *Walwins Wiles* (1649), sig. A3, pp. 5–7, in *Leveller Tracts*, pp. 288, 294–6.

[2] Brailsford, *The Levellers and the English Revolution*, p. 519. H. Denne, *The Levellers Design Discovered* (1649).

[3] Canne, having published a justification of Parliament's right to try and punish Charles I for treason in February 1649 (*The Golden Rule*), subsequently wrote a series of pamphlets defending the policy of the Commonwealth against the Presbyterians, the Irish, and the Scots, all of which were published 'by authority' (*The Snare is Broken*, May 1649, *The Improvement of Mercy*, August 1649, *Emmanuel, or God with us*, September 1650). The extent of Canne's responsibility for *The Discoverer* is unclear. Lilburne claimed that the first part was partly the work of Walter Frost, secretary to the Council of State, but 'principally' that of John Canne (*Legal Fundamentall Liberties*, p. 66): the anonymous author of *The Same Hand Again* claimed that Canne wrote the preface (sig. A2); Thomason noted on his copy of the second part of *The Discoverer* that it was by John Canne; and Perez Zagorin has noted that

disappointed man, had little but contempt left for 'that apostate John Canne' and the 'pretended churches of God, either Independent or Anabaptist'.[1]

9. 'A NEW HEAVEN AND A NEW EARTH': THE COMING MILLENNIUM

One further factor which contributed to the disruption of the Leveller–sectarian alliance remains to be considered: the growing conviction on the part of some Independents and Baptists that the Leveller proposals for a written constitution and a more representative political system were irrelevant at a time when the establishment of Christ's kingdom on earth could soon be expected. In the course of the Whitehall debates Colonel Thomas Harrison had objected to the *Agreement of the People* that it seemed 'to put power into the hands of the men of the world when God doth wrest it out of their hands', while Joshua Sprigge, Fairfax's Independent chaplain, doubted whether it was in their power to make a new constitution. They should, said Sprigge, wait upon God who 'will bring forth a new heaven and a new earth'.[2]

The widespread belief in the coming thousand-year reign of Christ was derived from the twentieth chapter of the Book of Revelation, in which the writer foresees 'an angel come down from heaven, having the key of the bottomless pit and a great chain in his hand, and he laid hold on the dragon, that old serpent, which is the Devil, and Satan, and bound him a thousand years'. The Roman Catholic Church condemned the concept of a future millennium as heretical, and Luther and other sixteenth-century Protestant reformers regarded the millennium as a thing of the past—the first thousand years of the Christian era. But under the impact of the wars of religion

---

'in style and language *The Discoverer* and Canne's signed works greatly resemble each other' (*Library*, 5th series, v. 182). On the other hand it is difficult to believe that Canne was the author of *The Discoverer*'s attack on private conventicles and the choice of ministers by their congregations (first part, pp. 3, 11), views which conflict violently with the opinions expressed by Canne both before and after 1649, and against which his whole life was a consistent testimony. There is also no obvious reason why Canne should have lapsed into anonymity when defending the Commonwealth against the Levellers when he was not afraid to use his name in defence of the Republic against its other enemies.

[1] Lilburne, *Legal Fundamentall Liberties*, pp. 39, 66.
[2] Woodhouse, *Puritanism and Liberty*, pp. 178, 136.

of the late sixteenth century, the Thirty Years War on the continent, and the Laudian persecution in England, some seventeenth-century Protestants reinterpreted the twentieth chapter of Revelation in terms of a future earthly reign of Christ.[1] Thomas Brightman, a Bedfordshire clergyman who died in 1607 but whose writings were published posthumously and exercised an important influence in the 1640s, postulated two millennia, the second of which, he argued, had begun about 1300, would continue for another 600 years, and would be marked in the near future by a Protestant occupation of Rome and the fall of Antichrist. Johann Alsted, professor of theology in the University of Herborn in Hesse-Nassau until the Thirty Years War drove him to take refuge in Transylvania, calculated that the thousand-year reign of Christ would begin in 1694. And Joseph Mede, Fellow of Christ's College, Cambridge, fell under Alsted's influence and attempted to synchronize the prophecies of what he regarded as the three distinct divisions of the Apocalypse. The sounding of the sixth trumpet in Revelation 9, suggested Mede, synchronized with the pouring of the seven 'vials of the wrath of God' of Revelation 16 and marked the stages of the fall of Antichrist. The pouring of the first three vials, representing the late-medieval heretics, the Lutheran reformation, and the defeat of the Spanish Armada, had already occurred, but the pouring of the last four, bringing about the destruction of the Holy Roman Empire, the papacy, the Turks, and Satan himself, had yet to be accomplished. The pouring of the seventh vial would coincide with the sounding of the seventh trumpet and would usher in the thousand-year reign of Christ.

Brightman, Alsted, and in particular Mede had a profound influence on the Independents of the 1630s and 1640s. Henry Burton followed Mede in believing that he was living in the time of the sounding of the sixth trumpet and that the sounding of the seventh would lead to the 'kingdoms of the world' deposing Antichrist and submitting 'their sceptres unto Jesus Christ by receiving his government over them . . . and he shall

---

[1] The following section is based on P. Toon, ed., *Puritans, the Millennium and the Future of Israel* (Cambridge, 1970), B. S. Capp, *The Fifth Monarchy Men* (Totowa, New Jersey, 1972), and P. K. Christianson, 'English Protestant Apocalyptic Visions, c. 1536–1642', University of Minnesota Ph.D. thesis, 1971.

reign for ever and ever'.[1] John Cotton looked forward to the coming millennium when men imbued with the spirit of the martyred Lollards and Huguenots would 'have crowns upon their heads and independent government committed to them'.[2] And Thomas Goodwin, who was credited by Robert Baillie with the authorship of the anonymous pamphlet *A Glimpse of Sions Glory*, acknowledged his debt to Thomas Brightman and suggested the 'probability' that Christ would soon reign 'gloriously for a thousand years'. The beginning of the millennium, he calculated, would date from 1650, though it would be another 'forty-five years before it comes to full head'.[3]

A Glimpse of Sions Glory constituted the text of a sermon preached to an exiled gathered church in the Netherlands, probably at Arnhem, and it was the pastor of the Jacobite church at Arnhem, John Archer, who produced the most detailed Independent exposition of the belief in the coming millennium, *The Personall Reigne of Christ upon Earth* (1642). The similarity between Goodwin's albeit cautious conclusions and Archer's more confident predictions is clear evidence of a mutual exchange of views. The basis of Archer's thesis was the seventh chapter of Daniel in which the prophet related his vision of 'four great beasts' which 'came up from the sea', the fourth with ten horns being 'dreadful and terrible, and strong exceedingly', and an additional 'little horn' with 'eyes like the eyes of man, and a mouth speaking great things'. The prophet had interpreted the vision in terms of the rise and fall of four kingdoms, with the ten horns representing ten kings who would arise out of the fourth kingdom and the little horn a ruler who would make 'war with the saints'. The power of the beasts would be destroyed with the coming of the Son of Man, who would be served by 'all people, nations, and languages' and would establish the rule of 'the saints of the most High, whose kingdom is an everlasting kingdom'. Archer interpreted Daniel's four beasts as the empires of Assyria–Babylonia, the Medes and the Persians, Alexander the Great, and Rome. The ten horns, he believed, were kingdoms which arose out of the ruins of the

---

[1] H. Burton, *The Sounding of the Two Last Trumpets* (1641), pp. 88, 90.
[2] J. Cotton, *The Churches Resurrection* (1642), p. 6.
[3] [T. Goodwin], *A Glimpse of Sions Glory* (1641), pp. 13–14, 32. R. Baillie, *A Dissuasive from the Errours of the Times* (1645), pp. 79–80.

Roman Empire, and the little horn, which persecuted the saints, was the papacy. Following Joseph Mede, Archer calculated that the reign of the papacy would last 1,260 years for, in Revelation 11: 2 it was stated that the holy city would be trodden under foot for forty-two months, which, if taken to mean lunar months, meant 1,260 days, and according to Numbers 14: 34 a day could represent a year. Since the bishop of Rome's assumption of papal power began around 406, the end of papal rule would come in 1666—a date which conveniently included the number of the beast of Revelation 13: 18. The fall of the papacy, according to Archer, would be preceded some ten years by the conversion of the Jews to Christianity, 1,290 years after the 'abomination that maketh desolate' of Daniel 12: 11, which Archer took to be the reign of Julian the Apostate around A.D. 366. On the basis of Daniel 11: 12 Archer concluded that forty-five years after the conversion of the Jews, that is around 1700, Christ would return to establish his personal rule, the fifth monarchy.[1]

Such apocalyptic expectation was not an exclusively Independent preoccupation and, as B. S. Capp points out, there were leading Presbyterians who also held millenarian views.[2] But, as Robert Baillie noted in 1645, for some Independents there was a specific connection between the founding of gathered churches and anticipation of the establishment 'of Christ's kingdom upon earth'.[3] Thomas Goodwin, in *A Glimpse of Sions Glory*, had taken as his text Revelation 19: 6, 'And I heard as it were the voice of a great multitude', and on the basis of this had argued that at 'the beginning of this glorious reign of Christ, the multitude of the people shall be the furtherers of it', that they would take precedence over the elders of the church. His exiled hearers in Arnhem, he told them, were 'beginning this despised work, gathering a church together, which way God will honour'.[4]

It was, though, in the wake of the execution of Charles I that the view gained widest currency among Independents that the setting up of gathered churches was but preparation for the coming millennium, that the end of the reign of the Stuarts

---

[1] J. Archer, *The Personall Reigne of Christ upon Earth* (1641), pp. 6, 42–7.

[2] Capp, *Fifth Monarchy Men*, pp. 38–9, 46–9.

[3] R. Baillie, *A Dissuasive from the Errours*, pp. 79–80. J. F. Wilson expands Baillie's suggestion in *Pulpit in Parliament* (Princeton, New Jersey, 1969), pp. 223–30.

[4] [Goodwin], *A Glimpse of Sions Glory*, pp. 5, 8, 33.

was the prelude to the inauguration of the reign of King Jesus. In February 1649, three weeks after the execution, 'many Christian people throughout the county of Norfolk and the city of Norwich' petitioned the Council of Officers with *Certain Quaeries*, the first manifesto of what was to become known as the Fifth Monarchy party. The petitioners, whose names are not known, suggested that 'a kingdom and dominion of the church, or of Christ and the saints' was to be 'expected upon earth', a fifth monarchy which would be 'external and visible' and whose authority would cover 'all persons and things universally'. The kingdoms and powers of the world, parliaments no less than kings, would have to be put down before the kingdom of Christ could be established, and the time for 'putting down that worldly government' was near, for the span allotted to the fourth monarchy, 1,260 years, was about to expire. The kingdom of Christ would be set up not by 'human power and authority, but by the Spirit of Christ, calling and gathering people into less families, churches, and corporations'. When these 'church societies and corporations (according to the Congregational way)' had 'increased and multiplied' they should 'combine into general assemblies or church-parliaments (according to the Presbyterian way)', and then would 'God give them authority and rule over the nations and kingdoms of the world'. In this way 'the churches' representatives' would rule until 'Christ the Head and King appears visibly'. 'How can the kingdom be the saints' when the ungodly are electors, and elected to govern?' asked the petitioners in conclusion. Is it not 'a straitening of the church's power to limit it only to spiritual matters?'[1]

The Norfolk petitioners' advocacy of government by the gathered churches in preparation for Christ's kingly rule drove a wedge between the extreme millenarian Independents on the one hand and the more conservative Independents on the other. It was a split which was more fundamental and did more damage to the Independent cause than the conflict over the Leveller proposals, for it was a dispute over matters which, by 1649, had become an integral part of the faith of the average Congregationalist, and it occurred at a time when

---

[1] *Certain Quaeries Humbly presented* (1649), reprinted in Woodhouse, *Puritanism and Liberty*, pp. 241–7.

Independents exercised greater political influence than at any other period of their history.

10. 'BY THE ARM OF FLESH' OR 'THE SPIRIT OF THE LORD'?: JOHN OWEN VERSUS THE FIFTH MONARCHISTS

The leadership of the conservative Independents fell to John Owen who, at mid-century, was emerging as the most influential Congregational minister in the country. Owen, a graduate of Queen's College, Oxford, and vicar of Coggeshall in Essex, had been a moderate Presbyterian until, in the mid-1640s, he had been converted to Independency by reading John Cotton's *Keyes of the Kingdom of Heaven.* His rise to eminence had begun in 1648 when, during the siege of Colchester, he had ministered to the parliamentary army and had won the friendship of both Fairfax and Ireton. He was invited to preach to the Commons on the day after the execution of Charles I in January 1649 and again in April, and these occasions brought him to the notice of Cromwell who saw in Owen a man who could make a distinctive contribution to the religious life of his country. Thereafter Owen rose rapidly in Cromwell's favour, accompanying him to Ireland in 1649 and to Scotland in 1650, securing appointments as preacher to the Council of State in 1650 and as dean of Christ Church, Oxford, in 1651, and finally, in 1652, being nominated vice-chancellor of the university. Owen was not a passionate man, and his personality left no deep impress either on his contemporaries or on his biographers, but the one thing he did care deeply about was the preservation and elucidation of the Puritans' theological heritage: he was, said his fellow Congregationalist Ambrose Barnes, 'the Calvin of England'.[1]

Owen preached frequently on apocalyptic themes between 1649 and 1652 and his sermons reveal a genuine sense of expectancy of the approaching establishment of Christ's kingdom. 'The Lord Jesus Christ by his mighty power,' he told the Commons in April 1649, 'in these latter days, as Antichristian tyranny draws to its period, will so far shake and translate the political heights, governments, and strength of the nations, as

---

[1] P. Toon, *God's Statesman, The Life and Work of John Owen* (Exeter, 1971), p. 173 and *passim.*

shall secure for the full bringing in of his own peaceable kingdom.' But Owen's concept of the kingdom was essentially
spiritual, not political, and he would have nothing to do with
the notion of 'the personal reign of the Lord Jesus on earth'.[1]
Herein lay the essential difference between Owen and the
Fifth Monarchy party. Whereas Owen urged his hearers to
prepare for the coming of the kingdom by spiritual means—
prayer, the provision of a godly ministry, the propagation of the
Gospel—the Fifth Monarchists sought to clear the way for the
approaching millennium by political measures—the dissolution of the Rump, the establishment of the rule of the saints,
and the reform of the country's institutions in accordance with
the precepts of the Old and New Testaments. While Owen was
content to wait on God to act in his own good time to bring in
the kingdom of Christ, the Fifth Monarchists wanted to give
God and history a shove. Owen and the conservative Independents were the Mensheviks of the English revolution; the
Fifth Monarchy men were the Bolsheviks.

The clash between Owen and the Fifth Monarchists was
postponed by the need to protect the revolution from the
Scottish Presbyterians' championing of the cause of Charles
II, and during the war with Scotland in 1650–1 Fifth Monarchists and radicals rallied loyally to the support of the Commonwealth. While Cromwell was in Scotland the command of the
army in England was entrusted to Thomas Harrison, a former
lawyer's clerk who, by dint of military prowess and religious
zeal had risen to become a major-general, was soon to become a
member of the Council of State, and was to emerge in the early
1650s as the most prominent of all the Fifth Monarchists. In
August 1650 Harrison was authorized by the Council to raise
forces from the Independent churches for the defence of the
Republic, and in the following year Welsh Congregational
preachers led troops of their congregations into north-west
England to defend the country against imminent Scottish invasion. Two of the preachers who thus assisted the Commonwealth's military effort, the itinerant evangelist Vavasor
Powell of Radnor and Morgan Llwyd of Wrexham, shared
Harrison's Fifth Monarchist views. Similarly London Baptists
recruited regiments for the defence of the capital, 'which

[1] J. Owen, *The Shaking and Translating of Heaven and Earth* (1649), pp. 16–17.

brigade of London sectaries was a grievous eye-sore to the classical [i.e. Presbyterian] ministers and people of the same city'.[1] But the defeat of the Scottish army at Worcester on 3 September 1651 and the final destruction of Charles II's hopes of overthrowing the Republic by military force removed the common danger to both Fifth Monarchists and supporters of the Rump and presented the former with the opportunity of implementing the next stage in the Norfolk manifesto of 1649: of following the execution of the king with the overthrow of Parliament as the prelude to the erection of the kingdom of Christ on earth.

In the months following the battle of Worcester there was an intensification of Fifth Monarchist activity, and in the autumn of 1651 three tracts appeared advocating the replacement of the Rump by a new assembly of saints: *A Cry for a Right Improvement of all our Mercies, A Model of a New Representative*, and Daniel Taylor's *Certain Queries*. The author of the first called for the restriction of membership of Parliament to those who were 'in church fellowship with some one or other congregation' or had 'engaged against the late invading Scots', while the second suggested that borough M.P.s should be replaced by 'two or more members' of the Congregational churches in their respective towns and that county M.P.s should be elected by the gathered churches of their shire. The author of the second tract even wanted the members of John Goodwin's church excluded from the franchise on the grounds that most of them were 'such high extollers of reason' that they would support no measure which was not 'grounded upon reason, though of never so spiritual a concernment'.[2]

Such views support the thesis of A. S. P. Woodhouse that a clear division of opinion appeared among the members of the gathered churches, between the followers of the Levellers who were 'democratic in tendency and ultimately secular in aim', and the Fifth Monarchists who emphasized 'not the rights of the people, but the privileges of the saints'.[3] Yet there were other

[1] *CSPD* 1650, p. 280, 1651–2, p. 579. C. Feake, *Beam of Light* (1659), p. 38. Richards, *Puritan Movement in Wales*, pp. 100–11. Tai Liu, 'Saints in Power: a Study of the Barebones Parliament', University of Indiana Ph.D. thesis, 1969, p. 208. Capp, *Fifth Monarchy Men*, pp. 54–5.

[2] *A Cry for a Right Improvement of all our Mercies* (1651), p. 9. *A Model of a New Representative* (1651), pp. 3–4.

[3] Woodhouse, *Puritanism and Liberty*, p. [18].

Independents whose views straddled both the Leveller and the Fifth Monarchist positions. Daniel Taylor was a member of John Goodwin's church and a member of the common council of the city of London. Though he would have been debarred from the franchise by the author of *A Model of a New Representative*, Taylor agreed with him that the right to vote should be restricted to the Congregational churches and to others who were 'well-affected . . . to this present power, and to real reformation'. Taylor recognized the fundamental flaw, from the point of view of the gathered churches, in the Leveller demand for a wider franchise and a freely elected parliament. It was 'unlikely, nay impossible, that multitudes should make any good choice at this time, considering that most men's spirits stand still opposite to a real and sound reformation', and a parliament elected by them would 'undo most of that which hath been already done by this Parliament . . . with the expense of so much treasure and blood for ten years or more past'. Yet the economic and social problems which had generated the Leveller protest remained, and while Taylor made recommendations typical of the 'saints' for strengthening legislation against 'adultery, whoredom, drunkenness, swearing, cursing, blasphemy, etc.', he coupled these with demands dear to the heart of John Lilburne. The salaries of customs-and excise-officers should be reduced for the benefit of the poor, the fees demanded by 'doctors of physic and surgeons ought to be regulated . . . considering that many drop into the grave for want of advice and means', monopolies should be ended and the law reformed, until this was done lawyers should be debarred from Parliament, and thieves, rather than be executed, should be set to work in workhouses in order to make restitution for their thefts.[1]

Other men who embraced, at different times, both Leveller and Fifth Monarchist ideas were William Allen and Edmund Chillenden, who were both army agitators in 1647, and John Lilburne himself had looked forward to the imminent return of Christ in glory in 1645.[2] Samuel Chidley, whose loyalty to Lilburne and the Leveller cause lasted longer than most men's,

---

[1] D[aniel] T[aylor], *Certain Queries* (1651), pp. 7–22.
[2] Capp, *Fifth Monarchy Men*, p. 92. J. Lilburne, *A Copie of a Letter to Mr. William Prinne* (1645), p. 5, in *Tracts on Liberty*, iii. 185.

defended his Leveller views in 1652 in terms of the return of Christ. 'If am a Leveller,' he wrote, 'I am no Leveller of the valleys, but a Leveller of the mountains, that the way of Jesus Christ may be prepared, that all flesh may see the salvation of our God.'[1] But the most significant person to hold both Leveller and Fifth Monarchist views was the Independent minister Christopher Feake. Feake had assisted the Levellers while he was vicar of All Saints, Hertford, in 1647, and two years later moved to London to become minister of Christ Church, New-gate, lecturer at St. Anne's, Blackfriars, and leader of the Fifth Monarchist cause in the metropolis. Both Leveller and Fifth Monarchist movements drew on a common stock of radical, sectarian ideas, ideas which were adapted to the needs of the moment, depending on whether the radicals were preoccupied by fear of Presbyterian tyranny or by exhilaration at the end of the monarchy and the defeat of the Scots.[2]

From the battle of Worcester in September 1651 to the fall of Barebone's Parliament in December 1653 radical and conser-vative Independents struggled for ascendency over the mind of Cromwell. Christopher Feake records that after Worcester some of the more radical sectaries tried to persuade Cromwell to hasten preparations for the establishment of the kingdom of Christ, but although the Lord General was at first willing to listen to them, after two meetings they came to the conclusion that they were wasting their time with him. Feake ascribed their failure to the growing influence over Cromwell of 'divers self-seeking officers' and of 'sectaries' who had obtained 'great preferments to honour, profit and other pleasing delights of this wicked old world'—a clear reference to Owen who had recently been appointed dean of Christ Church and was, in September 1652, to be nominated vice-chancellor of Oxford.[3]

Owen's prime concern in 1652 was to take advantage of the return to peace after the defeat of the Scots to create the right

[1] S. Chidley, *The Dissembling Scot set forth in his Colours* (1652), p. 3.

[2] Perez Zagorin's thesis that the Fifth Monarchy movement arose from the ruins of Leveller disillusionment has been challenged by B. S. Capp who suggests that few Levellers became Fifth Monarchists. Capp ignores, though, the significant example of Christopher Feake. P. Zagorin, *A History of Political Thought in the English Revolution* (1954), p. 105. Capp, *The Fifth Monarchy Men*, pp. 89–92.

[3] Feake, *A Beam of Light*, pp. 39–40.

conditions for the propagation of the Gospel. Such an objective was threatened on the one hand by the continued political agitation of Feake and his Fifth Monarchist followers, and on the other by the continuing growth of heretical ideas. As a former Presbyterian and disciple of John Cotton, Owen's Independency was of the conservative, non-separatist New England variety. His views on church government were very like those of his friend Henry Ireton, and like Ireton he believed it was the duty of the state to ensure 'that the truth of the Gospel be preached to all people', to protect the worship of all orthodox Protestants, irrespective of their views on ecclesiastical polity, and to prevent both the practice of Roman Catholic idolatry and the spread of Socinian heresy.[1] Owen abhorred the Leveller demand for complete religious freedom and was determined that Thomas Edwards's favourite thesis—that Independency was 'the mother, nurse and patroness of all other errors'— should not be proven.[2]

In January 1652 there was published in England a Latin edition of the Racovian Catechism, the confession of faith of the Socinian churches of Poland.[3] The anti-trinitarian doctrines of this document posed a much greater threat to Protestant orthodoxy than the heresies of Arminianism, Anabaptism, and Antinomianism with which Edwards had largely concerned himself, and in February Owen and nine other ministers, mainly Congregational, appealed to Parliament to prohibit the offending tract and to make better provision for a godly ministry. The Commons ordered that all copies of the Racovian Catechism be seized and burned and appointed a committee to consider recommendations for the propagation of the Gospel. Two years earlier Parliament had passed *An Act for the better Propagation and Preaching of the Gospel in Wales* in an attempt to meet the special needs of that spiritually desolate and politically royalist country: seventy-one lay commissioners had been appointed to eject scandalous clergymen and to appoint, with the approval of twenty-five ministers, men of 'approved piety and learning' to act as parish ministers and as itinerant

---

[1] J. Owen, *A Sermon Preached to the House of Commons* (1647), pp. 72, 77, 79. Jordan, *Religious Toleration*, iii. 425–35.

[2] Edwards, *Gangraena*, part i, § ii, p. 61.

[3] H. J. McLachlan, *Socinianism in Seventeenth-Century England* (Oxford, 1951), pp. 187–8.

evangelists.[1] Owen and fourteen ministerial colleagues proposed that a similar system now be extended to England, with the
important exceptions that ministers rather than laymen would
be given a predominant role, and that foot-loose evangelists
would not be appointed. 'A number of persons, ministers, and
others of eminency' were to be assigned to each of the six judi-
ciary circuits to eject ignorant and scandalous clergymen, while
committees of ministers and laymen were to be appointed in
every county to examine the worthiness of would-be preachers.
Furthermore, only seventeen months after Parliament had
repealed the Elizabethan statutes prescribing compulsory
church attendance Owen and his colleagues sought to reimpose
the requirement, except for 'such persons as through scruple of
conscience do abstain from those assemblies'. And while those
who dissented from the state religion should be permitted to
worship freely, providing that their meeting places were registered by the magistrate, this right should not be extended to
those who sought to 'promulgate anything in opposition' to the
'principles of Christian religion'.[2] Those principles they defined
in December 1652 in fifteen 'fundamental doctrines' which excluded Socinians by affirming that 'Jesus Christ is the true God'
and Roman Catholics by referring to justification by faith.[3]

It is significant, in view of what has been said above about the
common sectarian seed-bed of both Leveller and Fifth Monarchist ideas, that criticism of Owen's proposals should come both
from Major William Butler, who had supported the Levellers
in the Whitehall debates in January 1649, and from the Fifth
Monarchist Colonel Henry Danvers. In a tract called *The
Fourth Paper* they sought to show, with the support of a string
of Scriptural texts, that Christ's labourers should work without
financial reward, that the 'judgement and condemnation of . . .
false teachers and heretics' should be left to God, that 'for the
civil power to assume a judgement in spirituals' was 'against
the liberties given by Christ Jesus to his people'.[4] The objections
of sectarian radicals such as Butler and Danvers would not have

---

[1] Richards, *Puritan Movement in Wales*, pp. 81–9.

[2] *The Humble Proposals of Mr. Owen, Mr. Tho. Goodwin, Mr. Nye, Mr. Sympson and
other Ministers* (1652), printed in *TCHS* ix (1924–6), 22–6.

[3] J. Owen, *Proposals for the Furtherance and Propagation of the Gospel in this Nation*
(1653), pp. 11, 17.

[4] W. Butler, *The Fourth Paper* (1652), pp. 1–3.

impressed members of the Rump, and Owen's scheme appears to have been favourably received by Parliament.[1] But before his recommendations for the propagation of the Gospel in England could be implemented, the return to normality on which it was dependent was threatened by the renewal of war—this time, in June 1652, with the Dutch.

The outbreak of war revived the flagging apocalyptic hopes of the Fifth Monarchists and meetings were held at London House and St. Anne's, Blackfriars, 'publicly to own and plead that glorious cause of Christ's kingdom and interest in the nations'.[2] By October Owen had become seriously alarmed at the growth of Fifth Monarchist activity and in a sermon to the House of Commons attacked those who 'have degenerated into carnal apprehensions of the beauty and glory' of 'the rule of Christ'. 'The coming in of the kingdom of Christ', he emphasized, 'shall not be by the arm of flesh . . . but by the Spirit of the Lord of Hosts.' 'It is not the sons of men that, by outward force, shall build the new Jerusalem: that comes down from heaven adorned as a bride for Christ. . . . It shall be by the glorious manifestation of his own power, and that by his spirit subduing the souls of men unto it, not by the sword of men setting up a few to rule over others.'[3]

It was, though, 'by the sword of men' that England was a republic and John Owen vice-chancellor of Oxford, and Cromwell never forgot the fact if Owen did. When the failure of the Rump to reform the country's legal system and to reduce the burden of taxation on the poor led not only Fifth Monarchists but also 'most of the officers of the army' to demand the erection of 'a new representative', Cromwell was bound to take notice.[4] Radical dissatisfaction with the Rump intensified when, on 1 April 1653, the Commons resolved not to renew the Act for the Propagation of the Gospel in Wales, the instrument whereby Harrison and Powell had sought to extend their own, radical version of Christianity in that country, and pressure on Cromwell to be rid of the Rump increased. The Rump did intend to hold elections for a new parliament in November, but it

[1] Toon, *John Owen*, p. 87.
[2] Feake, *Beam of Light*, p. 45.
[3] J. Owen, *A Sermon Preached to the Parliament* (13 Oct. 1652), p. 19.
[4] *A Declaration of the Armie* (1652), pp. 4, 6.

also proposed to set itself up as judge of the fitness of M.P.s
to sit in the new House, and it was this issue which finally
threw Cromwell into the arms of the radicals. On 20 April,
while Parliament was debating its bill for a new representative,
Cromwell and Harrison dissolved the Rump with a party of
musketeers.[1]

II. 'JESUS CHRIST IS OWNED THIS DAY': BAREBONE'S PARLIAMENT

The dissolution of the Rump was regarded by the Fifth Monarchists as a further step towards the inauguration of the kingdom
of Christ. John Rogers, formerly pastor of an Independent
church at Dublin and now lecturer at St. Thomas Apostle's,
London, greeted Cromwell as 'the great deliverer of his people
. . . out of the house of Egypt'.[2] An unknown gathered church
urged Cromwell, 'whom we look upon as our Moses', to 'advance the sceptre of our Lord Jesus'.[3] And the army council
wrote to Charles Fleetwood, commander-in-chief of the forces
in Ireland, that 'we are not without hope that our Lord Jesus
Christ, who is the king of saints, will henceforth show himself to
be the king of nations also'.[4]

On 22 April Cromwell and the Council of Officers announced
their intention 'to call to the government persons of approved
fidelity and honesty', and were subsequently deluged with
advice as to how that end might be accomplished.[5] A hundred
and fifty-three members of Morgan Llwyd's Independent
church at Wrexham urged, as had the Norfolk petitioners of
1649, that the new representative should be elected by the
gathered churches.[6] The Fifth Monarchist John Spittlehouse
argued, on the contrary, that it was 'altogether improper' for
the Congregational churches 'to take upon them to rule the
nations . . . in a magistratical employment' lest they should thus
'make the spouse of Christ odious'; rather the new representa-

---

[1] Worden, *The Rump Parliament*, pp. 331–5.

[2] J. Rogers, *To His Excellency the Lord Gèneral Cromwell* (1653).

[3] *Severall Proceedings of State Affairs*, No. 187 (21–8 Apr. 1653), p. 2954.

[4] *The Fifth Monarchy, or Kingdom of Christ, in opposition to the Beasts, Asserted* (1659), p. 23.

[5] W. C. Abbott, *The Writings and Speeches of Oliver Cromwell* (Cambridge, Mass., 1945), iii. 7.

[6] J. Nickolls, *Original Letters and Papers of State, addressed to Oliver Cromwell* (1743), p. 120.

tive should be chosen by the commissioned officers in the army 'without the private soldiery'.[1] Edmund Chillenden's General Baptist church in Aldgate suggested that representatives should be chosen by lot from a short list of suitably qualified men drawn up by Cromwell, 'a way much owned by God in the Scriptures'.[2] John Rogers and his congregation at St. Thomas Apostle's also looked to the Scriptures for precedents and proposed that the country be ruled by a sanhedrin of seventy God-fearing men, chosen by Cromwell.[3] What united these diverse suggestions was their unanimous repudiation of the notion that representatives should be elected by the profane multitude. As John Spittlehouse commented, 'the real members of this Commonwealth are included in the Congregational churches, and the army and their well-wishers'.[4]

In the end the assembly which became known as Barebone's Parliament, after the Independent Fleet Street leather dealer who sat for London, was chosen by Cromwell and the Council of Officers from recommendations made by the gathered churches and other 'real members of the Commonwealth'. Initially Rogers's proposal that the representatives should number a sanhedrin of seventy was accepted, but the number was subsequently doubled to 140 to permit a more adequate representation not only of England and Wales, but also of Scotland and Ireland.[5] Austin Woolrych has disputed S. R. Gardiner's thesis that letters were sent by Cromwell and the Council of Officers to the gathered churches to invite nominations to the new representative,[6] but, whether or not invitations were sent, gathered churches from five counties and four towns are known to have submitted nominations for the new assembly, and it is probable that other churches made recommendations which have not survived. The nominations from Bedfordshire were signed by thirty-six men, including one of the Bedford gathered church's most recent converts, John Bunyan; the

[1] J. Spittlehouse, *The Army Vindicated, in their late Dissolution of the Parliament* (1653), pp. 6, 11.
[2] Nickolls, *Original Letters*, p. 121.
[3] Rogers, *To His Excellency the Lord General*.
[4] Spittlehouse, *The Army Vindicated*, p. 3.
[5] The number was subsequently increased to 144 by co-option.
[6] A. Woolrych, 'The Calling of Barebone's Parliament', *English Historical Review*, lxxx (1965), 492–513. S. R. Gardiner, *History of the Commonwealth and Protectorate* (1916), ii. 276.

nominations from Kent were signed by forty-nine men representing nineteen churches, and were accompanied by a plea that neither practising lawyers, nor impropriators of tithes, nor 'wilful rigid Presbyters' should sit in the new assembly; while the Gloucestershire churches were prompted to send in nominations 'by the example and encouragement of others the Lord's people'.[1] The recommendations of these gathered churches were not always accepted, but fifteen of their nominees are known to have sat in Barebone's Parliament and in addition Thomas Harrison used his position as head of the Commission for the Propagation of the Gospel in Wales to secure the return of religious radicals for that country and the border counties.[2] At least twenty-eight members of Barebone's Parliament can be clearly identified as members of Independent churches and another seven as Baptists.[3] Cromwell himself, in his opening speech to the new members of Parliament on 4 July, acknowledged that the gathered churches had played a part in their nomination:

Truly you are called by God to rule with him, and for him. And you are called to be faithful with the saints, who have been somewhat instrumental to your call. . . . I confess I never looked to see

[1] Nickolls, *Original Letters*, pp. 92, 95–6, 125.

[2] Woolrych, 'Calling of Barebone's Parliament', p. 506. Woolrych's thesis that Cromwell 'packed' Barebone's Parliament with moderate nominees in order to counter balance the influence of Harrison's supporters has been challenged by Tai Liu, 'The Calling of the Barebone's Parliament reconsidered', *JEH* xxii (1971), 223–36. By far the best account of Barebone's Parliament is Tai Liu's 'Saints in Power: a Study of the Barebone's Parliament', Indiana Univ. Ph.D. thesis, 1969.

[3] Louise F. Brown in *Baptists and Fifth Monarchy Men* (New York, 1911), p. 33n., gave the names of eleven supposed Baptists who sat in Barebone's Parliament, but her list includes a number of men, including Praise-God Barebone himself, who were never Baptists. I can find only seven men who were clearly Baptists at the time they sat in Barebone's Parliament: R. Bennett, H. Danvers, S. Highland, F. Langdon, H. Lawrence, S. Moyer, and A. Squibb. J. Carew, H. Courtney, and Thomas Harrison were subsequently baptized as believers, but were not Baptists in 1653. The fullest list of Independents in Barebone's Parliament is contained in Tai Liu's article, 'The Calling of the Barebone's Parliament reconsidered', pp. 232–4, and I have been able to supplement his list from other sources. My list is as follows: T. Baker, P. Barebone, J. Brown, W. Burton, E. Cater, J. Caley, J. Chetwood, J. Clark, H. Courtney, J. Crofts, R. Cunliffe, H. Dawson, R. Duckinfield, R. Duncon, J. Hewson, D. Hollister, D. Hutchinson, J. Ireton, A. Jaffray, J. James, H. King, R. Price, J. St. Nicholas, J. Stone, N. Taylor, R. Tichborne, J. Williams, and R. Wolmer. J. Desborough, W. Sydenham, and possibly J. Bingham became members of Independent churches subsequent to the meeting of Barebone's Parliament.

such a day as this—it may be nor you neither—when Jesus Christ should be so owned as he is, at this day, and in this work. Jesus Christ is owned this day by your call; and you own him by your willingness to appear for him. . . . And why should we be afraid to say or think that this may be the door to usher in the things that God has promised; which have been prophesied of; which he has set the hearts of his people to wait for and expect? . . . And we have some of us thought that it is our duty to endeavour this way; not vainly to look at that prophecy in Daniel, 'and the kingdom shall not be delivered to another people'.

Cromwell's speech indicates the extent to which he had been won over to the concept of the rule of the saints by Harrison and the Fifth Monarchists at the expense of the influence of more conservative men such as Owen. At this juncture Cromwell evidently shared the millenarian dreams of the Fifth Monarchists and emulated their apocalyptic rhetoric, but what he did not fully appreciate was the weight of opinion in favour of radical social, legal, and religious reform which lay behind the rhetoric. Though there were only a dozen clearly identifiable Fifth Monarchists in Barebone's Parliament,[2] these Fifth Monarchists in alliance with other radical Independents and Baptists constituted a formidable, if shifting, phalanx of men who would support drastic change. Barebone's Parliament was as embarrassed as its predecessor by the activities of John Lilburne—who had been sentenced to exile on pain of death in 1651, but returned to England in June 1653 to challenge the Act under which he had been banished and was found 'not guilty of any crime worthy of death'—but much of the legislation passed by Barebone's Parliament was of the sort about which Leveller, Fifth Monarchist, and radical sectary could agree. In six months the assembly of saints attempted wide-sweeping legal, administrative, and ecclesiastical reforms, the like of which would not be essayed again until the 1830s. It passed legislation providing for civil marriage, the national registration of births, marriages, and deaths, for the relief of debtors and poor prisoners, and for the protection of infants and the insane; it proposed that the excise be abolished; and it gave the second reading to a bill to abolish the notorious Court

---

[1] Abbott, *Writings and Speeches of Cromwell*, iii. 61, 63–4.
[2] Capp, *Fifth Monarchy Men*, p. 68.

of Chancery where, it was claimed, cases had been delayed for anything up to thirty years. But the most contentious issue with which Barebone's Parliament dealt, and the one which brought about its downfall, was that of the tithe.

One of the consequences of the collapse of royal and episcopal authority in the 1640s had been a widespread refusal to pay tithes, petitions for their abolition had poured into the House of Commons, and even the Rump had come within ten votes of stopping their payment.[1] There were, broadly speaking, three different views of the question: that tithes should be retained, that they should be replaced by some more equitable means of supporting ministers, and that they should be abolished along with the rest of the paraphernalia of the national church.

The first view was held by the more conservative Puritan clergy—Presbyterian, Independent, and those who eschewed party labels—and by their advocates in the legal profession. The Presbyterian William Prynne defended the payment of tithes by reference to the tenth which Abraham gave to Melchizedek, by 'God's special precepts and commands' which prescribed the payment of tithes to priests and levites in the Old Testament, and by Paul's instruction that 'they which preach the Gospel should live of the Gospel'.[2] The lawyer Nortcliffe added that the payment of tithes was sanctioned by both common law and statute law, that even with 'the casting off the popish yoke' in the reign of Henry VIII, 'these tithes of the parson stood firm, and [were] adjudged not superstitious'.[3] And the propertied classes in general supported tithes for fear that their abolition would be but the prelude to the abolition of rent, that the legal case for property in tithe was as strong— and as vulnerable—as the legal case for every other kind of property.[4]

The second view was held by middle-of-the-road Independents and by the conservative Baptist John Tombes. This group recognized the justice of the frequent criticisms which

[1] M. James, 'The Political Importance of the Tithes Controversy in the English Revolution', *History*, new series, xxvi (1941), 7–11.

[2] W. Prynne, *A Gospel Plea for the Lawfulness and Continuance of the Ancient Setled Maintenance and Tenthes of the Ministers of the Gospel* (1653), pp. 20, 57–8, 100.

[3] —— Nortcliffe, *An Argument in Defence of the Right of Patrons to Advowsons* (1653), pp. 5–7.

[4] James, 'The Tithes Controversy', p. 6.

werc made of the tithe: that it was an oppressive tax which bore heavily on the small farmer without doing much, in parishes where the tithe had been impropriated by laymen, to relieve the poverty of the poorer clergy. At the same time, though, this group did not want tithes abolished until alternative sources of revenue could be found to pay the clergy and to compensate the owners of impropriated tithes. This was the view of the Independent layman Daniel Taylor, who wanted farmers to purchase their freedom from tithes and the money thus raised to be used to support ministers and schools, and of John Tombes and the gathered churches of Herefordshire and Gloucestershire, who petitioned Parliament to appoint up to ten 'gospel preachers' for their counties, with 'a comfortable competence for their encouragement, some other way than by tithes'.[1]

Had the question been merely one of replacing the tithe by some more equitable means of public maintenance then it is possible that Barebone's Parliament would have found a solution to the problem. When the matter was first debated in Parliament on 13 July it was reported that 'it is the opinion of many, that if every parish was rated according to the poor book, to pay so much to the minister . . . and tithes be taken away, [this] would please both minister and people'.[2] But beyond the question of the tithe lay the question of whether ministers should receive any payment levied by compulsion, of whether in fact there should be state support for religion at all. It was this fundamental issue which divided conservative and moderate from radical Independents, which perpetuated the old dichotomy between Separatist and non-separatist, and which sealed the fate of Barebone's Parliament.

The case for the conservative and moderate Independents was stated by John Owen when he told the members of the Rump that it was incumbent on them 'to take care that the faith which you have received . . . be protected, preserved, propagated to and among the people which God hath set you over'. 'If once it comes . . . that you shall say, you have nothing to do with religion as rulers of the nation, God will quickly manifest that he will have nothing to do with you as rulers of

---

[1] D[aniel] T[aylor], *Certain Queries*, p. 14. Nickolls, *Original Letters*, p. 121.
[2] *Severall Proceedings of State Affairs*, No. 198, 7–14 July 1653, pp. 3134–5.

the nation.'[1] The case for the radicals was stated, and it was fitting that it should be, by the veteran Separatist John Canne. Since 1650 Canne had been living in Hull where he had fought a running battle with the Presbyterian John Shaw for the right to preach in the town's Holy Trinity church, had acted as chaplain to Colonel Robert Overton's garrison since 1652, and by 1653 was regaling them with Fifth Monarchist sermons. The execution of Charles I and the dissolution of the Rump, claimed Canne, proved 'that the Ancient of days hath set up his throne in England'; in 1655 there would be 'great revolutions' in Europe, in that year the Lord would 'most eminently appear, shaking the earth and overthrowing the thrones of kingdoms'.[2] But in embracing this new millenarian enthusiasm Canne did not abandon his old Separatist convictions. The national ministry and tithes, he told the garrison at Hull, were 'the institutions of popes' and ought to be abolished. 'If we follow the example and practice of our Saviour and apostles . . . the minister's maintenance is not any set portion of men's goods, nor to be taken from them by compulsion, but to be free.' But the abolition of tithes would not by itself be sufficient to purge the churches of 'superstition and will-worship': even if 'tithes be taken away, yet will the people do as they have done, go to these priests for marrying, burying, christenings, churchings, administering the Lord's Supper' and so on. 'The national ministry, commonly called the ministry of the Church of England . . . is a plant which the heavenly Father never planted, and therefore [should] be plucked up by the roots.'[3]

Canne's view was shared by the radical Independents and by the majority of Baptists, by Levellers and Fifth Monarchists alike. On 15 July the radicals in Barebone's Parliament attempted to stop 'the maintenance of ministers by tithes' from 3 November: it was their intention, so their opponents believed, to leave impropriators without compensation and clergy without salaries, to be supported henceforward either by the voluntary contributions of their congregations or by the labour of their hands. The attempt was defeated by 68 votes to 43, and

---

[1] Owen, *A Sermon Preached to the Parliament* (1652), pp. 36–7.

[2] *CSPD* 1650, p. 452, 1651–2, p. 211. J. Canne, *A Voice from the Temple to the Higher Powers* (1653), pp. 13–15, 29.

[3] J. Canne, *A Second Voice from the Temple* (1653), pp. 4, 8, 14.

the matter referred to a committee by 56 votes to 49.[1] It was these votes which enabled a contemporary, a week later, to classify the members of Parliament into two groups, according to whether they were for 'a godly learned ministry and universities' or supposedly against. Eighty-four members were classified as moderates and sixty as radicals. Seventeen of the twenty-eight known Independents and six of the seven Baptists in the assembly were listed in the ranks of the radicals.[2]

The committee on tithes had a majority of moderates; it was besieged by clergymen and their lawyers pleading for the preservation of the status quo; and when it reported to Parliament on 2 December it was with the conclusion that 'public preachers of the Gospel in the public meeting-places [should] have and enjoy the maintenance already settled by law'.[3] The committee further recommended the adoption of the scheme put forward by John Owen and the conservative Independents in the previous year, for the appointment of commissioners to go on circuit to eject ignorant and scandalous clergymen. The committee's report was anathema to the radical Independents and to the Baptists. Instead of the hoped-for measures to complete the Reformation by freeing the churches from the taint of popish superstition and placing religion on a voluntary basis, Parliament was being asked, as Vavasor Powell said, to maintain 'the old corrupt foundation still'.[4] Parliament refused. On 17 November the radicals had already scored an initial victory when they secured the passage of a resolution to abolish a patron's right to appoint clergymen to benefices, and on Saturday, 10 December, assisted, it would seem, by absenteeism amongst the moderates, they won their greatest triumph. By 56 votes to 54 they rejected the first clause of the report of the committee on tithes, that recommending Owen's scheme for the ejection of ministers.

It proved to be a Pyrrhic victory. Conservative opinion was

---

[1] *Journal of the House of Commons* (1742), vii. 285–6.

[2] The lists are printed in Gardiner, *Commonwealth and Protectorate*, ii. 308–10, and in H. A. Glass, *The Barbone Parliament* (1899), pp. 69–86. Six of the fifteen M.P.s who are known to have been recommended by gathered churches were moderates (Woolrych, 'The Calling of Barebone's Parliament', p. 506).

[3] J. Rogers, *Sagrir* (1653), epistle to the reader, sig. B3. Tai Liu, 'Saints in Power', pp. 158, 191. *Journals of the House of Commons*, vii. 361.

[4] Glass, *Barbone Parliament*, p. 111.

thoroughly alarmed, it being taken for granted, wrote Richard Baxter, 'that the tithes and universities would at the next opportunity be voted down'.[1] Two days later, on the morning of Monday 12 December, the moderate party got up early, arrived at the House before most of the radicals were present, and voted 'to deliver up unto the Lord General Cromwell the powers they have received from him'. Thereupon the majority vacated the House, leaving the radical minority to be expelled by soldiers. This was the end of the Commonwealth. Four days later Cromwell was installed as head of state with the title of Lord Protector, thus taking 'the crown off from the head of Christ', complained the Fifth Monarchist John Carew, and putting 'it upon his own'.[2]

Vavasor Powell and Christopher Feake attempted to stage a protest, and Powell, preaching from Feake's pulpit in St. Anne's, Blackfriars, on 19 December commanded his congregation to go home and pray, 'Lord, wilt thou have Oliver Cromwell or Jesus Christ to reign over us?'[3] But it was to no avail. Feake was imprisoned, Powell fled back to Wales, Harrison was deprived of his commission. The rule of the saints had been brought to an end by a mixture of fraud and force. Never again would Parliament come so near to disestablishing the Church of England. Not until the twentieth century would Dissenters from the established church again come so near to grasping the fulcrum of political power.

The reasons for the failure of the radicals are not difficult to fathom. Barebone's Parliament owed its existence to Cromwell and the army officers, whose constant quest it was throughout the Interregnum to find a broad base of support for their political power. 'I am as much for government by consent as any man,' said Cromwell, 'but where shall we find that consent?' At best it was a difficult task: it would become well nigh impossible if Cromwell could not retain the loyalty both of the army whose existence was a guarantee of religious toleration and of a proportion of the gentry and trading classes whose support was essential to the administration and financing of government. Consequently Cromwell, who had watched with growing concern the way in which the Rump had alienated the

---

[1] *Reliquiae Baxterianae*, part i, p. 70.
[2] Brown, *Baptists and Fifth Monarchy Men*, p. 82.   [3] Ibid., p. 45.

radicals in the army and the gathered churches in the latter part of 1652 and the first quarter of 1653, became even more alarmed as the radicals in Barebone's Parliament alienated conservative opinion in the summer and autumn of 1653. Cromwell shared the apocalyptic enthusiasms of the radicals only as long as they did not impinge on his responsibilities as England's most powerful country gentleman: once the radicals started to threaten the rights of patrons, the property of tithe owners, and the livelihood of the clergy, Cromwell's enthusiasm evaporated. He was 'more troubled now with the fool than before with the knave', he is reported to have said in 1653.[1]

If, in the end, the army leaders found their basis of support too narrow to maintain civilian government and had no recourse but to make way for the return of the Stuarts, how much narrower was the basis of support for the radicals in Barebone's Parliament. The radicals' attack on the national church was supported only by the Baptists (with notable exceptions), the more extreme Independents, the noisy but not numerous Fifth Monarchists, the dwindling band of Levellers, and the rising body of Quakers. They had against them the whole weight of propertied influence in the country, the vast majority of the parish clergy, and, apart from Harrison, the leading army officers. They also had against them the most influential of the Independent ministers who, under the leadership of John Owen, were at this juncture as firmly wedded to the established church as were the Presbyterians themselves. 'Tithes will be paid to the ministers as long as corn groweth', so Philip Nye is reported to have said.[2]

12. 'INDEPENDENCE AND STATE HIRE IN RELIGION': CONGREGATIONALISTS AND BAPTISTS UNDER THE PROTECTORATE

The Protectorate which was established on the dissolution of Barebone's Parliament was furnished with a written constitution, *The Instrument of Government*. Apart from its failure to proscribe anti-trinitarian opinions, its religious provisions were such as would have commended themselves to conservative Independents such as Owen and Nye. The *Instrument* provided for the

---

[1] *Calendar of the Clarendon State Papers* (Oxford, 1869), ii. 251.
[2] J. Spittlehouse, *An Explanation of the Commission of Jesus Christ* (1653), pp. 4–5.

'public profession' of the Christian religion and for the retention of tithes until some other 'provision, less subject to scruple
and contention' be found to support ministers. But no one was
to be compelled to conform to that 'public profession' and sects
which dissented from the established church, provided they
professed 'faith in God by Christ Jesus', were to be protected
in the 'exercise of their religion'. This liberty was not to be 'extended to popery or prelacy', but in practice Roman Catholics
were treated more leniently than they had been by the Stuarts,
Episcopalians continued to conduct services according to the
Book of Common Prayer, and Jews were permitted to settle in
England for the first time since 1290.[1] The legislation establishing Presbyterianism remained on the statute book, but even
in the Presbyterian strongholds of London and Lancashire
classical organization and discipline, bereft of penal sanctions,
languished in a state of decay;[2] and it was Cromwell's intention
that the Presbyterian clergy should share the ministry of the
established church with other Calvinists—the Independents
and the Particular Baptists. To this end two ordinances were
issued in March 1654 which put into operation a scheme similar
to that proposed by John Owen and the committee on tithes,
except that the roles of the national commissioners and the
county committees were reversed: under the government's
scheme the suitability of would-be incumbents was to be tested
by a commission of thirty-eight ministers and laymen, the
'Triers', while the ejection of scandalous clergymen was to
be entrusted to county committees. Of the thirty-eight
Triers, seventeen are known to have been Independents, eleven
Presbyterians, and four Baptists.[3] For the first and last time
in English history an official attempt was made to accommodate Independents and Baptists within the established
church.

The attempt revealed the difficulties involved in trying to

[1] Jordan, *Religious Toleration*, iii. 179–218.
[2] Shaw, *English Church*, ii. 98–142.
[3] The Independents were: Carter, Caryl, Cradock, Goff, Goodwin, Greenhill,
Lockyer, Nye, J. Owen, T. Owen, Peter, Sadler, Simpson, Slater, Sterry, Strong,
and Tichborn. The Presbyterians: Arrowsmith, Bamford, Cooper, Fairclough,
Horton, Manton, Marshall, Rous, Sedgwick, Tuckney, and Valentine. The
Baptists: Cresset, Jessey, Packer, and Tombes. C. H. Firth and R. S. Rait, *Acts and
Ordinances of the Interregnum* (1911), ii. 856.

graft the principle of the gathered church on to a national ecclesiastical system. Of the 2,029 clergy ejected in England and Wales at the Restoration, 194 were Congregationalists, of whom 154 held parochial livings, twenty-eight lectureships or chaplaincies, and thirteen academic posts.[1] In accepting livings within the established church the English Independents were following the precedent set by the Jacobites in the Netherlands and the Congregationalists of New England who had founded gathered churches recognized by and financed with the help of the magistrate. But in all three countries the attempt to combine separation from the world with support by the state led to anomaly and conflict. In the Netherlands the Dutch authorities, prompted by Archbishop Laud, had in 1634 insisted that state-supported Jacobite pastors should conform either to the Church of England or to the Dutch Reformed Church; in Massachusetts the colonial establishment provoked the anger of colonists who could not, or did not wish, to provide evidence of their regeneration by debarring them both from the sacraments of the church and the political privileges of the state; and in England those Congregationalists who tried to combine the duties—and emoluments—of a parish minister with the pastorate of a gathered church frequently incurred the hostility of their parishioners. It is not difficult to understand the resentment provoked by the Independent minister described by the Presbyterian Daniel Cawdrey who had 'a very great parish' and accepted his parishioners' financial support, but who would preach 'to them only in the morning . . . administering neither sacrament to them, for that he does in his own select congregation in the afternoon'.[2]

It was not only Independent ministers who were accused by disgruntled parishioners of maintaining too strict a control over admission to the sacraments. In the 1650s the parishioners of the Presbyterian John Shaw in Hull complained to the

[1] G. F. Nuttall, 'Congregational Commonwealth Incumbents', *TCHS* xiv (1940–4), 156–7. R. Tudur Jones and B. G. Owens, 'Anghydffurfwyr Cymru, 1660–2', *Y Cofiadur*, xxxii (1962), 3–91. Of the 154 Congregationalist incumbents, 130 held livings in England and 24 in Wales. One Congregationalist, Francis Howell, was both principal of Jesus College, Oxford, and incumbent of Llanrhaeadr-ym-Mochnant in Denbighshire.

[2] W. W. Briggs, 'The Controversy concerning Free Admission to the Lord's Supper', *TCHS* xvi (1949–51), 185, quoting D. Cawdrey, *Church Reformation Promoted* (1657), p. 107.

Council of State that he had 'erected a church government
without any authority known to us; and with the assistance of
some others who call themselves elders and church officers'
exercised 'an arbitrary and coercive power', refusing the
sacrament to those who would not 'come to the examination of
the said elders'.[1] But there was an essential difference between
the practice of even the strictest Presbyterians and the Independents. Whereas Roger Drake, one of the most rigid of
Presbyterians, laid down as the condition of admission to the
Lord's Supper 'visible worthiness, which consists in competent
knowledge, profession of piety, and immunity from scandal',
Independents required an applicant for church membership,
and hence for admission to communion, to give 'some experimental evidences of the work of grace upon his soul'.[2] The
Independents were more convinced than the Presbyterians
that they could distinguish the regenerate from the unregenerate, and the bounds they set to their gathered churches were
thus necessarily narrower than the limits the Presbyterians set
to their lists of communicants. Richard Baxter complained that
after Acton had been served successively by two Independent
rectors, Philip Nye and Thomas Elford, 'there remained but
two women in all the town and parish whom they admitted to
the sacrament', and in Lancashire the parishioners of Thomas
Jollie, the Independent curate of Altham, protested that he
declined to baptize their children and refused 'the Lord's
Supper to all the parishioners except three families'.[3]

In some cases aggrieved parishioners took action against their
incumbents. It was on the ground that he had refused to administer the sacraments indiscriminately that John Goodwin
had been deprived of his living at St. Stephen's, Coleman Street,
in 1645, though four years later the parish vestry invited him
back to his old pulpit and agreed to let his gathered church use
St. Stephen's for its communion services and its church meetings, and even to have half the collections for the poor.[4] But

---

[1] W. Whitaker, *Bowl Alley Lane Chapel, Hull* (1910), p. 24.
[2] R. Drake, *The Bar against Free Admission to the Lord's Supper Fixed* (1656), preface,
quoted by Biggs, 'Controversy concerning Free Admission', p. 181. J. Rogers,
Ohel or Beth-Shemesh. A Tabernacle for the Sun (1653), p. 354.
[3] A. G. Matthews, *Calamy Revised* (Oxford, 1934), p. 301. Nuttall, *Visible Saints*,
p. 137.
[4] Shaw, *English Church*, ii. 134–6.

other disputes were not settled so amicably. There was continuous trouble between John Loder, the Independent rector of St. Bartholomew Exchange, and his parishioners who refused to pay tithes when 'he refused to administer the sacrament and to christen children' and filled up the pews 'with strange congregations'.[1] The Congregationalist Thomas Weld, who had returned to England from Massachusetts with Hugh Peter in 1641, accepted the living as rector of Gateshead in 1650 only on condition that his duties as parish minister should not extend beyond preaching and visiting the sick. But when he refused to baptize his parishioners' children and would admit only eighteen of the parish's inhabitants to communion, the parish vestry and churchwardens retaliated by refusing to pay his removal expenses, declined to pay him his agreed salary, urged his parishioners to refuse to pay him tithes, and denied him the use of the parish church for the administration of the sacraments.[2] Some of the parishioners of Thomas Palmer, the Independent rector of Aston-upon-Trent in Derbyshire, of George Bound, the Presbyterian rector of Shenfield in Essex, and of several Lincolnshire ministers even went to the length of prosecuting them 'for not administering the Lord's Supper to all their parishioners, according to the statute of 1 Edward VI'. At the Lincoln assizes in 1658 Judge Windham told the defendants that it was 'a tyranny beyond that of prelacy for a minister to deny [the sacrament] to such as will not pin their faith to his sleeve', and added that it was lawful for parishioners to refuse tithes to such ministers. On two occasions, though, the government intervened on behalf of harassed ministers. In Gateshead in 1658 Thomas Weld's opponents were removed from office after he and his supporters had petitioned the Council of State. In Essex the prosecution against George Bound was stopped when it was found that the Act of 1 Edward VI had been repealed by the enactment of the Humble Petition and Advice in 1657, and the claimant was hauled before the Council of State to admit his error.[3] 'Independence and state hire in religion', commented John Milton, 'can never consist long or

---

[1] Ibid. ii. 132–3.

[2] T. Weld, *A Vindication of Mr. Weld* (1658), pp. 4–15.

[3] *CSPD* 1657–8, p. 251, 1658–9, pp. 69–70, 194–5, 210. R. Howell, *Newcastle upon Tyne and the Puritan Revolution* (Oxford, 1967), p. 265.

certainly together. For magistrates at one time or other will pay none but such whom by their committees of examination they find conformable to their interests and opinions.'[1]

Not all Independents, though, were prepared to work within the established church, and attitudes varied from the whole-hearted co-operation of conservative Congregationalists such as John Owen and Philip Nye to the total opposition of radical Separatists like David Brown and Samuel Chidley. Whereas Owen and Nye defended tithes, served as Triers, and urged the suppression of heresy, Brown and Chidley eschewed even the buildings of the established church as irremediably tainted with popish idolatry.[2] In between these two extremes lay a whole spectrum of opinions and practices: Independents whose views had been Separatist before 1642, but who were prepared to accept posts in the established church once episcopal control had been removed; Independents who denounced tithes and refused to accept benefices, but who were ready to serve as town lecturers or as army chaplains paid by the state; Independents who denounced the concept of a national church, but who tried to gain possession of its buildings; and, one suspects, Independents whose principal objection to tithes was that they were not in receipt of them.

Henry Burton had branded the Laudian church as antichristian and had believed it to be so tainted by popery as to be almost incapable of reform; but in 1642 he accepted a lectureship at St. Matthew's, Friday Street. James Forbes, the pastor of the Gloucester Congregational church, 'could not accept the call to be a parochial minister, for if I received the parish maintenance from all, all would expect to have me baptize their children, and administer the Lord's Supper to all', but he gladly accepted a lectureship at Gloucester cathedral since payment would come not from tithes but from the state.[3] Vavasor Powell denounced the payment of tithes, but not only received public maintenance from the Commission for the Propagation of the Gospel in Wales but also accepted money from the Committee for Plundered Ministers, which was in its

---

[1] W. Orme, *Life of John Owen* (1820), p. 137.

[2] D. Brown, *Two Conferences, passim.*

[3] W. Lloyd, *A Brief Account of the Foundation and History of the Protestant Dissenting Meeting House in Barton Street, Gloucester* (Gloucester, 1899), pp. 24–5.

turn derived from tithes.[1] William Bridge and Job Tookey, pastor and teacher respectively of the Congregational church at Great Yarmouth, similarly had no scruples about accepting payment from the state for their duties as town preachers, but when the corporation proposed to levy a rate for their main- tenance they both repudiated the attempt 'as being against the way of the Gospel' and their church 'desired that none of the brethren might have any hand in the acting of the same'.[2] David Davies, who held the living of Galligaer in Glamorgan, was said to have preached against tithes for three years and to have relied on voluntary contributions for his maintenance, but when he found that voluntary contributions were not yielding as much as tithes he began to advocate a return to the old ways.[3] Davies, admittedly, was a Baptist, but his attitude may not have been unique.

Geoffrey Nuttall has claimed that the Independent church at Bury St. Edmunds was 'Separatist to the core', for its church book begins with a covenant of 1646, witnessed by Katherine and Samuel Chidley, by which its eight signatories resolved to separate from 'the evil of the Church of England' and from those who communicate with it 'either publicly or privately'.[4] Two years later, though, the church appears to have been recon- stituted, for the original stridently Separatist covenant was replaced by a more typically Congregational document which was approved by the Congregational church at Norwich. Only three of the signatories of the 1646 covenant signed the 1648 covenant and all three were subsequently excommunicated for the various sins of theft, drunkenness, and quarrelling with the wife. However in 1656 the church ordained as its pastor a Cambridge graduate and former member of the Norwich church, Thomas Taylor, and not only did Taylor never hold a living in the established church but, under his guidance, the church approved a confession of faith which indicated a return to a Separatist position. The new confession asserted 'that all national, provincial, and parochial churches, though there be

---

[1] Richards, *Puritan Movement in Wales*, p. 164. Richards, *Religious Developments in Wales*, p. 227.

[2] Great Yarmouth Church Book, p. 98, DWL Harmer MSS. 76. 2.

[3] Richards, *Puritan Movement in Wales*, p. 164.

[4] Nuttall, *Visible Saints*, p. 27. Bury St. Edmunds Church Book, pp. 1–3, DWL Harmer MSS. 76.4. Browne, *Congregationalism in Norfolk and Suffolk*, p. 394.

some saints among them, are not the visible churches of Christ and of the lamb, but of Antichrist and the whore'. It was 'the duty of all the Lord's people to come out from among them and be separate, and not touch the unclean thing lest by partaking with Babylon in her sins they partake also in her plagues'. In radical Separatist tradition the church denied that the magistrate had any right 'to intermeddle with the matters of faith and conscience in such things as pertain unto the worship of God', and affirmed that the 'world's weapons of outward force and coercive power are too carnal and therefore too weak either to maintain or overthrow the truth and spiritual kingdom of Jesus Christ'. And early in 1660 the church excommunicated Elizabeth Inman for, among other offences, collecting money towards the minister's maintenance from people who were not members of the church, 'it being a thing most wicked and unreasonable that we should reap and require carnal things of them to whom we never sowed spiritual things'.[1]

But the Bury St. Edmunds church, in every other way so anxious to keep itself unsullied from the world, saw no inconsistency in twice petitioning Cromwell and the Council of State for assistance in finding a place in which to worship. The Independents complained that the Presbyterians in the town enjoyed 'the advantage of both the parish meeting-houses', that they themselves had 'to hire the shire house at a great rent, and to maintain a minister at their private charge', and requested that they be allowed the use either of one of the town's two parish churches, or at least of 'the chancel of Mary's parish' which could be divided off 'from the body of the meeting-house'.[2] What is even more surprising is the fact that the Bury church's Separatist confession of 1656 was approved by representatives from nine other East Anglian Independent churches, six of whose pastors held benefices within the established church.[3]

The complex influences at work on the church at Bury St. Edmunds indicates the way in which the Independency of the Interregnum inherited Brownist as well as Jacobite characteristics, was moulded by native Separatism as well as by the Con-

---

[1] Bury St. Edmunds Church Book, pp. 5–8, 17–19, 31–3.
[2] Browne, *Congregationalism in Norfolk and Suffolk*, pp. 395. 402–3.
[3] Bury St. Edmunds Church Book, p. 20.

gregationalism of the Netherlands and New England. While there may have been some 150 Independent churches whose pastors were also rectors or vicars of the local parish, there were other paedobaptist Independent churches which had no connection whatever with the established church. Neither the Independent church at Adisham in Kent, which dates back to 1649, nor that at Horningsham in Wiltshire, which was also probably founded before the Restoration, can be connected with any beneficed minister or parish lecturer.[1] The old Separatist church at Yarmouth, which dated back to at least 1624, maintained its separate existence until 1660, dissenting from the Cromwellian no less than from the Laudian establishment.[2] The London Separatist church to which John Canne and Samuel How had ministered in the 1630s lived on as an Independent church until 1705 without ever having ties with the state.[3] And it is probable, as Nuttall has pointed out, that there were other separatist Independent churches which, since they had no beneficed pastors to be ejected at the Restoration, have disappeared without trace.[4] John Canne himself was never appointed to a parish living and was a vigorous opponent both of tithes and of the national church, though in 1652 he did accept payment from the Council of State for his services as chaplain to Colonel Robert Overton's garrison in Hull.[5] After his acrimonious dispute with the Presbyterian John Shaw over the use of the town's Holy Trinity church Canne obtained the right to hold Independent services in the chancel, which was walled off from the rest of the church, until his Fifth Monarchist sympathies led the Council of State to order his removal from the town in 1656.[6] Canne forms a direct personal link between the Independency of the Interregnum and the Separatist church of Francis Johnson, Henry Barrow, and John

---

[1] M. Reeves, 'Protestant Nonconformity', *VCH Wiltshire* (1956), iii. 99. G. F. Nuttall, 'Dissenting Churches in Kent before 1700', *JEH* xiv (1963), 180–1. *Calamy Revised*, p. 365.

[2] Browne, *Congregationalism in Norfolk and Suffolk*, pp. 74–7. Burrage, *EED* ii. 309–10.

[3] 'The Hubbard–How–More Church', *TBHS* ii (1910–11), 30–52. F. Bate, *The Declaration of Indulgence* (1908), appendix, p. xxxviii.

[4] Nuttall, *Visible Saints*, p. 28.

[5] *CSPD* 1651–2, pp. 100, 211.

[6] *CSPD* 1650, p. 452, 1656–7, p. 41. J. G. Miall, *Congregationalism in Yorkshire* (1868), p. 288.

Greenwood, and, through Edith Bury, with Richard Fitz's church and the goldsmith's house congregation of 1568.

The Separatist strain in Independency would have been stronger had it not been for the fact that many Separatists were driven by the logic of their convictions to adopt a Baptist or even more extreme position. Radical Separatists such as Samuel Chidley who remained determined paedobaptists were probably the exception rather than the rule. Many Separatists would have appreciated the guileless logic of Thomas Wynell, vicar of Cranham in Gloucestershire, who argued against his local Separatists that if the ministry of the Church of England be false, so too must be its sacraments and baptism, with the result that some of the Separatists whom he had tried to persuade to return to the parish church instead 'fell upon this practice of sealing their covenant by baptism'.[1] In the 1650s a number of prominent religious radicals—Vavasor Powell, Thomas Harrison, John Carew, Hugh Courtney, and Richard Breviter—underwent believers' baptism, though Powell remained an Independent, believing that differing views on baptism could 'consist with brotherly love and Christian communion'.[2]

Far fewer Baptists than Independents retained links with the established church. By 1660 there were probably some 240 Baptist churches in existence, 130 Particular Baptist and 110 General Baptist, but only nineteen Baptist ministers were ejected from livings in 1660–2, eight in England and eleven in Wales.[3] Of those ejected in England one, Paul Hobson, was

[1] T. Wynell, *The Covenants Plea for Infants* (1642), sigs. A3, B.

[2] Brown, *Baptists and Fifth Monarchy Men*, p. 132. *Calamy Revised*, p. 71. R. Tudor Jones concludes from his study of Powell's attitude to baptism that while the evidence of whether he was or was not baptized as a believer is inconclusive, there is no doubt that he 'abandoned his belief in paedo-baptism'. R. Tudor Jones, 'Life, Thought and Work of Vavasor Powell', Oxford D. Phil. thesis, 1947, p. 179.

[3] W. T. Whitley attempted to compile a list of Baptist churches which had been founded before 1660 in *TBHS* ii (1910–11), 236–54, but his list needs to be treated with caution as it includes some churches, such as those at Bedford and Adisham, which were not Baptist but Congregational. W. K. Jordan, in his *Development of Religious Toleration*, iii, 457, put the number of Baptist churches in existence during the Interregnum at 297, but did not provide any detailed evidence to support his estimate. For the Baptists ejected in 1660–2 see Matthews, *Calamy Revised*, pp. 1, 186, 214, 269, 298, 303, 444, 487; Richards, *Religious Developments in Wales*, p. 361; and R. T. Jones and B. G. Owens, 'Anghydffurfwyr Cymru, 1660–62', *Y Cofiadur*, xxxii (1962), 11, 15, 19, 24, 45, 50, 58, 72, 73, 83. Of the other possible ejected Baptists listed in *Calamy Revised* Robert Brown did 'not renounce infant baptism',

chaplain of Eton College, two were lecturers, and of the five who held benefices two were themselves Triers. All the ejected Baptists were Particular Baptists, and can themselves be classified into two narrower categories. Seven of the eight Baptists who were ejected in England, together with one of those ejected in Wales, had connections with a small group of churches, led by the former Jacobite Independent, Henry Jessey, and the vicar of Leominster, John Tombes, which, in contrast to the practice of the overwhelming majority of Baptist churches, practised open membership—that is, while practising believers' baptism, they did not insist on it as a condition of membership and communion.[1] Similarly ten of the eleven Baptists ejected in Wales were at some time associated in the 'general meetings' initiated by John Miles of Ilston in 1650.[2] Miles, who had been educated at Oxford, had been baptized in 1649 by the Particular Baptist church which met in the Glaziers' Hall (the 'Glasshouse') in London, and had returned to Wales to found a Particular Baptist church at Ilston on the Gower peninsula. From Ilston Miles and his followers had disseminated Particular Baptist views to other parts of south Wales, and in the next three years churches were founded at Carmarthen, Abergavenny, Hay-on-Wye in Breconshire, and Llanharan in

and Daniel Dyke's Baptist connections seem to date from after 1660. Nor have I included the 'Catabaptist' Jenkin Jones among the Baptists ejected in Wales as his ecclesiastical connections appear to have been Congregational rather than Baptist.

[1] The connection between these eight men is best illustrated by the correspondence of the Particular Baptist church at Hexham which, unlike the more rigid Particular Baptist churches, recognized 'unbaptized churches and ministers for churches of Christ and ministers of Christ'. The churches of Henry Jessey, John Tombes, Paul Frewin, John Skinner, and William Kaye, all Baptists ejected at the Restoration, were all in correspondence and fellowship with the Hexham church (*Fenstanton Records*, pp. 344–6, 349, 353–5). Of the other Baptists who were ejected from livings in England Richard Adams 'was trained for the ministry by John Tombes' and Thomas Ewins was baptized by Henry Jessey (*Calamy Revised*, p. 1, *Broadmead Records*, p. 43). One of the Baptists ejected in Wales, John Abbot of Abergavenny, seconded Tombes in a debate on baptism in St. Mary's, Abergavenny, in 1653 (Richards, *Puritan Movement in Wales*, p. 153).

[2] The ten were John Miles, Walter Prosser, Thomas Proud, David Davies, John Edwards, Howell Thomas, Thomas Joseph, Morgan Jones of Llanmadock, Morgan Jones of Castellnewydd (Glamorgan), and Thomas Evans. *Association Records of the Particular Baptists of England, Wales and Ireland to 1660*, ed. B. R. White, i (1971), 3–17. For only one of the Baptists ejected at the Restoration. Paul Hobson, have I been unable to trace a connection with either the Jessey–Tombes group of churches or with Miles's general meetings.

Glamorgan.[1] Miles and his associated churches in south Wales, in sharp contrast to those English Baptist churches whose pastors held parochial livings, adopted a rigid closed membership position and would have communion only with baptized believers. When one of the future ejected Welsh Baptist pastors, Thomas Proud, embraced the open membership views of Jessey and Tombes in 1651, he was disowned by his fellow Welsh Baptists until he repudiated such 'destructive' opinions.[2]

Miles was incumbent at Ilston throughout the 1650s, and saw nothing incompatible in combining his duties as a Baptist pastor with the receipt of public maintenance. But the overwhelming majority of Baptists rejected what they regarded as Miles's, Tombes's, and Jessey's compromise with the Cromwellian state church. The Abergavenny church revolted against both the closed communion and the state connection of the Ilston church, and in July 1655 resolved to 'withdraw from all such ministers that do receive maintenance from the magistrates'.[3] Similarly in England in March 1656 representatives of the south Midland Particular Baptist churches, meeting at Tetsworth in Oxfordshire, condemned the payment of tithes and church rates as upholding the 'Babylonish and anti-christian' national church, while in the following month a meeting of the representatives of the West Country Particular Baptist churches at Wells resolved 'that a preacher of the Gospel ought not to accept a place of a minister to a parish, or lecturer, or chaplain, or to take a set maintenance from those' that were outside the church.[4] Admittedly the West Country Particular Baptists, like the Bury St. Edmund's Independents, saw nothing wrong in requesting the help of the magistrate in finding a suitable place in which to meet, and in March 1656 the Council of State instructed 'Colonel Desborough, major-general of county Devon, to take care that the Baptist church at Exeter have the best repaired public meeting place of the city which can conveniently be spared'.[5] But at another meeting at Tiverton in September 1657 the West Country Baptists agreed

[1] Richards, *Puritan Movement in Wales*, pp. 202–3.
[2] *Association Records*, i. 5–7.
[3] Richards, *Religious Developments*, p. 185.
[4] *Association Records*, ii. (1973), 62–3, iii. (1974), 151.
[5] *CSPD* 1655–6, p. 224.

to support those of their brethren who felt called to refuse payment of taxes levied 'in some cities and towns' for the maintenance of ministers, and resolved that Baptists 'ought to bear a public testimony against' such taxes 'as a soul offending and oppressing yoke'.[1]

Baptist criticism of the Cromwellian establishment was not confined to ecclesiastical matters. There was a good deal of opposition among Baptists to Cromwell's assumption of the title of Lord Protector: Paul Hobson, who acted as commissioner for Propagating the Gospel in the northern counties, suggested that all church members who signed loyal addresses to the Protector should be excommunicated: two other Baptists, Major John Bramston and Samuel Oates, now a chaplain in the army, were involved in a plot to place a third Baptist, Major-General Robert Overton, in command of the English army in Scotland; and a determined effort was made by the Fifth Monarchists to win over the Baptists of Norfolk and Suffolk.[2] When the Fifth Monarchist John Pendarves, pastor of the Abingdon Particular Baptist church, died in September 1656 Baptists and Fifth Monarchists came from places as far apart as Cornwall, Dartmouth, Totnes, Exeter, Norwich, London, and Hull (probably John Canne) to attend his funeral, and the government was so alarmed at the possibility of insurrection that eight troops of horse were dispatched to nearby Wallingford.[3] But despite the fears of one nervous pamphleteer, Abingdon did not prove to be a second Münster and most Baptists eschewed subversive activites. Particular Baptist churches in Hexham, Bradford, Derby, and Burton-on-Trent, in a loyal address to Cromwell, referred to the 'halcyon days of peace, plenty, and liberty' that they were enjoying under the Protectorate; the General Baptists, meeting in national assembly in 1654, repudiated the notion that 'the rule and government of the world should be put into' the hands of the saints before the return of the Lord; William Kiffin used his influence among the Particular Baptists of Ireland and the West Country

---

[1] *Association Records*, ii. 66–9.
[2] Brown, *Baptists and Fifth Monarchy Men*, pp. 71–3, 99–100.
[3] E. A. Payne, *The Baptists of Berkshire* (1951), pp. 27–30. B. R. White, 'John Pendarves, the Calvinistic Baptists and the Fifth Monarchy', *Baptist Quarterly*, xxv. (1974), 251–69.

to dissuade them from Fifth Monarchist activities; and Edmund Chillenden frustrated an attempt by Colonel Henry Danvers to get 'all the churches' to oppose Cromwell's new title.[1] Prominent Baptists who were loyal to the Protector got their reward: Henry Lawrence was made president of the Council of State, William Steele was appointed Lord Chancellor of Ireland, and William Kiffin, it was claimed, obtained from Cromwell concessions 'as to prohibited goods' and was 'thereby engaged to become his vassal'.[2]

The extent to which it is legitimate to classify the gathered churches of the Interregnum with the labels 'Particular Baptist', 'General Baptist', or 'Congregational' has been challenged by some historians. Christopher Hill has argued that it was a long time 'before clear-cut lines of sectarian division were imposed' on the fluid religious situation which arose after 1640. 'The disagreements among historians as to the exact sectarian classification of an individual or a congregation', he writes, 'is the best evidence that what they are trying to do is unsatisfactory because anachronistic.'[3] Claire Cross has similarly maintained that the religious history of the Interregnum 'can be studied meaningfully only if it is seen as the prehistory of the different denominations', and she criticizes those historians who, in her eyes, 'have been too eager to divide Commonwealth churches according to later theological distinctions that the churches themselves did not yet make'. To support her thesis Cross cites the examples of the gathered churches of Bristol and Bedford which contained both members who had undergone believers' baptism and those who had not, of the beneficed Baptist John Tombes 'who had far more in common with a Calvinist Independent minister of the stature of John Owen than he had with "mechanic" preachers of his own sect', and of the maverick John Goodwin who, though an Independent, held views on election similar to those of the General Baptists.[4]

---

[1] Nickolls, *Original Letters*, pp. 134–5, 159–60. *Minutes of the General Baptist Assembly*, i. 3. *The State Papers of John Thurloe* (1742), iv. 365. *Association Records of the Particular Baptists*, ii. 97.

[2] Tai Liu, 'Saints in Power', pp. 253–4.

[3] C. Hill, 'History and Denominational History', *Baptist Quarterly*, xxii (1967–8), 66–8.

[4] C. Cross, 'The Church in England', in *The Interregnum*, ed. G. E. Aylmer (1972), pp. 118–19.

It is true that the boundaries between the different denominations were sometimes indistinct in the 1640s and 1650s, but this was by no means a phenomenon peculiar to those two decades. Even in the eighteenth century it is not always easy to classify paedobaptist Dissenting churches and ministers as 'Congregational' or 'Presbyterian'; the phenomenon of Dissenters who occasionally conformed to the established church was well known for a hundred and more years after the Interregnum; and the existence of churches which refuse to make believer's baptism a condition for communion or church membership has continued to the present day. But this does not mean that one cannot give the overwhelming majority of gathered, and later Dissenting, churches their appropriate denominational label at any given period of their history. The examples given by Cross to support the thesis of a supposed lack of clear distinction between the denominations in the 1640s and 1650s are to a large extent exceptions which prove the rule. John Goodwin, in espousing Arminian opinions, was in a minority of one among Congregational ministers, and John Tombes, in holding a parochial living, occupied a position shared by fewer than twenty other Baptists. It is true that the Broadmead church, Bristol, and the church which became famous as the Bunyan meeting, Bedford, represented a larger number of churches which treated baptism as an open question.[1] But the very fact that such churches contained either a majority of members who upheld the validity of infant baptism or a majority who had undergone believers' baptism makes it possible, *pace* Christopher Hill, to classify such churches as either Congregational or Baptist. Both the Bedford church and the Bury St. Edmunds church contained members who questioned the validity of infant baptism, but neither church doubted that it was Congregational.[2] On the Baptist side the open-membership churches of the Jessey–Tombes group constituted but a tiny majority of Particular Baptist congregations. When Thomas Ewins, the pastor of the Broadmead church, decided to undergo believer's baptism in 1654 he went to Jessey's church

---

[1] Nuttall, *Visible Saints*, pp. 118–20.
[2] Church Book of Bunyan Meeting, typescript in DWL, MSS. 209. 2, p. 2. Bury St. Edmunds Church Book, DWL Harmer MSS, 76. 4, p. 10. Browne, *Congregationalism in Norfolk and Suffolk*, p. 395.

to receive the ordinance because he knew of no other church in London that had 'that latitude in their principles'.[1]

Against the few examples of men and churches which sat at the edge of denominational boundaries must be set the considerable amount of evidence which indicates the early existence of denominational ties and of denominational exclusiveness.[2] The five General Baptist churches in London, Lincoln, Coventry, Salisbury, and Tiverton had co-operated as early as 1626 in the abortive negotiations for union with the Dutch Waterlanders; thirty General Baptist churches in the Midlands came together in 1651 to draw up a confession of faith; and three years later General Baptist representatives from 'several parts of this nation' met in London in their first national assembly.[3] The Particular Baptists did not hold a similar national gathering until 1689, but as early as 1644 seven Particular Baptist churches in London co-operated in drawing up a confession of faith, and in other parts of the British Isles representatives of Particular Baptist churches met together in periodic 'general meetings' or associations. John Miles' South Wales Association first met in 1650; an association which came to include churches from Berkshire, Oxfordshire, Hampshire, Hertfordshire, Buckinghamshire, and Bedfordshire came together for the first time in 1652; in 1653 ten churches in Ireland wrote that they were 'united together'; the Western Association, comprising churches from Somerset, Devon, Dorset, Wiltshire, and Gloucestershire, also dates from 1653; and in 1655 the first meeting took place at Warwick of an association which included churches from the Midland counties of Warwickshire, Gloucestershire, and Derbyshire.[4] These associations kept in touch with each other and with the seven churches in

---

[1] R. Hayden, *The Records of a Church of Christ in Bristol* (Bristol Record Society, 1974), p. 29, citing T. Ewins, *The Church of Christ in Bristol Recovering her Veil* (1657), p. 57.

[2] Both Hill and Cross recognize the existence of much of this evidence, but they make no attempt to weigh its significance against the evidence they produce to support the thesis of a state of 'flux' in denominational relationships or of 'prehistory' in denominational life in the 1640s and 1650s.

[3] W. L. Lumpkin, *Baptist Confessions of Faith* (Philadelphia, 1959), pp. 171–88. *Minutes of the General Baptist Assembly*, i. 1–5.

[4] Lumpkin, *Baptist Confessions*, pp. 144–71. B. R. White, 'The Organisation of the Particular Baptists', *JEH* xvii (1966), 209–26. G. F. Nuttall, 'The Baptist Western Association, 1653–8', *JEH* xi (1960), 213–18.

London by personal contacts and by correspondence, and their records suggest not a state of flux or of denominational 'pre-history', but a determined attempt to establish and preserve denominational exclusiveness. The Western Association was of the opinion that believers' baptism was 'absolutely necessary to an orderly church communion', and lest any member be ensnared with the views of the General Baptists it resolved that 'a person holding general redemption, free will, and falling from grace' should be excommunicated; the Midland Association advised that it was 'very inconvenient and uncomfortable and dangerous' for a church member to marry a person who had not undergone believer's baptism; and both associations agreed that 'baptized believers ought not to hear the national ministers preach nor join with them in their public worship, their pretended ministry being Babylonish'.[1]

The Independents had neither the regional associations of the Particular Baptists nor, until representatives from over a hundred Congregational churches met at the Savoy palace in London in 1658, a national gathering comparable to those of the General Baptists. The preface to the Savoy Declaration, in which the Independents admitted that 'the generality of our churches have been . . . like so many ships . . . launched singly, and sailing apart and alone in the vast ocean of these tumulting times', might be adduced as evidence in support of the Hill-Cross thesis of lack of clear denominational distinctions for most of the Interregnum.[2] But this would be a most super-ficial reading of Independent history. Those Congregational church records which have survived from the Interregnum reveal a complicated nexus of ties by which Independent churches exchanged advice on, and gave approbation to, the drawing up of church covenants, practised intercommunion and gave and received the right hand of fellowship, sent representatives to each others' churches on the ordination of pastors, and transferred members from one church to another. Between 1649 and 1656 the church at Norwich gave advice to 'the Christians about North Walsham' on the correct pro-cedure on the setting up of a church; sent representatives to the

[1] *Association Records of the Particular Baptists*, i. 22, 25, ii. 57, 61, 63–4.
[2] *The Savoy Declaration of Faith and Order*, 1658, ed. A. G. Matthews (1959), p. 60.

gathering of churches at Bury St. Edmunds, Beccles, Wymond-
ham, Guestwick, Godwick, North Elmham, and Fritton, and
dismissed members to the churches at Yarmouth, Guestwick,
and Denton.[1] Even more significant are two items from the
records of the Yarmouth Congregational church which show
that when the original joint Yarmouth–Norwich church was
constituted in 1643 the members sought dismissal from and
approval of their former church at Rotterdam, and that in
1650 the Yarmouth church received into membership Elizabeth Edwards 'by the dismission from the church of Christ in
Salem, New England'.[2] The Congregational churches of England were in communion with, and influenced by, the churches
which, in the 1630s, had been set up in the Netherlands and
New England according to the principles of Henry Jacob and
William Ames. When the five Apologists returned from the
Netherlands in the early 1640s, when Hugh Peter and a score
of other Congregational ministers returned from Massachusetts, they brought with them the knowledge and experience
derived from putting those principles into practice.[3] Far from
emerging from a confused period of denominational 'prehistory'
during the Civil War and Interregnum, even the very earliest
Congregational churches set up in England in the 1640s were
the inheritors of an ecclesiastical system which had been tried
and developed in the Netherlands and New England during the
previous decade.

13. 'SAINTS BY CALLING':
THE SPIRITUAL EXPERIENCES OF THE INDEPENDENTS

It was the conservative Congregationalism of the Low Countries
and Massachusetts rather than the native radical Independent
tradition which inspired the Savoy Declaration of 1658. The
first draft of the declaration was drawn up by a committee
composed of John Owen, Thomas Goodwin, Philip Nye,

---

[1] Norwich Church Book, DWL Harmer MSS. 76. 1, pp. 16, 23–8, 33, 44.

[2] Browne, *Congregationalism in Norfolk and Suffolk*, pp. 209–10. Yarmouth Church
Book, DWL Harmer MSS. 76. 2, p. 27.

[3] The influence of the Congregationalism of Massachusetts on that of England is
the theme of R. F. Young's thesis, 'Good News from New England' (Michigan
State University, 1971). However Young overstates his case by minimizing the
influence of the English churches in the Netherlands, and ignoring that of the
English Separatists, on English Congregationalism.

William Greenhill, and Joseph Caryl, and although at least one radical Independent, Vavasor Powell, was invited to attend the conference, it is not known whether he or any other radicals were present.[1] The Savoy Declaration recognized that Congregational ministers might engage 'in the work of public preaching, and enjoy the public maintenance upon that account', but insisted that they were not thereby obliged to administer the sacraments to any but members of their own gathered churches.[2] That part of the declaration which concerned faith was modelled on the Presbyterians' Westminster Confession, but the section which dealt with church order distinguished Congregationalism from Presbyterianism by its insistence that Christ had delegated all 'power and authority' to particular, gathered churches, by its denial of authority to any higher 'synods or ecclesiastical assemblies', and by its belief that 'the work of preaching the word' should not be confined to pastors or teachers, but could be undertaken by others 'gifted and fitted by the Holy Ghost'.[3] But what most distinguished the Congregationalism of the Savoy conference from the Presbyterianism of the Westminster Assembly was the former's definition of, and qualification for, church membership. Whereas Presbyterians did not believe that it was possible to identify the elect with any certainty, argued that consequently the church on earth must include both the regenerate and the damned, and contented themselves with accepting a person's outward respectability and knowledge as a qualification for admission to communion, the Independents believed that church membership should and could be restricted to the elect. Church members, stated the Savoy Declaration, 'are saints by calling, visibly manifesting and evidencing . . . their obedience unto that call of Christ, who being further known to each other by their confession of the faith wrought in them by the power of God, declared by themselves or otherwise manifested, do willingly consent to walk together according to the appointment of Christ'.[4]

The point at which Independent churches began to expect

---

[1] Jones, *Congregationalism in England*, p. 35. F. Peck, *Desiderata Curiosa* (1779), ii. 507.

[2] *The Savoy Declaration of the Institution of Churches*, article xiv.

[3] Ibid., articles iv, v, vi, xiii, xxii.

[4] Ibid., article viii.

applicants for membership to give evidence of 'the faith wrought in them by the power of God' is a matter of dispute. Edmund Morgan, in his book *Visible Saints*, took up a suggestion of Robert Baillie that the Congregationalists imposed stricter qualifications for admission to church membership than did the Separatists, that they refused to admit not only those who were notorious for 'open profaneness', but those who exhibited 'want of true grace; yea . . . the want of convincing signs of regeneration'.[1] 'Nowhere', writes Morgan, 'did the Separatists charge that the English churches failed to inquire into the religious experiences of members in their effort to detect saving faith;' nowhere is there any suggestion that in the first Separatist churches 'members were subjected to a test for determining their possession of saving faith'. Morgan admits that Francis Johnson's Separatist church in Amsterdam, and most later Separatist churches, required applicants for membership to 'make confession of their faith', but he argues that what was implied by this formula 'was not saving faith but simply an intellectual understanding of it'. Indeed, so obsessed were the early Separatists with the purity of their members' lives that their opponents accused them of making works, not faith, the basis of church membership, and in order to meet this criticism Henry Ainsworth argued 'that people must be regenerate and born again, before they may be admitted into any particular church'. But, writes Morgan, it is unlikely that Ainsworth altered existing procedures for admission to church membership, and he suggests that the practice 'of testing prospective members of the church for signs of saving grace' originated not among the Separatists but 'in Massachusetts among the non-separating Puritans there, and spread from Massachusetts to Plymouth, Connecticut, New Haven, and back to England'. While the Separatists were preoccupied with the setting up and defending of 'churches formed, in their view, on the Scriptural pattern, Puritans who remained within the Church of England were primarily concerned with the individual rather than the church', with tracing 'the natural history of conversion in order to help men discover their prospects of salvation'.[2] In this

[1] Baillie, *Dissuasive from the Errours*, p. 156.
[2] E. S. Morgan, *Visible Saints* (New York, 1963), pp. 36–8, 52–7, 65–6. Quoted by permission of the New York University Press.

development the influence of William Perkins, the leading theologian of Elizabethan England, was paramount.

Morgan's thesis has been widely, though not universally, accepted among students of Separatist and early Congregational history. He admits that much of the evidence he adduces in support of his thesis is negative, and Raymond Stearns and David Brawner have argued that Morgan has misread the significance of the apparent absence of tests for 'saving faith' among the Separatists. The Separatists, they suggest, did not need to impose searching tests on applicants for membership to distinguish the regenerate from the damned, for only the elect would have sought to join churches membership of which involved exile, privation, and possibly death. It was only when membership of a gathered church came to offer social and political advantages, as in Massachusetts in the 1630s, that it became necessary to introduce stricter qualifications for church membership to distinguish hypocrites from the truly converted.[1]

The very notion of conversion, though, is one which is absent from the writings of the earliest Separatists. Robert Browne defined Christians as people who 'by a willing covenant made with our God, . . . are under the government of God and Christ, and thereby do lead a godly and Christian life'; to Henry Barrow the church was 'a company and fellowship of faithful and holy people gathered in the name of Christ Jesus'; John Greenwood's definition was similar—'a company of faithful people, separated from unbelievers and heathen of the land'.[2] It is only when we reach the seventeenth century and a generation of men—especially Cambridge men such as Ainsworth—who had fallen under the influence of William Perkins that Separatists start to speak of church membership in terms of regeneration and conversion. Not only Henry Ainsworth but the followers whom John Smyth left behind in Amsterdam spoke of members of the visible church as 'the regenerate', as new 'creatures'. As believers in free will these English Baptists emphasized the repentance of the believer rather than his election by God, but twenty years before the churches of

---

[1] R. P. Stearns and D. H. Brawner, 'New England Church "Relations" and Continuity in Early Congregational History', *Proceedings of the American Antiquarian Society* (April 1965), pp. 40–4.

[2] *Writings of Harrison and Browne*, p. 226. *Writings of Barrow, 1587–90*, p. 214. *Writings of Greenwood*, p. 98.

Massachusetts were asking applicants for membership to 'declare what work of grace the Lord hath wrought in them', the 'remainders of Mr. Smyth's company' were defining church membership in terms of the individual's relationship to God rather than of his fellowship with other Christians. 'The outward church visible', they wrote 'consists of penitent persons only, and of such as believing in Christ bring forth fruits worthy amendment of life [sic].'[1]

Morgan suggests that it was the religious revival which followed John Cotton's election as teacher to the Congregational church in Boston in 1633 which led the Massachusetts churches to require applicants for membership to give evidence of saving grace to the church, and if this was in fact the case the practice spread rapidly to the English churches in Europe, both Separatist and non-separatist.[2] When, in 1637, Sidrach Simpson sought to join William Bridge's church at Rotterdam he was required to make 'confession of his experience of the grace of God wrought in him', and two years later the Separatist Samuel How made a definite connection between conversion and church membership. 'Everyone's conversion', wrote the preaching cobbler, 'binds him to make speed to that church which consists of such as are faithful in Jesus Christ.'[3] In 1654 a general meeting of West Country Particular Baptists at Taunton considered the question of whether an applicant could be admitted to church membership on a 'bare confession' of faith, and concluded that no one should 'be admitted on such terms without a declaration of an experimental work of the Spirit upon the heart . . . being attended with evident tokens of conversion, to the satisfaction of the . . . church.'[4]

While the process by which Independent and Baptist churches came to require evidence of 'the work of grace upon the soul' from applicants for church membership is obscure, and is likely to remain so, the importance of one aspect of the question pointed to by Edmund Morgan cannot be disputed: the pervasive influence of William Perkins. William Ames, John Robinson, Henry Burton, and John Cotton all acknow-

---

[1] *Works of John Smyth*, ii. 744.
[2] Morgan, *Visible Saints*, pp. 98–100.
[3] Nuttall, *Visible Saints*, p. 111. How, *Sufficiencie of the Spirits Teaching*, sig. F.
[4] *Association Records of the Particular Baptists*, ii. 56.

ledged the impact on them of his preaching at Cambridge, Cotton in his unregenerate days rejoicing at the news of Perkins's death in 1602 since his sermons could trouble him no longer.[1] Perkins's teaching on conversion was a reflection of his own experience, of the repudiation of the 'wild liberties' of youth which, it seems, had issued in the birth of an illegitimate child. In a passage of dialogue which, though no doubt exaggerated, is probably autobiographical Perkins puts into the mouth of one of the characters remorse for the 'fervent lust' with which he had committed 'adultery, fornication, and suchlike uncleanness'. But when he 'heard the law [of Moses] preached', 'how that I ought to love and honour God with all my strength and might', it made him 'inwardly afraid' and his flesh 'began to tremble and quake'. He could not sleep at night; if he stayed in he feared the house would collapse; if he went out he thought 'every cranny of the earth would open itself wide and swallow me'. From this 'curse of the law' he was freed by 'a godly, learned preacher' who prayed with him and showed him 'the promises of mercy . . . in the book of God'. He came to realize that Christ's 'blood, his death, his patience in suffering rebukes and wrongs and the full wrath of God, his prayers and fastings, his meakness and fulfilling the uttermost points of the law, appeased the wrath of God, [and] brought the favour of God to me again'. This recognition did not, though, mean the end of doubts and temptations, which continued to assail him. Indeed, argued Perkins, the absence of doubt meant that one was damned: it was 'a grace peculiar to the man elect to try himself, whether he be in the estate of grace or not'. Only by being unsure of one's salvation could one be assured that one was saved. 'There is no man living that feels the power and virtue of the blood of Christ, which first hath not felt the pains of hell.'[2]

Apart from his teaching on the self-confirming value of perpetual doubt, which was rejected both by the Antinomians of the seventeenth century and by the Wesleyans of the eighteenth, the process of conversion as expounded by William

---

[1] Sprunger, *William Ames*, pp. 11, 145. Burgess, *John Robinson*, p. 48. Burton, *Narration of the Life*, p. 1. I. Breward, 'The Significance of William Perkins', *Journal of Religious History*, iv (December 1966), 128.

[2] I. Breward, ed., *The Work of William Perkins* (1970), pp. 6, 357, 362–72.

Perkins was upheld by English Evangelicals for three centuries as the normative Christian experience. It was the pattern of experience which the Independent and Baptist churches of the Interregnum regarded as the essential qualification for church membership. Two collections of such experiences, given by men and women in making application for membership of a gathered church, were published in the early 1650s by two Independent ministers, Henry Walker, the pastor of a London church, and John Rogers, the Fifth Monarchist, who from 1650 to 1652 was pastor of a church in Dublin.[1] Together they total ninety-nine personal accounts of spiritual doubts, fears, temptations, and ultimately conversion, and though the length and detail provided by each applicant varies considerably from person to person, and though their accounts have been subjected to a good deal of editorial interference by their pastors, they provide valuable insights into the process of conversion expected of members of gathered churches in the mid-seventeenth century.

Few of the spiritual autobiographies provide much information about the early life, home background, and upbringing of their subjects, but those that do bear witness to the abiding influence of the Puritan home. Eight of the converts claimed that they were brought up 'very religiously', while only one mentioned 'a wicked and profane' home background. But much more influential than the Puritan home, if these testimonies collected by two ministers can be taken at their face value, was the impact of the Puritan pulpit. Thirty-four of the converts specifically mentioned that their spiritual development had been influenced by listening to sermons, and women in particular appear to have been open to the influence of male preachers, for of those thirty-four twenty-three were female. From their pulpits Puritan preachers tried to impress on their congregations the importance of observing a strict moral code, the dangers of careless living, and the ultimate penalties of sin. Seventeen of the converts give details of the sins with which their consciences were burdened, all of them personal rather than social misdemeanours, apart from two men who as youths had disobeyed their parents and a girl who had got her sister

---

[1] [H. Walker], *Spiritual Experiences of Sundry Believers* (1652), J. Rogers, *Ohel or Beth-Shemesh, A Tabernacle for the Sun* (1653).

into trouble by lying. The actions for which the majority felt guilty were offences against the Puritans' moral and religious code: doubting the existence of God, questioning the truth of the Scriptures, blaspheming, swearing, gambling, drinking, taking tobacco, and breaking the Sabbath. One woman feared that she had offended God by gathering 'flowers in my garden on the Lord's day'; one man was tormented by the fear that, in telling a lie 'against conscience', he had committed the unforgivable sin against the Holy Ghost.[1]

For such offences, taught the Puritan preachers, the sinner deserved judgement and damnation. The listener was often made the more receptive to such threats by illness, bereavement, or the proximity of death, tribulations the incidence of which increased in the turmoil of the 1640s. Fourteen of the men and women whose testimonies Rogers and Walker published mentioned some such trial as an important factor in their spiritual development. When the Catholic rebellion broke out in Ulster in 1641 Major Andrew Manning's father was killed and his wife wounded, and at the siege of Drogheda he himself was left for dead on the field of battle with fifteen wounds; Francis Bishop was 'impeached upon an article of war' and came near to being shot; and another soldier 'had much experience of God's deliverance from enemies in the high places of the field'. When Frances Curtis heard what turned out to be a false report that her husband had been killed by the Irish rebels, she feared it 'was by my sins'; when a devoted daughter lost her father she concluded it was because she had 'omitted much good' and had 'committed much evil'.[2]

Personal tragedies such as these were frequently regarded as foretastes of future punishment and as warnings of hell. Fifteen of the testimonies mention fear of hell and damnation as a factor in the spiritual development of their subjects. John Bywater was tormented by thoughts of 'the horrors of hell' after witnessing a public execution; Francis Bishop, lying in prison under sentence of death, 'was in the apprehension of hell'; and Sarah Barnwell was 'struck deep to the heart' after hearing a Mr. Dunstable preach 'on the sad condition of some (even professors) that were

---

[1] Walker, *Spiritual Experiences*, pp. 53, 87.
[2] Rogers, *Ohel*, pp. 398, 412(2), 412(10). Walker, *Spiritual Experiences*, pp. 348–9, 161–4.

in hell howling'.[1] It is significant, though, that of these fifteen
testimonies eleven were published by Henry Walker and only
four, including his own, by John Rogers, for so horrific were
Rogers's own experiences at the hands of hell-fire preachers
that he deliberately refrained from similarly terrorizing his own
congregations.[2]

'When I was a school-boy in Essex,' wrote Rogers, 'I was
roused up by two men, Mr. Fenner and Mr. Marshall.' Fenner's
contribution was to ask, 'What wilt thou do when thou art
roaring in hell amongst the damned?', Marshall's to awaken the
schoolboy, who had been sleeping during his sermon, with 'his
powerful voice thundering against such as are drowsy . . . and
slumber away their salvation'. The young Rogers was so terrified that for ten years he followed an extraordinary course of
sermon repetition. He wrote down every sermon he heard, tried
to learn them all by heart, and for ten years repeated to himself
every Sunday night the sermon he had heard that morning, on
Monday night the sermon he had heard on Sunday afternoon,
on Tuesday, Wednesday, and Thursday nights sermons he had
heard in previous months and years, and on Friday and Saturday nights he returned to the sermons of the previous Sunday.
Yet all this excessive religiosity failed to give him peace, failed
to remove the ever-present fear of hell. Frequently he would
hide in barns or stables, 'to pray, sigh, weep, knocking my
breast . . . wishing I were a stone, any thing but what I was, for
fear of hell and the devils'. Sometimes the torment was so great
that he was tempted to commit suicide. But the greatest agony
of all came from reading Matthew 5: 20, 'except you exceed
the righteousness of the scribes and Pharisees, you shall in no
case enter into the kingdom of heaven'. He 'accounted God
most cruel to exact impossibilities of men . . . and to let so many
be damned . . . because they could not excel their righteousness'.
But release came soon afterwards. After a frenzy of despair
Rogers threw himself down on his bed and in a dream it came
to him that the righteousness of Christ, 'by faith made mine, did
excel the righteousness of the scribes and Pharisees'. 'When I
awaked', he concluded, 'I was so much changed I was amazed
at myself.'[3]

[1] Rogers, *Ohel*, pp. 394, 398, 415.
[2] Ibid., pp. 477–8.
[3] Ibid., pp. 419–31.

The extreme paroxysms of despair to which Rogers was driven were not peculiar to himself. Eight other men and women were tempted to commit suicide, and in twelve other cases conversion was assisted by a dream, vision, or voice. But at this point the similarity between the experiences collected by Rogers and those related by Walker ends, for the two men differed radically in their interpretation of what conversion meant in the life of the believer. For Rogers conversion was the ultimate religious experience, the decisive victory over sin, the final release from the bonds of legal religion. For Walker conversion was a crucial, but not final, battle in the continuing warfare against sin and doubt; the enemy was defeated but not annihilated. In the few cases in Rogers's book in which doubt and sin appeared to remain after conversion, it was because the initial conversion experience was not in fact genuine. The case of John Chamberlain, who had been a member of a gathered church but subsequently became a prey to drunkenness, is explained on the supposition that the gathered church which he first joined was not as strict as Rogers's church in Dublin, and that he was 'admitted without any great examination or trial'.[1] By contrast Henry Walker did not expect his converts to be free from doubt and temptation after their conversion experience. The members of Walker's church were afflicted by 'clouds of doubt', tempted by Satan to despair, troubled by the thought that religious devotion was motivated by fear of hell rather than love of God. 'Though I have many doubtings,' said one of Walker's subjects, 'yet sometimes I have more full assurance.'[2]

By regarding conversion as a milestone along, rather than the goal of, a Christian's pilgrimage, by recognizing that doubt and sin would continue after conversion, Walker was true to the teaching of William Perkins. But the fact that the convert's faith was still afflicted by doubt and 'ever assailed with desperation', as Perkins insisted it must, posed considerable pastoral problems for conscientious ministers.[3] They were faced with the need to console distraught members of their congregations who, despite their initial conversion experience, were still tormented

---

[1] Ibid., p. 412(8).
[2] Walker, *Spiritual Experiences*, pp. 4, 47, 275, 366.
[3] Breward, *Work of William Perkins*, p. 372.

by fear that they were damned. Not every member of Walker's flock found consolation in Perkins's assurance that worrying about one's salvation was itself a sign that one was saved. One woman gained some comfort from reading Perkins's *Grain of Mustard Seed* with its argument that 'a constant and earnest desire to be reconciled to God' was itself 'acceptation with God as reconciliation'. But her relief proved to be short-lived when, on reading another book, she came to the conclusion that just as a poor man knows 'that a desire to be rich and to be rich indeed, were two several things', so a desire to be saved, and salvation itself, were not the same.[1]

If concern for one's salvation was not itself a guarantee that one was saved, what other assurances could the believer expect? Most of the subjects whose testimonies were recorded by Henry Walker provided evidence which they regarded as proof that their conversions were genuine. Typical were the items listed by one woman: 'I find in my heart great love to God', 'I find frequently the power of the Spirit to subdue my heart not to submit to the flesh', 'I find in my heart a very great thirsting after the ordinances, and a great enlargement of heart, and comfort in the ordinances'.[2] It is this last point which most vividly distinguishes the testimonies collected by Walker from those related by Rogers. Rogers's own testimony, and those of eight other men and women in his book, is characterized by its insistence on the futility of trying to earn salvation by a ceaseless round of fasts, prayers, and sermon-tasting. 'I lay long under a legal sorrow and grief for sin, and I was then put upon work and duties hard for heaven, but I saw I could not get in that way', is a typical comment of one of Rogers's church members.[3] It is a theme which is largely absent from Walker's book. What Walker's subjects emphasize is not the futility of religious duties as a means to salvation but their value as confirmation of the reality of a conversion experience. More than half of the men and women whose conversions were recorded by Walker, thirty-four out of a total of sixty-one, cited their 'great affections to holy duties' or the comfort they derived from the sacrament as evidence of their conversion. But by emphasizing the impor-

---

[1] Ibid., p. 397. Walker, *Spiritual Experiences*, pp. 117–18.
[2] Walker, *Spiritual Experiences*, pp. 41–2.
[3] Rogers, *Ohel*, p. 415.

tance of continuing doubt, as did Perkins, and by stressing the value of religious duties, as did Walker, the two men opened the gates to a new legalism. One of Walker's subjects recognized that "'tis not duties, church-fellowship, ordinances, or anything that we conceive or propose to ourselves, which can give a soul rest, without living upon God in the spirit', but his was a solitary voice, likely to be drowned in the chorus of church members emphasizing the need for regular prayer, communion, and attendance at worship.[1] John Rogers saw the danger, and it was to avert it that he emphasized the futility of religious formalism, the finality of conversion. But in reacting against the legalism which threatened Walker's converts, in minimizing the importance of religious duties, in emphasizing 'the sweet doctrine of free grace' which made salvation independent of any action of the believer, Rogers opened himself to the accusation of Antinomianism.[2] The Independent and Baptist pastors of the Interregnum, in order to calm the fears and resolve the doubts of their congregations, had the difficult task of treading the exceedingly narrow path between legalism on the one hand and Antinomianism on the other. It was the failure of so many of them to do so which gave rise to the Ranters, the Seekers, and the Quakers.

14. 'NO LAW BESIDES':
ANTINOMIANS, RANTERS, AND SEEKERS

The accusation of Antinomianism, of being 'against the Law', has been levelled periodically throughout Christian history against individuals and groups who, in the eyes of their opponents, have emphasized Paul's teaching on salvation through grace to the point of effectively denying any need to obey the moral law. The heresy of Antinomianism was laid to the charge of Gnostic sects such as the Nicolaitans in the second century, was attributed by Luther to Johann Agricola, and in the seventeenth century was freely fostered on to Englishmen who sought to escape the bonds of legal religion and laid claim to a more spiritual relationship with God. The chief root of the alleged Antinomianism of seventeenth-century England lay in the desire of Puritan pastors to allay the fears of members of their

[1] Walker, *Spiritual Experiences*, p. 304.
[2] Rogers, *Ohel*, p. 15.

congregations who were worried about their election and prospects of salvation. It is significant that two of the most influential Antinomian writings of the 1640s were the posthumous
publications of Puritan ministers whose ministries had been
exercised in earlier decades of the century. John Eaton, vicar of
Wickham Market in Suffolk from 1604 to 1619, argued that
'the Law and the Gospel are two contrary doctrines', the former
consisting 'in exacting with threats, in doing by works', and
resulting in hypocrisy, the latter concerned with 'believing the
promise of God', 'in 'holy walking by love', and in making true
Christians.[1] Dr. Tobias Crisp, rector of Brinkworth in Wiltshire
from 1627 to 1642, took the disparagement of works much
further, maintaining that 'there is not one act of righteousness
that a person doth, but when that this righteousness is finished,
there is more transgression belonging to that person than before
he had performed that righteousness'.[2]

An Antinomian strain also permeated the preaching of Roger
Brerely, who was successively curate of Grindleton chapel in
the parish of Mitton in Craven and of Kildwick in Craven in
the West Riding in the first two decades of the seventeenth
century. Brerely taught that personal holiness and religious
duties could not purge man's conscience, 'but only the blood of
Christ, and man fixed thereon', for the 'doctrine of the Gospel
is not what we should do to God, but what we should receive
from him'. Though Brerely's sermons were not published until
1677, his preaching drew 'hearers from divers places about,
several miles distant', and his influence extended beyond the
bounds of his own cures.[3] It was Brerely's Grindletonianism, as
his teaching was called, which, according to Governor John
Winthrop of Massachusetts, inspired the Antinomianism of Mrs.
Anne Hutchinson, whose views racked the Bay Colony in the
later 1630s, though a more proximate source was John Cotton's
own insistence that moral behaviour was no indication of
justification.[4] Brerely's teaching also influenced the future Civil
War chaplain John Webster, who in 1634 succeeded to the

[1] J. Eaton, *The Honeycombe of Free Justification by Christ Alone* (1644), p. 214.
[2] T. Crisp, *Christ Alone Exalted* (1644), p. 214.
[3] R. Brerely, *A Bundle of Soul-Convincing, Directing and Comforting Truths* (1677),
pp. 38, 73, sig. A2.
[4] G. F. Nuttall, *The Holy Spirit in Puritan Faith and Experience* (Oxford, 1946),
p. 179.

curacy of Kildwick, which Brerely had left for Burnley three years earlier, and who in 1648 became vicar of Mitton. 'To a true believer', wrote Webster, 'the spirit of Christ is his ruler and conductor . . . and no law besides whatsoever.' To exhort men to obey the moral law 'for fear of punishment or hope of reward . . . is nothing else but to make clean the outside of the cup and platter, and to leave it within full of bribery and excess'.[1]

But if obedience to the moral law was irrelevant to a man's quest for salvation, what became of the time-honoured argument that religion was an essential preservative of the fabric of society? To conservative Puritans the Antinomianism of the 1640s, disseminated in the army by Webster and his fellow chaplains Saltmarsh, Dell, and Denne, was the harbinger of individual licentiousness and social anarchy. Tobias Crisp tried to argue that his doctrine would not encourage immorality. 'All that have this freedom purchased by Christ for them, they have also the power of God in them, which keeps them that they break not out licentiously.' But this was too like the hated doctrine that moral behaviour was evidence of election, and within a few pages Crisp was contradicting himself, arguing that if a 'free man of Christ' was guilty of even 'a scandalous failing into sin, Christ making a person free doth disannul . . . every curse and sentence that is in the Law . . . against such a transgression'.[2] Against the speculations of the Antinomians that their doctrine would not encourage licentiousness was the evidence collected by Thomas Edwards to show that it did.[3] John Sedgwick claimed that there were two sorts of Antinomians: those who were content with Antinomian doctrine, and those who sought to put doctrine into practice. The latter, wrote Sedgwick, 'break from the moral law by falling into forbidden courses, and yet they cry, they sin not; to be drunk, to whore, to lie, to steal, etc., with such persons is no sin to them'.[4] The truth of Sedgwick's analysis appeared to be substantiated by the Ranters.

The Ranter movement flourished for two brief years in the

---

[1] J. Webster, *The Saints Guide* (1653), pp. 10–12.
[2] Crisp, *Christ Alone Exalted*, pp. 177, 187.
[3] Edwards, *Gangraena*, part ii, p. 120.
[4] J. Sedgwick, *Antinomianisme Anatomized* (1643), pp. 29–30.

wake of the execution of Charles I. Whereas the deposition of
the House of Stuart encouraged Fifth Monarchists to expect the
imminent inauguration of the personal reign of Christ on earth,
it led other religious radicals to conclude that they were on the
threshold of the third dispensation prophesied by the twelfth
century Cistercian abbot Joachim of Fiore, the age of the Spirit
in which men would be directly inspired by God and would
attain perfection.[1] The sense of liberation which this interpretation of the revolutionary events of the 1640s inspired, coupled
with a mystical pantheism which taught 'that God is essentially
in every creature', induced the men who became known as
Ranters to take the teachings of the doctrinal Antinomians to
what they regarded as their logical conclusion. Since God was
in every man, the man who acknowledged that fact could not
sin. Sin, said Lawrence Clarkson, who had reached a Ranter
position after a pilgrimage from Presbyterianism through
Independency and Anabaptism, 'sin hath its conception only in
the imagination'.[2] The acts which the law condemned as
immoral, the behaviour which burdened scrupulous consciences with fears of damnation, the offences which Puritan
preachers argued fitted a man for hell, could all be performed
by the spiritual man with impunity. Indeed, argued Clarkson,
no action was sinful 'but as man esteemed it sin, and therefore
none can be free from sin till in purity it be acted as no sin'.[3]
To show that they were rid of sin, the Ranters proceeded to
flout the Puritans' moral code with a shamelessness which confirmed the worst fears of Edwards and Sedgwick. Clarkson
toured south-east England spreading Ranter doctrines and
entertaining a succession of women, counting it to his credit
that he continued to support his wife with money, 'only my
body was given to other women'. Abiezer Coppe, like Clarkson
a former Baptist, was said to spend much time 'in belching
forth imprecations, curses and other such like stuff' and to lie
'in bed with two women at a time'. And Thomas Webb, also a
former Baptist, who obtained the living of Langley Burrell in
Wiltshire in 1649, was said to have a 'man wife' and argued
that a man could sleep with any woman except his mother.

---

[1] J. F. McGregor, 'The Ranters', Oxford B. Litt. thesis, 1968, p. 39.
[2] A. L. Morton, *The World of the Ranters* (1970), p. 77.
[3] Ibid., p. 133.

'There's no heaven but women, nor no hell save marriage,' he is reported to have said.[1]

Ranter activity was brought to a speedy end by the Blasphemy Act of 1650 which, while tolerant of more usual heresies, prescribed six months' imprisonment, and for a second offence banishment, for claiming equality with God, denying the existence of heaven or hell, or maintaining the propriety of swearing, drunkenness, adultery, incest, or murder.[2] The doctrines of the Ranters were not such as would inspire martyrs and a few months in prison were sufficient to dampen the ardour of the most fervent Ranter. Abiezer Coppe recanted and went back to the Baptists, Webb was ejected from his Wiltshire rectory, Clarkson repudiated his Ranter beliefs and ended his days a disciple of the Muggletonian prophet John Reeve, who taught that the third dispensation had already begun with a revelation he had received in 1652.[3]

Only a tiny minority of those who embraced Antinomian doctrines used those doctrines to justify indulgence in Ranter-like excesses. The Antinomians, said Richard Baxter, 'were commonly Independents', and indeed John Rogers saw the contrast between the Independents' emphasis on free grace and what he regarded as the legalism of the Presbyterians as one of the main differences between the two groups.[4] It was not by persuading men to repudiate the Puritan moral code that Antinomianism acted as a dissolvent force on Independency, but by encouraging men to question the need for church covenants, ordinances, and the other external attributes of the gathered church. All too easily the reiterated theme of Independent preachers like John Rogers, that religious duties had no bearing on salvation, could lead men to the conclusion that religious duties had no point at all. The Antinomian army chaplain John Saltmarsh did not reject ordinances completely, but he did believe that they were of value only to Christians in a 'state of weakness and bondage, wherein God makes heavenly things appear by earthly, that men, as Thomas, may see and believe'.[5]

[1] Ibid., pp. 134, 81. McGregor, 'The Ranters', p. 93. C. Hill, *The World Turned Upside Down* (1972), p. 182.
[2] Jordan, *Religious Toleration*, iii. 135.
[3] McGregor, 'The Ranters', pp. 83–4, 106. Morton, *World of the Ranters*, pp. 138–9
[4] *Reliquiae Baxterianae*, part i, p. 111. Rogers, *Ohel*, p. 476.
[5] J. Saltmarsh, *Sparkles of Glory* (1648), Epistle to the Reader, sig. a3.

His fellow army chaplain William Erbery similarly argued that water-baptism and the breaking of bread were of but temporary relevance, designed to ease the transition of 'weak' believers from Judaism to Christianity. 'The strong, who were spiritual and perfect,' had no need of them.[1] Erbery's Antinomian friend John Webster was even more disparaging in his rejection of ordinances. They were the province of Satan, he told a London congregation in 1654, for they obscured the fact that salvation comes not from 'washings, nor disciplines, nor any external rules' but from 'God in us operating by his own almighty power'. One could undergo water-baptism and still be a sorcerer, as was Simon Magus. One could break bread with Christ and still be a devil, as was Judas Iscariot. 'You may talk of forms, and disciplines, and dippings, and of eating and drinking with Christ,' he told his congregation, but without the baptism of the Spirit what they preached was 'a lie and a delusion'.[2]

Webster and Erbery rejected all existing forms of church organization. Webster drew attention to what he regarded as the futility of the quest on which hundreds of men and women embarked during the Interregnum, the pilgrimage from Presbyterianism through Independency to Anabaptism in search of spiritual consolation. 'But when thou hast done all these things to find rest', he asked, 'dost thou think there is anything of Christ in all this?'[3] Erbery denied that the gathered churches had any Scriptural warrant for creeping 'together six or seven in a corner', drawing up covenants, and keeping 'the rest of the saints' waiting at their 'church-doors for admission'.[4] In 1653 the two men engaged in debate with two London ministers in All Hallows church in Lombard Street and Erbery told them 'that the wisest ministers and purest churches this day are befooled, confounded, and defiled by reason'.[5] The gathered churches, wrote Erbery in a pamphlet, were 'in Babylon, as dead dry bones, without breath or the spirit of life'. Why, he asked, do they 'pray for a way of propagating the Gospel, seeing

[1] W. Erbery, *The Welsh Curate* (1652), p. 3.
[2] J. Webster, *The Judgement Set, and the Bookes Opened* (1654), pp. 170, 239, 244, 249.
[3] Ibid., p. 243.
[4] Erbery, *Welsh Curate*, pp. 7–8.
[5] *Mercurius Politicus*, 13–20 Oct. 1653, pp. 1795, 1797.

the wise know it cannot be, but by the Spirit and power from on high, not yet appearing in the churches?'[1]

Erbery represented a position which contemporaries defined as that of a 'Seeker'. The essence of the Seeker position was a belief that the powers and authority granted to the apostles in the New Testament had been so corrupted and destroyed by the Church of Rome that no true church could be constituted until God had raised up a new race of apostles. As early as 1590 Henry Barrow had felt it necessary to counter the opinion that 'all extraordinary offices [in the church] have ceased, and so must all the building of Christ's church and the work of the ministry cease, until some second John the Baptist, or new apostles, be sent us down from heaven'.[2] Such views were attributed by the renegade Baptist Edmund Jessop to three brothers by name of Legate who lived—one can hardly say flourished— at the turn of the sixteenth and seventeenth centuries. All three met with unfortunate ends: Walter Legate was drowned 'while washing himself in a river' early in the seventeenth century; Thomas, who may at one time have been a member of Barrow's church, died in Newgate around 1607, where he had been confined for holding Arian views; and Bartholomew was burned at the stake at Smithfield for the same heresy in 1612. According to Jessop, John Wilkinson, the Separatist leader in Colchester, also shared their opinions.[3] But it was not until the ecclesiastical and spiritual turmoil of the 1640s that the view gained wide acceptance that 'there must be new apostles before there could be a true constituted church'. 'The sect of Seekers', reported Thomas Edwards in 1646, 'grows very much, and all sorts of sectaries turn Seekers; many leave the congregations of Independents [and] Anabaptists, and fall to be Seekers, and not only people, but ministers also.'[4] 'Very many of the Anabaptists are now turned Seekers', agreed Robert Baillie, including the future Ranter Lawrence Clarkson and the founder of Rhode Island, Roger Williams.[5] They met together, explained William Penn, 'not formally to pray or preach . . . but waited together

---

[1] W. Erbery, *The Bishop of London* (1653), p. 8.

[2] *Writings of Henry Barrow, 1587–90*, p. 443.

[3] E. Jessop, *A Discovery of the Errors of the English Anabaptists* (1623), p. 77.

[4] Edwards, *Gangraena*, part ii, p. 11.

[5] Garrett, *Roger Williams*, p. 147, citing R. Baillie, *Anabaptisme, the True Fountaine of Independency* (1647), pp. 96–7.

in silence, and as anything arose in any one of their minds, that
they thought savoured of a divine spring, so they sometimes
spoke'.[1] 'Though I speak sometimes unto men in the flesh,'
wrote William Erbery in 1652, 'yet my spirit is silent unto
God; thus I am wholly silent, waiting as one of the dry bones
in the dust, when the Lord will raise me with all his people out
of our graves, by revealing his glory in us.' The gatherings of
the Seekers in the early 1650s, like the meetings of the Fifth
Monarchists, were marked by a sense of expectation, but of
expectations very different from those entertained by the
millenarians. It was not 'a glory without' for which Erbery
waited, 'but a glory to be *revealed in us*, and that in this life'. 'I
looked and behold a whirlwind came out of the north,' Erbery
quoted from the Book of Ezekiel, 'a great cloud and a fire
unfolding itself.'[2] The prophecy was more apt than Erbery
could possibly know, for it was in that same year of 1652 that
George Fox came among the Seekers of the Pennine valleys and
fells. Within two years a whirlwind did indeed 'come out of the
north'.[3]

15. 'THE LIGHT ... WHICH LIGHTETH EVERY MAN': GEORGE FOX AND THE QUAKERS

George Fox was born in 1624, the son of a Puritan weaver in
the Leicestershire village of Drayton-in-the-Clay, now known
as Fenny Drayton. From his own account the young George
Fox appears to have been something of a prig, possessing 'a
gravity and staidness of mind and spirit not usual in children',
and when he was nearly nineteen and apprenticed to a shoemaker he was embarrassed by being in the company of two
Puritans who, when visiting a fair, asked him to join with them
in what turned out to be a drinking bout. This revelation of
disparity between religious profession and moral behaviour
came as a profound shock to the young apprentice and led him
to embark on a spiritual pilgrimage in search of perfection. He
left home in September 1643 and travelled southwards towards
London, only to find himself subjected to temptations 'which

---

[1] Braithwaite, *BQ*, p. 25.

[2] W. Erbery, *Apocrypha* (1652), pp. 4, 6.

[3] Erbery applied Ezekiel's prophecy not to the north of England but to the
'Northern (i.e. British) Isles', and in particular to his native Wales.

grew more and more' until he was 'tempted almost to despair'.[1] Fox does not specify the nature of these temptations, but it is probable that they were associated with the awakening of sexual desires. He refused, however, the advice of his family that he should marry, and in fact did not marry until he was forty-five, and then to the widowed Margaret Fell, ten years his senior, with whom he contracted 'a marriage as it was in the beginning before sin and defilement was'. To a man who protested that marriage was for the procreation of children, Fox replied, 'I judged such things below me'.[2]

In his struggles with temptation the youthful Fox, like so many of his contemporaries, became a seeker in a general rather than a specific sense, going from clergyman to clergyman in search of consolation. But he gained comfort neither from parish ministers nor from Separatist congregations. Calvinist theology assured the elect that they were predestined to enjoy eternal bliss, its Antinomian variant taught that behaviour was irrelevant to salvation, but Fox could never accept the implied divorce between religion and morality: for him there could be no assurance of salvation without tangible evidence of victory over sin. It was only when Fox stopped seeking other men's solutions to his problems, only when there was 'nothing outwardly' left that could help him, that he found the answer. Only then did he hear 'a voice which said, "There is one, even Christ Jesus, that can speak to thy condition"', and when he heard it his 'heart did leap for joy'. Peace came to him, he claimed, not through the Scriptures but by direct revelation of Christ. 'Christ it was who had enlightened me, that gave me his light to believe in, and gave me hope, which is himself, revealed himself in me, and gave me his Spirit and gave me his grace, which I found sufficient in the deeps and in weakness.'[3] It was an experience which took Fox far beyond the position of the Seekers: for him the new age for which others waited had now dawned. It was an experience which he could not keep to himself: soon afterwards he felt commanded by the Lord 'to go abroad into the world', to embark on the missionary crusade which was to occupy the remaining forty-odd years of his life.[4]

---

[1] J. L. Nickalls, ed., *The Journal of George Fox* (Cambridge, 1952), pp. 1–4.
[2] Ibid., p. 557. J. Sykes, *The Quakers* (1958), p. 94.
[3] *Fox's Journal*, pp. 11–12.   [4] Ibid., p. 33.

Fox's distinctive message was derived from the passage in the first chapter of John's Gospel in which John the Baptist is described as being sent 'to bear witness of the Light . . . which lighteth every man that cometh into the world'.[1] 'The Lord hath opened to me by his invisible power', wrote Fox, 'how that every man was enlightened by the divine light of Christ.' This revelation involved the total repudiation of the Calvinist doctrines of election and predestination, but it did not mean a blurring of the distinction between the saved and the damned, for not every man consented to be guided by the light that was within him. Some 'hated it, and did not believe in it [and] were condemned by it', but those who 'believed in it came out of condemnation and came to the light of life and became children of it'. Indeed, those men who followed the light could attain the state of perfection which had been the goal of Fox's own spiritual pilgrimage. 'The Lord showed me', he said, 'that such as were faithful to him in the power and light of Christ, should come up into that state in which Adam was before he fell.'[2] Against Puritans who were offended at the presumption of such a claim Fox triumphantly quoted the words of the first epistle of John, that 'he that is born of God sins not, neither can he sin, because his seed remaineth in him'.[3]

Fox claimed that his message was a direct revelation from God and declined to recognize or admit any debt to other men, or even to the Bible itself. That 'the Spirit of God was given to every man to profit withal', he said, was revealed to him not 'by the help of man, nor by the letter, though they are written in the letter, but . . . in the light of the Lord Jesus Christ, and by his immediate Spirit and power'.[4] We shall never be certain of the more mundane sources of his ideas. It was not untl 1675 that Fox dictated the account of his early spiritual development to his stepson-in-law Thomas Lower, and by this time he was unwilling to acknowledge, even if he could remember, what he must have owed to the religious radicals whom he met on his spiritual pilgrimage during the tumultuous years of the mid 1640s. Fox left behind at his death a library which contained

---

[1] John 1: 7–9. *Fox's Journal*, p. 16.   [2] *Fox's Journal*, pp. 33, 27.
[3] H. Barbour and A. O. Roberts, *Early Quaker Writings* (Grand Rapids, Michigan, 1973), p. 255.
[4] *Fox's Journal*, p. 34.

works by the mystic Sebastian Franck and by the Familist Henry Nicholas, but whether he ever read them, or at what stage in his life, it is impossible to say.[1] There are, though, few Quaker ideas which cannot be found in Thomas Edwards's catalogue of errors, published the year before Fox began his ministry. What Fox often claimed as direct revelations or 'openings'—that 'to be bred at Oxford or Cambridge was not enough to make a man fit to be a minister of Christ', that God 'did not dwell in temples made with hands'—were common-places among religious radicals and were clearly ideas which he picked up in the course of his wanderings.[2] Fox's teaching on the inner light was anticipated by the General Baptist Henry Denne, was paralleled almost exactly by the Antinomian John Webster, and was echoed by the Seeker William Erbery. 'The Spirit lighteth every man that cometh into the world', wrote Denne; the light of God 'is within thee, if thou wouldst let it shine out', exhorted John Webster; 'all men are in God, God in them, and they his off-spring', declared Erbery.[3] A variant of the same belief can be seen in the Ranter opinion that 'God is in all creatures', and although the pantheistic element in Ran-terism is largely absent from Fox's own teaching, he did on one occasion consent to put a pipe of tobacco into his mouth lest he be accused of denying 'unity with the creation'.[4]

Fox's claim that those who obeyed the light of Christ within them might attain perfection was also not new: the perfect-ability of man had been one of the tenets of the Family of Love, of the Antinomian William Dell, of William Erbery, of the Ranters, and perhaps of Roger Brerely and the Grindletonians. The early experience of Henry Nicholas, the sixteenth-century German Roman Catholic founder of the Family of Love, was very similar to that of George Fox, for he too was worried by the discrepancy between the church's claim that Christ had taken away sin and the obvious imperfections of those who claimed to be saved. To resolve the problem Nicholas had enunciated eight stages of religious development by following

[1] J. L. Nickalls, 'George Fox's Library', *JFHS* xxviii (1938), 3–21.
[2] *Fox's Journal*, pp. 7, 8.
[3] H. Denne, *Antichrist Unmasked, in three treatises, the third . . . the dragnet of the Kingdom of Heaven* (1646), p. 91. Webster, *The Judgement Set*, p. 246. W. Erbery, *Apocrypha* (1652), p. 2.
[4] Morton, *World of the Ranters*, pp. 70, 73–4. *Fox's Journal*, p. 110.

which, he argued, a man could attain a state of sinless perfection and mystical union with God. Nicholas's teaching was taken to England by a Dutchman named Christopher Vitells around 1550, and he appears to have won a number of adherents, especially in Cambridgeshire and East Anglia. However, the extent to which the Family of Love took root in England is difficult to judge for it was never a Separatist sect but rather a spiritual movement which was prepared to conform to established churches, whether Roman or Anglican.[1] Elizabeth's government made a determined attempt to suppress the movement in the late 1570s and evidence of its continued existence into the seventeenth century is scanty.[2] A petition from the Family of Love was presented to James I in 1604, claiming that the group had never departed from 'the established religion in this land'; in 1628 a clay-pipe maker by name of John Etherington was charged with holding the Familist view 'touching the perfect purity of the soul', a charge he vehemently denied; and in 1645 this same Etherington accused a deprived clergyman, Giles Randall of preaching Antinomian and Familist doctrines.[3] The Grindletonians were also charged with being Familists and with teaching that 'when God comes to dwell in a man, he so fills the soul that there is no more lusting', though there is no direct evidence of Familist influence on Roger Brerely and his published views on the question of perfectionism were more cautious.[4] But William Dell believed that 'as long as the Spirit of God dwells in the flesh, it will still be reforming the flesh to the Spirit . . . till all be perfected', and William Erbery affirmed 'that the Son and the saints make one perfect man, and that the fullness of the Godhead dwells in both in the same measure, though not in the same manifestation'.[5] The teaching of the early Quakers was in the same tradition. 'Christ my Saviour hath taken away my sin, and in him there is no sin', Fox

[1] W. N. Kerr, 'Henry Nicholas and the Familists', Edinburgh Ph.D. thesis, 1955, pp. 80, 118, 148, 165–6.

[2] N. A. Penrhyn-Evans, 'The Family of Love in England, 1550–1650', Univ. of Kent M.A. thesis, 1971, pp. 94–108.

[3] Kerr, 'Henry Nicholas', p. 245. S. Denison, *The White Wolfe* (1628), p. 33. J. Etherington, *The Defence of John Etherington against Stephen Denison* (1643), pp. 23–4. Etherington, *A Brief Discovery of the Blasphemous Doctrine of Familisme* (1645), pp. 1–5.

[4] Denison, *White Wolfe*, p. 38. Nuttall, *Holy Spirit*, p. 52.

[5] Solt, *Saints in Arms*, p. 33. *The Testimony of William Erbery* (1658), p. 8.

declared to the magistrates of Derby in 1650. The magistrates replied by committing him to prison for six months 'as a blasphemer and as a man that had no sin.[1]'

Fox's belief in the priority of the leading of the Spirit over the letter of Scripture was also anticipated by other religious radicals. 'Salvation is not bound up with the Scriptures' but with the 'word of God which is living, powerful and eternal . . . Spirit and no letter', wrote the sixteenth-century German Anabaptist Hans Denck. Denck's views were transmitted to mid-seventeenth-century Englishman through the writings of John Everard, sometime rector of St. Martin-in-the-Field, and Everard's *Gospel Treasures Opened* was in turn commended by John Webster, who held that the Gospel should be interpreted by 'the Spirit of Christ'.[2] Denck's belief in the supremacy of the Spirit over the letter was also echoed in the writings of the General Baptist pioneer John Smyth. It was because he held that 'a man regenerate is above all books and Scriptures whatsoever, seeing he hath the Spirit of God within him', that he rejected the use of books in public worship.[3] 'That their spirit is not to be tried by the Scripture, but the Scripture by their spirit', was one of the accusations levelled against the Grindletonians.[4] When, in 1649, Fox heard a preacher in St. Mary's church, Nottingham, claim 'that the Scriptures were the touchstone and judge by which they were to try all doctrines, religions, and opinions', he interrupted the sermon. 'Oh, no, it is not the Scriptures', protested Fox, it is 'the Holy Spirit, by which the holy men of God gave forth the Scriptures, whereby opinions, religions, and judgements were to be tried.'[5]

The consequences which Fox drew from this emphasis on the third person of the Trinity were similarly not original. He held that the church was 'a spiritual household which Christ was the head of, but he was not the head of a mixed multitude, or of an old house made up of lime, stones, and wood'; John Webster had likewise taught that the church was not 'a congregation of men and women assembled . . . together' nor 'a meeting place, built

[1] *Fox's Journal*, pp. 51–2.
[2] R. M. Jones, *Spiritual Reformers in the 16th. and 17th. Centuries* (1914), pp. 28, 243. Webster, *The Judgement Set*, p. 311. Webster, *The Saints Guide*, p. 10.
[3] *Works of John Smyth*, ii. 755.   [4] Denison, *White Wolfe*, p. 38.
[5] *Fox's Journal*, p. 40.

of bricks or wood or stone, but . . . the body of Christ'.[1] Fox argued that it was possession of the Holy Spirit, not possession of a university degree, which fitted a man to minister to others; but so too had the General Baptist John Murton, the cobbler Samuel How, the army chaplain John Saltmarsh, and even William Dell, who in 1649 was appointed master of Caius College, Cambridge. The Quakers repudiated all baptism, except that of the Spirit, and rejected all liturgical and sacramental forms as 'Babylonish and heathenish'; but in this they were merely following the example of Dell, Webster, and Erbery.[2] The two characteristics of Quaker meetings for worship—a readiness to listen to any Friend who was led by the Spirit to declare the 'things of God', but otherwise a willingness to 'sit silent in the tongue [and] worship God in Spirit and truth'—were inherited from the Separatists and Seekers respectively.[3] Even the Quaker repudiation of the democratic procedures of the majority of Separatist churches, and the attempt to seek the guidance of the Spirit through 'the sense of the meeting' had been anticipated by Henry Barrow.[4]

Similarly the customs and usages which in time came to be regarded as badges of Quaker distinctiveness were not initially peculiar to Friends. In insisting on using the familiar forms of 'thee' and 'thou' to men who considered themselves their social superiors, in refusing to take off their hats before magistrates, they were following the example already set by John Saltmarsh, who was said to have kept his hat on in the presence of Fairfax at the time of the Leveller mutiny in December 1647.[5] In rejecting the use of pagan names for days and months and in refusing to take oaths they were emulating the Baptists and other religious radicals. Only in their pacifism were the Quakers pioneers as far as English sects were concerned, and in this they were not agreed until after the Restoration. Though some Friends from the start believed that their new faith was incompatible with service in the

---

[1] Ibid., p. 24. Webster, *The Saints Guide*, p. 84.

[2] Barbour and Roberts, *Early Quaker Writings*, p. 95. Nuttall, *Holy Spirit*, p. 99. The attitude of Saltmarsh to ordinances was more equivocal. Though he spoke of baptism by water as 'legal baptism' and said that Christ had intended it 'to die out by degrees', he claimed he was not against all ordinances and he did not attack communion. *Sparkles of Glory*, Epistle to the Reader, and pp. 23, 63.

[3] Braithwaite, *BQ*, p. 510.

[4] Nuttall, *Holy Spirit*, p. 6, n. 8.

[5] Ibid., p. 83, n. 7. R. M. Jones, *Studies in Mystical Religion* (1909), p. 483.

armed forces, others protested vigorously when they were expelled from the army for refusing hat-honour to their commanders, and it was not until 1660 that Fox forbade his followers to take up arms on the ground that 'our weapons are spiritual and not carnal'.[1]

'He was an original, being no man's copy', was William Penn's tribute to Fox.[2] In terms of ideas Penn was wrong, but in terms of personality he was right. What was distinctive about Fox was not his opinions but the sense of spiritual power, the depth of insight, and the profound conviction of the reality of his own experience which he conveyed to other men. 'He had an extraordinary gift in opening the Scriptures,' wrote Penn, he spoke 'that which he had received of Christ', and 'above all he excelled in prayer'. Unlike so many of his contemporary preachers he spoke to his fellows, as Francis Howgill testified, 'with authority and not as the scribes'.[3] It was this which enabled him to convince the Seekers that he was the first of the new race of apostles for whom they waited. It was this which enabled him to guard against the licentious tendencies which had disgraced the Ranter movement and to impose on his followers a strict code of self-discipline. It was this which enabled him to weld his disparate band of disillusioned Baptists, former Seekers, and near Ranters into one of the most remarkable missionary movements in English history. 'The most awful, living, reverent frame I ever felt or beheld', added Penn, 'was his in prayer.' 'He knew and lived nearer to the Lord than other men.'[4]

Fox was the better able to convince men that he heralded a new apostolic dispensation by virtue of his outstanding psychic powers: like the first apostles he claimed to see visions, foretell events, and cure the sick. Men remarked on the piercing, perhaps hypnotic, power of his eyes, and Penn wrote that he was 'a discerner of others' spirits' just as he was 'very much a master of his own'.[5] The fall of the Rump, the death of Cromwell, and the fire of London were all events of which Fox claimed to have had premonitions, while on Pendle Hill and on Cader Idris he

---

[1] A. Cole, 'The Quakers and Politics', Cambridge Ph.D. thesis, 1955, p. 56. H. Barbour, *The Quakers in Puritan England* (New Haven, 1964), p. 221. Braithwaite, *BQ*, p. 462.

[2] *Fox's Journal*, p. xliii.

[3] Ibid., p. 107.   [4] Ibid., p. xliv.   [5] Ibid., pp. 108, 157, xliii.

had visions of the Quaker communities that were to arise in north-west England and in Merioneth.[1] When in Derby gaol in 1651 he met two men who were shortly to be put to death for minor thefts, and he was 'moved to admonish them for their theft and encourage them concerning their sufferings'; after the execution their spirits appeared to him and he 'saw the men were well'.[2] Most remarkable of all were the spiritual healings which Fox claimed to have effected: some 150 such cures were recorded in his 'Book of Miracles', and though the work was never published and the manuscript is now lost, its index was preserved and its contents have been skilfully reconstructed by Henry Cadbury.[3]

In a public ministry spanning more than forty years Fox's missionary journeys were to take him five times round England, to Wales, Scotland, Ireland, the Netherlands, Germany, and America, and to nine different prisons. His endeavours were made possible by a robust physical constitution which enabled him to endure strenuous journeys on foot and on horseback, the staves and stones of hostile mobs, nights in fields and hay-stacks under the rain and snow of mid-winter, and the filth and stench of insanitary prisons. He had a powerful voice, causing one judge before whom he appeared to complain that 'thou speakest so loud, thy voice drowns mine and the court's'. He dressed simply, in plain leather breeches and white hat, and wore his hair long, to the disgust of Puritans. He lived temperately, 'eating little and sleeping less, though a bulky person'.[4] His least attractive traits were his total lack of sense of humour and the violent and frequently vulgar language with which he lambasted his opponents. To one Presbyterian he gave the advice that 'thou must eat thy own dung, and drink thy own piss that comes from thee, for all that in thy book is but dung'.[5] The words are derived from the Book of Kings,[6] and such language was by no means confined to the Quakers in the outspoken, uninhibited controversies of the mid-seventeenth century; but it sounds singularly incongruous on the lips of one who claimed to divine the light of Christ in every man.

[1] Ibid., pp. 147, 350, 361, 104, 302.   [2] Ibid., p. 66.
[3] H. J. Cadbury, ed., George Fox's 'Book of Miracles' (Cambridge, 1948).
[4] Fox's Journal, pp. 467, xlviii.
[5] G. Fox, The Great Mistery of the Great Whore Unfolded (1659), p. 120.
[6] II Kings 18: 27.

Fox's first mission, begun in 1647, was to the Puritans, Independents, and Baptists of the north Midlands. At Nottingham he was thrown into prison for interrupting the sermon in St. Mary's, at Mansfield Woodhouse he was put in the stocks and stoned, at Derby he was imprisoned for six months on a charge of blasphemy. But he also had his triumphs: in Nottingham he convinced the sheriff and his family and in Derby his gaoler, at Skegby and Mansfield Woodhouse he cured epileptic women, and at Twycross in Leicestershire he cured 'a great man that had long lain sick and was given over by the physicians'.[1] It was at Derby that the magistrate Gervase Bennet first called Fox and his followers 'Quakers', since they made men 'tremble at the word of God', and in early Quaker meetings men and women experienced 'such a painful travail' of the soul that their bodies shook and they gave out 'groans, sighs, and tears'.[2] The Quakers' opponents claimed that Fox bewitched his listeners; comparison with the similar manifestations which accompanied the Methodist revival a century later suggests that it was fear of judgement and damnation which threw Fox's audiences into fits; but Fox himself was convinced that the 'quakings' were the work of God. People's hearts, he explained, 'had to be shaken before the seed of God was raised out of the earth'.[3]

For five years Fox travelled round the north Midlands and Yorkshire gathering 'divers meetings of Friends', but the real break-through in the expansion of Quakerism came in 1652 when he moved northwards into the Pennines and Westmorland. At the end of May, Fox came to Pendle Hill in Lancashire, overlooking the Craven parishes where Roger Brerely had exercised his ministry. He 'was moved of the Lord to go atop of it', which he did 'with much ado, it was so steep', and from the summit he 'saw Lancashire sea' and 'was moved to sound the day of the Lord; and the Lord let me see a-top of the hill in what places he had a great people to be gathered'. On descending Fox spent the night at an alehouse and had another vision, of 'a great people in white raiment by a river's side coming to the Lord'. The place Fox had seen in the vision proved to be

---

[1] *Fox's Journal*, pp. 40–57.
[2] Ibid., p. 58. Barbour, *Quakers in Puritan England*, p. 36.
[3] *Fox's Journal*, p. 22.

Sedbergh in north-west Yorkshire, beside the River Lune, and it was here, in the home of a magistrate, Gervase Benson, that Fox preached to a group of Seekers on Whit Sunday 1652, and they 'were generally convinced'. On the following Sunday morning the Seekers held a crowded meeting at Firbank chapel between Kendal and Sedbergh at which Francis Howgill, a local farmer, and John Audland, a linen draper, were preachers. Fox and many others could not get into the chapel, but after the meeting Fox announced that he would preach on the fellside that afternoon. For three hours he preached to a crowd of a thousand people from a rock near the chapel which is still known as 'Fox's pulpit'.[1] 'As soon as I heard [him] declare . . . that the light of Christ in man was the way to Christ,' recalled Howgill, 'I believed the eternal word of truth.' 'And so not only I, but many hundred more.'[2]

The Seekers of Sedbergh were associated with similar groups in northern Lancashire and Westmorland which met together in a monthly meeting at Preston Patrick chapel 6 miles south of Kendal. Three days after the gathering at Firbank Fox attended their monthly meeting and after the company had waited quietly 'upon God about half an hour' he 'stood up in the mighty power of God' and several hundred were said to have been convinced.[3] From Preston Patrick Fox passed to Kendal, Underbarrow, and Ulverston and finally came to Swarthmoor Hall, the home of the Puritan M.P. Judge Thomas Fell whose house was 'open to entertain ministers and religious people' and whose wife Margaret was convinced. Judge Fell himself never joined the Quakers, but he protected them from persecution and allowed them to use Swarthmoor Hall as the centre of their rapidly developing missionary movement.[4] Fox was again imprisoned, in Carlisle gaol for seven weeks on a charge of blasphemy, but his newly won converts roamed over the north of England and 'so great a convincement there was in Cumberland, Bishopric [Durham], Northumberland, Yorkshire, Westmorland, and Lancashire' that 'many of the steeple-houses' were emptied.[5]

[1] Ibid., pp. 103–4, 106–8. Braithwaite, *BQ*, p. 84.

[2] F. Howgill, *The Inheritance of Jacob Discovered* (1656), in *Early Quaker Writings*, p. 173.

[3] N. Penney, ed., *The First Publishers of Truth* (1907), p. 244.

[4] Braithwaite, *BQ*, pp. 100–4.   [5] *Fox's Journal*, pp. 168, 170.

'When the churches were settled in the north', wrote Fox, the Lord raised up seventy missionaries, after the manner described in Luke's Gospel, and sent them two by two into the southern counties in the summer of 1654.[1] The missionaries were supported by voluntary contributions to a central fund administered by Margaret Fell, who kept up a constant correspondence with missionaries in the field.[2] The former Seeker leader Francis Howgill and the nineteen-year-old Edward Burrough of Underbarrow went to London, rented a hall adjoining the Bull and Mouth Tavern in Aldersgate, and there preached to congregations of up to a thousand.[3] Two more former Seeker preachers, John Audland and the farmer John Camm, went to Bristol where they won over a congregation of Seekers and a quarter of the membership of the Broadmead gathered church, including Dennis Hollister who had represented the city in Barebone's Parliament.[4] Richard Hubberthorne, the son of a yeoman of Yealand in north Lancashire, and George Whitehead, another nineteen-year-old youth from Orton in Westmorland, went into East Anglia where Whitehead convinced two more men who had sat in Barebone's Parliament, Robert Duncon and Edward Plumstead.[5] Fox himself moved south again in 1654, addressed 2,500 people at Cinder Hill Green near Sheffield, was arrested at Leicester and taken to London where he was freed by Cromwell, and thence made his way to Cornwall where he was again arrested and thrown into the Doomsdale prison in Launceston, 'a nasty stinking place . . . where the prisoners' excrements had not been carried out for scores of years'.[6]

The Quakers did not confine their missionary endeavours to England. Fox himself traversed Wales from Glamorgan to Anglesey and visited the Scottish lowlands in 1657, while Edward Burrough and Francis Howgill visited Ireland in 1655 to win a number of converts among the parliamentary garrison. It was also in 1655 that Mary Fisher from Selby in Yorkshire and Ann Austin carried the Quaker message to Barbados and thence to Massachusetts, from which they were promptly expelled. And in the same year John Stubbs, a former

---

[1] Ibid., p. 174. Luke 10:1. E. E. Taylor identifies sixty-six of these missionaries in *The Valiant Sixty* (1951), pp. 40–1.

[2] Braithwaite, *BQ*, p. 135.   [3] Ibid., pp. 182–4.

[4] Braithwaite, *BQ*, pp. 165–70. *Broadmead Records*, p. 36.

[5] Braithwaite, *BQ*, pp. 155, 163–4.   [6] *Fox's Journal*, pp. 177, 191, 200, 252.

parliamentary soldier, and William Caton, who had been employed as a tutor at Swarthmoor Hall, paid the first of numerous visits to the Dutch Netherlands. William Ames, once a royalist soldier and later a Baptist, travelled widely over central Europe, visiting the Palatinate in 1657 and getting as far as Danzig in 1661, and other Quaker missionaries went even farther afield. In 1657 George Robinson of London visited Jerusalem; in the following year the intrepid Mary Fisher was given an audience by the Turkish sultan at his camp at Adrianople; and in 1661 John Stubbs and Henry Fell distributed pamphlets in the streets of Alexandria. Robinson and Mary Fisher were both treated by the Muslims with a good deal more civility than were other Quakers who fell into the hands of their supposed fellow Christians: John Luffe was seized by the Inquisition in Rome in 1658 and hanged; Katherine Evans and Sarah Chivers were taken by the Inquisition in Malta in 1659 and imprisoned for three and a half years; and four missionaries to Massachusetts, William Robinson, Marmaduke Stephenson, Mary Dyer, and William Ledra, refused to heed a sentence of banishment and paid for their stubbornness with their lives.[1]

These Quaker journeys produced few results outside the Netherlands and the English-speaking world, but none the less they constitute one of the most dramatic outbreaks of missionary enthusiasm in the history of the Christian church. How can the phenomenon be explained? In the first place the necessary conditions for the Quaker explosion were laid by the comparatively tolerant religious policy of the Commonwealth and Protectorate. The early Quakers themselves would have hardly conceded the point: they were charged with blasphemy under the Act of 1650 on the ground that they claimed equality with God, they were persecuted under an Elizabethan Act against vagabondage, they were prosecuted under Cromwell's proclamation of February 1655 against the disturbing of public worship, and they were imprisoned for declining to take the oath of April 1655 abjuring papal authority.[2] Above all they suffered for refusing to pay tithes, and of 123 Quakers in prison in 1658, sixty had been committed for this cause.[3] Quakers

---

[1] Braithwaite, *BQ*, pp. 212, 218, 401–33.
[2] Ibid., pp. 444–6. *Fox's Journal*, pp. 134–5, 238.
[3] Jordan, *Religious Toleration*, iii. 245.

suffered barbaric treatment at the hands of hostile magistrates and unsympathetic gaolers. Mary Fisher and Elizabeth Williams were flogged at Cambridge and Elizabeth Fletcher and Elizabeth Leavens were whipped at Oxford. At Maidstone John Stubbs and William Caton were put in the stocks and 'cruelly whipped with cords in a bloody manner'. At Evesham Margaret Newby and Elizabeth Cowart spent seventeen hours in the stocks, enduring the bitter cold of a November night. At Haverhill in Suffolk George Harrison was kicked and stoned by the mob and died from his wounds. James Parnell was thrown into 'the hole in the wall' in Colchester gaol, had to climb up by ladder and then by rope to reach his food, once failed to catch the rope 'and fell from a very great height down upon the stones' and died soon afterwards. And in Chester's Newgate prison it took four men to push the corpulent Richard Sale into a narrow hole called 'little ease', so that blood gushed from his nose and mouth, his body swelled up, and death came as a merciful release.[1] The Quakers claimed that they had suffered at least 2,100 imprisonments during the Interregnum, of which thirty-two had resulted in death.[2]

But for all this, persecution was localized and spasmodic. In the Quaker strongholds of Cumberland, Durham, London, and Bristol Friends preached their message largely unmolested,[3] and the persecuting ardour of local magistrates was frequently tempered by the central authorities. The Barebone's Parliament had sought to free Fox from Carlisle gaol in 1653, Cromwell secured his release in London in 1655, and the Council of State freed him from Launceston Castle in 1656; a month later the Council of State ordered the release of Quaker prisoners in Exeter, Dorchester, Colchester, Ipswich, and Bury St. Edmunds, went on to reprove magistrates for treating Quakers harshly in 1657, and freed a further forty-one Quaker prisoners in 1658.[4] The initial period of Quaker expansion was accompanied by real and often barbaric persecution, but before the Civil War it could not have taken place at all.

[1] Braithwaite, *BQ*, pp. 158–9, 187, 197, 367, 191, 127.
[2] Ibid., p. 581. Barbour, *Quakers in Puritan England*, p. 207.
[3] Braithwaite, *BQ*, p. 464.
[4] *Fox's Journal*, pp. 163, 200. Braithwaite, *BQ*, p. 240. Jordan, *Religious Toleration*, iii. 178, 244–5.

That the political conditions of the 1650s made possible the rapid growth of Quakerism does not explain, though, why it was that of all the religious sects which arose during the Interregnum—the Seekers, Ranters, Socinians, Muggletonians, and even more obscure sects whose existence, if indeed they ever existed, is known only from the writings of the heresy hunters—only the Quakers found lasting support and survived in any strength. Apart from those sects whose origins can be traced back before the Civil War—the Independents and the General and Particular Baptists—and the Presbyterians, who were not a sect at all, only the Quakers struck roots deep enough to survive both the turmoil of the Interregnum and the persecution of the Restoration in considerable numbers. Part of the explanation lies in the organizing genius of George Fox and the efficient central administration presided over by Margaret Fell at Swarthmoor Hall, but a prior and more fundamental explanation is to be found in the many autobiographies in which early Friends witnessed to what they regarded as 'the Truth'. These autobiographies are so remarkably consistent in the general picture of spiritual development they portray that one can be certain that the religious pilgrimages they describe were the common experience of a very large number of those mid-seventeenth-century English men and women who constituted the first generation of Friends.

Almost all the autobiographies of early Quakers begin, as does George Fox's own, with references to Puritan parents and a religious upbringing. John Beevan was 'bred up by my parents very exactly for refraining of gross evils', Edward Burrough was taken by his parents 'one day in seven to hear a man preach the word', John Whitehead was by his parents 'instructed in the strictest profession of religion'.[1] In retrospect, though, all such religion appeared purely formal, a ceaseless round of sermons, fasts, sacraments, and obedience to the Puritan moral code. Richard Farnworth gave up sports and pleasures as 'vain and heathenish', 'became very strict in observing what the priests did press me into', prayed and read the Scriptures three times a day, learnt 'many chapters by heart', and repeated sermons at

[1] J. Beevan, *A Loving Salutation to all People* (1650), p. 2. E. Burrough, *A Warning from the Lord to the Inhabitants of Underbarrow* (1654), p. 31. J. Whitehead, *The Enmitie between the Two Seeds* (1655), p. 2.

night.[1] But, as in the case of the Independents whose conversion experiences were recorded by John Rogers, all such performance of religious duties failed to provide assurance of salvation and indeed, by emphasizing the gap between profession and practice, often produced a crisis of despair. Stephen Crisp, John Crook, Richard Farnworth, Isaac Pennington, and Joan Vokins all listened to Calvinist preachers and agonized over whether they were among the elect.[2] John Crook was conscious that, despite his 'fervent devotion', he was still guilty of 'pride too much in my apparel ... wearing long hair, and spending my money in vain'. He concluded that he was a hypocrite and 'possessed with the devil', and was afraid to sleep with a knife in his room lest he be tempted to commit suicide.[3] Stephen Crisp regarded himself 'as one of the crucifiers' of Christ while he lived in sin, and wished 'I had never been born, or that my end might be like the beasts of the field ... for they had no such bitter combat here as I had'.[4] Thomas Forster also wished he had never been born, for he was taught both that 'the best of God's saints cannot be free from sin' and 'that the least sin deserved the torments of hell fire for ever'.[5] Richard Farnworth trembled in his 'heart for fear' when he took the sacrament, lest he be unworthy, and worried even more when he received from the ordinance no sign of 'divine operation' or 'spiritual change'.[6] Francis Howgill also feared that in taking communion unworthily he had committed the unforgivable sin against the Holy Ghost.[7] Thomas Symonds joined the parliamentary army, thinking that if he 'fought the Lord's battle ... there was laid up a sure reward for me', but he came to see that his 'iniquities were not yet blotted out'.[8]

In an attempt to resolve their spiritual conflicts the future Friends, like George Fox himself, 'tried all sorts of teachers and

[1] R. Farnworth, *The Heart Opened by Christ* (1654), pp. 1–2.

[2] S. Crisp, *A Journal of the Life of Stephen Crisp* (1694), in *Early Quaker Writings*, pp. 199–200. J. Crook, *A Short History of the Life of John Crook* (1706), p. 8. Farnworth, *Heart Opened by Christ*, p. 8. J. G. Bevan, *Memoirs of the Life of Isaac Pennington* (1807), p. 23. J. Vokins, *God's Mighty Power Magnified* (1691), p. 17.

[3] Crook, *Short History*, p. 8.

[4] Crisp, *Journal*, in *Early Quaker Writings*, p. 200.

[5] T. Forster, *A Guide to the Blind* (1659), sig. A4.

[6] Farnworth, *Heart Opened by Christ*, p. 8.

[7] Howgill, *Inheritance of Jacob*, in *Early Quaker Writings*, p. 120.

[8] T. Symonds, *The Voice of the Just* (1657), p. 2.

ran from mountain to mountain and from man to man, and from one form to another', yet still they failed to find the peace they sought.[1] William Bennitt attended the services of William Bridge's Independent church at Great Yarmouth, but came to the conclusion 'that many of their lives and conversations . . . were not consistent with what they professed in words'.[2] John Crook likewise joined the Independents in Bedfordshire and at first 'we had many refreshings together', but the church subsequently 'grew formal' and split over the question of baptism.[3] William Ames, John Beevan, Stephen Crisp, William Dewsbury, Thomas Forster, Francis Howgill, and Thomas Symonds were all associated with the Baptists at some time, but were ultimately repelled by what they came to regard as the Baptists' reliance on the letter rather than the Spirit.[4] William Bennitt, Francis Howgill, Thomas Symonds, and John Whitehead were then attracted by the Antinomian emphasis on free grace, but all found that the practical consequence of a doctrine which taught that conduct had no bearing on salvation was a widening of the gulf between profession and practice. Bennitt ran 'after the vanity, pleasures, and idleness of the world, delighting much in music and dancing, sporting and gaming, and so made merry over the pure witness of God, by sinning and rebelling against it'; Thomas Symonds found Antinomianism 'pleasing to the fleshyly mind', argued that 'it was the liberty of the saints to be merry cheery in the world', and 'delighted often to be in taverns, inns, and drinking-houses'; while John Whitehead was led by 'the mother of harlots' to believe that 'the saints had liberty to take pleasure and delights in the world' since though he sinned 'yet God did not impute it to me'.[5]

It was the glory of the Quaker message to resolve the conflict which racked the souls of John Crook and Stephen Crisp, to close the gap between profession and practice which disturbed the consciences of William Bennitt and Thomas Symonds. Fox

---

[1] E. Burrough, Epistle to the Reader, in G. Fox, *The Great Mistery of the Great Whore Unfolded* (1659), sig. B.

[2] W. Bennitt, *The Work and Mercy of God* (1669), p. 6.

[3] Crook, *Short History*, p. 19.

[4] See especially W. Ames, *A Declaration of the Witness of God* (1656), Forster, *Guide to the Blind*, sig. A4, and Howgill, *Inheritance of Jacob*, in *Early Quaker Writings*, p. 172.

[5] Bennitt, *Work and Mercy of God*, pp. 9–10. Symonds, *Voice of the Just*, pp. 3–4. Whitehead, *Enmitie between Two Seeds*, p. 5.

promised his followers victory over sin not at second hand, as did the Calvinists, through the imputed righteousness of Christ; he claimed victory over sin not by denying its existence, as did the Ranters; he offered victory over sin as a possibility—indeed a certainty—to every Christian who was obedient to the light within. When Fox rebuked Christians of other persuasions for 'pleading for sin, and for the body of sin and imperfection' he was not, as Christopher Hill suggests, taking a stance akin to that of the Ranters.[1] He was rebuking them for their lack of faith in the promise of John's Epistle, that he that abideth in Christ 'sins not'.[2]

Fox's conviction that every man was born with the light of Christ, a light which might be darkened by disobedience but never extinguished, a light which struggled through the barrier of sin to lead men ultimately to union with Christ, corresponded much more closely to the actual experiences of many men and women of the Interregnum than did the Calvinist doctrine that every man was saved or damned from birth, or the Independent and Baptist insistence on a single transforming experience. Six years before he became a Quaker William Dewsbury, having failed to find God among the Presbyterians, Independents, and Baptists, experienced Christ appearing 'to my soul . . . and my dead soul heard his voice and by his voice was made to live'.[3] Long before he joined the Friends and in 'extreme misery' John Crook heard a voice within 'saying, Fear not . . . I will help thee . . . with everlasting loving kindness will I visit thee'. And when, in later years, Crook, now a Bedfordshire magistrate,

---

[1] *Fox's Journal*, p. 70. Hill, *World Turned Upside Down*, pp. 135–6, 202. Hill's contention that it was the fall of Nayler in 1656 that 'helped to restore a sense of sin to the Quaker movement' can be disposed of by reference to four early Quaker writings: Farnworth, *Heart Opened by Christ*, p. 1, Whitehead, *Enmitie between Two Seeds*, pp. 3–5, E. Burrough, *The Visitation of the Rebellious Nation of Ireland* (1656), in *Early Quaker Writings*, p. 92, and Nayler's own letter *To All Dear Brethren and Friends in Holderness* (1653), in *A Collection of Sundry Books* (1716), p. 38. All these writings show that early Quakers had as profound a horror of sin as any Puritan. Hill is also wrong in stating that after his punishment Nayler gave up his belief that it was possible for a Christian to achieve perfection. In the very work that Hill cites to support his case (*What the Possession of the Living Faith is*, 1659) Nayler wrote 'that it is not the faith of Christ to believe that men could never be perfect' (*A Collection of Sundry Books*, p. 434).

[2] G. Fox, *Saul's Errand to Damascus* (1654), in *Early Quaker Writings*, p. 255.

[3] W. Dewsbury, *The Discovery of the Great Enmity of the Serpent against the Seed of Woman* (1655), pp. 17–18.

heard Dewsbury preach and was convinced, the Quaker message 'did not make void my former experiences of the love and mercy of God to my poor soul, nor in the least beget my mind into a contempt of his sweet refreshings in my wearied pilgrimage ... but on the contrary, brought all my former revivings that he gave me in my fore bondage fresh to my remembrance'.[1]

John Crook was one of several former Independents won over by the Quakers; an occasional Ranter, like John Chandler of Southwark, was convinced by Fox; and even an isolated Grindletonian, Thomas Bancroft, is known to have become a Friend.[2] The Seeker congregations centred on Preston Patrick chapel provided Fox with his first mass following, with the basis of his organization, and with many of his fellow missionaries; a company of Seekers prepared the way for Camm and Audland's success in Bristol; and in Kent and Sussex other Seeker communities came over to the Quakers.[3] But in general in central and southern England it was Baptist congregations which provided the most fruitful recruiting ground for the Quaker missionaries. Among Fox's earliest converts was 'a company of shattered Baptists' in Nottinghamshire; in Kent, Huntingdonshire, Dorset, Wiltshire, Somerset, and Radnorshire the Friends made serious inroads into Baptist churches; and the list of prominent early Friends who had once been Baptists is long.[4] 'Few experienced, humble, sober Christians' joined the Quakers, commented Baxter. They won their recruits from among 'the young, raw professors and women, and ignorant, ungrounded people that were but novices', and in particular from the 'Anabaptists or the members of some such sect, that by their division and error were prepared before'.[5]

---

[1] Crook, *Short History*, pp. 14, 24.

[2] R. Vann, *The Social Development of English Quakerism* (Cambridge, Mass., 1969), p. 24. *Fox's Journal*, p. 197. Braithwaite, *BQ*, p. 24. The evidence of Fox's *Journal* hardly supports the claim of C. Hill (*The World Turned Upside Down*, p. 192) that 'many Ranter groups ... ultimately became Quakers'. J. F. McGregor seems nearer the truth when he argues that 'there is little sign of a general [Ranter] absorption into the Quaker ranks'. 'The Ranters, 1649–60', Oxford B. Litt. thesis, 1968, p. 152.

[3] Braithwaite, *BQ*, pp. 95, 165, 395–7.

[4] *Fox's Journal*, p. 25. Braithwaite, *BQ*, pp. 386–7, 396–7, 399. *Fenstanton Records*, pp. 141, 146–7. Richards, *Puritan Movement in Wales*, p. 217. Vann, *Social Development*, p. 25, and above, p. 202.

[5] Braithwaite, *BQ*, pp. 193–4.

The Baptists, and especially the General Baptists, had certainly anticipated Quaker beliefs and practices in important respects. John Smyth had preceded George Fox in repudiating the Calvinist dogma of predestination and in opposing the taking of oaths; Henry Denne was preaching the inner light before Fox began his public ministry; and Denne, William Kiffin, and Hanserd Knollys were all said to have performed miraculous cures by baptizing or anointing with oil.[1] The General Baptists insisted, as did the Quakers, that the proper purpose of public worship was not to engage in formal prayer or to listen to preconcocted sermons, but to provide opportunity for the outpouring of the Spirit through the prophesying of inspired believers. Indeed the Baptist belief in the liberty of prophesying on several occasions provided the Quakers with a platform from which to win over their own followers.[2] But alongside, and in tension with, the General Baptist belief in the possibility of inspiration by the Holy Spirit existed an extreme literalism which may have been inherited from the Lollards and which, by the mid-seventeenth century, had superseded the earlier emphasis which John Smyth had placed on the supremacy of the Spirit over the letter. It was this literalism which was the chief cause of Baptist losses to the Quakers.

The Baptists of the Interregnum, following Smyth's own example, still searched through their Bibles for new rules of church order and in the process erected new legalisms in place of the old. Baptism itself had always threatened to become the Baptists' fetish: John Smyth and Roger Williams had both rejected infant baptism only to worry about the validity of their baptism as believers, and Walter Cradock, the Welsh Independent evangelist, related in 1648 how he had heard 'of some godly women' who 'made great doubt of their baptism'. 'They were baptized the first, and the second, and the third time', he wrote, 'and still they feared there was a fault, that they could not sleep in their beds, for horror of conscience lest there should be a nick, or flaw in the least, in their baptism, and so were still studying a way to do it better.'[3] It was a dispute about baptism

---

[1] Edwards, *Gangraena*, part i, § ii, pp. 44, 106, part iii. p. 19.
[2] Vann, *Social Development*, pp. 12–14.
[3] G. F. Nuttall, *The Welsh Saints* (Cardiff, 1957), p. 30, quoting W. Cradock, *Gospel-libertie* (1648), p. 142.

which rent the Independent church of which John Crook had
been a member, and so made him receptive to the Quaker
message of William Dewsbury. It seems probable that it was
similar disputes in the Broadmead church, Bristol, which led
Dennis Hollister to conclude that ordinances should be dispensed with and which prompted him to throw in his lot with
the Friends.[1]

Baptism was not the only issue which provoked controversy
and predisposed men towards Quakerism. By the 1650s many
General Baptists, ignoring Smyth's dying warning to put an end
to controversies about ceremonies, were anxious to add other
observances to baptism as a qualification for church membership. The laying on of hands on the newly baptized, the washing
of members' feet, the eating of a meal before the taking of
communion, were all held to be essential practices, and churches
quarrelled and divided over such issues.[2] For many new converts this obsession with ceremonies was intolerable, a denial of
the freedom they believed they had obtained by rejecting the
authority of the bishop and the Presbyterian classis. The Fenstanton General Baptist church in Huntingdonshire, which
Henry Denne had founded and of which his son, John Denne,
was pastor, was frequently troubled in the early 1650s by
members who gave expression to both Ranter and Quaker-like
sentiments. In January 1652 John Offley and his wife were excommunicated 'for denying all the ordinances of the Lord',
claiming 'that they were grown to perfection', 'slighting of the
Scriptures', 'for saying that all things are God, yea, that they are
gods', and for maintaining 'that there is no sin'. Two months
later four more members were excommunicated 'for denying
to be guided and ruled by the Scriptures; saying, that they were
in liberty, and they would not be brought into bondage again'.[3]
To many such Baptists, bowed down by the legal requirements

---

[1] Crook, *Short History*, p. 19. Hayden, *Records of a Church of Christ*, pp. 28–9, 31.

[2] *Fenstanton Records*, pp. 60–70, 202.

[3] Ibid., pp. 8, 12. It is possible that the spread of heretical views among the Fenstanton General Baptists was due to the influence of Thomas Moor of Lincolnshire,
whom Thomas Edwards describes as a 'manifestarian'. Edwards provides little
information about Moor's teaching, but it may be significant that five of the people
excommunicated by the Fenstanton church claimed to have had 'manifestations
of the Spirit'. Edwards, *Gangraena*, part i, § ii, p. 38. part ii, p. 86. part iii, p. 80.
Fenstanton Records, pp. 2, 41, 43, 46, 76.

of their new religion, the Quaker exaltation of the Spirit over the letter came as a heaven-sent release.

One further possible explanation of the Quaker appeal may be suggested: the meaning which the Quaker emphasis on realizing the kingdom of God within had for men and women whose hopes of establishing the kingdom of God on earth had been thwarted. William Dewsbury was serving in the parliamentary army when, he claims, 'the word of the Lord came unto me and said, put up thy sword into thy scabbard, if my kingdom were of this world then would my children fight'. He came to recognize 'that the kingdom of Christ was within, and the enemy was within and spiritual', and so he put up his 'carnal sword into the scabbard' and left the army.[1] Not all Friends were as clear as Dewsbury that their weapons should be entirely spiritual, and many Quakers, even Dewsbury himself, indulged in the apocalyptic rhetoric which marked the publications of other sects in the 1650s.[2] But there is some evidence that the disillusionment which followed the fall of Barebone's Parliament worked to the Quakers' advantage. The former Fifth Monarchist Morgan Llwyd broke with Vavasor Powell and began to emphasize the kingdom of God within, and although he remained minister of the Wrexham Independent church some of his leading followers, and those of Powell, were won over by the Quakers.[3] Five of the radical members of Barebone's Parliament subsequently joined the Quakers, including two of the representatives from Suffolk, and in 1656 Major-General Haynes reported from East Anglia that while many of the Fifth Monarchy men in Norfolk had turned Anabaptist, others 'had renounced that and all other ordinances and are turned Seekers, and feared by sober people will soon profess to be Quakers'.[4]

But the way in which Quakerism became a refuge for those whose political hopes had been eclipsed can be seen most clearly in the closing years of John Lilburne's tempestuous life. Despite

---

[1] Dewsbury, *Discovery of Great Enmity*, pp. 16–17.

[2] Hill, *World Turned Upside Down*, pp. 194–5. W. Dewsbury, *A True Prophecy of the Mighty Days of the Lord* (1655), in *Early Quaker Writings*, pp. 97, 102. Barbour, *Quakers in Puritan England*, pp. 182–8.

[3] Richards, *Religious Development in Wales*, pp. 263–4. Capp, *Fifth Monarchy Men*, p. 112. E. Lewis Evans, 'Morgan Llwyd and the Early Friends', *Friends Quarterly*, viii. 48–57.

[4] Braithwaite, *BQ*, p. 119, n. 3. *State Papers of Thurloe*, v. 187–8.

his acquittal at his trial in August 1653 Lilburne had continued to be held prisoner 'for the peace of this nation' and in March 1654 the government had him removed out of the reach of habeas corpus to the island of Jersey. Whereas Lilburne's first imprisonment, two decades earlier, had sharpened the cutting edge of his sword, his last imprisonment determined him to put up his sword for ever. He began to take an interest in the teachings of the Quakers and when, in October 1655, he was taken from Jersey to Dover Castle he sent for Quaker books and was visited by a Quaker shoemaker, Luke Howard. Lilburne was soon convinced, having at last, he wrote, 'really and substantially found that which my soul many years hath sought diligently after'. He recognized that his political battles had been futile, that Christ was the king of a 'spiritual kingdom', a kingdom which was not of this world. The laws of Christ's 'inward and spiritual kingdom', he now saw, 'are made in quite opposition against the laws of the mere glorious outside kingdom of the god and prince of this world'. And because carnal weapons had no place in this spiritual kingdom, he was resolved never again to 'be an user of a temporal sword ... nor a joiner with those that so do'. Lilburne was allowed out of prison on parole to preach for the Quakers in the towns of Kent, and to visit his wife and children at Eltham. It was there that he died in August 1657, at the age of forty-two.[1]

16. NEMESIS: JAMES NAYLER, THE RESTORATION, AND THE GREAT EJECTION

The Quaker message which thus brought peace to exhausted rebels and freedom to anxiety-ridden precisians had obvious merits. Yet at the same time Quakerism contained within itself the seeds of dangerous tendencies which grew to fruition in less than a decade. The critics of the Friends were not slow to point these out. There is no need to take seriously the frequent Puritan accusation that because the Quakers rejected both Calvinism and the supremacy of Scripture they were papists in disguise, but the opponents of Quakerism were on firmer ground when they criticized the Quaker assumption that the indwelling of the Holy Spirit guaranteed perfection to the believer. 'Can that

---

[1] J. Lilburne, *The Resurrection of John Lilburne* (1656), pp. 10, 12, 14. Gregg, *Free-born John*, pp. 332–5, 341–6.

man that hath one spark of grace believe that he hath no sin?'
asked Richard Baxter.[1] And the claim to complete possession by
the Holy Spirit led to an assertion of oneness with God which
opponents took as a claim to equality with God, and which was
the most frequent cause of the charge of blasphemy levelled
against the Friends. Fox was not without blame on this point,
for in a work published in 1653 he did write that 'he that hath
the same spirit that raised up Jesus Christ is equal with God'.[2]
But Fox's theological views were sufficiently grounded on the
Bible, though he refused to recognize the fact, to enable him for
the most part to avoid such extravagant expressions. The same,
though, cannot be said of all his followers. His future wife,
Margaret Fell, wrote of him as the 'fountain of eternal life' to
whom 'all nations shall bow'.[3] The martyred Richard Sale
addressed him in idolatrous language: 'Praise, praise, eternal
praises to thee for evermore, who was and is and is come, who is
god over all'.[4] Such sentiments, fortunately for Fox, were confined to private correspondence. More scandalous, because
more public, was the devotion paid to James Nayler by Martha
Simmonds, Dorcas Erbery, and Hannah Stranger.

James Nayler was the most eloquent of the early Quaker
leaders and contemporaries sometimes regarded him, mistak-
enly, as the leader of the movement. Rufus Jones, and following
him Christopher Hill, have suggested that Nayler represented
'the culmination of the Ranter tendency in Quakerism', while
Geoffrey Nuttall has conjectured that it was 'Familist teaching
which diverted Nayler from Apostolic Christianity'.[5] In fact
Nayler's published work shows that his teaching was no different
from that of other early Quaker publicists; he never gave the
least evidence of the libertinism which marked the Ranter
movement nor of the mystical language which was the chief
characteristic of Familism. Nayler's fall was occasioned not by
any peculiarity of doctrine but by the extravagance of his personality: by his failure to curb tendencies which were already

---

[1] Nuttall, *Puritan Spirit*, p. 115, quoting R. Baxter, *The Quakers Catechism*, p. 29.

[2] Braithwaite, *BQ*, p. 109.   [3] Ibid., pp. 105, 249.

[4] G. F. Nuttall, *Studies in Christian Enthusiasm* (Wallingford, Pennsylvania, 1948), p. 49.

[5] R. M. Jones, *Studies in Mystical Religion* (1909), p. 479. Hill, *World Turned Upside Down*, p. 199. G. F. Nuttall, 'James Nayler, A Fresh Approach', *JFHS*, Supplement (1954), p. 9.

implicit in the teachings and behaviour of other Friends, and by his reluctance, until it was too late, to repudiate the excesses of his followers.

Nayler came from Wakefield in the West Riding of Yorkshire where he had once been a farmer and a member of the Independent church at nearby Woodkirk, and for eight or nine years he had served in the parliamentary army. Nothing is known of the details of Nayler's early religious history and, like other Quakers, he claimed that his crucial experience came as a direct revelation from God. 'I was at the plough, meditating on the things of God, and suddenly I heard a voice, saying unto me, "Get thee out, from thy kindred, and from thy father's house".' So he joined the Quakers, gave up his farm and 'cast out' his money, and went 'out without bag or scrip or money into the most brutish parts of the nation, where none knew me, yet I wanted nothing'. His first service was in the north country and his most notable convert was the Durham magistrate Anthony Pearson, whose position facilitated the spread of Quakerism in the county.[1]

But in 1655 Nayler moved to London where his eloquence, charm, ruddy complexion, and long hair began to exercise a fatal fascination on the ladies, and in particular on Martha Simmonds, the wife of a Quaker printer. In July 1656 he went on to the West Country, followed by Mrs. Simmonds, and was thrown into Exeter gaol where women knelt before him singing 'Holy, holy, holy', Dorcas Erbery, the daughter of the Seeker William Erbery, claimed that Nayler had raised her from the dead, and Hannah Stranger wrote to him as the 'only begotten Son of God'. Even Fox sensed blasphemy in these proceedings, but Nayler was too proud and too weak a man to heed Fox's warnings, and on his release in October Nayler and his followers made their way to Bristol where they re-enacted Christ's entry into Jerusalem. Nayler rode into the city on horseback on a wet afternoon while Martha Simmonds, Dorcas Erbery, and Hannah Stranger spread out garments before him singing 'Holy, holy, holy, Lord God of Israel'. Nayler was arrested, told the local magistrates 'I am the son of God, but I have many brethren', and the perplexed magistrates referred

---

[1] J. Nayler, *A Collection of Sundry Books* (1716), pp. 12, 186. Braithwaite, *BQ*, pp. 61–2.

the matter to Parliament. Nayler was taken to London to be examined by a parliamentary committee set up to look into his 'great misdemeanours and blasphemies'. 'I was set up as a sign to summon this nation', he declared at the bar of the House of Commons, 'and to convince them of Christ's coming.'[1]

Even if Nayler were found guilty of blasphemy he could not, under the Blasphemy Act of 1650, suffer more than six months in prison for a first offence, and this was regarded as too trivial a punishment by the conservative Puritans and country gentlemen who made up the majority of the second Protectorate Parliament. For many M.P.s only the death penalty would be sufficient to purge Nayler's crime, and the case became a test of strength between Cromwell's supporters in Parliament, who were anxious to save Nayler from execution and to preserve what they could of the government's policy of religious toleration, and their conservative opponents.[2] If Parliament were to 'hang every man that says Christ is in you, the hope of glory', argued Henry Lawrence, the Baptist Lord President of the Council, then they would 'hang a good many'. In the end the proposal to exact the death penalty was lost by 96 votes to 82, but the House none the less took upon itself the unconstitutional power of acting as a judicial body and voted that Nayler be made to stand in the pillory, be whipped through the streets from Westminster to the Old Exchange, have his tongue bored through with a hot iron, and have his forehead branded with the letter 'B' for blasphemer.[3] Chastened by his sufferings, Nayler sent out from prison papers confessing his faults. He was guilty, he admitted, of 'spiritual adultery . . . against that precious pure life which had purchased me unto himself alone', and he condemned as idolatry 'all those false worships with which any have idolized my person in the night of my temptation'.[4] He was released from prison by the reinstated Rump Parliament in September 1659 and in the following January was publicly reconciled to Fox. In October 1660 he set out from

[1] Braithwaite, *BQ*, pp. 241–58.
[2] For the political implications of the Nayler episode see T. A. Wilson and F. J Merli, 'Naylor's case and the dilemma of the Protectorate', *University of Birmingham. Historical Journal*, x (1965–6), 44–59.
[3] Braithwaite, *BQ*, pp. 259–63. Jordan, *Religious Toleration*, iii. 223–35.
[4] Nayler, *Collection of Sundry Books*, pp. xli, lii.

London on foot to see his wife and children at Wakefield, but as he travelled through Huntingdonshire he was attacked and robbed and from this last ordeal he did not recover.[1]

The barbaric treatment meted out to Nayler by Parliament is a sharp reminder of the extent to which conservative Puritans deplored what they regarded as the religious anarchy of the 1650s. 'I have often been troubled in my thoughts to think of this toleration', said Major-General Skippon, who led the parliamentary attack on Nayler,[2] and it was an attitude of mind which prepared the way for the restoration of the Stuarts. Cromwell died in September 1658 and his son and successor Richard had neither his father's sense of divine calling nor the confidence of the army. He was moreover known to be sympathetic to the Presbyterians, and the brake which Oliver had exerted on the persecuting designs of the conservative majority in Parliament appeared thus to have been removed. When a new Parliament met in January 1659 M.P.s talked of disbanding the army, and in April they called for a general fast on account of the 'many blasphemies and damnable heresies' with which 'these nations are overspread'. Part of the fault, Parliament asserted, rested with magistrates who were failing in their duty of stamping out heresy.[3]

The threat to the army's authority and to religious liberty posed by Parliament led to the resurrection of the 'Good Old Cause'. Republicans who had deplored the drift towards monarchy under the late Protector now seized the opportunity of his death to try to return to what, in retrospect, came to be regarded as the pristine purity of the early days of the Commonwealth. In February 1659 William Kiffin and other worried 'Commonwealth's men, Levellers, [and] Fifth Monarchs' brought a republican petition to Parliament signed, it was claimed, by 40,000 Londoners.[4] A motion to thank the petitioners for their trouble was, though, defeated by a hundred votes, and more serious opposition to the new Protector centred on the gathered church founded by John Owen in London in March 1659, which included in its membership the republican

---

[1] Braithwaite, *BQ*, pp. 273–5.   [2] Ibid., p. 258.

[3] A. Woolrych, 'The Fall of the Protectorate', *Cambridge Historical Journal*, xiii (1957), 145. G. Davies, *The Restoration of Charles II* (1955), p. 69.

[4] Brown, *Baptists and Fifth Monarchy Men*, p. 174. *State Papers of Thurloe*, vii. 619.

army officers Charles Fleetwood, James Desborough, and John Lambert. These three officers, together with Owen had forfeited much of their influence over the old Protector when they had, in the spring of 1657, defeated the proposal that Cromwell should accept the crown, and they were now anxious to use the opportunity presented by the succession of his inexperienced son to restore their lost power. Both the church ministered to by Owen and the political group headed by Fleetwood took its name from Fleetwood's London residence, Wallingford House.[1]

The conflict between the Wallingford House party and Richard Cromwell came to a head in April 1659 when the Commons attempted to prohibit the meetings of the Council of Officers while Parliament was in session, and Fleetwood replied by summoning a general rendezvous of the army to St. James's. The Protector countered by ordering the army to Whitehall; the bulk of the army obeyed Fleetwood rather than Richard; and the officers were able to force the Protector to dissolve Parliament. The officers, apparently acting on Owen's advice, recalled the Rump of the Long Parliament, the Commonwealth was restored, and Richard Cromwell abdicated. The change of government was greeted by religious radicals with relief. The General Baptist Assembly, meeting at Aylesbury, welcomed the new regime, and when, in August, the Cheshire Presbyterian Sir George Booth led an abortive rising in the name of the king, the Independent churches in the city of London offered to raise three regiments for the defence of the Republic.[2] In return the government gave some evidence that the hopes placed in it would be fulfilled. A parliamentary committee was set up under the chairmanship of Sir Henry Vane to review the imprisonment of 'persons who continue committed for conscience-sake'; Baptists and radicals such as Hugh Courtney, John Carew, and Henry Danvers, and Quakers such as Anthony Pearson and Dennis Hollister, became commissioners for the militia; Quakers were invited to draw up lists of magistrates who had persecuted them and to submit names of Friends and others who might serve in their stead; and John Canne emerged from the oblivion to which he had been

---

[1] Toon, *God's Statesman*, pp. 109–13.
[2] Brown, *Baptists and Fifth Monarchy Men*, p. 180. B. Whitelocke, *Memorials of the English Affairs* (Oxford, 1853), iv. 357.

relegated by the Protectorate to become the government's official newswriter.[1]

But Canne's hope that the Lord would revive 'his work again in the midst of us' was doomed to disappointment. The failure of the first Commonwealth, the fate of Barebone's Parliament, above all the fact that the prophecies of the approaching millennium had not been fulfilled, militated against a return to the whole-hearted sectarian political activity of the early 1650s. When, in June, Owen's church at Wallingford House sought the advice of the Congregational church at Great Yarmouth on the country's future political development, it got the reply that 'concerning civil business the church, as a church, desires not to meddle with'.[2] Among the Quakers William Dewsbury opposed the proposal that Friends submit nominations for the magistracy on the ground that Christ alone should 'rule in the hearts and spirits of his people', and Francis Howgill was bitterly critical of Anthony Pearson's efforts to raise troops to put down Sir George Booth's rising.[3] The Rump, for its part, was as determined as the Parliaments of the Protectorate to retain tithes and bring the army under its control, and in October its members were for a second time ejected by troops.

The army, though, was no longer the body which had imposed religious toleration on a reluctant nation in the 1640s. Some of the religious enthusiasts whose Fifth Monarchist or republican sympathies endangered the Protectorate had been deprived of their commands,[4] and many more must have quietly gone home. They were replaced by men who were not so much religious crusaders as professional soldiers, chief of whom was General George Monck, who had fought for the king until 1644 and was now commander of the army in Scotland. When Monck heard of the expulsion of the Rump in October 1659 he determined to use his army to free England 'from that intolerable slavery of a sword government'. His design was supported by the garrison at Portsmouth, by the fleet, and by the army in Ireland, and in December Fleetwood

[1] Brown, *Baptists and Fifth Monarchy Men*, p. 182. Capp, *Fifth Monarchy Men*, p. 124. J. F. Maclear, 'Quakerism and the End of the Interregnum', *Church History*, xix. 255–7. Barbour, *Quakers in Puritan England*, p. 202.
[2] Browne, *Congregationalism in Norfolk and Suffolk*, p. 168.
[3] Maclear, 'Quakerism and the End of the Interregnum', pp. 260–1, 263–5.
[4] C. H. Firth, *Cromwell's Army* (1967), p. 339.

and the army leaders in London, conscious that power was slipping from them, restored the Rump. Monck, having purged his army of 'Anabaptist officers',[1] marched southwards in January and arrived unopposed in London on 3 February. He compelled the Rump to readmit the conservative M.P.s excluded by Pride's Purge in 1648, and Parliament proceeded to annul all Acts passed since that year, to attempt to enforce the legislation for the setting up of Presbyterian classes, and to prepare for new elections in April.

With the army leaders divided and the rank and file demoralized the 'Good Old Cause' was finished. Praise-God Barebone presented a petition to Parliament urging that no one be allowed to hold office in church or state without abjuring Charles Stuart, and Major-General John Lambert made a last attempt at military resistance. But Barebone's windows were smashed by the London mob, and the pathetic company gathered by Lambert surrendered without firing a shot.[2] The elections reduced the radicals in the House of Commons to a tiny minority, leaving the Presbyterians and Episcopalians almost equally balanced,[3] and when the Convention Parliament met on 25 April it took only a week to decide on the recall of Charles Stuart. The king landed at Dover on 25 May, to the relief of the majority of his subjects and to the fearful apprehension of a few.

Immediate steps were taken to seize the more notorious religious radicals. The three baptized Fifth Monarchists, Vavasor Powell, Thomas Harrison, and John Carew, had already been arrested at the end of April, and after the king's return George Fox was seized at Swarthmoor Hall and imprisoned at Lancaster.[4] Royalist mobs broke up Quaker meetings from Dorset to Norfolk, Baptists in Lincolnshire and Kent complained that their services were disrupted, the worshippers imprisoned, and their goods seized, and in London a Baptist meeting-house on St. Dunstan's Hill was destroyed by the mob.[5] On 12 August

[1] Brown, *Baptists and Fifth Monarchy Men*, p. 192.
[2] Ibid., p. 196.
[3] D. R. Lacey, *Dissent and Parliamentary Politics in England, 1661–89* (New Brunswick, New Jersey, 1969), p. 268, citing M. E. W. Helms, Bryn Mawr Ph.D. thesis, 'The Convention Parliament of 1660'.
[4] Richards, *Religious Developments in Wales*, p. 318. P. G. Rogers, *The Fifth Monarchy Men* (1966), p. 103. *Fox's Journal*, p. 375.
[5] A. Taylor, *History of the English General Baptists* (1818), i. 187, 268. W. T. Whitley, *A History of the British Baptists* (1923), p. 107. Braithwaite, *BQ*, p. 474.

John Miles conducted the last service of believers' baptism as the incumbent of Ilston and subsequently fled to New England, while old John Canne is reputed to have returned to the scene of his former labours in Amsterdam.[1] Not everyone escaped so lightly. Parliament excluded some fifty men from the general pardon which the king had promised to his father's opponents, and of these thirteen, charged with responsibility for the death of Charles I, were executed. Six can be identified as Congregationalists or Baptists. The first to suffer was Thomas Harrison who, unlike others who escaped execution, refused to apologize for his past. 'Maybe I might be a little mistaken', he said at his trial, 'but I did it all according to the best of my understanding, desiring to take the revealed will of God in his holy Scriptures as a guide to me.' He was sentenced to be hanged, cut down while still alive, disembowelled, and quartered, and on 13 October he was dragged on a sledge to the scaffold at Charing Cross, 'with a sweet smiling countenance, with his eyes lifted up to heaven'. Two days later John Carew met the same horrific fate, and on 16 October John Cook, who had conducted the prosecution of Charles I, and Hugh Peter were dealt with in similar manner. The head of Harrison was set on a pole and placed above Westminster Hall; that of Hugh Peter was displayed on London Bridge.[2]

Two more Independents who had sat in judgement on Charles I, Sir John Barkstead and Miles Corbet, escaped to the continent only to be betrayed by the renegade George Downing who, with the connivance of the Dutch authorities, had them seized and brought back to England. In April 1662 they, too, were hanged, drawn, and quartered, Barkstead's head being placed on the Traitor's gate in the Tower, Corbet's on London Bridge.[3] Finally Sir Henry Vane was brought to execution in 1662, beheaded on Tower Hill in June, though he had long since abandoned Calvinist Independency for his own singular variety of mysticism. Vane had opposed the trial and execution

---

[1] Richards, *Religious Developments in Wales*, p. 396. Rees, *Protestant Nonconformity in Wales*, p. 114. J. F. Wilson, 'Another Look at John Canne', *Church History*, xxxiii (1964), 34.

[2] C. V. Wedgwood, *The Trial of Charles I* (1964), p. 222. Rogers, *Fifth Monarchy Men*, p. 105. Stearns, *Strenuous Puritan*, pp. 413–19.

[3] Jones, *Congregationalism in England*, p. 51. Browne, *Congregationalism in Norfolk and Suffolk*, p. 233.

of Charles I, but he was, wrote the new king, 'too dangerous to let live'.[1]

Those Independents who had not been involved in the execution of the king could hope for no more from the Restoration religious settlement than that they would be allowed to continue to worship God as they saw fit, outside the established church. Even before the passing of the Act of September 1660, restoring ejected ministers to their livings, at least fifty Congregational ministers had voluntarily withdrawn from their rectories and vicarages,[2] and the Restoration destroyed for ever the Jacobite dream of reconciling the ideal of the gathered church with conformity to the established Church of England. Henceforward the successors of Henry Jacob were forced to adopt the position of the despised Robert Browne, and, as if to signify the coming together of the non-separating Congregationalists and the separatist Independents, in February 1660 the 'Old Separatist' church at Yarmouth united with the town's Congregational church, of which William Bridge had been pastor since 1643.[3]

While the Independents hoped for toleration, many Presbyterians, though by no means all, desired comprehension in the new religious establishment. The Independent desire for toleration and the Presbyterian aim of comprehension were not necessarily compatible. In August three leading Presbyterians, Edmund Calamy, Simeon Ashe, and Thomas Manton, wrote to their Scottish brethren recognizing that there was no hope of maintaining the Presbyterian establishment yet fearing the liberty which toleration would afford to papists and sectarians. Therefore, they concluded, 'no course seemeth likely to us to secure religion and the interest of Christ Jesus our Lord, but by making presbytery a part of the public establishment ... by moderating and reducing episcopacy to the form of synodical government'.[4] Initially the king seemed prepared to meet some of the Presbyterian requests: he appointed prominent Presbyterians as his chaplains, offered bishoprics to some and deaneries to others, and in the Worcester House Declaration of 25 October

---

[1] D. Ogg, *England in the Reign of Charles II* (2nd edn. Oxford, 1962), i. 180.

[2] Jones, *Congreationalism in England*, p. 48. Jones and Owen, 'Anghydffuryfwyr Cymru, 1660–2', *Y Cofiadur*, xxxii (1962), 11–93.

[3] Browne, *Congregationalism in Norfolk and Suffolk*, p. 77.

[4] *Calamy Revised*, p. x.

outlined a modified form of episcopacy in which bishops would exercise jurisdiction with the assistance of an advisory council made up of the cathedral chapters and presbyters elected by the clergy of the diocese. As further concessions to the Presbyterians admission to the Lord's Supper would be conditional on a profession of faith, changes in the Prayer Book would be considered by a commission of equal numbers of Episcopalian and Puritan clergy, and until such changes were agreed upon the use of the Prayer Book would not be enforced. Whether the king and his advisers were sincere in thus raising Presbyterian hopes of inclusion in a comprehensive national church is a matter of dispute: Robert Bosher maintains that the Declaration was merely a tactical move designed to placate the Presbyterians while they still had strong support in the House of Commons, while Anne Whiteman argues, less plausibly, that the proposals were sufficiently detailed to indicate a desire for a permanent settlement.[1] But whatever his original intentions, Charles II cannot have been pleased when the Presbyterian M.P.s tried to keep him to his word by committing the terms of the Worcester House Declaration to the statute book. The bill *For making the King's Declaration touching Ecclesiastical Affairs effectual* was opposed not only by the king's ministers and by Episcopalian M.P.s, but also by Independents who feared that the comprehension of the Presbyterians would lessen their own chances of toleration. The bill was rejected by 183 votes to 157, and Presbyterian hopes were dealt a mortal blow by the elections to the Cavalier Parliament in March 1661 which reduced Presbyterian strength in the Commons to no more than sixty.[2]

The Act of Uniformity which this Parliament subsequently passed in April 1662 compelled the Presbyterian clergy to choose between total submission to episcopacy and the loss of their livings. They were required, by St. Bartholomew's day 1662, to declare their 'unfeigned assent and consent' to everything in the Book of Common Prayer, to abjure the Solemn League and Covenant, and, if they had been ordained by their

[1] R. S. Bosher, *The Making of the Restoration Settlement* (1957), pp. 188–94, 217. A. Whitman, 'The Restoration of the Church of England', in *From Uniformity to Unity*, ed. G. F. Nuttall and W. O. Chadwick (1962), p. 71.

[2] F. Bate, *Declaration of Indulgence* (1908), p. 20. Lacey, *Dissent and Parliamentary Politics*, puts the figure rather lower at between thirty-seven and fifty, but this is on the basis of evidence of those who may have remained Presbyterians after 1662.

fellow presbyters, to seek reordination at the hands of a bishop. Conformity to the established church was similarly required of every university fellow, schoolmaster, and private tutor. To scrupulous Puritans the demand that they give unquestioning approbation to the rubrics against which they and their fore-fathers had contended for a century was tantamount to an order to disobey God. 'We will do anything for his majesty but sin', declared Robert Atkins, hitherto rector of St. John's, Exeter. 'We will hazard anything for him but our souls. We could hope to die for him, but we dare not be damned for him.'[1]

Nearly a thousand clergy gave up their livings rather than genuflect before the ghost of Archbishop Laud, and a total of 2,029 clergy, lecturers, and fellows were deprived of their posts between 1660 and 1662.[2] Of these 2,029, 194 are known to have been Independents and a further nineteen Baptists. Of the remaining 1,816 many were committed Presbyterians but per-haps a majority were, like Richard Baxter, mere Puritans who had hitherto eschewed sectarian labels. Their decision to lay down their ministry within the Church of England was taken with the utmost reluctance and often in the hope that the terms of the Act of Uniformity might soon be modified to enable them to conform. Yet expectations that the rifts of 1662 would soon be healed were never realized. Within a decade, wrote Baxter, 'some few Presbyterians, especially in London, who had large congregations and liberty and encouragement', had given up hope of returning to the Church of England.[3] Such men were prepared to join with the Independents in pressing for religious toleration, and as subsequent proposals for comprehension failed to reach the statute book in 1666–7, 1680, and again in 1689, those Presbyterians who could not conform were driven closer to Dissent.[4]

The Cavalier Parliament thus completed the work of Arch-bishops Parker, Whitgift, and Laud: it put an end to the

---

[1] *TCHS* i (1901–4), 86.

[2] The total of 2,029 is arrived at by adding to A. G. Matthews's figure for the ejected in England, 1,909, a further 120 for clergy who were ejected in Wales and not included in *Calamy Revised*. Matthews, *Calamy Revised*, pp. xiii–xiv. Jones and Owen in *Y Cofiadur*, xxxii. 3–91.

[3] *Reliquiae Baxterianae*, part iii, p. 100.

[4] R. Thomas, 'Comprehension and Indulgence', in *From Uniformity to Unity*, pp. 204–5, 208, 197–202, 226–30, 252–3.

Puritan dream of reforming the Church of England from within and in effect destroyed Puritanism itself. Sooner or later the Puritan had to choose between conformity and Dissent, and in so far as thousands chose the latter course the gain to Dissent was immense. To the spiritual descendants of John Smyth and the followers of George Fox were added the co-religionists not only of John Owen but also of Thomas Edwards. It had been difficult enough for the governments of Elizabeth and the early Stuarts to silence the handful of Separatists who had dissented from the state church; now that they were joined by the wealthy and influential Presbyterians it would be impossible. And although the immediate effect of the Restoration religious settlement was to bring persecution and suffering to those outside the established church, it can, in retrospect, be seen as a step towards the eventual and permanent liberation of Dissent.

III
'NO CROSS, NO CROWN':
THE PERSECUTION OF DISSENT,
1660–1689

I. VENGEANCE AND FEAR: THE CLARENDON CODE

In April 1660, while waiting at Breda in the Dutch Netherlands for the expected summons to England, Charles II issued a declaration promising 'a liberty to tender consciences . . . that no man shall be disquieted, or called in question, for differences of opinion in matters of religion which do not disturb the peace of the kingdom'. Whatever may be thought of the sincerity or otherwise of the proposals for comprehension offered to the Presbyterians in the Worcester House Declaration, there can be no question that the Declaration of Breda represented Charles's real desire for religious toleration. Indeed the court's opposition to the Presbyterian attempt to give the Worcester House Declaration the force of law may well have been influenced by the king's tolerant objective: for Charles, like the Independents, no doubt realized that the retention of the Presbyterians within the established church would weaken the chances of toleration for those left outside.[1]

Of the motives which lay behind Charles's desire for toleration it is less easy to be sure. Two explanations are possible: that the years of religious strife, involuntary exile, and the pursuit of pleasure had taught the king a worldly scepticism which looked on all religions with tolerant indifference; or, alternatively, that the king was a sincere, though secret, Roman Catholic who wanted toleration only because it would mean security for his hated co-religionists and would constitute a first step towards the restoration of papal influence in England, if need be by French arms. While the former theory corresponds the more closely to Charles's character, the latter provides the more coherent explanation of his actions. Perhaps character and conduct can be reconciled: as he lay on his deathbed he received the

---

[1] Dale, *English Congregationalism*, p. 402.

sacraments of the Roman Church, hoping thereby that the rites of death would absolve him from the sins of life.

Though Charles wanted religious toleration, he wanted the crown more, and in the Declaration of Breda his promised 'liberty to tender consciences' was qualified by the provision that such indulgence should be granted by Act of Parliament. But the Cavalier Parliament shared neither Charles's outward indifference to religious dogma nor his private sympathy with Roman Catholicism. What motivated the majority party in the Commons, apart from naked revenge, was loyalty to the Laudian conception of the church and fear that 1642 would come again, a belief that every Presbyterian was a potential rebel and every Independent a regicide at heart. And because the Restoration settlement did not leave the respective powers of king and Parliament clearly defined, the next dozen years were to see a struggle between the two in which Charles tried to keep the promises he had made at Breda, and Parliament endeavoured to set them at nought. But it was an unequal struggle: Parliament had shown in the recent past that it could rule without a king, Charles was soon to find that he could not rule for long without Parliament's money. And so the reign of the first English king to preach the virtues of religious toleration was marked by the calculated and often malicious persecution of Dissent.

After the initial wave of persecution which followed the election of the Convention Parliament in April 1660 and the return of the king in May, Dissenters were encouraged to believe that Charles would keep his promise of a liberty to tender consciences. For the Quakers, at least, the new regime promised to be a good deal more friendly than the old. In June the king assured Richard Hubberthorne, the former Lancashire Seeker, that 'you shall none of you suffer for your opinions or religion, so long as you live peaceably', and Fox and some 700 imprisoned Quakers were set at liberty. 'And then', said Fox, 'the Fifth Monarchy people rose and . . . made an insurrection in London.'[1]

The Fifth Monarchist rising was led by a wine-cooper named Thomas Venner who had been arrested while plotting an armed

---

[1] Braithwaite, *BQ*, pp. 476–7. *Fox's Journal*, pp. 391, 394.

insurrection against Cromwell in 1657 but had been spared to fight another day. For three days in January 1661 Venner and some fifty followers terrorized the city of London, killing twenty-two people until the train-bands and lifeguards put them to flight.[1] Venner's rising appeared to confirm the Cavalier view that the 'Good Old Cause' was not dead but only slumbering in Dissenting conventicles. It was in vain that Baptists dissociated themselves from Venner's activities and drew up declarations of loyalty to the king, that Quakers renounced 'all bloody principles and practices . . . with all outward wars and strife and fightings with outward weapons, for any end or under any pretence whatsoever'.[2] A royal proclamation of 10 January forbade all meetings of 'Anabaptists, Quakers, and Fifth Monarchy men', and within a few weeks 4,230 Quakers were in prison.[3] Baptists in London were dragged out of their beds at midnight by armed soldiers; John James, the pastor of a Sabbatarian Baptist church in Whitechapel, was arrested while preaching, accused of treason on the evidence of 'several profligate witnesses', and sentenced to be hanged, drawn, and quartered; and by the end of 1662 Newgate contained '289 Anabaptists and others taken at unlawful meetings'.[4]

The period of persecution is usually associated with the name of Charles's Lord Chancellor, the Earl of Clarendon, and with the series of enactments passed by the Cavalier Parliament and known as the Clarendon Code. The first such measure was the Corporation Act of December 1661, requiring all mayors, aldermen, councillors, and borough officials to swear loyalty to the king and to take 'the sacrament of the Lord's Supper, according to the rites of the Church of England'. The Act resulted not only in conscientious Dissenters losing their seats on borough councils, but also gave unscrupulous corporations an opportunity of replenishing their coffers by electing Dissenters to office and then fining them if they declined to take the Anglican sacrament in order to serve. Within twelve months of the passing of the Act the Coventry corporation tried to levy a fine of £100 on Nathaniel Hobson, who seems to have been a

[1] Rogers, *Fifth Monarchy Men*, pp. 81–7, 112–16.
[2] Whitley, *British Baptists*, p. 109. *Fox's Journal*, p. 399.
[3] Bosher, *Making of the Restoration Settlement*, p. 205. Braithwaite, *SPQ*, p. 9.
[4] Taylor, *General Baptists*, i. 244, 256–8. *CSPD* 1661–2, p. 605.

Baptist, because he refused to take the oath of supremacy to enable him to serve on the council, and Hobson was imprisoned for six weeks until he agreed to pay. The corporation subsequently relented and returned £85 to Hobson 'by reason of his old and decrepit age', but the precedent was followed by the corporations of Warwick, Stratford-upon-Avon, Southampton, Exeter, Bristol, and Norwich, and ultimately by the city of London itself.[1]

Local dignitaries intent on persecution did not, though, have to wait for new legislation before harassing Dissenters, for the restored Long Parliament of 1660 had abrogated the tolerant legislation of the Commonwealth and validated the earlier penal laws. In November 1660, six weeks before Venner's rising, John Bunyan, a member of the Bedford Congregational church, was arrested while speaking at an open-air meeting and sentenced to imprisonment under the terms of the notorious Act of 1593, *For Retaining the Queen's Subjects in their due Obedience*.[2] Though the initial sentence was for three months, Bunyan's continual refusal to conform led to twelve years in prison. The magistrates, had they wished, could have sentenced him to death, and such sentence was passed in 1664 on twelve General Baptists of Aylesbury, for refusing either to conform or abjure the realm under the terms of the Act of 1593. Only a royal pardon saved them from execution.[3]

Some Baptists and all Quakers were particularly exposed to persecution by reason of their refusal to take the oath of allegiance.[4] The penalty for a first refusal was imprisonment, for a second refusal the penalty was *praemunire*: imprisonment for life or at the king's pleasure, and forfeiture of property.[5] In the anxious months following Venner's rising, when, to quote W. Y. Tindall, 'both public and government were always finding

---

[1] J. J. Hurwich, 'Nonconformists in Warwickshire', Univ. of Princeton Ph.D. thesis, 1970, pp. 125, 156, 162–4. S. Stanier, *History of the Above Bar Congregational Church, Southampton* (1909), p. 30. A. Brockett, *Nonconformity in Exeter* (Manchester, 1962), p. 44. R. S. Mortimer, 'Quakerism in Seventeenth Century Bristol', Bristol Univ. M.A. thesis, 1946, pp. 346–7. Browne, *Congregationalism in Norfolk and Suffolk*, p. 176.

[2] J. Brown, *John Bunyan* (1928), pp. 132, 144–5.

[3] T. Crosby, *History of the English Baptists* (1739), ii. 180–5.

[4] For Baptists who refused the oath see A. C. Underwood, *A History of the English Baptists* (1947), p. 91.

[5] Braithwaite, *SPQ*, p. 14.

Fifth Monarchy men under the bed',[1] the Quaker refusal to swear allegiance seemed especially ominous to timid Cavaliers, and in May 1662 Parliament empowered magistrates to impose fines or imprisonment, and for a third offence transportation, on five or more Quakers who met together for worship. Quaker meetings were raided and hundreds thrown into prison.[2]

Two years later the provisions of the Quaker Act were extended to all Dissenters. In February 1663 the king attempted, and failed, to secure Parliament's consent to dispensing with the penal laws, and frustrated Dissenters in the north of England began to dream of overthrowing Clarendon and the bishops and of restoring religious toleration. In March an informer claimed that conspirators were meeting in the homes of Dissenters in Muggleswick Park in Derwentdale in Durham and plotting 'to murder all bishops, deans, and chapters, and all ministers of the church'. In August a plan to seize York Castle was frustrated by the arrest of the ring-leaders. And in October what had been planned as a nation-wide rising dwindled to a pathetic gathering of some 200 men at Farnley Wood near Leeds.[3] In January 1664 twenty-one conspirators were executed and in May Parliament used the plot as an excuse to pass the First Conventicle Act, forbidding five or more people from meeting together for worship except in accordance with the liturgy of the Church of England. For a first offence the penalty was a fine of £5 or three months' imprisonment; for a second offence a fine of £10 or six months' imprisonment; and for a third offence a fine of £100 or transportation for seven years.

It is possible to justify the Conventicle Act by reason of the Cavalier Parliament's fear of rebellion, but no such excuse can be offered in defence of the Five Mile Act of 1665. In the spring and summer of 1665 London was visited by the Great Plague: 70,000 of its half a million citizens fell victim to its ravages,[4] and the king, Parliament, and substantial citizens fled to Oxford and the country. Most of the parish clergy also fled, according to Baxter,

---

[1] W. Y. Tindall, *John Bunyan, Mechanick Preacher* (New York, 1964), p. 122.

[2] Braithwaite, *SPQ*, pp. 24–5.

[3] H. Gee, 'The Derwentdale Plot, 1663', *Trans. of the Royal Historical Society*, 3rd series, xi (1917), 124–42. W. G. Johnson, 'Post-Restoration Nonconformity and Plotting', Univ. of Manchester M.A. thesis, 1967, p. 173.

[4] D. Ogg, *England in the Reign of Charles II* (1956), i. 292.

and left their flocks in the time of their extremity: whereupon divers Nonconformists, pitying the dying and distressed people, that had none to call the impenitent to repentance, nor to help men to prepare for another world, nor to comfort them in their terrors, when about ten thousand died in a week, resolved that no obedience to the laws of any mortal men whatsoever could justify them for neglecting of men's souls and bodies in such extremities. . . . Therefore they resolved to stay with the people, and to go into the forsaken pulpits, though prohibited, and to preach to the poor people before they died; and also to visit the sick, and get what relief they could for the poor.[1]

The impudence of the Dissenting ministers in thus assuming the pastoral responsibility of the departed clergy evoked a sharp retort from Parliament, immune from plague in the safety of Oxford. In October it passed the Five Mile Act, imposing on all ejected clergy an oath not to endeavour at any time 'any alteration of government either in church or state'. Ministers who refused to comply were denied the liberty to come within 5 miles of any parish where they had exercised their ministry, any place where they had held conventicles, any city or corporate town, or any borough represented in Parliament. The penalty for disobedience was a fine of £40.

The fall of Clarendon in December 1667 brought some relaxation in the enforcement of laws against Dissent, and the First Conventicle Act expired on 1 March 1669.[2] But the relief thus brought to Dissenters was short-lived. In July the king was prevailed on to issue a proclamation ordering magistrates to continue to enforce the unexpired laws against Dissent, and though Charles was able to defeat a new Conventicle Bill by proroguing Parliament in November, shortage of money compelled him to summon Parliament again in February 1670. This time a second Conventicle Act passed into law. The fines for ordinary worshippers were reduced to 5s. for a first offence and to 10s. for each subsequent offence, but the fines imposed on preachers and the owners of meeting places were increased to £20 for a first offence and to £40 for subsequent offences. The fines were to be 'levied by distress and sale of the offender's goods and chattels', and if a worshipper's goods were too meagre to yield

---

[1] *Reliquiae Baxterianae*, part iii, p. 2.
[2] Jones, *Congregationalism in England*, p. 69n.

the required sum, the distress was to be levied on wealthier attenders at the same conventicle. To ensure that the Act was enforced, a third of the fines thus collected were to be paid to the informer, and magistrates who neglected to implement the Act were made liable to a fine of £100.

2. 'CONSTANCY AND SUFFERINGS' AND 'CREEPING INTO CORNERS': THE DISSENTING RESPONSE

The severity of the persecution depended on the extent to which Dissenters were prepared to abide by the law and compromise with the state. For this reason the Quakers suffered most, refusing to hide their light under a bushel and 'to dodge and shift' to avoid persecution.[1] When Quaker meeting-houses were closed or pulled down, Friends continued to meet in the street or amongst rubble. When, at Reading, all adult Quakers were thrown into gaol, the meeting was maintained by young women and children.[2] Fox epitomized the Quaker spirit of defiance. He was arrested at Swarthmoor in January 1664 and was imprisoned for refusing the oath of allegiance. When, at Lancaster assizes, he was handed a Bible on which to swear the oath, he turned to passages where Christ forbids swearing and 'wondered that the Bible was at liberty and that they did not imprison the book that forbids to swear'.[3] After an imprisonment of nearly three years in wretched conditions, first in Lancaster gaol and then in Scarborough Castle, he was freed in September 1666 by order of the king. But when the Second Conventicle Act came into force in May 1670 Fox deliberately attended the Quaker meeting in Gracechurch Street in London where he 'expected the storm . . . most likely to begin', and was again arrested.[4] Not all Friends were as resolute as their leader in the face of persecution, and when the Quakers at Preston Patrick were censured for meeting secretly two of their leaders, John Story and John Wilkinson, led a revolt against Fox's authority.[5] But tributes were paid to the Friends' constancy by men who had no love for their doctrines. Baxter regarded them

[1] C. G. Crump (ed.), *The History of the Life of Thomas Elwood* (1900), p. 181.
[2] Braithwaite, *SPQ*, pp. 75–6, 225–7.
[3] *Fox's Journal*, p. 282.   [4] Ibid., pp. 502, 560.
[5] Braithwaite, *SPQ*, pp. 294–323.

as 'poor deluded souls', but even he admitted that they bore the brunt of the persecution and so

did greatly relieve the sober people for a time: for they were so resolute, and gloried in their constancy and sufferings, that they assembled openly (at the Bull and Mouth near Aldersgate) and were dragged away daily to the common gaol . . . so that the gaol at Newgate was filled with them. Abundance of them died in prison, and yet they continued their assemblies still.[1]

Among the other Dissenting denominations there were widely differing attitudes towards the penal code. While the Norwich Congregational church resolved to meet in 'small parcels' in order to avoid infringing the Conventicle Act, the Bessell's Green General Baptist church in Kent excluded from membership one who endeavoured 'to make our knees feeble . . . by creeping into corners, and meeting by fours'.[2] In January 1682 the members of the Broadmead Particular Baptist church in Bristol, at the height of what they calculated to be their ninth and most severe persecution, resolved to meet privately, but their pastor, George Fownes, wrote from prison to urge them to continue to meet publicly till they 'were made to cease by force'.[3]

The widest differences of all, though, appeared among the Presbyterians. At the one extreme were ministers whose nonconformity consisted of nothing more than a refusal to exercise their ministry under the terms of the Act of Uniformity, but who continued to attend the services at their parish churches and even to receive communion there. Such were Richard Bell, who after ejection 'quietly set up his staff, and spent his time in profitable conversation', and Jerome Littlejohn, who lived 'very privately, never attempting anything against the peace and quiet either of church or state'.[4] Even Zachary Crofton, imprisoned in 1661 for his tirades against the bishops, went to 'common prayer in the Tower of London', and defended his action on the ground that the Church of England was like a degenerate vine which retained 'the name and nature of a vine' even though it brought forth 'little save sour grapes'.[5] Of the

---

[1] *Reliquiae Baxterianae*, part ii, p. 436.
[2] Browne, *Congregationalism in Norfolk and Suffolk*, p. 260. Taylor, *General Baptists*, i. 280.
[3] *Broadmead Records*, pp. 229, 253.   [4] *Calamy Revised*, pp. 46, 325.
[5] Ibid., p. 244. Z. Crofton, *Reformation not Separation* (1662), p. 7.

2,029 ejected clergy, 210 later conformed and at least another fifty were prepared to take the oath of non-resistance prescribed by the Five Mile Act.[1]

At the other extreme were Presbyterian ministers who from the time of their ejection refused to have anything more to do with the established church. William Alleine, reported an Anglican incumbent in 1665, 'never comes to church: but doth often keep private meetings for the sowing seeds of rebellion in the hearts of some of the people'; John Cole was opposed to occasional conformity and was imprisoned for eight years 'for expounding the Scripture and praying'; and Robert Collins kept conventicles on 'Sundays in time of divine service to the scandal of many' and was frequently fined and once imprisoned.[2] At least thirty-five of the ejected Presbyterian ministers were excommunicated during the Restoration period, often for failing to attend the parish church.[3]

Occupying a middle position were Presbyterian ministers who, while believing it their duty to attend their parish churches, at the same time continued to act as pastors to such of their former flocks as desired their services. Baxter, although he always disclaimed the name of Presbyterian, may be included in this group, for while living in Acton between the lapse of the First Conventicle Act and the passing of the second, he preached in his home to as many as cared to hear him, and after he had delivered his sermon he proceeded with his congregation to the parish church.[4] Similarly Oliver Heywood, ejected from the curacy of Coley near Halifax, encouraged those who came to hear him to attend their parish church as well, and even preached in his old pulpit when his successor was away.[5] Other Presbyterian ministers, while continuing to exercise their ministry, kept scrupulously within the law. After the passing of the Conventicle Act Adam Martindale divided his auditors into small groups and preached the same sermon four or five times a day. John Hieron 'preached twice a day in the biggest families, with four persons only besides; but as many under sixteen years of age as would come'. And Obadiah Grew,

---

[1] *Calamy Revised*, pp. xiii, lx. Jones and Owen in *Y Cofiadur*, xxxii. 8.
[2] *Calamy Revised*, pp. 8, 125, 129.
[3] Ibid., *passim*.
[4] *Reliquiae Baxterianae*, part iii, p. 46.
[5] J. Hunter, *Life of Oliver Heywood* (1842), pp. 163, 206.

when he lost his eyesight, kept an amanuensis to whom every
week he would dictate a sermon which was then sent 'to be
read to four or more writers in short-hand, every Saturday
night or Lord's day morning; and every one of these read it to
four new men who transcribed it also: and so it was afterwards
read at twenty several meetings'.[1]

The Quakers were scornful of the stratagems resorted to by
the other Dissenters to avoid persecution, but while such devices
may not have been heroic, they were up to a point effective.
According to Fox it was common practice for the Presbyterians
to hold services under the guise of feasts, and if they were disturbed 'they would put up their Bibles' and turn their attention
to 'tobacco pipes, flagons of drink, cold meat, bread and
cheese'.[2] Churches held meetings at times and places which
they hoped would enable them to elude discovery. The Nottingham Congregationalists met at 'night, or at two or three o'clock
in the morning'; their co-religionists in Stepney met when
necessary in a concealed room above the ceiling of their meeting
house; John Flavell, a Congregationalist ejected from a Dartmouth lectureship, held services on a rock in the Kingsbridge
estuary at low tide; Stephen Hughes and Rees Prytherch both
preached in caves in Carmarthenshire; the Dissenters at Olney
met at the 'three counties point' where Buckinghamshire,
Bedfordshire, and Northamptonshire converge, and when the
constables of one county approached they avoided arrest by
escaping into one of the other neighbouring counties.[3]

Particular care was taken to shield ministers from arrest,
both because they were the leaders of their congregations and
because they were liable to the severest penalties under the
Second Conventicle Act. Among the Presbyterians Richard
Chantrye went to meetings 'in the twilight to escape the
informers, with a Bible in his pocket and a fork on his shoulder';
when constables arrived to arrest Thomas Vincent while he was
preaching at Devonshire House his congregation sang a psalm

---

[1] *Life of Adam Martindale*, Chetham Society Publications, iv (1845), 176. *Calamy
Revised*, pp. 262, 236.

[2] *Fox's Journal*, pp. 517–18.

[3] Castle Gate Congregational church, Nottingham, Church Book, p. 2. C. E.
Whiting, *Studies in English Puritanism* (1968), pp. 73–4. *TCHS* i (1901–4), 166. Rees,
Nonconformity in Wales, pp. 224, 286. M. Hewett, 'John Gibbs', *Baptist Quarterly*, iii
(1926–7), 320.

while he made good his escape; and to enable William Wallace to escape in a similar situation 'several women big with child' obstructed the officers, trusting that their male chivalry would not permit them to remove the ladies by force.[1] The Congregationalists were no less resourceful. Joseph Oddy preached in a wood at night, seated on horseback to facilitate escape, while Thomas Jollie preached from a staircase to people gathered in his sitting-room, separated by a door which was cut in two and hinged, thus providing a pulpit while Jollie was preaching but a shutter which could quickly be closed to hide the preacher should the meeting be disturbed.[2] But it was the Dissenters of Bristol who had to exercise the greatest ingenuity in averting the law, for it was here that persecution was often at its fiercest. The Broadmead Baptists posted youths at the door of their meeting to warn of the approach of informers; when officers attempted to raid the meeting women sat on the stairs to impede their entry; and their minister preached from behind a curtain, so that any informer who had slipped into the congregation unnoticed should hear the preacher but not be able to identify him. Similar devices were adopted by the other Bristol Dissenters, and in 1675 the Presbyterian, Congregational, and two Baptist churches in the city agreed that one or other of them should hold an evening meeting on every day of the week except Saturday. As a result, 'through their granting of warrants, and sending their sergeants, and raising constables to suppress us in the evening, and the next morning receiving information and trials . . . the magistrates were tired and grew much weary, complaining that they could do little else . . . but matters about meetings'. And so the magistrates decided to confine the suppressing of conventicles to one day a week, and by this means, wrote Edward Terrill, the Baptist elder, 'the Lord many times gave us rest, and food for our souls'.[3]

Failure to avoid persecution meant fines, distraint, imprisonment, and sometimes death. The fines levied on Dissenters for worshipping God were frequently ruinous, and intended to be so. Thomas Tregoss, the ejected vicar of Mylor with Mabe in

---

[1] *Calamy Revised*, pp. 109, 507. *Fox's Journal*, p. 566.
[2] Jones, *Congregationalism in England*, p. 79. *Note Book of Thomas Jolly*, Chetham Soc. Publ., new series xxxiii (1894), p. xxi.
[3] *Broadmead Records*, pp. 98, 101–2, 109.

Cornwall, had paid £220 in fines by the time of his death in 1671, while Robert Collins of Ottery St. Mary in Devon was fined £60 in 1670, £20 in 1675, and £20 in 1682, and was at length compelled to flee to the Netherlands and to sell his house and estate 'to maintain his person and family in their distracted, shattered condition'.[1] By the terms of the Second Conventicle Act the fines were collected from the seizure and sale of the Dissenters' goods, and this often meant depriving a poor Dissenter of the tools of his trade or of the bed on which he lay down after a hard day's work. At Bedford Thomas Cooper, a heel-maker, was distrained upon for 'three cart-loads of wood, which was of more value than any of the household goods, he being a poor man, and living only upon making heels and lasts'. A blacksmith was deprived of his shovels and anvil, a pipe-maker of the wood with which he fired his kiln, a hatter of his stock of hats, and a widow of her 'tables, cupboards, chairs, irons, feather-beds, blankets, the very hangings of the room, and sheets off her bed'.[2] In Cornwall a Quaker widow was deprived of £35 worth of cattle to pay the £6 she owed in tithes; in Breconshire the last cow of Henry Gregory, a General Baptist pastor, was taken away, 'thus depriving his children of the milk they craved'; and when, in 1684, John Miller, the pastor of a General Baptist church at Minterne in Dorset was fined £220, the officers seized 'four hundred sheep, twenty cows, seven horses, six or seven hogs; all the hay, corn, and wool of the last year's produce; and even the malt and hops reserved for the use of the family'—goods worth nearly £500.[3] It was a traffic which brought handsome dividends to some informers: an inn-keeper of Richmond in Yorkshire collected £2,000 from seventy-nine meetings in fourteen months.[4]

The penal code was often enforced with quite unnecessary malice and brutality. In 1662 Quaker meetings at the Bull and Mouth were broken up by soldiers 'beating and kicking and hurling people on heaps and pushing them with the ends of their muskets', so that one Friend died of the wounds thus received.[5] Vavasor Powell complained that in Wales in the

---

[1] *Calamy Revised*, pp. 491, 129.   [2] Brown, *John Bunyan*, pp. 206–8.
[3] Whiting, *English Puritanism*, p. 149. T. Richards, *Wales under the Indulgence* (1928), p. 34. Taylor, *General Baptists*, i. 298.
[4] Braithwaite, *SPQ*, p. 79.   [5] Ibid., pp. 24–5.

same year 'poor and peaceable people [had] been dragged out of their beds and, without regard of sex or age [had] been driven some twenty miles to prison on their feet, and forced (though in the heat of the summer, till their feet were much blistered, and they were ready to fall with faintness) to run by the troopers' horses, receiving many blows and beatings'.[1] Again in 1662 an elderly Quaker was driven and dragged on foot by mounted soldiers from Evesham to Worcester and died as a result of his sufferings, while another Quaker, a poor shoemender, was imprisoned and whipped with rods for working on a Sunday.[2] The home of the Congregationalist John James of Flintham in Nottinghamshire was broken into 'in so furious a manner' that he not only lost nearly £500 in goods and cattle, but one of his children died of fright.[3] Benjamin Keach, a General Baptist tailor from Winslow in Buckinghamshire, was sentenced to prison and the pillory in 1664 for adopting 'damnable positions contrary to the Book of Common Prayer' in his *Child's Instructor*; all the copies of the book were destroyed and he wrote it again from memory.[4] And Francis Smith, a General Baptist printer who published much of Bunyan's work, maintained that it was the practice of government agents to seize his books as seditious or unlicensed and to sell them again for their own profit; in this way he claimed to have lost £1,400.[5]

Not even for the bereaved and the deceased had the persecutors respect. Edmund Tucker, the ejected curate of Halwell in Devon, was on one occasion fined £30 'for praying with three gentlewomen who came to visit his wife, and comfort her upon the death of her son and only child, who was drowned at sea'.[6] At Amersham in 1665 a Quaker funeral was disrupted by a magistrate who collected a crowd of constables and 'rude fellows', assaulted the bearers, and threw the coffin to the ground.[7] At Croft in Lincolnshire the body of a General Baptist was taken out of its grave in the parish burial-ground and dragged on a sledge to the gate of his home and left outside, while in Breconshire the body of a young Baptist woman was

---

[1] D. Davies, *Vavasor Powell* (1896), p. 117.
[2] Whiting, *English Puritanism*, p. 211. *Life of Thomas Ellwood*, pp. 102–3.
[3] A. R. Henderson, *History of Castle Gate Congregational Church, Nottingham* (1905), p. 69.
[4] Underwood, *English Baptists*, p. 111   [5] Taylor, *General Baptists*, i. 343.
[6] *Calamy Revised*, p. 495.   [7] *Life of Thomas Ellwood*, pp. 139–40.

dug up out of the churchyard 'and buried at the cross-roads like a common suicide'.[1]

The worst sufferings, however, were endured by those Dissenters who experienced life inside Restoration gaols. Conditions varied enormously from prison to prison, depending on the generosity or vindictiveness of the local magistrates and gaoler, the extent to which the prisoner was permitted and able to pay for reasonable accommodation and food, and the help he was allowed to receive from his church, family, and friends. At best life in prison was fairly comfortable and control over the prisoner's conduct remarkably lax. Prisoners whom a friendly gaoler knew he could trust were often allowed out to visit their families or even to preach at conventicles, provided that they returned to gaol at night. William Jones, the ejected rector of Cilmaenllwyd in Carmarthenshire, who subsequently became a Baptist, was imprisoned at Haverfordwest for preaching at a conventicle, but the gaoler allowed him out of prison to fulfil a preaching engagement arranged before his commitment.[2] Bunyan was a prisoner in Bedford county gaol from 1660 to 1672, but he was allowed out of prison to attend church meetings in 1661, 1668, 1669, and 1670, and was elected to the pastorate of the Bedford Congregational church in January 1672 while still a prisoner.[3] Even Vavasor Powell was allowed out of the Fleet prison to preach on one occasion in 1669, and was often permitted to preach in the prison to people who came to hear him.[4] Charles Lloyd of Dolobran in Montgomeryshire, the patriarch of a famous Quaker family, was held prisoner in Welshpool from 1662 to 1672, but from May 1663 he and his fellow Quakers were allowed to 'have a house at the end of the town to themselves, and they had quietness at that house to meet to worship God as often as they pleased'.[5] John Farroll, imprisoned in the Marshalsea at Southwark for six months in 1669 for breaking the Five Mile Act, found prison to be 'one of the most comfortable parts of his life, through the kindness of

---

[1] Taylor, *General Baptists*, i. 202. Richards, *Wales under the Indulgence*, p. 33.

[2] Rees, *Nonconformity in Wales*, p. 230.

[3] Brown, *John Bunyan*, pp. 187, 192, 213. W. T. Whitley, 'Bunyan's Imprisonments', *TBHS* vi (1918–19), 7, 14.

[4] Davies, *Vavasor Powell*, p. 151. T. Richards, *Wales under the Penal Code* (1925), p. 82.

[5] H. Lloyd, *The Quaker Lloyds in the Industrial Revolution* (1975), p. 19.

friends who God raised up to administer relief to him'.[1] And Baxter, who was imprisoned for a short time in 1670 for holding conventicles, experienced no great hardship, for he had a kind gaoler, 'a large room, and the liberty of walking in a fair garden', and the company of his wife who 'brought so many necessaries that we kept house as contentedly and as comfortable as at home'.[2]

But if some gaols were tolerable and some gaolers kind, many prisons were stinking holes and their keepers brutes. Thomas Ellwood, a young Quaker convert who was arrested at the Bull and Mouth in 1662, drew a sharp contrast between conditions in Bridewell, where the Quakers were allowed out to visit other imprisoned Friends and, on their release, made a collection for their gaolers as an appreciation of their kindness, and Newgate, where the Quaker shared overcrowded, suffocating, disease-ridden quarters with pickpockets and prostitutes, and where the felons made sport with the heads of three executed men.[3] The filthy, congested, foul-smelling Restoration gaols, unheated in winter and sweltering in summer, the breeding-ground of fever, plague, and smallpox, took a fearful toll of Quaker lives.[4] Richard Hubberthorne, to whom Charles II had held out such hopes of toleration in June 1660, died in Newgate two years later at the age of thirty-four. Edward Burrough, who had helped to launch the Quaker mission at the Bull and Mouth, succumbed to fever in Newgate in February 1663, only twenty-eight years old, his last days spent on a damp straw mattress next to an open drain.[5] His fellow evangelist Francis Howgill died in Appleby gaol in 1669; John Audland, who had taken the Quaker message to Bristol, contracted a lung disease while in Banbury gaol and died in 1663; and Thomas Stordy of Moorhouse in Cumberland, imprisoned for life for refusing the oath of allegiance, languished in gaol for twenty-two years till his death in 1684.[6]

Even when Friends escaped from prison with their lives, it was often with their health permanently impaired. Such was the

---

[1] *Calamy Revised*, p. 192.   [2] *Reliquiae Baxterianae*, part iii, pp. 50–1.
[3] *Life of Thomas Ellwood*, pp. 107, 113–14, 126–7.
[4] For detailed descriptions of prison life under Charles II see G. R. Cragg, *Puritanism in the Period of the Great Persecution* (Cambridge, 1957), ch. 4.
[5] Cragg, *The Great Persecution*, p. 107.
[6] Whiting, *English Puritanism*, pp. 147, 149–50.

experience of William Dewsbury, who had already spent more than a year in York Castle and Northampton gaol during the Interregnum. He was imprisoned in York Castle again in 1661, in Newgate in 1662, and spent nineteen of the twenty-three years from 1663 to 1686 in Warwick gaol, four of them in close confinement. He was freed in 1686, but lived to enjoy only two years of liberty.[1] Not even George Fox's iron constitution could remain unaffected by three years in appalling conditions in Lancaster gaol and Scarborough Castle. In Lancaster he 'was put in a smoky tower where the smoke of the other rooms came up' so that he could scarcely see a candle, and where it rained in upon his bed; in Scarborough he was put into a room again open to the rain and to the east winds blowing in from the North Sea. 'The water came over my bed and ran about the room . . . and when my clothes were wet I had no fire to dry them; so that my body was numbed with cold, and my fingers swelled, that one was grown as big as two.' When he was eventually released the joints of his body were so stiff that he could scarcely bend his knees or get on his horse, 'nor hardly endure fire nor eat warm meat: I had been so long kept from it'.[2]

Friends were also liable to transportation under the Quaker Act of 1662, though only a score of such sentences appear to have been carried out. Fifty-five Quakers were put on board the *Black Eagle* in 1665, but twenty-eight died of the plague while the ship lay at anchor in the Thames, and the rest were ultimately set at liberty after the ship had been captured in the Channel by a Dutch privateer.[3] It is impossible to know exactly how many Quakers suffered by fines, imprisonment, and transportation during the reign of Charles II, but W. C. Braithwaite made a reasonable estimate of 15,000, of whom 450 paid for their convictions with their lives.[4]

The Quakers, by reason of their refusal of the oath of allegiance, suffered longer and more rigorous terms of imprisonment than the other Dissenters, but they did not suffer alone. Of the ejected clergy and fellows in England 215 suffered imprisonment between the Act of Uniformity and the death of Charles II,[5] 12·4 per cent of the total of those who did not afterwards

---

[1] Ibid., pp. 205–6. Braithwaite, *SPQ*, pp. 449–50.
[2] *Fox's Journal*, pp. 484, 491, 510. [3] Braithwaite, *SPQ*, pp. 47–8, 50.
[4] Ibid., p. 115. [5] *Calamy Revised*, p. lix.

conform. Most of these imprisonments were for fairly short terms, but the Congregationalist Francis Holcroft was imprisoned at Cambridge for nine years, the Presbyterian John Cole was imprisoned at Colchester and Chelmsford for eight years, and the Congregationalist Richard Worts was imprisoned for seven years, for part of the time with six other prisoners in a 'hole in the wall' in Norwich Castle 'which had neither door, window nor chimney, and room for but one truckle-bed', and where the prisoners were almost suffocated by the smoke from burning charcoal.[1] Seven of the ejected clergy died in prison, among them John Thompson, the minister of the Bristol Congregational church, whose death in 1675 aroused accusations of ill-treatment which his gaoler countered with the ludicrous claim that he had died of a surfeit of eating and drinking.[2] As in the case of the Quakers, many of the ejected clergy who did not die in prison suffered permanent injury to their health. John Cromwell, imprisoned for three years in Newark gaol, emerged suffering from asthma, scurvy, and dropsy; John Hoppin, after six months in 'a very cold chamber' in the Southgate prison, Exeter, 'thereby got such a rheumatism as rendered him a perfect cripple to the day of his death'; and Henry Jessey, the Particular Baptist leader and former Cromwellian Trier, who had known imprisonment under Charles I, was again arrested in 1661 and died in September 1663, six months after his release.[3]

A separate group of sufferers were Commonwealth regicides and radicals who had escaped the scaffold in 1660. Three Independents who had sat in judgement on Charles I, and who at their own trials had pleaded ignorance in extenuation of their guilt, died in prison: Isaac Pennington and Owen Rowe, both members of John Goodwin's church, died in the Tower in 1660 and 1661, and Robert Tichborne, once lord mayor of London and a member of George Cockayn's church, lingered in the Tower until 1682. Robert Lilburne, the Leveller leader's Baptist brother, also died in prison in 1665; so too did another Baptist, the former Major-General Robert Overton, in 1668; and in October 1670 there occurred in the Fleet prison the death of the Welsh evangelist Vavasor Powell, 'in the eleventh

[1] Ibid., pp. 271–2, 125. S. Palmer, *Nonconformist's Memorial* (1778), ii. 192.
[2] *CSPD* 1675–6, p. 94.   [3] *Calamy Revised*, pp. 147, 277, 298.

year of his imprisonment and in the fifty-third of his age'.[1]
Edward Bagshaw, an ejected clergyman who had shared
Powell's captivity in Southsea Castle, and was soon to follow
him to the grave, composed these lines for his friend's tomb in
Bunhill Fields:

> In vain oppressors do themselves perplex,
> To find out acts how they the Saints may vex,
> Death spoils their plots, and sets the oppressed free,
> Thus Vavasor obtained true liberty,
> Christ him released and now is joined among
> The martyred souls, with whom he cries how long? [2]

3. 'THE GOOD FRUIT OF THIS PRESENT PERSECUTION': JOHN BUNYAN AND WILLIAM PENN

The verse which Edward Bagshaw penned on the death of
Vavasor Powell expresses the conviction of all Dissenters that
whatever their present sufferings, their ultimate victory was
assured. 'If you suffer with Christ, you shall reign with him',
wrote Ralph Ward to his Congregational church at York, from
which he had been separated by the Five Mile Act.[3] Evidence of
that ultimate victory, the Dissenters believed, was being daily
supplied. The Great Plague and the fire of London, which
Quaker seers claimed to have foretold, were interpreted by
more sober Dissenters as God's judgement on an apostate
nation.[4] Nonconformist writings abound in stories of disasters
which befell individual persecutors. A man of property in
Lincolnshire named Radley attempted to molest a congregation
of General Baptists; he subsequently became bankrupt and
died of the plague, leaving his widow and children to be
assisted by the very Baptists he had sought to persecute.[5]
William Swinton, the sexton of St. Cuthbert's, Bedford, and an
informer, fell from his bell-tower and was killed.[6] David Morrice,
a Montgomeryshire magistrate who 'had been very bitter
towards Dissenters', was thrown from his horse into a ditch and

[1] Underwood, *English Baptists*, p. 90. Rogers, *The Fifth Monarchy Men*, p. 121.
Davies, *Vavasor Powell*, p. 159.
[2] Davies, *Vavasor Powell*, p. 159.
[3] Palmer, *Nonconformist's Memorial*, ii. 264.
[4] *Fox's Journal*, p. 503. J. W. Graham, *Psychical Experiences of Quaker Ministers*
(1933), p. 17. *Diaries and Letters of Philip Henry*, ed. M. H. Lee (1882), p. 193.
[5] Taylor, *General Baptists*, i. 197.   [6] Brown, *John Bunyan*, p. 211.

drowned.[1] And Thomas Robinson, the M.P. for Helston in Cornwall, on the day that he intended 'to go a fanatic-hunting' was gored by a bull and died from his injuries.[2]

When the plague visited the just no less than the unjust, and Dissenters were rotting in prisons, it was difficult to maintain that God's mercies, no less than his judgements, were effective in this life as well as in the next.[3] But one case of what was regarded as direct divine intervention on behalf of a Dissenter passed into Welsh Nonconformist folk-history. Henry Williams, an itinerant evangelist of Ysgafell near Newtown in Montgomeryshire, spent nine years in prison, during which time his persecutors burned his house to the ground and murdered his aged father. 'They seized the stock upon the land and seemed resolved to leave nothing behind them for the future subsistence of the family', but they left untouched a newly sown field of wheat which they did not consider it worth their while to destroy, and the crop produced by this field became the 'common talk and wonder of the whole country . . . [and] amounted to more than double the value of what the persecuting plunderers had carried off'. For two centuries the field was remembered as 'Cae'r fendith', 'the field of blessing', and 'two stalks of the miraculous harvest' were preserved and shown to the curious.[4]

At the deepest level the Dissenters derived from the Restoration period a spiritual experience such as only a time of persecution can provide. Three of the most cherished of all Dissenting works were started in prison in this time, William Penn's *No Cross, No Crown*, Bunyan's *Grace Abounding to the Chief of Sinners*, and *The Pilgrim's Progress*. By birth and upbringing the two men were separated by a wide gulf. William Penn was the son of Admiral Sir William Penn, a successful careerist and political weathercock who had sailed for Parliament and the Commonwealth and, in return for distinguished service in the battle of the Downs in 1652, had been rewarded with an estate in the south of Ireland. But by 1660 Sir William was an enthusiastic royalist: as a member of the Convention Parliament he

---

[1] *Diaries of Philip Henry*, p. 274.
[2] *Fox's Journal*, p. 447. *Calamy Revised*, p. 439.
[3] *Reliquiae Baxterianae*, part iii, p. 1.
[4] Rees, *Nonconformity in Wales*, pp. 159–60. Davies, *Vavasor Powell*, pp. 120–1.

was sent to escort Charles II back to England, and as a commissioner of the navy he became the close friend of the king's brother, James, Duke of York. Bunyan's father was a brazier or tinker of the village of Elstow near Bedford, a man who went from house to house and village to village mending household utensils. William Penn was educated at Christ Church, Oxford, where he was 'perverted' by John Owen and sent down for nonconformity in 1661, and at Lincoln's Inn, and was then sent to Ireland to take care of his father's estate.[1] Bunyan, 'notwithstanding the meanness and inconsiderableness of my parents', did go to school, but he claimed that he soon lost the little that he learned, and after service in the parliamentary army he followed his father's humble trade.[2]

By temperament, too, Penn and Bunyan were utterly different. The former had all the self-confidence of a rich young man sent down from Oxford, 'a most modish person' and 'a fine gentleman' in the opinion of Mrs. Pepys.[3] His spiritual pilgrimage, from his refusal to conform at Christ Church to his resolve to become a Quaker preacher in 1668, was marked by a series of intellectual decisions, and only once did it take the form of an emotional experience, when, at the age of twenty-two, he attended a Quaker meeting in Cork and the message of the evangelist Thomas Loe moved him to tears.[4] Bunyan, by contrast, was from childhood afflicted by 'dreadful visions', 'apprehensions of devils and wicked spirits', and 'thoughts of the fearful torments of hell-fire'. His experience closely paralleled those of his fellow Independents whose spiritual autobiographies were recorded in the 1650s by Henry Walker and John Rogers. He was tortured by the fear that he was not among the elect; he was stricken with terror at the thought that he had committed the unforgivable sin against the Holy Ghost; like John Rogers he wished he was not a man but a dog that 'had no soul to perish under the everlasting weights of hell for sin'. For two and a half years, while in his early twenties, Bunyan experienced alternating moods of spiritual ecstasy and black depression until he appropriated to himself the words 'Thy righteousness is in

[1] C. O. Peare, *William Penn* (Philadelphia, 1957), *passim*.

[2] J. Bunyan, *Grace Abounding to the Chief of Sinners*, ed. R. Sharrock (Oxford, 1962), p. 5.

[3] *Diary of Samuel Pepys* (Everyman edn., 1906), i. 513.

[4] Peare, *William Penn*, pp. 56–7.

heaven', realizing that Christ's 'righteousness was mine, his merits mine, his victory also mine'.[1] But for Bunyan this liberating experience did not mean, as it did for the Antinomian or for the Quaker, that henceforward there would be no more doubt or sin. *The Pilgrim's Progress*, which he began during his twelve-year-long imprisonment in Bedford county gaol, was an allegory not of instantaneous conversion, but of continual warfare with the powers of darkness.[2]

Theologically Penn and Bunyan were poles apart. The latter was an orthodox Calvinist, worried about his election, whose first literary venture was a vigorous attack on 'the Quakers' delusions', 'the same that long ago were held by the Ranters'.[3] In churchmanship he was a Congregationalist, and though he underwent believer's baptism he did so in the belief, which he shared with Vavasor Powell, that 'differences in judgement about water-baptism [were] no bar to communion'.[4] By contrast Penn, as a Quaker, not only rejected Calvinism, but in a work published in 1668, for which he was committed to the Tower, attacked the contemporary understanding of the Trinity as 'a fiction' and denied the orthodox Calvinist doctrines of the vicarious atonement 'and the justification of impure persons by an imputative righteousness'.[5] But for all their differences, the prison messages of the two men were essentially the same: that the way of salvation is narrow, and reached only through suffering and renunciation of the world. 'As receiving of Christ is the means appointed by God to salvation', wrote Penn, 'so bearing the daily cross after him is the only true testimony of receiving him.'[6] To turn back from the journey to the celestial city, says Bunyan's pilgrim when told that lions bar his way, 'is nothing but death; to go forward is fear of death, and life everlasting beyond it: I will yet go forward'.[7]

The Dissenters expected their sufferings to be rewarded not only by their own eternal happiness in the life to come, but also in

---

[1] Bunyan, *Grace Abounding, passim.*

[2] R. Sharrock, *John Bunyan* (1968), pp. 70–3, argues that Bunyan began *The Pilgrim's Progress* between 1666 and 1672.

[3] G. Offord, ed., *The Works of John Bunyan* (1859), ii. 133, 183.

[4] This was the title of a pamphlet which Bunyan published in 1673. *Bunyan's Works*, ii. 616.

[5] Peare, *William Penn*, pp. 80–1.

[6] W. Penn, *No Cross, No Crown* (1849), pp. 17–18.

[7] J. Bunyan, *The Pilgrim's Progress* (Nelson's Classics), p. 47.

the future prosperity of their cause here on earth. Visions of the millennium receded, but hopes of the less spectacular advancement of Christ's kingdom on earth took their place. Thomas Hardcastle, the pastor of the Broadmead Baptist church, Bristol, 'seven times imprisoned for Christ and a good conscience', was convinced that his winter of suffering was but the prelude to seed-time and harvest. 'It has been our great error', he wrote from prison to his congregation, 'that we have not trusted in the power of God. We have reasoned about the worst that men can do, but have not believed the best that God can do. . . . We are sowing for posterity; the generation coming on will have the good fruit of this present persecution.'[1]

There is some evidence that Thomas Hardcastle's optimism was not unfounded. By comparison with the host of Dissenters who suffered for their faith, the recorded instances of apostasy are remarkably few. Anthony Pearson, the Durham magistrate who had been converted to Quakerism through the testimony of James Nayler, returned to the Church of England after the Restoration; the Bedford Congregational church had to exclude from membership Humphrey Merrill, for charging the church with rebellion, and Robert Nelson, for receiving confirmation at the hands of a bishop; the Nailsworth Congregational church in Gloucestershire lost thirty members through persecution in the 1680s; and a Gloucester Quaker who had been in prison for two years conformed after the bishop entertained him to dinner.[2] But such examples are comparatively rare. The members of the Broadmead church were constantly harried by persecution and expressed concern in 1665 that some of their number were neglecting to attend services for fear of the consequences, but Edward Terrill's very full transcripts of the church's records for the whole of the Restoration period reveal only one case of a person excluded or refused membership for conformity to the established church.[3] And although the church lamented in 1675 that meetings were 'grown very poor and lean through fines, imprisonments, and constant worrying of us every day', membership none the less increased from 100 in 1671 to 166 in 1679.[4]

---

[1] *Broadmead Records*, pp. 180, 324–5.

[2] Braithwaite, *BQ*, pp. 112–14. Brown, *John Bunyan*, pp. 193–6. A. Gordon, *Freedom after Ejection* (Manchester, 1917), p. 44. *CSPD* 1667–8, p. 301.

[3] *Broadmead Records*, pp. 57, 169.   [4] Ibid., pp. 144, 73, 205.

As for the Friends, Baxter was of the opinion that 'many turned Quakers, because the Quakers kept their meetings openly and went to prison for it cheerfully', while the researches of Richard Vann suggest that in Buckinghamshire and Norfolk the number of Friends also increased between 1662 and 1689.[1]

There must, of course, have been cases of backsliding in the face of persecution which went unrecorded, and it is likely that the penal code was more effective in rural than in urban areas. John Browne calculated that of the thirty-six Congregational churches founded in Norfolk and Suffolk before 1660, only fourteen survived the Restoration.[2] But in many such cases Independency had owed its position during the Interregnum not to local support but to the zeal of individual Congregationalist incumbents, and their ejection from their parishes in reality marked a strengthening, not a weakening, of Dissent. Similarly the later conformity of 210 of the ejected Puritan clergy can scarcely be accounted apostasy when the Puritans had always upheld the concept of a national church. Much more significant was the way in which many Presbyterians, who had held this Puritan position before 1662, came by degrees to share the outlook of the other Dissenters. After the Five Mile Act, wrote Bishop Seth Ward of Exeter, there was a 'sweet concurrence . . . betwixt the Presbyterians and Independents in the principles of rebellion', and in Bristol the Presbyterians for a time cooperated with the Baptists and Congregationalists by joining a committee to search for legal ways of resisting persecution, uniting for prayer, and holding their meetings on different evenings of the week.[3] In 1671 Joseph Williamson, the future Secretary of State, wrote that had the Presbyterians been allowed to stay within the established church, there would have been not a fanatic left in England. As it was Presbyterian 'congregations are now come to ride their teachers, and make them do what they will . . . all the Presbyterians are growing to Independents, and so must the teachers'.[4]

[1] *Reliquiae Baxterianae*, part ii, p. 437. Vann, *Social Development*, pp. 93–5.
[2] Browne, *History of Congregationalism in Norfolk and Suffolk*, p. 171.
[3] Brockett, *Nonconformity in Exeter*, p. 27. *Broadmead Records*, pp. 95, 109, 113–14.
[4] *CSPD* 1671, p. 496.

4. 'MONGREL JUSTICES' AND THE KING'S PREROGATIVE: THE FAILURE OF PERSECUTION

The survival, invigoration, and, in many respects, strengthening of Dissent during the period of persecution was due not only to the Dissenters' own spiritual resources, and to the strength which came to old Separatism through the alliance with new Nonconformity, but also to the reluctance of many Anglicans to pursue their fellow Protestants with the ferocity with which French Catholics were to harass the Huguenots in the 1680s. The absence, in England, of a strong centralized administration on the French pattern made the full implementation of the penal code wellnigh impossible. A Warminster magistrate wrote to the Secretary of State in 1661 that there were 'many mongrel justices that were for Oliver, who proceed coldly and neglect duty', Bishop Seth Ward complained that at least fourteen magistrates in Devon were 'arrant Presbyterians',[1] and until the Second Conventicle Act imposed fines of £100 on justices who declined to enforce the laws against Dissenters, many cases of magisterial mercy were recorded. When a company of Quakers was arrested at the home of Isaac Pennington at Chalfont St. Peters in Buckinghamshire in 1661 the local magistrate, Sir William Bowyer, made every conceivable excuse to justify his releasing them.[2] When George Fox was arrested at Tenterden in Kent in 1663 he persuaded the magistrates that the Quaker Act was aimed only at those who 'met to plot and contrive insurrections against the king' and they set him free.[3] When Francis Soreton, an ejected minister, was arrested at Exeter in 1666 for violating the Five Mile Act the high sheriff of Devon, Sir William Courtenay, 'got him released and conveyed him, in his own coach, to his own house', where he lived until his death in 1689.[4] At Chester in 1666 the Dissenters were 'so linked into the magistracy by alliance' that it was 'very difficult to bring them to punishment'; at Newcastle in 1668 it was reported that 'the mayor slights the informers when they give notice of the meetings'; and at Bristol in 1670 the election of a new mayor who 'winked' at the conventicles brought a welcome

---

[1] *CSPD* 1661–2, p. 155. H. P. R. Finberg, *West Country Historical Studies* (Newton Abbot, 1969), p. 202.

[2] *Life of Thomas Ellwood*, pp. 77–80.   [3] *Fox's Journal*, p. 439.

[4] *Calamy Revised*, p. 452.

respite from persecution.[1] The Bishop of Lichfield wrote in despair to the Archbishop of Canterbury in 1669 to request the quartering of troops in Coventry since 700 Dissenters gathered every Sunday in Leather Hall and the mayor 'says he does not know how to help it'; and in London, even after the Second Conventicle Act, magistrates were reluctant to act on the evidence of informers and 'Alderman Forth got an informer bound to the behaviour for breaking in upon him in his chamber against his will.'[2]

But it was at Yarmouth that the persecution was most successfully frustrated. The Congregationalists were particularly strong in a town which had had a Separatist church as early as 1624 and where William Bridge had ministered from 1643 until compelled to leave by the Five Mile Act. The Congregationalists were expelled from the chancel of the parish church in 1661 by Sir Thomas Meadows, who was subsequently chosen as bailiff and ensured that the penal laws were enforced.[3] But in 1666 Presbyterians and 'moderate Episcopalians' gained control of the town council, they had no desire to suppress conventicles since 'so many of their wives flock to them', and new bailiffs were elected who were sympathetic to the Dissenters.[4] 'The magistrates do not put the least check on the conventicles', wrote the government informant Richard Bower in December 1667, 'and the numbers flocking thither increase daily.'[5] William Bridge returned to the town, people came to hear him 'in such numbers that by 7 a.m. there [was] no room to get in', and in 1669 the Congregationalists 'fitted up a place for public meetings . . . where at least 1,000 meet'.[6] The Dissenters were silenced for a time in March 1675, but by August the Congregationalists and Presbyterians were meeting together 'in greater numbers than formerly', and in 1676 it was reported that they had 'both the civil and military power' in the town in their hands.[7]

The suppression of conventicles, wrote Bower despairingly,

> may with ease be done in the country, where the gentry live and the people have a dependence on them . . . but in corporations it will

---

[1] *CSPD* 1666–7, p. 12; 1668–9, p. 342. *Broadmead Records*, p. 67.
[2] *CSPD* 1668–9, p. 655. *Reliquiae Baxterianae*, part iii, p. 165.
[3] *CSPD* 1668–9, p. 100.   [4] *CSPD* 1667–8, pp. 88, 145.
[5] *CSPD* 1667–8, p. 97.   [6] *CSPD* 1667–8, p. 277; 1668–9, p. 221.
[7] *CSPD* 1675–6, pp. 18, 275; 1676–7, p. 155.

never be carried through by the magistrates or inhabitants, their
livelihood consisting altogether in trade, and this depending one
upon another, so that when any of these shall appear to act in the
least measure, their trade shall decline, and . . . their credit with it.[1]

Even where the local magistrates and officers were bent on
carrying out the law, their actions could be frustrated by public
sympathy for the persecuted. In Lincolnshire soldiers 'struck by
[the] innocent deportment' of the Baptists they had been sent to
arrest, refused to interfere with them; in London and Bristol
it was almost impossible to get sea captains and sailors to trans-
port Quakers to the colonies.[2] When a Bedford churchwarden
attempted to levy distress on a man 'whom the whole town knew
to be a just and harmless man' the common people fixed the tail
of a calf to his back, 'and deriding him with shouts and hollos,
he departed without taking any distress'.[3] The roughest treatment, however, was reserved for the informers, 'men of sharp
wit, close countenances, pliant tempers, and deep dissimulation'
who were universally despised.[4] At Colchester two informers
were stoned by 'the rabble' and had to take refuge in the town
gaol; in London in 1670 a Roman Catholic who had procured
the arrest of George Fox was attacked by a crowd and had to be
rescued by soldiers who got him into a house where 'he changed
his periwig and vest'; and at Wrentham in Norfolk two informers were 'dragged through a foul hog sty, and from thence
through a pond' with the result that one of them died.[5]

In one important respect public sympathy for the Dissenters
was of more than temporary significance. On several occasions
juries refused to convict Dissenters—at Canterbury, for
example, where 'most of the grand jury are fanatics'—but the
judge could in return fine the jurymen for bringing in a verdict
in defiance of the evidence.[6] A crucial case occurred in 1670
when the Quakers were locked out of their Gracechurch Street
meeting-house by soldiers and met in the street outside. Two of
their number, William Penn and William Meade, were indicted
for riot, but at their trial at the Old Bailey the jury found
Meade 'not guilty' and Penn 'guilty of speaking in Gracious

[1] *CSPD* 1675–6, p. 1.
[2] Taylor, *General Baptists*, i. 197. Braithwaite, *SPQ*, pp. 42–3, 46.
[3] Brown, *John Bunyan*, p. 205.   [4] *Life of Thomas Ellwood*, p. 171.
[5] Braithwaite, *SPQ*, pp. 80–1. *Fox's Journal*, pp. 561–3. *CSPD* 1673–5, p. 396.
[6] *CSPD* 1665–6, p. xxx; 1663–4, p. 560.

Street', which was no crime, but not guilty of unlawful and tumultuous assembly. The judge refused to accept the verdict and the jury was locked up for the night 'without meat, drink, fire, and tobacco' and not 'so much as a chamber pot'. The following day the jury returned the same verdict and was again locked up for the night. On the third day they returned a simple verdict of 'not guilty'. Despite the verdict Penn was kept in prison for contempt of court and each of the jurymen was fined and four were imprisoned. But they sought a writ of habeas corpus and in *Bushel's Case*, named after their ringleader, the jurymen obtained a verdict in the Court of Common Pleas that a jury cannot be punished for its verdict.[1]

'Never thing since the king's return', wrote Baxter of the verdict in *Bushel's Case*, 'was received with greater joy and applause by the people.'[2] And of all the men who conspired to defeat the intentions of the penal code, none played a greater part than Charles II himself. On several occasions in the early years of his reign he intervened to save Dissenters from the consequences of the law. In 1661 he put a stop to the execution of Quakers in Massachusetts[3] and three years later saved the Baptists of Aylesbury from similar fate. He intervened to free the first Edmund Calamy from Newgate in 1663 and secured Fox's release from Scarborough Castle in 1666.[4] But the king's most important intervention on behalf of the Dissenters was his Declaration of Indulgence of March 1672, suspending 'all manner of penal laws in matters ecclesiastical'. Henceforward Dissenters would be able to meet freely for worship provided that they had a licence for their meeting place and for their preacher.

The Declaration of Indulgence, issued while Parliament was prorogued and by virtue of the royal prerogative, and allowing Roman Catholics to worship in private houses, was received by Dissenters with mixed feelings. Had they known that it was part redemption of Charles's promise to Louis XIV to declare himself a Roman Catholic, in return for French money, their misgivings would have turned to outright oppositon. As it was Alderman William Love, Presbyterian M.P. for the city of London, was

---

[1] Braithwaite, *SPQ*, pp. 69–73. Peare, *William Penn*, pp. 109–23.
[2] *Reliquiae Baxterianae*, part iii, p. 87. [3] *Fox's Journal*, pp. 411–14.
[4] *CSPD* 1663–4, p. 64. *Fox's Journal*, p. 502.

soon to declare that 'I had much rather see the Dissenters suffer by the rigour of the law, though I suffer with them, than see all the laws of England trampled under foot of the prerogative.'[1] And many Dissenters feared that the information they had to supply about their meeting-places and preachers in order to obtain licences would one day be used against them. The Quakers as a body declined to take out licences on the ground that the state had no more right to give, than to take away, religious liberty, and many Baptists and Congregationalists adopted the same position.[2]

None the less a total of 1,610 licences were issued for preachers, of whom 939 were named, not always accurately, as Presbyterians, 458 as Congregationalists or Independents, and 210 as Baptists.[3] The more conservative Presbyterians had their own reasons for disliking the Indulgence for, as always, toleration's victory meant comprehension's defeat. Philip Henry of Malpas in Cheshire feared that the sanctioning of separate places of worship would help to overthrow what he still called 'our parish-order',[4] and a group of Yorkshire Presbyterians explained that in taking out licences they were not proposing 'to set up any distinct or separate churches in opposition to those already established', nor intending to preach at times when services were held in the parish churches.[5]

But for all such protestations the Declaration of Indulgence gave an important stimulus to Dissent. At Northowram near Halifax the Presbyterian Oliver Heywood formed his hearers into a regular church and got them to subscribe to a declaration of faith not unlike an Independent covenant; Presbyterian ordinations, of which only one example is recorded between the Act of Uniformity and the Indulgence, began again; and the Presbyterians of Leeds and Sowerby even went so far as to erect their own meeting-houses.[6] There was thus some justice in

---

[1] Brown, *John Bunyan*, p. 243.

[2] Jones, *Congregationalism in England*, p. 92. 'The Baptist Licences of 1672', *TBHS* i (1908–9), 156–76.

[3] G. Lyon Turner, *Original Records of Early Nonconformity* (1914), iii. 732–6.

[4] *Diaries of Philip Henry*, pp. 250–1.   [5] Hunter, *Life of Oliver Heywood*, p. 229.

[6] J. H. Turner, ed., *The Rev. Oliver Heywood: his Autobiography, Diaries, Anecdote and Event Books* (Brighouse, 1882), ii. 21. Hunter, *Life of Heywood*, pp. 241, 244, 255. The only known Presbyterian ordination between 1662 and 1672 took place at Exeter in 1666. C. G. Bolam and J. Goring, 'Presbyterians in Separation', in Bolam, *et al.*, *The English Presbyterians* (1968), p. 86.

the Anglican taunt that the Presbyterians were beginning to look like 'Independent apes'.[1] And the Independents of Yarmouth, whether simian-like or not, seized the opportunity presented by the Indulgence to open a subscription-list for a new meeting-house, 'their old one having become too little for them'. By January 1673 they had raised £800 and the meeting-house was soon built, complete with galleries.[2] As for the Quakers, although they refused to take out licences for their meetings they were no longer harassed: the king granted a general pardon to 491 imprisoned Dissenters, the majority of whom were Friends but including also John Bunyan, while William Penn used the respite from persecution to undertake a missionary journey through Kent, Sussex, and Surrey.[3] Needless to say all this was alarming to staunch upholders of the established church. The meetings of Dissenters 'are already grown so full', it was reported from Chester in December 1672, 'that our episcopal congregations look very thin'; 'both Presbyterians and Anabaptists with the Quakers are exceedingly increased', complained the Bishop of Lincoln; 'many left the Church' after the Indulgence, wrote the Archdeacon of Canterbury four years later, 'who before did frequent it'.[4]

5. POPISH PLOTS AND PROTESTANT UNITY: THE EXTREMITY OF PERSECUTION AND THE MAKING OF THE TOLERATION ACT

Though shortage of money obliged the king to recall Parliament in February 1673, and Parliament compelled the king to withdraw his Indulgence in March, the results of the twelve month's toleration could not be completely eradicated. On the one hand the Dissenters faced the future with increased confidence, on the other Parliament itself began to look more kindly on their plight. From 1673 onwards many Anglicans became increasingly alarmed at the signs of growing Catholic influence at court, and especially at the prospect of Charles II's being succeeded by his brother, the now openly Roman Catholic James,

[1] Bolam, *English Presbyterians*, p. 89.
[2] *CSPD* 1672–3, p. 462; 1673–5, p. 396.
[3] Braithwaite, *SPQ*, p. 84. Peare, *William Penn*, p. 149.
[4] *CSPD* 1672–3, p. 300. Bate, *Declaration of Indulgence*, p. 103. T. Richards, 'The Religious Census of 1676', *Transactions of the Honourable Society of Cymmrodorion* (1925–6), supplement, pp. 2–3.

Duke of York, and as Anglican fears of Catholicism increased, so their hostility to Dissent abated. The Anglican opponents of the Declaration of Indulgence emphasized that their main objection was to the toleration of popery, not of Dissent,[1] and to substantiate the point the Commons even passed a Bill for the Ease of Protestant Dissenters. The bill would have allowed Dissenters who subscribed to the doctrinal sections of the Thirty-nine Articles and took the oaths of allegiance and supremacy to absent themselves from church and to attend conventicles, but the Lords wrecked it with an unacceptable amendment to allow the king to limit or extend this concession by proclamation.[2]

Charles attempted to allay Anglican fears of popery and to put Parliament in generous mood by issuing, in February 1675, an Order of Council commanding the enforcement of the penal laws against Catholics and Protestant Dissenters alike. But the Dissenters responded to the renewed outburst of persecution not only by the well tried means of evasion but also by direct political action. Hitherto Dissenting representation in the Cavalier Parliament had been negligible. If fifty or sixty Presbyterian M.P.s had been elected to the Commons in 1661, many of them must have severed all connection with Presbyterianism once the Act of Uniformity had reduced it to the level of the other Dissenting sects. Douglas Lacey has been able to find only fifteen certain and ten probable or possible Presbyterians in the House of Commons in 1674, and no representatives of the other Nonconformist denominations.[3] Even these figures may be too high, for the fact that an M.P. employed an ejected clergyman as his chaplain, while indicating an obvious sympathy with Dissent, does not necessarily mean that the M.P. himself was a Dissenter. As Lacey himself points out, very few of his 'Presbyterian' M.P.s are known to have attended public Nonconformist services.[4] As for the House of Lords, only one peer, Philip, Lord Wharton, is known to have ever attended Dissenting meetings, and although the Countess of Bedford was apprehended at a conventicle at which Thomas Manton was

[1] K. H. D. Haley, *The First Earl of Shaftesbury* (Oxford, 1968), p. 319.
[2] N. Sykes, *From Sheldon to Secker* (Cambridge, 1959), pp. 77–8.
[3] Lacey, *Dissent and Parliamentary Politics*, pp. 476–9.
[4] Ibid., p. 405.

preaching in 1675, and the Countess of Anglesey was arrested at a service conducted by John Owen in 1684, their husbands were conspicuously absent.[1]

From 1675, though, encouraged by growing Anglican hostility to the court, the Dissenters made a determined effort to influence the composition and mind of Parliament. In March 1675 Richard Bower reported from Yarmouth that the Dissenters of Norfolk were making 'great endeavours to make Sir Robert Kempe knight for this county' and he was subsequently elected.[2] In Durham in June 'all the sectaries' helped to secure the return of Thomas Vane, son of the late Sir Henry Vane, though he died of smallpox within a few days of the election.[3] In October the Dissenters of Dorset supported the wealthy Presbyterian Thomas More, the candidate favoured by the Earl of Shaftesbury, soon to emerge as the leader of the country opposition or Whig party.[4] And in 1677 Sir Robert Cann was elected for Bristol with the support of 'the Presbyterians, Independents, Anabaptistical, and Quakers' party'.[5] Meanwhile in May 1675 the Morning Meeting of Quaker ministers in London advised Friends to obtain from the parliamentary candidates they favoured a written undertaking to support 'a general liberty of conscience', and in October of the same year the Quaker Meeting for Sufferings was set up to lay before Parliament evidence of the 'gross sufferings' of Friends and to attempt to secure redress. A 'Book of Sufferings' was presented to Parliament in March 1677, and in the following year the Meeting for Sufferings organized the lobbying of M.P.s and urged Quaker Quarterly Meetings to supply their M.P.s with evidence of persecution.[6]

But all this Dissenting political activity had little immediate effect, for only two of the candidates they supported, Kempe and Cann, were able to take their seats in Parliament and neither was himself a Dissenter.[7] It is sometimes maintained that Dissenters were kept out of Parliament by the Test Acts,[8] but

---

[1] Ibid., pp. 460, 464, 473.   [2] *CSPD* 1675–6, p. 54.   [3] Ibid., p. 184.
[4] Ibid., p. 59.   [5] *CSPD* 1677–8, p. 426.
[6] Braithwaite, *SPQ*, p. 90 Lacey, *Dissent and Parliamentary Politics*, p. 106. N. C. Hunt, *Two Early Political Associations* (Oxford, 1961) pp. 3–6.
[7] Lacey, *Dissent and Parliamentary Politics*, p. 110.
[8] e.g. A. Browning, ed., *English Historical Documents* (1966), p. 360; A. R. Vidler, *The Church in an Age of Revolution* (1961), p. 41.

the Act of 1673 which imposed a sacramental test on all holders of civil and military offices under the crown did not apply to M.P.s, while the Act of 1678, which did apply to M.P.s, required only that they take the oaths of allegiance and supremacy and subscribe to a declaration against transubstantiation and the adoration of the Virgin Mary and the saints. The only occasion on which a sacramental test was applied to M.P.s was at the opening of the Cavalier Parliament in 1661, and there was subsequently no legal obstacle to a Dissenter taking his seat in Parliament, provided that he did not have scruples about the taking of oaths. It was in securing legal election to Parliament that the Dissenters' difficulties lay, for they possessed neither sufficient numbers in popular constituencies nor the necessary influence in closed constituencies to make much impact on Parliament. Even in a town such as Yarmouth where they were comparatively strong they failed to secure the return of their candidate Richard Huntington against their old enemy Sir Thomas Meadows in 1678,[1] and they were at an especial disadvantage in constituencies where the M.P. was elected by the borough corporation. On two occasions the Cavalier Parliament nullified the election of a Dissenting M.P. on the ground that his supporters had violated the Corporation Act by not taking the Anglican sacrament.[2]

The Dissenters were thus powerless by themselves to influence political events and could achieve their ends only in alliance with sympathetic Anglicans. This was to remain true for the next two and a half centuries, for as long as the Dissenters were to have distinctive political aims, and in the later 1670s it meant alliance with Shaftesbury and his nascent Whig party. Shaftesbury, for his part, was conscious of the importance of securing Dissenting support, but conscious, too, of the danger of alienating moderate Anglican opinion by putting forward Dissenting 'fanatics' as candidates.[3] The patronizing attitude adopted by the first Whigs towards the Dissenters was also to last for nearly two centuries, until the Dissenters no longer needed Whig patronage.

The alliance between Shaftesbury and the Dissenters appeared to be bearing fruit when, in an attempt to save his chief

[1] *CSPD* 1678, pp. 1–2.   [2] Lacey, *Dissent and Parliamentary Politics*, pp. 101–2.
[3] Halley, *First Earl of Shaftesbury*, p. 500.

minister Danby from the consequences of impeachment, Charles II dissolved the Cavalier Parliament in January 1679 and in the subsequent elections the opposition won a majority of nearly two to one.[1] Of the 300 members whom Shaftesbury claimed as his supporters, twenty-one were, according to Lacey's calculations, definite Dissenters, and a further twenty-one possible or probable Dissenters.[2] Though the vast majority of Dissenting M.P.s were still Presbyterians, they were now joined by the Congregationalist Sir John Hartopp, a member of John Owen's church, and by John Braman, who may have retained the Independent views he had held during the Civil War.[3]

The opposition owed its victory, at least in part, to the stories of a Popish Plot to assassinate Charles II and place his Catholic brother on the throne which had been circulated by Titus Oates, the disreputable son of Samuel Oates, the General Baptist preacher of the 1640s. The prime objective of the opposition thus became the exclusion of James from the succession to the throne, and all thirty-eight M.P.s present who have some claim to be regarded as Dissenters voted with the majority who supported the Exclusion Bill in May 1679.[4] But by thus supporting the opposition against the king's brother the Dissenters forfeited the goodwill of Charles for the rest of the reign. Whereas until 1673 it had been Parliament which had persecuted the Dissenters and the king who had tried to alleviate their sufferings, from 1679 onwards these roles were reversed. The First Exclusion Parliament was dissolved in July and the second, elected in August and September, was not allowed to meet until October 1680. When it did the Exclusion Bill was defeated in the Lords and a bill to repeal the Act of 1593 against Dissenters, though it was passed by both Houses, failed when the king ordered the clerk not to present it for his signature.[5] The Second Exclusion Parliament was dissolved in January 1681 and the third, which met in Oxford in March, lasted only a week.[6] For the rest of the

---

[1] Ibid., p. 500.
[2] Lacey, *Dissent and Parliamentary Politics*, pp. 476–9.
[3] Ibid., pp. 408–9, 384.   [4] Ibid., p. 131.
[5] Halley, *First Earl of Shaftesbury*, p. 619.
[6] Lacey calculates that there were twenty-five definite and twenty-seven possible Dissenters in the Second Exclusion Parliament, and twenty-five definite and twenty-one possible Dissenters in the Oxford or Third Exclusion Parliament. *Dissent and Parliamentary Politics*, pp. 476–9.

reign Charles, now in receipt of French subsidies, could afford to do without Parliament and the Dissenters were left to suffer the full force of royal vengeance.

The persecution which thus began with the dissolution of the Oxford Parliament was the most severe of the Restoration period. In April Francis Smith, the General Baptist printer whose news-sheet, *Smith's Protestant Intelligence*, had played a leading part in the Whig election campaign earlier in the year, was committed to Newgate on a charge of treason.[1] In December at Southwark fines amounting to £9,680 were imposed on twenty-two Dissenting ministers, among them John Owen, Samuel Annesley, and the second Edmund Calamy.[2] In the following year Benjamin Agas was fined £840 for holding conventicles at St. Giles-in-the-Fields and Arthur Barham was fined £600 for similar offences at Hackney.[3] In October 1682 the informer John Hilton stated that he was employing more than fifty men every Sunday in tracking down conventicles, and claimed that in six months he had obtained convictions which had cost Dissenters over £10,000 in the city of London and another £7,000 in Westminster.[4] By December so many Norwich Quakers were in prison that their Monthly Meeting had to be held in Norwich gaol.[5] And, most tragic of all, Newgate continued to take its toll of Dissenting lives. Francis Bampfield, an ejected clergyman who had adopted Seventh-day Baptist views and spent ten years in prison, died there in 1684, as did Thomas Delaune, together with his wife and children, imprisoned for publishing *A Plea for the Nonconformists*.[6]

The renewed persecution was particularly intense in Bristol where, in December 1681, a mob headed by an attorney named John Hellier wrecked the Presbyterian, Quaker, and two Baptist meeting-houses, causing damage estimated at £200.[7] By January 1682 all the Bristol Dissenters, apart from the Quakers, had decided to give up their public services and meet secretly in fields and woods, but this did not deter Hellier and his followers who on one occasion chased a Presbyterian minister named

---

[1] Ibid., p. 115. Halley, *First Earl of Shaftesbury*, p. 640.
[2] *CSPD* 1680–1, p. 613.   [3] *Calamy Revised*, pp. 3, 28.
[4] *CSPD* 1682, p. 520.
[5] A. J. Eddington, *The First Fifty Years of Quakerism in Norwich* (1932), p. 181.
[6] *Calamy Revised*, p. 26. Whiting, *English Puritanism*, pp. 127–8.
[7] *Broadmead Records*, pp. 218–19, 221.

Knight and a mercer named Ford into the River Avon, so that the mercer drowned and the minister died soon afterwards.[1] Meanwhile the pastor of the Broadmead Baptist church, George Fownes, was thrown into Gloucester gaol where he died in November 1685, after nearly three years in prison.[2] As for the Bristol Quakers, by June 1682 150 were in prison and the meetings were maintained by their children who met outside their nailed-up meeting-house until they were put into the stocks and beaten by Hellier 'with a twisted whale-bone stick'.[3] In 1684 two prominent Bristol Dissenters were prosecuted under the Elizabethan Act of 1593. Dr. Ichabod Chauncey, a Congregationalist physician, agreed to take the oath abjuring the realm and fled to the Netherlands, but Richard Vickris, a Quaker merchant, refused to take the oath and lay under sentence of death until William Penn used his friendship with the Duke of York to obtain a reprieve.[4] Finally, in 1685, the city council, anxious to make good a deficit in the corporation finances, resorted to what was for Bristol a novel form of persecution: that of electing Dissenters to the council and then fining them if they declined to take the oaths of loyalty and the Anglican sacrament in order to serve. The Quakers in particular were selected for this dubious honour, and three fines of £200, two fines of £100, and other fines of £50 were levied.[5]

The severity of the persecution in the years after 1681 is nowhere better illustrated than in the sufferings of Richard Baxter. Baxter was the most reluctant of all Dissenters, in reality the last of the Puritans, a man of 'no sect or party' who repudiated the name of Presbyterian and conscientiously took the sacrament at his parish church.[6] Apart from a brief period in prison in 1670 he had hitherto largely escaped persecution, but towards the end of 1682, when he was 'newly risen from extremity of pain', he was surprised at his home in Bloomsbury by an informer and constables who sought to arrest him for breaking the Five Mile Act and to fine him £190 'for five sermons'. Baxter's physician persuaded the magistrates that the old Puritan 'could not go to prison without danger of death' and,

---

[1] Ibid., pp. 228, 236, 238, 250, 253.   [2] Ibid., pp. 248, 274.
[3] Braithwaite, *SPQ*, pp. 102–3.   [4] Ibid., p. 107. *Broadmead Records*, p. 272.
[5] Mortimer, 'Quakerism in Seventeenth Century Bristol', p. 347.
[6] *Reliquiae Baxterianae*, part ii, pp. 387, 436.

with the king's consent, imprisonment was postponed, but Baxter was deprived of his cherished books and even of the bed that he 'lay sick on'. Two years later his home was again raided and he was compelled to put down a bond of £400 as a guarantee of his good behaviour; and in February 1685 he was arrested again, on the ground that he had published a veiled attack on the bishops in his *Paraphrase of the New Testament*. By now a very sick man, aged beyond his sixty-nine years and 'nothing but skin and bones', Baxter was tried before Judge Jeffreys who abused him as 'an old schismatical knave, a hypocritical villain'. He was found guilty of sedition and sent to prison, from which he scarcely hoped to emerge alive.[1]

Dissenters could not look to Parliament, as they had done between 1675 and 1681, for relief from persecution. Charles II, illegally, called no Parliament between the dissolution of the Oxford Parliament and his death in February 1685, and in the Parliament called by James II for May 1685 court influence, the forfeiture of the borough charters, and fear of rebellion kept the number of opposition M.P.s, according to James's own estimate, down to forty and the number of Dissenting M.P.s down to three or four.[2] Some Dissenters so despaired of obtaining redress for their grievances by legal means that they resorted to violence. Robert Ferguson, an ejected Presbyterian minister, and three Baptists and former Cromwellian officers, Richard Rumbold, Abraham Holmes, and Thomas Walcot, were involved in the abortive Rye House plot of 1683 and accused of designing to kill Charles II and his brother on the way back from the races at Newmarket.[3] More Dissenters gave their support to the Duke of Monmouth's rebellion against James II in June 1685. A declaration promising annual parliaments, no standing army without Parliament's consent, and equality for all Protestants was drawn up by Robert Ferguson and issued by Monmouth, and after his landing at Lyme Charles's illegitimate son received the support of numerous Dissenters from Devon and Somerset as he marched to defeat at Sedgemoor.[4] Dis-

[1] Ibid., part iii. pp. 191, 198–200. J. M. Lloyd Thomas, ed., *The Autobiography of Richard Baxter* (1931), pp. 257–64.

[2] Lacey, *Dissent and Parliamentary Politics*, p. 165. F. C. Turner, *James II* (1948), pp. 253–6.

[3] Underwood, *English Baptists*, pp. 107–8.

[4] Lacey, *Dissent and Parliamentary Politics*, pp. 168–72.

senters figured prominently among the 150 or so who were executed for their part in the rebellion. Richard Rumbold and Abraham Holmes who, unlike Thomas Walcot, had escaped the consequences of their involvement in the Rye House plot, were now caught and executed. So, too, were the ejected Presbyterian minister John Hicks, Samuel Lark, the pastor of Lyme Baptist church, and two grandsons of William Kiffin, the venerable pastor of the Devonshire Square Particular Baptist church in London. The most pathetic victim of royalist vengeance was, however, Elizabeth Gaunt, a Baptist who kept a chandler's shop in Whitechapel and who, according to Bishop Burnet, devoted herself to 'visiting gaols and looking after the poor of every persuasion'. A rebel to whom she had given shelter saved his own neck by informing against her, and Judge Jeffreys had her burnt at the stake at Tyburn.[1]

Then, in 1686, came a dramatic reversal in royal policy. James II's dispensation of the Test Act to enable Roman Catholics to hold high office, the maintenance of a standing army on Hounslow Heath, and the establishment of an ecclesiastical commission to enforce a pro-Catholic policy on the Church of England, so antagonized Anglicans that the king conceived the plan of uniting Protestant Dissenters and Roman Catholics against the persecuting state church. In March 1686 James issued a general pardon to Dissenters imprisoned for breaches of the penal code, some 1,200 Quakers were freed, and in November Baxter was released after seventeen months in prison.[2] In April 1687 this policy was completed by a Declaration of Indulgence suspending both the penal laws and the Test Acts.

Some contemporaries and some historians have maintained that James was a sincere believer in religious toleration.[3] Prominent among James's contemporary apologists was William Penn, whose father had won James's friendship when they had both served in the admiralty. Penn had campaigned for the exclusionist and future Whig martyr Algernon Sidney in both

---

[1] Underwood, *English Baptists*, pp. 108–9. *Calamy Revised*, p. 260. *DNB* vii. 951–2.

[2] Lacey, *Dissent and Parliamentary Politics*, pp. 176, 339. Thomas, *Autobiography of Richard Baxter*, p. 264.

[3] e.g. Whiting, *English Puritanism*, p. 180. M. P. Ashley in *Historical Essays, 1660–1750, presented to David Ogg*, ed. H. E. Bell and R. L. Ollard (1963), p. 202.

elections of 1679, but by 1686 he was desperately anxious to earn royal favour in order to retain the charter for his colony of Pennsylvania, a charter which he had obtained from Charles II in 1681 in payment of a debt owing to his father.[1] James, for his part, saw the importance of using Penn's influence among the Quakers in support of royal policy, and even used him to gain approval of his policy from his son-in-law William of Orange. In May 1687 Penn headed a deputation from the Friends' Yearly Meeting to express their thanks to the king for his Indulgence, and a total of eighty such addresses were presented by various Baptist, Congregational, and Presbyterian ministers and churches.[2]

On the other hand, as in 1672, there were many Dissenters who disliked a toleration granted by royal prerogative, and more who distrusted the motives of a Catholic king. It was only seventeen months since Louis XIV had revoked the Edict of Nantes and destroyed the last vestiges of liberty enjoyed by French Huguenots, and English Protestants, both Dissenting and Anglican, found it difficult to believe that James II's policy would not issue in similar conclusion. The Presbyterian Daniel Williams persuaded a meeting of London Dissenting ministers not to present an address of thanks to the king, arguing that 'it were better for them to be reduced to their former hardships, than declare for measures destructive of the liberties of their country'.[3] William Kiffin, broken-hearted by 'the death of my poor boys', used his influence among the Baptists to the same end.[4] And Baxter, explaining why he, too, could not support an address to the king, wrote that for thirty-five years he had 'made love, concord, and peace the main study of my life; and . . . dare not violate it causelessly with the body of conforming clergy'.[5]

Baxter's comment is significant, for one of the consequences of the king's pro-Catholic policy was, as in 1673, the appearance

---

[1] Peare, *William Penn*, pp. 205, 209–13. Lacey, *Dissent and Parliamentary Politics*, p. 182.

[2] Braithwaite, *SPQ*, p. 133. Lacey, *Dissent and Parliamentary Politics*, p. 341.

[3] Dale, *English Congregationalism*, p. 451.

[4] *Remarkable Passages in the Life of William Kiffin*, ed. W. Orme (1823), p. 83. Underwood, *English Baptists*, p. 110.

[5] Quoted by R. Thomas in *From Uniformity to Unity*, ed. G. F. Nuttall and W. O. Chadwick (1962), p. 237.

of a more tolerant attitude towards Dissent on the part of moderate Anglicans. In April 1688 James reissued his Declaration of Indulgence and ordered the bishops to circularize it throughout their dioceses and have it read in every parish church on two successive Sundays. There followed the refusal and petition of the seven bishops, their imprisonment in the Tower, their trial for seditious libel, and their acquittal. But in declining to publicize the Indulgence the bishops obtained the prior agreement of Dissenting ministers in London and in their petition to the king the bishops disclaimed 'any want of due tenderness towards the Dissenters'.[1] On his release from the Tower Archbishop Sancroft issued instructions to his clergy 'to have a very tender regard to our brethren the Protestant Dissenters', 'to visit them at their houses and receive them kindly at their own', and to assure them 'that the bishops of the Church are really and sincerely irreconcilable enemies to the erroneous superstititions, idolatries, and tyrannies of the Church of Rome'.[2]

The luckless James II thus not only gave the Dissenters freedom of worship for the last two years of his reign, he broke the back of Anglican intolerance and made possible the permanent toleration of Dissent once William of Orange had landed at Torbay and James himself had fled to France. In the election to the Convention Parliament in February 1689 the number of M.P.s who may have been Dissenters increased to thirty,[3] and on 28 February the Tory Earl of Nottingham introduced into the Lords the bill which three months later became law as the Toleration Act. By the terms of the Act Protestant Trinitarian Dissenters who took the oaths of allegiance and supremacy and obtained a licence for their meetings were exempt from the penalties of the Elizabethan Act of 1593 and the Conventicle Act of 1670, and Nonconformist ministers who subscribed to thirty-six of the thirty-nine articles were exempt from the penalties of the Act of Uniformity and of the Five Mile Act. Baptist ministers were also excused subscription to the article on infant baptism and Quakers were allowed to make a declaration

[1] Thomas in *From Uniformity to Unity*, p. 239. Lacey, *Dissent and Parliamentary Politics*, p. 210.

[2] T. Birch, *The Life of Dr. John Tillotson* (1752), pp. 165–6.

[3] Lacey, *Dissent and Parliamentary Politics*, pp. 224, 476–9. Lacey estimates that nineteen were definite Dissenters and eleven possible or probable Dissenters.

instead of taking the oaths. But Roman Catholics and any who denied the doctrine of the Trinity were specifically excluded from the benefits of the Act.

The 'Glorious Revolution' thus gave orthodox Dissenters statutory freedom to worship in their own way, but it did not give them civil equality. In March 1689 William III urged Parliament to remove the obstacles to Protestant Dissenters entering public service, but there was a furious Tory reaction, even talk of preventing Dissenters from sitting in Parliament, and attempts to remove the sacramental test from the Test Act of 1673 and to repeal the Corporation Act both failed.[1] So, too, did a last attempt to remove Presbyterian objections to the Act of Uniformity: a Comprehension Bill had been introduced into the Lords on 27 February, but the Tories in the Lords tried to make it less generous to the Nonconformists, the Whigs in the Commons tried to make it less acceptable to the Anglicans, and the bill finally disappeared when the Whigs agreed to drop it in return for Tory support for the Toleration Bill.[2]

The Revolution thus marked the victory of the Independent concept of toleration over Presbyterian hopes of comprehension. It also completed the metamorphosis of Presbyterianism from the religion of a national church to that of a Dissenting sect. After James's Declaration of Indulgence the cautious and conservative Cheshire Presbyterian Philip Henry had continued to attend Anglican services 'whenever there was preaching' and preached at his own house only when there was not, but after the passing of the Toleration Act 'he was at last prevailed with to preach at public time every Lord's day', and continued to do so until his death seven years later.[3]

The Revolution was also a vindication of Independent political theory. A century earlier Robert Browne had argued from the right of a church to elect and dismiss its pastor and elders to the right of citizens to choose and reject their rulers, and this theory was now given classic expression by John Locke, who as an Oxford undergraduate in the 1650s had listened to John Owen's sermons and had been taught by the future Congrega-

---

[1] Lacey, *Dissent and Parliamentary Politics*, p. 233. Dale, *English Congregationalism*, p. 466.

[2] Thomas in *From Uniformity to Unity*, pp. 245–53.

[3] *Diaries of Philip Henry*, pp. 328–9.

tional minister Thomas Cole. Whereas the Independents saw the origin of a church as a covenant between men to serve God, so Locke saw the origins of civil society as a covenant between men to protect life, liberty, and property. And just as the Independents taught that a church could exist without a pastor, so Locke taught that the existence of society was prior to its choice of a ruler.[1] Even the great ambiguity of Locke's work, his failure to reconcile the rights of property with the rule of the majority, reflects the difficulty involved in transferring democratic theories from a voluntary church to a coercive state, a problem experienced by the Congregationalists of Massachusetts in their attempts to legislate both for the reprobate and for the elect.

Finally, the Revolution of 1688 marked the end of the heroic age of Dissent. One by one their greatest leaders were passing from the stage. John Owen had died in 1683, aged sixty-seven, leaving, as he said, 'the ship of the church in a storm, but while the great Pilot is in it, the loss of a poor under-tower will be inconsiderable'.[2] John Bunyan died in August 1688, at the age of fifty-nine. In his last years both his preaching and his writing had earned him fame: 3,000 people were said to have come to hear him preach in a London meeting-house, of whom half had to be turned away through lack of room, and 100,000 copies of *The Pilgrim's Progress* alone had been sold. But now Bunyan 'desired nothing more than to be dissolved and to be with Christ'.[3] George Fox followed him to the grave in January 1691, aged sixty-six, spending his last hours, 'as if death were hardly worth notice or a mention', in arranging 'the despatch and dispersion of an epistle just before written to the churches of Christ throughout the world'.[4] And Richard Baxter also died in 1691, in December, having lived, despite nearly a lifetime of ill health, to the age of seventy-six. 'Weakness and pain', he had written, had helped him 'to study how to die'. He had 'talked in the pulpit', commented the third Edmund Calamy, 'with great freedom about another world, like one that had been there and was come as a sort of express from thence to make a report concerning it'.[5]

[1] Nuttall, *Visible Saints*, pp. 76–7, 85–6.
[2] Jones, *Congregationalism in England*, p. 101.
[3] Tindall, *John Bunyan*, pp. 210–11. Brown, *John Bunyan*, p. 374.
[4] Penn's preface to *Fox's Journal*, p. xlviii.
[5] Thomas, *Autobiography of Richard Baxter*, pp. xiii, xviii.

The period of persecution had enabled the Dissenters to reveal their greatest qualities: their faith, their courage, their largely unwavering loyalty to God rather than to the state. But whether they had the qualities necessary to survive the ensuing period of toleration remained to be seen. Eight days before his death George Fox had issued a warning. He contrasted the present ease enjoyed by the Quakers with their earlier hardships, and 'complained of many Demases and Cains who embrace the present world and encumber themselves with their own businesses and neglect the Lord's and so are good for nothing'.[1]

[1] Braithwaite, *SPQ*, p. 437.

IV

'A PLAIN CALLED EASE': THE
TOLERATION OF DISSENT, 1690–1730

I. 'THE MERCIES OF THE LORD':
THE LAST STUART AND THE FIRST HANOVERIAN

In Bunyan's vision of *The Pilgrim's Progress* the way to the
Celestial City lay through Vanity Fair. It was a place where
Christian and his companion Faithful were subjected to violent
abuse, beaten up by the mob, chained in irons, and thrown into
a cage as a public spectacle. Faithful was charged with denying
the validity of the town's religion, inciting disloyalty to its
rulers, and speaking contemptuously of its nobility. He was
sentenced to be scourged and burnt at the stake. But Christian
escaped from Vanity Fair and 'came to a delicate plain, called
Ease' where he travelled 'with much content'. This was not,
though, the end of his trials: 'at the farthest side of that plain
was a little hill called Lucre, and in that hill a silver mine'. And
beyond the hill lay Doubting Castle.

Such, in epitome, was the history of Dissent from the persecution of the Restoration period, through the relief of toleration, to the material prosperity yet spiritual decline of the early
eighteenth century. Toleration was not irrevocable after 1690.
The trust deeds of meeting-houses built in the reigns of William
and Mary and of Anne contained provisions that, in the event of
the proscription of Dissenting worship, the buildings should be
sold and the proceeds used for the benefit of the poor.[1] The
arrogant and vindictive High Churchman Henry Sacheverell,
himself the grandson of an ejected Presbyterian minister who
had died in Dorchester gaol, railed against Dissenters as 'mis-
creants begat in rebellion, born in sedition, and nursed in
faction'.[2] For satirizing such views in *The Shortest Way with*

---

[1] A. G. Cumberland, 'Protestant Nonconformity in the Black Country', Birmingham University M.A. thesis, 1951, pp. 37–8. W. Whitaker, *Bowl Alley Lane
Chapel, Hull* (1910), pp. 77–8.

[2] H. Sacheverell, *The Perils of False Brethren* (1709, reprinted in Exeter, 1974),
p. 36.

Dissenters the Presbyterian Daniel Defoe was sentenced in 1703 to stand in the pillory. In the previous year a Tory mob had celebrated the death of William III by attacking the Dissenting meeting-house at Newcastle-under-Lyme, and eight years later similar mobs, inflamed by the nectar of Bacchus and the impeachment of Sacheverell, plundered and burned meeting-houses in London, Bristol, Gainsborough, and Walsall. Further riots followed the accession of George I when, in 1715, Jacobite mobs marked the Pretender's birthday by wrecking some thirty Dissenting meeting-houses, eleven of them in Staffordshire and six in Lancashire.[1] The Toleration Act failed to make clear the legal position of Dissenting schools and academies, so that Dissenting schoolmasters could still be prosecuted in both ecclesiastical and civil courts for teaching without an episcopal licence. As late as 1733 the chancellor of the diocese of Peterborough prosecuted Philip Doddridge for conducting his Northampton academy without licence, though the case did issue in a victory for the Dissenters.[2] Other loop-holes in the law provided would-be persecutors with the pretexts on which to harass Dissenting ministers. In 1738 an attempt was made to compel the Presbyterian Samuel Bourn to leave his pastorate at Coseley in Staffordshire on the ground that he might 'become chargeable to the parish', and in 1712 the Congregationalist Matthias Maurice was even seized by the press-gang at Haverfordwest and transported in a man-o'-war to London.[3] But all such incidents were, after 1690, the exception rather than the norm: for the most part Dissenters were now able to go about their daily business without fear of the informer, the constable, and the magistrate.

Though they had been obliged to concede religious liberty to

---

[1] G. Holmes, *The Trial of Doctor Sacheverell* (1973), pp. 162–74, 235. E. Calamy, *An Historical Account of My Own Life* (1829), i. 46. D. Bogue and J. Bennett, *History of Dissenters* (1808–12), i. 257. A. G. Matthews, 'Some Notes on Staffordshire Nonconformity', *TCHS* xii (1933–6), 7–9. John Evans, List of Dissenting congregations and ministers, 1715–29, DWL MS. 38. 4, p. 150. W. I. Williams, 'Some Aspects of Non-Conformity in the North-West of England, 1650–1750', Univ. of Wales M.A. thesis, 1973, p. 51.

[2] A. G. Cumberland, 'The Toleration Act of 1689 and Freedom for Protestant Nonconformists', London Ph.D. thesis, 1957, pp. 144–8. J. D. Humphreys, ed., *The Correspondence and Diary of Philip Doddridge* (1830), iii. 127–9, 139–40.

[3] J. Toulmin, *Memoirs of the Rev. Samuel Bourn* (Birmingham, 1808), pp. 243–8. Rees, *Nonconformity in Wales*, p. 303.

Dissenters, rigid Anglicans were most reluctant to extend to them civil equality. Quakers continued to suffer fines and imprisonment for non-payment of tithes and for refusing oaths, and although an Act of 1696 allowed Quakers to make an affirmation rather than swear on oath, many Friends refused to make the affirmation on the ground that the words used were tantamount to an oath.[1] But the chief source of contention between High Churchmen and Dissenters in the thirty years following the passing of the Toleration Act was the practice of some Presbyterians and a few Congregationalists, though not of the Baptists and Quakers, of taking the Anglican sacrament in order to qualify for office under the terms of the Test and Corporation Acts. From the point of view of the Presbyterians at least the practice was theologically defensible, and some Presbyterians had continued to communicate with the Church of England after 1662, as Calamy said, 'with a design to show their charity towards that church'.[2] But the sight of the Presbyterian Sir Humphrey Edwin, lord mayor of London in 1697, attending parish communion in the morning and a Dissenting service in the afternoon, and of Sir Thomas Abney, another Presbyterian, taking the Anglican sacrament so that he could serve as lord mayor of London in 1700, was an affront to High Church consciences.[3] 'To qualify themselves for a paltry place', complained Sacheverell, 'these crafty, faithless, and insidious persons ... slyly creep to those altars they proclaim idolatrous.'[4]

A bill to prevent all Dissenters, whether occasional conformists or not, from serving on borough corporations or in offices under the crown was rejected by the Commons in February 1702, but the accession of Queen Anne in the following month and the Tory victory in the subsequent elections encouraged the High Church party to persist in its efforts. A bill to prevent occasional conformity passed the Commons in November 1702 but was wrecked in the Lords, thanks to the Whig peers and bishops created by William III, and similar bills were again thrown out by the Lords in 1703 and 1704.[5] The Whigs won a majority in

[1] Braithwaite, *SPQ*, pp. 181–9.   [2] Calamy, *Historical Account*, i. 473.
[3] Ibid. i. 400. Dale, *English Congregationalism*, pp. 487–8.
[4] Holmes, *Trial of Sacheverell*, p. 53.
[5] Dale, *English Congregationalism*, pp. 489–91. P. M. Scholes, 'Parliament and the Protestant Dissenters, 1702–19', London M.A. thesis, 1962, pp. 23–32.

the elections of 1705 and the occasional conformists obtained a temporary reprieve, but the Tories were victorious again in 1710 in the wake of Sacheverell's impeachment, and this time, as part of a bargain with dissident Tories led by the Earl of Nottingham, the Whigs dropped their opposition and in 1711 the Bill for Preventing Occasional Conformity became law.

The Act did not, however, have the expected effect. The Whigs and Hanoverian agents in England urged Dissenting office-holders to abstain temporarily from public worship rather than resign their posts, and most followed the example of Sir Thomas Abney who held on to both his offices and his convictions by holding private services in his own home, conducted by his friend Isaac Watts.[1] The High Church party consequently resumed the attack on Dissent, and chose as its target the Dissenting academies which Sacheverell declared to be the breeding ground of 'Atheism, Deism, Tritheism, Socinianism, with all the hellish principles of Fanaticism, Regicide, and Anarchy'.[2] In 1714 Parliament passed a bill 'to prevent the growth of schism' by forbidding anyone who attended Dissenting meetings from teaching on pain of three months in prison, a measure which struck at the very heart of Presbyterianism in particular by seeking to destroy its hopes of perpetuating an educated ministry. But on the very day that the Schism Act was to come into force, Sunday, 1 August 1714, Thomas Bradbury, the pastor of the Congregational church meeting in Fetter Lane, met the Whig Bishop Burnet in Smithfield. Bradbury was on his way to conduct morning service, the bishop was going to the royal palace where Queen Anne lay dying. If she died during the morning, Burnet promised, he would send a messenger to Bradbury's meeting-house and he woud indicate the passing of the queen by dropping a handkerchief from the gallery. While the service was in progress the messenger arrived and the agreed signal was given. Bradbury finished his sermon and in his closing prayer 'implored the divine blessing upon his majesty King George and the house of Hanover'.[3]

[1] Calamy, *Historical Account*, ii. 245–6.
[2] Sacheverell, *Perils of False Brethren*, p. 25.
[3] W. Wilson, *History and Antiquity of Dissenting Churches in London* (1808–14), iii. 513.

The accession of George I meant the triumph of the Whigs and the eclipse of the Tories. Dissenters gave loyal support to the new dynasty: when the Jacobites rebelled in the north of England in 1715 the North Shields Presbyterian meeting in Northumberland raised a hundred men in the name of the new king; in Lancashire John Turner, Presbyterian minister at Preston, and 'many of the younger part of his congregation' were used as scouts by government troops; and James Wood, minister at Chowbent, 'headed a body composed of all the hale and hearty men of his congregation, armed with all the instruments of husbandry, and marched to Preston, and secured the possession of Walton bridge' against the rebels.[1] The Whigs, in return, remedied the Dissenters' more recent grievances. The Riot Act of 1715 made the destruction of meeting-houses a felony and Dissenters received £5,000 from the Treasury as compensation for the damage done to their property; the Act for Preventing Occasional Conformity and the Schism Act were both repealed in 1719; and in 1722 the words of the affirmation were altered to meet the objections of the more scrupulous Quakers.[2] Well might Thomas Bradbury's congregation, on that Sunday morning in August 1714, end their service with the singing of the eighty-ninth Psalm. 'I will sing of the mercies of the Lord for ever'.

2. THE EVANS MANUSCRIPT:
THE GEOGRAPHIC DISTRIBUTION OF DISSENT

It is likely that it was the need to secure an early repeal of the Schism Act which in 1715 prompted a committee of London ministers to set in motion a survey of Dissenting congregations throughout the country. This Committee of the Three Denominations, consisting of four Presbyterians, three Congregationalists, and three Baptists, had been set up in 1702 to protect Dissenting interests from Tory designs on the accession of Queen Anne,[3] and after her death it was decided to write to correspondents

---

[1] Evans list, p. 90. B. Nightingale, *Lancashire Nonconformity* (1890–93), i. 11. E. D. Bebb, *Nonconformity and Social and Economic Life* (1935), p. 80, n. 2.

[2] Calamy, *Historical Account*, ii. 369. Braithwaite, *SPQ*, pp. 202–3.

[3] Calamy, *Historical Account*, i. 460. J. Ivimey, *History of the English Baptists* (1811–30), iii. 42. In 1717 the size of the committee was increased to sixteen, comprising six Presbyterians, six Congregationalists, and six Baptists. Scholes, 'Parliament and the Protestant Dissenters', p. 127.

throughout England and Wales, asking for the location of every Dissenting congregation, the name of its minister, the number and quality of his 'hearers', and the number of votes the congregation could command. The results were for the most part collected in by 1718, though further information continued to be added until 1729, and at least two records of the survey were compiled: one by the Congregationalist Daniel Neal, author of *The History of the Puritans*, and the other by the secretary of the Committee of the Three Denominations, Dr. John Evans, the minister of the Hand Alley Presbyterian meeting in London. Neal's list is now lost, though a copy was made by a retired Baptist minister, Josiah Thompson, when he made a further survey in 1772–3. The much fuller Evans list is preserved in Dr. Williams's Library in London.[1] The task of interpreting the Evans list bristles with difficulties, but it is the most detailed and comprehensive survey we have of Dissenting strength before the religious census of 1851, and some attempt must be made to assess the information it contains.

The Evans manuscript purports to list every Presbyterian, Independent, and Baptist congregation in England and Wales. As far as the paedobaptist congregations are concerned the list appears to be fairly complete, but W. T. Whitley subjected the list to close scrutiny on behalf of the Baptists sixty years ago and found some seventy-odd churches not listed by Dr. Evans, and local studies are revealing other gaps in the list.[2] Dr. Evans had no correspondence with Quakers, and most of his correspondents made no attempt to assess the strength of Quakerism in their areas, but it is possible to calculate the number of Quaker particular meetings existing in the early eighteenth century from the 'Index to Meetings for Church Affairs', compiled by Edward Milligan and deposited in the Friends House library, and by supplementing this index from contemporary material.[3] On the basis of these various sources it is possible to estimate the

---

[1] Evans list, DWL MS. 38.4. Josiah Thompson list, DWL. MS. 38. 5, 6. There are two slightly different versions of the Thompson list.

[2] *TBHS* ii (1910–11), 95–109. M. Reeves, 'Protestant Nonconformity', in *VCH Wiltshire*, iii (1956), 108–15.

[3] In particular, 'The Account of the Severall Meetings in the Eight Western Counties', 1696, Friends House library, Dix MS. I. 1B, and D. M. Butler, 'Meeting Houses Built and Meetings Settled', *JFHS* li (1965–7), 174–211. I am indebted to Edward Milligan for transcribing the 1696 'Account' for me.

total number of Dissenting congregations in England and Wales in the second decade of the eighteenth century, as shown in Table I.

TABLE I

Dissenting congregations, 1715–1718

	England (including Monmouthshire)	Wales	Total
Presbyterians	637	25	662
Independents	203	26	229
Particular Baptists	206	14	220
General Baptists	122	0	122
Seventh-day Baptists	5	0	5
Quakers	672	24	696
	1,845	89	1,934

Dr. Evans's correspondents not only supplied him with the location of Dissenting congregations, many of them also furnished him with an estimate of the number of 'hearers' who frequented their services, and although the accuracy of such estimates has sometimes been questioned, comparison with early-eighteenth-century church-membership lists, with episcopal visitation returns for the first half of the century, and with contemporary Presbyterian and Congregational baptismal registers, suggests that at least as far as England is concerned the statistics in the Evans list are a reliable base from which to estimate the number of Presbyterian, Independent, and Baptist adherents.[1] As for the Quakers, it is possible to calculate their numbers both from episcopal visitation returns, where these exist, and from the transcripts of Quaker burial registers in Friends House. One can thus arrive at an estimate for the total number of Dissenters in the early eighteenth century, and by calculating the population of England on the basis of Davenant and Houghton's lists of households at the end of the seventeenth century, the number of Dissenters can be expressed as a proportion of the total population.[2] The results of these calculations are given in Table II.

[1] See Appendix, pp. 491–504.
[2] For the details of these calculations see Appendix, pp. 505–510.

TABLE II

Total number of Dissenters in early-eighteenth-century England

	Estimated numbers	Percentage of total population
Presbyterians	179,350	3·30
Independents	59,940	1·10
Particular Baptists	40,520	0·74
General Baptists	18,800	0·35
Quakers	39,510	0·73
All Dissenters	338,120	6·21
Total population (including Monmouthshire)	5,441,670	

The Evans-list figures for Wales are more suspect than those for England, and the Quaker registers for most Welsh counties in the early eighteenth century are lost, but what figures I have been able to collect for the principality are given in Table III.

TABLE III

Total number of Dissenters in early-eighteenth-century Wales

	Estimated numbers	Percentage of total population
Presbyterians	6,080	1·96
Independents	7,640	2·47
Particular Baptists	4,050	1·31
All Dissenters	17,770	5·74
Total population	309,750	

The same method can be used to plot the geographic distribution of Dissent.[1] The Presbyterians appear to have constituted more than 8 per cent of the population of Lancashire, more than 7 per cent of Cheshire, Devon, and the city of Bristol, more than 6 per cent of Somerset, more than 5 per cent of Dorset and Northumberland, and more than 4 per cent of Berkshire, Derbyshire, Essex, Nottinghamshire, and Staffordshire. They were also numerous in Carmarthenshire, where they had seventeen congregations, though the Evans-list figure of 4,750

---

[1] See maps on pp. 272–6 and Tables XII and XIII on pp. 509–10.

Presbyterian hearers in the county, which gives a proportion to the total population of more than 13 per cent, is probably exaggerated.[1]

The heavy concentration of Presbyterians in these areas can usually be explained by one or more of four factors, which themselves were often interrelated: a Puritan tradition going back well before the Civil War; the presence either of a large number, or of particularly energetic, ejected ministers after 1662; deficiencies in the parochial organization of the Church of England; and the existence of a large population which earned its living either by trade or by manufacture, especially of textiles. The foundations for the numerous Presbyterian congregations of Lancashire, Cheshire, and Devon had been laid in the reign of Elizabeth, whose governments had tolerated Puritanism to counter the continuing influence of Roman Catholicism in those distant counties.[2] In Lancashire and Cheshire Elizabeth's Privy Council had approved and even encouraged the holding of ministerial conferences at a time when prophesyings were forbidden in the province of Canterbury, and no attempt was made to root out Puritanism until the 1630s, by which time it was too late.[3] In Devon Puritanism had been fostered in the Elizabethan period through the patronage of Francis Russell, Earl of Bedford, and had been reinforced during the reigns of James I and Charles I by the influence of Exeter College, Oxford, whose rector, John Prideaux, had attempted to preserve the college as an island of Calvinism amidst the rising sea of Arminianism. Sixty-four of the ministers ejected after the Restoration had been educated at Exeter College, and a total of 121 ministers were ejected from Devonshire livings, the highest figure for any county.[4] In Northumberland Presbyterian influence can possibly traced back to visits which John Knox paid to Newcastle and Berwick in the early 1550s and it was certainly strengthened by the arrival of Scottish exiles in the 1580s,

---

[1] T. Richards, 'Nonconformity from 1620 to 1715', in *A History of Carmarthenshire*, ed. Sir John Lloyd (Cardiff, 1939), ii. 174–6.

[2] Finberg, *West Country Historical Studies*, pp. 196–8. R. Halley, *Lancashire: its Puritanism and Nonconformity* (1869), i. 129. R. C. Richardson, 'Puritanism in the Diocese of Chester', Manchester Ph.D. thesis, 1968, pp. 406–11.

[3] Collinson, *Elizabethan Puritan Movement*, pp. 210–11. Richardson, 'Puritanism in the Diocese of Chester', p. 300.

[4] *Calamy Revised*, pp. xii, lxi.

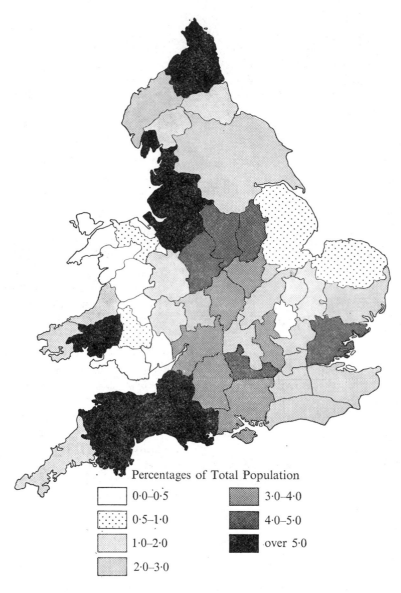

Percentages of Total Population

0·0–0·5		3·0–4·0	
0·5–1·0		4·0–5·0	
1·0–2·0		over 5·0	
2·0–3·0			

MAP 1. Distribution of Presbyterians, 1715–1718.

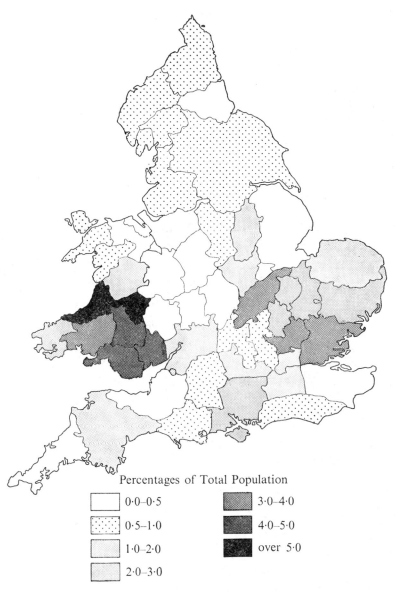

Percentages of Total Population

0·0–0·5	3·0–4·0
0·5–1·0	4·0–5·0
1·0–2·0	over 5·0
2·0–3·0	

MAP 2. Distribution of Independents, 1715–1718.

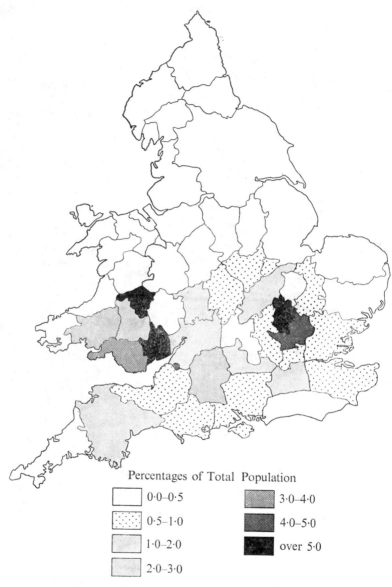

Percentages of Total Population

0·0–0·5
0·5–1·0
1·0–2·0
2·0–3·0
3·0–4·0
4·0–5·0
over 5·0

Map 3. Distribution of Particular Baptists, 1715–1718.

Percentages of Total Population

0·0–0·5

0·5–1·0

1·0–2·0

MAP 4. Distribution of General Baptists, 1715–1718.

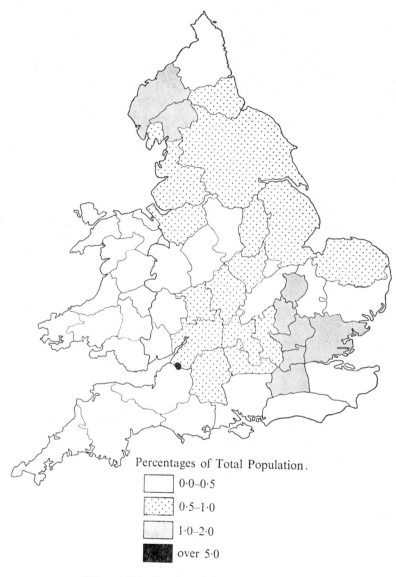

Percentages of Total Population.

         0·0–0·5

         0·5–1·0

         1·0–2·0

         over 5·0

MAP 5. Distribution of Quakers, 1700–1709

though the incursions of the Scottish army in the 1640s probably did more harm than good.[1] In Essex the strength of post-Restoration Presbyterianism probably owed a good deal to the appointment, in 1625, of the Earl of Warwick as lord lieutenant of the county. Warwick held the right of presentation to twenty-two benefices in the county, and during the episcopate and archiepiscopate of Laud shielded Essex Puritans from persecution. Ninety-nine ministers were ejected from Essex parishes after the Restoration, a figure exceeded only in Devon and Yorkshire.[2]

The survival of Presbyterianism in the north of England after 1662 was guaranteed by the inadequate parochial structure of the established church. Parishes in the dioceses of Chester, Durham, and Carlisle covered, on average, areas four times as large, and parishes in Yorkshire areas as twice as large, as parishes in southern and central England.[3] In Northumberland there were only fifty-four rectories and vicarages in the whole of the county, and Lancashire had but sixty-four parishes, six of them covering more than fifty square miles.[4] The Church of England's parochial organization had taken shape some seven or eight centuries earlier when the country's population was concentrated in the south and east,[5] and by the early eighteenth century it had been rendered obsolete by the growing population of the industrial towns of Lancashire, Northumberland, the West Riding, and north-east Cheshire. The growth of the coal and ship-building industries of Newcastle-upon-Tyne had boosted the town's population to around 18,000 by the beginning of the eighteenth century, but it was served by only four parish churches and the Evans list records the existence in the town of four Presbyterian meetings with a total of 1,900 adherents.[6] The growth of the sugar and slave trades raised the

---

[1] R. Howell, *Newcastle-upon-Tyne and the Puritan Revolution* (Oxford, 1967), pp. 78–80, 250.

[2] C. Holmes, *The Eastern Association* (1975), p. 19. *Calamy Revised*, p. xii.

[3] A. D. Gilbert, 'The Growth and Decline of Nonconformity in England and Wales', Oxford D. Phil. thesis, 1973, p. 272.

[4] Howell, *Newcastle and the Puritan Revolution*, p. 65. Richardson, 'Puritanism in the Diocese of Chester', p. 2.

[5] G. W. O. Addleshaw, *The Development of the Parochial System from Charlemagne to Urban II*, St. Anthony's Hall Publications, No. 6, 1954, pp. 13–15.

[6] F. J. C. Hearnshaw, *Newcastle-upon-Tyne* (1971), p. 74. Howell, *Newcastle and the Puritan Revolution*, p. 70.

population of Liverpool to 12,500, the development of the cotton industry raised that of Manchester to 8,000, and that of Bolton to 5,500.[1] But in the second decade of the eighteenth century Liverpool and Manchester had only two parish churches and Bolton only one, and in each town the Presbyterians claimed over 1,000 hearers. By the 1730s the inhabitants of the cutlery town of Sheffield numbered nearly 10,000, but it too had only one parish church and the Evans list credited the town's Presbyterian meeting with 1,163 adherents, a figure fully substantiated by the meeting's baptismal registers.[2] In north-east Cheshire a piece of land at Hyde was given to the Presbyterians in 1708 'to build a chapel thereupon . . . for the benefit of old people and children of the inhabitants of the three towns of Hyde, Werneth, and Haughton by reason that these three towns are so far distant from their parish churches'.[3]

Similar situations existed in parts of the Midlands, the West Country, and Wales. Nottingham, the centre of the hosiery industry, had three parish churches for a population of 8,000 and a Presbyterian meeting which claimd 1,400 hearers, again a claim which is largely confirmed by the church's baptismal registers.[4] Taunton, Somerset's principal clothing town, had two parish churches for some 9,000 inhabitants, and its Presbyterians boasted both the largest Dissenting congregation and the largest Dissenting meeting-house in the country.[5] In Somerset's second clothing town, Frome, the Presbyterians claimed 1,000 hearers in a town whose rapid population growth led Daniel Defoe to place it in the same category as Liverpool and Manchester.[6] Even in rural Carmarthenshire the Church of England was ill served by its antiquated machinery. In 1710 Archdeacon Tenison's visitation returns recorded that in the parish of Abergwili Dissenters were most numerous 'in that part of the

---

[1] The population figures for Liverpool, Manchester, and Bolton are derived from the number of families listed in Bishop Gastrell's *Notitia Cestriensis* (Chetham Society Publications, xiv (1849), 6, 57, and xxi (1850), 190), assuming an average family size of 4·5 persons.

[2] E. R. Wickham, *Church and People in an Industrial City* (1957), pp. 20, 41.

[3] T. Middleton, *A History of Hyde Chapel* (Manchester, 1908), pp. 4, 12.

[4] J. D. Chambers, 'Population Change in Nottingham, 1700–1800', in *Studies in the Industrial Revolution presented to T. S. Ashton* (1960), p. 122.

[5] Holmes, *Trial of Sacheverell*, p. 28. D. Defoe, *A Tour Through England and Wales* (1927), i. 267.

[6] Defoe, *Tour*, i. 280, ii. 262.

parish next Llanegwad' where the Anglican chapel was decayed.[1]

In Lancashire and the West Riding attempts had been made to remedy the deficiencies in the Church of England's parochial structure by building chapels of ease to serve remote parts of large parishes, and by 1650 Lancashire had nearly twice as many chapels of ease as it had parish churches.[2] But from the point of view of the established church such efforts proved largely self-defeating for chapelries were poorly endowed and irregularly served, and in at least twenty such chapels in Lancashire and the West Riding services were maintained during the reigns of Charles II and James II by Presbyterian ministers.[3] Most of the Dissenting congregations were ejected in the two decades after 1689, when licences were refused to them under the Toleration Act and the ecclesiastical authorities attempted to regain possession of the chapels, but by this time the Presbyterian ministers in such places were established in the affections of the people and appear to have acted virtually as parish ministers to the surrounding population. In 1710 an Anglican curate complained that the Presbyterian minister at Walmsley was encroaching upon his 'liberty of christening children'; four years later it was reported from Darwen that a 'great many of the inhabitants frequent a Presbyterian meeting-house' when there was no service in the Anglican chapel; and although the Presbyterians of Horwich were deprived of their chapel of ease in 1716, four years later no services were being performed there because 'the contributions of the Episcopal inhabitants are so small'.[4]

The failure of the Church of England to adapt its parochial organization to the changing economic and demographic

---

[1] Lloyd, *History of Carmarthenshire*, ii. 162.

[2] P. J. W. Higson, 'A Neglected Revolution Family: the Lancashire Lords Willoughby of Parham and their Associations with Protestant Dissent, 1640–1765', Liverpool Ph.D. thesis, 1971, p. 23.

[3] Williams, in his thesis on 'Non-Conformity in North-West England', pp. 30–1, claims that twenty-six chapels of ease were occupied by Dissenters in Lancashire alone. See also Cumberland, 'Toleration Act', pp. 139–43. Miall, *Congregationalism in Yorkshire*, pp. 294–5, 320–1. F. T. Wood, *History of Underbank Chapel, Stannington* (Sheffield, 1944), pp. 24–38. Stannington is listed as Independent in the Evans list.

[4] Nightingale, *Lancashire Nonconformity*, ii. 251, iii. 55. Higson, 'Lords Willoughby of Parham', pp. 57–8.

structure of the country provided Presbyterian ministers with fine opportunities for poaching on what Anglican clergymen regarded as their own preserves, and in three areas—the West Riding of Yorkshire, the Peak district of Derbyshire, and Carmarthenshire—such opportunities were exploited by ejected ministers of unusual zeal and energy. In 1662 Oliver Heywood was ejected from the curacy of Coley chapel near Northowram in the parish of Halifax. Halifax, in the opinion of Daniel Defoe, was the most populous parish in England, 'a monster', its rapid growth due to the great demand for its 'kersies for clothing the armies abroad'.[1] The parish covered 124 square miles and comprised twenty-six townships, and to serve this vast agglomeration the established church provided but one parish church and twelve chapels of ease. In 1743 the vicar of Halifax estimated that there were 6,200 households in his parish—which would mean a population of nearly 28,000—but the usual number of communicants at the parish church was but 160.[2] It was this situation, which had been developing since the later years of the previous century, which enabled Oliver Heywood to establish a strong Presbyterian presence in the area. When the Five Mile Act compelled him to leave his home he embarked on an itinerant mission to neighbouring towns and villages, preaching at Presbyterian meetings and in chapels of ease, and travelling on average 900 miles a year for the next thirty-five years.[3] By the time of his death in 1702 there were seven Presbyterian meetings in the parish of Halifax with a combined total of adherents which the Evans list put at over 2,000.

Presbyterian strength in Derbyshire similarly owed a good deal to the evangelistic zeal of William Bagshaw, who until 1662 was vicar of Glossop. After his ejection he had retired to his father's country residence at Ford Hall and thenceforward preached 'both at his own house and from house to house' in the Peak district, 'prudently changing the locality almost every Lord's day, that he might not expose his [congregation] to the lash' of the penal laws.[4] From the passing of the Toleration Act

---

[1] Defoe, *Tour*, ii. 197–8.

[2] S. L. Ollard and P. C. Walker, *Archbishop Herring's Visitation Returns* (Yorkshire Archaeological Society Record Series, 1927–31, vols. lxxi-ii, lxxv, lxxvii, lxxix), ii. 32–3.

[3] Hunter, *Life of Heywood*, pp. 174–94. *Heywood's Autobiography*, ii. 227–8.

[4] W. H. G. Bagshawe, *A Memoire of William Bagshaw* (1887), pp. 9–10.

until his death in 1702 at the age of 74 'the Apostle of the Peak' preached regularly to ten congregations, the continuing existence of at least six of which is recorded in the Evans list.[1] Likewise in Carmarthenshire much of the Presbyterian influence of the early eighteenth century can be traced to the labours of Stephen Hughes, ejected from Meidrim. Hughes's particular concern was that the people of Wales should be taught in their native tongue and he both published Welsh translations of the Puritan classics and co-operated with Thomas Gouge, also an ejected minister, in the trust which made possible the printing of 8,000 Welsh Bibles. On most Sundays until his death in 1688 Hughes rode to preach to scattered congregations throughout Carmarthenshire, and at least eight of the meetings recorded in the Evans list claimed to be founded by him.[2]

In London and the counties to the north of the capital Presbyterianism had perforce to share the Puritan inheritance with Congregationalism. In England the Independents were strongest in those counties which had provided the heart of the Puritan movement in the reign of Elizabeth and which had sustained the parliamentary cause during the Civil War. Congregationalists appear to have constituted more than 3 per cent of the population of Essex, Hertfordshire, and Northamptonshire, nearly 3 per cent of Bedfordshire and Cambridgeshire, and more than 2 per cent of Huntingdonshire, Suffolk, and Hampshire. This suggests that it was only in those counties where Protestantism was well established, and which during the Civil War had for the most part lain safely behind the parliamentary lines, that the more radical Puritans had felt sufficiently secure to push their views on church government to the point of Independency. In those counties which had been in the front line in the contest with popery in the previous century, and which had seen most of the fighting during the Civil War—Yorkshire, Lancashire, the north Midlands, the West Country—Puritanism could not so easily afford the luxury of internal dispute and the Dissent of those areas in the early eighteenth century remained predominantly Presbyterian. There is one important

[1] R. Mansfield, 'The Development of Independency in Derbyshire', Manchester M.A. thesis, 1951, pp. 118, 124.

[2] E. Calamy, *An Account of the Ministers . . . . ejected after the Restoration* (1713), ii. 718. Rees, *Nonconformity in Wales*, p. 222. For Gouge's trust see M. G. Jones, *The Charity School Movement* (Cambridge, 1938), pp. 228–9.

exception to this generalization—south Wales and Monmouthshire—where, apart from Carmarthenshire, Presbyterianism
was never well represented and where, if the figures in the
Evans-list can be trusted, Congregationalism was propor-
tionately stronger than anywhere in England. The work of
Vavasor Powell and his fellow 'propagators of the Gospel in
Wales' appears to have born fruit throughout the southern half
of the principality, not least in Powell's native Radnorshire; the
strength of Independency in Monmouthshire and Glamorgan
reflected the influence of the Congregational church which
William Wroth had founded at Llanfaches in 1639; and the
firm foothold which Congregationalism had in Breconshire was
a tribute to the zeal of Henry Maurice, who had resigned an
Anglican living in 1671 to devote the rest of his life to the
evangelization of Wales and the care of his scattered Breconshire church.[1]

The Particular Baptists tended to be best represented in the
same counties as the Independents from whom they had originally sprung. Indeed, the Particular Baptists outnumbered the
Congregationalists in Monmouthshire, Radnorshire, and Bedfordshire, where they constituted at least 5 per cent of the
population, and in Bristol and Hertfordshire where they comprised more than 4 per cent of the population. They were also
more numerous than the Independents in Wiltshire, where they
constituted nearly 3 per cent of the population and occupied an
important social position in the cloth-making towns of Bradford-on-Avon, Trowbridge, and North Bradley.[2] 'The finest
medley Spanish cloths, not in England only, but in the whole
world, are made in this part', wrote Daniel Defoe,[3] and in the
valley of the Wiltshire Avon it was the Particular Baptists who
benefited from the failure of the established church to cater for
the needs of a manufacturing community. In the late seventeenth century Bradford-on-Avon constituted the largest parish
in the county, both in terms of area and of population, and
Southwick did not have an Anglican church of its own until the
late nineteenth century.[4] This part of Wiltshire had seen a

---

[1] W. T. Pennar Davies, 'Episodes in the History of Brecknockshire Dissent', in
Brycheiniog, iii (1957), 27–9.

[2] Evans list, p. 125.   [3] Defoe, *Tour*, i. 281.

[4] B. Williams, 'The Church of England and Protestant Nonconformity in Wiltshire, 1645–65', University of Bristol M.Litt. thesis, 1971, pp. 9–10. W. Doel,

number of prosecutions for Lollardy in the 1510s,[1] and it is possible that the Particular Baptists of the eighteenth century were the inheritors of the Lollard traditions of the area, consolidated during the Interregnum by the evangelistic activities of Thomas Collier.

It was, though, the General Baptists who were the principal heirs of the Lollards. They were most numerous in Kent, Buckinghamshire, and Lincolnshire, though in none of these counties do they appear to have exceeded 2 per cent of the population, and in Sussex and Cambridgeshire where they may have constituted about 1 per cent of the population. It is possible that the General Baptist cause in Lincolnshire had its origin in John Smyth's connections with the county, for a General Baptist church is known to have existed in Lincoln as early as 1626, and by the late 1630s it was apparently extending its influence to other parts of the county.[2] The willingness with which a minority of the inhabitants of both the Lincolnshire Fens and the Isle of Axholme embraced the General Baptist message was probably related to the intense hostility provoked by the drainage and enclosure of common land in these areas in the 1620s and 1630s. The two districts were notable for their loyalty to the parliamentary cause during the Civil War, and political and religious radicalism were doubtless connected.[3] It was during the Interregnum that the main Baptist expansion took place in Lincolnshire, when the influence of the Lincoln church in the north and centre of the county was supplemented in the south by the missionary activities of Henry Denne. Denne was one of the first General Baptists to be appointed to the denomination's distinctive post of 'Messenger', with a Commission 'to preach the Gospel where it is not known; to plant churches where there is none; to ordain elders in churches remote, and to assist in dispensing the holy mysteries'.[4] Apart from his brief period of service in the army between 1646 and 1649, culminating in the ignominious role he played in the

---

Twenty Golden Candlesticks . . . a History of Baptist Nonconformity in Western Wiltshire (1890), p. 3.

[1] Thompson, *The Later Lollards*, pp. 49–51.

[2] J. Plumb, 'Early Nonconformity in Lincolnshire', University of Sheffield M.A. thesis, 1940, pp. 23–4.

[3] B. Manning, *The English People and the English Revolution* (1976), p. 188.

[4] Underwood, *English Baptists*, p. 120.

Leveller mutiny at Burford, Denne devoted himself throughout most of the Interregnum to preaching and to establishing General Baptist churches in Huntingdonshire, Cambridgeshire, Lincolnshire, and Kent.[1]

The most satisfactory explanation of General Baptist strength in early-eighteenth-century Kent, Sussex, and Buckinghamshire is, though, that it represents the legacy of fifteenth- and early-sixteenth-century Lollardy. General Baptists were particularly numerous, as were the Lollards, in the Chilterns and the Weald, and it is likely that the common characteristics of these forest areas—large parishes, weak manorial structure, and opportunities for squatters[2]—assisted the survival of radical religious views from the fifteenth to the eighteenth century. In Buckinghamshire the very names of the persecuted Lollards of the first two decades of the sixteenth century reappear in General Baptist records a century and a half later.[3] In Kent a continuous tradition of radical Dissent is suggested by the persecution of Lollards in the Tenterden, Maidstone, and Ashford areas in 1511,[4] the activities of the Anabaptist martyr Joan Boucher in the 1540s, the anti-predestinarian conventiclers who were questioned by the Privy Council in 1551 and burned at Canterbury four years later, and the Separatist congregation in the Maidstone and Ashford district which troubled Laud in the 1620s and 1630s. This radical tradition was strengthened in the 1640s by the activities of William Jeffery of Bradbourne, who was said to have had a hand in the formation of more than twenty General Baptist churches, and by the conversion to General Baptist views of Francis Cornwell, vicar of Marden.[5] Even the General Baptists of Lincolnshire and the Fens probably owed something to Kent, for the Dennes were a Kentish family.[6]

The Quakers were strongest in three distinct areas: the coun-

---

[1] *Fenstanton Records*, pp. 72–81.

[2] A. Everitt, 'Nonconformity in Country Parishes', in *Agricultural History Review*, supplement, xviii (1970), 189–91.

[3] W. H. Summers, *The Lollards of the Chiltern Hills* (1906), pp. 85. 133. A. H. J. Baines, 'The Signatories of the Orthodox Confession of 1679', *Baptist Quarterly*, xvii (1957–8), 43.

[4] Thompson, *The Later Lollards*, pp. 187–9.

[5] T. Crosby, *History of the English Baptists* (1738–40), iii. 98. G. F. Nuttall, 'Dissenting Churches in Kent before 1700', *JEH* xiv (1963), 185.

[6] A. Everitt, *The Community of Kent and the Great Rebellion* (Leicester, 1966), p. 177.

ties of Cumberland and Westmorland and the Furness district of
Lancashire, where they built on their Seeker heritage and set
up their first headquarters at Swarthmoor Hall; the city of
Bristol; and London and the counties to the north—Bedfordshire, Hertfordshire, Huntingdonshire, and Essex. The early
successes and continuing strength of the movement in the north-
western counties—the Galilee of Quakerism, as Thomas Hodg-
kin called them—like that of the Presbyterians elsewhere in the
north, can in part be explained by the inadequate parochial
machinery of the established church: the parish of Kendal
included half the Lake District, the parish of Dalton-in-Furness
comprised twenty villages, that of Ulverston nine.[1] Their comparative strength in Bristol and the counties to the north of
London can be attributed to their original success in decimating
Independent and Baptist congregations, and so invalidates
Hugh Barbour's thesis that 'the real heartland of Puritanism'
was peculiarly cold to the first Friends.[2] But what is most
remarkable about the geographic distribution of the Quakers in
the early eighteenth century is the fact that, although they were
less numerous than the Presbyterians or Independents, they had
more particular meetings and were more evenly distributed over
the country than any of the other Dissenting denominations. Of
the five major groups of Dissenters only the Quakers had meetings in every English county, a tribute both to the missionary
enthusiasm and to the organizational ability of the first Friends.

The evidence of the Evans list, the episcopal visitation
returns, and the Quaker burial registers all suggests that
Dissent was more urbanized than the population at large. Of
the 1,238 Presbyterian, Independent, and Baptist congregations
which are known to have existed in the years 1715–18, more
than half met in places which are described in the Evans list as
cities, boroughs, or market towns.[3] Moreover, the town congregations were usually much larger than the village congregations,
and on the basis of the Evans list it is possible to calculate that in
England 63·2 per cent of Presbyterians, 69·5 per cent of Independents, 58·0 per cent of Particular Baptists and 61·3 per cent of
General Baptists worshipped in cities, boroughs, or market towns.

[1] Barbour, *Quakers in Puritan England*, p. 42.
[2] Ibid., pp. 79–80.
[3] See Table IV on p. 286.

TABLE IV

Dissenting congregations in urban and rural areas

	Congregations meeting in cities, boroughs or market towns	Congregations meeting in other townships or villages
Presbyterians	336	326
Independents	133	96
Particular Baptists	105	115
General Baptists	55	67
Seventh-day Baptists	3	2
Totals	632	606

The visitation returns, which give estimates of the number of Dissenters in the parishes in which they lived rather than in the meetings in which they worshipped, provide even firmer evidence that a higher proportion of Dissenters than of the population at large lived in towns. For example, 11·9 per cent of the Dissenters of Leicestershire are recorded as living in Leicester itself, but only 6·8 per cent of the total population of the county lived in the county town; 19·4 per cent of the Dissenters of Lincolnshire lived in the four towns of Lincoln, Boston, Gainsborough, and Spalding, but these towns accounted for only 7·9 per cent of the county's population; and in Oxfordshire 39 per cent of the county's Dissenters lived in the four towns of Banbury, Chipping Norton, Henley, and Witney, though these towns cannot have comprised more than 10 per cent of the total population of the county.[1] The evidence of the Quaker burial registers points to the same conclusion. Nearly 20 per cent of all the Quakers in England lived in London and Middlesex in the first decade of the eighteenth century, compared with only 10 per cent of the total population. Friends were also heavily concentrated in Bristol, as were Dissenters in general: nearly 20 per cent of the city's population was Nonconformist, 6 per cent of it Quaker.

Rural Dissenters could be subjected to pressures to conform which did not exist in the towns. We have noted how Richard Bower of Yarmouth complained in 1675 that conventicles could

[1] These calculations are based on the Speculum Dioceseos Lincolniensis in the custody of the Lincolnshire Archives Committee and on *Bishop Secker's Visitation Returns*, Oxfordshire Record Society (1957).

not be suppressed as easily in towns as in villages, where the people were dependent on the Anglican gentry for their livelihood, and the contrast between town and country was evident in periods of toleration as well as in times of persecution. The minutes of the General Baptist church in Fenstanton in Huntingdonshire record how, in 1653, a farmer who wished to be baptized 'desired liberty to hear the priests of England as often as he should think fit' because he had 'hired a farm of Mr. Bendich, and if he should know that he was baptized he would turn him out'.[1] John Bunyan complained in 1658 of 'rich ungodly landlords that so keep under their poor tenants, that they dare not go out to hear the word for fear their rent should be raised, or they turned out of their houses'.[2] But in urban areas pressures could be exerted in the opposite direction. Thomas Edwards alleged in 1646 that a 'godly' London citizen had been deprived of work by an Independent woollen draper for 'whom he had worked almost twenty years . . . because the night before this citizen had argued against Independency'.[3] And in 1716 Dr. Evans recorded the opinion of an Exeter merchant, John Vowler, that 'the influence of trading Dissenters' in the city was 'very extensive over their dependants in business'.[4]

The tendency for Dissenters to live in urban rather than rural England intensified as the religious enthusiasm of the Interregnum and the exhilaration of the challenge of persecution gave place to the ordered devotional life of the age of toleration. Churches formed as a result of missionary endeavour and itinerant preaching among scattered villages would often draw their membership from a large area. The members of the Fenstanton General Baptist church came from more than thirty different towns and villages in Huntingdonshire, Cambridgeshire, and Bedfordshire in the 1650s; the members of the Rothwell Congregational church in Northamptonshire were drawn from more than sixteen different places in the reign of Charles II; the members of the Arnesby Particular Baptist church in Leicestershire lived in more than thirty-five towns

[1] *Fenstanton Records*, p. 82.
[2] M. Spufford, *Contrasting Communities: English Villages in the Sixteenth and Seventeenth Centuries* (Cambridge, 1974), p. 307, citing J. Bunyan, *Sighs from Hell* (1666), pp. 101–2.
[3] Edwards, *Gangraena*, part ii, p. 7.   [4] Evans list, p. 31.

and villages in Leicestershire, Northamptonshire, and Warwickshire in 1706.[1] But such Dissenters often had far to travel to worship, like the woman member of the Bedworth Congregational church in Warwickshire who journeyed to 'church meetings seventeen long miles, twelve times in a year, and that on foot', and it would require an uncommon degree of zeal and devotion for such a person to retain his or her church membership.[2] Unless rural Dissenters could be united with other of their co-religionists in the same or neighbouring villages, they were likely to drift back to the Church of England or into indifference. As early as 1654 the Fenstanton church had to send two members to inquire of Jasper Dockwra why he no longer attended the meetings of the church, and were told that while 'he was the same which he had formerly been for matter of faith . . . he being alone a long time was much discouraged, and at length did go to the Church of England'.[3]

Even where village meetings were established, they often could not survive the loss of leading members, the death or removal of a minister, or the loss of their place of meeting. The Presbyterians, who insisted that the presence of a trained and educated minister was essential to the existence of a properly constituted church, in particular experienced the slow attrition of many of their rural congregations in the course of the eighteenth century. But even the Quakers, whose lay leadership and itinerant ministry to some extent cushioned them against such factors, suffered from the fact that a marginal loss of membership which might be imperceptible in an urban meeting could be fatal for a rural one. The Friends of the Upperside Monthly Meeting, Buckinghamshire, were in the late 1680s confronted with the loss of their usual meeting places at both Great Missenden and Rowsham. Joseph Graveney and his wife offered the use of their home at nearby Prestwood for the meeting of Great Missenden Friends, but 'inasmuch as the number of Friends thereabouts is but small, it was thought fit to

---

[1] *Fenstanton Records*, pp. 251–4. N. Glass, *The Early History of the Independent Church at Rothwell* (Northampton, 1871), p. 28. Arnesby Particular Baptist Church Book, i. 210–12, Leicestershire County Record Office. G. Jackson, 'The Evangelical Work of the Baptists in Leicestershire', University of London M.A. thesis, 1955, p. 26.

[2] J. J. Hurwich, 'Nonconformists in Warwickshire, 1660–1720', Princeton University Ph.D. thesis, 1970, p. 275.

[3] *Fenstanton Records*, p. 99.

be held there but once in a month only, and the Friends to repair to other adjacent meetings on the other days'. In the case of the Rowsham meeting it was decided that since it was so poorly attended it should be united with that at Aylesbury.[1] Such was to become an increasingly familiar story in the experience of both Quaker and other rural Dissenting congregations in the first half of the following century.

3. HARMONY AND DISCORD:
THE HAPPY UNION AND THE ANTINOMIAN CONTROVERSY

It was primarily the need to relieve impoverished Dissenting ministers and to assist congregations who could not support ministers from their own resources, of which the majority were in rural areas, that led in 1690 to the setting up of the Common Fund by a group of Presbyterian and Congregational ministers in London.[2] The establishment of the Common Fund was one of a long series of attempts to secure some degree of co-operation between the two denominations. Even before the Restoration the Presbyterian and Independent ministers of Lancashire had agreed to meet periodically and preach to each other's congregations, though the agreement was destroyed by Sir George Booth's Presbyterian rising against the Rump in August 1659.[3] But once the Act of Uniformity had cast ministers of both persuasions out of the established church co-operation became more feasible. Presbyterians and Congregationalists co-operated in providing a lecture at Hackney in 1669 and in giving a weekly lecture, financed by a group of merchants, at Pinners' Hall in the city of London in 1672; in Yarmouth they combined to raise money for their ministers in 1668, and in 1675 met together for worship; in Northowram in 1672 they united for 'all ordinances . . . and both parties were willing to overlook any matters of difference'; and around 1678 a group of City laymen drew up 'An Essay for an Accommodation betwixt the Ministers of the Presbyterians and the Congregational Way'.[4]

---

[1] B. Snell, ed., *The Minute Book of the Monthly Meeting of the Society of Friends for the Upperside of Buckinghamshire, 1669–1690* (High Wycombe, 1937), pp. 181–4, 209–11.
[2] A. Gordon, *Freedom after Ejection* (Manchester, 1917), p. 158.
[3] *Life of Adam Martindale* (Chetham Society Publications, 4, 1845), pp. 128–31.
[4] Gordon, *Freedom after Ejection*, p. 154. *Reliquiae Baxterianae*, part iii, p. 103. *CSPD* 1667–8, p. 186; 1675–6, p. 275. *Heywood's Autobiography*, iii. 109, 152. *DWL Occasional Paper* No. ix, 1960.

It apparently found favour with most of the London ministers of both denominations, but the intensification of persecution in the early 1680s prevented its implementation, and no action was taken until the failure of the Comprehension Bill of 1689 finally destroyed any lingering hopes the Presbyterians may have entertained of returning to the established church.

Thereafter schemes for union were set on foot in various parts of the country. At Bristol in June 1690 a meeting of ministers from Somerset, Gloucestershire, Wiltshire, and Dorset subscribed to the 'Essay of Accommodation'; in London in July the Common Fund was set up; and, most ambitious of all, in March 1691 the so-called 'Happy Union' was formed with the adoption of a set of proposals known as the 'Heads of Agreement' by most of the 'United Ministers in and about London, formerly called Presbyterian and Congregational'.[1] These proposals were in their turn subsequently endorsed by associations of ministers in Devon, Hampshire, Cheshire, Lancashire, the West Riding, and probably elsewhere.[2]

As far as external organization was concerned, it was not difficult for the Presbyterians and Congregationalists to come to an agreement in 1691. The Presbyterians made no attempt either to set up a hierarchy of church courts on the Scottish model or to resurrect the system of classes which the Long Parliament had established in 1646 and subsequent years. During the period of persecution, as Baxter noted, the Presbyterians had been 'forced to forbear all exercise of their way; they durst not meet together (synodically) unless in a gaol' and their congregations became, of necessity, 'of independent and separating shape'.[3] But though the Presbyterian meetings were independent, they were not congregational, and the Presbyterian minister, freed from the control of superior church courts, had far greater authority than his Congregational brother who was subjected to the rule of the church meeting. And after the passing of the Toleration Act the Presbyterian ministers had no

---

[1] *DWL Occasional Paper* No. vi, 1957, pp. 2, 5, 12.

[2] *DWL Occasional Paper* No. vi, 1957, pp. 15–16. A. Brockett, ed., *The Exeter Assembly, Minutes 1691–1717* (Devon and Cornwall Record Society, new series, vi, 1963), p. 4. G. F. Nuttall, 'Assembly and Association in Dissent', *Studies in Church History*, ed. G. J. Cuming and D. Baker (Cambridge, 1971), vii. 297. Hunter, *Life of Heywood*, pp. 373–5.

[3] *Reliquiae Baxterianae*, part iii, p. 43.

inclination either to subject that authority to higher ecclesiastical jurisdiction or to share it with lay elders. Their ideal was rather a voluntary association of ministers such as Baxter had established in Worcestershire in 1653, and which had been copied in other counties during the Interregnum.[1] The Heads of Agreement were thus able to satisfy the Presbyterian need for a regular meeting of ministers without infringing the Congregationalists' belief in the independence of the local church. Though the word 'classis' was revived to describe the gatherings of ministers in Cheshire and in four parts of Lancashire (Manchester, Warrington, Bolton, and Northern), these classes contained no lay elders and confined their activities largely to licensing candidates for the ministry, arranging ordinations, and giving advice on the removal and settlement of ministers.[2]

There were, however, other issues which continued to divide Presbyterian from Congregationalist, and which the Heads of Agreement failed to resolve. While the Presbyterian meetings retained the marks of their birth as parochial congregations, often describing themselves as 'societies' rather than 'churches', and ruled by an educated ministry, the Congregationalists clung to their conception of the gathered church, composed only of true believers and self-governing under the lordship of Christ. While the Presbyterians admitted to communion all who lived respectably and had some knowledge of the Christian religion, the Congregationalists restricted communion and church membership to those who were able 'to give an account of the work of grace' in their souls.[3] While the Presbyterians followed Baxter in believing 'that education is God's ordinary way for the conveyance of his grace', the Congregationalists were more impressed by the direct action of the Holy Spirit on the heart, even of the ignorant.[4] And while the Presbyterians restricted their ministry to the well-educated, and devised a rigorous ordination procedure to keep out of the ministry 'unlearned, conceited, pragmatical persons and mechanics of the lowest

---

[1] Ibid., part iii, pp. 148–50, 167.
[2] Gordon, *Freedom after Ejection*, p. 157. A. Gordon, ed., *Cheshire Classis Minutes* (1919), *passim*. A. Holt, 'Minutes of the Warrington Classis, 1719–22', *TUHS*, vii (1939–42), 12–17.
[3] Hunter, *Life of Heywood*, pp. 99–102, 416, 422.
[4] *Reliquiae Baxterianae*, part i, p. 7. Hunter, *Life of Heywood*, p. 39.

station',[1] the Congregationalists, though not despising education, defended the right of the spiritually gifted, if academically deficient, brethren to preach the Gospel.

Within months of the consummation of the Happy Union Presbyterians and Congregationalists were quarrelling over such issues. In March 1690 Richard Davis, a fiery thirty-one-year-old Welshman with 'a good voice and a thundering way of preaching', had been ordained pastor of the Congregational church at Rothwell in Northamptonshire.[2] Even at his ordination service Davis had given offence to some of his neighbouring ministers by inviting them to the service but declining to let them take part in the ordination, which was performed by the officers of the church according to strict Congregational practice.[3] And he subsequently gave greater offence by embarking on a vigorous evangelistic campaign in which it was claimed that he took the Gospel to eleven counties within an 80-mile radius of Rothwell and founded seven new churches.[4] Presbyterians such as Oliver Heywood, William Bagshaw, and Stephen Hughes had initiated similar campaigns and had not fallen foul of their fellow Dissenting ministers, but their activities had taken place in co-operation with those ministers in areas where Dissenters would otherwise have been thin on the ground, and in so doing they had incurred the hostility only of the clergy of the established church. By contrast Davis was operating in an area where scores of Dissenting ministers were already at work, and they complained, as bitterly as did Anglican clergymen of Presbyterians in Lancashire, that the Welshman was poaching on their territory. Justification for Davis's activities can be found in the survey conducted by the managers of the Common Fund in 1690 which showed that in Northamptonshire Dissenting congregations were disintegrating for want of ministers.[5] But whereas the answer of the London ministers to the problem was to raise sufficient funds to educate and main-

---

[1] A. Lincoln, *Some Political and Social Ideas of English Dissent, 1763–1800* (Cambridge, 1938), p. 14.

[2] Glass, *Independent Church at Rothwell*, pp. 33, 100.

[3] T. Coleman, *Memorials of the Independent Churches of Northamptonshire* (1853), p. 54.

[4] Glass, *Independent Church at Rothwell*, pp. 35, 54, 111. H. G. Tibbutt, introductory note to Rothwell Church Book, DWL MS. 201. 42.

[5] Gordon, *Freedom after Ejection*, p. 77.

tain men who were 'devoted to and exercised in the ministry as their fixed and only employment', Davis's solution was to send out as evangelists 'shoemakers, joiners, dyers, tailors, weavers, farmers', and other such laymen.[1] And it hardly commended Davis's activities to sober Dissenters that his evangelism, like the Quaker enthusiasm of the 1650s and the Methodist revivalism of the following century, induced hysterical fits in some of his female hearers.

Dissenting opinion of Richard Davis did not divide along strictly denominational lines: John King, minister of the neighbouring Congregational church at Wellingborough, took the initiative in arousing opposition to Davis, and the Bedworth Congregational church in Warwickshire was split between supporters and opponents of the Welsh evangelist.[2] But the issues raised by Davis's campaign, the use of lay preachers, the lack of respect for the 'parish' boundaries of other ministers, the emphasis on emotional conversion rather than on an educated faith, were the very questions at issue between the Presbyterians and Congregationalists which the Heads of Agreement had attempted to obscure. And even more serious were the theological issues raised by Davis's activities, for his opponents accused him of Antinomianism and the beginning of his evangelistic campaign coincided, in 1690, with the republication of the works of the early-seventeenth-century Antinomian Tobias Crisp. These two events rekindled something of the embers of theological controversy left over from the conflagration of the 1640s and 1650s, and the last decade of the seventeenth century, far from removing differences between Presbyterians and Congregationalists, saw a wedge driven between the two denominations which was to force them ever wider apart in the following century.

On and off for forty years conservative Puritans such as Richard Baxter had suspected individual Independents of Antinomianism, while Congregationalists had on occasion retaliated by charging Baxter with Arminianism. Baxter's first published work, *Aphorismes of Justification* (1649), was written with an 'eye upon the Libertines, commonly called Antinomians',

---

[1] Ibid., p. 199. 'P. Rehakosht', *A Plain and Just Account of the Most Horrid and Dismal Plague, begun at Rowel, alias Rothwell, in Northamptonshire* (1692), p. 1.

[2] R. Davis, *Truth and Innocency Vindicated* (1692), pp. 3–4. Hurwich, 'Noncomformists in Warwickshire', pp. 279-80.

whom he regarded as a greater danger than either the papists
or the Socinians. The Antinomians, wrote Baxter, insinuate
themselves 'with the weaker sort of godly people . . . by the
advantage of the name of free-grace' and so lead men into
'so easy a way, which flesh and blood hath so little against,
as being too consistent with men's carnal interest'. 'To be
revenged on me for calling them Antinomians,' he complained,
'they have resolved to call me Arminian, Socinian, Papist, and
Jesuit,'[1] and in 1672 the charge of Arminianism was again raised
against him as a result of his contribution to the joint Presbyterian–Congregational lectures at Pinners' Hall. The republication of Tobias Crisp's sermons in 1690 reawakened Baxter's
long hostility to Antinomianism and he immediately rushed
out his *Scripture Gospel defended . . . against the Libertines*. In this
work the fears contracted during the upheavals of the Interregnum erupted once again. If the Antinomians 'prevail to
make England believe that elect wicked infidels are as righteous
as Christ', he stormed, 'and that it is impossible that any sin
should hurt them . . . I should have more hope of the Turks and
heathens, than of the land that receiveth and practiseth these
principles'.[2]

This was almost Baxter's parting shot against his old adver-
saries, for he died in December of the following year, but his
crusade was continued by Daniel Williams, John Evans's predecessor at the Hand Alley Presbyterian meeting, who in May
1692 published his *Gospel-Truth Stated and Vindicated*. The
essential dispute between the Baxterians and the Antinomians,
argued Williams, was that whereas Crisp taught that the
operation of the covenant of grace was not conditional on any
action on the part of man, the Baxterians taught that the
covenant of grace was conditional on man's repentance from
sin and faith in Christ. In contrast to the Antinomian view that
a man's obedience to the moral law and performance of religious
duties had no bearing on his ultimate salvation, Williams maintained that 'true holiness, sincere obedience, or good works,
and perseverance, are the way to heaven, and so necessary
to the salvation of a believer that without them he cannot be

---

[1] R. Baxter, *Richard Baxter's Confession of his Faith* (1655), pp. 2–3, 6.
[2] R. Baxter, *The Scripture Gospel defended . . . against the Libertines*, book ii, *A Defence of Christ and Free Grace* (1690), sig. A.

saved'.[1] One did not need to be an Antinomian to regard such sentiments as a betrayal of the Reformation doctrine of justification by faith alone. Williams, commented Richard Davis, was 'lashing' at 'the orthodox professors [of religion] over the shoulders of Dr. Crisp'.[2]

Conflict between the two expatriate Welshmen came into the open in that same month of May 1692 when Davis went up to London to meet the leading ministers of the Happy Union and Williams charged him with Antinomianism.[3] Support for Williams's accusation was provided by the anonymous author of *A Plain and Just Account of a Most Horrid and Dismal Plague begun at ... Rothwell* who claimed that Davis taught that 'to preach marks of sanctification is a doctrine of an old covenant strain', that 'the law sets persons a thousand times further off from Christ', and that 'such as preach up qualifications are legal preachers [who] keep people in bondage'.[4] And support for the Presbyterian view that such teaching encouraged immorality is provided by the records of the Bedworth Congregational church. The church's minister, Julius Saunders, had initially welcomed Davis and his evangelistic methods and members who were critical of Davis had either withdrawn from membership or had been excommunicated. But in 1693 the Bedworth church had to expel two members for adultery, 'both of them deeply tainted with Antinomianism', and their failings, Saunders was forced to admit, were due to 'Mr. Davis and his notions'.[5]

Other Congregationalists, though, rallied to Davis's support. In November 1692 some of the London ministers went to Kettering to investigate Davis's activities further and the Rothwell minister refused to meet them, claiming that their purpose

[1] D. Williams, *Gospel-Truth Stated and Vindicated* (1692), pp. 57–60, 120, 132.

[2] Davis, *Truth and Innoecency*, p. 6.   [3] Ibid., p. 38.

[4] 'P. Rehakosht', *Plain and Just Account*, pp. 6–7. Davis conceded that these statements reflected his views, *Truth and Innocency*, pp. 15–20. Alexander Gordon, in *Freedom after Ejection*, p. 186, suggested that 'P. Rehakosht' was John King, minister of the Wellingborough Congregational church. But Gordon provided no evidence for this identification and 'Rehakosht' described himself as 'inhabiting on the east side of the seat of the plague' whereas Wellingborough is to the south of Rothwell. The Rothwell church itself placed at least part of the blame for the *Plain and Just Account* on a 'Mr. Pain of Oundle' who was apparently a member of the Kettering Independent church and whom the Rothwell church charged with 'handing the libel to the press' (Rothwell Church Book, DWL, pp. 36–7). Oundle does lie to the east of Rothwell.

[5] Hurwich, 'Nonconformists in Warwickshire', pp. 279–81.

'was to hook away judgement from a particular church of Christ and fix it in a Presbyterian classis'.[1] Davis was supported by John Langston, minister of the Ipswich Congregational church, who had known the Welshman for seventeen years and wrote a testimony to his godliness.[2] Isaac Chauncey, minister of the Mark Lane Congregational church, attacked Daniel Williams as the 'grand assertor of a new Law, and the doctrine of justification by works', and protested at the London ministers' attempt to exercise 'synodical jurisdiction'.[3] And Nathaniel Mather, pastor of the Lime Street Congregational church, in criticizing Williams's *Gospel-Truth*, expressed surprise 'that any pretending to be a Protestant should lick up that popish self-justiciaries vomit'.[4] The theological consensus which for thirty years had ostensibly united the Presbyterianism of the Westminster Confession and the Congregationalism of the Savoy Declaration was thus shattered. Presbyterian charged Congregationalist with Antinomianism, Congregationalist charged Presbyterian with 'Arminianism or even Socinianism',[5] and the Happy Union disappeared in acrimonious controversy. In Daniel Williams's home town of Wrexham members of the united Presbyterian–Congregational church who sympathized with the pastor of Hand Alley seceded in 1691 to form a separate Presbyterian meeting.[6] In London in 1694 Williams was voted out of the Pinners' Hall lecture and the rest of the Presbyterian lecturers left to start a rival lecture on the same day in the Salters' Hall. And not content with this some of Williams's more headstrong opponents levelled accusations of immorality against him, accusations which were taken seriously enough for a committee of ministers to be set up to conduct an eight weeks' inquiry before vindicating him of the charges.[7] Finally in 1695 the Congregationalists left the Common Fund to the Presbyterians and set up a denominational fund of their own. It was not until nearly 300 years later, in 1972, that the union of Con-

---

[1] Davis, *Truth and Innocency*, p. 40.   [2] Ibid., p. 26.
[3] I. Chauncey, *Neonomianism Unmask'd* (1692–3), part i, Epistle Dedicatory, part iii, p. 98.
[4] N. Mather, *The Righteousness of God through Faith* (1694), p. 22.
[5] Calamy, *Historical Account*, i. 337.
[6] A. N. Palmer, *A History of the Older Nonconformity in Wrexham and its Neighbourhood* (1884), p. 54. The Wrexham Old Meeting subsequently became Baptist.
[7] Calamy, *Historical Account*, i. 351, 356.

gregationalists and Presbyterians in England was effected, and by that time few of the Presbyterian churches involved could claim descent from the English Presbyerians of the seventeenth century.

Something was salvaged from the wreck of the Happy Union. In Devon Congregationalists and Presbyterians continued to meet together until the middle of the eighteenth century,[1] and the demarcation lines between the two denominations were often a good deal more blurred in the provinces than they were in London. Presbyterian meetings invited Congregationalists to minister to them, and vice versa; members of the two denominations worshipped together in Canterbury, Chester, Chesterfield, and Leicester; in Hull Presbyterian and Independent ministers baptized each other's children; in the records of the Worcester Dissenters the terms 'Presbyterian' and 'Independent' are used interchangeably; and in drawing up deeds or applying for licences under the Toleration Act congregations often described their meeting-houses as for the use of 'Protestant Dissenters' or people 'of the Presbyterian or Independent persuasion' rather than for the exclusive use of either denomination.[2] But as far as the London-based leaders of the two denominations were concerned, co-operation was henceforward restricted to the furtherance of the political interests of Dissent.

4. CENTRALIZATION AND DIVISION: THE CAFFYN CONTROVERSY AND THE WILKINSON–STORY SEPARATION

It is significant that Presbyterian–Independent relations were often more cordial at congregational than at associational level, for ecclesiastical centralization increased the tendency of Dissenting denominations to quarrel and divide. The Congregationalists, whose independent principles precluded their meeting in national assembly between the Savoy conference of

[1] Brockett, *Nonconformity in Exeter*, p. 65.
[2] Hunter, *Life of Heywood*, pp. 300–1. Jones, *Congregationalism in England*, pp. 124–5. Evans list, pp. 53, 64. G. Bolam, 'Presbyterianism in Derbyshire, Leicestershire and Nottinghamshire', Nottingham M.A. thesis, 1957, pp. 475–8. J. C. Warren, 'From Puritanism to Unitarianism at Lincoln', *TUHS* ii (1919–22), 16. Whitaker, *Bowl Alley Lane Chapel*, p. 102. W. Urwick, *Nonconformity in Worcester* (1897), p. 84.

1658 and the formation of the Congregational Union in 1832, were seldom troubled by disputes of denominational importance. While individual congregations were often rent by unseemly quarrels, and contentious issues such as the disputed choice of a pastor would sometimes lead to a church's dividing, it was rare for a controversy among Congregationalists to assume more than local significance. The most important theological dispute among Independents between the Restoration and the French Revolution—the controversy over Matthias Maurice's *Modern Question* in the mid-eighteenth century—did not split the denomination. Similarly the Particular Baptists, who closely resembled the Congregationalists both in theology and polity and whose annual assemblies from 1689 to 1692 were the first and last to be held before 1813, suffered but little from denominational strife. The controversy provoked by the opposition of the elder Robert Hall and of Andrew Fuller to High Calvinism in the late eighteenth century did not lead to denominational fissure until the early nineteenth century when a comparatively small number of Strict Baptist churches seceded from Particular Baptist county associations.

By contrast with the comparative peace reigning within the Independent and Particular Baptist denominations, the General Baptists and Quakers, who both had annual national assemblies and paid less regard to the independence of local churches, both experienced major schisms in the last quarter of the seventeenth century. Admittedly the General Baptist Assembly, which first met in 1654, was not consistent in the authority it claimed. In 1656 it presented its decisions to its constituent churches only that they might 'seriously consider and examine them by the Scriptures of truth', but forty years later the Assembly voted that the churches had to abide by its decisions and that the independence of churches was 'very dangerous and detrimental'.[1] It was, though, easier to pass such resolutions than to enforce them and churches which disliked the Assembly's decisions had only to withdraw from membership. This is precisely what happened during the prolonged controversy over the views of Matthew Caffyn which racked the denomination from the 1670s to 1731.

Caffyn had been born in 1628, the son of a yeoman farmer of

[1] *Minutes of the General Baptist Assembly*, i. 9, 42.

Horsham in Sussex, and while at Oxford during the first Civil War he had adopted Baptist views and had been expelled. He returned to Horsham to farm and to become pastor of the town's General Baptist church and Messenger with responsibilities for evangelism in Sussex and Kent. The area of Caffyn's origin and influence is significant, for in the 1670s he became the centre of a controversy which had its roots in the ancestry of the General Baptist movement. Whereas the radicals of south-east England had in the previous century come under the influence of continental Anabaptism, the General Baptists of Buckinghamshire and the south Midlands seem to have inherited their religious radicalism from native Lollardy in isolation from continental influences, and the different heritages of the General Baptists of these two areas go far to explain the divisions of the late seventeenth and early eighteenth centuries. That Anabaptist influence persisted in the south-east is strongly suggested by the fact that Caffyn was attracted to the Christological views of Melchoir Hofmann, but such views were vigorously repudiated by the General Baptists of Buckinghamshire and the south Midlands. In 1673 Thomas Monck, a Messenger from Berkhamstead in Hertfordshire, published *A Cure for the Cankering Error of the New Eutychians* in order to warn his fellow General Baptists against the Melchiorite heresy 'that our blessed mediator did not take his flesh of the Virgin Mary, neither was he made the seed of David according to the flesh'. Six years later Monck's stand was endorsed by fifty-four General Baptist Messengers and pastors, forty-four of whom came from Buckinghamshire.[1] These Buckinghamshire General Baptists, faced with the apparent threat to Protestant England from the Popish Plot, published in 1679 *An Orthodox Confession* in which they sought to minimize the theological differences between themselves and the Calvinists. They followed Thomas Helwys in holding that while no one was predestined to death, some were predestined to life; they agreed with the Calvinists on original sin and final perseverance; above all they rejected Melchior Hofmann's teaching on the incarnation of Christ. Christ, they wrote, is both 'coequal, coessential, and coeternal with the Father', and was 'formed of the only seed, or substance

[1] A. H. J. Baines, 'Signatories of the Orthodox Confession of 1679', *Baptist Quarterly* xvii (1957–8), 35–6.

of the Virgin Mary'. 'The denying of baptism is a less evil than
to deny the divinity or humanity of Christ.'[1]

The subsequent course of the dispute is obscure, for the
records of the General Assembly for the years of persecution are
lost, but it appears that in the mid 1680s Joseph Wright, a
Messenger from Maidstone, accused Caffyn of denying not only
the humanity but also the divinity of Christ, and tried to secure
his condemnation by the General Assembly.[2] The accusations
were repeated in 1693, but though the Assembly condemned
Melchiorite views it acquitted Caffyn of subscribing to them and
when, three years later, it refused to reopen the question a
minority of churches seceded and met in 1697 as a rival General
Association.[3] For the next thirty-four years there were virtually
two General Baptist denominations, the more orthodox drawing
its support from Buckinghamshire and the Midlands, the more
heterodox from Kent, Sussex, Essex, and the West Country.[4] It
was not until 1731, when Caffyn had been dead seventeen years,
that the two groups reunited on the basis of 'the six principles of
the doctrine of Christians as contained in Hebrews 6: 1, 2' and
even then the Buckinghamshire and Northamptonshire Associations remained unhappy about the terms of agreement.[5]

The Quakers, who began by emphasizing more than any
other sect the possibility of the individual believer's direct
inspiration by the Holy Spirit, ended, perhaps for that reason,
with a more complex and more centralized organization than
any other Dissenting denomination. In origin Quaker organization probably owed something both to the Westmorland Seekers
and to the General Baptists, for among both groups it was
common for separate congregations to unite together for
monthly meetings for worship, discipline, and the relief of the
poor.[6] Among the General Baptists it was often these joint
meetings, rather than those of particular congregations, which
constituted meetings of the church, and they were in their turn
linked to quarterly county associations and to the General

---

[1] Lumpkin, *Baptist Confessions of Faith*, pp. 297–334.
[2] Crosby, *History of the English Baptists*, iii. 280–1.
[3] White's Alley General Baptist Church Book, i. 157. Guildhall Library.
Minutes of the General Baptist Assembly, i. 39–40, 43.
[4] *Minutes of the General Baptist Assembly*, i, p. xxii.
[5] Ibid. ii. 2, 13–14, 32–4.
[6] Braithwaite, *BQ*, p. 140.

Assembly.[1] But the General Baptist county associations were frequently ephemeral[2] and the denomination's churches were too concentrated in the south and east Midlands and in south-east England to develop anything that could be called a national organization. Above all, the General Baptists possessed no nationally recognized leader able to leave the impress of his organizational genius on the denomination. By contrast the Quakers, under the guiding hand of Fox, evolved a hierarchy of meetings rising from the particular meetings for worship to the Monthly Meetings for discipline, the county Quarterly Meetings and the national Yearly Meeting, a pyramidal structure which bore a closer resemblance to the organization of the Scottish kirk than to the polity of any other English Dissenting denomination. And to this structure the Quakers added what no other Nonconformist denomination had until the nineteenth century, an executive committee.

It has been argued by Arnold Lloyd that it was the necessity of organizing 'for legal protection against persecution' which led to the contrast between Quaker and Baptist organization,[3] but this is true only in a very limited sense. In support of Lloyd's contention is the fact that it was the Meeting for Sufferings, established in 1675 to secure relief from persecution, which became the executive committee of English Quakerism. But the Meeting for Sufferings was not the only Quaker institution capable of developing such a role, and had it not been set up its functions would probably have been assumed by the Morning Meeting of Ministers, which met on Mondays from 1673 onwards to exercise censorship over Quaker publications and to arrange for the allocation of ministers to London meetings on the following Sunday.[4] The crucial development of Quaker organization had in fact already taken place in the 1660s when Fox, after his release from Scarborough Castle, had determined to travel round England to 'order and establish the men's and women's Monthly and Quarterly Meetings in all the nation'.[5] His purpose was not to resist persecution but to impose some sort of order on the movement after the Nayler

---

[1] Taylor, *General Baptists*, i. 267. W. T. Whitley, ed., *The Church Books of Ford and Amersham* (1912), *passim*.

[2] Taylor, *General Baptists*, i. 458.

[3] A. Lloyd, *Quaker Social History* (1950), p. 175.

[4] Ibid., p. 124.   [5] *Fox's Journal*, pp. 511–12.

episode and the dissension caused in the early 1660s by the insistence of John Perrot and his supporters at keeping their hats on during prayer. The excessive individualism of which the early Quakers were accused by their opponents led, by way of reaction, in the 1670s to what many Friends regarded as excessive authoritarianism.

The leaders of the protest against the developing authoritarianism of Quaker organization were two pioneer Quaker ministers from Westmorland, John Story and John Wilkinson, who had been engaged in missionary work in the West Country where they had built up a large following. They objected to the practice of compelling Friends who had been disciplined to draw up a self-condemnatory paper; they resented the censorious attitude adopted towards Friends who tried to avoid persecution; they wished to stop itinerant ministers from other parts of the country from interfering in the affairs of the local Monthly and Quarterly business meetings; above all, they objected to Fox's determination to set up separate business meetings for women with the power to grant or refuse permission for marriage.[1] And beyond specific grievances lay a fundamental objection to what William Mucklow called 'Foxonian unity', depriving 'us of the law of the Spirit' and bringing 'in a tyrannical government'.[2] Story and Wilkinson set up a separate business meeting in Westmorland in 1675 and won considerable support from Quakers in Bristol, Wiltshire, Reading, and Buckinghamshire. But Story died in 1681 and William Rogers, a Bristol merchant who succeeded him as chief spokesman of the protest movement, attacked Fox and other leading Quakers with such venom that he alienated his own supporters.[3] The separatist movement gradually disintegrated and the last remaining separatist meeting, that at Reading, reunited with the main body of Quakers in 1716.[4]

The Wilkinson–Story separation was the most serious, but not the only, Quaker schism in the last quarter of the seventeenth century. The refusal of the Yorkshire Quarterly Meeting to allow a Friend to marry a second time led to the establishment of a separate meeting at York in 1684, and a further schism occurred in 1695 when the London Yearly Meeting condemned

[1] Braithwaite, *SPQ*, pp. 297–8.   [2] Ibid., p. 292.
[3] Ibid., pp. 319, 366.   [4] Ibid., p. 473.

George Keith, a Scottish Friend who had charged his fellow Quakers with so emphasizing the spirit of Christ that they neglected his historic mission and sacrifice.[1] It would be wrong, though, to assume that even the Quakers spent most of their time in internal squabbles. For the religious interest of most Dissenters was focused not on Quarterly and Yearly Meetings, not on General Assemblies and Unions, happy or otherwise, but on their own local church and meeting-house.

5. 'JOIN ALL THE GLORIOUS NAMES': MEETING-HOUSES AND WORSHIP

For most Dissenters before 1689 their place of worship was not a specifically constructed meeting-house but a private dwelling, barn, or rented room. In London Dissenters often hired the halls of the city guilds, and many congregations dating from the seventeenth century bore names such as Pewterers' Hall, Haberdashers' Hall, and Joiners' Hall. Apart from the ever reckless Quakers, who throughout the reign of Charles II had built their own meeting-houses, and had rebuilt them when they were pulled down, few Dissenting congregations had deemed it wise to advertise their presence to would-be persecutors by constructing their own places of worship. A few Dissenting meeting-houses were erected in London after the Restoration: in 1666 a wooden meeting-house was constructed for Thomas Doolittle in Bunhill Fields, soon to be superseded by a large brick building with galleries in Mugwell Street, and in 1669 Samuel Annesley was reported to be preaching in Spitalfields 'at a new house built for that purpose' to a congregation which included the young Daniel Defoe.[2] But some of these meeting-houses were seized by the established church after the Great Fire had destroyed many of the parish churches, and others were closed down in 1670 by Christopher Wren in his capacity as surveyor general of works.[3] Again, a number of meeting-houses are known to have been erected after Charles II's Declaration of Indulgence in 1672,[4] and at least a score of Dissenting congrega-

[1] Ibid., pp. 476, 484–6.
[2] Gordon, *Freedom after Ejection*, pp. 201, 254. J. R. Moore, *Daniel Defoe, Citizen of the Modern World* (Chicago, 1958), p. 17.
[3] Wilson, *Dissenting Churches in London*, i. 399, 462, ii. 189. J. Waddington, *Surrey Congregational History* (1866), pp. 63–4.
[4] Wilson, *Dissenting Churches in London*, i. 212, 363, ii. 532.

tions, mainly in Lancashire and Yorkshire, made use of chapels of ease. But elsewhere Dissenters met in secular buildings, and some of the more humble General Baptist churches of south-east England never possessed specifically constructed meeting-houses.[1] Meeting in private homes and hired barns did, though, have its disadvantages, apart from the obvious one of size. People who allowed their homes to be used for Dissenting meetings could be the target for persecution and riot, and in 1686 the Dover General Baptist church found it necessary to resolve 'that if any person do suffer any damage upon the account of our meeting at their house' the members would make good the damage 'according to our abilities'.[2] Services held in private houses could also lack the dignity and reverence of services held in meeting-houses, and on Christmas day 1702 the Speldhurst General Baptist church complained of members who came late to meeting and slept through the proceedings, of those who brought with them 'too many children', and of some who so crowded round the fire that others could not get warm.[3] Consequently once the Toleration Act had legalized Nonconformist worship most Dissenting churches sought to provide themselves with permanent places of worship, and in Nottingham the foundation stone of the Congregationalists' Castle Gate meeting-house was laid only five days after the Act received the royal assent.[4] Over the next twenty years meeting-houses sprang up in most of the towns and many of the villages of England and Wales, visible and permanent reminders of the failure of the established church to extinguish or comprehend Dissent.

The meeting-houses which have survived from the seventeenth century are not obviously ecclesiastical buildings, except that they are sometimes surrounded by graveyards. What is probably the oldest surviving Congregational chapel, that at Walpole in Suffolk, consists of two converted cottages; the oldest Quaker meeting-house, at Broad Camden in Gloucestershire, was converted from 'two bays of housing'; the second oldest, at

---

[1] W. H. Burgess, 'The Church Book of the General Baptist Church of Turners Hill', *TUHS* i (1917–18), 195.

[2] Dover General Baptist Church Book, 30 Sept. 1686. DWL MS. 38. 208.

[3] Speldhurst General Baptist Church Book, fo. 34v, British Museum Add. MS. 36. 709.

[4] Castle Gate Congregational Church Book, Nottingham, historical notes by Richard Preston.

Portishead in Somerset, was originally a thatched cottage; and the oldest Baptist meeting-house, at Tewkesbury, is from the outside scarcely distinguishable from the neighbouring dwellings. With their dark oak woodwork and furnishings, set against whitewashed walls and plain-glass windows, they have all the charm and simplicity of the domestic architecture of the period. Pews were arranged along three sides of the building, facing, except in Quaker meeting-houses, a raised pulpit and, in front of it, a central communion table. In contrast to the converted cottages is the meeting-house built for the Norwich Congregationalists in 1693, a rectangular building with a double row of tall windows separated by delicate brick pilasters and topped by stone corinthian capitals. But even this building has the appearance of a substantial town house rather than an ecclesiastical structure, and the contrast between Norwich Old Meeting and Walpole is a contrast between the resources of a prosperous city community and the functional needs of their less wealthy rural brethren, rather than a contrast of any ecclesiological significance.[1]

Horton Davies has pointed out that whereas the Anglicans followed Luther in believing that while Scripture was authoritative in matters of doctrine, it need not be treated as binding in matters of worship, the Dissenters, like Calvin, held that 'the books of the New Testament contain divine directions in all the most important parts of worship and discipline'.[2] In practice, though, the Dissenters inherited two rather different traditions of worship, the Separatist and the Puritan, and the resultant pattern of worship was an amalgam of the two. From the Separatists the Dissenters inherited their opposition to set forms of prayer, an attitude which had not been shared either by the Puritans of the sixteenth century or the Presbyterians of the Westminster Assembly.[3] Robert Browne had castigated Angli-

---

[1] These early meeting-houses are described with affection and illustrated by K. Lindley, *Chapels and Meeting-houses* (1969), pp. 44–8. Quaker meeting-houses are attractively illustrated in K. H. Southall, *Our Quaker Heritage, Early Meeting Houses* (York, 1975). The claim of the thatched Congregational chapel at Horningsham in Wiltshire to be the oldest in the country has been disputed. C. Stell, 'Our Architectural Heritage', *Journal of the United Reformed Church History Society*, i (1975), 166.

[2] H. Davies, *Worship of the English Puritans* (1948), pp. 3, 16. Bury Street Records, *TCHS* vi (1913–15), 333.

[3] Davies, *Worship of the English Puritans*, pp. 48, 111–12.

can services as 'stinted', 'their tossing to and fro of psalms and sentences . . . like tennis-play where to God is called a judge who can do best and be most gallant in his worship', and his views were echoed by John Owen and the Congregationalists in the following century.[1] The General Baptists and the Quakers, following the example of the London Separatists of the 1580s and 1590s, took their opposition to set forms of prayer to the extent of proscribing even the Lord's Prayer.[2] And in reacting against Parliament's attempt to impose the Prayer Book on the nation in 1662, the Presbyterians, too, came to share the Separatist hostility to liturgies and to set prayers.[3]

In the case of preaching the reverse happened, and it was the Puritan rather than the Separatist tradition which proved the more durable. For the Puritan the sermon was the crucial point of the service, the moment at which, to quote Baxter, the pastor stood 'up in the face of [the] congregation, [to] deliver a message of salvation or damnation, as from the living God, in the name of our Redeemer'.[4] The Separatists had a more democratic tradition of preaching, a belief in the liberty of prophesying which meant that any member of the congregation who felt moved by the Holy Spirit could rise and deliver his message to the church. But prophesying was not always compatible with reverent worship. The meetings of the 'ancient' Separatist church at Amsterdam were disturbed by 'prophets' who 'openly contradicted and quarrelled with each other',[5] and we have seen the horrified fascination with which Thomas Edwards described the 'disputes and wranglings' in Thomas Lamb's Bell Alley church in 1646. Consequently prophesying fell into disuse in the second half of the century. Some congregations continued to hold meetings for prophecy on mid-week evenings and the practice was revived by Richard Davis's church at Rothwell in 1700,[6] but, apart from the Quakers, no Dissenting church appears to have retained

---

[1] *Writings of Harrison and Browne*, p. 415. G. F. Nuttall, 'The First Nonconformists', in *From Uniformity to Unity*, p. 168.

[2] Speldhurst General Baptist Church Book, fo. 17. Burrage, *EED* ii. 43, 56. *Writings of Greenwood*, pp. 261–2, 295.

[3] Davies, *Worship of the English Puritans*, pp. 102–8, 161.

[4] Ibid., p. 183, quoting Baxter, *The Reformed Pastor* (1860), p. 128.

[5] Powicke, *Barrow*, p. 236.

[6] Taylor, *General Baptists*, i. 431. Glass, *Independent Church at Rothwell*, p. 69.

prophesying as part of its Sunday worship after 1660. When Thomas Brade of the Speldhurst General Baptist church in Kent interrupted the sermon of Reuben Coppis in 1695, because he had spoken too long and strayed too far from his text, the church reproved Brade since his action 'would open a door to the discontented that it would become hard for any man to preach a sermon without interruption'.[1] Even the Quakers, who have retained prophesying as an essential part of worship to the present day, on occasion experienced its inconveniences. In the 1670s the meetings of the Bristol Quakers were disturbed by the 'babbling' of a certain William Davis and 'the crazy woman' Katherine Wellsteed, and in 1681 a door-keeper was paid 10s. a quarter to keep them out of the meeting.[2] During the Wilkinson–Story controversy another Bristol Quaker, Elizabeth Stirredge, claimed that she was moved by the Holy Spirit to interrupt John Story while he was speaking and to cry 'woe to that pot that the scum remains in it, for it is the broth of abominable things'.[3] Early in the eighteenth century the meetings of the Hertford Friends were disturbed by the interruptions of the 'troublesome, malicious, and vexatious' Susan Featherston.[4] And in 1691 the Norwich Quakers disowned James Duncks for persisting in 'speaking in our public meetings' despite the judgement of Friends that he was not qualified.[5]

The Norwich Friends' treatment of James Duncks is an illustration of the extent to which even Quaker worship was becoming formalized by the end of the seventeenth century. Although the Quakers did not have an ordained ministry, as did other denominations, they did have 'public Friends', or 'recorded ministers' as they came to be called in the eighteenth century, who were acknowledged to have a special gift of utterance by their Monthly Meeting, and who were often given leave to undertake itinerant journeys to other gatherings of Friends. By the late seventeenth century Quaker meetings were relying increasingly on these 'public travelling Friends' to provide the

---

[1] Speldhurst Church Book, fo. 19v.

[2] *Minute Book of the Men's Meeting of the Society of Friends in Bristol*, ed. R. Mortimer, Bristol Record Society, xxvi (1971), 87, 144–5, 158.

[3] Mortimer, 'Quakerism in Seventeenth Century Bristol', p. 115.

[4] V. A. Rowe, *The First Hertford Quakers* (Hertford, 1970), pp. 45–6.

[5] Eddington, *Quakerism in Norwich*, p. 56.

spoken ministry and in their absence meetings were frequently held in silence.[1] It was one of William Mucklow's complaints against the Quaker leadership in 1673 that 'public Friends' monopolized the meetings, and that other Quakers came only as 'hearers, neglecting the gift in themselves, only waiting upon their lips'.[2] The change that was coming over Quaker meetings was reflected in their seating arrangements, with benches ranged along three sides of a square facing a raised bench or 'gallery' on the fourth side which was occupied by recorded ministers.[3]

In one important respect the Dissenters of the age of toleration were not content with their Separatist or Puritan inheritances, but made a major contribution of their own to English worship. At the time of the passing of the Toleration Act the singing of hymns was largely unknown to English congregations, whether they met in parish churches or in Dissenting meeting-houses. Anglican and Presbyterian congregations sang metrical versions of the psalms, usually in the literal translations of Sternhold and Hopkins, but Anglicans no less than Dissenters followed Calvin instead of Luther in rejecting the use of hymns of the ground that they were of human rather than of divine composition. Some Dissenting churches eschewed congregational singing altogether. Both the General Baptists and the Quakers, though they did not in theory object to the singing of psalms by individuals during worship, were opposed to singing by the whole congregation on the ground that this required such 'carnal formalities' as the use of rhyme and metre and would involve unconverted persons in singing the praises of God.[4] Among the Particular Baptists and Congregationalists practice varied from congregation to congregation, but in both denominations there was a strong movement in favour of congregational singing once the Toleration Act had made it safe for churches to advertise their presence by song. In 1690 the Bedford Congregational church agreed that 'the public singing of psalms be practised by the church with a caution that non

---

[1] Mortimer, 'Quakerism in Seventeenth Century Bristol', p. 115.

[2] Braithwaite, SPQ, p. 293.

[3] Lindley, Chapels and Meeting-houses, p. 63. Lloyd, Quaker Social History, pp. 129–31.

[4] Minutes of the General Baptist Assembly, i. 27. Davies, Worship of the English Puritans, p. 169. Burgess, John Smith, p. 174.

others perform it but such as can sing with grace in their hearts'.[1] And it was in the Congregational and Particular Baptist churches of the late seventeenth and early eighteenth centuries that the crucial evolution from psalm-singing to hymn-singing took place.

The first English hymn-book, consisting largely of translations of German Lutheran hymns, was published by Miles Coverdale in the reign of Henry VIII, but the book was banned by the king and had no enduring significance. Nearly a century later the Puritan poet George Wither published his *Hymnes and Songs of the Church* (1623) and obtained from James I a patent ordering it to be bound up with the psalms of Sternhold and Hopkins, but this so aroused the antagonism of the Stationers' Company that the patent was withdrawn in 1634 and Wither's hymns likewise had little subsequent influence. Later in the seventeenth century collections of hymns were issued by the London music publisher John Playford (1671) and by the eccentric Anglican clergyman and millenarian preacher John Mason (1683), but the Roman Catholic provenance of Playford's hymns militated against their acceptance, and Mason's hymns won greater favour among the Dissenters than among his fellow Anglicans.[2] Some Dissenters, including John Bunyan, Richard Baxter, and Vavasor Powell, themselves wrote hymns; John Goodwin's Coleman Street church sang hymns to celebrate Cromwell's victories at Dunbar and Worcester; and John Rogers's Independent church in Dublin also sang hymns in the 1650s.[3] But it was not until the first half of the eighteenth century that the practice of congregational hymn-singing became firmly established among English Dissenters, while among Anglicans hymns did not meet with universal approval until well into the nineteenth century.

In a number of Dissenting churches in the late seventeenth century the ground was prepared for the acceptance of hymn-singing in full congregation by the introduction of a hymn at the close of the communion service, for which the precedent of the

[1] Brown, *John Bunyan*, p. 400.
[2] L. F. Benson, *The English Hymn* (New York, 1915), pp. 25, 66, 71, 75. C. S. Phillips, *Hymnody Past and Present* (1937), pp. 151, 157–8, 161.
[3] R. Tudur Jones, 'The Life, Work, and Thought of Vavasor Powell', Oxford D. Phil. thesis, 1947, p. 306. Kirby, 'The Parish of St. Stephen's, Coleman Street', p. 160. Rogers, *Ohel or Beth-Shemesh*, Epistle Dedicatory, p. 91.

Last Supper could be cited.[1] Richard Davis of Rothwell published in the 1690s a collection of 168 *Hymns composed on several subjects and on divers occasions* which included a number of hymns found in the study of his predecessor, Thomas Browning, 'and used by him at the Lord's table'. Joseph Stennett, the pastor of a Seventh-day Baptist church which met in Curriers' Hall, began to use his own hymns at the Lord's Supper in the 1690s and published them for the use of other congregations in 1697.[2] But the transition from communion to congregational hymn-singing was not always accepted without protest, and the need for caution on the part of the advocates of hymn-singing is seen in the career of Benjamin Keach. Once the pastor of a General Baptist church in Southwark, Keach had joined the Particular Baptists in 1672 and founded a new church at Horsleydown. Soon after the church's formation he began the practice of singing a hymn at the close of the communion service, but it was not until 1691 that he persuaded the church to agree to the singing of a hymn at the end of its Sunday services, and even then the innovation provoked furious opposition. Members who had hitherto tolerated singing by their fellow church members at the Lord's Supper were not prepared to countenance what Isaac Marlow, a London merchant, described in a pamphlet as singing by 'a promiscuous assembly of professors and profane men and women'. Disaffected members of Keach's church distributed copies of Marlow's pamphlet to other members and argued against congregational singing on the grounds that it involved 'such close communion with the world' and the singing of women in the church 'contrary to the word of God'. Keach's chief opponents were excommunicated and they and their supporters founded a new Particular Baptist church in Fleur de Lys Yard, Tooley Street (later Maze Pond), which maintained its opposition to singing until 1736.

Dissension over singing troubled other Baptist churches. When, in 1692, the Bow Street General Baptist church, Covent Garden, allowed its minister 'to sing a psalm or hymn after the work of preaching and praying' it was criticized by the rest of the London General Baptist churches and declared itself 'free and independent of the other churches'. The Particular

---

[1] Matthew 26:30.
[2] Benson, *The English Hymn*, pp. 100, 104–5.

Baptist church which met first in Petty France and then in Artillery Lane, Spitalfields, suffered secessions over the question of hymn-singing in 1700 and again in 1706. And in 1703 the Tiverton Particular Baptist church reprimanded Thomas Brabham for attempting to 'set up singing' in the neighbouring Cullompton church, and did not relinquish its opposition to singing until 1732.[1]

Keach published a volume of 300 hymns in 1691, but his verses were too uncouth to gain wide acceptance in the Augustan age, and it was not until Isaac Watts published his *Hymns and Spiritual Songs* in 1707 that the advocates of congregational hymn-singing had an effective weapon with which to overcome the objections of their opponents. Watts was the son of a prosperous Southampton cloth-maker who also kept a school and was deacon of the town's Congregational church. In 1674, the year in which Isaac was born, his father's Dissent led to his imprisonment in Southampton gaol, and it was said that the baby Isaac was often suckled on the prison steps as his mother waited to visit her husband. Isaac obtained an early start in education from his father, learning Latin at the age of four, Greek at nine, French at ten, and Hebrew at thirteen, and at the age of seven he was already composing respectable verse. When he was sixteen he entered the academy run by the Congregationalist Thomas Rowe in Little Britain in the city of London and he subsequently succeeded Isaac Chauncey as minister of the Mark Lane Congregational church. Charitable to those who disagreed with him on points of theology, generous in his use of money, and though suffering from chronic ill-health, and sometimes of hasty temper, Watts was a popular preacher and under his leadership his church soon outgrew its Mark Lane premises, moving first to Pinners' Hall and then to a new meeting-house in Bury Street, built in 1708 to house a congregation of 428.[2] But it is as a hymn-writer that Watts is remembered today when many other excellent pastors are forgotten.

[1] Maze Pond, Southwark, Particular Baptist Church Book, 1691–1745, pp. 31–49 Baptist Church House. Crosby, *History of the Baptists*, iv. 298–301. H. Martin, 'The Baptist Contribution to Early English Hymnody', *Baptist Quarterly*, xix (1961–2), 199–207. Wilson, *Dissenting Churches in London*, iv. 286. C. Woollacott, *Brief History of the Baptist Church in Little Wild Street* (1858), p. 12. H. B. Case, *The History of the Baptist Church in Tiverton* (Tiverton, 1907), pp. 25–6, 31.

[2] A. P. Davis, *Isaac Watts* (1943), pp. 2–8, 29, 219.

Watts objected to the monopoly which Jewish psalms occupied in Christian praise, 'with confessions of sins you never committed, with complaints of sorrows which you never felt; cursing such enemies as you never had; giving thanks for such victories as you never obtained; or leading you to speak . . . of things, places, and actions you never knew'.[1] His *Hymns and Spiritual Songs* contained both paraphrases of New Testament passages and verses of his own composition, and twelve years after the appearance of this volume, in 1719, he published *The Psalms of David imitated in the language of the New Testament* in which he sought 'to teach my author to speak like a Christian'. The latter collection contained such well-known paraphrases a 'Jesus shall reign where e'r the sun', 'Our God, our help in ages past'. 'How pleas'd and blest was I'; the former included 'I'm not ashamed to own my Lord', 'Join all the glorious names', and one of the greatest of all Christian hymns, 'When I survey the wondrous cross'.[2] By expressing the central tenets of the Christian faith in simple, direct, and often beautiful language which the ordinary believer could apply to his own experience, Watts set the pattern for the 'flowering of English hymnody' over the next century. At the time of his death in 1748 sixteen editions of his hymns and seven editions of his psalms had been published.[3] They were being used in Congregational, Presbyterian, and Particular Baptist meeting-houses, and although most General Baptist churches maintained their opposition to the singing of 'men's composures with tuneable notes and a mixed multitude', a minority of General Baptist churches were using hymns by 1733 and in that year the General Assembly agreed that such peccadilloes were undeserving of censure.[4] Only the Quakers remained untouched by Watts's hymns.

The order of service in Watts's Bury Street meeting-house was described in 1723 in the following terms:

In the morning we begin with singing a psalm, then a short prayer follows to desire the divine presence in all the following parts of worship; after that, about half an hour is spent in the exposition of some portion of Scripture, which is succeeded by singing a psalm or an hymn. After this the minister prays more at large, for all the

[1] Davies, *Worship of the English Puritans*, pp. 176–7.
[2] Ibid., pp. 177–9.   [3] Davis, *Isaac Watts*, p. 207.
[4] *Minutes of the General Baptist Assembly*, ii. 18.

variety of blessings, spiritual and temporal, for the whole congregation, with confessions of sins, and thanksgivings for mercies. ...
Then a sermon is preached, and the morning worship concluded
with a short prayer and the benediction.

A second service was held in the afternoon, in which the same
order was followed, except 'that we omit the first short prayer
and the exposition, and sing the psalm or hymn just after the
sermon'. And on the first Sunday of every month the Lord's
Supper was celebrated, usually following the afternoon sermon,
but sometimes in winter at noon, to enable members to return
home before the light faded.[1] Services were long by today's
standards: sermons usually lasted an hour, and the prayers, psalms,
and exposition of Scripture would take up another. Nor was the
afternoon service the end of the day's devotions. In many
Dissenting homes Sunday evening was set aside for family worship, during which time sermons heard during the day were
repeated either from notes or from memory.[2] And in most pious
homes not only Sunday but every day began and ended with
family devotions. 'If the worship of God be not in the house',
wrote Philip Henry, then 'write "Lord have mercy on us" upon
the door, for there is a plague, a curse in it.'[3]

Sunday, wrote A. G. Matthews, 'retained its lonely splendour
as his sole red-letter day of the Puritan calendar'.[4] Robert
Browne regarded Christmas, Easter, and Whitsuntide as 'dung
... received from Baal'; the Westminster Assembly resolved
that 'festival-days, vulgarly called holy-days, having no warrant
in the word of God, are not to be continued'; and Dissenting
hostility to such occasions lasted well into the nineteenth
century.[5] The Presbyterian Oliver Heywood devoted Christmas
day 1671 to fasting; the Congregationalist Thomas Jollie spent
25 December 1673 'in mourning for the sin of the time privately
and in prayers'; and the Quakers with characteristic iconoclasm
opened their shops on Christmas day.[6] In Bristol in 1663 the

---

[1] Bury Street Records, *TCHS* vi. (1913–15), 334.
[2] Bogue and Bennett, *History of Dissenters*, ii. 105.
[3] *Diaries and Letters of Philip Henry*, p. 73.
[4] Davies, *Worship of the English Puritans*, p. 41, quoting A. G. Matthews in *Christian Worship*, ed. N. Micklem (1936), p. 173.
[5] *Writings of Harrison and Browne*, p. 168. Davies, *Worship of the English Puritans*, p. 140.
[6] *Heywood's Autobiography*, i. 285. *Notebook of Thomas Jolly*, p. 12.

servants of Quaker shop-owners who worked on 25 December were seized by soldiers and 'tied neck and heels together with half hundredweights and muskets hanging about their necks'; in Monmouth in 1668 two Friends were imprisoned for keeping their shops open on Christmas day; in Weymouth in 1671 constables celebrated the birth of Christ by raiding Quaker shops and throwing their stock into the streets; and in Norwich in 1676 Quakers were attacked with snowballs and the windows of their shops broken, 'upon the 25th. day of the 10th. month . . . for opening their shops upon that day'.[1] The one day in the year which some Dissenters did permit themselves to celebrate with unaccustomed festivity was 5 November, the anniversary both of Parliament's escape from Roman Catholic treachery in 1605 and of William of Orange's landing in Tor Bay in 1688. Thomas Bradbury preached political sermons on that day and then withdrew to a tavern to join in the singing of 'The Roast Beef of Old England'.[2]

But when Dissenters usually wished to mark a special occasion they did so not by feasting but by fasting. Fasts were held frequently, on days set apart for the election and ordination of church officers and on occasions of national or personal crisis. Oliver Heywood kept, on average, thirty-five fasts a year: on the anniversary of his ejection on St. Bartholomew's day 1662, at the time of the plague in 1665, when a young man at Wakefield was 'judged to be possessed', when a woman was concerned 'for her mother's soul', and so on.[3] The Broadmead church, Bristol, spent two days in prayer in 1673 at the home of John Fry who had fallen into a fit, 'raving and striking them that came to hold him', so that he had to be bound to his bed, and blaspheming 'against the whole Deity'. He recovered, and three years later was still in a 'gracious frame of spirit'.[4] Similarly in 1697 the General Baptist church at Fair Street, Southwark, kept a day of fasting and prayer from eight in the

---

[1] Mortimer, 'Quakerism in Seventeenth Century Bristol', p. 33. T. Mardy Rees, *The Quakers in Wales* (Carmarthen, 1925), p. 74. Whiting, *English Puritanism*, p. 162. Eddington, *Quakerism in Norwich*, p. 94.

[2] E. Bushrod, 'The History of Unitarianism in Birmingham from the middle of the eighteenth century to 1893', Birmingham Univ. M.A. thesis, 1954, p. 82. C. Robbins, *The Eighteenth-Century Commonwealthman* (Cambridge, Mass., 1959), p. 236.

[3] *Heywood's Autobiography*, i. 190–1, 197–8, 199, 271–2, 281. ii. 43, 227.

[4] *Broadmead Records*, pp. 84–6.

morning till six in the evening at the home of a member whose daughter lay 'in a deplorable condition'. At the next church meeting a day of thanksgiving was set aside for the girl's restoration to health.[1] In August 1713, in the last critical year of Queen Anne's reign, the Abergavenny Congregational church appointed a day of fasting and prayer in which they petitioned for 'Brother Bagehot in his afflictive circumstances', for Sister Watson's 'disordered daughter', and for 'God's over-ruling the present elections for the ensuing Parliament'. Three more fast days were held in the winter of 1713–14 for 'our civil and religious concerns', but in October 1714 the church was able to hold 'a day of solemn thanksgiving' for God's 'delivering us from our late fears . . . by settling the king on the throne in peace'.[2]

6. RITES OF INITIATION: THE ORDINATION OF MINISTERS AND THE ADMISSION OF MEMBERS

Meetings for worship, the celebration of the Lord's Supper, days set apart for fasting and prayer, assumed a similar pattern, except for the vexed question of singing, among Presbyterians, Congregationalists, and General and Particular Baptists alike. But the emphasis placed on other ordinances varied from denomination to denomination and reflected the differing polities of the four denominations. The Presbyterians vested greater authority in their pastors than did the other Dissenters and for them the examination and ordination of the minister was an event of supreme importance. By contrast, in the Congregational and Baptist churches authority rested in the last resort with the members, and in these denominations corresponding attention was paid to the examination of applicants for church membership, and, among the Baptists, to the rite of believers' baptism.

The method of appointing a Presbyterian minister varied from meeting to meeting: the decision could lie either with the trustees of the meeting-house, or with those who made a regular financial contribution to the cause, or with 'the greater number

[1] Taylor, *General Baptists*, i. 430.
[2] Abergavenny Church Book, PRO RG 4 1241.

of the usual auditors, being housekeepers'.[1] On occasion the pastor of a large meeting could even take it upon himself to appoint his own assistant and eventual successor.[2] But however appointed a Presbyterian minister was not, like a Congregational or Baptist pastor, subject to the control of a regular church meeting—there were only two church meetings in the thirty-two years that Thomas Reynolds was minister at the King's Weigh House[3]—and consequently he was less easily removed. Great care thus had to be taken that only proper persons were admitted to the ministry and the formidable ordination procedure devised by the Westminster Assembly was designed to secure this end. When, for example, three candidates were ordained in Yorkshire in 1687 the proceedings took two full days. On the first day the candidates were examined by three ministers on their knowledge of the Greek and Hebrew Scriptures, philosophy, and divinity, and on the second they were each required to present and defend a theological thesis. The first two candidates presented their theses in Latin but the third, 'who begged leave to deliver himself in English' left the examiners dissatisfied and a special plea concerning his 'pious conversation' had to be entered on his behalf. The candidates were then required to make a confession of faith, and were examined on their beliefs, their motives for entering the ministry, and their abilities as pastors. After all this the three men were ordained by the laying on of hands, a sermon was preached, and the proceedings ended with the singing of a psalm.[4]

Among the Congregationalists and Baptists ordination was a much simpler procedure. When Isaac Watts was ordained to the pastorate of the Mark Lane church in 1702 only one day of fasting and prayer was set aside, and after a neighbouring minister had begun the day with prayer a deacon of the church asked the members whether they were agreed in their choice of Watts as their pastor, 'to which a vote was given by every brother present in the affirmative'. Watts replied by accepting the office, and other ministers followed with prayers and an

[1] Brockett, *Nonconformity in Exeter*, p. 105. Bolam, 'Presbyterianism in Derbyshire, etc.,' p. 478.

[2] Calamy, *Historical Account*, i. 361.

[3] E. Kaye, *History of the King's Weigh House Church* (1968), p. 29.

[4] Hunter, *Life of Heywood*, pp. 284–6.

appropriate sermon.[1] There were some Congregationalists, as we have seen in the case of Richard Davis, who refused to allow other ministers to play any part in the ordination, and when the covenant of the Burwell and Soham Congregational church in Cambridgeshire was renewed in 1707 it was with the specific condition that the church would not surrender its powers of ordination 'to a classis of ministers'.[2] Although such rigid attitudes do not appear to have persisted long into the eighteenth century,[3] Congregational ordinations remained primarily a transaction between a church and its chosen pastor rather than, as among the Presbyterians, a transaction between ministers.

The Congregationalists and Baptists examined prospective members with almost as much care as the Presbyterians examined prospective ministers. Indeed, some would argue that the Congregationalists and Baptists exercised more care, for what concerned them was not an applicant's knowledge of philosophy or facility in Latin, but his spiritual experience. Among the Presbyterians a person was admitted to communion either on the sole authority of the minister, or after the minister had informed the existing communicants that an application for admission to communion had been received, and would be granted if no objection was forthcoming.[4] By contrast the Congregationalists and Baptists used an elaborate procedure to guarantee that only those who could give some account of their faith and experience were admitted to the church. Once again the practice of Isaac Watts's church can be cited as typical. When a person indicated a wish to join the church, Watts talked with him 'concerning his knowledge of the things of God . . . his hearty profession of repentance toward God, and faith toward our Lord Jesus Christ', and if satisfied with his spiritual state the pastor informed one or two deacons who would then accompany the pastor in a second interview. If this second interview also proved satisfactory the application was laid before the church, 'that they may have a month's time for more public inquiry into his behaviour in the world; whether his character be unblemished and honourable'. If after this

---

[1] 'Dr. Watts's Church Book', *TCHS* i (1901–4), 36–8.
[2] *TCHS* vii (1916–18), 7.
[3] Bogue and Bennett, *History of Dissenters*, iii. 354.
[4] A.B. 'A View of the Dissenting Interest in London', 1732, DWL MS. 38. 18, pp. 94–5.

time 'nothing blameable or offensive' could be discovered about the applicant the pastor would give an account of his profession of faith to the church and the church was required to say whether or not they were prepared to accept him into membership. If accepted, the candidate was admitted to membership of the church at the next celebration of the Lord's Supper. It is significant that whereas Watts's church was prepared to accept into membership applicants who had been members of other Congregational or Baptist churches simply on the basis of a recommendation from the applicant's former church, in the case of a person who had been a member of a Presbyterian meeting it required in addition 'some account of the reasons of his hope'.[1]

Baptists, of course, besides examining the applicant's spiritual state and character, normally expected him to undergo believer's baptism before being admitted to church membership. Baptism was by total immersion, and in the early eighteenth century only a handful of meeting-houses, such as those belonging to the Particular Baptists of Norwich or to the Baptists of Paul's Alley, Barbican, had specifically constructed baptistries sunk into the meeting-house floor.[2] When the Paul's Alley baptistry was built in 1716 at the expense of the Hollises, a family of wealthy drapers, the meeting-house was also provided with three changing rooms, for the minister and candidates of both sexes, a lead water pump, a stove to keep the candidates warm, two new black gowns and a dressing gown for the minister, eight cinnamon-coloured serge coats for the candidates and four serge petticoats for the women.[3] The baptistry was used by other Baptist churches in London, and candidates were expected to pay 2s. each to offset the running costs, but outside London the vast majority of baptisms in the late seventeenth and early eighteenth centuries were held out of doors. Baptist records often carry accounts of out-door baptisms being performed in conditions of 'hard frost and deep snow', with the candidates emerging none the worse for their experience. 'Let none be afraid to venture into the water when the season is cold', commented John Cropper, senior elder of the Fenstanton

[1] Bury Street Records, *TCHS* vi (1913–15), 336–9.
[2] C. B. Jewson, *Baptists in Norfolk* (1957), p. 81.
[3] Paul's Alley General Baptist Church, Baptistry book, DWL MS. 38. 75.

General Baptist church, 'lest they be laid in their graves before the weather be warm.'[1]

Not all Baptist churches insisted on baptism as a condition of church membership, and in the seventeenth century a dozen or so Calvinist gathered churches are known to have treated baptism as an open question and to have included advocates of both infant and believers' baptism in the same fellowship.[2] But such agreements to differ did not always prove durable, and while some churches, such as College Lane, Northampton, carried their traditions of open membership into the nineteenth century,[3] others became either purely paedobaptist or entirely Baptist: in Wales open-membership Baptist churches tended to become Congregational, whereas the Broadmead church, Bristol, which had treated baptism as an open question since 1653, 'though for the most part baptized' by 1674, became exclusively Baptist in 1733.[4] The most famous of all open membership churches, the Bunyan Meeting, Bedford, has not always found it easy to accommodate Baptists and paedobaptists in the same fellowship, and while the conversion of its minister to Baptist views led to the secession of part of its Congregational membership in 1773, twenty years later the appointment of a Congregational minister led to the loss of nineteen of its Baptist members.[5]

7. RIGHTS OF MEMBERS: THE POSITION OF WOMEN AND THE EXERCISE OF DISCIPLINE

Once admitted to the membership of a Baptist or Congregational church, the new member was able to take a full part in the business meetings of the church—providing he was male. From the early days of the Separatist movement women had usually outnumbered men in Dissenting congregations,[6] Episcopalian and Presbyterian pamphleteers had lamented the presence of

---

[1] *Broadmead Records*, pp. 61–2. *Fenstanton Records*, p. 264.

[2] Nuttall, *Visible Saints*, pp. 118–20.

[3] E. A. Payne, *The Fellowship of Believers* (2nd edn., 1955), p. 79.

[4] Richards, *Wales under the Indulgence*, p. 39. *Broadmead Records*, pp. 35, 92, 305.

[5] H. G. Tibbutt, *Bunyan Meeting Bedford* (Bedford, 1950), pp. 35, 43. Thompson List DWL MS. 38. 6.

[6] K. Thomas, 'Women and the Civil War Sects', in *Crisis in Europe*, ed. T. Aston (1965), pp. 320–1.

women preachers in Separatist conventicles in the 1640s, and women had figured prominently in the Quaker missionary movement, both in England and abroad. But for all this, women were not accorded equality with men. The early Separatists and later Nonconformists, searching their Bibles for every detail of church government, not surprisingly endorsed Paul's prohibition of women speakers. Francis Johnson believed that women should confine their talents to domestic matters; John Smyth refused to allow women to prophesy and was not sure that they should be allowed to vote; and Bunyan dismissed the claim of women to speak in church with the comment, 'When Miriam began to perk it before Moses, God covered her face with a leprous scab'.[1] It was customary in the meeting-houses of the late seventeenth and early eighteenth centuries for men and women to sit apart, the men's side distinguished by a row of wooden pegs for their hats, and although women were usually allowed to attend church business meetings, they were not normally permitted to speak.[2] Women might speak in a church meeting in order to make a profession of faith, the Midland Particular Baptist Association agreed in 1656, but for the rest they should acknowledge 'the inferiority of their sex' by keeping quiet.[3] The Particular Baptist church which met in Fleur de Lys Yard in Southwark in 1694 regarded the sisters of the church as 'being equally with the brethren members of the mystical body of Christ' and accorded them the right to vote 'by lifting up of their hands', but at the same time it insisted that women should be excluded 'from prayer, prophesying, and giving of thanks' and from 'all church offices'.[4] The one office which women were permitted to hold in some churches was one which appeared to have Pauline sanction: widows over the age of sixty were given special responsibility for the care of the sick.[5]

The Quakers, relying on the inspiration of the Spirit rather than on the letter of Scripture, gave their womenfolk a larger, though still not equal, part in the worship and government of

[1] Ibid., p. 322. *Works of John Smyth*, ii. 256. Lloyd, *Quaker Social History*, p. 107.

[2] Lindley, *Chapels and Meeting-houses*, p. 36. Browne, *Congregationalism in Norfolk and Suffolk*, p. 240.

[3] *Association Records of the Particular Baptists*, i. 28.

[4] Maze Pond Particular Baptist Church Book, 1691–1745, p. 109, Baptist Church House.

[5] *Association Records*, i. 11. *Broadmead Records*, pp. 187–8.

the church. Women Friends were permitted to prophesy and to become itinerant ministers, and in the 1670s Fox secured the establishment of separate business meetings for women, meetings which came to have special responsibilities for the relief of the poor. But responsibility for major issues of finance remained with the men's meetings, and women were excluded from the executive bodies of the Friends, the Morning Meeting of Ministers and the Meeting for Sufferings, and from the business sessions of the Yearly Meeting.[1] If a dispute arose between a men's meeting and a women's meeting, it was the latter which had to climb down. When, at the beginning of the eighteenth century, women ministers in London started to hold meetings on Saturdays to determine which meetings they should attend the following day, the men's Morning Meeting put a stop to it. Women ministers, they said, spoke too long.[2]

One of the chief tasks of the Quaker Monthly Meeting and of Independent and Baptist church meetings was the exercise of discipline. Before the Civil War Puritans had complained of the laxity of discipline in the Church of England, and after the Restoration Dissenters could scarcely be more liberal than an established church which continued to exclude persons from communion for adultery, fornication, and drunkenness, and which until the end of the eighteenth century expected women found guilty of fornication to do public penance 'bareheaded, barefooted, and barelegged' and draped in a white sheet.[3] Among the Dissenters, though, the exercise of discipline varied from denomination to denomination and even from church to church. An anonymous Congregationalist who penned a 'View of the Dissenting Interest in London' in 1732 claimed that 'the Presbyterians very rarely if ever as a church enquire into the conduct and behaviour of their members', that it was almost as rare for them to expel any of their members 'for heresy or disorderly walking', and that 'for want of proper discipline immoral persons are continued in their societies'.[4] The accusation is obviously partisan, and there is some evidence to suggest

---

[1] Braithwaite, *SPQ*, p. 286.
[2] Lloyd, *Quaker Social History*, p. 118.
[3] *Archbishop Herring's Visitation Returns*, vol. i, p. xviii, vol. iii, p. 226. A. C. Wood, 'Nottinghamshire Penances, 1590–1794', *Trans. of the Thoroton Society of Nottinghamshire*, xlviii (1944), 52–63.
[4] 'View of the Dissenting Interest', p. 96.

that Presbyterian discipline could be as strict as that of the Congregationalists or Baptists. In the 1690s the Presbyterian meeting in Nottingham suspended Elizabeth Gee 'for lying, slandering, [and] talebearing', Margaret Hancock for 'notorious lying', William Field for drunkenness, and Deborah Short for 'too great familiarity with . . . her paramour'.[1] Vincent Alsop, the pastor of the Tothill Street Presbyterian meeting in London, refused communion to Titus Oates after a member of the congregation had questioned his fitness, but the General Baptist church in Virginia Street admitted Oates to membership around 1698, only to regret it almost immediately when he became involved in an unsavoury dispute over the will of a member of the church.[2]

It is, however, difficult to generalize about the nature of Presbyterian discipline since it was usually exercised by the minister, either on his own authority or in consultation with the committee which managed the church's secular affairs, and there was consequently no need for acts of discipline to be recorded as they were in the minute books of Baptist or Congregational church meetings. Apart from the entries in the records of the Presbyterian meeting in Nottingham, which were restricted to the space of four years, I have come across only two sets of Presbyterian records in which cases of discipline were systematically minuted. In the first, the minutes of the Devon and Cornwall association of ministers, the largely Presbyterian Exeter Assembly, it was ministers, or candidates for the ministry, rather than laymen who were disciplined. John Edwards, pastor to the Presbyterian meeting at Honiton, was disowned by the Assembly because his wife had given birth to a child only 'twenty weeks after they were married'; the ordination of Thomas Edgley of Totnes was postponed on account of his supposed 'indecent carriages towards women'; and John Prew, a ministerial candidate, was disowned for 'immoral and scandalous practices'.[3] Only once between 1691 and 1717 did the Exeter Assembly concern itself with the disciplining of a layman, when it advised that 'a professor that hath been scan-

---

[1] High Pavement Registers, 1690–1723, p. 21. Transcripts in Nottingham University Library.
[2] Calamy, *Historical Account*, i. 120–1. Crosby, *English Baptists*, iii. 169–80.
[3] *Exeter Assembly Minutes*, pp. 28, 45, 60.

dalously flagitious' should make open confession of his sin and 'be for some considerable time afterward kept from off the sacrament'.[1]

The only other Presbyterian records I have examined which provide evidence of the regular disciplining of members are those of the meeting at Brentford in Middlesex. Between 1701 and 1713 two men and two women were charged with un-Christian behaviour: William Badger was said to have been drunk in the Red Lion at Southwark; Elizabeth Stevenson was accused of deserting her husband and 'keeping a disorderly house' in a coffee-house in Falcon Court, Southwark; Goodman Kirby was charged with stealing a Scotsman's pack of cloth 'which was said to be lost or fallen into the Thames'; and Mary Caton was said to be pregnant by the 'coachman to Mr. Kingsford and . . . she was not married to him'. But in only two of these cases was any action taken: 'William Badger was required to appear before the brethren of the church' and to promise 'greater circumspection for the future', and Goodman Kirby was suspended from communion until he expressed sorrow for his action. But since Elizabeth Stevenson refused to attend meetings or answer the minister's letters, and since Mary Caton was said by her sister to be 'now living at Newington in Surrey', the cases against both women were dropped.[2] It is inconceivable that a Congregational, Baptist, or Quaker meeting would have thus allowed matters to rest without passing judgement on the offenders, and the Brentford records lend support to the Independent accusation that Presbyterian discipline was lax in application and infrequent in incidence. And in so far as the argument from silence carries weight, the dearth of information about discipline in other Presbyterian records points to the same conclusion. Only one person is known to have been disciplined by the Presbyterian meeting which met over the King's Weigh House in Little Eastcheap in the whole of the thirty-two years from 1695 to 1727 that Thomas Reynolds was its minister, and there is no record of any case of discipline during the fifteen-year pastorate of his successor James Wood.[3]

[1] Ibid., p. 50.

[2] Brentford Presbyterian (later Congregational) Church Book, 9 Apr.–16 Apr. 1701, 5 Sept. 1703, 4 Oct. 1713. Greater London County Record Office.

[3] Kaye, *History of the King's Weigh House*, p. 29. King's Weigh House Church Book, 1699–1795. DWL MS. 209. 1.

By contrast with the paucity of evidence concerning Presbyterian discipline, there is ample material to illustrate the way in which the gathered churches—and here the term includes the Quakers—felt obliged to support their claim to be separate from the world by guaranteeing the purity of their members' lives. But once again generalizations can be misleading, for the frequency with which disciplinary measures were resorted to varied a good deal among Congregational and Baptist churches. The rigour of a church's discipline was determined by the location of the congregation, the theological views of its minister, the evangelistic zeal of its members, and the nature of the constituency from which members were recruited. A growing rural church whose members were drawn from tightly knit communities in which everyone's personal failings were public knowledge, led by a pastor who sought to apply rigorously the moral precepts of the New Testament, a church engaged in continuous evangelistic activity and so constantly recruiting new members from the world, was likely to adopt, and indeed to need, more severe standards of discipline than an established, urban church whose members could live their lives with a degree of privacy, whose minister was tainted by liberalism, and whose membership was recruited largely from the children and grandchildren of former members, men and women whose personal code of conduct had been long determined by a life-time's association with the meeting-house. The Fenstanton General Baptist church in Huntingdonshire was founded by Henry Denne in 1645 and by 1656 178 people had been baptized, but of these fifty-three were at some time excommunicated.[1] Seven hundred and ninety-five members were added to the Rothwell Congregational church during the ministry of Richard Davis (1690–1714), but 199 were excommunicated during the same period.[2] By contrast not a single case of discipline was recorded in the minute book of the Fetter Lane Congregational church in London between 1703 and 1722, and by the 1730s the Nightingale Lane Congregational church was holding but one church meeting a year, and that only for the purpose of electing two deputies to 'manage the civil interests

[1] *Fenstanton Records*, pp. 251–4.
[2] Glass, *Independent Church at Rothwell*, pp. 61, 66.

of the Protestant Dissenters'.[1] When the cultivated and moderate Philip Doddridge was invited to the pastorate of the Pershore church in Worcestershire in 1723, composed of a mixture of Independents and Baptists, he declined in part because 'their method of church discipline [is] so very severe, that I am afraid I should be a little uneasy with them'.[2]

When Congregational and Baptist churches did attempt to discipline their members they sought to follow the rule laid down by Christ in Matthew's Gospel. If possible private sins were to be dealt with between brother and brother, and only if the offender was impenitent or the sin was 'commonly known' was the matter brought before the church.[3] If this happened the church would examine the evidence and if the offence was proved and regarded as particularly grave the offender would be excommunicated. But in most cases the offence would not be deemed serious enough to warrant such summary action and the offender would be admonished and urged to repent. If the admonition was heeded and the church was convinced of the offender's sincere repentance, he or she would be allowed to remain in communion with the church. If the admonition was ignored it would sometimes be repeated two or three times before hope of repentance was despaired of and sentence of excommunication was pronounced. In such cases, in the words of Paul, the sinner was delivered 'unto Satan for the destruction of the flesh, that the spirit may be saved in the day of the Lord Jesus'.[4] Even then the church would be prepared to restore the offender to membership and communion if, in the future, evidence of genuine repentance and a reformed life was forthcoming.

In general Quaker discipline was exercised in similar manner, though in detail Quaker practice sometimes differed from that of the Baptists and Congregationalists. Friends did not, at this period, keep formal lists of members and of course had no communion from which to excommunicate offenders. But in securing evidence of repentance the Quakers were even more

---

[1] Fetter Lane Congregational Church Book, Greater London Record Office. Nightingale Lane Congregational Church Book, Guildhall Library, London.

[2] *Correspondence of Doddridge*, i. 269.

[3] Matthew 18:15–17. Davies, *Worship of the English Puritans*, p. 237. Vann, *Social Development*, p. 96.

[4] I Corinthians 5:5.

exacting than the other denominations, and the penitent sinner was frequently required to draw up and sign a paper of self-condemnation before his contrition was accepted by his meeting. The first such paper of which we have evidence was that drawn up by James Nayler in 1659, confessing his faults 'in the night of my temptation . . . that all burdens may be taken off with the truth, and the truth cleared thereby',[1] and so notorious was the Nayler episode, and so determined was Fox that Friends should never again fall into such excesses, that it is likely that Nayler's confession served as the model for all subsequent Quaker papers of self-condemnation. Later Friends were sometimes required to give evidence of their repentance not only to their fellow Quakers but also to the world in the place where the offence had occurred. Thus when John Crew of Bristol was involved in a drunken brawl he was 'advised for his inward peace toward God and the clearing Truth from the reproach brought on it thereby, to go to the public house where the offence was given and condemn himself before all that may be there present'.[2] Failure to produce adequate evidence of repentance led to disownment by the Monthly Meeting, until such time as the offender might 'come to repentance and acknowledgment of the Truth from which he hath departed'.[3]

From the seventeenth to the nineteenth century the most common offences requiring the censure of Independent and Baptist churches were neglect of worship, drunkenness, and sexual lapses. Members who failed to attend Sunday services or who absented themselves from the Lord's Supper were reprimanded, and persistent absenteeism issued in expulsion. Congregationalists and Baptists who attended services at their parish church were also likely to be disciplined for their 'sin in joining in with false worship and therein going a whoring from Christ', and the Speldhurst General Baptists even admonished a member who dared to attend a Presbyterian service.[4]

---

[1] Nayler, *A Collection of Sundry Books*, p. liv.

[2] Mortimer, 'Quakerism in Seventeenth Century Bristol', p. 177.

[3] *First Minute Book of the Gainsborough Monthly Meeting of the Society of Friends, 1669–1719*, ed. H. W. Brace, Lincoln Record Society, xxxviii, xl, xliv (1948–51), ii. 148.

[4] Arnesby Particular Baptist Church Book, i. 75. Speldhurst General Baptist Church Book, fo. 20*r*.

Inns, unlike parish churches, were not out of bounds to Independents and Baptists, and Dissenters of the seventeenth and eighteenth centuries were not teetotal. Those members of the Presbyterian congregation at Hyde in Cheshire who travelled some distance to worship on Sundays brought their dinner with them and ate it in a room at the local inn; the Luton Particular Baptists similarly provided beer for members of their congregation who came from outlying villages and stayed 'all Lord's day'; and Peter Walkden, minister to two Presbyterian meetings in the Forest of Bowland, frequently refreshed himself at a local hostelry after he had ridden his horse through the Pennine valleys to take a Sunday service, and after the service would drink 'a penny pot of ale' before returning home.[1] But all Dissenting churches abhorred drunkenness, for it led to behaviour which brought the Gospel into disrepute, and in the gathered churches the drunkard had to mend his ways or be disowned. Thus John Rush, a member of the Bedford Congregational church, who was drunk 'above the ordinary rule of drunkenness', was summarily excommunicated after he had had to 'be carried home from the Swan' with 'the help of no less than three persons'.[2] Walter Horn of the Rothwell Congregational church was first admonished and then excommunicated 'for being drunk and found in the stocks'.[3] And Thomas Jacob of the Broadmead church, Bristol, admonished for being drunk and keeping bad company, was excommunicated twelve months later for fighting in the street and hitting his wife.[4] Even the selling of strong drink was deemed an unsuitable occupation for Christians by the Broadmead church and by the Quakers of Bristol and Exeter.[5]

Church members who got themselves involved in sexual scandals also brought discredit to the whole fellowship. It is hardly surprising, for example, that the Great Yarmouth Congregational church should expel Thomas Staunton for 'having

---

[1] T. Middleton, *A History of Hyde Chapel* (Manchester, 1908), p. 12. C. E. Freeman, 'A Luton Baptist Minute Book', *Publications of the Bedfordshire Historical Record Society*, xxv (1947), 160. W. Dobson, ed., *Extracts from the Diary of the Rev. Peter Walkden* (Preston, 1866), pp. 7, 10, 64, 102.

[2] Bunyan Meeting Church Book, p. 53. DWL MS. 209.2.

[3] Rothwell Church Book, pp. 62, 70. DWL MS. 201.42.

[4] *Broadmead Records*, pp. 156–8, 172.

[5] Ibid., p. 90. *Minute Book of the Society of Friends in Bristol*, p. 98. Brockett, *Nonconformity in Exeter*, p. 112.

three wives', or that the Turner's Hill General Baptist church in Sussex should cast out John Potter who 'did beget a child on his own daughter'.[1] Similarly the White's Alley General Baptist church in London had little choice but to excommunicate Ben Adams, who was found guilty 'of picking up harlots in the streets', or to dispense with the services of its pastor, Joseph Taylor, who admitted trying to pick up five different women and keeping company 'with a common whore in a common bawdy house'.[2] The Nightingale Lane Congregational church was likewise obliged to take action against a Rotherhithe man who 'had raised a very great scandal by having a child by his servant-maid under promise of marriage, which when born was said to be dropped in' the night-cart which collected the refuse.[3] But even in this latter case the culprit was given an opportunity to humble himself before the church meeting—which he refused—before excommunication was agreed to, and in other churches severity was frequently tempered by compassion. In 1688 Mary Boreman was expelled from the Speldhurst General Baptist church on account of her 'whorish' behaviour, and she subsequently 'brought forth a bastard child', but six years later, having returned to the worship of the church 'as a proof of her constant and unfeigned humility', she was again 'granted her free communion'.[4] In 1704 John Johnson of the Kimbolton Independent church was found guilty 'of drunkenness and too much familiarity with a woman that is reported to be a common whore', but after he had 'declared his repentance for his sins with great brokenness of spirit ... he was restored into the affections and bosom of the church with more than ordinary joy to all present'.[5] And concern for the future welfare of the excommunicated person was shown by the Broadmead church in 1679 when it had to deal with the case of Mary Smith, a servant girl and member who was pregnant by William Ship, a yeoman and widower. The church, on the advice of its ruling elder,

[1] Great Yarmouth Congregational Church Book, p. 240. DWL MS. 76.2. Turner's Hill General Baptist Church Book, p. 8. DWL MS. 38.84.

[2] White's Alley General Baptist Church Book, i. 12, 202, 207. Guildhall Library, London.

[3] Nightingale Lane Congregational Church Book, 3 June 1724, Guildhall Library, London.

[4] Speldhurst General Baptist Church Book, fo. 16.

[5] Kimbolton Independent Church Book, pp. 18, 21. DWL MS. 201.32.

Edward Terrill, decided that in so scandalous a case the girl should be excommunicated 'without previous admonitions'. But Terrill was not content merely to censure Mary Smith's moral behaviour. He attempted to repair the damage which had been done to her life by riding over to William Ship's farm, persuading him that it was his duty to marry her, and then going off to find a parish priest to marry them before Ship could change his mind.[1]

Matrimonial problems of a different kind occupied a good deal of the attention of those churches which, again following Paul, insisted that their members marry 'only in the Lord'.[2] Many Congregational churches, most Particular Baptist churches, and all General Baptist churches and Quaker meetings tried to ensure that their members married only within the faith. John Smyth had laid down that church members 'may not marry any of the profane or wicked godless people of the world', and the General Baptist Assembly adopted the same position in 1656.[3] George Fox insisted that before Quakers were married they should obtain the consent both of the men's and women's meetings to which they belonged, and Friends who, impatient of this procedure, went off to be married by an Anglican priest were reprimanded if not disowned.[4] The Broadmead church admonished members 'for not marrying in the Lord'; the Arnesby Particular Baptist church excommunicated members 'for going to Babylon to be joined together according to the wicked way of the Church of England'.[5]

Marriage regulations, though, often proved to be the most unsatisfactory part of a church's discipline: they were difficult to enforce, were frequently flouted, and caused a good deal of resentment among Dissenters who could not find eligible partners in their own local meeting. Women were at a special disadvantage in churches where there were often twice as many female as male members, and when in 1698 the Rothwell Congregational church admonished Sarah Uffington for befriending a man of the world, she replied 'that if the church would provide her an honest man, she would possibly renounce the company

---

[1] *Broadmead Records*, pp. 195–9.   [2] I Corinthians 6:39.
[3] *Works of John Smyth*, ii. 749. *Minutes of the General Baptist Assembly*, i. 6.
[4] *Fox's Journal*, p. 519.
[5] *Broadmead Records*, pp. 214–15. Arnesby Particular Baptist Church Book, i. 97.

of the carnal man, but she thought there were but few honest men in the church'.[1] In practice the theoretical objection to members marrying outside the church was often modified in the interests of retaining the support of otherwise unexceptionable people. The ruling of the General Baptist Assembly that a member who married an unbeliever should be excommunicated was somewhat softened by the provision that the offending member might be readmitted if, though still married, he or she displayed 'unfeigned repentance', and by 1744 the chairman of the Assembly, Matthew Randall, was giving his personal opinion that it was not always prudent to exclude those who married outside the church, since they might never return.[2] Similarly Quaker meetings were initially prepared to forgive Friends who 'married out of Truth' or were married by a priest, providing that they gave evidence of contrition after the event.[3]

Those churches which tried to insist on rigorous obedience to the Pauline commandment 'be ye not unequally yoked together with unbelievers' had to pay a heavy price in falling numbers and a contracting community. When, in 1700, Joseph Jacobs, the pastor of the Congregational church in Horsleydown, Southwark, attempted to persuade his members to pledge themselves to marry only within the faith, the result was the disruption and dissolution of the church.[4] For half a century the Arnesby Particular Baptist church automatically excommunicated those who married unbelievers and those who were married in the parish church, so that by 1751 this once flourishing church was bemoaning that 'our number is but few and circumstances low'.[5] Quaker disownments for 'disorderly marriages' became more frequent after the printing of marriage rules in 1754 and the general tightening up of discipline in the 1760s.[6] Of the 1,025 Friends disowned by the six Monthly Meetings in London between 1750 and 1794, 425 were dis-

[1] Rothwell Congregational Church Book, p. 98.

[2] *Minutes of the General Baptist Assembly*, i. 23, ii. 73–4.

[3] *Minute Book of the Society of Friends in Bristol*, pp. 23, 91–2. *Minute Book of the Gainsborough Monthly Meeting*, ii. 52, 55, 101. *Minute Book of the Upperside Monthly Meeting*, pp. 13–14.

[4] Waddington, *Surrey Congregational History*, p. 158.

[5] Arnesby Particular Baptist Church Book, i. 133.

[6] Jones, *LPQ*, i. 143.

owned for offences arising out of their marriages, and by the early nineteenth century the rigid enforcement of the marriage rules was having a disastrous effect on Quaker numbers.[1]

The churches' surveillance over family life did not end with the marriage ceremony. Where necessary disputes between man and wife were brought before the church meeting and judgement pronounced. Thus John Christmas of the Warboys General Baptist church in Huntingdonshire was 'withdrawn from . . . for not loving Ann his wife as he ought, and for speaking hateful and despising words against her', and John Stanton of the Bedford Congregational church was excommunicated for 'abusing his wife and beating her often for very light matters'.[2] Nagging wives and bitchy women were similarly subject to the church's discipline. The Carlton Independent church in Befordshire suspended Elizabeth Knott from communion on account of her unkindness to her 'old and crazy' husband by trying to force him to go out to work.[3] The East Kent General Baptist Association took up the case of a poor man from Dover who was compelled by his wife to add to his income by shaving men on Sundays, since she 'would fall into a passion and speak evil' of him and his church if he did not comply.[4] The White's Alley General Baptist church reprimanded the wife of James Morris for falsely spreading the rumour that her husband 'was a common tippler and drunkard, and . . . suspected to have the pox', and it tried to resolve a quarrel between Thomas Bastin and his mother-in-law Alice Bottley, who claimed that while her daughter lay on her deathbed Bastin was already courting another woman.[5] The Bromsgrove Particular Baptist church excommunicated Mary Crowe for taunting the 'widow Cook that her face or herself was handsomer than hers, intimating as if Thomas Cook was more taken with her than with his own wife'.[6] And it is pleasant to read in 1663, in a decade which saw an increase in the trial and execution of women for witchcraft, that the Warboys church

---

[1] W. Beck and T. F. Ball, *London Friends' Meetings* (1869), p. 123.

[2] *Fenstanton Records*, p. 278. Bunyan Meeting Church Book, p. 68.

[3] H. G. Tibbutt, 'Some Early Nonconformist Church Books', *Bedfordshire Historical Record Society*, li (1972), 53.

[4] East Kent General Baptist Association records, p. 17. DWL MS. 38.79a.

[5] White's Alley Church Book, ii. 79, 83, 336, 338, iii. 10, 12.

[6] *Bromsgrove Baptist Church, Church Record Book* (1975), i. 57.

excommunicated Ellen Burgess 'for lying and slandering of her relations, counting them and her mother witches, which we have no ground to believe'.[1] Such rumour-mongering was not an exclusively feminine trait, for in 1689 the Friends of the Upperside Monthly Meeting in Buckinghamshire disowned Edward Lered of Amersham for 'heathenish superstition' in accusing a local woman of bewitching his child.[2]

Some churches tried to regulate relations between masters and servants in the same way that they watched over relations between husband and wife. In 1655 the Fenstanton church excommunicated Joan Parker not only for absenting herself 'from the assembly of the congregation' but also for 'running from her service, without the consent either of her master or dame', while in the early 1690s the Rothwell Congregational church admonished Elizabeth Campion for being 'a disobedient servant' and Brother Geeson for slandering his master and mistress.[3] On the other hand the Speldhurst General Baptists tried to ensure that masters treated their servants, and even their animals, with proper concern. In 1701 both Thomas Benge and William Hadlow were suspended from communion: the former for 'being provoked into an unreasonable passion in which he beat his apprentice and broke his head that the blood came', the latter for failing to provide 'sufficient provender for some of his cattle, especially his horse which was almost starved, nor food for his servant'.[4]

Quarrels between church members over business matters were also occasionally placed before the church, and some fellowships sought to implement the Pauline objection to brother going to law with brother.[5] In the view of William Bridge, the pastor of the Great Yarmouth Congregational church, such matters were too trivial to occupy the church's time, and after one such dispute had disturbed the church in 1650 he requested 'if any difference be among brethren about buying and selling and merchandise, that such things ... be made up by the brethren, and not to trouble the church with them'.[6] But the Speldhurst General Baptists had no such inhibi-

---

[1] *Fenstanton Records*, p. 278. G. N. Clark, *The Later Stuarts* (1955), p. 418.
[2] Vann, *Social Development*, p. 136.
[3] *Fenstanton Records*, p. 169. Rothwell Church Book, pp. 29, 35.
[4] Speldhurst Church Book, fo. 27v.   [5] I Corinthians 6:6.
[6] Great Yarmouth Church Book, p. 48.

tions about adjudicating in business matters: in 1698 they tried to resolve a dispute between William Hollamby and Richard Martin over the delivery and payment of goods, and when they failed and the two members resorted to 'un-Christian fighting with each other and going before the magistrates' they were both suspended from communion.[1]

Churches could sometimes be precipitate in the judgement they passed on supposedly erring members. In the late seventeenth century the Speldhurst church excommunicated 'Sister Willard . . . for being under a bad report to the scandal of the truth of her having that loathsome disease the French pox'. But when several years had passed and no symptoms of the disease had appeared in either her husband or her children, and the unfortunate woman continued to wait humbly 'on the church's pleasure', the church was convinced of her innocence and in 1695 she was restored to communion.[2] More often, though, churches showed surprising patience in their discipline of offenders. The case of Andrew Brothers, charged with 'neglecting the necessary care of his family' and 'spending too much of his time in tippling-houses', was first brought before the Buckinghamshire Quakers' Upperside Monthly Meeting in September 1686, but he was not disowned until May 1690, after more than a dozen visits by leading Friends had failed to exact any lasting evidence of repentance or reformation.[3] For more than thirty years the Speldhurst church was troubled by the wayward antics of Reuben Coppis who maintained the 'schismatical, heterodox notion' that the church should use the Lord's Prayer, contrary to General Baptist practice; refused to accept the judgement of the church when it went against him; delivered 'unsavouring grating and railing speeches' against a fellow member who employed his son as apprentice without his permission; was frequently drunk; and kept company 'with a whorish woman'. Five times Coppis was suspended from communion, yet five times he was subsequently restored, and he appears to have ended his days a loyal member of the church.[4]

[1] Speldhurst Church Book, fos. 22v–24r.
[2] Ibid., fo. 19v.
[3] *Minute Book of the Upperside Monthly Meeting*, pp. 179–228.
[4] Speldhurst Church Book, fos. 17, 18, 25, 28, 38, 39, 42, 43, 44, 46.

The Speldhurst church, which could be so charitable towards an erring member who was prepared to admit his faults and attempt reformation, could at other times exhibit the most bigoted literalism in its exercise of discipline. In 1710 the church was called to pass judgement on Hannah Harrison, who was said to have broken both the Levitical commandment against the eating of beasts which had died from natural causes and the apostolic injunction to abstain from eating strangled food.[1] The woman's crime was to have accepted the gift of a hen, which had died from drowning, from a neighbour who was herself too scrupulous to eat the dead bird. The church resolved, in all seriousness, that since there was no question that the hen had met its end 'as if it died of itself', and since Hannah Harrison's 'eating of it had occasioned a very great reproach in the neighbourhood', there was no alternative but to suspend her from communion.[2]

The Speldhurst church, in common with other Dissenting churches, adopted the same harsh attitude to those of its members who engaged in what others would have regarded as harmless pastimes. In 1721 it agreed that 'going to horseraces, cricketing, and playing at cards etc. is not to be practised nor no ways allowed of by the professors of the Gospel'.[3] The Kimbolton Independent church reprimanded Ann Hawking 'for her heinous evil in going to see . . . a puppet play', and decided that its women members should not be seen wearing 'fashionable hoops'.[4] And the Rothwell Congregational church disciplined members for travelling on Sunday, 'spending the Lord's day altogether at home with carnal relations', playing at cards, cudgels, and ninepins, jumping for wagers, dancing and conforming to the fashions of the world, and for 'encouraging fiddling and vanity, and singing vain songs'.[5] Was any recreation permitted to conscientious Dissenters? William Penn produced a list of suggestions which included the study of 'profitable arts' such as 'arithmetic, geometry, husbandry, gardening, handicraft, medicine', and, as befitted the son of an admiral, navigation. For women he recommended spinning, sewing, knitting,

---

[1] Leveticus 11:39. Acts of the Apostles, 15:20, 29.
[2] Speldhurst Church Book, fo. 44v.   [3] Ibid., fo. 36r.
[4] Kimbolton Independent Church Book, pp. 41–2.
[5] Rothwell Church Book, pp. 35, 52, 73, 74, 88, 91, 106, 113, 115. Glass, *Independent Church at Rothwell*, pp. 75–7.

weaving, and helping those 'who for want are unable to keep servants'. But for Penn the chief recreations were frequenting 'the assemblies of religious people', visiting 'sober neighbours to be edified, and wicked ones to reform them', and ministering to the needs of the sick and the imprisoned.[1]

The attitude of some Presbyterians to amusements was less rigid. Roger Lowe, Presbyterian mercer's apprentice of Ashton-in-Makerfield in Lancashire in the 1660s, rode in a horse race, lost 12 pence at a 'bowling alley', and spent much time in ale-houses where he contended for presbytery against episcopacy and 'talked about trading and how to get wives'.[2] Samuel Merivale, minister to the Presbyterian meeting at Tavistock in the mid-eighteenth century, after enjoying a substantial dinner at a neighbour's home consisting of 'a leg of mutton boiled, a turkey very nicely roasted, a cheek of pork, delicate minced pies, an apple pie, and Gloucestershire cheese', washed down by 'brandy and rum . . . three sorts of wine, and a noble bowl of arrack punch', sat down to 'a very innocent game at cards'.[3] James Clegg, who succeeded William Bagshaw as minister of Malcoffe chapel in the Peak district in 1702, 'joined his friends in fishing and coursing, played a game at bowls or shovel-board' and 'spent a festive evening in a tavern'. When he was nearing the end of his life he sought to provide for the continuance of the Presbyterian cause in that remote part of Derbyshire by purchasing a ticket in the Irish lottery, hoping that providence would 'favour me with a prize'.[4] But strict Dissenters such as Penn felt no need 'to drive away that, by foolish divertisements, which flies away so swiftly of itself; and when once gone, is never to be recalled'.[5]

One aspect of early Dissenting discipline will strike the modern reader as particularly harsh: the attitude adopted towards bankrupts. Bankruptcy was regarded as a breach of Paul's command to 'owe no man any thing', as evidence that a man had conducted his business without proper concern for others, and bankrupts were usually excommunicated from the gathered

[1] W. Penn, *No Cross, No Crown* (1849), pp. 205–6, 208.
[2] W. L. Sachse, ed., *The Diary of Roger Lowe* (1938), pp. 27, 33, 37, 52.
[3] A. W. Merivale, *Family Memorials* (Exeter, 1884), p. 22.
[4] H. Kirke, ed., *Extracts from the Diary and Autobiography of the Rev. James Clegg* (1899), pp. 6, 101.
[5] Penn, *No Cross, No Crown*, p. 208.

churches and disowned by the Quakers.[1] In some cases, though, the rule against bankruptcy was exercised with compassion. A general meeting of West Country Particular Baptists in 1654 advised that it was a church's duty to pay the debts of any member who had fallen into financial straits, 'provided it doth not disable them in the performance of more necessary duties, such as respect both family and church'.[2] The Castle Hill Congregational church, Northampton, attempted to distinguish between bankrupts whose fall was due to their 'own sin and folly' and those who were victims of 'the afflicting hand of God', and when the latter appeared to be the case the church was prepared to 'vindicate, comfort, and assist' the person concerned.[3] And in 1739 the Lime Street Congregational church, London, restored a bankrupt to communion despite the fact that fourteen years earlier he had embezzled £70 of the money the church had collected for the relief of the poor, and could not hope to repay it since 'he had nothing for subsistence but charity'.[4]

8. MATTERS OF FINANCE: THE RELIEF OF THE POOR AND THE PAYMENT OF MINISTERS

Many Dissenting churches accepted a measure of responsibility for the care of their own poor, but the degree of charitableness varied enormously from church to church and from denomination to denomination. Those denominations which stood farthest from the established church, as did the Quakers, were the most reluctant to allow their poor members to accept parish relief and consequently were most obliged to provide alternative assistance. Whereas George Fox insisted that none of his followers 'should be chargeable to their parishes',[5] the Presbyterians had no such objection to parish relief and appear to have made no special provision for their own poor. The Congregationalists and Baptists did on the whole accept responsi-

---

[1] Romans 13:18. Henderson, *Castle Gate Congregational Church, Nottingham*, pp. 100–1. Davis, *Isaac Watts*, p. 38. Lloyd, *Quaker Social History*, p. 72.

[2] White, *Association Records of the Particular Baptists*, ii. 55.

[3] Coleman, *Independent Churches in Northamptonshire*, p. 22.

[4] Lime Street Congregational Church Book, pp. 108–10. Guildhall Library, London.

[5] *Fox's Journal*, p. 375.

bility for their poor, and unlike the Presbyterians they elected
deacons who were charged with responsibility for the financial
affairs of the church in general and for the relief of the poor in
particular.[1] When John Gifford, the founder and first pastor of
the Bedford Congregational church, was nearing his death in
1655, he counselled his church to 'let your deacons have a constant stock by them to supply the necessities of those that are in
want'.[2] But five years earlier the Great Yarmouth Congregational church had seen nothing wrong in accepting parish
relief on behalf of its poor, and when discussing the maintenance of the orphaned children of deceased members had concluded that since church members paid 'the town towards the
poor . . . we should have help from them'. The church did,
though, agree to supplement the amount paid in poor relief
should it prove to be insufficient.[3]

Baptists were usually reluctant to counsel their members to
seek parish relief, but they too were prepared to advise their
poor to accept it when the church itself could not raise sufficient
funds. When, in 1654, a member of the Fenstanton church lost
his barns and outhouses 'with all his hay and grain' in a fire,
the church resolved that he should not go to the local magistrates for permission to appeal to the inhabitants of the county
for reparation, and instead asked seven neighbouring churches
to help in making good his loss.[4] But in 1698 the Speldhurst
church decided, reluctantly, that since 'the church is again in
debt and the number of the poor to be wholly chargeable so
increased' the deacons would have to seek the help of the parish
officers on behalf of the poor, though the church would make up
what was wanting for 'their comfortable being, more than what
the parish provideth'.[5] Even the Quakers of Norwich agreed in
1676 to seek the assistance of the parish overseers in the case of
'Nicholas Wharloe and his mother, to relieve their necessity,
being in great distress', though it is possible that the two concerned were not regarded by Friends as being of their number.[6]
Certainly the Norfolk Quarterly Meeting resolved in 1714 that
while the poor who occasionally attended Quaker meetings but

---

[1] Great Yarmouth Church Book, pp. 217–18.
[2] Bunyan Meeting Church Book, p. 4.   [3] Great Yarmouth Church Book, p. 52
[4] *Fenstanton Records*, pp. 103–5.   [5] Speldhurst Church Book, fo. 22v.
[6] Eddington, *Quakerism in Norwich*, p. 236.

were not 'owned as members' should be relieved by the parish, 'all such as are members of us, ought to be relieved by us . . . and not by the parish'.[1]

While some Dissenting churches were on the one hand prepared to allow their poor members to accept parish relief, they were on the other hand willing to contribute to public charities sanctioned by the state. After the passing of the Toleration Act charity briefs authorized by royal letters patent often contained provisions for collections to be taken in Dissenting congregations, and an Act of 1705 which sought to reform the collection of money for charity briefs included a clause providing that all such briefs should be distributed to Dissenting meeting-houses.[2] Though the reform of 1705 was not fully implemented and the system of charity briefs fell into decay, there is evidence to suggest that in the early decades of the eighteenth century Dissenters contributed generously to appeals from outside their congregations. The Congregationalists of Wrentham in Suffolk raised 2s. 5½d. for the victims of fire in Dorchester in 1714, 5s. 3d. for sufferers from storm in Staffordshire in 1720, and 11s. 1d. for the victims of floods in Lancashire in 1722. Their generosity was especially stirred by the plight of foreign Protestants, and in 1716 they contributed £7. 9s. 6d. to a fund for the Reformed churches of Poland whose members were being persecuted for their collaboration with Charles XII of Sweden.[3] Dissenters frequently contributed more than Anglicans to such briefs, and in 1703-4 the Dissenters of Colchester raised £31. 5s. 1½d. for the Protestants of the principality of Orange, who were being forced into exile by Louis XIV, and £4. 5s. 10¼d. for the widows and orphans of seamen drowned in the great storm of 27 November 1703. In both cases this was three times the amount raised by the Anglicans in the same town.[4]

The chief beneficiaries of Dissenting charity were, though, the poor and unfortunate of their own churches. If a Baptist, Congregationalist, or Quaker suffered imprisonment for his faith, was unable to work through old age, ill health, or bad trade, or lost his goods by fire, he could usually expect the

[1] Vann, *Social Development*, p. 146.
[2] T. L. Auffenberg, 'Organized English Benevolence: Charity Briefs, 1625–1705', Vanderbilt University Ph.D. thesis, 1973, p. 54.
[3] Wrentham Congregational Church Book, pp. 50–4. DWL MS. 76.7.
[4] Auffenberg, 'English Benevolence', pp. 55–6.

assistance of his church. When a father died and left orphaned children behind him the Lime Street Congregational church arranged for their education and apprenticeship; when a poor widow died leaving no relations and few goods, the church saw that she received a decent burial.[1] The Stepney Congregational church gave sums of 30s., 40s., and £4 to three poor women to enable them to pay their rent, and gave £5 to Sister Manley who was 'under some straits by reason of a loss by fire'.[2] The Bromsgrove Particular Baptist church gave a guinea to Sister Pike to enable her to pay a doctor's bill, and 2s. 'to buy corn and capons for Sister Phillips'.[3] The Speldhurst General Baptists paid for Elizabeth Foild to stay with Thomas Benge for six weeks so that she could drink the waters at Tunbridge Wells, and in 1703 collected 30s. to repair the damage done to Brother Archer's house 'in the late dreadful and amazing high wind'.[4] When Sam Lawrence was taken prisoner by the French during the War of the Spanish Succession the White's Alley General Baptists took up a collection for him, and when he was released from captivity the church agreed to pay up to 30s. to get him into Greenwich Hospital.[5] The Bristol Quakers gave 50s. to enable a widow to fit out her two sons who were going to sea; 18s. to help a poor man to pay his rent; and 10s. to a man whose wife was expecting her sixth child.[6] The Norwich Quakers arranged apprenticeships for the sons of poor Friends and paid for them to fitted out with new clothes.[7] One of the most generous churches was the Maze Pond Particular Baptist church in Southwark, which in the late 1710s was distributing over £30 a year to the poor.[8] Even the tight-fisted Great Yarmouth Congregationalists held collections in the 1650s for a poor man who had lost 32s. and for a recently widowed woman. But in 1656 William Bridge warned them 'that if any that were poor

[1] Lime Street Congregational Church Book, pp. 78, 97.
[2] A. T. Jones, *Notes on the Early Days of Stepney Meeting* (1887), pp. 45, 48.
[3] *Bromsgrove Baptist Church Book*, i. 68.
[4] Tunbridge Wells (Speldhurst) General Baptist Church, Deacons Book, 1708. DWL MS. 38.71. Speldhurst General Baptist Church Book, fo. 34v. BMAdd MS. 36.709.
[5] White's Alley Church Book, iii. 51, 76.
[6] *Minute Book of the Society of Friends in Bristol*, pp. 4, 137, 162.
[7] Eddington, *Quakerism in Norwich*, pp. 128–9.
[8] Maze Pond Particular Baptist Church, Poors' Book, 1716–32. Baptist Church House.

offered themselves to the church to observe whether they were industrious or not, because poverty with industry was to be honoured, the contrary not'.[1]

The problem of distinguishing between the deserving poor and the idle was recognized by other churches, and in some cases aid was given not as a financial dole but with the aim of providing the needy with the means of once again earning their own living. Thus when the case of Mary Whittock was brought before the Fenstanton General Baptists, that she 'is destitute of harbour, and her mother being very sick, and her children small, and the ways dirty, she is not able to travel from place to place as she hath been accustomed', the pastor of the church, John Denne, agreed to provide her with accommodation and the church voted to give her 20s. to enable her to start up in trade again.[2] Similarly the Stepney Congregationalists gave 'Sister Murrell the sum of £3 towards putting her into a way to get a livelihood for herself and family'.[3] The Bristol Quakers provided John Brewer with work as a gravedigger, lent the baker Edward Payne £5 to help him buy corn, gave John Verrick 4 cwt. of iron to enable him to continue as a black-smith, and helped to keep James Sterridge and William Cole in work as shoemakers by agreeing to buy from them a dozen shoes a week for twelve months.[4] And in 1675 the Friends of the Upperside Monthly Meeting in Buckinghamshire agreed to assist the husband of Ellen Hawks 'with a little money to pay for some birch which he had bought, that so he might have work whereby to earn something to maintain them'. But in this case the Friends added the caution 'that he should not be trusted with much at a time'.[5]

From 1677 to 1684 the London Quakers bought flax to enable poor Friends to earn their living by spinning, and during the last four years of the scheme's operation its accounts were kept by John Bellers, a London cloth-merchant who in 1695 produced his *Proposals for Raising a Colledge of Industry*. Bellers suggested that as a means of relieving poverty institutions should

---

[1] Great Yarmouth Church Book, pp. 78, 92, 94.

[2] *Fenstanton Records*, pp. 82–3, 86.

[3] Jones, *Early Days of Stepney Meeting*, p. 48.

[4] *Minute Book of the Society of Friends in Bristol*, pp. 16, 41, 50, 110. Mortimer, 'Quakerism in Seventeenth Century Bristol', pp. 283, 308.

[5] *Minute Book of the Upperside Monthly Meeting*, p. 35.

be set up in which the poor could work for their mutual benefit.[1] Attempts were made to implement Beller's proposals by the Quakers of Bristol in 1696 and by those of London in 1701, but neither experiment was entirely successful. In order to persuade Friends to enter the workhouse the Bristol Quakers had to stop out-door relief, but even then it proved difficult to attract inmates, and there must have been many Quakers who shared the objections of a Bristol mother who would not let her children enter the workhouse and 'be bred so slavish'.[2] The workhouse established by the London Friends at Clerkenwell similarly had little attraction for the able-bodied, and it became essentially a home for the elderly and an orphanage for children too young to be apprenticed. The Clerkenwell workhouse must have been a grim place, with an open drain from a pigsty running through the cellars of the building, bedsteads infested with vermin, and a largely starch diet, but in 1735 the Quakers could claim with some satisfaction that in twenty-five years only thirteen children, out of a total of probably around 300, had died there.[3] Bellers had intended that his 'colleges of industry', once established, should be self-supporting, but in most years after 1735 the finances of the Clerkenwell workhouse showed a deficit which had to be made good by the London Quarterly Meeting. In 1701 a sum of £1,888 had been raised for starting the project, and a further subscription of £1,085 was raised in 1760.[4]

That the Friends were able to contribute so generously to the care of the poor is partly explained by the fact that, unlike other Dissenters, they had no paid ministry to support. For the Presbyterians, of course, an educated and professional ministry was essential to the work of the church, and the Congregationalists and Particular Baptists too believed that pastors should, if possible, have 'a comfortable supply, without being . . . entangled in secular affairs'.[5] The General Baptists, in this as in so much else, anticipated the Quaker objections to a wholly professional ministry, and in 1651 the Midland General Baptists declared that while ministers might be supported by

[1] A. R. Fry, ed., *John Bellers, his Writings Reprinted* (1935), pp. 40–1.
[2] Mortimer, 'Quakerism in Seventeenth Century Bristol', pp. 241–2.
[3] Beck and Ball, *London Friends' Meetings*, pp. 363–73.
[4] Ibid., pp. 363, 374.
[5] Lumpkin, *Baptist Confessions of Faith*, p. 288.

the 'cheerful contribution of those that acknowledge themselves members of the same fellowship', they should 'be content with necessary food and raiment, and to labour with their hands'.[1] But by the end of the seventeenth century the General Baptists were beginning to fall in line with the other denominations, and the pastors of some urban churches at least were being paid.[2]

The remuneration paid to Dissenting ministers varied enormously from congregation to congregation. When the Presbyterians and Congregationalists set up their Common Fund in 1690 they instituted an inquiry into the condition of their ministers and churches throughout England and Wales, and the information thus collected showed that stipends ranged from the £5, and in 'some years not above 40s.' paid annually to Anthony Sleigh by the Congregationalists of Threlkeld in Cumberland, to £100 a year paid to James Hannot by the Independents of Great Yarmouth.[3] But most stipends were in the £20–£40 range, sums which would provide for a minister's basic necessities and perhaps enable him to buy a few books, but which would leave no margin for luxuries. When Philip Doddridge accepted an invitation to the pastorate of the Kibworth Congregational church in Leicestershire in 1723 he did so in the knowledge that his salary would not 'amount to above £35 a year', but this he regarded as adequate for a single man 'since provisions are pretty cheap in that country' and he could 'board for about £10 a year'. He lodged with a family who were members of his church and soon fell in love with his landlady's daughter, but their engagement was broken off when his fiancée was threatened with the loss of legacies from two rich Tory uncles in London, and she came to the conclusion that she could not face life on a Dissenting minister's salary.[4]

The stipends paid to Dissenting ministers in the early eighteenth century were comparable to the incomes of the poorer Anglican clergy,[5] with the important differences that most Dissenting ministers, unlike their Anglican counterparts, were not provided with a house and had no security of tenure. The

[1] Ibid., p. 184.
[2] White's Alley Church Book, i. 124, 134.
[3] Gordon, *Freedom after Ejection*, pp. 22, 74.
[4] *Correspondence of Doddridge*, i. 217, 220, 389. ii. 48, 58–9, 84, 86.
[5] B. Williams, *The Whig Supremacy* (1952), p. 78.

minister of the Presbyterian meeting in Chesterfield was a privileged exception, for in 1695 he was appointed 'for his natural life', and from 1697 was provided with a manse,[1] but the majority of Dissenting pastors had to pay for their accommodation out of their limited incomes and could be dismissed if their congregations grew tired of their preaching. The experiences of the few churches which did provide their pastors with manses in the early eighteenth century did not always encourage others to follow their example. In 1713 the Kettering Congregational church dismissed John Wills from the pastorate on account of 'his lying and other scandalous sins', but he claimed that the manse with which the church had furnished him was his private property and he sold it and kept the proceeds.[2] In 1721 the Guestwick Congregational church in Norfolk resolved to build a manse both for its present aged pastor and 'for the encouragement of succeeding ministers', but it only succeeded in encouraging a man who was attracted by the material comforts rather than by the spiritual challenge of the post. Within ten years the church found itself saddled with one Jacob Astley who borrowed large sums of money 'to support an extravagant way of living', accumulated debts of over £100 which he could not repay, and was accused of offering money to a maid at the Bull Inn in Norwich if she would go to bed with him. Not surprisingly the church decided to dispense with his services, but it proved difficult to get him out of the manse and it was not until the church paid him £15 in lieu of salary that he left Guestwick and entered the ministry of the established church.[3]

There was no necessary connection, though, between a comfortable pastorate and an unsatisfactory pastor, and some of the most distinguished ministers of the later seventeenth century had private estates or private fortunes which made them independent of the contributions of their congregations. A hundred or so of the ejected ministers of 1660–2 had means of this sort.[4] John Owen inherited a legacy of £500, married a wealthy second wife, lived in comfort in villas in Kensington and Ealing, and

[1] D. W. Robson, *The Story of Elder Yard Unitarian Chapel, Chesterfield* (revised by A. W. Valance, 1967), pp. 7, 9.
[2] F. C. Goodman, *The Great Meeting. The Story of Toller Congregational Church, Kettering* (1962), pp. 15–16.
[3] Guestwick Congregational Church Book, pp. 76, 80–95. DWL MS. 76.6.
[4] *Calamy Revised*, p.lv.

kept a carriage.[1] The evangelistic activities of the 'apostles' both
of the Peak and of Carmarthenshire were made possible by the
absence of financial worries: William Bagshaw inherited considerable private estates, and Stephen Hughes, after his ejection, married a woman 'whose portion, frugality, and industry
contributed much to his comfortable subsistence'.[2] Of the next
generation of Dissenting pastors Thomas Baddy, Presbyterian
minister at Denbigh, 'was a gentleman of some property' who
'occasionally wore silver spurs, which gave offence to some of his
congregation', while Daniel Williams acquired great wealth
through two fortunate marriages and on his death in 1716 left
£50,000 in trust for religious and educational purposes and for
the founding of the library which bears his name.[3]

At the other extreme were ministers who had been reduced to
poverty by their ejection from the established church, men such
as Joseph Chadwick, once vicar of Winsford in Somerset, who
'had little but brown rye bread and water for himself, his wife,
and many children, and when his wife was ready to lie in, was to
be turned out of door, for not paying his house-rent'.[4] But apart
from the aged and the infirm, who were often in a very sorry
state before the Common Fund came to their rescue in 1690,
Dissenting ministers whose stipends were inadequate, or who
were expected by their churches to labour with their hands,
were usually able to support themselves and their families by
taking up other occupations. Despite the provisions of the Act of
Uniformity, 101 of the ejected ministers at some time kept
schools, while fifty-nine practised medicine, forty-seven became
chaplains or tutors in well-to-do households, ten took to farming and nine to trade.[5] Similar occupations were followed by
succeeding generations of Dissenting ministers, except that the
demand for private tutors and chaplains declined as the noble
and gentle families which had once been sympathetic to Dissent
found their way back to the established church. Thus James
Clegg, William Bagshaw's successor at Malcoffe, kept a farm
and practised medicine; Anthony Sleigh of Threlkeld also
farmed in order to supplement his ministerial stipend of £5 a

[1] Jones, *Congregationalism in England,* p. 72.
[2] Calamy, *Account of the Ministers Ejected,* ii. 718.
[3] Rees, *Nonconformity in Wales,* pp. 301–2, 296. Gordon, *Freedom after Ejection,*
p. 384.
[4] *Reliquiae Baxterianae,* part iii, p. 4.   [5] *Calamy Revised,* p. lvi.

year; Thomas Dixon and Ebenezer Latham both combined the duties of Presbyterian minister, academy tutor, and medical practitioner; and John Turner, who became pastor of the Liverpool Particular Baptist church in 1730, was an apothecary who on occasion was summoned from his pulpit to attend patients and left his congregation to pray and sing until his return.[1]

By the early eighteenth century the lot of the poorer minister had to some extent been eased by the setting up of the Common Fund, followed by the establishment of the Congregational Fund in 1695, the Particular Baptist Fund in 1717, and the General Baptist Fund in 1726.[2] In 1732 the author of the 'View of the Dissenting Interest' estimated that the Common Fund, which was not officially described as Presbyterian until 1771 and which continued to assist Congregationalists, was raising over £2,000 a year, that the Congregational Fund was raising over £1,700, and the Particular Baptist Fund perhaps £500.[3] Initially, at least, by far the most generous contributions to the Common Fund came from men who were themselves ejected ministers,[4] but prosperous laymen also made special provision for poor ministers, often by means of bequests. These could range from the £40 per annum for fourteen years bequeathed by John Lancaster, a Chester ironmonger, in 1676, to £12,000 left in 1725 by a Fleet Street haberdasher named Barnes.[5]

But the prime responsibility for finding a minister's stipend remained with the local church. The sacrifice that this could entail on the part of a conscientious fellowship is revealed in the records of the Broadmead church, which in 1671 invited Thomas Hardcastle to become its pastor at a salary of £80 a year and drew up a list of those who would promise to contribute annually to guarantee that sum. The church had one prosperous member, its lay elder Edward Terrill, a merchant in the sugar trade who had married a wealthy widow, wrote the

---

[1] Kirke, *Diary of James Clegg*, p. 8. H. McLachlan, *Essays and Addresses* (Manchester, 1950), pp. 136, 149. Halley, *Lancashire*, ii. 327.

[2] White's Alley Church Book, iii. 239, 243. An earlier attempt to set up a General Baptist Fund in 1704 had proved abortive.

[3] 'View of the Dissenting Interest', pp. 88–9, 91–2, 100. Gordon, *Freedom after Ejection*, p. 184.

[4] Gordon, *Freedom after Ejection*, pp. 164–6.

[5] *Diaries and Letters of Philip Henry*, pp. 271–2. Calamy, *Historical Account*, ii. 486.

earlier part of the church records, and left the bequest which
led to the foundation of the Bristol Baptist academy. But of the
other 100 members only half could afford to give anything at all.
None the less the £80 was guaranteed, in sums ranging from
6s. to £6, and in some cases the amounts given must have
entailed real hardship. Thus 'one aged brother named Henry
Pierce, a very mean poor man to appearance . . . and by
profession . . . but a journeyman shoemaker, that lived up in a
cock-loft' gave 20s. a year, and Margaret Webb who 'had two
children to maintain' and 'lived very mean' gave 40s. 'Which
examples', commented Terrill, 'did provoke, if not shame, not
many others.'[1]

9. THE SOCIAL STRUCTURE OF DISSENT: ECONOMIC INDEPENDENCE AND COMMERCIAL MORALITY

The example of the Broadmead church, containing within the
same fellowship the prosperous Edward Terrill and the lowly
Henry Pierce, illustrates the difficulties involved in attempting
to generalize about the social and economic condition of
Dissent. There are four possible sources from which such
generalizations might be made for the late seventeenth and
early eighteenth centuries: the few Dissenting registers of births,
marriages, and deaths which provide information about the
occupation of the men whose names are entered therein;
the Evans manuscript, which contains observations about
the 'quality' of Dissenting congregations in some counties; the
hearth-tax returns from 1662 to 1688; and the records of the
persecution of Dissenters in the reigns of Charles II and James II.
All four groups of records have major drawbacks as reliable
bases from which to assess the economic strength and social
structure of Dissent. Most Dissenting registers are silent about
occupation, and where such information is provided it is invari-
ably incomplete. The Evans list is an even more uncertain
guide: although it contains a good number of random com-
ments about the condition of Dissenters, usually in an effort to
prove their economic worth, the categories it employs are too
vague and the data it provides too sparse to enable it to be used
for any meaningful statistical analysis. The hearth-tax returns
have been used by Margaret Spufford to establish the economic

[1] *Broadmead Records*, pp. 76–9.

position of Dissenters in two Cambridgeshire villages,[1] but the possibility that this line of inquiry will yield much information about the economic condition of Dissent on a wider scale is limited by the fact that so very few Dissenting membership lists, apart from the Quaker marriage and burial registers, have survived from the period for which hearth-tax returns are available. Judith Hurwich has tried to overcome this problem in her unpublished study of Warwickshire Dissenters by using the hearth-tax returns in conjunction with court records from the period of persecution and other local records. She has thereby attempted to identify as many Dissenters as possible who lived in Warwickshire between 1660 and 1720 and to discover their occupation and social status, but, as she admits, the nature of her sources makes it inevitable 'that Quakers, preachers and leaders, persons of high social status, and residents of towns should be over-represented'.[2]

For all their imperfections, the Dissenting registers thus constitute the most reliable guide to the economic condition of Dissent, and Table V summarizes both the fruits of Alan Cole's researches into the Quaker registers for Bristol, Buckinghamshire, Gloucestershire and Wiltshire, Lancashire, London, and Yorkshire, and the results of my own researches into the Presbyterian and Congregational baptismal registers in the Public Record Office.[3] For purposes of comparison with the population at large I have also included a summary of Gregory King's estimate of the social status of all heads of households in England in 1688, an analysis of the occupations of 400 men who were married in St. James's church, Duke's Place, Aldgate, London, in the twelve months from July 1698 to June 1699, and a breakdown of the occupations of the male residents of the city of Norwich who were married in Norwich cathedral between 1698 and 1706.[4] I have not used the results of Richard Vann's

[1] Spufford, *Contrasting Communities*, pp. 300–6.

[2] Hurwich, 'Nonconformists in Warwickshire', p. 41.

[3] W. A. Cole, 'The Quakers and Politics, 1652–60', Cambridge Ph.D. thesis, 1955, pp. 294–318, summarized in Cole, 'The Social Origins of the Early Friends', *JFHS* (1957), pp. 99–118. The list of non-parochial registers available in the PRO has been published by the List and Index Society, vol. 42 (1969).

[4] W. I. W. Phillimore and G. E. Cockayne, *London Parish Registers* (1901), vol. iii, marriages at St. James's, Duke's Place, 1691–1700, pp. 310 ff. *Marriages recorded in the Register of the Sacrist of the Cathedral Church of Norwich, 1697–1754* (Norwich, 1902), pp. 6–31.

study of the Quaker registers for Buckinghamshire and Norfolk
since his method of analysis makes it impossible to compare his
figures with the more extensive findings of Cole.[1] Nor have I
included the fruits of Judith Hurwich's researches into the
occupations of the Warwickshire Dissenters since her results are
distorted by her sources and are too heavily weighted in favour
of the more prosperous Dissenters to justify comparison with the
more representative samples provided by the Dissenting
registers.[2]

What, at first sight, appears to be the most striking feature of
the accompanying analysis of Dissenting occupations is the comparative absence of labourers and servants and the high proportion of tradesmen and artisans.[3] Little reliance, though, can be
placed on the contrast between the evidence of the Dissenting
registers and the estimates of Gregory King, for King was
primarily concerned with income, not with occupation, and he
appears to have relegated the majority of artisans to the rank of
labourer. The apparent contrast between the almost total
absence of labourers in the register of the Norwich Presbyterian
meeting and nearly 20 per cent of labourers among the men
who were married in the city's cathedral is also misleading. In

[1] Vann has tried to distinguish those Quakers who were 'convinced' before 1662
from those who are not known to have been Friends until after that date. In so
doing he has challenged Cole's contention that 'the early Friends were mainly
drawn from the urban and rural *petite bourgeoisie*', and has argued that 'it was the
middle to upper bourgeoisie, rather than the *petite bourgeoisie*, which was strikingly
prominent among the early Quakers'. However, Vann's sample is too small, and
Buckinghamshire Quakers probably too atypical, for much confidence to be placed
in his conclusions. R. Vann, 'Quakerism and the Social Structure in the Interregnum', *Past and Present*, xliii (1969), 72.

[2] e.g. Hurwich's figures suggest that 12 per cent of Warwickshire's Presbyterians were gentlemen and a further 20 per cent merchants, statistics which result
from the fact that she has been able to provide evidence for the occupation of only
209 Presbyterians over a period of sixty years. 'Nonconformists in Warwickshire',
p. 210.

[3] I have placed apprentices in the same occupational category as their masters
rather than with 'servants' as does B. S. Capp, *Fifth Monarchy Men*, pp. 84–6.
Though, as Capp says, apprentices often 'lacked both money and personal freedom
in their current situation' and could consequently become, as in the 1640s, a
disruptive influence, it seems no more appropriate to classify them with servants
who could not hope to rise out of their positions than it would be to classify the
undergraduates of today among the unemployed. The London apprentices of 1642
insisted that they were not 'of the base and mechanic scum of the people' but
'have trades and callings, the most of them young men of good parentage'. B.
Manning, *Politics, Religion, and the English Civil War* (1973), p. 117, quoting *A
Declaration of the Valiant Resolutions of the Famous Prentices of London* (1642).

December 1702 responsibility for keeping the cathedral register passed from the precentor to the sacrist, and while, between 1698 and 1702, the precentor had recorded thirty labourers among the hundred Norwich men whose occupations he registered, from December 1702 to 1706 the sacrist recorded the occupations of fifty-seven Norwich men, and among them not a single labourer. The sacrist of Norwich cathedral, in taking more trouble than his predecessor to ascertain the precise occupations of the men whose marriages he registered, thus eliminated the category of labourer, as did those Dissenting ministers who recorded the occupations of the fathers whose children they baptized. Without those thirty questionable labourers, the evidence from Norwich suggests that the occupational structure of Presbyterianism in the city was very like that of the population at large. A similar conclusion was reached by Judith Hurwich when she analysed the occupations of the freemen in the city of Coventry. She found that the proportion of Dissenters who were engaged in the cloth industry 'was almost exactly the same as that of the general population', though Dissenters were 'more closely associated with the old heavy-woollen industry' and less active in the newer manufactures of worsteds and silk.[1]

The contrast between the handful of men who were noted as having been seamen, soldiers, or servants in the baptismal records of the Hand Alley Presbyterian meeting, Bishopsgate, and the 28 per cent of men in those categories who were married in St. James's church, Duke's Place, is a stronger indication of Dissent's lack of appeal to the unskilled, for the two places of worship were only a quarter of a mile apart. But even here the evidence is not conclusive, for the difference in the occupational structure of the two groups may be explained almost as well by Hand Alley's proximity to the silk-weaving district of Spitalfields, and St. James's proximity to the river, for it was the weavers of Hand Alley and the mariners and servants of St. James's who accounted for the differences, not the labourers, who constituted only 2 per cent of the men married in Duke's Place. In the early eighteenth century men who are accurately described as 'general labourers' were confined largely to rural areas, and it is only in those country districts covered by the

---

[1] Hurwich, 'Nonconformists in Warwickshire', p. 248.

TABLE V

OCCUPATIONS OF MALE DISSENTERS ACCORDING TO THE DISSENTING REGISTERS

compared with the occupations of the male population at large

(all figures are percentages)

	Gentlemen	Merchants	Professions	Yeomen Freeholders	Farmers Husbandmen	Tradesmen		Artisans			Seamen, soldiers	Labourers, servants
						Food Consumption goods	Textile trade	Textile manufactures	Tailors, shoemakers, etc.	Mechanic trades		
The general population												
All heads of household according to Gregory King, 1688	1·2	0·7	4·0	13·2	11·0	2·9		4·4			6·2	56·2
Men married in St. James's, Duke's Place, London, 1698–9	3·9	1·0	2·7	2·2	3·2	11·8	1·2	5·9	9·3	30·7	15·5	12·8
Male residents of Norwich married in Norwich cathedral, 1698–1706	0·6	0·0	3·8	0·0	0·6	7·6	0·0	53·2	3·8	10·5	0·6	19·1
Presbyterians												
Chesterfield, 1732–5	2·9	0·0	5·7	0·0	20·0	14·3	2·9	11·4	11·4	20·0	0·0	11·4
London, Hand Alley, 1705–11	0·0	0·0	1·1	0·0	0·0	11·1	6·7	51·1	10·0	13·3	5·6	1·1
Norwich, 1701–20	1·7	1·5	6·3	0·0	2·5	7·9	4·2	59·0	7·8	7·1	0·8	1·2
Nottingham, 1703–22	1·8	0·0	2·3	0·0	1·6	15·5	0·9	31·7	16·9	26·4	0·4	2·6
Southwark, Court Yard, 1729–35	0·0	0·0	2·6	0·0	2·6	18·4	2·6	2·6	5·3	60·5	0·0	5·3
Independents												
Bury St. Edmunds, new members 1670–91	0·0	0·0	4·2	0·0	8·3	12·5	0·0	33·3	16·7	25·0	0·0	0·0
Great Yarmouth, 1705–25	0·0	8·5	2·9	0·0	0·0	5·7	0·0	0·0	17·1	5·7	6·0	0·0
Haverfordwest, 1706–11	0·0	0·0	15·4	7·7	0·0	0·0	23·1	3·8	26·9	11·5	7·7	3·8

Quakers

Bristol, 1657–88	0·0	10·1	2·4	0·0	0·6	17·3	4·2	16·1	23·2	22·0	3·6	0·6
Buckinghamshire, 1689–1725	3·4	1·3	0·7	12·7	21·5	23·5	1·3	2·0	12·1	18·1	0·0	3·4
Gloucestershire and Wiltshire, 1656–88	0·0	1·1	0·0	20·2	5·3	7·4	3·2	29·9	6·4	23·4	1·1	2·1
Lancashire, 1652–88	0·6	0·0	1·7	14·6	18·5	5·6	4·5	19·6	16·4	16·8	0·6	1·2
London and Middlesex, 1715–19	0·5	6·5	3·0		5·6	17·7	10·6	11·6	10·0	26·7	5·1	2·5
Yorkshire, 1652–88	0·0	0·0	0·8	7·4	9·0	9·8	4·1	21·3	18·1	16·6	12·1	0·8

Sources

The Presbyterian and Independent figures are all based on baptismal registers in the Public Record Office, apart from those for Bury St. Edmunds which are derived from the church book in Dr. Williams's Library. The Quaker figures are taken from W. A. Cole's Cambridge Ph.D. thesis, 'The Quakers and Politics, 1652–60' (1955), pp. 294–318. The figures for St. James's, Duke's Place, are derived from W. P. W. Phillimore and G. E. Cockayne, *London Parish Registers* (1901), iii. 310 ff, and those for Norwich cathedral from *Marriages recorded in the Sacrist of the Cathedral Church of Norwich, 1697–1754* (Norwich, 1902), pp. 6–31.

Method

No allowance has been made for men who had no occupation recorded against their name, and in the case of the Yorkshire Quakers the sample from which the above figures were derived constituted only 10 per cent of all male Yorkshire Friends. Multiple counting has been avoided by recording the name of each father entered into a baptismal register and by counting his occupation once only. Where a father was recorded as having two different occupations, each occupation was counted as half.

Definitions

Tradesmen in food and consumption goods includes bakers, brewers, butchers, chandlers, grocers, malsters, tobacconists, etc.

Textile trade denotes those whose principal occupation was the buying and selling either of raw material or of finished cloth, such as woolmen, flaxmen, mercers, and drapers.

Textile manufactures comprise woolcombers, weavers, fullers, dyers, and stockingers.

Tailors, shoemakers, etc. include a small number of other workers engaged in making clothes, such as bodice-makers, feltmakers, glovers, and hatters.

Mechanic trades include blacksmiths, carpenters, clockmakers, coopers, ironmongers, joiners, glaziers, masons, tanners, etc.

Quaker registers that the comparative absence of labourers is really significant.

While Gregory King's analysis of the status of heads of households in 1688 is a guide to income but not necessarily to occupation, the descriptions of occupation in the Dissenting registers are not necessarily an accurate guide to income or wealth. More than a quarter of the men whose occupations are given in the High Pavement, Nottingham, registers are listed as stockingers, and by the mid-eighteenth century the poverty of Nottingham stockingers was proverbial, but among the High Pavement stockingers was Samuel Fellows, who built up 'one of the most successful silk hosiery businesses in Nottingham'.[1] Judith Hurwich has attempted to relate occupation to wealth by comparing the occupations of Warwickshire Dissenters with the hearth-tax returns and has found that 'husbandmen and artisans were nearly as poor as labourers', thus providing some justification for Gregory King's classification of artisans as labourers, given his prime concern with income.[2]

Judith Hurwich has also used the Warwickshire hearth-tax returns to compare the wealth of the county's Dissenters with that of the population in general, and has concluded that Dissenters were more prosperous than the community as a whole, that this was due to the greater concentration of the 'middling sort of people' among Dissenters, and that Dissent claimed few adherents from the ranks of either the very rich or the very poor.[3] Her statistics, though, must be treated with caution in view of the nature of her sources, and it may be significant that the distribution of hearths among the Quakers of Warwickshire, the denomination for which her information is most complete, was very similar to the distribution of hearths among the Warwickshire population at large.[4] Margaret Spufford's similar researches into the distribution of hearths among the Dissenters of two Cambridgeshire villages have failed to yield any firm conclusion: while in Orwell Dissenters were 'distri-

---

[1] G. Henson, *The Civil, Political, and Mechanical History of the Framework-knitters* (Nottingham, 1851), i. 101. S. D. Chapman, 'The Genesis of the British Hosiery Industry, 1600–1750', *Textile History*, iii (1972), 17. Richard Vann makes a similar point about the Gurneys of Norwich, *Social Development*, p. 70.

[2] Hurwich, 'Nonconformists in Warwickshire', pp. 231, 234. She was unable to use the hearth-tax returns for Coventry, which are incomplete.

[3] Ibid., p. 234.   [4] Ibid., p. 236.

buted throughout every layer of village society', in Willingham they came from the 'relatively comfortable and substantial middle section' of the community.[1] However her generalizations concerning Orwell are based on the evidence of only twelve Dissenting households, and it is possible that Willingham, a fenland village of small-sized farms and comparatively few landless labourers, was the more typical of rural communities in which Dissent flourished.[2] In general Dissent appears to have been comparatively strong in those rural areas such as the Fens of Lincolnshire, Cambridgeshire, and the Isle of Ely, which were characterized by the predominance of small farms and the absence of large ones, and whose inhabitants were relatively free from the social and economic pressures which induced conformity on the part of large landowners and landless labourers alike.[3]

The evidence concerning the occupations and economic worth of Dissenters in the late seventeenth and early eighteenth centuries is thus sparse and fragmentary, and even the most sophisticated methods elaborated by scholars to interpret it are open to objection. What evidence there is, though, points to two different, but not incompatible, conclusions. In the first place late Stuart and early Hanoverian Dissent, like Elizabethan Separatism and Lancastrian Lollardy, appealed chiefly to the economically independent—to men who were dependent neither on the favour of the king and his ministers for social and political advancement, nor on the parson or squire for their daily bread. Such people were to be found in some rural areas such as the Fens, but the association between economic and religious independence was chiefly a characteristic of urban areas. However, the second conclusion to emerge from the work which has been done on Dissenting occupations suggests that in those urban areas in which Dissent flourished, such as Norwich and Coventry, the social composition of Dissent was very like that of the surrounding community. In other words, the presence of trade and industry, by freeing men from the social and economic pressures of the countryside, created conditions which were favourable to the growth and survival of

[1] Spufford, *Contrasting Communities*, pp. 301–3.
[2] Ibid., p. 148.
[3] J. Thirsk, *Fenland Farming in the Sixteenth Century* (Leicester, 1953), pp. 41–4.

Dissent, but within those manufacturing and commercial communities in which Nonconformity thrived, Dissenters were not distinguished by occupation or social status from the population at large.

This was most obvious in the case of the clothing towns. While the evidence from Norwich and Coventry suggests that the proportion of Dissenters who were employed in textiles was roughly the same as that of the general population of those cities, this does not detract from the massive weight of evidence which shows that Dissenters were much more heavily concentrated in clothing towns than was the population of the country as a whole. The most impressive fact to emerge from the analysis of occupations recorded in the Dissenting registers is the high proportion of male Dissenters who earned their living in one of the clothing trades. Seventy per cent of the Norwich Presbyterians, two-thirds of the Hand Alley Presbyterians, half the Congregationalists of Haverfordwest and Bury St. Edmunds, nearly 50 per cent of the Nottingham Presbyterians, and 40 per cent of the Quakers of Bristol, Lancashire, Yorkshire, and Gloucestershire and Wiltshire were employed either in textiles, in occupations such as tailoring and shoemaking, or in trade connected with these manufacturers. Weavers constituted nearly half of the male Norwich Presbyterians, over a third of the Hand Alley Presbyterians, and nearly a quarter of the Friends of Gloucestershire and Wiltshire, while more than a quarter of the Nottingham Presbyterians were stockingers.

This close connection between religious radicalism and the clothing trade has continental parallels in Anabaptism and the Family of Love, and in England can be traced back to the Lollards of the fifteenth and sixteenth centuries.[1] It is probable that the mobility and degree of economic independence provided by the woollen industry in particular was an important factor in the growth of radical Dissent after the Reformation. Two of the first Dissenters from the post-Reformation Church of England, the Bocking conventiclers of 1550, were clothiers, and the comings and goings of radical religious leaders between northern Essex and Kent in the mid-sixteenth century suggests a connection with the cloth trade: in the following century

---

[1] J. F. Davis, 'Lollard Survival and the Textile Industry in South-east England', in *Studies in Church History*, ed. G. J. Cuming (Leiden, 1966), pp. 191–201.

we know that raw wool was shipped from Faversham to Colchester.[1] The religious radicalism of the clothing towns of northern Essex, it has been suggested above, survived in the General Baptist congregations of the seventeenth and eighteenth centuries; the early-sixteenth-century Lollards of the clothing towns in the valley of the Wiltshire Avon may have prepared the way for the unusual concentration of Particular Baptist numbers and wealth in those same towns two centuries later; a clothier, John Fort, was fined £500 for Anabaptism at Tiverton in 1639, and was evidently a leader of what was one of the earliest General Baptist churches in the West Country; and it was a clothier's apprentice, Hugh Evans, who having migrated from his native Radnorshire to Coventry in the 1640s, made contact with the city's General Baptist church and returned to Radnorshire to establish the General Baptist cause in Wales.[2]

The haven which the Netherlands provided for English Puritans and Separatists in the late sixteenth and early seventeenth centuries, and the stimulus which the Low Countries gave to English Dissent, were also in part made possible by the cloth trade. The churches of the Merchant Adventurers in the Netherlands provided employment for radical Puritans such as Francis Johnson at Middelburg in the early 1590s, and for John Forbes and Thomas Hooker at Delft in the 1620s and 1630s. The Arian martyr Bartholomew Legate was engaged in the cloth trade with Zeeland in the early seventeenth century, and was thereby brought into contact with the Dutch Mennonites.[3] And when William Bridge fled from Norwich to Rotterdam in the late 1630s he is said to have taken with him 'wealthy citizens and clothiers' whom the Rotterdam authorities encouraged to remain in the city by providing them with a place of worship and their minister with public maintenance.[4]

The wealthy clothiers who are reputed to have accompanied William Bridge to Rotterdam and, for example, the weavers

[1] Burrage, *EED* ii. 5. P. J. Bowden, *The Wool Trade in Tudor and Stuart England* (1962), p. 66.

[2] *CSPD* 1640, pp. 391, 399. Richards, *Puritan Movement in Wales*, p. 209. It is possible that the 'John Fort' of the State Papers was 'James Topp', pastor of the General Baptist church at Tiverton. Burrage, *EED* i. 275–6.

[3] Jones, *Studies in Mystical Religion*, p. 454.

[4] Edwards, *Antapologia*, pp. 57–8.

and wool-combers who made up the bulk of the adherents of the Norwich Presbyterian meeting seventy years later, though they both earned their living from textiles, were of course in terms of wealth poles apart. And it must be emphasized that while the majority of Dissenters shared certain economic characteristics, of which the most important was a degree of independence, Dissent was not socially homogeneous. The Evans list and Judith Hurwich's work on the Warwickshire hearth-tax returns suggest that in general Presbyterians were more prosperous than Independents, and Independents more prosperous than Quakers or Baptists, but social distinctions between denominations were less significant than social distinctions within denominations and within individual congregations. The Presbyterian congregations of Cumberland listed by Dr. Evans included not only that at Whitehaven, which contained 'one merchant worth above £20,000' and 'four merchants more worth each about £4,000', but also that at Salkeld, composed, apart from one gentleman, of 'the meaner sort of yeomen and poor farmers'.[1] And whereas the Particular Baptists of Hengoed in Glamorgan numbered only two gentlemen among eighty-five farmers and 140 labourers, those of the clothing towns of Wiltshire included four 'very rich' gentlemen at Trowbridge, five 'worth £500 at least' at Bradford-on-Avon, and ten 'worth at least £500' in North Bradley.[2]

Such social divisions inevitably led to the formation of governing élites within the churches. The Committee of Thirteen which was responsible for the financial affairs of the three Exeter Presbyterian meetings comprised, in 1718, a freeman of the city, two serge manufacturers, four wholesale grocers, and five substantial merchants, but it would be wrong to assume that they were typical of the congregations they served.[3] Similarly the most assiduous attenders at the business meetings of the Buckinghamshire Quakers were 'gentlemen, rich yeomen, and wholesale traders'.[4] Although any male Friend in good standing could be chosen to represent his particular meeting at the relevant Monthly Meeting, or the Monthly Meeting at the county Quarterly Meeting, and

[1] Evans list, p. 19.   [2] Ibid., pp. 141, 125.
[3] Finberg, *West Country Historical Studies*, p. 210. There was one vacancy in 1718.
[4] Vann, *Social Development*, p. 118.

although Baptist and Congregationalist church meetings were in principle open to all members, in reality attendance was restricted by the common practice of holding such meetings during the hours of daylight before the advent of gas lighting early in the nineteenth century. While this did not in theory exclude the attendance of the majority of male Dissenters, who as yeomen, husbandmen, tradesmen, or artisans were still free to decide when they could stop work, in practice blacksmiths and weavers were more reluctant to leave their forges and looms than merchants to leave their counting-houses for meetings at ten o'clock on Wednesday mornings or at two o'clock on Tuesday afternoons.[1]

A more obvious form of social distinction arose out of the problem of financing the building and maintenance of meeting-houses. While a minister's stipend was usually provided by regular subscriptions collected quarterly, and the cost of building a meeting-house was met where possible by a special appeal, any remaining deficit and the cost of maintaining the fabric was often provided for by allocating seats in the meeting-house to individuals in return for a regular pew-rent.[2] Thus when the Congregational church of which Isaac Watts was pastor built their new meeting-house in Bury Street in 1708, the cost of £650 was met partly by subscription and partly by charging for pews at prices ranging from 40s. for four seats in front of the pulpit on the ground floor to 7s. 6d. for five seats at the back of the gallery. Although accommodation was provided for the apprentices and servants of pew-holders, and for those in 'low circumstances' to have 'places assigned them gratis', it was not apparently felt necessary to make special provision for occasional worshippers. Such a system could, though, lead to abuse, and the Bury Street Congregationalists were aware that in some meeting-houses pew-holders had laid claim 'to the boards and materials' with which the pews were constructed, and even to 'the spot of ground on which the seats stood'.[3] The pews in the Benn's Garden Presbyterian meeting in Liverpool were regarded as the property of the pew-holders, to sell or to bequeathe to others;

[1] Lloyd, *Quaker Social History*, p. 7. Browne, *Congregationalism in Norfolk and Suffolk*, p. 228.
[2] Brockett, *Nonconformity in Exeter*, pp. 54, 99, 101. A. Holt, *Walking Together, a Study in Liverpool Nonconformity* (1938), p. 109.
[3] *TCHS* iii (1907–8), 117–24.

the Presbyterian meeting-house at Rivington near Chorley was dominated 'by the tall canopied pews of the Willoughby family'; and in the Tockholes meeting-house near Blackburn the pews of the Hoghton family were distinguished by the family monogram carved on the door.[1] The Abergavenny Congregational church was troubled by 'persons pretending a right to the timber' with which the pews were made, and had to insist in 1725 that 'the rights to the timber' belonged to the 'trustees and the whole church'.[2] Similarly the Bury Street Congregationalists laid down that if a pew-holder died or was absent from worship for more than six months his place should revert to the trustees. And when the Luton Particular Baptists provided their new meeting-house with pews in 1733, they stipulated 'that none of the pews shall have any locks put upon the doors, and that if at any time the place is full, and any room to spare in the pews, the owner shall freely offer a place for standers to sit in the pews'.[3]

This practice of dividing meeting-houses up according to ability to pay aroused no more comment in the eighteenth century than does the similar practice in the theatres and cinemas of today, and in extenuation of the Dissenters' practice it should be pointed out that in some meeting-houses a place of honour was provided for elderly and poor men at the 'table-pew' which was placed in the front of the building next to the communion table.[4] It needs also to be emphasized that Dissent, unlike conformity, made considerable and continuous demands on the worshipper's purse: more than one eighteenth-century Nonconformist minister suggested that 'some sordid people' left Dissent for the established church 'merely to save their subscriptions'.[5]

Fortunately, for the eighteenth-century Dissenters, the cost of paying their ministers and building their meeting-houses was partially offset by their rising prosperity. In the forty years

---

[1] Holt, *Walking Together*, p. 109. Higson, 'The Lords Willoughby of Parham', p. 51. Halley, *Lancashire*, ii. 299.

[2] Abergavenny Congregational Church Book, PRO RG4 1241.

[3] Freeman, 'Luton Baptist Minute Book', *Publications of the Bedfordshire Historical Record Society*, xxv (1947), 152.

[4] Halley, *Lancashire*, ii. 299–300. Brown, *John Bunyan*, p. 398.

[5] Browne, *Congregatinalism in Norfolk and Suffolk*, p. 194. *The Theological and Miscellaneous Works of Joseph Priestley*, ed. J. T. Rutt, xxii (1823), 274–5.

following the Act of Uniformity this had seemed an unlikely prospect. There were, it is true, some members of the aristocracy and gentry who had helped the ejected ministers of 1662: the Earls of Anglesey and Denbigh, the Countess Dowager of Clare, the Countesses of Exeter and Manchester, the Lords Wharton, Holles, and Delamere, had all allowed ministers into their homes as chaplains or tutors, and Lord Wharton and Lady Hewley in particular had given generous financial support to Presbyterian ministers and congregations.[1] The Countess Dowager of Clare and the Countesses of Bedford and Manchester had attended services conducted by the Presbyterian Thomas Manton, while the Congregationalist John Owen numbered among the members of his church the Countess of Anglesey, Sir John and Lady Hartopp, and the Ladies Abney, Dethick, Thompson, and Vere Wilkinson.[2] But by the beginning of the eighteenth century most of these aristocratic and gentle patrons of Dissent were dead, and their places in the meeting-houses were seldom taken up by their sons and daughters. No member of the upper class gave greater support to Dissent than Philip, Lord Wharton, but his son and heir Thomas earned a reputation as a rake and a duellist;[3] John Shute, Viscount Barrington, was regarded as the political leader of Dissent in the early eighteenth century, but his son became Bishop of Llandaff; and while Sir Edward Harley attended the services of Richard Baxter and had his son Robert educated in a Dissenting academy, it was this son Robert who, as Earl of Oxford and Lord Treasurer, sat embarrassed while his colleague Bolingbroke, who may also have been educated at a Dissenting academy, pushed through the Schism Bill of 1714 for the closing of all such educational institutions.[4] By the mid-eighteenth century there was only one Dissenting peer left, Lord Willoughby of Parham, and he not only held his barony in error but had to have the income from his modest estates supplemented by a government grant of £600 a year in order to maintain his

---

[1] *Calamy Revised*, pp. 2, 3, 286, 296, 342, 343, 355, 487. Hunter, *Life of Heywood*, pp. 382, 423–4. Miall, *Congregationalism in Yorkshire*, p. 113.

[2] Whiting, *English Puritanism*, p. 416. *TCHS* i. 27–9.

[3] J. Carswell, *The Good Old Cause* (1954), pp. 44–6.

[4] A. McInnes, *Robert Harley, Puritan Politician* (1970), p. 165. For a discussion of the obscure question of Bolingbroke's education see H. T. Dickinson, *Bolingbroke* (1970), pp. 2–4.

dignity as a peer.[1] 'Pray for me', said Sir Henry Hoghton, the last of the Hoghton baronets to attend the Presbyterian meeting-house at Tockholes, to its minister, 'for there are very few in my situation that go to heaven.'[2]

For most members of the aristocracy and gentry association with a Dissenting conventicle was incompatible with their social and political aspirations, whether as justices in the counties or as office-holders at court. On the rare occasions that Dissenters were named in commissions of peace, as they were in Lancashire in the 1690s, they were drawn from the legal profession and from trade, not from the landed classes who usually filled up the magistrates' bench.[3] It is significant that what support the Dissenters did enjoy among the upper classes in the later seventeenth century came largely from wives and widows, not from husbands who had to worry about the political consequences of their actions. Richard Vann has concluded from his study of the Buckinghamshire and Norfolk Quakers that 'the converts made after 1670 were generally of lower social status than the original ones', and that the heads of landed families were the most difficult to recruit and the first to defect.[4] The Quaker experience reflected that of the Lollards of the late fourteenth and early fifteenth centuries and of the Separatists of the sixteenth and early seventeenth centuries, and is likely to have been shared by all the other Dissenting denominations after 1662.

The failure of the Dissenters to win any appreciable support from the landed interest did, however, in time have compensation. Both the geographic distribution of Dissent and the evidence of the Dissenting registers suggests that a much higher proportion of Dissenters than of the population at large were engaged in commerce or manufactures as merchants, tradesmen, or self-employed artisans, and the social and legal pressures of the eighteenth century helped to confine Dissenters to such occupations. For the most part they were outcasts from polite society, excluded from the English universities, and, if they were Baptists, Quakers, or strict Independents, forbidden

---

[1] Higson, 'The Lords Willoughby of Parham', *passim.*
[2] Halley, *Lancashire,* ii. 430, n.
[3] Higson, 'The Lords Willoughby of Parham', pp. 171–6.
[4] Vann, *Social Development,* pp. 73–8.

to serve king or corporation without compromising their consciences. Some Dissenters refused to serve the persecuting state and resigned their offices even before required to do so by the Test Act: Captain Samuel Taverner, for example, the governor of Deal Castle, joined the General Baptist church at Dover in 1663 and two years later resigned his commission to become a grocer.[1] The Quakers in particular were subjected to pressures which helped to channel their energies into trade and industry, for the fines and distraints imposed on Quaker farmers who refused to pay tithes made farming an expensive and uncertain business,[2] and the Quakers, unlike the Presbyterians and Congregationalists, had no professional ministry to provide employment for their most gifted sons. To some extent the same was true of the Baptists before the Particular Baptists could afford to pay for full-time pastors and the General Baptists dropped their objections to a paid ministry.

It is not difficult to see why the stern self-discipline preached by William Penn, the strict morality enforced by the gathered churches, and the disgrace associated with bankruptcy, could lead to success in business and to the careful husbanding of the rewards thus won. But one does not need to invoke an elaborate theory of the connection between 'the Protestant ethic and the spirit of capitalism'[3] to explain the evolution of Baptist tradesmen and Quaker ironmongers into Baptist merchants and Quaker ironmasters in a period when the country's trade was increasing and Parliament was removing monopolistic restrictions from commerce and industry. It could be argued, for example, that the success of the Baptist merchant William Kiffin is a perfect illustration of the Weber thesis. Born in London in 1616, Kiffin lost most of his family through plague when he was only nine years old and at the age of thirteen he was apprenticed 'to a mean calling' in which he befriended his fellow apprentice John Lilburne. In 1638 Kiffin joined a Separatist church,[4] four years later he became a Baptist and suffered a short term of imprisonment, and in 1643 he embarked on a trading venture with the Dutch which laid the foundation of his

---

[1] Taylor, *General Baptists*, i. 277.

[2] A. Raistrick, *Quakers in Science and Industry* (1950), pp. 39, 53.

[3] M. Weber, *The Protestant Ethic and the Spirit of Capitalism* (1930).

[4] B. R. White, 'How did William Kiffin join the Baptists?', *Baptist Quarterly*, xxiii (1969–70), 201–7.

future fortune. For nearly sixty years, until his death in 1701, Kiffin was pastor of what became the Devonshire Square Particular Baptist church, but he was not paid for his services and he found time to become M.P. for Middlesex in 1656 and to become one of the richest of London merchants. It is said that on one occasion Charles II asked Kiffin for a loan of £40,000, and that Kiffin replied that while he could not lend so large an amount, which he knew he would probably never get back, he would make the king a gift of £10,000. In this way, claimed Kiffin, he saved £30,000.[1] But there is no evidence that the man who showed such business acumen felt 'called' to his trade. Rather he had engaged in commercial ventures out of sheer necessity, at a time when imprisonment and ill health had reduced him to destitution. Even after his first successful trading venture he neglected 'the opportunity of proceeding in that trade' and devoted his time chiefly to 'studying the word of God', until he had spent most of what he had earned and was obliged to return to commerce.[2]

When success came to Dissenting traders and craftsmen, it was not because they had been conditioned by their religion to make profits, but because they applied their minds and hands to the tasks which they and their Separatist forbears had always pursued. It was in this way that in the first half of the eighteenth century a number of Dissenters helped to pave the way for the industrial revolution. Thomas Newcomen, a Dartmouth ironmonger who was for twenty years pastor of the town's Particular Baptist church, and his Baptist assistant John Calley, supplied tools to the tin miners of south Devon, and, impressed by the 'heavy cost of lifting water by means of horses', invented in 1712 a 'fire-engine', the progenitor of the modern steam engine, a discovery which was to be of major importance in the growth of the coal industry.[3] Four years earlier a crucial step in the development of the iron industry had been taken when Abraham Darby, a Quaker ironmaster faced with a shortage of charcoal for the smelting of iron, transferred his activities from

---

[1] Orme, *Life of Kiffin, passim.* It is a major weakness of Weber's thesis that his evidence is drawn from the writings of theoreticians and not from the lives of men who were actually engaged in 'capitalist' enterprises.

[2] Orme, *Life of Kiffin*, pp. 22–3.

[3] *TBHS* ii (1910–11), 118–20, L. T. C. Rolt, *Thomas Newcomen* (Dawlish, 1963), pp. 51–2.

Bristol to Coalbrookdale in Shropshire and discovered a means of using coke instead of charcoal.[1] The tin-plate industry of south Wales owed its origin to another Quaker ironmaster, John Hanbury, who began the manufacture of tin-plate at Pontypool in 1720 in works which had been in his family for a century and a half.[2] The Quaker chemist Edward Wright perfected a furnace for smelting lead with coke, and in order to implement his discovery engaged in mining activities and, with the assistance of other Friends, founded in 1705 the Quaker Lead Company, which for two centuries 'continued as the largest mining corporation in the country'.[3] The same response to an immediate problem led the Quaker watch-maker Benjamin Huntsman of Doncaster, when faced with the unreliability of springs made from poor-quality steel, to discover how to improve its strength by casting it in crucibles in a molten condition.[4] And it was doubtless a similar logical development which led the grocer John Freame to inaugurate the financial services which were to evolve into Barclays Bank. Like another Quaker grocer, Henry Coward of Lancaster, Freame's credit would have been such 'that any who had money to dispose of lodged it with him, to put out to interest or make use of it'.[5]

The success of Dissenting tradesmen and manufacturers was assisted by the network of business connections and relationships which arose out of their denominational ties. Thomas Newcomen received the chance to set up his first successful steam engine near Dudley Castle in Worcestershire through the intermediary of a Bromsgrove Baptist, Humphrey Potter, and it was another Bromsgrove Baptist, Joseph Hornblower, who erected three more Newcomen engines near Chacewater and St. Austell in Cornwall between 1725 and 1727.[6] Joseph's two sons and four of his grandsons followed in his footsteps as engineers, and it was one of these grandsons, Jonathan Hornblower, also a Baptist, who in 1781 invented the double-cylinder compound steam engine, of which ten were erected in

[1] A. Raistrick, *Dynasty of Ironfounders* (1953), pp. 23–40.
[2] Raistrick, *Quakers in Science and Industry*, pp. 146–8.
[3] Ibid., pp. 56, 163, 170.
[4] Ibid., pp. 200–1.
[5] Ibid., pp. 167, 321. J. D. Marshall, ed., *The Autobiography of William Stout of Lancaster* (Manchester, 1967), p. 75.
[6] Rolt, *Thomas Newcomen*, pp. 60, 64, 90.

Cornwall in the 1790s despite the claims by Boulton and Watt that it infringed their patent.[1] Among Quakers the regular round of Quarterly and Yearly Meetings brought Friends from different areas into regular contact with each other and facilitated the formation of both business and matrimonial alliances. The foundations of the prosperity of the Quaker dynasty of Lloyd were laid in the 1690s when three of the children of Charles Lloyd of Dolobran in Montgomeryshire married into the families of two Midland ironmongers—the Crowleys of Stourbridge and the Pembertons of Birmingham. Sampson Lloyd I moved from his Herefordshire farm to Birmingham in 1698 to take up the ironmongering trade of his newly acquired relatives, and thirty years later his sons Charles and Sampson Lloyd II bought a corn mill from yet another family of Birmingham Quakers and adapted it for the rolling and slitting of iron for the making of nails. The desire of the second Sampson Lloyd to provide adequate employment for his sons led in turn in 1765 to his joining with a Presbyterian button-maker named John Taylor to found the bank which a century later became Lloyds.[2]

Not all Quaker enterprises met with equal success. The elder brother of Sampson Lloyd I, Charles Lloyd II, engaged in iron production in his native Montgomeryshire and brought shame to his family and to his religious profession by becoming bankrupt in 1727.[3] But the rising prosperity of the Quaker community as a whole cannot be doubted, and is substantiated by a comparison which W. Beck and T. F. Ball made of 250 marriages recorded by London Friends around 1680 with the same number of marriages a century later. The number of bankers had increased from none to seven, the merchants from fourteen to twenty, and the substantial tradesmen, manufacturers, brewers, goldsmiths, coal merchants, and so on from eighteen to fifty-nine. By contrast, the number of craftsmen, carpenters, shoemakers, tailors, masons, basket-makers, and weavers had fallen from 112 to thirty.[4]

George Fox had an explanation of Quaker business success

[1] L. A. Fereday, *The Story of the Falmouth Baptists* (1950), pp. 37–9. D. B. Barton, *The Cornish Beam Engine* (Truro, 1966), pp. 23–6, 137–8, 271.

[2] H. Lloyd, *The Quaker Lloyds in the Industrial Revolution* (1975), pp. 41, 70, 74, 101, 168. Bushrod, 'Unitarianism in Birmingham', pp. 212, 215.

[3] Lloyd, *Quaker Lloyds*, pp. 56–7.

[4] Beck and Ball, *London Friends' Meetings*, p. 90.

which had nothing to do with their 'capitalist spirit', but rather the reverse:

> At the first convincement when Friends could not put off their hats to people nor say 'you' to a particular, but 'thee' and 'thou' . . . many Friends, being tradesmen of several sorts lost their custom . . . [and] could hardly get enough money to buy bread. But afterwards people came to see Friends' honesty and truthfulness and 'yea' and 'nay' at a word in their dealing . . . and they knew and saw that, for conscience sake towards God, they would not cozen and cheat them. . . . So then things altered so that all enquiry was, where was a draper or shopkeeper or tailor or shoemaker or any other tradesman that was a Quaker; insomuch that Friends had double the trade, beyond any of their neighbours.[1]

Far from devoting all their energies to maximizing their profits, some Dissenters sought, through their churches, to uphold a high standard of commercial morality. Early in the seventeenth century John Smyth's church was accused of excommunicating a tailor 'for taking 7*s*. for making a doublet and hose' when 'another tailor said he ought to have had but 5*s*'.[2] The Bedford Congregational church expelled Richard Dean in 1671 for, among other offences, 'selling to several persons deceitful goods'.[3] Thirty years later the Kimbolton Independent church reprimanded Thomas Woodham for 'not sending as good barley as he sold, and wanting measure according to [his] bargain to the man at Croydon'.[4] In 1693 the Stevington Particular Baptist church in Bedfordshire investigated the case of Sister Fowler who was charged with using light weights, but she claimed she had acted in ignorance and the church gave her the benefit of the doubt.[5] Similarly the Rothwell Congregational church looked into an accusation against a Mrs. Charlton that she was selling butter under weight, but she, too, was vindicated.[6]

The Quakers attempted to enforce the principle of a fixed price and to eschew the common practice of setting an inflated price on an article as a basis from which to haggle. Quaker meetings in Devon and Somerset ordered Friends to pay their

[1] *Fox's Journal*, pp. 169–70. [2] Burgess, *John Smith*, p. 96.
[3] Brown, *John Bunyan*, p. 195.
[4] Kimbolton Independent Church Book, p. 17.
[5] Tibbutt, 'Some Early Nonconformist Church Books', p. 37.
[6] Glass, *Independent Church at Rothwell*, p. 77.

employees in money and not in goods, and in Southwark Quaker coopers were ordered to have their casks measured for their true capacity.[1] The stern attitude which all Dissenting churches adopted towards bankruptcy was designed to prevent excessive speculation in the search for excessive profits, and the Quakers in particular were likely to find that profitable lines of trade were closed to them by the ban which their denomination placed on the manufacture and selling of luxury articles.[2] The General Baptist Assembly advised its constituent churches in 1656 to be 'exceeding careful that persons do not leave their proper callings and undertake such dealings as far exceeds their ability to manage', an attitude hardly designed to encourage commercial enterprise.[3] They even had doubts about the propriety of taking out patents for new inventions, for when Richard Haines, a member of Matthew Caffyn's church at Horsham, was granted a patent in 1672 for a process he had discovered for cleaning hop-clover, he was excommunicated by his church and was only restored to membership eight years later after an appeal to the General Assembly.[4] Nor was Haines a grasping capitalist without a social conscience, for he published at least seven pamphlets on the relief of the poor and in a pamphlet of 1671 he outlined *Proposals for Building in every County a Working-Almshouses or Hospital* which foreshadowed John Bellers's later plans for 'colleges of industry'.[5]

10. 'FREEDOM OF INQUIRY':
THE CONTRIBUTION OF THE DISSENTING ACADEMIES

If the chief Quaker contribution to the secular life of England in the eighteenth century lay in the fields of commerce and technology, that of the Presbyterians and Congregationalists was primarily in the sphere of education. The Presbyterians in particular could not conceive of a well-ordered church without an educated ministry, and since the statutes of Oxford and Cambridge after the Restoration closed the one university to Dissenters and debarred them from graduating at the other,

---

[1] Brockett, *Nonconformity in Exeter*, p. 112. Braithwaite, *SPQ*, p. 562. Beck and Ball, *London Friends' Meetings*, p. 231.

[2] I. Grubb, *Quakerism and Industry before 1800* (1930), pp. 94–5.

[3] *Minutes of the General Baptist Assembly*, i. 8.

[4] Ibid. i, pp. xii–xv.

[5] Bebb, *Nonconformity and Social and Economic Life*, p. 129.

Nonconformists who wanted their sons to receive higher education had to seek it either in Scotland or the Netherlands or in institutions of their own. Although the Act of Uniformity imposed a penalty of £40 on any Dissenter who ventured to earn his living by teaching, at least twenty ejected ministers braved the law by establishing academies at which they sought to provide higher education for the sons of Dissenters. Entry into such institutions was not necessarily confined to students who intended to study for the ministry. Of the twenty-three academies in existence in 1690 at least half were open to students who had careers other than the ministry in mind, and of the 303 students educated at the largest academy, Richard Frankland's, only 110 became pastors.[1] When Philip Doddridge proposed to admit only potential ministers to his Northampton academy in 1732, his fellow minister David Jennings remonstrated 'that the support of our interest comes from the laity, and . . . they will not be constrained to bring up all their sons either as ministers or dunces'. There was no sense, argued Jennings, in driving the sons of Dissenters 'who are designed for physicians, lawyers, or gentlemen, to Oxford or Cambridge, or to make them rakes in the foreign universities', and Doddridge heeded his advice.[2]

The Dissenting academies had their deficiencies. Their resources were for the most part inadequate, their library facilities limited, and their locations determined by the changing needs of their tutors. If a tutor changed his pastorate or, in the period of persecution, moved his residence to avoid prosecution, his pupils were likewise obliged to uproot themselves. If a tutor died, his academy was all too likely to come to an end. The first generation of Dissenting tutors had themselves been educated at Oxford or Cambridge, and for the most part attempted to perpetuate the traditions of classical education in which they had been reared.[3] Little attention was paid to modern languages in the academies of the later seventeenth and early eighteenth centuries, and although Doddridge studied French at Kibworth it was without regard to 'the pronunciation

[1] H. McLachlan, *English Education under the Test Acts* (Manchester, 1931), pp. 6–15. Cragg, *Puritanism in the Period of the Great Persecution*, p. 189.
[2] *Corresopndence of Doddridge*, iii. 115–16.
[3] J. W. Ashley Smith, *The Birth of Modern Education* (1954), pp. 10–11.

with which Mr. Jennings was not acquainted'.[1] At Timothy
Jollie's Attercliffe academy philosophy was taught badly and
mathematics not at all, since Jollie believed it fostered 'scepticism and infidelity', while Strickland Gough resented the time
'wasted in old systems of logic and metaphysics'.[2] But subsequent generations of tutors were less bound by the example of
the past and encouraged both a spirit of critical inquiry in their
students and an interest in contemporary developments in the
natural sciences. At a time when the reputations of Oxford and
Cambridge were at their nadir, their universities like two
'enormous hulks confined with mooring-chains, everything
flowing and progressing around them', the education at the
Dissenting academies could hardly have been worse and in
many instances was vastly superior to anything provided beside
the Isis and the Cam.[3]

The most progressive of the early academies was that run by
the Congregationalist Charles Morton at Newington Green
(*c.* 1675–85), the excellence of which was testified by two of its
most distinguished students, Samuel Wesley and Daniel Defoe.
Wesley, the son and grandson of ejected ministers, ultimately
conformed to the established church and as rector of Epworth
became a bitter critic of Dissent, but even he could not fail to
bestow praise on Morton's academy for its 'fine garden, bowling
green, fish pond, and within a laboratory and some not inconsiderable rarities with air pump, thermometers, and all sorts
of mathematical instruments'.[4] It was at mathematics, said
Wesley, that Morton excelled, while Defoe added that he studied
'natural philosophy, logic, geography, and history', 'politics as
a science', 'went through a complete course of theology', and
emerged from Morton's academy the 'master of five languages'.
That Morton was able to achieve so much is no doubt largely
explained by the fact that, unusually for a late-seventeenth-
century tutor, whether Dissenting or Anglican, he gave all his
instruction in English.[5]

---

[1] *Correspondence of Doddridge*, ii. 463.

[2] McLachlan, *English Education*, pp. 107–8. S. Gough, *An Enquiry into the Causes of the Decay of the Dissenting Interest* (1731), p. 43.

[3] V. H. H. Green, *A History of Oxford University* (1974), p. 107.

[4] S. Wesley, *A Letter from a Country Divine . . . concerning the Education of Dissenters in their Private Academies* (2nd edn., 1704), p. 6.

[5] McLachlan, *English Education*, p. 79. Smith, *Modern Education*, pp. 57–8.

Morton's practice of teaching in English did not become common form in the Dissenting academies for another half-century, when Philip Doddridge at Northampton (1729–51) set an example which other tutors were soon to follow. Like Morton, Doddridge provided his students with a broad curriculum which typified the Dissenting academies at their best. In the first year of their four-year course students were required not only to improve the Latin and Greek they had acquired at school and to learn sufficient Hebrew to enable them to read the Old Testament in the original tongue, but also to study logic, rhetoric, geography, metaphysics, geometry, and algebra. They then proceeded to the study of 'trigonometry, conic sections, and celestial mechanics, consisting of a collection of important propositions taken chiefly from Sir Isaac Newton', and to a course of 'natural and experimental philosophy', which comprised physics and astronomy and 'was illustrated by a neat and pretty large philosophical apparatus'. Anatomy, natural and civil history, and especially the history of Dissent, were taught, and 'polite literature' was 'by no means neglected'.[1]

In addition to lecturing to his own students on the natural sciences Doddridge also joined the Northampton Philosophical Society and read to its members papers on pendulums and on 'the laws of the communication of motions'.[2] Among other Dissenting teachers who encouraged the study of scientific subjects was John Horsley, who was minister of the Presbyterian meeting in Morpeth from the early years of the eighteenth century until his death in 1732. Horsley kept a school in Morpeth, lectured on natural philosophy in the town and in Newcastle, was elected a Fellow of the Royal Society, wrote a monumental work on Roman Britain, and collected extensive scientific apparatus which passed after his death to Caleb Rotheram, who kept an academy at Kendal from 1735 to 1752.[3] Rotheram lectured on 'the nature of matter, the laws of motion, mechanics . . . heat . . . optics, light and colours, and astronomy', and after his death his experimental apparatus passed in turn to the Warrington academy which was founded

---

[1] Bogue and Bennett, *History of Dissenters*, iii. 306–8.
[2] A. E. Musson and E. Robinson, *Science and Technology in the Industrial Revolution* (Manchester, 1969), pp. 382–3.
[3] *DNB* ix. 1276.

in 1757.[1] It was probably on this apparatus that Joseph Priestley, who became a tutor at Warrington in 1761, conducted his first experiments, and it was in this way that the Dissenting academies made their most important contribution to original scientific research. But the overriding purpose of the academies' courses on the natural sciences was to deduce arguments in favour of the wisdom and power of the Creator. The principal object of study at the Northampton academy was always Doddridge's 'system of divinity', comprising the nature of the human mind, 'the proof of the existence and attributes of God', 'evidence of the immortality of the soul', and 'the genuineness, credibility, and inspiration' of Scripture.[2]

The education provided by the academies was not only broad in terms of the curricula but also liberal by virtue of the tolerance which many tutors displayed towards divergent opinions. Thomas Rowe, who conducted an academy at Newington Green from 1678 until 1705, encouraged 'freedom of enquiry' by his students, and his most distinguished pupil, Isaac Watts, wrote in 1696 that he had sometimes 'carried reason with [him] even to the camp of Socinus', though Paul had borne him back again 'almost to the tents of John Calvin'.[3] The future Archbishop Thomas Secker wrote of Samuel Jones's academy at Gloucester in 1711 that the tutor allowed his students 'all imaginable liberty of making objections against his opinion, and prosecuting them as far as we can'. Among the books studied was 'the greater part' of Locke's *Essay Concerning Human Understanding* with its insistence that knowledge is derived from experience and that 'revelation must be judged by reason'.[4] John Jennings, who taught at Kibworth and Hinckley from 1715 to 1723, also introduced his students to Locke's *Essay*, and as his most celebrated pupil, Doddridge, bore witness, he encouraged 'the greatest freedom of inquiry' among his students, insisting 'that the Scriptures are the only genuine standard of faith'. In his divinity course, wrote Doddridge while still a student at Kibworth, 'Mr. Jennings does not follow the doctrines or phrases of any particular party; but is some-

---

[1] Musson and Robinson, *Science and Technology*, pp. 90, 103.

[2] Bogue and Bennett, *History of Dissenters*, iii. 306–8.

[3] Davis, *Isaac Watts*, pp. 13–14. Rowe's academy was a separate institution from Morton's academy, which was also situated at Newington Green.

[4] Bogue and Bennett, *History of Dissenters*, iii. 85–8.

times a Calvinist, sometimes an Arminian, and sometimes a Baxterian, as truth and evidence determine him.' 'He furnishes us with all kinds of authors upon every subject, without advising us to skip over the heretical passages for fear of infection', and Doddridge was to continue the same liberal tradition in his own academy at Northampton.[1]

Doddridge himself remained immune to infection from heresy, but not all students at Dissenting academies at the turn of the seventeenth and eighteenth centuries were so protected. James Clegg, who entered John Chorlton's academy in Manchester in 1698, read the works of Socinus in Chetham's public library and although he claimed that these writings made little impression on him, at the same time he admitted that he could never again 'be entirely reconciled to the common doctrine of the Trinity, but then began to incline to that scheme which long after Dr. Clarke espoused and published'.[2] Such was to be the experience of many English Presbyterians in the eighteenth century.

11. ART THOU 'A THREEFOLD DEITY'?: EXETER AND SALTERS' HALL

Two forms of anti-trinitarianism flourished in eighteenth-century England, Arianism and Socinianism. Both schools of thought regarded Christ as subordinate to the Father, but whereas the Arians acknowledged the pre-existence of Christ, looked upon him as in some sense divine, and retained the concept of the atonement, the more radical Socinians denied both the divinity and the pre-existence of Christ and rejected the doctrine of vicarious atonement.[3] Arianism took its name from the fourth-century Alexandrian priest whose views were condemned by the Council of Nicaea in 325, Socinianism from a sixteenth-century Italian, Fausto Sozzini or Socinus, who had been associated with a group of anti-trinitarian Anabaptists at Rakow in Poland in 1580. Arian views did not gain wide currency in England until the first half of the eighteenth century,

---

[1] *Correspondence of Doddridge*, i. 155–6, 198.

[2] Kirke, *Diary of James Clegg*, p. 23.

[3] Socinus, unlike Englishmen who bore his name, did though believe that Christians had the authority of the New Testament for the 'adoration' of Christ as one set over the Church by God. H. J. McLachlan, *Socinianism in Seventeenth Century England* (Oxford, 1951), pp. 13–15.

but Socinianism attracted a number of Englishmen during the intellectual turmoil of the 1640s and 1650s. Among them were Paul Best, who had fought in the army of Gustavus Adolphus during the Thirty Years War and brought anti-trinitarian views back with him to England, and John Biddle, a Gloucestershire schoolmaster who published an English translation of the Racovian Catechism in 1652 and spent nearly ten years in prison for propagating Socinian doctrines. Biddle died in one of Charles II's gaols in 1662, but he left behind a handful of converts, of whom the most important was the wealthy London silk merchant and philanthropist Thomas Firmin, and it was Firmin who financed the publication of a series of anti-trinitarian tracts which appeared in the late 1680s and 1690s. The first, *A Brief History of the Unitarians, called also Socinians*, published in 1687, was written by Stephen Nye, rector of Little Hormead in Hertfordshire, the Anglican grandson of that Philip Nye who, as a leading Congregationalist of the Interregnum, had joined with John Owen in seeking to proscribe the Racovian Catechism thirty-five years earlier.

The bishops of the 1690s were as alarmed as the Congregationalists of the 1650s at the dissemination of anti-trinitarian views, and Unitarians were both excluded from the benefits of the Toleration Act and, under the Blasphemy Act of 1698, liable to three years' imprisonment for propagating their beliefs. Such measures, though, failed to halt the growth of heresy. Among the pamphlets published in reply to Stephen Nye's *Brief History* was *A Vindication of the Doctrine of the Trinity* by William Sherlock, dean of St. Paul's, who so overstated his case that he unsettled the orthodoxy of two Dissenters, William Manning, an ejected minister of Peasenhall in Suffolk, and his friend Thomas Emlyn, pastor to a Presbyterian meeting in Dublin. Manning embraced the very Socinian views which Sherlock had sought to refute and persuaded Emlyn to go part way with him along the road from orthodoxy. Emlyn 'could never be brought to doubt . . . the pre-existence of our Saviour' but he did adopt Arian views, and when he acknowledged his heterodoxy in 1702 he was dismissed from his Dublin pastorate. But before returning to England he defended his position in *An Humble Inquiry into the Scripture Account of Jesus Christ* for which he was prosecuted, found guilty of issuing a blasphemous libel, and suffered two years in prison.[1] It was Emlyn's Arianism rather than Manning's Socinianism which became the prevailing heresy of the early eighteenth century. In 1710 William Whiston, professor of mathematics at Cambridge, was deprived of his chair and expelled from the university for holding the Arian opinions which he published in the following year in his *Primitive Christianity Revived*. And in 1712 Samuel Clarke, rector of St. James's, Westminster, in attempting to explain *The Scripture-doctrine of the Trinity*, also came to conclusions which his critics branded as Arian.[2] Clarke denied the charge, and when Convocation threatened him with prosecution for heresy he agreed to publish no more on the subject. But his book on the Trinity was widely read, not least among Dissenters.

That some Dissenters were receptive to the views of Whiston and Clarke is not difficult to understand. Though the Westminster Assembly had defined the theological beliefs of Presbyterians in Calvinist terms, in practice they had maintained with Chillingworth that the Bible and 'the Bible only, is the religion of Protestants'. 'If there be nothing against Socinianism in Scripture', wrote Baxter in 1668, 'it is no heresy: if there be (as sure there is enough and plain enough) judge them by that rule, and make not new ones.'[3] This attitude was shared by the General Baptists, among whom the question of the Trinity had been raised during the Caffyn controversy. In 1697 the General Baptist Assembly resolved that if members debated the Trinity, they must do so 'in Scripture words and terms and in no other terms', and the Assembly held to that position consistently throughout the following century.[4] The Bible, though, nowhere mentions the Trinity and the one passage in the Authorized Version which appeared to refer to the doctrine, I John 5: 7, 8, was in 1715 rejected as a spurious interpolation by Richard Bentley, professor of theology at Cambridge.[5] Locke was teaching Dissenters to test revelation by reason, not by the theological schemes of Athanasius or Calvin, and when they did so they not infrequently came up with unorthodox answers.

---

[1] T. Emlyn, *Works* (1746), i, p. xiii. Browne, *Congregationalism in Norfolk and Suffolk*, pp. 528–9. *DNB* vi. 774–8, xii. 958.
[2] J. H. Colligan, *The Arian Movement in England* (Manchester, 1913), p. 37.
[3] *Reliquiae Baxterianae*, part iii, p. 65.
[4] *Minutes of General Baptist Assembly*, i. 43, ii. 27, 141, 186.
[5] O. M. Griffiths, *Religion and Learning* (Cambridge, 1935), p. 119.

Among the first Presbyterians to be influenced by the views of Whiston and Clarke were James Peirce, minister to one of Exeter's three Presbyterian congregations, and the students at Joseph Hallet's academy in the same city. Peirce had known Whiston when he had held a pastorate at Cambridge, and he was led by reading Clarke's book on the Trinity to the opinion that he must either 'part with some beloved opinions, or else quit my notion of the authority of the Holy Scriptures'.[1] Initially Peirce tried to keep his doubts about the Trinity to himself, but towards the end of 1716 it became known in Exeter that at 'the house of a layman, who boarded some of Mr. Hallet's pupils, the divinity of Christ was disputed', and one of the students, Hubert Stogdon, let it be known that he had been converted to Clarke's views. As a result Peirce himself came under suspicion and was asked to preach on the deity of Christ, but he delivered the crucial part of his sermon too fast for the heresy-hunters in his congregation to take down his words, and when he and Joseph Hallet signed a certificate commending Stogdon for ordination, the fears of the orthodox seemed confirmed.[2] In September 1718 the Devon and Cornwall association of ministers, the Exeter Assembly, demanded that every member should declare his position on the Trinity, which Peirce did by stating that he believed 'the Son and Holy Ghost to be divine persons, but subordinate to the Father';[3] and in November the Committee of Thirteen laymen which was responsible for the financial affairs of the Presbyterian meetings in Exeter asked the city's four Presbyterian ministers for a statement of their orthodoxy. But the Committee of Thirteen got 'no satisfaction' from three of its four ministers and, at a loss to know what to do next, they appealed to Presbyterian ministers in London for advice.[4] Peirce also appealed to sympathizers in London, and the upshot was that the Committee of the Three Denominations decided to call a meeting of all Dissenting ministers in London to debate the 'advices' they should send to Exeter.

[1] Brockett, *Nonconformity in Exeter*, p. 79.
[2] Ibid., p. 80. J. Eveleigh, *An Account of the Reasons why many citizens of Exon. have withdrawn from the ministry of Mr. Joseph Hallet and Mr. James Peirce* (1719), p. 4.
[3] J. Murch, *A History of the Presbyterian and General Baptist Churches in the West of England* (1835), p. 395.
[4] Brockett, *Nonconformity in Exeter*, pp. 88–90.

The London ministers met at Salters' Hall on 19 and 24 February 1719 and on a crucial division it was resolved by 57 votes to 53 'that no human compositions, or interpretations of the doctrine of the Trinity, should be made a part of those articles of advice'.[1] Two years earlier Bishop Hoadly of Bangor had earned the wrath of his own communion by denying the authority of the Church to enforce religious belief, and now he rejoiced that at Salters' Hall, for the first time since the apostolic age, an assembly of divines had 'carried a question for liberty'.[2] The vote, though, had no effect on events in Exeter. The trustees of the Presbyterian meeting-houses, on the advice of orthodox local ministers, closed their doors to Peirce and Hallet, and in 1720 the ejected ministers opened a new meeting-house where, notwithstanding the laws against Unitarianism, they preached to a congregation of about 300, undisturbed 'by the magistrate'.[3]

Meanwhile, in London, the controversy continued, and at a further meeting at Salters' Hall on 3 March the defeated minority subscribed their names to a Trinitarian declaration which led henceforward to the two sides being known as Subscribers and Non-subscribers. The issue between them was not, ostensibly, their orthodoxy or heresy on the question of the Trinity. The Non-subscribers disowned Arianism, expressed their belief in 'the doctrine of the blessed Trinity, and the proper divinity of our Lord Jesus Christ', and agreed that there were errors in doctrine which, if preached by a minister, justified a congregation in withdrawing its support. But at the same time they insisted on 'the Protestant principle that the Bible is the only and perfect rule of faith', and refused 'to condemn any man upon the authority of human decisions, or because he contents not to human forms or phrases'.[4] And in time the fears of the Subscribers that the attitude adopted by the Non-subscribers would lead to Unitarianism were justified.

Of the seventy-eight London Dissenting ministers who are

[1] Anon., *An Account of the late proceedings of the Dissenting ministers at Salters' Hall* (1719), p. 10.

[2] R. Thomas, 'Presbyterians in Transition', in *The English Presbyterians*, p. 161. The connection between the Bangorian controversy and the Salters' Hall dispute is brought out by Thomas in 'The Non-subscription controversy among Dissenters in 1719', *JEH*. iv (1953), 180–4.

[3] Murch, *Presbyterian Churches in the West of England*, p. 401 n.

[4] Anon., *An Authentick Account of Several Things Done and Agreed upon by the Dissenting ministers lately Assembled at Salters' Hall* (1719), pp. 5, 8, 15.

known to have been Subscribers at Salters' Hall, thirty were Presbyterians, twenty-eight Congregationalists, fourteen Particular Baptists, one General Baptist, and five of unknown affiliation. Of the seventy-three Non-subscribers there were forty-seven Presbyterians, nine Congregationalists, fourteen General Baptists, two Particular Baptists, and one of uncertain affiliation.[1] In other words, the majority of Presbyterian and General Baptist ministers took their stand on the sufficiency of Scripture, the majority of Congregationalists and Particular Baptists insisted on subscription to a Trinitarian creed. And within a century most Presbyterian meetings and many of the General Baptist churches connected with the General Assembly had become Unitarian, while the Congregational and Particular Baptist churches not only remained Trinitarian, but continued to honour the theology of John Calvin.

How can we account for the divergent paths taken by the Presbyterians and General Baptists on the one hand, and by the Congregationalists and Particular Baptists on the other? The literalism which led the General Baptists to practise the washing of feet and anointing with oil—customs which were to continue well into the eighteenth century[2]—also made them suspicious of doctrinal statements not based on Scripture. And their neo-Arminianism predisposed them to look more favourably than their Calvinist brethren on liberal trends in theology. For many Presbyterians, too, Arminianism proved to be a halfway house between Calvinism and Arianism. During the Civil Wars Presbyterians had deplored what they regarded as the Antinomian tendencies of some Independents, and had feared that Antinomianism would undermine order and morality in society in the same way that Independency was producing, in their eyes, anarchy in the church. The Presbyterians had lost the struggle against Independency and by virtue of their exclusion from the established church had themselves been forced into an independent position, but the fight against Antinomianism had been maintained, first by Richard Baxter and then by Daniel Williams. But in denouncing what he regarded

[1] Jones, *Congregationalism in England*, p. 136 n. R. Thomas in *The English Presbyterians*, p. 163.

[2] The Lewes and Ditchling General Baptist church was still practising feet-washing in 1767, and the Turner's Hill church, Sussex, as late as 1785. *Baptist Quarterly*, iv (1928-9), 71. *TUHS* i (1916-18), 212-13.

as the irrationality of Antinomianism Baxter had modified Calvinism in a way which opened him to the charge of Arminianism, and among the next generation of Presbyterian ministers were those who insisted on free will as well as free grace to an extent which made nonsense of the Calvinist scheme.[1] By 1732, according to the author of the 'View of the Dissenting Interest in London', the thirty-one Congregational ministers in the metropolis were Calvinists 'almost to a man', but the forty-four Presbyterians were classified as nineteen Calvinists, thirteen Arminians, and twelve who followed Baxter's 'Middle Way'.[2] It was, moreover, the younger Presbyterian ministers who were most 'inclined to the Arminian scheme', and their acceptance of Arminianism led, as it did in the case of many General Baptists, to a readiness first to tolerate and then to embrace Arian views. The Salters' Hall episode was thus a seismic forecast of the theological chasm which would ultimately open up between the Presbyterian and Congregational denominations, the first cracks of which had appeared at the time of the Richard Davis case thirty years before.[3]

To the Unitarian historian Alexander Gordon the upshot of all this was that 'in process of time, the old denominational labels seemed almost to have changed places. Independent, which under the Commonwealth had stood for toleration and variety, now came to mean theological conservatism. Presbyterian, which, theologically speaking, had meant doctrinal consensus, now stood for latitude.'[4] The paradox is, however,

---

[1] R. Thomas, 'The Break-up of Nonconformity' in *The Beginnings of Nonconformity*, pp. 49–50.

[2] 'View of the Dissenting Interest in London', pp. 87–92.

[3] R. E. Richey has argued that 'the social foundations of Unitarianism' are to be found 'in the community called Protestant Dissent' rather than in Presbyterianism alone ('The Origins of English Unitarianism', Princeton University Ph.D. thesis, 1970, p. 121). There is, as will be seen, a good deal of evidence which can be adduced to support Richey's thesis, but he overstates his case by failing to pay adequate attention to the way in which the ecclesiastical traditions of Presbyterianism favoured the growth of rationalism while those of Congregationalism assisted the preservation of Calvinism. 'The denominational affiliation of a chapel had meaning really only internally,' writes Richey (p. 94), but it was precisely here that the crucial difference between Presbyterianism and Congregationalism in the eighteenth century lay. Richey's thesis is summarized in his article 'Did the English Presbyterians become Unitarian' in *Church History*, xlii (1973), 58–72.

[4] A. Gordon, *Historical Account of Dukinfield Chapel* (1896), p. 47.

explained by the differing ecclesiastical traitions of the two denominations, which showed greater continuity than might at first sight appear. Though the Presbyterian ministers of the Interregnum had always been intolerant of separatism outside the established church they had, as Calvinist parish clergy, always maintained that the church on earth must consist of both saved and damned, for God's decrees of election and reprobation could not be known to men. The church at Corinth, said the Presbyterian John Geree in defending the concept of a national church, consisted both of those who 'denied the Resurrection' and those who 'had not repented of their uncleanness, fornication, and lasciviousness'.[1] Though the Presbyterians of the early eighteenth century set higher moral standards than the church at Corinth, they, too, were tolerant towards those of heterodox beliefs. There were some Presbyterian ministers, wrote the Congregationalist author of the 'View of the Dissenting Interest', who 'admit all sorts of persons that will but say they are Christians into their communion, be they Arminians, Calvinists, Freethinkers, Arians, or Socinians, it is all one to them, and their pulpits too are ready to receive ministers of the same make'.[2]

On the other hand the Independents' reputation for toleration, to which Gordon alluded, can be misconstrued. As far as the Congregational wing of Independency was concerned, their advocacy of toleration was a product not of their theology but of their circumstance: when in a position of power, as in Massachusetts, the Congregationalists showed themselves as ready as the Presbyterians to use the authority of the state to enforce outward religious conformity. But the Congregationalists were more confident than the Presbyterians that they could distinguish between the elect and the reprobate on earth, and were always determined in their efforts to restrict church membership to the former. By insisting on religious experience as the condition for church membership, rather than on 'a degree of knowledge' which the Presbyterians used as the test for admission to communion, the English Congregationalists for the most part succeeded in keeping out of their churches people who might seek to judge Calvinist orthodoxy at the bar

[1] Geree, *Judah's Joy at the Oath*, appendix, *Vindiciae Voti*, sig. D3.
[2] 'View of the Dissenting Interest in London', p. 87.

of reason.[1] And should heretics inadvertently be admitted, or existing members acquire heretical views, the disciplinary machinery for dealing with such cases was at hand. In 1704 the Kimbolton Independent church excommunicated Brother Hall for 'drinking in erroneous doctrines'; in 1727 the Hertford Congregational church expelled James Santeen and Susanna Lobb for denying 'the proper Godhead of Christ'; and in 1736 the Castle Gate Congregational church in Nottingham excommunicated John Rawson for holding Arian views.[2] Three years later the Nottingham church took a further step to safeguard its doctrinal purity by resolving that people who had joined the High Pavement Presbyterian meeting since 1735 would not be admitted to membership at Castle Gate 'without giving in their experience'. The English Independents thus largely avoided the fate not only of the English Presbyterians but also of the New England Congregationalists, whose state-supported churches were under constant pressure to liberalize their requirements for church membership, and many of which were to become Unitarian in the early nineteenth century.[3]

In England the Presbyterians and Congregationalists also differed both in the way they chose and removed their ministers, and in the control they exercised over them once they were installed. The Presbyterian minister, answerable neither to bishop or ecclesiastical court on the one hand, nor to an inquisitorial church meeting on the other, was in a relatively privileged position, free, as the younger Calamy said, 'to pursue his

---

[1] For an example of Presbyterian insistence on 'a degree of knowledge' as a qualification for admission to communion see Calamy, *Historical Account*, ii. 132.

[2] Kimbolton Independent Church Book, p. 17. W. Urwick, *Nonconformity in Hertfordshire* (1884), p. 545. Castle Gate Congregational Church Book, pp. 14–55, 26.

[3] Stearns and Brawner produce evidence which suggests that as early as the 1640s the requirements for church membership in the Congregational churches of Massachusetts were more liberal than in the Congregational churches in England. The Cambridge platform of 1648 denied that 'faith in the heart' was essential to church membership 'because that is invisible'—a position the English Presbyterians would have approved. R. P. Stearns and D. H. Brawner, 'New England Church "Relations" and Continuity in Early Congregational History', *Proceedings of the American Antiquarian Society* (April, 1965), pp. 26–8. David Kobrin also shows that by the 1650s the churches of New England were insisting on a profession of faith rather than an account of conversion as a qualification for church membership. 'The Expansion of the Visible Church in New England, 1629–50', *Church History*, xxxvi (1967), 206.

commission, to teach whatever Christ commanded'.[1] True, orthodox trustees could, as at Exeter, close their meeting-house doors to heterodox ministers, but for the most part the respectable merchants, manufacturers, and wholesale traders who acted as Presbyterian trustees were as much opposed to 'enthusiasm', and were as sympathetic to a rational approach to religion, as were their ministers. Consequently when, in the second half of the eighteenth century, a Presbyterian minister interpreted his commission 'to teach whatever Christ commanded' in the light of the theology of Arminius, Arius, or even Socinus, rather than of Athanasius or Calvin, he might suffer the departure of a large and orthodox section of his congregation, but he was likely to retain the confidence of the select group of laymen who held the deeds of his meeting-house and hence the key to his chief source of income. The contrast between prosperous, sophisticated oligarchs who were sympathetic to liberal views, and simple-minded humble democrats who remained Calvinists can be overdrawn, for the theological development of the General Baptists—probably the poorest of all the Dissenting denominations—was similar to that of the Presbyterians. But it is significant that one of the very few Particular Baptist churches to become Unitarian—that at Trowbridge in Wiltshire—was also one of the wealthiest.[2]

It would similarly be a mistake to exaggerate either the illiberalism of the Congregationalists or the liberalism of the Presbyterians. Neither of the two leading Congregationalists of the first half of the eighteenth century—Isaac Watts and Philip Doddridge—adopted positions which were entirely pleasing to strictly orthodox Independents. Doddridge not only referred students in his academy 'to authors on both sides of every question', but sympathized with the Non-subscribers in the Salters' Hall dispute, and in 1728 refused an invitation to the pastorate of the heresy-conscious Castle Gate church in Nottingham where there was 'some uneasiness at the free declaration I had made of my catholic sentiments on the head of the Trinity'.[3] As for Isaac Watts, he not only reached a Baxterian position in attempting to mitigate the rigours of Calvinism, but spent his

---

[1] Thomas, 'Presbyterians in Transition' in *The English Presbyterians*, p. 128.
[2] Reeves, 'Protestant Nonconformity', *VCH* Wiltshire, iii. 126.
[3] *Priestley's Works*, vol. i (i), p. 23. *Correspondence of Doddridge*, ii. 335, v. 263.

last years worrying about the Trinity, praying almost despairingly that God would show him 'whether he be one pure and simple being or whether thou art a threefold deity'.[1]

In the case of the Presbyterians it must be emphasized that the process by which many meetings passed from Calvinism through Arminianism to Unitarianism was one of slow evolution, not revolution, and that although the development had begun well before 1730, the outcome was by no means obvious by that date. Thus the writer of the 'View of the Dissenting Interest' of 1732 knew of thirteen Arminians and twelve Baxterians among London's Presbyterian ministers, but of none deserving the name Arian or Socinian. When a Presbyterian minister embraced heretical views he did not normally risk ejection or the disruption of his congregation by regaling them with his new opinions, and the need for caution is illustrated by contrasting careers of Thomas Emlyn and Martin Tomkins on the one hand, and of Nathaniel Lardner on the other. After his dismissal from his Presbyterian congregation in Dublin and his imprisonment for propagating Arian views, Emlyn retired to London where, even after the Salters' Hall dispute, none of the Dissenting ministers dared ask him to preach from their pulpits, apart from the heterodox ministers of the liberal Baptist church at the Barbican.[2] Tomkins was also dismissed from his pastorate of the Presbyterian meeting at Stoke Newington in 1718 on account of his Arian views, and twenty years later was complaining that his opinions prevented his being acceptable to any other Presbyterian congregation.[3] By contrast Nathaniel Lardner, a former Congregationalist who was assistant pastor of the Crutched Friars Presbyterian meeting from 1729 to 1751, repudiated Arianism and committed himself to the more radical Socinian position in his *Letter concerning . . . the Logos* which he wrote in 1730. But Lardner delayed publishing his book until 1759, eight years after he had resigned from his pastorate, and in 1732 the author of the 'View of the Dissenting Interest' accounted him a 'Middle Way' man.[4] The writer of the 1732 manuscript similarly concluded that most General Baptist

---

[1] Davis, *Isaac Watts*, pp. 108–9, 121.   [2] Emlyn, *Works*, i, p. lxii.
[3] Griffiths, *Religion and Learning*, pp. 128, 132.
[4] Wilson, *Dissenting Churches in London*, i. 100. 'View of the Dissenting Interest', p. 89.

ministers in London were Arminians rather than Socinians, and in 1735 the General Baptist Assembly reaffirmed, in admittedly ambiguous terms, its belief 'in the doctrine of the Trinity, as contained in the Scripture'.[1] The Presbyterian and General Baptist denominations were thus not Unitarian by 1730, though they had opened the door to Unitarianism. 'I believe ... the doctrine of the ever-blessed Trinity', wrote Matthew Towgood, Presbyterian minister at Shepton Mallet, in 1734, but 'I am thoroughly persuaded that no Christians of any denomination ought to be trusted with a power of imposing creeds on others, being sensible that all ... from the inborn propensions of human nature, won't fail more or less to abuse it; so by the grace of God, I propose henceforth to call no man master on earth.'[2]

12. 'THE DECAY OF THE DISSENTING INTEREST': SECT TO DENOMINATION?

There were, indeed, some Presbyterians for whom the process of liberalization was too slow. In 1730 there appeared an anonymous pamphlet which caused a considerable stir in Dissenting circles, *An Enquiry into the Causes of the Decay of the Dissenting Interest*. It was written, it was later revealed, by Strickland Gough, a somewhat shallow young man who had just emerged from one of the Dissenting academies with excessive self-confidence and an imperfect knowledge of Dissenting history. But the title of his pamphlet, if not its contents, gave expression to the growing uneasiness with which many Dissenters

---

[1] 'View of the Dissenting Intererest', p. 102. The writer claims that there were seven Arminian Baptist ministers in London (including one Seventh-day Baptist) and three Socinian Baptists (Burroughs and Foster of Paul's Alley, Barbican, and Morris of Glasshouse Yard). The classification of the Barbican church is open to dispute. Whitley, in his *History of the British Baptists*, insisted that it 'was never associated with the General Baptists' but was 'the most learned, the wealthiest, the most progressive of the London Particular Baptist churches' (p. 201). It was in fact the product of the amalgamation of a Particular Baptist church (the Barbican) and a General Baptist church (Turners' Hall) in 1695, and as early as 1698 it had requested its Sunday-morning lecturer, Joseph Stennett, to refrain from preaching Calvinist doctrines 'contrary to the sentiments of the church'. Since the church was clearly not Calvinist in 1717, when its co-operation with the Particular Baptist Fund was refused, for statistical purposes I have counted it as General Baptist. *TBHS* iv (1914–15), 46, 52. Barbican Church Book, i., 26 May 1698, Baptist Church House.

[2] Griffiths, *Religion and Learning*, pp. 132–3.

regarded the state of their churches, their principles, and their religion.

What Strickland Gough understood by 'the decay of the Dissenting interest' was not so much loss of numbers or lack of zeal, but a departure of ministers who could not subscribe to creeds which their congregations sought to impose on them, and of gentlemen who 'are ashamed of our interest'.[1] Gough was under the impression that 'the spirit of the good old Puritans was nothing else but a spirit of liberty', that 'the fundamental principle of the Dissenters . . . is a liberty for every man to form his own sentiments', and that failure to adhere to those principles by the Subscribers at Salters' Hall was the cause of the present malaise.[2] To remedy the situation he recommended that ministers pay less heed to the needs of the humble members of their congregations and more to the tastes of 'people of wit and politeness'.[3] Money from the Common Fund should not be spent on educating the children 'of low and mechanical persons'; the number of congregations should be reduced, even if it meant leaving some villages without a meeting, so that ministerial stipends could be increased and gentlemen would not be 'ashamed to breed up their children to the ministry'; and at the academies dancing masters should be employed 'to prune off all clumsiness and awkwardness that is disagreeable to people of fashion'.[4]

Strickland Gough was evidently more concerned with respectability than with liberty and he subsequently became a clergyman of the established church, but his pamphlet is an unintended caricature of an attitude of mind which led to the decline of many a Presbyterian congregation in the course of the eighteenth century. As the Congregationalist Doddridge pointed out in his *Free Thoughts on the Most Probable Means of Reviving the Dissenting Interest*, 'plain people of low education and vulgar taste . . . constitute . . . nine parts in ten of most of our congregations', and a minister who acted on Gough's advice would soon find himself 'entertained with the echo' of his own voice.[5] In Doddridge's view 'the generality of Dissenters' were 'persons of

---

[1] Gough, *Decay of the Dissenting Interest*, pp. 28, 36.
[2] Ibid., pp. 4–5, 6, 28.　　　[3] Ibid., pp. 33–4.
[4] Ibid., pp. 42–4.
[5] P. Doddridge, *Free Thoughts on the Most Probable Means of Reviving the Dissenting Interest* (1730), pp. 11, 13.

serious piety' who had 'been deeply impressed with the pecu-
liarities of the Gospel-scheme' and had experienced the conflict
between 'Satan, and the corruptions of [their] own heart on the
one hand, and the operations of the Holy Spirit of God on the
other'. This was 'the great support of our interest', not Gough's
'rational and generous principles of liberty'.[1] Just as Gough's
pamphlet foreshadows the eventual decline of Presbyterianism,
so does that of Doddridge indicate the reason for the ultimate
success of eighteenth-century Congregationalism.

For the moment, though, it could scarcely be disguised that
all was not well with Dissent. Some support for Strickland
Gough's point of view was provided by the anonymous author
of *Some Observations upon the Present State of the Dissenting Interest*
(1731) who estimated that fifty Dissenting ministers had conformed to the established church since 1714, presumably
reasoning that since they could not continue as Dissenters
'without submitting to some . . . impositions' they might as well
submit to the Thirty-nine articles and the Book of Common
Prayer.[2] The younger Edmund Calamy could not understand
the logic of such persons, but he had to admit that the ministers
and students who had seceded to the Church of England were
for the most part men 'of sobriety and unblemished character',
among them Joseph Butler, the future Bishop of Durham and
author of *The Analogy of Religion*, and Thomas Secker, the future
Archbishop of Canterbury.[3] Doddridge believed that the number of Dissenters in many Leicestershire and Northamptonshire
congregations had 'greatly increased within these twenty years',
but he too had to acknowledge that 'many . . . have quitted us',
some in the hope of secular advancement, some on marrying into
Anglican families, and 'many more . . . from a secret dislike of
piety'.[4] It was the view of Isaac Watts that religion had fallen
'under a general and remarkable decay', and that Dissenters, by
wasting time at plays, gaming-tables, and dances, were losing
their reputation for 'superior virtue, and merit'.[5] Abraham
Taylor, Congregational minister at Deptford, bemoaned 'the

[1] Doddridge, *Free Thoughts*, pp. 19–21.
[2] Anon., *Some Observations upon the Present State of the Dissenting Interest* (1731), pp.
8, 10.
[3] Calamy, *Historical Account*, ii. 505–6.   [4] Doddridge, *Free Thoughts*, pp. 19–21
[5] I. Watts, *An Humble Attempt towards the Revival of Practical Religion among Christians* (1735, first published 1731), pp. 1, 233–5.

growth of error and the great decay of practical religion', by which he meant that family worship was neglected, that prayer was offered but once a day, and that on Sundays it was becomeing fashionable to attend public worship once only and, 'on the least pretence in the world, not to attend at all'.[1] And the Independent author of the 'View of the Dissenting Interest' believed that while the population of London had increased by 'about a sixth part' since 1695, the number of persons who attended Dissenting worship in 1731 'are rather less than what they were in 1695'.[2]

Nor was concern at the decline of Dissent confined to Congregationalists. As early as 1704 the Kent General Baptist Association referred to 'the great decay, sinking and languishing condition' of all the churches in the county, and in 1711, 1714, 1719, and 1724 the General Assembly appointed days of fasting and prayer on account of the 'great decay of religion'.[3] Similarly among the Friends the Devonshire House Monthly Meeting in London complained of 'coldness of zeal' in 1731, 'declension and remisness' in 1741, and 'diverse evils to the dishonour of truth' in 1748.[4] And in 1751 Samuel Bownas, who had been born in Westmorland way back in 1676 and had been a Quaker minister for fifty-four years, wrote that he had had better success in the first twenty years of his ministry than he had 'since had for a long time'.[5]

That this was not just a matter of old men looking back to the golden days of their youth is confirmed by the episcopal visitation returns of the 1730s and 1740s. Ten Oxfordshire clergymen reported to Bishop Secker in 1738 that the number of Dissenters in their parishes had 'of late years considerably decreased'. In Oxford itself the Presbyterian congregation was 'scarce half so numerous as it was fifteen or sixteen years ago'; in Bicester the number of Presbyterians was 'much lessened of late years by the death of some of the principal of them, and by the good influence of the charity school'; and in Wroxton the Baptist meetinghouse had not been used for fifteen years, ten former Baptists had been christened by the vicar, and 'the rest have been yearly

---

[1] A. Taylor, *Of Spiritual Declensions* (1732), pp. iii, 29–30.

[2] 'View of the Dissenting Interest', pp. 81–2.

[3] *Minutes of the General Baptist Assembly*, i. 95–6, 114, 118, 124, 135.

[4] Beck and Ball, *London Friends' Meetings*, p. 188.

[5] Braithwaite, *SPQ*, pp. 239–40.

dying off'.[1] Similar situations were reported from Nottingham-shire in 1743, with disused Presbyterian meeting-houses in Calverton, Woodborough, and Windmerpool, and from Devon in 1744, where the demise of Presbyterian meetings was noted in Bovey Tracey, Buckerell, Malborough, and North Molton. The vicar of Collumpton reported that in eight years the number of Dissenters had 'considerably decreased', that he had 'baptized thirty-two adults who had been Anabaptists or Quakers', and that some Presbyterians, for twelve months without a minister, had also conformed.[2]

To what are we to attribute 'the decay of the Dissenting interest'? In part the explanation is supplied by the passage from *The Pilgrim's Progress* with which this chapter opened. Toleration had brought with it, as Bunyan feared it might, material benefits which threatened to sap the spiritual zeal of Dissent. This was particularly true of the Presbyterians who, as is evident from the episcopal visitation returns, were failing to recruit men for the ministry in adequate numbers and were losing many of those they did recruit to the established church. But without an educated, professional ministry Presbyterianism would die, and by the 1740s the situation was becoming critical for congregations in villages and small towns which could not hope to vie with larger urban meetings in the competition for Dissenting ministers. In 1744 the vicar of Brixham reported to Bishop Claggett that the town's Presbyterian meeting was served by Samuel Adams of Dartmouth and his son John, but, he added, the meeting 'must inevitably sink when either of these die, by reason the survivor will be confined to the meeting-house at Dartmouth, there being no probability of raising sufficient here for the maintenance of another who hath no foreign support'.[3]

That the fall in recruits for the ministry was not the only factor in the decline of Dissent is, though, illustrated by the case of the Quakers who were not dependent on a professional ministry yet experienced a similar loss of enthusiasm and of

[1] *Bishop Secker's Visitation Returns, 1738*, Oxfordshire Record Society (1957), pp. 18, 22, 30, 32, 44, 78, 121, 145, 174, 180.
[2] *Archbishop Herring's Visitation Returns*, iv. 176, 174, 163. Bishop Claggett's Visitation Returns, 1744, Devon Record Office, Exeter. I am indebted to the Revd. Dr. A. Warne for providing me with this information.
[3] Bishop Claggett's Visitation Returns.

numbers. The Quaker registers of births, marriages, and deaths are not an infallible guide to Quaker strength in the eighteenth century, and a decline in the numbers they record can indicate a growing carelessness in record keeping as well as a fall in real strength. But it is none the less probably significant that in the 1740s the Quakers registered 3,530 fewer births, 3,349 fewer deaths, and 1,118 fewer marriages than in the first decade of the century, and more significant that in every decade from the 1670s to the 1790s the number of registered Quaker deaths exceeded the number of registered births.[1] Quaker missionary endeavours had begun to slacken as early as the 1660s, when many of their leaders were confined to prison and Fox had turned his attention to the setting up of Monthly and Quarterly meetings, and although Quaker ministers continued to itinerate in the eighteenth century they no longer attempted to convert the sultan or to brave the Inquisition, and their mission was largely to other Friends. The Quakers of the 1650s had seized every opportunity to debate their principles with parish ministers, and from the 1650s to the 1670s had taken part in heated pamphlet exchanges and public confrontations with the Baptists, but in 1696 the Bristol Yearly Meeting cautioned Friends to avoid 'disputings and public contentions with wrangling persons'.[2] The Friends of the Interregnum had not been afraid to warn their fellow countrymen of the disasters which would fall upon their apostate land, and the Great Plague and fire of London had appeared to justify their warnings, but when in 1693 John Hall warned the Quakers of Bristol that the Lord would visit their city with 'a most terrible earthquake' the prosperous Bristol Friends tried to stop the publication of his prophecy.[3] And whereas George Fox had claimed to have effected some 150 cures by spiritual means, by the end of the century his claims were regarded as something of an embarrassment by the sober Quakers of the Augustan age, and the 'Book of Miracles' which he left them to publish never saw the light of day.[4]

[1] J. S. Rowntree, *Quakerism Past and Present* (1859), pp. 79, 82.
[2] T. L. Underwood, 'The Controversy between the Baptists and the Quakers in England, 1650–89', London Ph.D. thesis, 1965, pp. 46–52. Mortimer, 'Quakerism in Seventeenth Century Bristol', p. 367.
[3] Mortimer, 'Quakerism in Seventeenth Century Bristol', pp. 124–5.
[4] Cadbury, *Fox's 'Book of Miracles'*, pp. 39–40, 98.

By the early eighteenth century the Quaker ethos had shifted from an emphasis on individual inspiration to conformity to the social *mores* of the group. In an attempt to preserve their distinctive witness in an age which distrusted fanaticism, Friends no longer interrupted sermons in parish churches or went naked in the streets, but stressed the virtues of plain speech and plain dress and the evils of china tea-services, painted calicoes, black hats, coloured shoes, scarlet stockings, 'and petticoats made short to expose 'em'.[1] They became far more punctilious than the General Baptist churches from which many of their forefathers had seceded in the 1650s, and it was in vain that Fox's widow, the former Margaret Fell, protested against the 'silly, poor gospel' that 'we must be all in one dress and one colour'. 'Legal ceremonies are far from gospel-freedom', she wrote in 1698, but hers was the voice of a bygone age, silenced four years later when she died at the age of eighty-eight.[2]

It is tempting to describe the changes which Quakerism in particular and Dissent in general underwent between 1690 and 1730 as the evolution, in sociological terms, from 'sect' to 'denomination'. 'By its very nature', writes H. Richard Niebuhr, 'the sectarian type of organisation is valid only for one generation.' In subsequent generations the wealth of the sect increases as it 'subjects itself to the discipline of asceticism in work and expenditure', compromise with the world follows, an official clergy replaces lay leadership, and 'children are born into the group and infant baptism or dedication becomes once more a means of grace'.[3] Bryan Wilson rightly criticizes Niebuhr's account as an oversimplification, and in particular insists that sectarian characteristics can persist over several generations, but in distinguishing between 'sect' and 'denomination' he has a similar process in mind. A sect Wilson defines as a voluntary association in which membership is 'by proof . . . of some claim to personal merit', 'exclusiveness is emphasized', expulsion is 'exercised against those who contravene doctrinal, moral, or organizational precepts', and in which there is a 'high level of lay participation'. By contrast he sees a denomination as a voluntary association in which procedures of admission are formalized and adherents accepted without the 'imposition of

---

[1] Braithwaite, *SPQ*, pp. 511–12.   [2] Ibid., pp. 518–19.
[3] Niebuhr, *Social Sources of Denominationalism*, pp. 19–20.

traditional prerequisites of entry', in which conventional standards of morality are accepted and expulsion is rare, in which 'services are formalized, spontaneity is absent', and worship is led by a 'trained professional ministry', and in which the 'education of the young is of greater concern than the evangelism of the outsider'.[1]

That some of the changes which Dissent underwent in the later seventeenth and early eighteenth centuries can be characterized in these terms as the evolution from 'sect' to 'denomination' will be obvious from the foregoing pages. Only the Quakers retained prophesying as a part of public worship and even they came to acknowledge a separate, if unpaid, ministry; lay pastorates appear to have been rare among the Congregationalists and even the General Baptists came to accept a paid ministry; Quakers for the most part ceased to preach in places where non-Quakers gathered, and General Baptist Messengers confined their activities largely to General Baptist congregations. The General Baptists of south-east England did send two missionaries to Virginia in 1714, one of whom died on the voyage, and three more were sent out in 1715, but the Kent and Sussex General Baptist Association found it difficult to support the mission either financially or with further recruits.[2] The Congregationalists could still produce aggressive evangelists, as the activities of Richard Davis in Northamptonshire bear witness, but Davis was frowned on by some of his co-religionists and his zeal was exceptional, not the rule. In east Lancashire and west Yorkshire in the 1690s the Particular Baptists William Mitchell and David Crossley evangelized towns and villages in the Pennine valleys from their base at Rossendale and laid the foundations of scores of future Baptist churches, but again their exploits were exceptional: they were converts to the Baptist tradition, not products of it.[3]

A shift of emphasis from evangelism to education was noted regretfully by the Cumberland Quaker Thomas Story in 1716 when he attended a meeting at which there were many young people who had 'not yet arrived at a sufficient sense of Truth . . .

---

[1] B. Wilson, *Patterns of Sectarianism* (1967), pp. 22–4.

[2] *TBHS* iv (1914–15), 56. Kent and Sussex General Baptist Association Minute Book, 4 Oct. 1720. DWL MS. 38.83.

[3] F. Overend, *History of the Ebenezer General Baptist Church, Bacup* (1912), pp. 22–4.

but think themselves safe, having had their education in the form'.[1] Richard Vann has estimated that by the mid-eighteenth century between 80 and 90 per cent of Quakers were themselves the children of Friends, and he concludes that the 'bias of Quaker institutions was against the conversion of the world and in favour of the organization of family life for the conversion of Quaker children'.[2] Among Congregationalists there was a movement to ease the rigorous requirements for the baptism of children and for entry into church membership. In 1683 the Altham and Wymondhouses church resolved that the 'children of godly parents' who were not members of the church might none the less be baptized, and similar provisions were made by the churches at Great Yarmouth and Woodbridge in 1694 and 1709.[3] The Woodbridge church also recommended 'that much tenderness . . . be allowed in admission of church members, that none of whom there was reason to hope they were truly gracious might be excluded', and both the Yarmouth and Nightingale Lane churches agreed that since 'many good pious Christians through weakness or disability of mind or speech, may not be willing' to give an account of their religious experience to a full church meeting, an applicant should be accepted for membership if he satisfied the church's pastor with his 'reasons of hope'.[4] By 1735 the affairs of the Nightingale Lane church were being conducted not only by 'the brethren of the church' but also, in Presbyterian fashion, by 'the gentlemen that contributed to the ministry of the place', and in 1745 the Lime Street Congregational church put on record what appears to have become established practice, that not only church members but also their children should be admitted to church meetings. Five years later, in an attempt to halt the declining attendance at such gatherings, the Lime Street church further resolved that church meetings should be open, in addition, to any 'pious Christians as should please to attend'.[5] In such

---

[1] Braithwaite, *SPQ*, p. 539.

[2] Vann, *Social Development*, pp. 166, 196.

[3] *Altham and Wymondhouses Church Book*, Chetham Society Publications, new series, xxxiii (1894), 138. Great Yarmouth Congregational Church Book, p. 172. Woodbridge Congregational Church Book, pp. 7–8 DWL MS. 76.5.

[4] Nightingale Lane Congregational Church Book, 1719. Guildhall Library, London.

[5] Ibid. 1735. Lime Street Congregational Church Book, pp. 152, 189. Guildhall Library.

churches, with shrinking membership figures and a dearth of recruits, both the need and the incentive to prune membership lists further by the rigorous exercise of discipline were not surprisingly lacking.

Having said all this, though, it none the less remains true that Congregational and General and Particular Baptist churches continued to expect evidence of religious experience from prospective church members, and many of them to discipline and if necessary expel members whose lives brought discredit on the whole fellowship. In the late seventeenth and early eighteenth centuries the minute book of the Bury St. Edmunds Congregational church carried accounts of the conversion experiences of applicants for church membership which were reminiscent of those collected by John Rogers and Henry Walker amid the excitement of the Interregnum half a century earlier.[1] As for the Quakers, Richard Vann argues that although they might draw 90 per cent of their recruits from the ranks of their own children, they continued to expect evidence of conversion from those children, and he challenges the accepted view that the Quakers adopted the concept of 'birth-right membership' in 1737 by pointing out that the rules of settlement of that year had no spiritual significance but were merely an attempt to resolve controversies concerning responsibility for the relief of poor Friends.[2] Only the Presbyterians, with their exclusively professional ministry, their liberal requirements for admission to communion, and their rarely exercised discipline, correspond entirely to the sociologists' definition of a 'denomination' as opposed to a 'sect', and the Presbyterians had never claimed to be a gathered community, but rather an alternative national church.

It was not only the 'hill called Lucre' which confronted Christian as he crossed the plain of Ease; beyond the hill lay Doubting Castle. And beyond the problems of social adjustment which faced the Dissenters in the age of toleration lay more serious problems of religious adjustment raised by the transition from the enthusiasm of the mid-seventeenth century to the

---

[1] Bury St. Edmunds Congregational Church Book, pp. 71–2, 106, 116. DWL MS. 76.4.
[2] Vann, *Social Development*, pp. 145–53. Vann argues, in ch. VI, that the evolution of Quakerism during the first century of its existence was from 'movement to sect'.

rationalism of the early eighteenth. In so far as Dissenters were now looking to Locke rather than to Calvin for intellectual support for their faith, in proportion to their readiness to seek inspiration from the spirit of reason rather than the Spirit of God, their zeal flagged and their congregations dwindled. The reaction against Calvinism which had begun with Baxter and had led to the Salters' Hall dispute did not end there, and by the 1730s it was becoming clear that more than just the doctrine of the Trinity which was at stake. When Christians begin to apostatize, wrote the author of the 'View of the Dissenting Interest', 'it is very often first manifested in their attacking the divine decrees, by explaining the doctrine of universal redemption as a sentiment that is full of benevolence; from thence they appear fond of pleading the cause of the heathens, and of the possibility of salvation merely by the light of nature'.[1] Four years later John Ball, the Presbyterian minister at Honiton, criticized his fellow Presbyterian, Henry Grove of Taunton, for 'urging charity' towards the heathen. He upbraided Grove for teaching respect for 'the genius of the age' when both Sir Isaac Newton and Samuel Clarke had given their opinion 'that the torments of hell were not eternal', and Locke speculated that 'the wicked should after death have no sense . . . nor being'. 'When men are got clear of the dread of everlasting torments,' added Ball, 'they will be easy to entertain strange doctrines, and be weary of striving to enter in at the straight gate, and find out an easier religion, when there remains no fear of hell after death.'[2] Even Isaac Watts, who believed that pastors were commissioned to warn the impenitent of 'the torments and agonies of hell', had not the heart to condemn children of the unregenerate who died in infancy to eternal punishment and believed that their souls would be annihilated.[3]

The Dissenters were thus torn between a Calvinism which was rejected by the leading thinkers of the age and which even some of its nominal adherents were attempting to moderate, and a rationalism which, as Doddridge realized, had no popular appeal. Was there any alternative route that Dissent could take, or was it doomed to wither away? In 1731 the Quaker John

[1] 'View of the Dissenting Interest', pp. 82–3.
[2] J. Ball, *Some Remarks on a New Way of Preaching* (1736), pp. 11, 20–2.
[3] Watts, *Revival of Practical Religion*, p. 103. Davis, *Isaac Watts*, p. 109.

Kelsall, formerly clerk to the Lloyd iron-works at Dolobran in Montgomeryshire, noted sadly the way in which toleration was blunting the edge of Quaker criticism of the 'wicked practices in the great and the lifeless superstitious ministry of the priests'. 'The Government and better sort of people', he wrote, 'are very kind and civil to Friends', with the result that 'too many Friends, being unwilling to give them offence . . . are too easy towards them in respect to religious matters.' Not until God raised up 'a people out of Friends or others, who will be commissioned to strike at the root and branch of antichrist' would there be 'any considerable addition to the Church'.[1]

Such a people were, indeed, soon raised up, but they came not from the ranks of the Friends, basking in their newly won respectability, nor from the Presbyterians or General Baptists, racked by theological dissension, nor from the Congregationalists or Particular Baptists, whose independent polity and Calvinist theology prevented, at least initially, much in the way of evangelism. The revival of religion in England and Wales, and ultimately of Dissent itself, was to come, paradoxically, from the ranks of the established church.

[1] Braithwaite, *SPQ*, pp. 636–7.

V

'THE WAY TO HEAVEN': THE REVIVAL OF DISSENT, 1730–1791

1. 'JUSTIFICATION BY FAITH ALONE': THE EVANGELICAL REVIVAL

The eighteenth-century Evangelical revival was an international and intercontinental phenomenon. In Germany, in America, and in England and Wales it was an attempt to return, after the spiritual lethargy of the late seventeenth century, to the religious fervour of an earlier age, to the Reformation emphasis on justification by faith and to William Perkins's insistence on personal conversion. The earliest manifestations appeared in the English colonies in America, 'the beginner of the great work', in Whitefield's words, Theodorus Frelinghuysen, a minister of the Dutch Reformed Church. Frelinghuysen became pastor to four churches in the Raritan valley in New Jersey in 1719 and, faced with the conventional religion of his congregations, challenged them with Evangelical preaching which was soon producing frequent converts.[1] His success inspired Gilbert Tennent, who became minister of the Presbyterian church in New Brunswick in 1726, to emulate his example, and Tennent began attacking the 'presumptuous security' of formal Christians who rested their hopes of eternal salvation on 'a dead form of piety, resulting from a religious education'. By 1729 he, too, was gaining converts, his work supported by his father and two brothers, all in the Presbyterian ministry.[2] And five years later, in 1734, in the remote town of Northampton in western Massachusetts, the

---

[1] *George Whitefield's Journals* (Banner of Truth edn., 1960), p. 352. L. J. Trinterud, *The Forming of an American Tradition* (Philadelphia, 1949), p. 54. W. S. Hudson, *Religion in America* (New York, 1965), p. 62. The traditional view of Frelinghuysen has been challenged by H. Harmelink, 'Another Look at Frelinghuysen and his Awakening', *Church History*, xxxvii (1968), 423–7. But while Harmelink succeeds in showing that Frelinghuysen's behaviour did not accord with the traditions of the Dutch Reformed Church, and indeed that his conception of the church came close to that of the Congregationalists, he fails to dislodge Frelinghuysen from his accepted position in the history of American revivalism.

[2] Trinterud, *American Tradition*, pp. 57–9.

pastor of the town's Congregational church, Jonathan Edwards, preached a sermon on 'justification by faith alone' which had an electrifying effect on the community: the town's inhabitants talked of little but 'spiritual and eternal things', 300 people' were savingly brought home to Christ . . . in the space of half a year', and the revival spread to neighbouring towns and settlements.[1]

A second focus of the revival was the religious community which grew up at Berthelsdorf in Saxony on the estate of the eccentric, arrogant, yet much loved Count Nicholas von Zinzendorf. Zinzendorf had been educated at the University of Halle under August Francke, the organizing genius of the devotional movement known as Pietism which had developed in Germany in the last quarter of the seventeenth century in reaction to the arid scholasticism of contemporary Lutheranism. Pietism, with its emphasis on personal conversion and its appeal to the emotions rather than the intellect, was a precursor of eighteenth-century Evangelicalism, and under Francke's influence Zinzendorf determined to devote his life to religion.[2] He was initially deflected from his course by his family's insistence that he take up a secular career, but in 1722 an opportunity of furthering the Pietist cause presented itself when representatives of the persecuted remnant of the Unitas Fratrum, the ancient Protestant church of Bohemia and Moravia, sought refuge on Zinzendorf's estate at Berthelsdorf and he allowed them to establish the settlement which became known as Herrnhut. It was partly to resolve the quarrels between the disparate refugees who now began to flock to Herrnhut, and partly to reconcile the Moravian tradition with conformity to the Lutheran church, that in 1727 Zinzendorf asserted his authority over the community and insisted that it abide by the Pietist principle of 'ecclesiola in ecclesia'—a church within the church. The task of the 'Moravians', in Zinzendorf's view, was not to set themselves up as a new denomination but to revitalize existing churches, acting as the yeast to leaven the lump of Christendom, and under his leadership the band of quarrelling refugees was transformed into a body of dedicated evangelists. Soon

[1] J. Edwards, *A Faithful Narrative of the Surprising Work of God in the Conversion of Many Hundred Souls* . . . (1737), pp. 10–12, 18–19, 25.

[2] K. S. Pinson, *Pietism as a Factor in the Rise of German Nationalism* (New York, 1968), pp. 13–25.

missionaries from Herrnhut were going out to the West Indies (1732), Greenland (1733), to the Indians of Surinam (1734), to the Hottentots of South Africa (1737), and to the Gold Coast and Ceylon (1737).[1]

The American revival and the outburst of Moravian missionary enthusiasm were independent of each other and of the third revivalist movement which began in Wales in 1735. On Palm Sunday of that year a twenty-one-year-old Anglican layman of Trevecca in Breconshire, Howell Harris, was alarmed by his vicar's warning that 'if you are not fit to come to the Lord's table . . . you are not fit to live, nor fit to die'. For eight weeks he was in spiritual turmoil until on Whitsunday, at the sacrament, he was convinced 'that Christ died for me, and that all my sins were laid on him'. As soon as he was certain of forgiveness he 'felt some insatiable desires after the salvation of poor sinners', so he started family worship in his mother's house, invited the neighbours to come and hear him read to them 'concerning the sacrament and church attendance', and then went from house to house in his own and near-by villages, 'exhorting all those with whom I had formerly sinned'. 'The word', he wrote, 'was attended with such power that many on the spot cried out to God for pardon of their sins', and towards the end of 1736 he began to organize his converts into religious societies.[2]

Meanwhile, and again independently, towards the end of 1735 an Anglican curate of Llangcitho in Cardiganshire, Daniel Rowland, attended a service conducted by Griffith Jones, the rector of Llanddowror in Carmarthenshire. Jones was struck by Rowland's vain appearance, offered a prayer on his behalf, and this public reproof resulted in a conversion experience which transformed Rowland into a compelling revivalist preacher.[3] Rowland and Harris met for the first time in August 1737. The two men were very different characters: Harris austere, humourless, imperious, yet passionately devoted

[1] J. E. Hutton, *A History of the Moravian Church* (2nd edn., 1909), pp. 177–245.

[2] B. La Trobe, *A Brief Account of the Life of Howell Harris, extracted from papers written by himself* (1791), pp. 10–24. R. Bennett, *The Early Life of Howell Harris* (English translation by G. M. Roberts, 1962), p. 31.

[3] R. W. Evans, 'The Eighteenth Century Welsh Awakening, with its Relationship to the Contemporary English Evangelical Revival', Edinburgh Ph.D. thesis, 1956, p. 51.

to the salvation of his fellow men, Rowland quick-tempered yet light-hearted, too easy-going for Harris's exacting tastes.[1] In time this difference of personality would cause a deep division between the two men, but for the moment they agreed to work together for the conversion of Wales.

Harris flayed his own body in his exertions to bring the Gospel to his fellow countrymen. At first he tried to combine school-teaching in the day with 'exhorting' in the evening, making do with two hours' sleep at night or none at all. But at the end of 1737 the school managers issued an ultimatum: either he must stop 'exhorting' or he must leave the school. Harris left, and was thereby freed to devote the next twelve years to itinerant evangelism, first in south Wales, then in north Wales, finally in England.[2] In thirty-three days early in 1747, he wrote, 'I travelled about 600 miles and have visited part of five counties in Wales and have been through the west of England, through Bristol, Bath, Exeter, Plymouth dock, and Cornwall, and came home at two in the morning last Sunday after travelling last week about 250 miles'.[3] The constant punishment Harris inflicted on his body eventually took its toll, and the irritability which resulted combined with his natural arrogance and conflicts over theology and personalities to produce a break with Daniel Rowland and most of his followers in 1750. But by then there were 433 religious societies in Wales and the borders,[4] and Harris, more than any other man, had begun a revolution in the religious life of Wales which was to determine the character of its people for 200 years.

These three independent revivalist movements—the American, the Moravian, and the Welsh—were brought into contact with each other through the medium of a group of Oxford graduates and students who, from 1729, had been in the habit of meeting together for study, prayer, and good works and who had been branded by their scornful contemporaries as 'Methodists . . . from their custom of regulating their time and planning the business of the day every morning'.[5] The first of the Oxford

---

[1] W. G. Hughes-Edwards, 'Development and Organisation of the Methodist Society in Wales 1735–50', University of Wales M.A. thesis, 1966, pp. 329–30.

[2] Bennett, *Early Life of Harris*, pp. 88–9, 149.

[3] Evans, 'Welsh Awakening', p. 12.

[4] Hughes-Edwards, 'Methodist Society in Wales', p. 97.

[5] *Whitefield's Journals*, p. 48.

Methodists to join the ranks of the revivalists was George
Whitefield, the son of the keeper of the Bell Inn at Gloucester.
Whitefield's mother had been widowed when he was two years
old and George helped her in the menial tasks of running a
public house until, in 1732, he entered Pembroke College as a
servitor, paying his way through the university by waiting on
'gentlemen' undergraduates. Notwithstanding his early environment, Whitefield took a serious interest in religion. At Oxford
he joined the Methodists' 'Holy Club', and after sharing in their
ascetic life and fasting to the point of emaciation, he experienced
conversion around Easter 1735.[1] He was ordained deacon in
1736 and resolved to answer a call to the infant colony of
Georgia, but while waiting for his departure he spent much of
1737 in fulfilling preaching engagements and was soon attracting large and excited congregations in Bristol, Gloucester, and
London. 'The doctrine of the new birth and justification by
faith in Jesus Christ', he wrote of his early sermons in Bristol,
'made its way like lightning into the hearers' consciences. The
arrows of conviction stuck fast; and my whole time, between
one lecture and another, except what was spent in necessary
refreshment, was wholly occupied in talking with people under
religious concern.'[2]

Apart from three years from 1738 to 1741 when he was
nominally parish minister of Savannah in Georgia, Whitefield
was free from the ties of a parochial charge and was able to
devote the rest of his life to itinerant evangelism. Passionate,
eloquent, theatrical, Whitefield was the greatest popular
preacher of the Evangelical revival. He brought something of
the bar-room manner to religion: his answer to the problem of
a small boy 'not above four years of age' who refused to say the
Lord's prayer was to deal him 'several blows', and Samuel
Johnson dismissed him as a mob orator who compared un-
favourably with a mountebank.[3] But other men of culture
thought differently. Bolingbroke declared him to possess 'the
most commanding eloquence I ever heard in any person', while
David Hume thought it 'worth going twenty miles to hear him'.[4]
For more than thirty years Whitefield held vast audiences with

---

[1] Ibid., p. 57.   [2] Ibid., p. 81.
[3] Ibid., p. 146. L. Tyerman, *Life of George Whitefield* (1876), i. 221.
[4] Tyerman, *Whitefield*, ii. 194 n.

his melodic voice and transfixed them with his eyes—aided by a squint, the result of measles, which led his hearers to feel that they could not escape his stare.[1] During his early sermons in Bristol 'people hung upon the rails of the organ loft, climbed upon the leads of the church, and made the church itself so hot with their breath, that the steam would fall from the pillars like drops of rain'.[2] When the crowds grew too large for the churches and hostile incumbents refused Whitefield their pulpits, he preached out of doors, thus reaching 'ten times more people than I should if I had been confined to churches'.[3] Like Harris, Whitfield burnt himself out in his master's service. In July 1770 he travelled 500 miles through the American colonies and preached every day; in August and September he continued his preaching tour though getting progressively weaker; on 29 September he preached to a large open-air audience in Exeter, New Hampshire. 'How willingly', he said, 'would I live for ever to preach Christ. But I die to be with him.' The following morning he was dead.[4]

Whitefield provided the link between the English, American, and Welsh revivals. He crossed the Atlantic thirteen times, preaching for the Presbyterian Tennents for the first time in November 1739 and for the Congregationalist Jonathan Edwards in October 1740.[5] Whitefield shared with the Tennents and with Edwards not only their passion for evangelism but also their Calvinist theology, and this was also a common bond with Howell Harris. Whitefield appears to have embraced Calvinism partly as a result of his correspondence with the Scottish Presbyterian minister Ralph Erskine; Harris was influenced by his contacts with Welsh Particular Baptists.[6] The two men met for the first time in March 1739: 'when I first saw him,' wrote Whitefield of his meeting with Harris, 'my heart was knit closely to him', and for the next ten years they made common cause.[7] Whitefield, ever restless for new fields of evangelism, had neither Harris's taste nor his talent for organization, and although Whitefield had a wooden meeting-house built in

---

[1] A. D. Belden, *George Whitefield, the Awakener* (2nd edn., 1953), p. 29.
[2] *Whitefield's Journals*, p. 84.   [3] Ibid., p. 233.
[4] Tyerman, *Whitefield*, ii. 596–7.   [5] *Whitefield's Journals*, pp. 347, 377.
[6] A. A. Dallimore, *George Whitefield* (1970), i. 405. Bennett, *Early Life of Harris*, pp. 114–15.
[7] *Whitefield's Journals*, p. 229.

London in 1741—Moorfields Tabernacle—it was Harris who took charge there during Whitefield's frequent absences in America and Scotland.[1] Similarly although the first joint Association of English and Welsh Calvinistic Methodists, which met at Watford in Glamorgan in 1743, chose Whitefield as its moderator, a post he held for six years, it was largely an honorary position and it was again Harris, as superintendent of the Welsh societies, who bore the brunt of the organization. The contrasting attitudes of Harris and Whitefield to organization is reflected in the contrasting fortunes of Welsh and English Calvinistic Methodism. Whereas there were 433 Welsh Calvinist societies in existence by 1750, in 1747 there were only twenty-nine English Calvinistic Methodist societies and a further twenty-three preaching stations.[2]

Some attempt to give English Calvinistic Methodism a degree of permanence was made by Selina, Countess of Huntingdon, who was converted in the 1730s through the agency of her husband's sister, Lady Margaret Hastings.[3] Lady Huntingdon appointed Evangelical clergymen, among them Whitefield, as her private chaplains, provided opportunities for them to preach to members of the aristocracy in her Leicestershire and London homes, built chapels for them in fashionable resorts such as Brighton, Bath, and Tunbridge Wells, and in 1768 opened an Evangelical training college for ministers at Trevecca. But Lady Huntingdon's authority over her Connexion was moral rather than legal and not until it was too late did she attempt to provide it with an organization that would out-live her. In 1790, the year before her death, she drew up a 'plan of association' to give the sixty-four chapels of her Connexion an organization comparable to that of the Welsh Calvinistic Methodists. But the scheme was opposed by her confidante, Lady Anne Erskine, who regarded herself as Lady Huntingdon's heiress apparent and who realized that the plan would deprive her of any authority in the Connexion. The 'plan of association' was therefore dropped and all Lady Huntingdon was able to do was to leave the seven chapels which were her own

[1] Evans, 'Welsh Awakening', pp. 94, 162.
[2] C. E. Welch, *Two Calvinistic Methodist Chapels* (London Record Society publications xi, 1975), pp. 16–17.
[3] Anon., *Life and Times of Selina, Countess of Huntingdon* (1839), i. 14–15.

private property to the care of four trustees.[1] In any case Lady Huntingdon's mission to the upper classes was no substitute for Whitefield's failure to organize his converts among the lower classes. Whitefield's unconcern with organization guaranteed that English Methodism would become almost entirely Arminian in its theology.

The conversions of the Wesleys did not take place until May 1738, three years after Whitefield and Harris had gone through their own transforming experiences, and twelve months after Harris had founded his first permanent religious society at Wernos in Breconshire and Whitefield had filled the churches of Bristol to overflowing. The grandfathers of John and Charles Wesley, John Westley and Dr. Samuel Annesley, had been among the parish ministers ejected at the Restoration, but the parents of the Wesley brothers had both deserted Dissent for High Anglicanism and, in the case of Susanna Wesley, for Jacobite politics. It was Charles Wesley who had founded the Methodist 'Holy Club' at Oxford in 1729, but it was John, his elder and dominant brother, a Fellow of Lincoln College, who became its spiritual guide. In the winter of 1735–6 the two brothers sailed to Georgia to minister to the colony and to convert the Indians, but the rigid discipline they sought to impose on their flocks provoked the resentment of the colonists, and instead of converting the Indians they came to doubt whether they were themselves converted. Their doubts were first sown by a group of Moravians, migrating from Europe to the New World, whom the Wesleys encountered on the outward voyage. In Oxford John had devoted himself to 'visiting the prisons, assisting the poor and sick in town, and doing what other good I could . . . to the bodies and souls of all men'. He 'carefully used, both in public and in private, all the means of grace at all opportunities'. He 'omitted no sort of self-denial which [he] thought lawful', and fasted on two days a week. But all this abstinence and activity gave him no comfort nor 'any assurance of acceptance with God', and the Moravians endeavoured to show the Wesleys 'a more excellent way', of reliance on faith in Christ alone for forgiveness.[2]

Charles returned to England in the autumn of 1736, depressed

[1] Ibid. ii. 484–92.
[2] *The Journal of the Rev. John Wesley*, ed. N. Curnock (1909–16), i. 467–9.

at the failure of his mission, and John followed him early in 1738, 'with the sentence of death in my own soul'.[1] John's path crossed with that of Peter Böhler, a young Moravian missionary who was in London *en route* to Carolina, and it was Böhler who convinced both Wesleys that they lacked 'that faith whereby alone we are saved', a faith that could be attained only through 'instantaneous conversion'.[2] Charles was the first to experience such conversion. On Whitsunday, 21 May 1738, while he lay ill in bed with pleurisy, a woman entered his room and declared, 'In the name of Jesus of Nazareth, arise, and believe and thou shalt be healed of all thy infirmities'. He got up from his bed, found himself 'at peace with God', and, in the words of one of his best-loved hymns,

> My chains fell off, my heart was free,
> I rose, went forth, and followed thee.[3]

'His bodily strength returned also from that hour', noted his brother John in his *Journal*.[4] Three days later, on 24 May, John himself

went very unwillingly to a [religious] society in Aldersgate Street, where one was reading Luther's preface to the *Epistle to the Romans*. About a quarter before nine, while he was describing the change which God works in the heart through faith in Christ, I felt my heart strangely warmed. I felt I did trust in Christ, Christ alone, for salvation; and an assurance was given me, that he had taken away *my* sins, even *mine*, and saved *me* from the law of sin and death.[5]

Though the Wesleys both experienced Evangelical conversions in May 1738, experiences which resolved their spiritual crises and redirected their lives, they retained the theological beliefs in which they had been nurtured, and these beliefs guaranteed that, unlike Harris and Whitefield, they would never be attracted by the eternal decrees of the Calvinist system. Instead John became the priest, Charles the poet, of a distinct Arminian Methodist organization. The personalities of the two brothers enabled them to complement each other's efforts: while Charles was emotional, warm-hearted, impulsive,

---

[1] T. Jackson, *Life of the Rev. Charles Wesley* (1841), i. 107. *The Letters of the Rev. John Wesley*, ed. J. Telford (1931), i. 239.
[2] *Wesley's Journal*, i. 442, 454, 459. Jackson, *Charles Wesley*, i. 125–7.
[3] Jackson, *Charles Wesley*, i. 134–5. [4] *Wesley's Journal*, i. 464.
[5] *Wesley's Journal*, i. 475–6.

gregarious, content to take second place in the Methodist hierarchy, John was a natural leader, single-minded, autocratic, somewhat detached from his fellows, a man 'with a mind as exact as a calculating-machine'[1] who would never allow personal relationships to interfere with what he came to see as his chief task of evangelism. In March 1739 Whitefield, soon to return to Georgia and not yet estranged by the Wesleys' Arminianism, invited John to take over his evangelistic work in Bristol. John accepted, and although at first he could 'scarce reconcile' himself to Whitefield's 'strange way of preaching in the fields', on 2 April he 'submitted to be more vile, and proclaimed in the highways the glad tidings of salvation, speaking from a little eminence in a ground adjoining to the city'.[2] In next thirty years, he calculated in 1770, he rode 'above a hundred thousand miles' on horseback,[3] and he still had twenty years of travelling in front of him, though for these latter years he was compelled to leave the horse for the coach. On his seventy-first birthday he attributed his good health to his practice of rising at four, preaching at five, and 'never travelling less, by sea or land, than 4,500 miles in a year'; on his eighty-first birthday he claimed that he was as strong as he had been at the age of twenty-one.[4] He went round England annually until his death in 1791, paid twenty visits to Scotland and another twenty to Ireland. He was ever restless, anxious to get on to the next town or village, anxious more souls to save. Though 'his conversation is good . . . he is never at leisure', complained Samuel Johnson. 'He is always obliged to go at a certain hour. This is very disagreeable to a man who loves to fold his legs and have his talk out as I do.'[5] Even while riding he employed his time usefully. 'History, poetry and philosophy I commonly read on horseback, having other employment at other times.'[6]

John Wesley possessed something of Whitefield's oratorical gifts, yet held these gifts in conjunction with an appreciation of the importance of the more humdrum tasks of pastoral care and

---

[1] The expression was John Hutton's, quoted in R. Knox, *Enthusiasm* (Oxford, 1950), p. 442.
[2] *Wesley's Journal*, i. 167, 172–3.   [3] Ibid., v. 361.
[4] Ibid., vi. 29, 521.
[5] J. Boswell, *Life of Johnson* (Oxford, 1934), iii. 230.
[6] *Wesley's Journal*, v. 360.

organization which Whitefield so conspicuously lacked. He shared Harris's passion for itinerant evangelism and for the formation of religious societies, while at the same time, as an ordained clergyman, he had an authority over such societies which Harris, as a layman, did not enjoy. Wesley, in reply to a friend who protested that he was violating parish boundaries, declared that he looked 'upon all the world as my parish'. It was, he explained, his 'bounden duty to declare unto all that are willing to hear, the glad tidings of salvation'.[1] But 'the world' was his parish not only to evangelize, but also to educate, discipline, encourage, and reprove. Wesley was not content merely to preach to men and women, but went on to organize those who desired 'to be saved from their sins' into societies, to divide the societies into bands and classes, and to keep strict control over the admission of new members and the behaviour of old ones by issuing and renewing membership tickets four times a year. As far as was humanly possible Wesley kept the discipline of the societies in his own hands, or in the hands of assistants appointed by him, and his visits to the societies were frequently followed by large-scale expulsions. Yet, notwithstanding the frequent purges, by the time of Wesley's death in 1791 there were 72,000 Arminian Methodists in the British Isles and a further 60,000 in North America. 'My brother Wesley acted wisely', wrote Whitefield towards the close of his life. 'The souls that were awakened under his ministry he joined in class, and thus preserved the fruit of his labour. This I neglected, and my people are a rope of sand.'[2]

Wesley might regard the world as his parish, but Anglican clergymen resented the claim and the Methodists, Arminian and Calvinist alike, had to contend with the furious opposition of clergymen who objected to the invasion of itinerant preachers into their parishes, and of mobs enraged by the Methodists' assurance that they were saved and other men were damned. They assert 'that they and none others are the elect', complained twelve Caernarvonshire clergymen to Griffith Jones in 1743, 'and damn all others in order to terrify the illiterate into their faction. They assure them that their fathers and grandfathers are in hell: and that they see visible marks of damnation in the faces

---

[1] *Wesley's Letters*, i. 286.
[2] Quoted in W. Sargant, *Battle for the Mind* (Pan Books, 1959), p. 197.

of such as will not become Methodists.'[1] Such as would not become Methodists often retaliated with violence. At Machynlleth in 1739 Howell Harris was prevented from preaching by a mob which 'continued hollowing, threatening, swearing, and flinging stones', and one of whose number fired a pistol at him; at Newport in Monmouthshire in 1740 he was pelted with apples and dirt and had his coat sleeves and his wig torn off; at Bala in 1741 he and John Cennick were squirted with water from a fire-engine and deluged with buckets of water and mud.[2] John Wesley too suffered indignities: at St. Ives in Cornwall in 1743 a mob burst into the room in which he was preaching and he received a blow on the side of the head; in Staffordshire a few months later the rival mobs of Darlaston and Walsall fought a pitched battle for the privilege of tormenting the Methodist leader; in Falmouth in 1745 the house which he was visiting was besieged by a mob and he had to escape by sea.[3] His brother Charles found that when he attempted to address a congregation in Sheffield in 1743 the mob demolished the Methodists' preaching-house; when he tried to preach in the market-place in Walsall in 1744 he was assaulted with dirt and stones; and while he was in Devizes in 1747 the mob turned a fire-engine on to the house in which he was preaching, broke the windows, and flooded the rooms.[4] Most of the first Methodist preachers had similar experiences. At Stepney in 1772 a group of sailors 'swore they would hear no such doctrine as damnation', placed a Methodist preacher in a wheelbarrow, and tipped him into a pond; at Pateley Bridge in Yorkshire in 1752 Thomas Lee was dragged through the common sewer; John Nelson, while preaching at Hepworth Moor in Yorkshire in 1747, was felled to the ground by a brick which hit him on the back of the head; and the stone which hit William Seward at Hay in Breconshire in 1742 proved to be fatal.[5]

Nor was persecution confined to the leaders of the movement.

---

[1] Jones, *Charity School Movement*, p. 307.

[2] La Trobe, *Life of Harris*, pp. 29, 44, 49, 56. E. R. Hassé, *The Moravians* (1911), p. 80.

[3] *Wesley's Journal*, iii. 93, 98–103, 188–92.

[4] Jackson, *Charles Wesley*, i. 329–30, 366–7, 464.

[5] R. F. Wearmouth, *Methodism and the Common People of the Eighteenth Century* (1945), p. 158. T. Jackson, ed., *The Lives of Early Methodist Preachers* (3rd edn., 1865), iv. 158, i. 160.

In some places Methodists who tried to maintain societies in their own localities were more exposed to danger than were itinerant evangelists who could often elude hostile mobs by passing on to their next destination. In February 1744 the Methodists of Wednesbury in Staffordshire were attacked by the Darlaston mob: their homes were systematically ransacked, their windows broken, their possessions looted, and what furniture could not be removed was broken up. Not even women were safe: in Wednesbury 'William Sitch's wife was lying in, but . . . they pulled away her bed too, and cut it in pieces'; John Nelson's pregnant wife was assaulted as she was walking home from Wakefield to Birstal and lost the child she was carrying; and in Exeter in 1745 rioters entered the Calvinistic Methodist meeting-house, women had their clothes torn from their backs, and one lady had to jump from the gallery to avoid being raped.[1] Methodist men were frequently victims of the press-gang, Methodist artisans were deprived of work on account of their religion, Methodist farmers were evicted from their holdings. To the Methodists, though, such trials were but trifles when viewed in the light of their ultimate reward. Richard Hughes, evicted from his farm in Anglesey for his Methodism, left with the comment, 'Whoever is willing to sell an everlasting kingdom and a glorious crown for a poor farm at a high rent, it is not I'.[2]

2. 'ARTLESS, SIMPLE PEOPLE': SOCIOLOGICAL AND PSYCHOLOGICAL EXPLANATIONS OF THE REVIVAL

How can the Evangelical revival be explained? To the Evangelicals themselves it was sufficient to attribute the awakening to the workings of the Holy Spirit—an interpretation strengthened by the fact that the beginnings of Jonathan Edwards's revival and the conversions of George Whitefield and Howell Harris occurred quite independently of each other in Massachusetts, Oxford, and Breconshire between December 1734 and Whitsunday 1735. But even if this explanation is accepted, it does not tell us why men and women were more open to the influence

---

[1] *Wesley's Journal*, iii. 118. *Early Methodist Preachers*, i. 79. Tyerman, *Whitefield*, ii. 115.
[2] W. Williams, *Welsh Calvinistic Methodism* (1872), p. 72.

of the Holy Spirit in the 1730s than in the previous decades. Nor does it explain why the conversions of the 1730s transformed not only the lives of certain individuals, but proved to be the first stirrings of a mass movement which was to have a profound effect on the history of England, Wales, and what was soon to become the United States of America.

Richard Niebuhr has interpreted the revival in sociological terms, arguing that since the Quakers had been 'prevented from becoming a really inclusive church of the disinherited by the persecutions which isolated them and drove them back upon themselves to form a narrow sect', the Methodists took their place as the missioners to the poor.[1] There were certainly striking resemblances between the Friends of the seventeenth century and the Methodists of the eighteenth. They placed the same emphasis on itinerant evangelism, preached as readily on hillsides as within buildings, organized their travelling preachers on similar plans, and, in the cases of Fox and John Wesley especially, on occasion produced similar outbreaks of hysteria from their audiences. They shared a common disdain for rank, apart from Whitefield, who adopted an obsequious attitude to the Countess of Huntingdon,[2] and the Methodists, like the Quakers, achieved some of their greatest successes in the large parishes of northern England where the influence of the clergy declined as the distance from the parish church increased. 'I bear the rich and love the poor; therefore I spend almost all my time with them', commented John Wesley.[3] And as Maldwyn Edwards has pointed out, most of the Arminian Methodist leader's work was done along lines connecting the three centres of London, Bristol, and Newcastle, with frequent forays into Cornwall. Wesley 'confined himself mainly to the coal-mining area of Newcastle, the industrial region of the north, the seaport of Bristol and its adjacent collieries, and the tin mines of Cornwall'.[4]

The biographies of forty-one of the eighteenth-century Wesleyan evangelists were published by Thomas Jackson in the nineteenth century under the title of *The Lives of Early Methodist*

[1] Niebuhr, *Social Sources of Denominationalism*, p. 53.
[2] e.g. *Life of Countess of Huntingdon*, i. 90.
[3] *Wesley's Letters*, iv. 266.
[4] M. Edwards, 'John Wesley', in *A History of the Methodist Church in Great Britain*, ed. R. Davies and G. Rupp (1965), i. 257.

Preachers, and in thirty-one cases there is some evidence of the occupation followed by the preacher before he devoted himself to full-time evangelism. Six of the preachers had been employed in the manufacture of textiles, five had served in the army in the ranks, one was a tin-miner, one a china-clay factory worker, and eleven were engaged in, or apprenticed to, some trade such as building, carpentry, or baking. In only seven of the thirty-one cases is there any hint of education or employment above the level of artisan: William Hunter followed his father's occupation of farming; John Valton, who went to grammar school, and Joseph Cownley were both clerks; Thomas Walsh stayed at school until he was nineteen and became a teacher; Thomas Payne served the East India Company on St. Helena; George Story managed a printing-office; and John Pritchard's father was sufficiently prosperous to be able to send him to the Academy for Drawing at Dublin. W. G. Hughes-Edwards has made a similar analysis of the occupations of eighty Welsh Calvinistic Methodist exhorters for whom biographical information is available before 1750 and has found a few men of higher social standing: four members of the lower squirearchy, two merchants, a prosperous builder, a physician, an apothecary, and a veterinary surgeon. But twenty-three of the eighty exhorters were artisans, including six blacksmiths, five carpenters, and four shoemakers; another five were farm labourers; fifteen were schoolmasters who were in the main employed by Griffith Jones's circulating schools and would be men of humble social standing; and nineteen were farmers who were as likely to be tenants as freeholders.[1]

The Welsh Calvinistic Methodists from the start drew wider support from the countryside that did the English Arminian Methodists, but both the main Methodist movements recruited a substantial proportion of their preachers from those artisan classes which were already preponderant in Dissenting meeting-houses. They were overwhelmingly men of modest means and humble circumstance, but to describe them as 'the disinherited' is wrong, for the term obscures the skills, the potential for economic advancement, and, in the case of masters, the economic independence which distinguished artisans from mere labourers. Alan Gilbert has suggested that the appeal of

---

[1] Hughes-Edwards, 'Methodist Society in Wales', pp. 131, 143.

Methodism, and of Nonconformity in general, to the artisan classes during the early years of the Industrial Revolution was in part due to their 'capacity for satisfying the profound associational and communal demands of people experiencing anomie (social disorganization) and social insecurity in a period of rapid social change'.[1] While Gilbert's thesis remains to be tested for the late eighteenth and early nineteenth centuries, it fails when applied to the early Methodist preachers. Not one of the preachers whose biographies were collected by Thomas Jackson appears to have been the victim of 'social disorganization', and a high proportion seem to have enjoyed secure family life, steady work, and modest prosperity. Even the five future Methodist preachers who enlisted in the army did so not from economic pressure but from a desire to escape from the humdrum existence of civilian life. Indeed, *The Lives of the Early Methodist Preachers* suggest than in so far as security entered into their thoughts in their pre-conversion days, it was something to be escaped from rather than something to be sought. Matthias Joyce and Thomas Taylor both ran away from their masters; Sampson Staniforth and George Shadford both enlisted despite the pleadings of their friends and relations; and Thomas Payne sought to join 'General Burgoyne's light regiment of dragoons' because he had 'an inclination to see the world'.[2]

Sociological explanations of human behaviour are, in any case, in the words of R. H. Thouless, ultimately dependent 'on the facts of individual psychology'.[3] And a thesis which attempts to link sociology with psychology in explaining the Methodist revival was advanced earlier in the present century by F. M. Davenport in his *Primitive Traits in Religious Revivals*. 'The natural result of assembling men in crowds', wrote Davenport, 'especially when skilful speakers engage their attention and play upon the chords of imagination and emotion, seems to be the weakening of the power of inhibition in each individual, and the giving of free rein to feeling and imitation.' In this way the mind of the crowd becomes 'strangely like that of primitive man', 'reason is in abeyance', and imagination unlocks 'the

[1] A. D. Gilbert, *Religion and Society in Industrial England* (1976), p. 89.

[2] *Early Methodist Preachers*, iv. 231, v. 5, iv. 111, vi. 140, ii. 178–9.

[3] R. H. Thouless, *An Introduction to the Psychology of Religion* (Cambridge, 1923), p. 144.

flood-gates of emotion, which on occasion may become wild enthusiasm or demonic frenzy'.[1] Davenport supports his case by comparing the hysteria and paroxysms which often accompanied eighteenth- and nineteenth-century religious revivals with the contagious shaker and ghost-dance religions which affected some Red Indian tribes at the end of the last century.[2] And William Sargant, in his *Battle for the Mind*, notes similar phenomena among the adherents of Voodoo in Haiti.[3]

It is certainly true that the eighteenth-century revivalists found their most appreciative audiences among unsophisticated communities. Jonathan Edwards explained that the people of Northampton, Massachusetts, had been sheltered from error and vice by reason of their 'being so far within land, at a distance from sea-ports, and in a corner of the country'.[4] John Wesley had a particular affection for the colliers of Kingswood, near Bristol, men who before the Methodists preached to them were notorious 'for neither fearing God nor regarding man; so ignorant of the things of God that they seemed but one remove from the beasts that perish'. He felt his heart 'exceedingly enlarged' towards the inhabitants of Chowden, near Newcastle, the 'Kingswood of the north', where 'twenty or thirty wild children ran round us' who 'could not properly be said to be either clothed or naked'.[5] When Wesley wished to pass favourable comment on a people, the word 'artless' frequently sprang to his mind. The inhabitants of the Isle of Man, he discovered, had the same qualities which Jonathan Edwards admired in the people of Northampton. The island was 'shut up from the world, and having little trade, is visited by scarce any strangers', so that the 'natives' were 'a plain, artless, simple people, unpolished, that is unpolluted'.[6] This lack of sophistication was not just a matter of poverty or poor education: no eighteenth-century Englishman had less affectation or a stronger belief in witches and ghosts than John Wesley, Fellow of Lincoln College, Oxford.

The physical manifestations which so surprised Wesley and which have perplexed historians first occurred in London in

---

[1] F. M. Davenport, *Primitive Traits in Religious Revivals* (1905), pp. 10, 26–7.
[2] Ibid., pp. 32–44.   [3] Sargant, *Battle for the Mind*, pp. 93–6.
[4] Edwards, *Faithful Narrative*, p. 2.   [5] *Wesley's Journal*, ii. 322, iii. 68–9.
[6] Ibid. vi. 321.

January 1739. 'While I was expounding in the Minories', wrote Wesley in his *Journal*, 'a well-dressed, middle-aged woman suddenly cried out, as in the agonies of death.'[1] But it was in Bristol in April that the convulsions became contagious. Wesley was praying at a meeting of a religious society when a woman 'cried out aloud, with the utmost vehemence, even as in the agonies of death', then two more people 'were seized with strong pain', and finally a man 'called upon God, as out of the belly of hell'.[2] The phenomena continued to attend Wesley's preaching in Bristol throughout 1739, and culminated in hysterical fits of laughter which disrupted his meetings in May 1740.[3] Similar outbreaks occurred when Wesley preached in London in June 1739 and August and October 1740, in Epworth in June 1742, and in the Newcastle area in November 1742 and March 1743. Nor was Wesley alone in producing such phenomena. Whitefield, having protested against the 'outward signs' which attended Wesley's preaching, himself found in Bristol in July 1739 that 'no sooner had he begun . . . to invite all sinners to believe in Christ, than four persons sunk down close to him, almost in the same moment'.[4] Two years later, again in Bristol, when Charles Wesley preached 'on death and judgement' at the grave of a dead Methodist, 'many trembled' and 'one woman cried out in horrible agony'.[5] Whitefield produced 'outcries, faintings, and the like' in Northampton, Massachusetts, in 1741; the preaching of John Berridge, the Evangelical vicar of Everton on the border of Bedfordshire and Huntingdonshire, was attended by similar convulsions in 1759; and the Methodist preachers William Hunter and John Watson also produced paroxysms in their hearers in Weardale in the winter of 1771–2.[6] Howell Harris wrote in 1743 that it was 'very common for scores to fall down by the power of the word' when listening to Daniel Rowland, and three years later an anonymous writer claimed to have witnessed incredible scenes at a Calvinistic Methodist service at Llangeitho. Rowland's sermon, he wrote, 'flung almost the whole society into the greatest agitation and confusion possible—some cried, others

[1] Ibid. ii. 131.   [2] Ibid. ii. 180.
[3] Ibid. ii. 346–7.   [4] Ibid. ii. 240.
[5] Jackson, *Charles Wesley*, i. 288–9.
[6] Knox, *Enthusiasm*, p. 526. *Wesley's Journal*, iv. 318–22, v. 467–72.

laughed, the women pulled one another by the caps, embraced each other, [and] capered like, where there was any room'. 'I never saw greater instances of madness,' commented the observer, 'even in Bedlam itself.'[1]

What explanation can be offered for the convulsions, trances, and hysteria which the revivalists thus produced? To describe the communities in which such phenomena occurred as unsophisticated or primitive, to examine the uninhibited nature of crowd behaviour, is to explain the conditions but not the cause of such phenomena. Wesley himself was initially content merely to describe the outbreaks, convinced that they were of divine origin and content to leave 'God to carry on his own work in the way that pleaseth him'.[2] But in December 1742 and March 1743 he began to look more closely into the cases of people in Newcastle who 'cried out aloud during the preaching'. Several of those he interviewed in December 'said they were afraid of the devil'. Others 'gave a more intelligible account of the piercing sense they then had of their sins . . . of the dread they were in, of the wrath of God and the punishment they had deserved, into which they seemed to be just falling, without any way to escape'. And one person explained, 'I felt the very fire of hell already kindled in my breast, and all my body was in much pain as if I had been in a burning fiery furnace'.[3] By March Wesley had come to the conclusion that their cries and agonies were not the work of God at all, but were due to 'Satan tearing them, as they were coming to Christ', that he might thus 'discredit the work of God, and . . . affright fearful people from hearing that word whereby their souls might be saved'.[4]

Henceforward physical manifestations are rarely mentioned in Wesley's *Journal*, and those which are recorded were the product of other men's preaching, not of his own. Was he reluctant to record what he had come to regard as the work of the devil? Or did he tone down his sermons so that his hearers were no longer frightened into convulsions? Whichever the case, it seems certain that Wesley had found the chief cause of the phenomena in his interviews in Newcastle in December 1742:

---

[1] Tyerman, *Whitefield*, ii. 52. Hughes-Edwards, 'Methodist Society in Wales', p. 56.

[2] *Wesley's Journal*, ii. 240. [3] Ibid. iii. 59–60. [4] Ibid. iii. 69.

those who had cried out in pain and dropped to the floor as though dead had been terrified by fears of damnation and hell. And Wesley's interviews provide us with an explanation not only of the convulsions, but with one of the keys to the success of the Evangelical revival itself.

The paroxysms themselves were of little long-term significance, and there is some evidence to suggest that the more spectacular conversions were not always permanent. Wesley noted that the effects of the Weardale revival of 1771–2 were short-lived, and Thomas Taylor, the most perceptive of the *Early Methodist Preachers*, wrote of a 'noisy' and ephemeral revival in Halifax in the 1790s that 'very many of those hasty converts have proved like the stony-ground hearers, in the time of temptation they have fallen away'.[1] Few of the deepest Evangelical conversions can be ascribed to 'the unrestrained tendency of the psychological crowd'.[2] In thirty-six of the biographies of Wesleyan itinerants preserved in the *Early Methodist Preachers* there is a description of the process of conversion, but in only six cases did the crucial moment come while the convert was listening to a sermon, and in only one of these cases, that of George Shadford, was conversion accompanied by any sort of physical disturbance.[3] In seven cases conversion took place while the future preacher was engaged in prayer with a few companions, in four cases it was described as a gradual process, and in one case it was the giving out of the words of a hymn which gave the convert an assurance of forgiveness. But in half the thirty-six cases assurance came when the convert was alone— while reading the Bible or some other religious book, while at private prayer, or, in the cases of Joseph Cownley and Duncan Wright, while lying in bed. Thomas Taylor's experience was typical:

One Lord's-day evening I retired to my apartment for my usual exercise of reading and prayer. While I was calling upon the Lord, he appeared in a wonderful manner, as with his vesture dipped in blood. I saw him by the eye of faith, hanging on the cross; and the sight caused such love to flow into my soul that I believed that moment, and never since gave up my confidence.[4]

[1] Ibid. iv. 25. *Early Methodist Preachers*, v. 86–7.
[2] Davenport, *Primitive Traits*, p. 31.   [3] *Early Methodist Preachers*, vi. 149–50.
[4] Ibid. v. 11.

A psychological factor of far greater importance than the emotional and imitative influence of the crowd was fear of death, judgement, and damnation. Twenty-four of the *Earl Methodist Preachers* recorded that they experienced such fears at some time before their conversions. John Furz of Wilton, for example, 'began to be afraid of death and hell' when he was ten years old. At some subsequent date he attended a Presbyterian meeting, and a remark by the preacher so terrified him at the thought that his Bible lay covered in dust, that he went home 'afraid the earth would open and swallow me up, or that infernal spirits would be permitted to drag me to the bottomless pit'. After a night of terror he 'leaped down stairs and fell to the ground' and 'heard a small, still voice saying, "Thy sins are forgiven thee"'.[1] Not all the *Early Methodist Preachers* had such terrifying experiences: William Hunter was deeply affected by the preaching of Christopher Hopper, 'not with terror but with love', and George Story's conversion was the culmination of a search for happiness which the pursuit of pleasure failed to bring.[2] But the fear of John Furz was the more common pre-conversion experience.

The extent to which Evangelical preachers played on their audiences' fears of death and hell varied a good deal. In America Gilbert Tennent and Jonathan Edwards terrorized their congregations with their hell-fire preaching, and Edwards's sermons on 'The justice of God in the damnation of sinners' and 'Sinners in the hands of an angry God' help us to understand why the inhabitants of Northampton were unable to sleep at night.[3] Whitefield, like Edwards, preached on *The Eternity of Hell Torments*, warned his hearers against 'everlasting burnings', and refused the sacrament to a man whom he found to believe in the annihilation of the wicked rather than in their eternal punishment.[4] And when the Welsh Calvinistic Methodist David Morris preached on the day of judgement his hearers screamed, fainted, and, on one occasion in Bridgend, Glamorgan, 'ran wildly through the town, thinking that the solemn day had actually come'.[5]

[1] Ibid. v. 108, 112–13.   [2] Ibid. ii. 241, v. 224, 228–9.
[3] Edwards, *Faithful Narrative*, p. 33.
[4] G. Whitefield, *The Eternity of Hell Torments* (1783), p. 20. *Whitefield's Journals*, pp. 123, 157–8.
[5] Rees, *Nonconformity in Wales*, pp. 393, 403.

It has, though, been claimed that Wesley made less use of 'impassioned appeals to terror' and that he doubted the effectiveness of trying to frighten men with the prospect of hell.[1] Wesley did publish a sermon on hell, a place where there is 'no light but that of livid flames' and 'no music but that of groans and shrieks',[2] but it is true that he did not dwell on the sufferings of the damned to the extent that Tennent and Edwards did. When, at Studley in Warwickshire in 1745, he met a poor man who swore 'almost at every sentence' he rebuked him not with threats of judgement but with the love of God.[3] This does not mean, though, that fear of damnation was not an important factor in Wesley's winning of converts. Most eighteenth-century Englishmen appear to have believed in hell as a place of real physical torment. It was common practice, said Wesley, 'to say to a child, "Put your finger into that candle: can you bear it even for one minute? How then will you bear hell-fire?" '[4] And it is thus unfair to blame the Methodists, as did Lecky, for erecting an 'appalling system of religious terrorism' to unhinge tottering intellects and embitter sensitive natures.[5] Only eccentrics, such as William Whiston, publicly denied eternal punishment in the eighteenth century,[6] and Wesley did not need to spell out the fact that when he spoke of the need for salvation, he meant salvation from hell. The whole purpose of Wesley's ministry was other-worldly: Christianity, for him, was 'the way to heaven'.[7]

Why were eighteenth-century Englishmen and Welshmen so susceptible to appeals to escape from the wrath to come? The ever-present threat of death was of crucial importance here. When Harris, Whitefield, and the Wesleys commenced their ministries in the 1730s smallpox was still a major killer, death from starvation was still a real threat to the poor, as frequent bread riots bore witness,[8] and in 1739 England, after a genera-

---

[1] Davenport, *Primitive Traits*, p. 167. S. G. Dimond, *Psychology of the Methodist Revival* (1926), p. 148. D. D. Wilson, 'The Importance of Hell for John Wesley', *Proceedings of the Wesley Historical Society*, xxxiv (1963–4), p. 14.

[2] *Works of John Wesley* (3rd edn., 1829–30), vi. 383.

[3] *Wesley's Journal*, iii. 177.   [4] *Wesley's Works*, vi. 388.

[5] W. H. H. Lecky, *A History of England in the Eighteenth Century* (1878), ii. 582.

[6] D. P. Walker, *The Decline of Hell* (1964), pp. 96–103.

[7] Quoted by R. Davies, 'The People called Methodists—our Doctrine', in *History of the Methodist Church*, i. 147.

[8] Wearmouth, *Methodism and the Common People*, pp. 19–76.

tion of peace, was plunged into war which was to occupy sixteen of the next twenty-four years. Literature which had death as its theme had a considerable vogue, much of it making its first appearance in the 1740s: for example, John Blair's *The Grave*, of which forty-seven editions were published between 1743 and 1798, and James Hervey's *Meditations among the Tombs*, which was republished twenty-five times between 1745 and 1791.[1]

There is ample evidence of the way in which the proximity of death increased a person's readiness to embrace the Evangelical message. Jonathan Edwards's revival in Northampton, Massachusetts, had been preceded by the untimely deaths of a young man and a young woman which 'seemed much to contribute to the solemnizing of the spirits of many young persons'.[2] An important step towards Wesley's own conversion was the fear he experienced during a storm at sea while returning from Georgia in January 1738, fear which contrasted with the courage displayed by the Moravians during a similar storm on the outward voyage.[3] And the death of a child from smallpox in the Methodist school at Kingswood, wrote Wesley, enabled God to touch the hearts of many of his school-fellows 'in a manner they never knew before'.[4] Much of the Methodists' effort was directed towards saving the souls of condemned criminals. Public executions were frequently used by preachers as occasions on which to impress sightseers with the brevity of life and the wages of sin, and even children were taken to witness these spectacles that they might learn the consequences of evil-doing.[5] The stress which the Evangelicals placed on the penal theory of the atonement would have seemed particularly relevant in a society in which the most petty of crimes incurred the death penalty. The fear experienced by British troops in the battles of Dettingen and Fontenoy made them, too, receptive to Methodist teaching, and while the army was stationed in Flanders in 1743–4 John Haime formed a Methodist society among the troops which soon had 300 members and seven preachers.[6] Indeed, it is probable that the series of shocks experienced by the public in

---

[1] G. R. Taylor, *The Angel-Makers* (1958), p. 118.
[2] Edwards, *Faithful Narrative*, pp. 8–9. [3] *Wesley's Journal*, i. 142–3, 417–18.
[4] Ibid. v. 31. [5] Taylor, *The Angel-Makers*, p. 312.
[6] *Wesley's Journal*, iii. 155–6. *Early Methodist Preachers*, i. 284, iv. 128.

the middle years of the century—the War of the Austrian Succession, the Jacobite rebellion of 1745, the London earthquakes of 1750, the catastrophic Lisbon earthquake of 1755— inclined people to take religion more seriously than usual. When Charles Stuart invaded England in November 1745 John Nelson was in Bristol and noted that 'many trembled for fear of the calamities that were expected . . . and attended the word and prayer, though they used not to attend before', and when a national fast was proclaimed in the following month John Wesley observed from London that 'such a solemnity and seriousness everywhere appeared as had not been lately seen in England'.[1] Five years later, when London was shaken by a series of earthquakes, Charles Wesley noted that he had 'scarce ever seen so many at intercession'; 'fear filled our chapel', he recorded on 4 April, 'occasioned by a prophecy of the earthquake's return this night'.[2]

What was the nature of the sins which caused the Methodists to fear, before their conversions, that they would be damned and cast into hell? Two of the *Early Methodist Preachers* appear to have been real rogues before their conversions. Thomas Olivers of Montgomeryshire was for four or five years 'greatly entangled with a farmer's daughter', but then he appears to have jilted her, certainly he 'was a means of driving her almost to an untimely end', and such was the anger of the people of the neighbourhood that he set off for England and travelled from inn to inn, usually without paying his debts, until he heard Whitefield preach in Bristol and was converted.[3] Sampson Staniforth had a similarly chequered career: the son of a Sheffield cutler, he was apprenticed to a baker from the age of fourteen to seventeen, but got into bad company, gambled and drank, and then enlisted in the army to the sorrow of his mother. While in Perth he slept with a woman whom he then refused to marry, escaped an attempt by her enraged relations to kill him, and in 1743 served in Flanders and Germany where he stole bullocks from the villagers and plundered 'all the country' until he started to attend the preaching of John Haime and the Methodist soldiers and was converted.[4] But the other

---

[1] *Early Methodist Preachers*, i. 144. *Wesley's Journal*, iii. 228.
[2] Jackson, *Charles Wesley*, i. 549–50.   [3] *Early Methodist Preachers*, ii. 50–6.
[4] Ibid. iv. 110–18.

Early Methodist Preachers, though all came 'short of the glory of God', were guilty of more commonplace sins: drinking, swearing, gambling, dancing, card-playing, and Sabbath-breaking were the usual misdeeds they attributed to their unregenerate days.

Edward Thompson has suggested that 'the objective component' of pre-conversion sin was often masturbation, and there is some evidence to support his point of view.[1] It is a topic about which one would expect the Methodist convert to be reticent, but in the case of three prominent preachers we have fairly clear references to the habit. George Whitefield, in his sixteenth year, 'fell into abominable secret sin' and asked why God had given him such passions when he was not permitted to gratify them; Thomas Walsh, also in his sixteenth year, found that 'the desire of the flesh . . . raged in his nature' and spoke darkly of his 'besetting sin'; and John Nelson, when he was about nineteen, found himself 'in great danger of falling into scandalous sins' and prayed that God would give him a wife.[2] Indeed, Nelson's account of his temptations and of his restless search for spiritual consolation is reminiscent of the experiences of George Fox nearly a century earlier and probably had similar cause. Feelings of guilt arising from masturbation had contributed to the spiritual development of other religious men in the seventeenth century, among them the Puritan Richard Norwood, the Quaker William Ames, and the Exeter Presbyterian minister George Trosse, and their experiences are likely to have been much more common than the records suggest.[3]

One does not need to accept Thompson's view that the early Methodists saw Satan as a 'phallic image'[4] to appreciate the way in which sexual guilt or repression often played a part in their religious development. It is significant that a high proportion of the membership of some early Welsh Calvinistic Methodist societies was unmarried: in eight north Pembrokeshire and south Cardiganshire societies in the 1740s, for example,

---

[1] E. P. Thompson, *The Making of the English Working Class* (Penguin Books, 1970), p. 403.

[2] *Whitefield's Journals*, pp. 41, 43. *Early Methodist Preachers*, i. 8, 17, iii. 22.

[3] P. Delany, *British Autobiography in the Seventeenth Century* (1969), pp. 59, 68. W. Ames, *A Declaration of the Witness of God* (1659), sig. A. A. W. Brink, ed., *The Life of the Reverend George Trosse* (Montreal, 1974), p. 62.

[4] Thompson, *Making of the English Working Class*, p. 43.

out of 200 members 111 were single women and fifty-eight single men.[1] Similarly Wesley, in commenting on the decline of Weardale Methodism, noted that 'most of the liveliest in the society were the single men and women', several of whom 'in a little time contracted an inordinate affection for each other'.[2] In such cases Methodism offered young people both relief from guilt feelings concerning sex and the chance of finding partners for marriage.

Howell Harris and John Wesley themselves were both inhibited by their upbringing and their religious preoccupations from developing satisfactory relationships with persons of the opposite sex, and their inadequate sex lives were in turn compensated for by their devotion to evangelism. Two years after his conversion Harris became interested in a lady and was on his way to see her when, 'becoming filled with zeal for my master's cause', he put off the visit.[3] Three years later the Welsh revivalist was attracted to a thirty-five-year old widow, Mrs. Elizabeth James, but George Whitefield was also looking for a wife, 'not for lust' but as a 'helpmeet' to assist in the running of his orphanage in Savannah, and after one lady had rejected his unromantic overtures he, too, turned his attentions to Mrs. James.[4] Harris claimed that Mrs. James much preferred himself to the Englishman,[5] but at the same time he felt that God had chosen her 'for Brother Whitefield and the orphan house' and the reluctant Mrs. James was married to Whitefield in November 1741. Five days later, on the rebound from Mrs. James, Harris proposed to Miss Ann Williams and they were married in May 1744. It was hardly an ideal match: Mrs. Harris refused to accompany her husband on his evangelistic tours, he took with him in her place the wife of a Caernarvonshire squire, and the indignant squire replied by threatening to kill the Welsh Methodist leader.[6]

John Wesley's love affairs were even more unfortunate. Such was the dominant personality of Susanna Wesley that John was left with a mother-fixation which crippled him in his dealings with other women for the rest of his life. After a brief romance

---

[1] Hughes-Edwards, 'Methodist Society in Wales', pp. 170–3.
[2] *Wesley's Journal*, vi. 25.   [3] Bennett, *Early Life of Harris*, p. 117.
[4] Tyerman, *Whitefield*, i. 367–9, 530.
[5] D. E. Jenkins, *Calvinistic Methodist Holy Orders* (Caernarvon, 1911), p. 36.
[6] Evans, 'The Welsh Awakening', pp. 99–101, 187, 194.

when he was twenty-three years old he vowed he would never again touch a woman's breasts, and looked forward to his mission to Georgia since he thought that there he would 'see no woman but those which are almost of a different species'.[1] But Georgia was not empty of English women and possessed the alluring charms of Sophy Hopkey. John fell in love with her, but with the irresolution he so often displayed in affairs of the heart he could not decide whether or not to marry her, and postponed any decision until he had 'been among the Indians'. Sophy thereupon married a rival and the jilted clergyman caused a scandal by refusing her the sacrament. Twenty years later, when he was forty-five, he fell in love again, with the homely Grace Murray, a thirty-three-year-old widow who kept the Methodist orphanage in Newcastle. But Grace was already the recipient of the attentions of one of Wesley's lay preachers, John Bennett, and Charles Wesley, apparently under the mis-apprehension that Grace and John Bennett were virtually engaged, was alarmed lest her marriage to John Wesley would cause a scandal among the Methodists. He rode from Bristol to Newcastle to prevent the marriage between his brother and 'so mean a woman', Grace married John Bennett, and John Wesley endured what he described as one of the worst trials of his life with little outward recrimination. 'Why should a living man complain? a man for the punishment of his sins.'[2]

Finally, in 1751, John contracted a disastrous marriage to a forty-one-year-old widow, Molly Vazeille. He was to find, as Howell Harris had already discovered, that marriage was scarcely compatible with the life of an itinerant evangelist. In the first year or so of marriage Mrs. Wesley did on occasion accompany her husband on his journeys, but she soon tired of the hardships of continual travel, and as she and John spent less and less time with each other so she grew increasingly jealous of her husband's friendship with his female converts.[3] She was particularly incensed when, in 1757, John tactlessly appointed as the housekeeper of his Kingswood school a converted bigamist named Sarah Ryan who had three husbands, all of them living.[4] In retaliation Molly Wesley opened her husband's

---

[1] V. H. H. Green, *The Young Mr. Wesley* (1961), p. 106. *Wesley's Letters*, i. 189.
[2] *Wesley's Letters*, iii. 19–20.   [3] Ibid. iii. 87, 94.
[4] L. Tyerman, *Life of the Rev. John Wesley* (1871), ii. 285–7.

correspondence, stole his papers, and continually charged him with living in adultery.[1] On one occasion she is said to have vented her rage on her husband by dragging him across the floor of a room by his hair.[2] She left John in 1758, there followed a temporary reconciliation, but she left him finally in 1775, and when she died six years later he was not even informed of her funeral until after the event.[3] As relations with his wife deteriorated John increasingly derived satisfaction from his correspondence with his female followers, and especially with Ann Bolton of Witney, to whom he confessed his love. 'I have often examined myself . . . with respect to you', he wrote to her defensively when he was seventy years old, 'and I find "no fever's heat" . . . but a steady, rational affection.'[4] Ann herself did not marry until Wesley was dead.[5]

The connection between an unhappy sex life and successful evangelism was noted by John Berridge, the Evangelical vicar of Everton. 'Matrimony has quite maimed poor Charles [Wesley]', he wrote to the Countess of Huntingdon in 1770, 'and might have spoiled John [Wesley] and George [Whitefield], if a wise master had not graciously sent them a brace of ferrets.' Eight or nine years earlier, added Berridge, he had thought 'of looking out for a Jezebel myself' until he 'besought the Lord to give me a direction'. Letting his 'Bible fall open of itself', his eyes lighted on II Esdras 10:1, 'When my son was entered into his wedding chamber he fell down and died'.[6]

3. PIOUS PARENTS AND CHARITY SCHOOLS: THE HISTORICAL ROOTS OF THE REVIVAL

The unsophisticated nature of the communities to which the Methodists preached helps to explain the conditions which favoured the Evangelical revival, while the ever-present threat of death, feelings of guilt arising from sexual desires and breaches of a strict moral code, and the fears of judgement and damnation which these provoked, offer psychological insights into the minds of the people who responded to the Methodist message. But these factors do not explain why the Evangelical revival

---

[1] *Wesley's Letters*, iv. 21, 52–3, 61, vi. 99–102, 273–4.
[2] Tyerman, *John Wesley*, ii. 110.   [3] *Wesley's Journal*, vi. 337.
[4] *Wesley's Letters*, vi. 73, 85, 279.   [5] Ibid. viii. 254.
[6] *Life of Countess of Huntingdon*, i. 389.

occurred when it did, nor do they explain why some people were attracted by the Methodist movement while others living in the same communities were unaffected or repelled. The answer to these problems lies in the homes, schools, and churches of the first converts: the Evangelical revival did not spring from uncultivated soil, but was the fruit of years of careful husbandry of the spiritual life of a section of the nation.

John Wesley put his finger on one of the crucial factors in the Evangelical revival when he recorded the result of a visit he paid to Rothwell in Yorkshire in 1780. He 'inquired what was become of that lovely class of little girls, most of them believers', which he had met three years before, and found that those who 'had pious parents remain to this day, but all of them whose parents did not fear God are gone back into the world'.[1] That the home environment could be of cardinal importance in determining a person's future religious development is evident from the careers of John and Charles Wesley themselves: Susanna Wesley reared her family on the principle that, since 'self-will is the root of all sin and misery', the mother who seeks to conquer her child's will 'works together with God in renewing and saving a soul'.[2] The importance of upbringing in conditioning men to receive the Evangelical message is similarly revealed in the biographies of the *Early Methodist Preachers*. In thirty-seven of the biographies we have information about the future evangelist's early life, and in thirty-one of these it is clear that the convert to Methodism was brought up in a religious atmosphere. Twenty-two were raised in the Church of England, three in the Church of Scotland, and three in the Roman Catholic Church, while one was brought up by the Particular Baptists, one by the English Presbyterians, and one had alternated between his father's parish church and his mother's Presbyterian meeting. In eighteen cases the home was mentioned as the primary source of religious impressions, in seven cases school appears to have been the more important influence. Sampson Staniforth, in this as in much else, was the exception to the rule: 'While I was young', he wrote, 'I heard nothing about either religion or morality.'[3] But the typical upbringing

---

[1] *Wesley's Journal*, vi. 273. [2] Ibid. iii. 36.
[3] *Early Methodist Preachers*, iv. 110.

was that of John Pawson, whose parents 'constantly attended public worship' and taught their children 'to say our prayers and repeat the church catechism, obliged us constantly to go to church, and would not suffer us to run into open sin'.[1] 'I heartily thank God for a pious education,' wrote Thomas Payne of his Particular Baptist upbringing, 'which laid a foundation for a future reformation.'[2]

If the foundations of the Evangelical revival were laid in the homes of humble Christian parents, the first stage of the super-structure was added by the charity schools. The charity-school movement had its origin in the alarm felt by devout Anglicans at the end of the seventeenth century at the extent of irreligion among the poor. By the 1690s many Anglicans had come to the conclusion that the reaction against strict attitudes to morals and religion which had accompanied the restoration of Charles II had gone too far, and there took place what was in effect a revival of 'puritanism', in a devotional and moral, rather than in an ecclesiastical, sense within the established church. As early as 1678 'several young men of the Church of England, in the cities of London and Westminster', inspired by the preaching of Dr. Anthony Horneck in the Savoy chapel, were 'touched with a very affecting sense of their sins, and began to apply them-selves in a very serious manner to religious thoughts and pur-poses'.[3] Thus was launched the first of the Anglican Religious Societies which Howell Harris was to claim as the model for his own societies in the later 1730s, and which were to provide Whitefield, the Moravians, and the Wesleys with some of their earliest audiences and their first converts.[4] The formation of the Religious Societies was followed in the 1690s by the setting up of Societies for the Reformation of Manners which were con-cerned with the enforcement of laws against drunkenness, blasphemy, prostitution, gambling, and 'Sabbath-breaking', some of which dated back to the reign of Henry VIII. In forty-four years the London societies alone claimed responsi-bility for 101,683 prosecutions, but their use of paid informers

---

[1] Ibid. iv. 1.   [2] Ibid. ii. 278.

[3] J. Woodward, *An Account of the Religious Societies in the City of London* (4th edn., 1712, reprinted Liverpool, 1935, ed. D. Jenkins), p. 32.

[4] La Trobe, *Life of Harris*, p. 24. J. D. Walsh, 'The Origins of the Evangelical Revival', in *Essays in Modern English Church History in Memory of Norman Sykes*, ed. G. V. Bennett and J. D. Walsh (1966), pp. 144–8.

was bitterly resented and to the reformers vice seemed as prevalent in the 1730s as it had been in the 1690s. Support for the societies dwindled and the last was dissolved in 1738.[1]

The attempt to make Englishmen moral by compulsion was followed by the attempt to make them religious by education. The causes of vice, not its symptoms, were to be tackled. When Dr. Thomas Bray founded the Society for Promoting Christian Knowledge in 1699 it was in the belief that 'the growth of vice and debauchery is greatly owing to the gross ignorance of the principles of the Christian religion, especially among the poorer sort', and the new society proceeded to encourage parish clergymen and laymen to set up charity schools and to print Bibles, catechisms, and other devotional works for their use.[2] By 1723 the SPCK was claiming that 23,421 scholars were being instructed in 1,329 schools under its auspices.[3]

Wales posed a particular problem to the SPCK. Although the Society had ninety-five schools in the principality between 1699 and 1737, thirty-one of these were in Pembrokeshire and there appears to have been some reluctance to provide Welsh-speaking schools for Welsh-speaking areas.[4] Moreover in some Welsh counties parents were reluctant to send their children to school because, according to the dean of Bangor, 'they must go ever and anon to beg for victuals, there being no poor rates settled in these parts'.[5] These deficiencies were made good by the circulating schools launched in 1737 by Griffith Jones, the rector of Llanddowror in Carmarthenshire. Jones's objective was to teach not only children but also 'hired servants, day-labourers, and married men and women' to read the Scriptures and recite the catechism. He recognized that such people could spare little time for learning, especially in a foreign language, and so he collected a team of itinerant teachers, each of whom would hold a school in a village for three or four months, instructing the inhabitants in their native tongue, before moving on to the next. There was no time to teach the poor to write, and in any case it was 'by no means the design of this spiritual

---

[1] D. W. R. Bahlman, *The Moral Revolution of 1688* (New Haven, 1957), pp. 14, 62–6.

[2] Jones, *Charity School Movement*, pp. 38–41.

[3] Ibid., p. 24.

[4] Ibid., p. 389. M. Clement, *The SPCK and Wales* (1954), p. 10.

[5] F. A. Cavenagh, *The Life and Work of Griffith Jones* (Cardiff, 1930), p.34.

kind of charity to make them gentlemen, but Christians and heirs of eternal life'.[1] At the time of Griffith Jones's death in 1761 it was claimed that 3,498 circulating schools had existed at some time in the previous twenty-four years, and that 158,237 pupils had been instructed.[2]

From the start there was a close, if uneasy, connection between Griffith Jones and the Welsh Methodist movement. It was Jones who had been instrumental in the conversion of Daniel Rowland in 1735, and two years later Howell Harris had served as superintendent of the circulating schools.[3] There were many other schoolmasters who combined teaching in the circulating schools with exhorting in Methodist meetings, and although Griffith Jones dismissed some of his schoolmasters for exhorting in 1741, two years later twelve Caernarvonshire clergymen complained that his itinerant teachers, though pretending to be Church of England people, spoke at night at Methodist meetings and accused the clergy of not preaching the Gospel.[4] A comparison of the geographic distribution of the circulating schools and Methodist societies in Wales in 1740 shows that they were flourishing in the same counties: Breconshire, Cardiganshire, Carmarthenshire, Glamorgan, and Monmouthshire.[5]

The teaching in the charity and circulating schools was based on the Bible, the catechism of the Church of England, and on devotional books of which *The Whole Duty of Man* appears to have been by far the most widely used. This book, first published in 1658 and frequently reprinted, was probably the work of Richard Allestree, who had fought on the royalist side in the Civil War and after the Restoration was successively professor of divinity at Oxford and provost of Eton.[6] 'The only intent of this ensuing treatise', wrote Allestree on his first page, 'is to be a short and plain direction to the very meanest readers to behave themselves so in this world that they may be happy for ever in the next.'[7] 'The benefits purchased for us by Christ', he ex-

---

[1] Cavenagh, *Life of Griffith Jones*, pp. 38, 52–3.

[2] Jones, *Charity School Movement*, pp. 302, 309.

[3] Bennett, *Early Life of Harris*, p. 139.

[4] Hughes-Edwards, 'Methodist Society in Wales', p. 317. Cavenagh, *Life of Griffith Jones*, p. 45.

[5] Clement, *SPCK and Wales*, p. 100.

[6] The authorship of *The Whole Duty of Man* is discussed by P. Elmen in *The Library*, 5th series, vi (1951), 19–27.

[7] R. Allestree, *The Whole Duty of Man* (1739), p. v.

plained, 'are such as will undoubtedly make the soul happy . . .
but because these benefits belong not to us till we perform the
condition required of us, whoever desires the happiness of his
soul must set himself to the performing of that condition . . . the
hearty, honest endeavour of obeying the whole will of God.'[1]
The will of God, though, contained 'under it many particulars',
and the 'short and plain direction' developed into over 400
pages of advice on trusting in God, observing the Lord's day,
honouring God's word, reverencing the sacraments, praying
and fasting, being humble, sober, and temperate, avoiding
time-wasting in recreation and immodesty in apparel, performing duties to one's neighbour, and 'abstaining from all kinds of
uncleanness, not only that of adultery and fornication, but all
other more unnatural sorts of it, committed either upon ourselves or with any other'. Failure thus to obey the will of God,
warned Allestree, would involve 'endless misery'. 'If a small
spark of fire, lighting on the least part of the body, be so
intolerable, what will it be to have the whole cast into the
hottest flames, and that not for some few hours or days, but for
ever? So that when you have spent many *thousands* of years in
that unspeakable torment, you shall be no nearer coming out of
it than you were the first day you went in.'[2]

That this was the staple diet of children, and in Wales of
adults as well, who were being taught in the charity and circulating schools established in the first half of the eighteenth
century goes far to explain both the timing and the success of
the Evangelical revival. The SPCK and Griffith Jones laid the
tinder to which the Methodists set the spark.

The author of *The Whole Duty of Man* painted in lurid pictures
the consequences of failing to secure eternal happiness, yet at the
same time laid down conditions which it was impossible for
ordinary sinful men and women to fulfil. And there is abundant
evidence that this was true of much of the teaching of the
Church of England in the early eighteenth century. Such was
the case of William Law, whose *Practical Treaties on Christian
Perfection* and *A Serious Call to a Devout and Holy Life* so influenced
John Wesley.[3] 'Religion is a state of labour and striving', wrote
Law, and, 'many will fail of their salvation, not because they
took no pains or care about it, but because they did not take

---

[1] Ibid., p. 1.   [2] Ibid., p. ix.   [3] *Wesley's Journal*, i. 467.

pains and care enough.'[1] Similar teaching was listened to by John Nelson in his years of spiritual wandering. 'Man', he was told, 'could not perfectly fulfil the will of his maker; but God required him to do all he could, and Christ would make out the rest: but if man did not do all he could, he must unavoidably perish.' From this Nelson concluded that 'Not only I, but every soul must be damned, for I did not believe that any who have lived to years of maturity had done all they could'.[2]

Far from being responsible for this 'system of religious terrorism', as Lecky maintained, the Methodists offered a way of escape. Howell Harris's conversion was preceded by his reading of *The Whole Duty of Man*, by which he 'was convinced that in every branch of my duty to God, to myself and to my neighbours I was guilty and had fallen short'. 'I began to humble myself by fasting and denying myself in every outward comfort', he wrote, 'but knew as yet nothing of the inward self-denial which our Saviour enjoins' until convinced 'that Christ died for me, and that all my sins were laid on him'.[3] George Whitefield similarly sought to absolve his sins by 'a round of duties, receiving the sacrament monthly, fasting frequently, attending constantly on public worship' and even by wearing 'woollen gloves, a patched gown, and dirty shoes' until, at his conversion, he experienced deliverance 'from the burden that had so heavily oppressed me'.[4] And John Wesley, according to his own testimony, attempted to win salvation by practising and preaching good works for ten years and found no peace until, at his conversion, he recognized 'that the death and righteousness of Christ are the whole and sole cause' of our justification.[5] The Evangelical revival, like the Antinomian and Quaker movements of the previous century, was a reaction against a legalistic religious system which made impossible demands on the moral and spiritual resources of the ordinary believer, and the Methodist preachers, like the Antinomians and early Friends, brought relief and joy to men and women whose consciences were tormented by the memory of unfor-

---

[1] W. Law, *A Serious Call to a Devout and Holy Life* (Methuen, 6th edn., 1920), p. 31.
[2] *Early Methodist Preachers*, i. 12.
[3] La Trobe, *Life of Harris*, pp. 12–13.
[4] *Whitefield's Journals*, pp. 44, 53, 57.
[5] *Wesley's Journal*, ii. 262, 275.

given sins and whose lives were burdened by the over-scrupulous performance of religious duties.

4. PREDESTINATION AND PERFECTION: THE RIFT BETWEEN CALVINIST AND ARMINIAN METHODISM

In the mid-seventeenth century the Antinomians and Quakers had provided two possible means of escape for people whose lives were made miserable by their attempts, and their failure, to meet the rigorous demands of contemporary Puritanism, but the escape routes they offered led off in two different directions. The Antinomians, by emphasizing the sovereignty of God and the free grace of Christ, rendered the question of an individual's salvation independent of his moral behaviour: not even the most heinous sin could disannul the elect's predestination to eternal life. The Quakers, by contrast, sought to resolve the religious dilemma of their contemporaries not by asserting that sin was no barrier to salvation, but by promising them victory over sin: those who were obedient to the light within, they claimed, would attain a state of sinless perfection. The same division reappeared among the Methodists of the eighteenth century. The Wesleys, like the Quakers, rejected predestination, loathed the Antinomian tendencies of Calvinism, and set before their followers the hope of Christian perfection. The Calvinists emphasized election and reprobation, regarded Arminianism as a blasphemous denial of the sovereignty of God, and looked upon sinless perfection as a dangerous delusion. From the late 1730s until the end of the century the Evangelical movement was rent in two by these opposing theological systems.

In the eyes of the Calvinists, John Wesley's conversion in May 1738 was a superficial, short-lived experience which made no difference to his fundamental theological beliefs. The influences of his High Church upbringing and of the ascetic William Law were temporarily set aside when they failed him in the moment of spiritual crisis, but once the example of the Moravians and the writings of Luther had served their purposes they, too, were set aside and the earlier, pre-conversion influences reasserted themselves. In September 1739 Wesley defined his belief in justification by faith in terms which would have delighted any Calvinist. 'No good work', he wrote, 'can be previous to justification, nor, consequently, a condition of it . . .

we are justified (being till that hour ungodly, and, therefore, incapable of doing any good work) by faith alone, faith without works, faith . . . including no good work.'[1] But in little more than three months Wesley had abandoned this extreme position on justification and had begun to move back to his earlier emphasis on the observance of religious duties and the performance of good works. In October 1739 there arrived in England a disciple of Count Zinzendorf, Philip Molther, who brought with him the doctrine of 'stillness', that the way to attain faith is not by attending church or receiving the sacrament, but by being still and waiting for Christ. Wesley recoiled with horror from a doctrine which rendered superfluous the ministry of the Church of England and the truth of which was at variance with his own experience. In conversation with Molther Wesley maintained that public worship, private devotions, fasting, and communion were 'means of grace' which 'do ordinarily convey God's grace to unbelievers'. Whereas Molther denied that there was any value in the unconverted performing works of charity or endeavouring to do 'spiritual good', Wesley countered that the unbeliever should 'do all the temporal good he can' and even 'spiritual good', for 'many fruits of the Spirit are given by those who have them not themselves'.[2] The Moravians, complained Wesley in a letter to them in 1740, taught that salvation by faith 'does not imply the proper taking away our sins, the cleansing our souls from all sin, but only the tearing the system of sin in pieces'. They preached unashamed Antinomianism, that 'one who is saved through faith is not obliged or bound to obey' the commandments of God.[3] In 1738 Wesley had attributed his conversion to the reading of Luther's preface to the *Epistle to the Romans*, but three years later he found Luther's *Comment on the Epistle to the Galatians* 'muddy and confused', the German reformer's denigration 'of good works and of the law of God . . . the real spring of the grand error of the Moravians'.[4]

If Wesley's approbation of Luther was short-lived, his antipathy towards Calvin was enduring. He never departed from the sentiments expressed in a letter to his mother in 1725, that the proposition that the 'vast majority of the world were only born to eternal death, without so much as a possibility of

---

[1] *Wesley's Journal*, ii. 275.   [2] Ibid. ii. 329–30.   [3] Ibid. ii. 491.
[4] Ibid. ii. 476.

avoiding it', was not consistent 'with either the divine justice or mercy'.[1] But George Whitefield had embraced Calvinist views shortly after his conversion in 1735, and by 1741 his disagreement with Wesley over the question of predestination was threatening 'to make an open (and probably irreparable) breach' between them.[2] Within a month of accepting Whitefield's invitation to take over his evangelistic work in Bristol in April 1739 Wesley was preaching 'strongly and explicitly' against what he called 'the horrible decree', and Whitefield was soon writing to Wesley to express concern at reports that a Methodist had been excluded from the society in Bristol 'because he holds predestination', and that Wesley was 'about to print a sermon' on the subject.[3] 'Silence on both sides will be best', Whitefield advised, but Wesley went ahead with publication and in the summer of 1739, while Whitefield was on his way to America, Wesley's sermon on 'Free Grace' appeared.

'The doctrine of predestination', argued Wesley, renders 'all preaching vain', tends to destroy holiness, militates against 'our zeal for good works', and makes the Christian revelation unnecessary. Worst of all, 'it represents the most holy God as worse than the devil, as both more false, more cruel, and more unjust'.[4] Whitefield was no match for Wesley when it came to theological controversy, and his reply, written on Christmas eve, 1740, went far to prove Wesley's case. On the one hand he argued that only those who held the doctrine of election could 'have a comfortable assurance of eternal salvation', on the other that such a doctrine did not undermine holiness because no one could be certain whether he was saved or not. In reply to Wesley's contention that the doctrine of predestination represented God as more cruel than the devil, Whitefield maintained that 'after Adam fell, and his posterity with him', God could with justice have condemned the whole of mankind to 'everlasting burnings'. You dishonour God by denying election,' Whitefield concluded. 'You plainly make salvation depend not on God's free-grace, but on man's free-will.'[5]

When Whitefield's reply to Wesley was printed, and when the Arminian Methodist leader found copies being distributed

---

[1] *Wesley's Letters*, i. 22.   [2] *Wesley's Journal*, ii. 441.

[3] *Wesley's Letters*, i. 303. Tyerman, *John Wesley*, i. 277, 312.

[4] *Wesley's Works*, vii. 373–86.   [5] *Whitefield's Journals*, pp. 571–88.

among his hearers at the Foundry in London, he picked one up and dramatically tore it in pieces before his congregation.[1] But in fact the two evangelists had too much respect for each other, and shared too common a purpose, to continue the dispute openly, and in the autumn of 1741 they were reconciled through the mediation of Howell Harris.[2] It was not until thirty years later, when Whitefield's restraining hand was about to be removed by death, that disagreements between the Arminian and Calvinist Evangelicals degenerated into bitter controversy. In 1768 the expulsion of six Calvinistic Methodists from St. Edmund Hall, Oxford, led to a pamphlet war in which Calvinists and Arminians both contended that theirs was the doctrine of the Church of England; the death of Whitefield in September 1770 occasioned further controversy when, in the course of a memorial sermon preached at Moorfields Tabernacle, Wesley spoke of the dead evangelist's 'fundamental doctrines' without mentioning election; and at the annual Wesleyan Methodist Conference in August of the same year Wesley defined his attitude to the relationship between faith and works in terms which the Calvinists characterized as 'the very doctrines of popery'.[3] 'Whoever desires to find favour with God should "cease from evil, and learn to do well"', read the Conference minutes. 'Whoever repents, should do "works meet for repentance".' The Christian was not saved by the merit of his works, but works were a condition of salvation.[4] To Calvinists such was not only Arminianism, it was rank Pelagianism, and Wesley even went so far as to defend the reputation of the fifth-century British heretic, 'a wise and an holy man'.[5] To Augustus Toplady, the Calvinist rector of Blagdon in Somerset, Wesley was worse even than Pelagius himself, without exception 'the most rancorous hater of the gospel system that ever appeared in England'.[6]

As the Calvinist controversy developed Wesley retraced his steps part way back to the convictions of his youth. 'I am often in doubt whether it would not be best for me to resume all my

---

[1] *Wesley's Journal*, ii. 421–2.   [2] Tyerman, *John Wesley*, i. 349.
[3] Ibid. iii. 77, 91.
[4] *Minutes of the Methodist Conferences* (1812), i. 96.
[5] *Wesley's Letters*, iv. 158, vi. 175. B. Semmel, *The Methodist Revolution* (1974), pp. 83–6.
[6] Tyerman, *John Wesley*, iii. 159.

Oxford rules, great and small,' he wrote to his brother Charles in 1772. 'I did then walk closely with God and redeem the time.'[1] 'What is usually called gospel preaching is the most useless, if not the most mischievous; a dull, yea or lively, harangue on the sufferings of Christ or salvation by faith without strongly inculcating holiness.'[2] The Wesleyan leaders do not 'talk of being accepted for our works', he assured another correspondent in 1774, 'but we all maintain we are not saved without works, that works are a condition (though not a meritorious cause) of final salvation'.[3] Such sentiments placed Wesley not only at loggerheads with the Moravians and Calvinists, they also caused friction between himself and his own followers. 'The doctrine of justification and salvation by faith are grievously abused by many Methodists,' he wrote to John Fletcher in 1775, and he was not thinking of the Calvinists.[4]

For Wesley the assurance of salvation was not the end of Christian experience but the beginning, the ultimate goal was entire sanctification, the hope of Christian perfection. Perfection he defined as 'the one undivided "fruit of the Spirit"', 'another name for universal holiness'.[5] While Christians could not be free from ignorance, error, 'slowness of understanding', or 'incoherency of thought', he argued, they should be 'free from outward sin'.[6] How can a man attain perfection while dwelling in a corruptible body? By ' "loving the Lord his God with all his heart, and with all his soul, and with all his mind". This is the sum of Christian perfection: it is all comprised in that one word, love.'[7] Wesley did not claim that he himself was perfect, and on one occasion explained that in the case of most Christians the soul attained perfection only in death,[8] but the aim of perfection was one which he sought constantly to keep before his converts less their assurance of salvation degenerate into Antinomian apathy. The ideal was derived partly from William Law and partly from Jeremy Taylor's *Rules of Holy Living and Dying*,[9] and is one of the many points of similarity between the views of Wesley and those of George Fox.

A month before his heart-warming experience in Aldersgate

---

[1] *Wesley's Letters*, vi. 6.   [2] Ibid. v. 345.   [3] Ibid. vi. 76.
[4] Ibid. vi. 175.   [5] *Wesley's Works*, vi. 413–14.   [6] Ibid. vi. 4–7.
[7] Ibid. vi. 413.   [8] *Wesley's Letters*, v. 38–9, 42.   [9] Ibid. iv. 298–9.

Street in 1738 Wesley had been persuaded by Peter Böhler of the need both for saving faith and for instantaneous conversion, and three weeks later he had written a reproachful letter to William Law in which he claimed that for two years he had been seeking to live by Law's *Christian Perfection*, only to find that it was 'a law by which a man cannot live'. Law, Wesley complained bitterly, had never told him of the need for saving faith, and suggested that the reason lay in the fact that 'you had it not yourself'.[1] But in subsequent years, partly as a reaction to his disputes with the Moravians in 1739–40, partly as a result of his own evangelistic experience, Wesley came increasingly to question the value of instantaneous conversion without subsequent pastoral care, even to doubt whether he had really been unconverted when he went to Georgia in 1736.[2] Significantly the qualification required of applicants for membership of the Wesleyan Methodist societies was not evidence of conversion but simply 'a desire to flee from the wrath to come', and in the case of four of the *Early Methodist Preachers*, Peter Jaco, Robert Roberts, Thomas Walsh, and Matthias Joyce, conversion was experienced after they had been admitted to Wesleyan societies and not before.[3] By 1767 Wesley had come to the opinion 'that a man may be saved who has [no] clear conceptions' of imputed righteousness, that even 'a mystic who denies justification by faith' may be saved, even Mr. Law.[4]

Wesley came to regard Christian perfection as the distinctive Wesleyan Methodist doctrine, but it was a legacy of his pre-conversion days, the logical development of an emphasis on works rather than faith, and as such it caused much heart-searching among his followers. 'The doctrine of perfection', complained one of his correspondents in 1758, 'has perplexed me much since some of our preachers have placed it in so dreadful a light: one of them affirming a believer till perfect is under the curse of God and in a state of damnation.'[5] But Wesley's chief problem was not with preachers who thus distorted his teaching but with preachers who ignored his

---

[1] Ibid. i. 239–40.   [2] *Wesley's Journal*, i. 422, n. 2.
[3] L. F. Church, *The Early Methodist People* (2nd edn., 1949), p. 185. *Early Methodist Preachers*, i. 268, iii. 59, iv. 240–1.
[4] *Wesley's Journal*, v. 243–4.   [5] *Wesley's Letters*, iv. 10.

insistence on Christian perfection altogether, and in few areas did he find it so difficult to enforce his authority on his followers. 'The more I converse with the believers in Cornwall, the more I am convinced that they have sustained great loss for want of hearing the doctrine of Christian perfection clearly and strongly enforced,' he complained in 1762.[1] But matters got worse rather than better. 'Shall we go on in asserting perfection against all the world', he asked his brother in 1768, 'or shall we quietly let it drop?'[2] Four years later he virtually admitted the battle was lost. 'I find almost all our preachers in every circuit have done with Christian perfection. They say they believe it; but they never preach it, or not once in a quarter.'[3]

In the eyes of rank-and-file Methodists there was no necessary connection between their conversion experiences and Wesley's teaching on Christian perfection, and they preferred the simple Evangelical message of justification by faith to their leader's constant exhortations to strive towards the goal of High Church ascetics. In theory Wesleyan Methodism, with its emphasis on the importance of good works and its hope of Christian perfection, and Calvinist Methodism, with its belief in predestination and its emphasis on free grace, were poles apart. But in practice the messages of the two branches of the movement were very similar, with the Arminians largely ignoring their leader's perfectionist teaching and the Calvinists, despite their predestinarian theology, in effect offering the Gospel to all their hearers.[4] 'Few of the Methodists are now in danger from imbibing error from the Church ministers', wrote Wesley in 1778, 'but they are in great danger of imbibing the grand error—Calvinism—from the Dissenting ministers.'[5]

5. THE 'OLD PURITAN FANATICISM REVIVED': METHODISM AND DISSENT

Wesley's failure to carry his followers back with him to the perfectionist ideal of William Law helps us to resolve the question posed by John Walsh in his essay on the 'Origins of the Evangelical Revival', of whether the movement owed more to 'High Church piety' or to 'the traditions of seventeenth century

---

[1] *Wesley's Journal*, iv. 529.　　[2] *Wesley's Letters*, v. 93.　　[3] Ibid. v. 314.
[4] Cf. Semmel, *The Methodist Revolution*, pp. 103–9.
[5] *Wesley's Letters*, vi. 326.

Puritanism'.[1] As far as John Wesley himself is concerned a case can be made out for either proposition, and there is truth both in V. H. H. Green's contention that 'theologically he remained a High Churchman to his dying day', and in A. Skevington Wood's argument that his spiritual development marked a 'reversion to type', to the Puritan and Dissenting tradition of his grandfathers.[2] Wesley grafted on to the High Church stock from which he was reared the Evangelical scions of conversion and justification by faith, and for most of his life both original stock and new graft grew side by side to the puzzlement of contemporaries and the perplexity of historians. But Wesley's spiritual development was unusual in this respect, and few of his followers retained or appreciated his continued respect for High Church devotional aspirations. For most early Methodists their indebtedness to High Church piety was by way of reaction, their obligations to Puritanism and Dissent were by way of example. The trustees of the charity schools and many of the Anglican clergy shared with William Law and the parents of the Wesleys a common high churchmanship which placed supreme importance on the attainment of holiness and at the same time made no secret of the awful penalties which awaited those who failed to reach that goal. But the religion thus instilled into a significant section of the population, and especially into children, aroused fears and spiritual aspirations which could not be satisfied by the observance of taboos and the performance of religious duties, and which could be met only by reverting to the Reformation emphasis on justification by faith. The biographies of eighteenth-century Evangelicals record the same attempts to live up to the requirements of a legalistic religion, the same agonies suffered by the failure to do, and the same relief provided by the realization that salvation comes through faith alone, as do the conversion experiences of the Independents collected by the Henry Walker and John Rogers in the middle of the previous century. In four cases the conversion of one of the *Early Methodist Preachers* was preceded by the reading of Puritan and Dissenting classics—especially Bunyan's *Grace Abounding* and Joseph

---

[1] *Essays in Modern English Church History*, pp. 138–60.

[2] V. H. H. Green, *John Wesley* (1964), p. 108. A. Skevington Wood, 'John Wesley's Reversion to Type', *Proceedings of the Wesley Historical Society*, xxxv (1965–6) 88.

Alleine's *Alarm to the Unconverted*.[1] And Wesley himself abridged and republished works by Puritan and Dissenting divines, praised them for their emphasis on 'evangelical repentance', and read with sympathy Daniel Neal's *History of the Puritans* and Edmund Calamy's *Abridgement of Mr. Baxter's Life*.[2] He had been brought up, he confessed, to call 'Presbyterian' anyone who claimed it was possible to have 'constant peace from a sense of forgiveness'.[3]

Contemporaries frequently commented on the similarities between Methodism and Puritanism or Dissent. Methodism, complained Bishop Warburton, was the 'old Puritan fanaticism revived'.[4] Thomas Jones, the Evangelical vicar of Cwm Iau in Monmouthsire, wrote enthusiastically to Whitefield in 1739 that the latter's teaching on the new birth 'is the good old Puritan doctrine that to my great concern I thought had quite forsaken the land till about fourteen months ago I met with some of your sermons'.[5] As for the American colonies, the revival there began among Presbyterian and state-supported Congregational churches which, more than either the established or Dissenting churches in England, preserved the true traditions of early-seventeenth-century Puritanism. When Jonathan Edwards's *Faithful Narrative* was introduced to English readers by the Congregational ministers Isaac Watts and John Guyse in 1737, it was with the comment that the doctrine preached by Edwards during the Northampton revival was 'the common plain Protestant doctrine of the Reformation, without stretching towards the Antinomians on the one side, or the Arminians on the other'.[6]

Why, then, when the revival crossed the Atlantic, did it begin not among the Dissenting churches but with the laymen and clergymen of the Church of England? Part of the answer lies in the terms of the Toleration Act, which gave the Dissenters liberty to hold services only in places licensed by a bishop, archdeacon, or magistrate, and such licence was unlikely to be granted to Dissenters to engage in the sort of field preaching

---

[1] *Early Methodist Preachers*, i. 273–4, ii. 111, iv. 8, v. 7, 9–10.
[2] J. A. Newton, *Methodism and the Puritans* (1964), pp. 8–9, 12.
[3] *Wesley's Journal*, i. 471.
[4] L. E. Elliott-Binns, *The Early Evangelicals* (1953), p. 120.
[5] Bennett, *Early Life of Harris*, pp. 57–8.
[6] I. Watts and J. Guyse, preface to Edwards, *Faithful Narrative*, p. vii.

which contributed so greatly to the Methodists' success.[1] But the Methodists had other, more important, advantages as members of the established church, advantages which they shared with the state-supported Congregationalists of New England but which were denied to the Welsh and English Dissenters. In England and Wales, where the turmoil of the Civil War was not forgotten and people still reflected with horror on the execution of Charles I, it was of considerable importance that Harris, Whitefield, and the Wesleys could present themselves to their audiences as loyal members of the Church of England. As it was, the evangelists had to suffer rough treatment at the hands of hostile mobs and indignities before unsympathetic magistrates, but such opposition would have increased tenfold had Howell Harris been a Baptist or John Wesley a Quaker. Whitefield recognized the advantage he had as an Anglican clergyman, and when he heard to his dismay that a fellow Evangelical clergyman proposed to resign his living he remonstrated that 'my being a minister of the Church of England, and preaching its Articles, is a means, under God, of drawing so many after me.'[2] John Wesley similarly argued that if the Methodists left the established church 'it would hinder multitudes of those who neither love nor fear God from hearing us at all'.[3] And when in 1753 he heard that one of his preachers had become a Congregational minister, he greeted the news with the comment, 'Did God design that this light should be hidden under a bushel? In a little, obscure, Dissenting meeting-house?'[4] There is a striking similarity between the spiritual experiences, the personalities, and the evangelistic zeal of Vavasor Powell and Howell Harris, and a marked contrast in the results they achieved. Powell left behind him a strong Congregational church in his native Radnorshire and perhaps another dozen churches throughout central Wales, but the Independents cannot have accounted for more than 3 per cent of the country's total population half a century later: Harris founded what was to become the principality's largest religious denomination. Part of the explanation lies in the fact that the way for Harris was prepared by the

---

[1] As late as the 1790s a Congregational minister was threatened with prosecution for preaching out of doors. R. F. G. Calder, 'The Congregational Society for Spreading the Gospel in England', *TCHS* xix (1960–4), 250.

[2] *Whitefield's Journals*, p. 256.   [3] *Wesley's Works*, xiii. 93.

[4] Jones, *Congregationalism in England*, p. 151.

charity schools, but also important is the fact that Powell, unlike Harris, represented a strange ecclesiastical organization supported by an unpopular political regime. The English and Welsh Methodists, in the middle third of the eighteenth century, had as Anglicans a potential constituency fifteen times the size of the Dissenting community. When Wesley noted in 1739 that the inhabitants of Wales 'are indeed ripe for the Gospel', it was of Anglican Wales that he was thinking: 'many of them can say both the Lord's Prayer and the Belief', he wrote, 'and some all the Catechism'.[1]

Could revival have come from the Dissenting denominations, even had the opportunity been there? There were, in addition, both organizational and theological factors which help to explain the failure of Dissent to contribute much to the initial impetus of the Evangelical revival. Neither the independent polity cherished by the Congregationalists and the Particular Baptists, nor the *de facto* independency of the Presbyterians, was geared to evangelism as was the connexional polity and circuit system of the Wesleyans. The author of the 'View of the Dissenting Interest' of 1732 complained of the London Congregationalists that 'there is not a church of this denomination [which] will encourage any others, one congregation only excepted',[2] and when Richard Davis had attempted to evangelize a large part of the south-east Midlands in the 1690s he had encountered the hostility of many of his fellow Dissenting ministers. Theologically, too, Dissent was handicapped: on the one hand by a Calvinism which saw evangelism as an attempt to alter the predestined decrees of a sovereign God, on the other by a rational Arminianism which was inclined to treat Christianity as a philosophy to be debated rather than as a faith to be shared.

That this is not the whole explanation, though, is obvious when it is remembered that Calvinism did not inhibit the evangelistic zeal of the Tennents, Edwards, Harris, or Whitefield, that Arminianism in the hands of the Wesleys did not threaten to become a rationalist creed. More important was the habit of mind the Dissenters had inherited from the Elizabethan Separatists, a habit of mind fostered by a century or more of persecution and fifty years of legalized but still restricted tolera-

---

[1] *Wesley's Journal*, ii. 296.
[2] 'A View of the Dissenting Interest', p. 92.

tion. The impulse behind Elizabethan Dissent was a desire not to convert the world but to separate from it, and it was an attitude which persisted into the eighteenth century, expressed, as Tudor Jones has pointed out, in the lines of Isaac Watts:

> We are a garden wall'd around
> Chosen and made peculiar ground.[1]

By withdrawing from the parish system the Dissenters had gained much, but something had also been lost. Unlike the Anglican Methodists they did not readily acknowledge a responsibility to men and women outside their own congregations. No early-eighteenth-century Dissenter regarded the world as his parish.

Though Harris and Whitefield shared the Calvinist beliefs of the Congregationalists and Particular Baptists, and the Wesleys held Arminian views similar to those of the Quakers, General Baptists, and many Presbyterians, they had arrived at them by different routes and they were to issue, at least initially, in far more dramatic results. The Calvinism and Evangelical Arminianism of the Methodists were not, as in the case of the Dissenters, intellectual creeds inherited from their forefathers, they were beliefs forged in the fires of deep spiritual tension and experience. Harris and Whitefield became Calvinists after, not before, their conversions, because they felt that Calvin's theology best explained the experiences through which they had passed.[2] And the word 'felt' is used deliberately, for the Methodists insisted that their faith was a matter not just of intellectual conviction but also of emotional experience. 'Although I had but little knowledge of the way of salvation by faith', wrote Howell Harris of his conversion, 'yet I was happy by feeling the blessedness of it in my own heart.'[3] The 'inward fruits of the spirit . . . must be *felt*', Wesley emphasized in 1739.[4] 'People begin not only to discern but to feel the doctrines of the Gospel,' wrote Whitefield of a visit to Exeter in 1743.[5] Geoffrey Nuttall, in distinguishing the Arminianism of the General Baptists and Presbyterians from that of the Wesleyan Methodists, contrasts

[1] Jones, *Congregationalism in England*, p. 109.
[2] Cf. Walsh, 'Origins of the Evangelical Revival', in *Essays in Modern English Church History*, p. 155.
[3] La Trobe, *Life of Harris*, p. 20.   [4] *Wesley's Journal*, ii. 251.
[5] Brockett, *Nonconformity in Exeter*, p. 120.

what he calls 'Arminianism of the head' and 'Arminianism of the heart'.[1] The contrast is important, but it is also important to realize that there was a similar contrast between Calvinism of the head and Calvinism of the heart. 'We preach mainly to the heart and spirit,' wrote Howell Harris in 1746. 'Unless God has your heart', he is reported to have said, 'he will cause the devils to maul you—body and soul, when the hour of death and the day of judgement comes.'[2]

It was thus not because they were Arminians, as Nuttall argues, but because they had undergone deeply emotional experiences that the Methodists were concerned with evangelism. Once they had been converted the early Methodists, Calvinist and Arminian alike, felt, as Howell Harris said, 'some insatiable desires after the salvation of poor sinners'.[3] In part the evangelistic impulse was a product of the growing benevolence of the age. Earlier Calvinists had not always been troubled by the prospect of the non-elect writhing in hell, but now Whitefield, passing 'a stage built for the cudgellers and wrestlers', 'could not bear to see so many dear souls for whom Christ died, ready to perish'.[4] There would come a time, though, when the descendants of the eighteenth-century Evangelicals would be too kind to believe that even 'cudgellers and wrestlers' would be consigned to hell, and then the missionary impulse would decline.

The Evangelical revival was initially an Anglican, not a Dissenting movement, but it was Dissent, not the Church of England, that reaped the ultimate benefit. The position of the eighteenth-century Methodists was not unlike that of the early-seventeenth-century advocates of non-separatist gathered churches, Henry Jacob, William Bradshaw, and William Ames. These Jacobites, like Harris and Wesley, protested their loyalty to the Church of England, shared in its communion, and asked only for the freedom to put into practice their distinctive religious views within the framework of the established church. But, as happened in the case of Henry Jacob, Harris's and the Wesleys' protestations of loyalty were not always believed by the rulers of the church, and their non-separating principles were not always accepted by their own followers. The logic of the

---

[1] Nuttall, *Puritan Spirit*, p. 78.
[2] Hughes-Edwards, 'Methodist Society in Wales', pp. 48, 50.
[3] La Trobe, *Life of Harris*, p. 14.   [4] *Whitefield's Journals*, p. 310.

situation was ultimately to drive the Methodists, as it had driven many of the Jacobites, out of the established church.

Harris and the Wesleys fought against this logic as long as they lived. Initially Harris had received a good deal of support from Dissenting ministers in south Wales and he felt a greater spiritual affinity with Nonconformists than with many of his own church.[1] In the later 1730s and early 1740s he was under considerable pressure from his Dissenting allies to separate from the Church of England. William Herbert, a Baptist minister of Tresgoed in Breconshire, claimed that Harris's good work would be undone by the Anglican church: he likened the Welsh Methodist leader to a farmer who laboured 'hard to cure many scabby sheep of the rot', but, when he had made them almost well, turned ''em to a field full of scabby ones which made 'em as rot and scabby as ever'.[2] 'I am tossed to and fro by people of different views,' exclaimed Harris in his diary,[3] but in the end he remained loyal to the church of his fathers. During the 1740s Welsh Calvinistic Methodism became an almost exclusively Anglican movement. Whereas at its first Association meeting at Dugoedydd in Carmarthenshire in 1742 it was resolved that members were at liberty to communicate either in their parish churches or with the Dissenters,[4] in 1745 an exhorter was told to stop his activities until he had made up his mind whether he was a Methodist or a Dissenter, and three years later Nonconformist ministers were prevented from speaking in Methodist societies in north Wales and Methodist exhorters were forbidden to preach in Dissenting meetings. The Calvinistic Methodists, wrote Harris, were resolved not to call themselves 'a church or sect', but to remain 'in the established church till turned out'.[5]

There was even less likelihood of the Wesleys' joining the Dissenters. John Wesley did not share Harris's sympathy with Quakers and Baptists—the former feature in the *Journal* chiefly as potential converts, the latter are referred to consistently by the opprobrious and inaccurate name of 'Anabaptist' —and he disliked both the Calvinism of the Congregationalists

[1] Bennett, *Early Life of Harris*, p. 149.
[2] Evans, 'The Welsh Awakening', pp. 68–9.
[3] Bennett, *Early Life of Harris*, p. 105.
[4] G. M. Roberts, ed., *Selected Treveka Letters, 1742–7* (Caernarvon, 1956), i. 1.
[5] Hughes-Edwards, 'Methodist Society in Wales', pp. 301, 305.

and the Socinian tendencies of the Presbyterians.[1] The Church of England, John Wesley believed, 'is nearer the Scriptural plan than any other in Europe',[2] and Charles was even more unswerving in his loyalty to the established church. Charles constantly worried that John was allowing himself to be pushed into separation from the Church of England, and wrote in 1772 that whereas 'my brother's first object was the Methodists, and then the Church; mine was first the Church and then the Methodists'.[3] But John believed that the essence of conformity lay in attending the services and participating in the communion of the established church: like Harris he tried to insist that Methodist meetings should be held only at times at which they did not conflict with the services of the parish church, and that Methodists who had been brought up as Anglicans—as were the vast majority—should receive the sacrament only at the hands of clergymen of the Church of England.

But in thus insisting on conformity to the established church, Harris and the Wesleys often strained the loyalty of their own followers. Men and women who had worshipped in parish churches for years without finding relief from their guilt or freedom from their fears did not always see the point of continuing to worship and communicate in those churches now that the Methodists had pointed the way of salvation. Nor was the attitude adopted by many Anglican bishops and clergy one to encourage continued adherence to the Church of England. Whitefield frequently found Anglican pulpits closed to him, and in 1739 the chancellor of Bristol even threatened him with excommunication.[4] In Wales Howell Harris was refused ordination by the Bishop of St. David's in 1736 and twice in 1739; William Williams, the greatest Welsh hymn writer and author of 'Guide me, O Thou Great Jehovah', was ordained deacon in 1740 but was never ordained priest; and Peter Williams was similarly refused ordination as a priest.[5] Daniel Rowland, who never rose above the status of curate, was deprived of his position at Llangeitho in 1763, and Thomas Charles, the most celebrated of the second generation of Welsh

[1] *Wesley's Works*, xiii. 198.   [2] *Wesley's Letters*, vii. 28.
[3] F. Baker, *John Wesley and the Church of England* (1970), p. 207.
[4] *Whitefield's Journals*, p. 218.
[5] Evans, 'The Welsh Awakening', p. 65, Hughes-Edwards, 'Methodist Society in Wales', pp. 42, 45.

Calvinistic Methodist leaders, was ejected from his curacy at Llan ym Mawddwy in Merioneth in 1784 and found it impossible to secure another post in the established church in north Wales.[1]

A few clergymen incited riots against the Methodists, others refused them the sacrament, more lambasted them from their pulpits.

I fain would prevent the members here from leaving the church [wrote Wesley of his native Epworth in 1788] but I cannot do it. As Mr. G[ibson] is not a pious man, but rather an enemy to piety, who frequently preaches against the truth, and those that hold and love it, I cannot, with all my influence, persuade them either to hear him, or to attend the sacrament administered by him. If I cannot carry this point even while I live, who then can do it when I die? And the case of Epworth is the case of every church where the minister neither loves nor preaches the Gospel.[2]

In spirit the Methodists of Epworth were already Dissenters and, as Wesley recognized, their position was typical of many Wesleyan societies throughout the country. From the point of view of organization the Wesleyan Methodists and the Dissenters had little in common. True, from 1740 Wesley made use of lay preachers and organized them on a circuit system not unlike that of the Quakers, but Wesley maintained an autocratic control over his societies in a way which was quite foreign to the spirit of Old Dissent. Membership of the societies was regulated either by Wesley personally or by assistants appointed by him, society leaders and stewards were appointed and dismissed in the same way, itinerant preachers were nominated and stationed by Wesley alone, and the governing body of Wesleyanism, the annual Conference, was composed of those preachers whom Wesley saw fit to invite. 'As long as I live', wrote Wesley in 1790, 'the people shall have no share in choosing either stewards or leaders among the Methodists. . . . We are no republicans, and never intend to be.'[3] When it was complained that Wesley had too much power, he retorted that he summoned preachers to Conference 'of my own free choice . . . to *advise*, not *govern* me'. At no time, he said, had he divested himself of that power

---

[1] Evans, 'The Welsh Awakening', p. 210. D. E. Jenkins, *Life of Thomas Charles* (Denbigh, 1908), i. 477.
[2] *Wesley's Journal*, vii. 414.   [3] *Wesley's Letters*, viii. 196.

'which the providence of God had cast upon me, without any design or choice of mine'.[1]

Howell Harris, as a layman, never had the authority over the Welsh Calvinistic Methodists which Wesley had over the Arminians, and he lost control of the Association in 1750. The Welsh Methodists also lacked a national ruling body comparable to the Wesleyan Conference: there were separate Associations for north and south Wales and it was not until 1864 that an annual General Assembly for the whole principality was established.[2] But the Welsh Calvinistic Methodists, like the Wesleyans, repudiated independency, and a hierarchy of meetings was set up comparable to that of the Quakers and the Scottish kirk. Each exhorter in charge of a society had to present a report of its spiritual condition to the Monthly Meeting for the county, the Monthly Meeting had to report to the Quarterly Association for north or south Wales, and it was the Quarterly Association which became the most powerful organ of Calvinistic Methodism: it gave and took away the right to exhort, appointed exhorters to societies and superintendents over groups of societies, and acted as a court of appeal.[3]

While the polity of the Methodists was less democratic than that of Dissent, in matters of discipline the Methodists were much closer to the stricter Dissenters than they were to their fellow Anglicans. Although the condition for membership of a Wesleyan society was not, as among the Baptists or Congregationalists, evidence of conversion but merely a desire for salvation, members had to prove the sincerity of their quest by their conduct: by doing good works, by attending public worship, and by observing a long list of negative rules. Wesleyan Methodists were expected to avoid drunkenness and the drinking of spirits, 'putting on of gold or costly apparel', 'taking such diversions as cannot be used in the name of the Lord Jesus', 'singing those songs or reading those books which do not tend to the knowledge of the love of God', 'giving or taking things on usury', 'laying up treasures upon earth', and 'profaning the day of the Lord'.[4] That such rules were obeyed was guaranteed by

[1] *Minutes of the Methodist Conferences*, i. 60.

[2] Williams, *Welsh Calvinistic Methodism*, pp. 215–16.

[3] Ibid., p. 201. Hughes-Edwards, 'Methodist Society in Wales', pp. 246–7, 266, 281.

[4] Church, *Early Methodist People*, pp. 185–6.

dividing the societies into bands and classes—the former for those who claimed to have 'remission of sins', the latter for all members of the society. Bands could be composed of as few as four people, classes of as many as twelve: both met weekly under the leadership of a man or woman who was entrusted with the task of inquiring into the spiritual life of his members. The class-meeting developed into a fellowship for prayer, consolation and advice, but the band-meeting was a much more forbidding occasion at which members were asked to relate the temptations they had met with since the previous meeting, the sins they had committed, and the victories they had won.[1] Among the Welsh Calvinistic Methodists conditions of membership were even more rigorous: an applicant had to produce evidence not only of a holy life but also of conversion, and in addition had to agree publicly to a Calvinist creed.[2] Discipline was maintained by means of the reports which the exhorters in local societies had to pass on to the Monthly Associations, reports which in the early years of the movement often detailed the spiritual development of each individual member.[3]

6. 'A NEW SECT OF PRESBYTERIANS': THE BREAK WITH THE CHURCH OF ENGLAND

The strictly disciplined, tightly knit, exclusive Methodist societies thus had a close affinity with the gathered churches of the Baptists and Congregationalists and, notwithstanding the protestations of Harris and the Wesleys, stood in direct contradiction to the Anglican principle of the identity of church and nation. And bit by bit the Methodists, like the non-separating Congregationalists before them, were forced into a Separatist position. Except in parishes where the clergyman was sympathetic, as at Llangeitho while Daniel Rowland was still curate, they had to erect their own meeting-houses: Wesley laid the foundation stone of his first 'preaching-house' at Bristol in May 1739, in November he took possession of the ruinous cannon foundry in Moorfields which was to become his London headquarters, and in 1742 the first Welsh Calvinistic Methodist

---

[1] Ibid., pp. 150–6.
[2] Hughes-Edwards, 'Methodist Society in Wales', p. 221.
[3] Williams, *Welsh Calvinistic Methodism*, p. 33.

society-house was built at Groeswen in Glamorgan.[1] But such places were exposed to prosecution under the Conventicle Act unless they were registered under the Toleration Act, and although Wesley argued initially that since Methodists did not dissent from the established church they did not need the Toleration Act, by the 1750s he had come to recognize that in some cases registration was necessary.[2] From the late 1750s onwards it became increasingly common for Methodist preaching-houses to be registered under the Toleration Act, and although Wesley tried to insist that when his followers made application for licences they did not do so as 'Protestant Dissenters', in some cases magistrates would grant licences only if the offending words were used.[3] In the last year of his life Wesley was troubled by the case of a poor Lincolnshire man, whom he supposed 'was not worth twenty shillings', who was fined £20 under the Conventicle Act on the ground that 'Methodists could have no relief from the Act of Toleration because they went to church'.[4]

Having got their own meeting-houses, Methodists were increasingly reluctant to attend the ministrations of clergymen who ridiculed their work, denounced their teaching, and refused them communion. As early as 1745 the Calvinistic Methodists at Groeswen insisted on holding communion services in their new society-house and broke away from the Association to form a Congregational church.[5] A possible solution to the problem, which Harris contemplated but did not like, was for the sacrament to be administered in the meeting-houses by sympathetic Anglican clergymen.[6] Ever since 1739 the Wesleys had felt obliged to administer the sacrament in private homes and preaching houses to Methodists who had been refused communion in their parish churches, and Howell Davies followed their example in Pembrokeshire in the 1750s.[7] But it was a solution which became increasingly in-

[1] *Wesley's Journal*, ii. 197, 316, 319 n. Tyerman, *John Wesley*, i. 271–3. Hughes-Edwards, 'Methodist Society in Wales', p. 102.

[2] *Wesley's Works*, viii. 113. Baker, *Wesley and the Church of England*, pp. 95, 174.

[3] Baker, *Wesley and the Church of England*, pp. 198–9.

[4] *Wesley's Letters*, viii. 231.

[5] Hughes-Edwards, 'Methodist Society in Wales', p. 120.

[6] Jenkins, *Calvinistic Methodist Holy Orders*, p. 145.

[7] L. F. Church, *More About Early Methodist People* (1949), pp. 256–7. Jenkins, *Calvinistic Methodist Holy Orders*, p. 148.

adequate as the number of Methodist societies grew and the number of clergymen prepared to serve them declined. In 1760 three Methodist preachers in Norwich provoked a crisis in the Wesleyan movement by taking it upon themselves to administer the Lord's Supper, and on numerous occasions in the last thirty years of his life Wesley had to intervene to stop his societies from leaving the Church of England.[1] At Deptford in 1787 he only got his way by telling the local Methodists that if they insisted on holding services at the same time as those in the parish church they would never see his face again.[2] The Wesleyan Conference itself repeatedly declined to separate from the established church, but such determination, Wesley feared, would last only until he was 'removed into a better world'.[3]

It is not true, though, as Ronald Knox maintained, that the Methodists were solely responsible for their eventual secession from the Church of England.[4] Over two important issues—the right of Anglican clergymen to assist the Methodists outside their own parishes, and the ordination of Methodist preachers— they were pushed towards Dissent by the attitude of the Anglican establishment. Until the last quarter of the century it was assumed that sympathetic Anglican clergymen were free to preach at Methodist meetings and to officiate at their communion services, but in 1777 doubt was thrown on the legality of the actions of clergymen who helped the Methodists in this way. In that year two Evangelical clergymen began preaching in a chapel in Spa Fields in London, but the local incumbent, a pluralist named William Sellon, disputed their right to preach in a parish without the consent of its minister and in a building which had not been consecrated by a bishop. Sellon's view was upheld in the Bishop of London's Consistorial Court and the chapel was closed. In order to maintain the work the Countess of Huntingdon intervened and purchased the chapel in the belief that her domestic chaplains would be safe from Sellon's antipathy. Sellon though, challenged Lady Huntingdon's right to allow her domestic chaplains to officiate at public services and again his view was upheld by the Consistorial Court. As a result

---

[1] Baker, *Wesley and the Church of England*, pp. 175–9. *Wesley's Journal*, v. 245, vi. 90, vii. 60, 217.
[2] *Wesley's Journal*, vii. 232.   [3] Ibid. vii. 192.   [4] Knox, *Enthusiasm*, p. 506.

Lady Huntingdon's leading preachers broke away from her Connexion and those that remained seceded from the established church. Henceforward Lady Huntingdon's chapels were licensed as Dissenting meeting-houses and from 1783 the Connexion ordained its own ministers.[1]

Even before Sellon questioned the right of Anglican clergymen to preach and officiate in other men's parishes, the number of clergymen prepared to co-operate with the Wesleyans was dwindling. An attempt by John Wesley to secure a union of Evangelical clergy in 1764 came to nothing, and after the publication of the minutes of the Wesleyan Conference of 1770, with its declaration that works were a condition of salvation, relations between the Wesleyans and the Evangelical clergy, who were for the most part Calvinists, deteriorated rapidly. Ties between the Wesleyans and the established church could have been strengthened had the bishops been prepared to ordain itinerant Methodist preachers to the ministry, but this even the most sympathetic of the bishops consistently refused to do, and matters came to a head with the outbreak of the War of American Independence in 1776. The subsequent return to England of most Anglican clergymen in the colonies left some 15,000 American Methodists without facilities for communion or baptism, and the recognition of American independence in 1783 created the further problem of organizing Methodism in a country where the king's writ no longer ran. As early as 1746 Wesley had been convinced by Lord King's *Enquiry into the Constitution . . . of the Primitive Church* that 'bishops and presbyters are (essentially) of one order', and after the Bishop of London had declined to ordain a Methodist preacher for service in America Wesley took the matter into his own hands. In 1784 he published a revised and drastically reduced version of the Prayer Book for use by the American Methodists, ordained Richard Whatcoat and Thomas Vasey as presbyters, and 'set apart' Thomas Coke as superintendent of American Methodism. Wesley followed this up by ordaining three preachers for Scotland in 1785, and in 1788 ordained Alexander Mather for service in England.[2]

Despite Charles Wesley's protests that the Arminian Metho-

[1] *Life of Countess of Huntingdon*, ii. 305–13, 436.
[2] Baker, *Wesley and the Church of England*, pp. 180–96, 241–4, 259–80.

dists were now no more than 'a new sect of Presbyterians', John insisted that his ordinations did not involve separation from the Church of England, and that many of his followers shared his view is confirmed by the fact that after his death they continued to dispute whether they should or should not continue to communicate with the established church. In 1792 Wesleyan preachers in the West Riding, east Midlands, and on Teesside voted to remain in the Church of England, but the preachers of Newcastle 'resolved to administer the ordinance [of holy communion] to such of their community as shall desire'.[1] Divisions ran so deep at the Conference of that year that members resorted to drawing lots to preserve the peace, but the lot chosen, 'that the sacrament should not be administered in our Connexion for the ensuing year', merely postponed a decision. By 1793 Conference recognized that if it did not allow those societies which wanted to receive the Lord's Supper from their own preachers to do so, it would lose them, and it sanctioned the administration of the sacrament in places 'where the society is unanimous for it'. But this concession failed to satisfy the radicals, especially when accompanied by the entreaty that Wesleyan Methodists remain in the Church of England, and Conference met in 1795 apprehensive that the Connexion was near to disruption. A committee of nine was elected to try to end the crisis, and after long arguments running through six evenings it produced a 'Plan of Pacification' which was accepted unanimously by the Conference. It was agreed that the Lord's Supper might be administered in any chapel where a majority of trustees on the one hand, and a majority of stewards and leaders on the other, were in favour, and in other chapels where it was already the custom.[2] The 'Plan of Pacification' did not in fact bring peace, but it guaranteed that the Wesleyan Methodists of the early nineteenth century, if not exactly Dissenters, would for the most part not be Anglicans either.

The Welsh Calvinistic Methodists were the last of the Methodist bodies to sever their formal links with the established church. They had been more successful than either Lady Huntingdon's Connexion or the Wesleyans in retaining the

---

[1] Wearmouth, *Methodism and the Common People*, p. 127.
[2] *Minutes of the Methodist Conferences*, i. 262, 279–80, 321–3.

services of a small group of episcopally ordained clergymen—in the first decade of the nineteenth century they still had the support of about nineteen clergymen, all but three of whom were in south Wales[1]—and this fact explains why the Welsh Calvinistic Methodists were the most reluctant of all the Methodists to break with the Church of England. But the question of the right of the Connexion's preachers to administer the sacraments was raised at the South Wales Association at Fishguard in 1808, and the issue was dramatized by a confrontation which is alleged to have taken place at the North Wales Association at Bala in June 1810. Ebenezer Morris of Cardiganshire is said to have challenged the moderator Thomas Charles, hitherto an opponent of the ordination of lay preachers, 'Which is the more important, preaching the Gospel or administering the sacraments?' 'The most important work is preaching the Gospel', replied Thomas Charles. 'Then,' said Morris, 'we are one.'[2] Charles's biographer, D. E. Jenkins, has questioned whether it was Morris's intervention which changed Charles's mind. Other factors, he suggests, were at work: the failure of the Welsh clergy to support the British and Foreign Bible Society, in whose foundation he had had a major share, and the threat posed to itinerant Methodists by Lord Sidmouth's proposal that only preachers in charge of a congregation should enjoy the benefits of the Toleration Act.[3] But whatever the cause, both Charles and the North Wales Association agreed to the ordination of Methodist preachers in June 1810, the South Wales Association followed suit in November, and the first ordinations took place at Bala in June 1811. Ten Anglican clergymen and a handful of societies seceded from the Associations, but the vast majority of Calvinistic Methodists followed the lead of the Associations out of the established church.[4]

7. 'A FRENZICAL KIND OF ZEAL': THE IMPACT OF THE REVIVAL ON OLD DISSENT

The Evangelical revival not only produced new Nonconformist denominations, it also had a revitalizing effect on some sections

---

[1] Williams, *Welsh Calvinistic Methodism*, pp. 182, 200.
[2] Ibid., p. 192. Jenkins, *Thomas Charles*, iii. 258–9.
[3] Jenkins, *Calvinistic Methodist Holy Orders*, pp. 180–1, 186–8.
[4] Ibid., p. 206. Williams, *Welsh Calvinistic Methodism*, pp. 198–9.

of Old Dissent. Initially the disdain with which the Wesleys in particular regarded Dissent was reciprocated. Calvinist Dissenters distrusted the Wesleys' Arminianism, liberal Dissenters suspected the Methodists of Antinomianism, and Dissenters of all shades of opinion disliked Methodist 'enthusiasm'.[1] Presbyterian ministers, even Calvinist Presbyterians, denounced Whitefield and his followers as 'false prophets', and Congregational and Baptist churches refused membership and communion to people who attended Methodist meetings.[2] In Dudley and Devizes Dissenters were said to have stirred up the mob against the Methodists, and John Bennett complained that at Woodley in Cheshire Dissenters tried to press-gang Methodists into the army.[3] Of the prominent Dissenting ministers Philip Doddridge was unusual in his friendship with John Wesley and the Countess of Huntingdon,[4] and more typical, at least in the early years of Methodism, was the attitude of Samuel Newton, Independent minister at Norwich, who complained to his fellow Congregationalists in 1766 that for twenty years the Methodists had thinned their congregations, disturbed the order of their churches, and infected numbers of their hearers 'with a frenzical kind of zeal that has raised them above sentiment and instruction'.[5]

In the long run, though, Samuel Newton's pessimism proved to be unwarranted. Although some Dissenting churches may have suffered the loss of members who were attracted by the novelty of Methodism in the 1740s and 1750s, by the 1770s it was becoming clear that these losses were being more than compensated for by the influx into the ranks of Dissent of Evangelicals who could not reconcile their conversion with continued membership of the established church. The refusal of Howell Harris and the Wesleys to break with the Church of England and disagreements over theology led to frequent secessions to Dissent. In Wales the Calvinistic Methodist society at Brychgoed near Defynnog in Breconshire seceded in 1742, that

---

[1] Kirke, *Diary of James Clegg*, pp. 75–6. *Broadmead Records*, pp. 309–10.

[2] Tyerman, *Whitefield*, ii. 113–14. *Baptist Quarterly*, iv (1928–9), 70; x (1940–1), 283. *Broadmead Records*, p. 306.

[3] Jackson, *Charles Wesley*, i. 363, 416, 464.

[4] *Wesley's Journal*, iii. 206.

[5] S. Newton, *The Causes and Reasons of the Present Declension among the Congregational Churches* (1766), pp. 9–10.

at Groeswen followed three years later, and several of the early exhorters—Evan Williams, Milbourn Bloom, Morgan John Lewis—received from the Dissenters the ordination denied them by the Methodists.[1] In England John Wesley had frequent occasion to lament Methodist losses to the Baptists: at Wednesbury and Tipton in 1751, in Horncastle, Heptonstall, Bingley, and Haworth in 1766, at Yarmouth in 1769.[2] Dissatisfaction with Wesley's Arminianism led to secessions in Leeds, Halifax, Rotherham, and Whitby which resulted in the foundation of Congregational churches, while John Bennett, the man who defeated John Wesley in the race to marry Grace Murray, also turned Calvinist and was responsible for transforming the Methodist society at Bolton into a Congregational church.[3] At least a score of the converts of the Evangelical clergymen Henry Venn of Huddersfield, William Grimshaw of Haworth, and Thomas Jones of Creaton ended up as Dissenting ministers; four Congregational churches in Yorkshire, at Huddersfield, Holmfirth, Honley, and Brighouse, owed their origins to Venn's converts, and a fifth, that at Booth, to those of Grimshaw; while in the West Country the Congregational churches at Truro and Malmesbury were similarly the products of the zeal of Evangelical Anglican clergymen.[4] But the most fruitful sources of Dissenting recruits were the Methodist societies founded by Whitefield, Lady Huntingdon, and independent evangelists such as David Taylor and Captain Jonathan Scott.

Whitefield always enjoyed better relations with Dissent than did either Harris or the Wesleys: early in his career he irritated his critics by his 'free conversation with many of the serious Dissenters', he was on particularly good terms with the Quakers of the Bristol area, and in 1764 he did not scruple to register his Moorfields Tabernacle and Tottenham Court chapel as 'In-

---

[1] Hughes-Edwards, 'Methodist Society in Wales', pp. 302, 141. Evans, 'The Welsh Awakening', p. 135.

[2] *Wesley's Journal*, iii. 519, v. 165, 179, 180, 347.

[3] Miall, *Congregationalism in Yorkshire*, pp. 267, 305, 341–2, 379–80. Tyerman, *Whitefield*, ii. 257 n. E. A. Payne, 'A Yorkshire Story', *Baptist Quarterly*, xix (1961–2), 367–8. Halley, *Lancashire*, ii. 443 n. Jones, *Congregationalism in England*, p. 155.

[4] J. D. Walsh, 'Methodism at the end of the Eighteenth Century', in *History of the Methodist Church*, i. 294. Miall, *Congregationalism in Yorkshire*, pp. 150, 232. J. Kent, *Jabez Bunting, the last Wesleyan* (1955), p. 8. *VCH Wiltshire*, iii. 131.

dependent' meeting-houses.[1] His failure to unite his societies by any strong connexional ties, coupled with his Calvinism, ensured that sooner or later most of the societies he founded would become Congregational churches: the Calvinistic Methodist societies at Rodborough and Dursley in Gloucestershire became Independent churches in 1774 and 1784, the societies at Plymouth and Devonport both became Congregational churches in 1797, the Portsmouth Tabernacle became the seat of the first Independent church in the town, the Moorfields Tabernacle had become Congregational by the end of the eighteenth century, and the Tottenham Court chapel was to become the home of one of the leading Congregational churches of the metropolis.[2] Similarly the failure of the Countess of Huntingdon's plan to provide her Connexion with an organization comparable to that of the Welsh Calvinistic Methodists facilitated the passage of many of her chapels and ministers to Congregationalism. Her societies in Chichester, Mevagissey, Peterborough, Preston, Reading, West Bromwich, Wigan, and York all became Congregational churches; many of the students of Trevecca College passed into the Independent ministry; and by converting, training, and ordaining William Roby, Lady Huntingdon's Connexion was responsible for the early spiritual development of the man who was to revitalize Lancashire Congregationalism.[3] Jonathan Scott, who claimed descent from the Scottish king John Balliol and was a captain in the dragoons, was also converted in one of Lady Huntingdon's chapels—by William Romaine at Oathall in Sussex around 1765.[4] He sold his commission in 1769 and went to live at his wife's home at Wollerton in Shropshire where he gathered an Independent church, and from his base at Wollerton went out on evangelistic tours which contributed to the founding of twenty-two

[1] *Whitefield's Journals*, pp. 90, 234–7. C. E. Watson, 'Whitefield and Congregationalism', *TCHS* viii (1920–3), 242.

[2] C. E. Welch, 'Andrew Kinsman's Churches at Plymouth', *Report and Transactions of the Devonshire Association*, xcvii (1965), 233–4. Welch, *Two Calvinistic Methodist Chapels*, p. xv. Jones, *Congregationalism in England*, pp. 149–50. Belden, *Whitefield*, p. 81.

[3] Halley, *Lancashire*, ii. 467, 469. T. Coleman, *Memorials of the Independent Churches in Northamptonshire* (1853), p. 352. Miall, *Congregationalism in Yorkshire*, p. 388. A. G. Matthews, *Congregational Churches of Staffordshire* (1924), p. 143. Walsh in *History of the Methodist Church*, i. 295.

[4] *Life of Countess of Huntingdon*, i. 317–18.

Congregational churches in Shropshire, Staffordshire, Cheshire, and Lancashire.[1]

The Baptists, too, benefited from Lady Huntingdon's activities. One of her servants at Donnington Park, a man named David Taylor, was converted, probably by the Moravians, in 1741, and was encouraged by the countess to go out to preach to the farmers and labourers of the neighbouring Leicestershire villages. So impressed was Lady Huntingdon by David Taylor's efforts that she released him from his duties at Donnington Park to enable him to devote his time fully to evangelism, and he travelled into Derbyshire, Cheshire, Lancashire, and Yorkshire and by November 1743 had joined the Moravians.[2] But he left behind him in Leicestershire a group of converts who organized themselves into a religious society and in 1745 built a meeting-house at Barton-in-Fabis near Market Bosworth which they registered as 'Independent'.[3] The Barton society, though, was independent by virtue of its isolation from other churches rather than from conviction, and its leaders, the blacksmith Joseph Donisthorpe, the farm labourer and wool-comber Samuel Deacon, and the schoolmaster William Kendrick, consulted the Bible rather than the traditions of any existing denomination when they drew up rules for their society. In 1755 they came to the conclusion that infant baptism was unscriptural, and so Donisthorpe baptized Kendrick, Kendrick baptized Donisthorpe, and they then administered the ordinance to the rest of their members.[4] From Barton evangelists went out to the neighbouring towns and villages and by 1760 the membership had so grown that it was decided to divide into five separate churches with centres at Barton, Melbourne, Kegworth, Loughborough, and Kirkby Woodhouse.[5]

The Barton Baptists, perhaps because of the Moravian influence of David Taylor, were Arminian rather than Calvinist in their theology. So, too, was another Taylor, Dan Taylor, a collier from Northowram near Halifax and a former Wesleyan

---

[1] D. Macfadyen, 'The Apostolic Labours of Captain Jonathan Scott', *TCHS* iii (1907–8), 48–66.

[2] Taylor, *General Baptists*, ii. 3–4. Hassé, *The Moravians*, p. 72. *Wesley's Journal*, iii. 112.

[3] Taylor, *General Baptists*, ii. 16, 18.

[4] Ibid. ii. 31.   [5] Ibid. ii. 44–54.

preacher. Dan Taylor had broken with Wesley over unspecified questions of discipline and theology and in 1762 became preacher to a group of Methodist seceders who met at Wadsworth near Heptonstall in the West Riding. Like the Barton Baptists, Taylor and his followers had nothing but the Bible to guide them in the ordering of their society and they too came to see the necessity for believers' baptism. The local Particular Baptist minsters refused to baptize Taylor as he was an Arminian, but he received baptism at the hands of the pastor of a General Baptist church at Gamston in Nottinghamshire, joined the Lincolnshire Association of General Baptists, and in 1764 helped to build a meeting-house at Birchcliffe, labouring 'daily at the work with his own hands'.[1] But Taylor, the erstwhile Methodist, found both the conservative customs and the liberal theology of many of the General Baptists uncongenial. He had much more sympathy with the evangelistic fervour of the Barton Baptists, with whom he came into contact around 1765, and he resolved to unite the Evangelical churches of the existing General Baptist denomination with the Barton Baptists and their associated churches in a new organization. In Whitechapel in June 1770 eight preachers connected with the Barton Baptists and their satellites met with Dan Taylor and nine ministers of old General Baptist churches to form the New Connexion of General Baptists. Six articles were drawn up eschewing Calvinism on the one hand and Unitarianism on the other, and all ministers who joined the Connexion were required to subscribe to the articles and to give an account of their religious experience.[2]

Several attempts were made to heal the breach between the New Connexion and the old General Baptists. Difficulties arose because ministers of the New Connexion accused members of the old of denying 'the proper atonement of Christ'; because the old General Baptists insisted that the new should abstain from the eating of blood and should practise the laying on of hands when admitting new members.[3] In 1786, though, the New Connexion appears to have agreed to send a representative to the old

---

[1] Ibid. ii. 70–6. J. H. Wood, *A Condensed History of the General Baptists of the New Connexion* (1847), p. 182.

[2] Taylor, *General Baptists*, ii. 134–43.

[3] Ibid. ii. 216. *Minutes of the General Baptist Assembly*, ii. 183.

General Baptist Assembly, and Dan Taylor attended most assemblies between 1787 and 1802 and even took the chair on five occasions.[1] But when, in 1802, William Vidler, a Unitarian and an advocate of universal restoration, was admitted to the General Baptist Assembly, Dan Taylor and the New Connexion severed all relations with the old.[2]

Despite the rupture of 1802, the New Connexion of General Baptists owed a good deal to the denomination of Helwys and Murton. By June 1817, seven months after Dan Taylor had died at the age of seventy-seven, the New Connexion had 6,846 members in seventy churches, of which twenty-two were old General Baptist foundations and a further four had been constituted as a result of secessions from old General Baptist churches.[3] Those twenty-two churches included some of the oldest in the denomination, among them the church at St. Ives in Huntingdonshire, the descendant of the Fenstanton church founded by Henry Denne in 1645, and the church in Whitechapel which traced its lineage back to a congregation which had met on Tower Hill during the Interregnum, and of which Dan Taylor was pastor from 1785 until his death.[4] Despite the Moravian and Methodist influences on many of their churches, the New Connexion churches were independent in polity, and although they held annual associations, as did the old General Baptists, such associations claimed no authority over individual churches. The annual association which met at Boston in 1816 reaffirmed that membership of the Connexion should be dependent on adherence to the six articles of 1770,[5] but in practice this did not prevent liberal views from gaining ground in the New Connexion as they had gained ground in the old.

The Evangelical revival also had important consequences for the Particular Baptists. Some Particular Baptist ministers owed their conversions to Wesleyans, more had been awakened by Whitefield,[6] but the most decisive Evangelical influence on the Particular Baptists was that of Jonathan Edwards. By the middle of the eighteenth century Particular Baptists were

---

[1] *Minutes of the General Baptist Assembly*, ii. 188.

[2] Ibid. ii. 250, 256.

[3] Taylor, *General Baptists*, ii. 452. Wood, *General Baptists*, pp. 181–5, 191–3, 205–9.

[4] Taylor, *General Baptists*, i. 168.   [5] Ibid. ii. 459.

[6] O. C. Robison, 'Particular Baptists in England, 1760–1820', Oxford D. Phil. thesis, 1967, pp. 145–7, 159.

being widely influenced by the High Calvinism of Joseph Hussey and John Gill. Hussey had been appointed pastor of the Presbyterian meeting in Cambridge in 1691, but in the developing quarrel over Antinomianism and Arminianism Hussey sided with the Independents and in 1694 persuaded his church to become Congregational. Hussey took his Calvinism so seriously that he denied that God's grace should be offered to the non-elect; his teaching had a profound effect on a member of his church, John Skepp, who subsequently became a Baptist pastor; and Skepp in his turn relayed Hussey's views to John Gill, who for more than half a century, from 1719 to 1771, was minister to the Particular Baptist church at Horselydown, Southwark, and one of the most influential men in the denomination.[1]

Hussey's views did not, though, go unchallenged among his fellow Congregationalists, and in the middle years of the century they were agitated by what became known as the 'Modern Question'. The controversy took its name from a pamphlet published in 1737 by Matthias Maurice, who in 1715 had succeeded to the pastorate of the Rothwell Congregational church in Northamptonshire on the death of Richard Davis. Maurice's pamphlet, *A Modern Question Modestly Answer'd*, posed the question of whether it was 'the duty of poor unconverted sinners, who hear the Gospel preached or published, to believe in Jesus Christ', and answered it in the affirmative.[2] To many Calvinists Maurice's answer was a negation of the doctrine of election and a betrayal of the principles for which Richard Davis had contended against the Baxterian Daniel Williams.[3] But although Maurice died in 1738 he received posthumous support from Dr. Abraham Taylor, minister of the Deptford Congregational church, and the pervasive influence of Philip Doddridge was thrown behind Maurice and Taylor,[4] thus preparing the Congregationalists for co-operation with the Evangelical Calvinism of Whitefield.

Among the Particular Baptists the High Calvinism of Hussey

---

[1] P. Toon, *The Emergence of Hyper-Calvinism in English Nonconformity* (1967), pp. 70–88, 97–9.

[2] M. Maurice, *A Modern Question Modestly Answer'd* (1737), p. 3.

[3] G. F. Nuttall, 'Northamptonshire and *The Modern Question*', *Journal of Theological Studies*, new series, xvi (1965), 110.

[4] Nuttall, 'Northamptonshire and *The Modern Question*', p. 119.

and Gill took deeper root. Gill's voluminous works, wrote the younger John Fawcett, were 'considered as almost an essential part of the library, not only of ministers, but of private Christians of the [Particular] Baptist denomination' and 'were read almost exclusively, to the neglect of other works on divinity'.[1] For Gill, as for Hussey, faith was a gift bestowed only on the elect and it was therefore unscriptural to urge the vast majority of mankind to have a faith which they could never possess.[2] Andrew Fuller, writing of the Particular Baptist preaching to which he listened in the late 1760s and early 1770s, commented that nothing was said to the 'unregenerate' 'in the way of warning them to flee from the wrath to come, or inviting them to apply to Christ for salvation'.[3] Gill's views did not, though, enjoy a monopoly, even among the Particular Baptists. In 1752 Alvery Jackson, a Particular Baptist minister of Barnoldswick in Yorkshire, entered the controversy over the 'Modern Question' with *The Question Answered* which supported Maurice's position, and in 1768 Abraham Booth, pastor of Goodman's Fields Particular Baptist church and a former General Baptist, published *The Reign of Grace* in which he maintained that 'complete provision is made for the certain salvation of every sinner, however unworthy, who feels his want and applies to Christ'.[4]

But the centre of Particular Baptist opposition to Gill's views lay in that part of England where Matthias Maurice and Philip Doddridge had spent the greater part of their ministries and where the 'Modern Question' was a continuing topic of debate. In 1764 six Particular Baptist churches had formed the Northamptonshire and Leicestershire Association, and the Association subsequently expanded to comprise churches stretching from Nottinghamshire to Hertfordshire. The Northamptonshire Association's circular letter of 1770 has usually been taken as indicative of a movement away from High Calvinism,[5] but this seems unlikely in view of the fact that its author, John Martin, was subsequently an opponent of Andrew Fuller. The circular letter's statement that 'every soul that comes to Christ

---

[1] J. Fawcett, Jnr., *An Account of the Life, Ministry and Writings of the late Rev. John Fawcett* (1818), p. 97.

[2] Robison, 'Particular Baptists', pp. 22–3.

[3] J. Ryland, *Life and Death of the Rev. Andrew Fuller* (1833), p. 51.

[4] Robison, 'Particular Baptists', p. 46. Underwood *English Baptists*, p. 179.

[5] Underwood, *English Baptists*, p. 160.

to be saved from hell and sin by him, is to be encouraged' was carefully qualified by the explanation that 'the coming soul need not fear that he is not elected, for none but such would be willing to come and submit to Christ'.[1] Perhaps the crucial moment came in the mid-1770s when the younger John Ryland, pastor of the College Lane church, Northampton, read Jonathan Edwards's *Inquiry into the Freedom of the Will* and two sermons on the subject by another American, John Smalley. He lent Smalley's sermons to the elder Robert Hall, pastor of the Arnesby Particular Baptist church in Leicestershire, with the comment that Edwards's 'distinction between natural and moral inability . . . would lead us to see that the affirmative side of the Modern Question was fully consistent with the strictest Calvinism'. According to Ryland's account Robert Hall was initially sceptical, but by the time they met again Hall had come round to Ryland's point of view.[2] In 1779 Hall preached a sermon before the Northamptonshire Association which was greeted with relief by Particular Baptists trying to reconcile their Calvinism with the evangelistic commands of the New Testament. Four hundred and sixty-eight grateful Calvinists contributed to a public subscription to enable Hall's sermon to be published, and it appeared in print in 1781 with the title *Help to Zion's Travellers*. 'The way to Jesus', said Hall, 'is graciously open for everyone who chooses to come to him.'[3]

The elder Robert Hall 'took particular delight in the writings of President Edwards'[4] and it was he who introduced Andrew Fuller to the works of the Massachusetts divine. The son of a Cambridgeshire farmer, Fuller was a big, broad-shouldered man with heavy eyebrows and deep-set eyes, a man who later reminded William Wilberforce of a village blacksmith, though Wilberforce at the same time paid tribute to his 'considerable powers of mind'.[5] Fuller was brought up in the Particular Baptist church at Soham under John Eve who 'had little or nothing to say to the unconverted' but whose Calvinism was not high enough for some of his congregation, and when he suggested that men were sufficiently free agents to 'keep themselves

---

[1] Ibid., p. 160.   [2] Ryland, *Life of Fuller*, pp. 9–10 n.
[3] Robison, 'Particular Baptists', p. 57. Underwood, *English Baptists*, p. 160.
[4] Robison, 'Particular Baptists', p. 166.
[5] R. and S. Wilberforce, *Life of William Wilberforce* (1838), iii. 389.

from open acts of sin' the protests of his members led to his resignation.[1] Fuller himself became pastor of the church in 1775, at the age of twenty-one, but was troubled by the memory of the contentions which had led to Eve's resignation, and by the fact that Dr. Gill's system of divinity did not seem consistent with the writings of Bunyan and other seventeenth-century Calvinists. His doubts about High Calvinism were strengthened by reading Abraham Taylor's pamphlet on *The Modern Question* and finally, on the advice of Robert Hall, he followed John Ryland in reading Jonathan Edwards's *Inquiry into the Freedom of the Will*.[2] Fuller was convinced by Edwards that evangelism and Calvinism could be reconciled, he started to put his thoughts on paper, and in 1785, by which time he had become pastor of the Kettering Particular Baptist church, he published *The Gospel Worthy of All Acceptation*. Fuller's contention that there was no contradiction between the 'peculiarity of design in the death of Christ, and a universal obligation on those who hear the gospel to believe in him'[3] did not satisfy Arminian critics such as Dan Taylor, but it was accepted by the majority of Particular Baptists and 'Fullerism' became the new orthodoxy of the denomination.

The breach with High Calvinism was not the limit of Edwards's influence on the Particular Baptists. In April 1784 John Sutcliff, the pastor of the Olney church, read Edwards's *Humble Attempt to Promote Explicit Agreement and Visible Union of God's People in Extraordinary Prayer* and was so moved that when representatives of the twenty or so churches which comprised the Northamptonshire Association met in Nottingham in June Sutcliff proposed that the churches should set aside the first Monday of every month for prayer for the revival of religion. The proposal was adopted and the prayer movement spread from Northamptonshire and the surrounding counties to the Particular Baptist churches of Warwickshire, Yorkshire, and the West Country. The Northamptonshire Association's circular letter of 1784 urged the churches not to confine their petitions to their own societies or their own denomination, but to remember 'the whole interest of the Redeemer' and to request 'the

---

[1] Ryland, *Life of Fuller*, pp. 17, 39–41.   [2] Ibid., pp. 58–60.
[3] E. F. Clipsham, 'Andrew Fuller and Fullerism', *Baptist Quarterly*, xx (1963–4), 217.

spread of the Gospel to the most distant parts of the habitable globe'.[1] Eight years later their prayers were answered with the founding of the Particular Baptist Society for the Propagation of the Gospel among the Heathen. Thus did the writings of the Congregational pastor of Northampton, Massachusetts, lead to religious revival among the Particular Baptists of Northamptonshire, England, and set in train the dispersion of the principles of English Dissent to the four corners of the world.

The Quakers, too, were affected by the Evangelical revival, though later than either the Congregationalists or the Baptists. Quakerism in the mid- and later eighteenth century was dominated by the phenomenon of quietism, an attitude of mind which owed a good deal to the seventeenth-century Scottish Quaker Robert Barclay. Quietism was not Calvinism, but it was the closest the Friends ever got to Calvinism, and while Barclay did not preach election or reprobation he did emphasize original sin and deny that 'the natural man' can have 'any place or portion in his own salvation'. For him salvation was dependent on obedience to the inner light, and this obedience came from passive waiting on God.[2] Consequently, under Barclay's influence, eighteenth-century Quakers came to place great emphasis on silent meetings, spoken ministry became the exception rather than the rule, and, like High Calvinism among the Particular Baptists, quietism made Quakerism introspective and helped to stifle the original evangelistic zeal of the movement.

The widespread influence of quietism guaranteed that the Friends would not experience the full impact of the Evangelical revival until half a century or so after the Congregationalists and Baptists. Initially some Quakers had welcomed the Methodists and a number of Methodist converts had become Friends: in 1748 John Wesley felt it necessary to publish *A Letter to a Person lately join'd with the People call'd Quakers*, and in 1772 he urged Mary Stokes, a Wesleyan leader at Bristol, to read it in a vain attempt to prevent her from joining the Friends.[3] But the numbers involved in Methodist secessions to the Quakers were

---

[1] E. A. Payne, *The Prayer Call of 1784* (1941), *passim*.

[2] E. Isichei, *The Victorian Quakers* (1970), p. 18.

[3] F. Baker, 'The Relations between the Society of Friends and Early Methodism', *London Quarterly and Holborn Review*, clxxiii (1948), 315–21, clxxiv (1949), 243–4.

small—a dozen at Worcester in 1756 and twenty at Lough-borough in 1775 seem to have been the largest[1]—and it was not until the 1820s and 1830s that Evangelicalism replaced quietism as the major influence among the Friends.[2]

The triumph of Evangelicalism was in part a reaction against the liberal views of the American Quakers Hannah Barnard and Elias Hicks. Hannah Barnard, who travelled to Quaker meetings throughout the British Isles from 1798 to 1800, was silenced by the London Yearly Meeting for questioning the historical accuracy of parts of the Bible, and Elias Hicks, whose views led to schisms in the Yearly Meetings of Philadelphia, New York, Baltimore, Ohio, and Indiana, denied the doctrine of Christ's vicarious atonement.[3] Faced with these challenges to Christian orthodoxy, Quakers such as Henry Tuke and John Bevans were at pains to emphasize their belief in the infallibility of Scripture and in the vicarious sacrifice of Christ, and Isaac Crewdson, in *A Beacon to the Society of Friends* (1835), went so far as to denounce the doctrine of the inner light as 'delusive' and to maintain that there is no way of salvation but by the Scriptures.[4] Crewdson's position was too extreme to win the approval of most Quakers, and when, in an attempt to calm the storm aroused by his book, a committee of inquiry appointed by the London Yearly Meeting advised Crewdson to refrain from public ministry, he and some fifty supporters resigned to found the short-lived sect of Evangelical Friends.[5] But Crewdson's secession did not halt the growth of Evangelicalism among the Friends, for Evangelical Quakers had a more moderate and more influential leader in the wealthy, handsome, and learned Norwich banker, Joseph John Gurney.

The roots of Gurney's Evangelicalism, as of the early Methodist leaders, lay in the frustration he experienced as he tried to measure up to the impossible standards—intellectual and spiritual—which he set himself.[6] Relief came when, as he explained, 'I lay in bed one night [and] light from above seemed to beam upon me and point out in a very explicit

[1] Baker, *London Quarterly*, clxxiv (1949), 242–3.
[2] E. Grubb, *The Evangelical Movement and its Impact on the Society of Friends* (Leominster, 1924), pp. 12–13.
[3] Jones, *LPQ* i. 302–5, 449–80.   [4] Ibid. i. 491–2.
[5] Ibid. i. 506–8.
[6] D. E. Swift, *Joseph John Gurney* (Middletown, Connecticut, 1961), pp. 36–9.

manner the duty of submitting to decided Quakerism'. Three weeks later he took his stand for his faith when, on going to a dinner party 'at the house of one of our first country gentlemen', he entered the drawing-room 'in a Friend's attire, and with my hat on'.[1] Gurney received no more invitations to such dinner parties, but his position as owner of Earlham Hall enabled him to mix on equal terms with leading Evangelical Anglicans. Edward Edwards, the Evangelical vicar of St. Margaret's, Kings' Lynn, was a friend of the family, five of Joseph John's sisters joined the Church of England, and Gurney himself had an enduring friendship with the Evangelical Anglican Charles Simeon.[2] During nearly thirty years in which he was a Quaker minister, from 1818 to 1847, Gurney's influence helped to swing the denomination decisively from quietism to Evangelicalism. In 1816 he persuaded the Quaker school at Ackworth in Yorkshire to adopt a systematic course of Bible study. In 1825 he published his *Essays on Christianity* which declared the Bible to be 'the only authorized record' of divine truth. And in 1836, after Crewdson's secession, he persuaded the London Yearly Meeting to declare that since the Scriptures 'rest on the authority of God . . . there can be no appeal from them to any other authority whatsoever'.[3] There were some contemporary Friends, such as the venerable Sarah Grubb, who feared that the Society was returning to those 'things which our community, in the beginning, suffered much in coming out of';[4] and most twentieth-century Friends would probably agree with her grandson, Edward Grubb, that Gurney tried to change the basis of the Society's authority from the inward revelation of the Spirit to outward reliance on the letter;[5] but as long as the Norwich banker lived, Evangelicalism remained a dominant influence on English Quakerism.

Sarah Grubb, and those Friends who shared her views, were not the only Dissenters who wished to repudiate the influence of the Evangelical revival. A minority of Particular Baptists, led by William Gadsby who was minister of the Back Lane church in Manchester from 1805 until his death in 1844, refused to follow

---

[1] Jones, *LPQ* i. 496–7.
[2] Swift, *J. J. Gurney*, pp. 118–19, 124–6.
[3] Ibid., pp. 57–61, 128, 180. [4] Ibid., p. 181.
[5] Grubb, *The Evangelical Movement and Society of Friends*, pp. 33–4. cf. Jones, *LPQ* i. 500.

the Northamptonshire Association on the road which, they foresaw, would lead from Fullerism to Arminianism, and, holding fast to the principle of closed communion, became known as Strict Baptists.[1] At the other end of the Baptist spectrum the General Baptist Assembly, by admitting the Unitarian William Vidler to membership in 1802 and thus forfeiting the support of Dan Taylor, in effect turned its back on the Evangelical revival, a decision which led to a century of decline and of tension between the Baptist and Unitarian elements in the denomination until, in 1916, its few remaining churches were divided between the Baptist Union and the British and Foreign Unitarian Association.[2] But the most important group of Nonconformists to remain aloof from the Evangelical revival were those who prided themselves on being 'rational Dissenters', men whose churchmanship was largely, though not exclusively, Presbyterian.

8. 'THE ETERNAL LAW OF REASON': RATIONAL DISSENT AND THE PRESBYTERIAN SCHISM

The slow process of liberalization among the Presbyterians, which had begun with Baxter's moderate Calvinism, had continued with the Arianism of Peirce and Hallet at Exeter, and had been condoned if not approved at Salters' Hall in 1719, accelerated after 1730. Until 1730 the Dissenting churches of Wales, apart from the diminishing number of Quakers, were exclusively Calvinist in theology, but in the late 1720s an Independent, Jenkin Jones, had begun to preach Arminianism, in 1733 he built a meeting-house at Llwynrhydowen in Cardiganshire in which to propagate his views, and by the time of his death in 1742 his opinions were shared by 'six or seven influential' Presbyterian ministers in the principality.[3] In Devon the Exeter Assembly, which had imposed a Trinitarian test on all ordination candidates since 1719, voted in 1753, by 14 votes to 10, to drop the test.[4] And whereas the author of the 'View of the Dissenting Interest' of 1732 had listed nineteen Calvinists among the forty-four Presbyterian ministers of London, by 1750 John

[1] Underwood, *English Baptists*, pp. 185–8.
[2] I. Sellers, 'The Old General Baptists', *Baptist Quarterly*, xxiv (1971), pp. 30–8, 74–85.
[3] Rees, *Nonconformity in Wales*, pp. 272–4.
[4] Brockett, *Nonconformity in Exeter*, p. 108.

Barker of Salters' Hall was 'almost the only London minister who continued to regard himself as both a Calvinist and a Presbyterian'.[1] Barker's sense of isolation is reflected in a letter he wrote to Doddridge in 1744 in which he complained that the Dissenting interest he had known and loved was now scarcely recognizable. 'Primitive truths and duties are quite old fashioned things', he sighed; 'one's ears are so dinned with reason, the *great law* of Reason, the *eternal law* of Reason, that it is enough to put one out of conceit with the chief excellency of our nature'.[2]

In the progress, or declension, of Presbyterianism from Baxter's 'Middle Way' through Arminianism to Arianism, a crucial part was played by the Dissenting academies. It was the incipient Arianism of the students at Joseph Hallet's Exeter academy which had led to the controversy at Salters' Hall in 1719, but the number of students educated at Exeter was small and the academy came to an end in 1719 when the Exeter Assembly withdrew its financial support. Of far greater importance as a seminal influence was the academy over which Thomas Dixon presided, first at Whitehaven and then at Bolton, from 1708 to 1729.[3] Dixon himself was a Baxterian, but the Baxterian of one generation was likely to foster the Arians or Socinians of the next, and Dixon numbered among his students George Benson, who was deprived of his pastorate at Abingdon in 1729 on account of his Arminian views and subsequently became a Socinian;[4] John Taylor, Presbyterian minister at Norwich from 1733 to 1757, whose *Scripture Doctrine of Original Sin* (1740) was believed by John Wesley to shake 'the whole frame of scriptural Christianity';[5] and Caleb Rotheram, who in his turn directed, from 1735 to 1752, the academy at Kendal which supplied Arian ministers to Lancashire pulpits.[6] In the Midlands a liberal influence was provided by Ebenezer Latham's academy at Findern near Derby (1720–54), which was said to have educated between 300 and 400 students, many of whom became Arian ministers;[7] in the West Country the

---

[1] 'A View of the Dissenting Interest', pp. 87–92. J. Goring, 'The Break-up of Old Dissent', in *The English Presbyterians*, p. 204.

[2] *Correspondence of Doddridge*, iv. 359.

[3] H. McLachlan, *Essays and Addresses* (Manchester, 1950), pp. 131–46.

[4] Goring in *The English Presbyterians*, p. 182.

[5] *Wesley's Journal*, iii. 374.   [6] Halley, *Lancashire*, ii. 394–5.

[7] McLachlan, *Essays*, pp. 157–64.

academy at Taunton under the Baxterian Henry Grove (1706–38) and the Arian Thomas Amory (1725–59) continued the heretical tradition of Exeter; and in Wales suspicions of the heterodoxy of Samuel Thomas led the Congregational Fund to withdraw its support from the Carmarthen academy in 1757 and to establish a Calvinist institution at Abergavenny.[1]

The Kendal academy died soon after Caleb Rotheram in 1752, Findern perished with Ebenezer Latham in 1754, and Taunton closed its doors when Thomas Amory moved to London in 1759. But new institutions arose to take their places. A second academy which opened at Exeter in 1760 inherited both the library and the traditions of Taunton, for of its three tutors Micaijah Towgood, himself a product of Taunton, was an Arian and Samuel Merivale became a Socinian.[2] And the gap left by the demise of Kendal was filled in 1757 by the establishment of an academy at Warrington, largely as a result of the energetic advocacy of John Seddon, the Presbyterian minister at Warrington, a former student of Caleb Rotheram and a Socinian.[3] The first head of the Warrington academy was John Taylor, whose denial of original sin had so alarmed Wesley, and when Joseph Priestley joined the staff at Warrington in 1761 he found that all three of its tutors were Arians.[4] It was some consolation to the orthodox that of the 393 students educated at Warrington between 1757 and 1786, only fifty-five were divinity students.[5]

Even some academies whose foundation was Congregational rather than Presbyterian had a liberalizing influence. Of the three tutors at the Hoxton academy between 1762 and 1784 Abraham Rees was an Arian and Andrew Kippis a Socinian, and Kippis was himself a product of Doddridge's Northampton academy.[6] After the death of Doddridge in 1751 the work of the Northampton academy was continued by Caleb Ashworth at Daventry, and when Priestley entered Daventry as a student in 1752 he found that Ashworth was perpetuating the open-

---

[1] McLachlan, *English Education*, pp. 73–4, 54.
[2] Ibid., pp. 230–1. Brockett, *Nonconformity in Exeter*, p. 139.
[3] H. McLachlan, *Warrington Academy* (Chetham Society publications, cvii, 1943), p. 11.
[4] *Autobiography of Joseph Priestley*, ed. J. Lindsay (Bath, 1970), p. 91.
[5] McLachlan, *English Education*, p. 209.
[6] Ibid., pp. 122–4.

minded approach to education which Doddridge had himself inherited from John Jennings. 'The general plan of our studies', wrote Priestley, 'which may be seen in Dr. Doddridge's published lectures, was exceedingly favourable to free inquiry, as we were referred to authors on both sides of every question.' Free inquiry was further assisted by the fact that the two tutors 'were of different opinions; Dr. Ashworth taking the orthodox side of every question, and Mr. [Samuel] Clark, the sub-tutor, that of heresy'.[1] This spirit was maintained by Thomas Belsham, who was tutor at Daventry from 1770 to 1778 and principal from 1781 to 1789. Belsham was initially a Calvinist and lectured on the person of Christ with 'the hope of putting a speedy termination' to the Unitarian controversy, but in presenting Biblical texts on both sides of the argument he converted first some of his students and finally himself to Socinian views.[2]

In the academies Calvinists like Caleb Ashworth and heretics like Samuel Clark were often able to work together in comparative harmony, respecting though regretting opposite points of view. But once Arminians, Arians, or Socinians moved from the academies to the meeting-houses dissension frequently followed. In the second half of the eighteenth century it became a common occurrence for the arrival of a new, unorthodox minister to a Presbyterian pulpit to be followed by a secession of the Calvinists in the congregation, who then formed themselves into, or joined, a Congregational church. During the ministry of the Arian John Smith at Chapel Lane, Bradford, the meeting continued the practice of repeating sermons on Sunday evenings, but the man responsible for the task, a Mr. Swaine, instead of repeating Smith's sermons often substituted those of his predecessors, 'of which he had taken notes years before, deeming them of far superior excellence'. Orthodox members of the congregation who could no longer endure Smith's preaching walked to Leeds to hear John Edwards, a Calvinistic Methodist whose congregation eventually became an Independent church.[3] At Dukinfield in Cheshire William Buckley added to the sin of Arianism the crime of wearing a silk gown and powdered wig in the pulpit, actions which resulted in a secession

---

[1] *Priestley's Autobiography*, pp. 74–5.
[2] T. Belsham, *Memoirs of Theophilus Lindsey* (1820), pp. 218–22.
[3] Miall, *Congregationalism in Yorkshire*, pp. 235–6.

of Calvinists who joined the Congregational church at Ashton-under-Lyne.[1] And in Wolverhampton it was the arrival of a Trinitarian pastor, William Jameson, that led to the heterodox trustees locking the doors of the Presbyterian meeting-house against him, and again to the founding of an Independent church.[2] In at least a score of other towns Congregational churches were constituted as a result of Calvinist secessions from Presbyterian meetings before the end of the eighteenth century.[3]

In some meetings strife between the orthodox and heretical parties was so bitter that the issue had to be settled by legal action. A dispute in the Batter Street meeting, Plymouth, over the appointment of a minister—with the trustees wanting an Arian and a majority of the congregation an orthodox preacher—was resolved in the King's Bench in 1762 in favour of the orthodox party.[4] A similar dispute at Leek between 1782 and 1784 was taken to the Staffordshire assizes and also issued in a victory for the orthodox claimant to the pulpit, while at Sutton-in-Ashfield in Nottinghamshire in 1791 legal action resulted in the heterodox Jacob Brettell being deprived of his pastorate by his orthodox congregation.[5] Most Presbyterian meetings which remained orthodox, with or without a struggle, ultimately came to describe themselves as Congregational churches. James Miall, in his *Congregationalism in Yorkshire*, listed twenty Congregational churches which had begun as Presbyterian meetings, among them the meeting which Oliver Heywood had founded at Northowram in the 1670s.[6] Robert Halley discovered another five in Lancashire, Marjorie Reeves has also

---

[1] A. Gordon, *Historical Account of Dukinfield Chapel* (1896), pp. 57–8, 113.

[2] W. H. Jones, *History of the Congregational Churches of Wolverhampton* (1894), p. 8.

[3] The following Congregational churches were formed as a result of secessions from Presbyterian meetings: Warminster (1719), Bradford-on-Avon (1730s), Maidstone (1745), Carr's Lane, Birmingham (1747), Warwick (*c.* 1750), Sherborne (1754), Poole (1760), Walsall (1763), Hinckley (1763), Morley, West Riding (1763), Shrewsbury (1767), Chester (1768), Ilkeston (1770), Honiton (1771), Chesterfield (1772), Macclesfield (1772), Liverpool (1776), Warrington (1779), Wolverhampton (1782), Stourbridge (1788), Stand, Lancashire (1791), Bury (1792), Exeter (1795), Tavistock (1796), Beaconsfield (1797), Sandwich (1798), Dukinfield (1805), Preston (1808).

[4] S. Griffin, *A History of the Batter Street Congregational Church* (1944), p. 3.

[5] Matthews, *Congregational Churches of Staffordshire*, p. 151. G. C. Bolam, 'Presbyterianism in Derbyshire, etc.', p. 558.

[6] Miall, *Congregationalism in Yorkshire*, pp. 225–389.

counted five in Wiltshire, and W. H. Summers listed six in the area of the future Berkshire, South Oxfordshire, and South Buckinghamshire Congregational Association.[1] The Presbyterian meeting at Milborne Port in Somerset became Congregational in 1744 when a new minister persuaded a majority of its members to subscribe to a covenant.[2] In London the King's Weigh House church was persuaded by its minister, John Clayton, to transfer its contributions from the Presbyterian to the Congregational Fund in 1784 on the ground that Presbyterian ministers were preaching 'another Gospel'.[3] The Presbyterian meeting in Kidderminster took a decisive step towards Congregationalism in 1782 when the appointment of an orthodox minister led to the secession of Arian members, although the church did not become fully Congregational until control over the meeting-house was transferred from the trustees to the church meeting in 1849.[4] And Chinley meeting in Derbyshire, the fruit of the labours of William Bagshaw, also became Congregational after the appointment of a Calvinist pastor in 1782.[5] The paradoxical consequence of the liberalization of Presbyterianism, as of the growth of English Calvinistic Methodism, was thus a considerable strengthening of Congregationalism, not least in those parts of the country, such as Lancashire, Yorkshire, the north Midlands, and the West Country, where Independency had hitherto been weak.

The Congregational denomination itself, though, was not free from the taint of heresy, and at least half a dozen Independent churches ultimately became Unitarian. The Dissenting meeting in Gloucester was originally Congregational, but in 1712 the church elected an Arminian, Joseph Denham, as its pastor with the result that three years later Calvinist members seceded to form a new Independent church and in the Evans list Denham's

---

[1] Halley, *Lancashire*, ii. 420–7. Reeves, 'Protestant Nonconformity', *VCH Wiltshire*, iii. 134. W. H. Summers, *History of the Congregational Churches in the Berkshire, South Oxfordshire and South Buckinghamshire Association* (Newbury, 1905), pp. 9, 36, 39, 42, 94, 200.

[2] E. R. Pitman, *Memorials of the Congregational Church at Milborne Port* (1883), pp. 48–51.

[3] Kaye, *History of the King's Weigh House*, p. 53.

[4] G. Hunsworth, *Memorials of the Old Meeting Congregational Church, Kidderminster* (Kidderminster, 1874), pp. 46–7, 65–6.

[5] R. Mansfield, 'Development of Independency in Derbyshire', Manchester M.A. thesis, 1951, p. 145.

church is described as Presbyterian.[1] The Congregational church at Great Yarmouth similarly split over the alleged Arminian views of its pastor in 1732 and the liberal party remained in possession of the meeting-house, though the seceding Calvinists claimed to have a majority of church members behind them and received £700 from the church funds with which to build a new meeting-house.[2] The Congregational church at Walthamstow, which virtually owed its existence to the wealthy Calvinist merchant and benefactor William Coward, also attracted a succession of liberal ministers from 1737 onwards, resulting in a secession of Calvinist members in 1786.[3] The Gloucester, Yarmouth, and Walthamstow Old Meetings all subsequently became Unitarian, as did the Independent churches at Bridport, Framlingham, Leeds, and Swansea, but such cases were very much the exception rather than the rule.[4] Whereas a Presbyterian minister who embraced Arminian, Arian, or Socinian opinions was likely to retain the support of the trustees of his meeting-house,[5] though he would lose the adherence of the Calvinist members of his congregation, a minister raised among the Independents who espoused heretical views was far less likely to find a Congregational church which would welcome or retain his services. The Socinian Nathaniel Lardner was initially a Congregationalist, but he preached to a Presbyterian congregation for the latter part of his ministerial career; when Richard Rees, minister of the Cwm-y-glo Independent church, Merthyr Tydfil, embraced Arminian views, the church split and Rees and his supporters were forced to leave and to establish, in 1747, the new church of Cefn-coed-cymer; and when the Great Yarmouth Congregational church found

---

[1] W. Lloyd, *A Brief Account of the Foundation and History of the Protestant Dissenting Meeting-house in Barton Street, Gloucester* (1899), pp. 17–18.

[2] J. E. Clowes, *Chronicles of the Old Congregational Church at Great Yarmouth* (Great Yarmouth, 1960), p. 53.

[3] H. D. Budden, *The Story of Marsh Street Congregational Church, Walthamstow* (Margate, 1923), pp. 22–30. J. Goring, 'The Break-up of the Old Dissent', in *English Presbyterians*, p. 210.

[4] Densham and Ogle, *Congregational Churches of Dorset*, pp. 50–1. *TCHS* i. (1916–18), 91. Leeds Arian Independent Church Register, PRO RG4 3724. W. T. Jones, *The Rise and Progress of Religious Free Thought in Swansea* (1900), pp. 35–9.

[5] Heterodox Presbyterian ministers were excluded by orthodox trustees at Exeter in 1719, Abingdon in 1729, and Bridlington *c.* 1773. By contrast at Poole in 1759 Arian trustees locked an orthodox minister out of his pulpit. Densham and Ogle, *Congregational Churches of Dorset*, p. 196.

in 1764 that for a second time it had saddled itself with a heretical pastor—this time an Arian—it was the minister who was now obliged to go.[1] Jenkin Jones, the pioneer Arminian preacher in Wales, was admittedly a Congregationalist, but unlike other Congregational preachers he was economically and ecclesiastically independent, for he had married a rich wife and his meeting-house at Llwynrhydowen was built on his own estate.[2] The most celebrated of all the rational Dissenters, Richard Price and Joseph Priestley, both came from Congregational families, and both spent their pastoral careers entirely in the service of Presbyterian congregations.

9. FREEDOM AND NECESSITY: RICHARD PRICE AND JOSEPH PRIESTLEY

The careers and interests of Price and Priestley had much in common, and though important theological and philosophical issues divided them, for the last twenty-five years of Price's life they were firm friends. Richard Price was the elder, born in 1723 the son of Rees Price, an Independent minister of Cildeudy near Bridgend in Glamorgan.[3] Rees Price was a rigid Calvinist and when he found his son, still a schoolboy, reading a volume by Samuel Clarke he grabbed it from him and threw the heretical book into the fire. But Richard was converted to Arianism, and after completing his education at John Eames's Moorfields academy he was for twelve years chaplain to a wealthy Stoke Newington Dissenter, then preacher to Presbyterian congregations in Poor Jewry Lane and Stoke Newington, and finally, from 1770 to his death in 1791, minister to the Gravel Pit Presbyterian meeting in Hackney.

Joseph Priestley similarly rejected the Calvinism of his family. He was born ten years later than Richard Price, the son of a cloth-worker of Fieldhead near Birstal in the West Riding. His mother died when he was seven years old and he was subsequently brought up by an aunt, a Mrs. Keighley, who was a

---

[1] Nuttall, *Puritan Spirit*, p. 71. Great Yarmouth Church Book, p. 272.

[2] Rees, *Nonconformity in Wales*, p. 272.

[3] C. B. Cone in his biography of Richard Price, *Torchbearer of Freedom* (Lexington, 1952), p. 10, describes Rees Price as a Presbyterian, but he is listed as an Independent in the Evans manuscript and he was supported by the Congregational Fund. Evans list, p. 141, R. Thomas, *Richard Price* (1924), p. 6.

member of the Heckmondwike Congregational church. Mrs. Keighley was a Calvinist, 'but was far from confining salvation to those who thought as she did on religious subjects', and her home 'was the resort of all the Dissenting ministers in the neighbourhood', irrespective of their theological views. In this way Priestley came under the influence of two local ministers who held Baxterian opinions, and when he applied for admission to membership of the Heckmondwike church he was refused because he 'appeared not to be quite orthodox, not thinking that all the human race (suppose them not to have any sin of their own) were liable to the wrath of God'. Already an Armin-ian, he entered Caleb Ashworth's Daventry academy in 1752 where he became an Arian, and after pastorates at Needham Market in Suffolk and at Nantwich in Cheshire, he spent six years as languages tutor at the Warrington academy. In 1767 he accepted the pastorate of the Mill Hill Presbyterian meeting in Leeds, and soon after his settlement in Leeds he read Lard-ner's *Letter concerning ... the Logos* which converted him to Socinianism.[1]

Price and Priestley were both men of wide intellectual interests. Price acquired from his tutor John Eames an interest in mathematics which led to a study of life assurance and of public finance: he was adviser to the Society for Equitable Assurance, published life expectancy tables, was consulted by both Lord Shelburne and the younger Pitt when they were head of the ministry, and put forward the proposals for a sinking fund to reduce the national debt which Pitt afterwards adopted.[2] Priestley was a universal genius, the Leonardo da Vinci of Dissent. He claimed to know Latin, Greek, Hebrew, French, Italian, Dutch, Chaldee, and Syriac before he went to the Daventry academy and he taught languages at Warrington;[3] his *Theological and Miscellaneous Works* fill twenty-six volumes; he made an original contribution to chemistry, discovered ammonia, sulphur dioxide, and oxygen, and invented soda-water by impregnating water with carbon dioxide.[4] Most significant of all, Priestley was a strenuous advocate of the study

[1] *Priestley's Autobiography*, pp. 70–93.
[2] Cone, *Torchbearer of Freedom*, pp. 40–3, 137–49.
[3] *Priestley's Autobiography*, pp. 70, 72.
[4] F. W. Gibbs, *Joseph Priestley* (1965), pp. 69, 94.

of history, for it was history which provided, for Priestley, the key to both science and theology. He recommended the study of history, and 'especially the important objects of civil policy ... demonstrated from history', as an essential part of the education of the sons of gentlemen and of prospective lawyers, soldiers, and merchants; at Warrington he gave an extended course of lectures on the sources, methods, and objects of history; and he published chronological and biographical charts to facilitate its study.[1] His first serious work in science was his *History and Present State of Electricity* (1767), in the course of writing which he sought 'to ascertain several facts which were disputed' and was thus led into the 'field of original experiments'.[2] And his approach to theology, too, was historical, essaying to strip Christianity of the corruptions of time in an endeavour to discover its original message.[3]

Price and Priestley first met in January 1766 when Price, already a Fellow of the Royal Society, took Priestley to one of its meetings and helped to secure his election as a Fellow later in the same year.[4] In the following year Price published a volume of sermons, *Four Dissertations*, which earned him the acquaintance of the Earl of Shelburne, and it was Price who obtained for Priestley the offer of the post of librarian to Shelburne in 1773. With a house and a stipend of 100 guineas a year at Leeds Priestley was one of the best paid of Dissenting ministers, but he complained that this was 'not quite sufficient' for his family, that it did not enable him to make provision for them after his death, and he was tempted away by Shelburne's offer of £250 a year for life, whether he continued in Shelburne's service or not.[5] That Priestley succumbed to Shelburne's offer, when Andrew Fuller, for example, was struggling along at Soham on £21 a year in the late 1770s, is indicative that Priestley's Christian ministry was somewhat lacking in zeal.[6] And when he left Shelburne's household at Calne and became co-pastor of the New Meeting in Birmingham in 1780 it was on the understanding that, in order to enable him to continue his

---

[1] *Theological and Miscellaneous Works of Joseph Priestley*, ed. J. T. Rutt (1817–31), vol. xxiv, *passim*, especially p. 11.
[2] *Priestley's Autobiography*, pp. 89–90.   [3] *Priestley's Works*, v. 8.
[4] Gibbs, *Joseph Priestley*, pp. 26, 29.
[5] Cone, *Torchbearer of Freedom*, p. 35. *Priestley's Autobiography*, p. 98.
[6] Ryland, *Life of Andrew Fuller*, p. 71.

'philosophical and other studies', baptisms and sick-visiting would be left to his fellow minister and Priestley's own duties would be confined to Sundays.[1] Price's wide intellectual interests also militated against his effectiveness as a pastor. On one occasion James Boswell, in depressed mood, turned to Price for consolation. But Price 'obliged me with the rate of an annuity on money sunk'.[2]

Yet despite their friendship and the similarity of their careers Price and Priestley were not alike, for Price was a more humble, more generous, more down-to-earth character than the somewhat arrogant Priestley, and with differences of personality went important differences of theology and philosophy.[3] Price remained faithful to the Arianism he had learnt from Samuel Clarke, believing in the pre-existence of Christ and, while denying his deity, refusing to accept the doctrine of his 'simple humanity'.[4] Priestley, in passing from Arianism to Socinianism, adopted an aggressive creed which regarded Jesus as a man like anyone else, 'though honoured and distinguished by God above all other men', and which went much further than Faustus Socinus in rejecting the worship of Christ as idolatrous.[5] While Price wrote of the atonement in terms which approached orthodoxy—Christ 'by humbling himself to death . . . acquired the power of destroying death'—Priestley saw no necessity for any doctrine of atonement, since 'it is a great dishonour to God to suppose that his mercy and grace takes its rise from anything but his own essential goodness'.[6] Priestley came to regard Arianism, as much as Athanasianism, as one of the 'capital corruptions' of Christianity; in Price's opinion Christianity was degraded by the 'Socinian scheme'.[7]

The philosophical gulf between the two men was revealed by the *Free Discussion* between them which was published in 1778. While he was a student at Daventry Priestley had read the recently published *Observations on Man* (1749) by the physician David Hartley, and the book became the corner-stone of his own philosophical system. Hartley's work was based on a suggestion of Isaac Newton that impressions of the senses are

---

[1] *Priestley's Autobiography*, p. 121.   [2] Cone, *Torchbearer of Freedom*, p. 56.

[3] For an example of Priestley's arrogance see his attitude to his congregation at Nantwich, *Autobiography*, p. 86.

[4] Cone, *Torchbearer of Freedom*, p. 164.   [5] *Priestley's Works*, ii. 414.

[6] Ibid. iv. 62, ii. 398.   [7] Ibid. iii. 200, iv. 71.

carried to the brain by means of vibrations along the nerves, and from this he concluded that complex thought is merely a combination of such vibrations and that 'passions and affections can be no more than aggregates of simple ideas united by association'.[1] This meant, wrote Priestley, that 'the business of thinking' is dependent 'upon mere matter', and from this he deduced two further principles, 'the system of materialism' and 'the doctrine of necessity'. Priestley shocked his contemporaries by suggesting that 'man does not consist of two principles . . . matter and spirit' but is 'wholly material'. And this materialist view of man, he argued, involves a mechanistic interpretation of human actions: man's will 'is never determined without some real or apparent cause, foreign to itself'.[2]

Although he was denounced as an atheist, Priestley believed that materialism and necessity were not only consistent with Christianity, but placed Christianity on a sound philosophical foundation. He revived the 'mortalist' heresy propounded by the Leveller Richard Overton in the previous century, and like Overton argued that the doctrine of the immortality of the soul had been foisted on to Christianity through Platonic influence, whereas the New Testament taught the resurrection of 'the whole man at some distant period'.[3] The concept of necessity, he argued, strengthened belief in the providence and prescience of God, for 'if man be possessed of a power of proper self-determination the Deity himself cannot control it . . . and if he does not control it, he cannot foresee it'.[4] By emphasizing man's dependence on his environment and God's all-pervading influence Priestley foreshadowed both the biological and economic determinism and the theological immanentism of the nineteenth century. 'Nothing', he wrote, 'is without the sphere of a properly divine, though regular and constant influence.'[5] And this meant, as Priestley admitted, 'that God is the author of sin'.[6]

Richard Price dissented vigorously from Priestley's philosophical position. The Welshman's most celebrated work was his *Review of the Principal Questions in Morals*, first published in 1758, in which he had argued that without liberty, the power

---

[1] *Priestley's Works*, iii. 175–6, 178. *Priestley's Autobiography*, p. 34.
[2] *Priestley's Works*, iii. 181–2, 220, 462.
[3] Ibid. iii. 386.   [4] Ibid. iii. 471.   [5] Ibid. xv. 85.
[6] Ibid. iii. 510.

of self-determination, 'there can be no moral capacities'.[1] The
right to choose between right and wrong, Price maintained, lay
in the understanding and was not, as Locke had argued, the
result of sense perception. 'Sense sees only the *outside* of things,
reason acquaints itself with their *natures*.'[2] Priestley's theories
thus struck at the very root of Price's philosophy, and the latter
replied by exposing the weaknesses of Priestley's own system.
When Priestley argued that 'we have no more reason ... to
conclude that a man can move himself, that is, that he can will
without motives, than that a stone can move itself', Price
retorted that a man can choose between contradictory motives.[3]
When Priestley maintained that man's soul, no less than his
body, is extinguished at death, Price asked, 'If I am to lose my
existence at death, will not my resurrection be the resurrection
of a non-entity, and therefore a contradiction?'[4] Most important
of all, Price put his finger on the great weakness of Priestley's
theological system, his neglect, if not denial, of the work of the
Holy Spirit. For the previous two centuries the great innovators
in English religious history—John Smyth, George Fox, the
Wesleys—had all placed great emphasis on the work of the
Spirit, but Priestley wrote that the Deity 'has no local presence'
and took Bishop Warburton to task for maintaining 'that the
Spirit of God abides with the Church for ever'.[5] 'It is ... the
notion of spirit', complained Price, 'which is combated through
the greatest part of Dr. Priestley's work.'[6]

Among the rational Dissenters of the late eighteenth century
Priestley's aggressive Socinianism had a greater appeal than
Price's more cautious Arianism. Priestley claimed that as late as
1770 he did not know more than half a dozen Dissenting ministers who were Socinians, but when the Unitarian Society for
Promoting Christian Knowledge was set up in 1791 it was
established on a narrowly Socinian basis and scrupulous
Arians were excluded by rules which repudiated the worship of
Christ as 'idolatrous'.[7] Arianism survived into the nineteenth
century, especially among the Presbyterians of Ireland, and in
1826 a monthly magazine, the *Christian Moderator*, was launched

[1] R. Price, *A Review of the Principal Questions in Morals* (Oxford, 1948), p. 181.
[2] Ibid., pp. 17–20.   [3] *Priestley's Works*, iv. 72, 94.
[4] Ibid. iv. 50.   [5] Ibid. iv. 43, xv. 86.   [6] Ibid. iv. 54.
[7] Ibid. x. 490–1. Belsham, *Memoirs of Lindsey*, pp. 227–8. J. Williams, *Memoirs of Thomas Belsham* (1833), pp. 435–40.

to propagate Arian views. But England's leading Arian ministers—Hugh Worthington of Salters' Hall, Dr. Abraham Rees of Jewin Street, Robert Lewin of Liverpool, the General Baptist John Evans—all died in the second and third decades of the century, the *Christian Moderator* ceased publication in 1828, and by 1869 Robert Halley was able to write that he did not know of an Arian minister anywhere in England.[1]

What happened to the Arians? There were undoubtedly many ministers and many meetings for whom Arianism was merely a resting-place on the road from Trinitarianism to Socinianism, but in other cases Arianism appears to have been but a temporary deviation from orthodoxy. Among the twenty Presbyterian meetings in Yorkshire which became Congregational were three, at Cleckheaton, Idle, and Low Row, which did so only after long and apparently successful pastorates by Arian ministers.[2] In both Cleckheaton and Idle the death or resignation of an Arian Presbyterian minister was followed immediately by the choice of a Calvinist Congregationalist. In Manchester many members of the large Presbyterian congregation at Cross Street who had listened contentedly to the Arian Thomas Barnes for nearly forty years (1771–1810), refused to sit under his Socinian successors and joined local Congregational churches.[3] And in Preston in the first decade of the nineteenth century William Manning Walker, the minister of the town's Presbyterian meeting, moved from Arianism to Evangelicalism and resigned in 1807 to found a Congregational church.[4] Thomas Morgan, minister of Morley Presbyterian meeting in the West Riding, was said to have 'associated much with the Unitarians, till roused by the extreme opinions of Dr. Priestley', and there were no doubt other liberal Dissenters who were similarly affronted by Priestley's blunt Yorkshire language.[5] Trinitarianism, said Priestley, is as idolatrous as transubstantiation, and Jesus 'is as much a creature of God as a loaf of bread'.[6] When faced with a choice between Trinitarianism and Unitarianism expressed in such terms, many liberal Dissenters must

[1] Halley, *Lancashire*, ii. 417.
[2] Miall, *Congregationalism in Yorkshire*, pp. 249, 295, 312.
[3] Halley, *Lancashire*, ii. 435.
[4] Nightingale, *Lancashire Nonconformity*, i. 48.
[5] Miall, *Congregationalism in Yorkshire*, p. 323.
[6] *Priestley's Works*, ii. 414.

have preferred to keep their doubts about the Trinity to themselves and retained their membership of churches whose theology was officially Calvinist.

10. THE 'NATURAL RIGHTS AND LIBERTIES OF MANKIND': THE AMERICAN AND FRENCH REVOLUTIONS

Priestley, as might be expected, viewed the Evangelical revival with mixed feelings. He assured the Methodists of his 'brotherly love' and rejoiced at the signs of tension between the Wesleyans and the hierarchy of the established church: at a time when Old Dissent was declining, he wrote, the Methodists were raised up by divine providence 'as a barrier against the encroachments of ecclesiastical tyranny'.[1] But Priestley, who in his youth had worried about his failure to experience conversion, came to the conclusion that the doctrine of new birth was unscriptural, deceitful, and a 'dangerous delusion'.[2] 'The work of conversion and reformation', he wrote, 'takes place according to the usual course of nature.'[3] And starting from different theological and ecclesiastical standpoints, Priestley and Wesley came to different political conclusions. To Priestley, with his determinist philosophy, goodness and happiness were synonymous: 'the good and happiness of the members, that is, the majority of the members of any state, is the great standard by which everything relating to that state must finally be determined'.[4] It was this passage that inspired Jeremy Bentham to adopt 'the greatest happiness of the greatest number' as the key to his own Utilitarian philosophy. Wesley, by contrast, was concerned not with the temporal happiness of the majority, but with their eternal salvation. Though Priestley was not in favour of universal suffrage, he believed that 'the great natural rights and liberties of mankind are best secured when the supreme magistracy is in the hands of persons chosen by the people, and when they are entrusted with that power for a limited time'.[5] Wesley disagreed. If a man had religious liberty and protection for his life and property, he could not conceive what other rights he should want. 'What liberty can you reasonably desire', he asked his fellow countrymen in 1772, 'which you do not already enjoy?'[6]

---

[1] *Priestley's Works*, xxv. 333, xii. 293.
[2] *Priestley's Autobiography*, p. 71. *Priestley's Works*, xv. 83, 97.
[3] *Priestley's Works*, xv. 85.　　　　[4] Ibid. xxii. 13.　　　　[5] Ibid. xxii. 385.
[6] *Wesley's Works*, xi. 41–3.

Consequently, on most of the political issues which divided Englishmen in the last third of the eighteenth century, Wesley and the rational Dissenters took opposite sides. The one exception was the question of the slave-trade. It was the Quakers who first aroused the consciences of Englishmen against the traffic in human beings: the London Yearly Meeting censured Friends who engaged in the slave-trade as early as 1727, and in the 1760s the Philadelphia Quaker Anthony Benezet started publishing the series of books which marked the first shot in the anti-slavery campaign.[1] Early in 1772 John Wesley read Benezet's *Historical Account of Guinea* which convinced him that the slave-trade was the 'execrable sum of all villainies',[2] and two years later he made his own contribution to the anti-slavery cause with his *Thoughts on Slavery*. By the 1780s rational and Evangelical Dissenters were united in their condemnation of the slave-trade: Congregationalists, Particular Baptists, and Old General Baptists passed resolutions against the traffic, Richard Price urged the Americans to free their slaves over a period of time, and in January 1788 Priestley wrote from Birmingham that on the following Sunday the town's ministers were to preach against the slave-trade, in 'churches and meeting houses alike'.[3]

But on other issues Wesley and the rational Dissenters were far apart. Wesley attempted to justify the House of Commons' action in expelling Wilkes from Parliament in 1769; Priestley believed that the Commons, in refusing to allow Wilkes's Middlesex constituents 'to judge of the fitness of the person who shall represent them in Parliament', were violating the Bill of Rights.[4] When the War of American Independence broke out in 1775 most of the leaders of Old Dissent, Congregationalists and Baptists no less than rational Dissenters, supported their co-religionists on the other side of the Atlantic, where fear of the establishment of state-supported episcopacy had been a contributory factor to the colonial revolt.[5] One of the most influential defences of the colonists' position was Richard

[1] Jones, *LPQ* i. 317–20.   [2] *Wesley's Journal*, v. 445–6.
[3] Browne, *Congregationalism in Norfolk and Suffolk*, p. 201. *VCH Wiltshire*, iii. 137. *Minutes of the General Baptist Assembly*, ii. 188. Payne, *Prayer Call of 1784*, p. 6. Cone, *Torchbearer of Freedom*, p. 113. *Priestley's Works*, vol. i, part ii, p. 7.
[4] *Priestley's Works*, xxii. 390. *Wesley's Works*, xi. 21.
[5] Hudson, *Religion in America*, p. 91.

Price's *Observations on the Nature of Civil Liberty*, published in February 1776, in which the minister of the Gravel Pit meeting argued that 'in every free state every man is his own legislator, all taxes are free-gifts for public services', and all laws 'regulations established by common consent for gaining protection and safety'.[1] Sixty thousand copies of Price's pamphlet were sold and within two years it had brought forth forty more tracts, either in support or in opposition, among them Wesley's own *Observations on Liberty*. Although Wesley had, in the previous year, urged the government to make concessions to the colonists, and three days before the battle of Bunker Hill had questioned whether it was 'common sense to use force toward the Americans', he was subsequently persuaded by reading Samuel Johnson's *Taxation no Tyranny* of the justice of the government's case.[2] 'The greater share the people have in the government', replied Wesley to Price, 'the less liberty, either civil or religious, does the nation enjoy.' 'There is most liberty ... under a limited monarchy; there is usually less under an aristocracy, and least under a democracy.'[3] It followed that the rational Dissenters would support, and Wesley oppose, the movement for parliamentary reform. Dissenters were among the chief supporters of Wyvill's County Association movement of 1779–83, especially in Yorkshire and Cambridgeshire; Richard Price joined Cartwright's Society for Constitutional Information; and Robert Robinson, who managed to combine the pastorate of the Cambridge Particular Baptist church with a belief in the unity of God, founded the Cambridge Constitutional Society.[4] All this activity Wesley could scarcely comprehend. Nine in ten people 'throughout England have no representative, no vote', he wrote in an attempt to calm the agitation of the American colonists, yet 'they enjoy both civil and religious liberty to the utmost extent'.[5]

Most significant of all, rational Dissenters and official Wesleyan Methodism conflicted in their opinions of the French

[1] R. Price, *Observations on the Nature of Civil Liberty* (1776), pp. 6–7.
[2] *Wesley's Letters*, vi. 155–64. *Wesley's Works*, xi. 80.
[3] *Wesley's Works*, xi. 105.
[4] A. Lincoln, *Some Political and Social Ideas of English Dissent* (Cambridge, 1938), p. 47. Cone, *Torchbearer of Freedom*, pp. 152–3. G. W. Hughes, *With Freedom Fired, the Story of Robert Robinson* (1955), p. 48.
[5] *Wesley's Works*, xi. 81.

Revolution. On 4 November 1789, the eve of the anniversary of the landing of William of Orange at Torbay and five months after the proclamation of the French National Assembly, Richard Price, now sixty-six years old and suffering from ill health, preached his most famous sermon. It was delivered in the Old Jewry meeting-house to the Society for Commemorating the Revolution in Great Britain and was later printed under the title *A Discourse on the Love of our Country*. Price was largely concerned with what he regarded as the domestic implications of 1688—that George III is 'almost the only lawful king in the world, because [he is] the only one who owes his crown to the choice of his people'—but in his peroration he linked the English Revolution with the 'two other Revolutions, both glorious', the American and the French, and warned 'all ye oppressors of the world' that they could no longer 'hold the world in darkness'. The effort involved in preaching the sermon so exhausted Price that he had to return home to bed, but by the evening he was sufficiently recovered to attend the society's dinner at the London Tavern and to propose that the company send to the French National Assembly 'their congratulations on the Revolution'. The motion was carried and the message was sent, together with the hope that the French example would 'encourage other nations to assert the unalienable rights of mankind'.[1]

It was Price's sermon and the Revolution Society's message to the National Assembly that provoked Burke into publishing his *Reflections on the Revolution in France*. Nothing like Price's sermon, wrote Burke, had been heard in English pulpits since 1648 when Hugh Peter demanded judgement on Charles I. It was 'nonsense' to maintain that the king owed his crown to the will of the people, for the Revolution of 1688 had been but 'a small and temporary deviation from the strict order of a regular hereditary succession' and George III 'holds his crown in contempt of the choice of the Revolution Society'. Burke was anxious, he wrote, to protect both the French and the British from a 'double fraud' whereby 'counterfeit wares' were exported to France 'in illicit bottoms, as raw commodities of British growth though wholly alien to our soil, in order afterwards to

---

[1] R. Price, *A Discourse on the Love of our Country* (5th edn., 1790), pp. 25, 49–51, appendix, p. 13. Cone, *Torchbearer of Freedom*, p. 180.

smuggle them back again into this country, manufactured after the newest Paris fashion'.[1]

Evangelical Dissenters were divided in their attitude to the French Revolution. John Clayton, who in 1784 had taken the King's Weigh House meeting out of the Presbyterian Fund and into the Congregational denomination, went out of his way to dissociate himself from 'the theological and political sentiments of those who ... style themselves rational Dissenters', and emphasized *The Duty of Christians to Magistrates*.[2] But among the Particular Baptists Joseph Kinghorn of Norwich rejoiced 'at the destruction of that most infamous place, the Bastille', Mark Wilks, a Calvinistic Methodist turned Baptist, saw the hand of God in the capture of Louis XVI at Varennes, and the younger Robert Hall, exultant that 'the empire of darkness and despotism [has] been smitten with a stroke which has sounded through the universe', replied to John Clayton with his *Christianity Consistent with a Love of Freedom*.[3] For those Methodists who were loyal to the principles of John Wesley, though, there could be only one response to the events in France. The Methodists, wrote Samuel Kenrick of Bewdley in 1792, 'are the most violent anti-revolutionists we have'.[4]

II. REACTION: THE CAMPAIGN AGAINST THE TEST AND CORPORATION ACTS, THE BIRMINGHAM RIOTS, AND THE ECLIPSE OF RATIONAL DISSENT

One consequence of the reaction which followed the outbreak of the French Revolution was the destruction of Dissenting hopes of an early repeal of the Test and Corporation Acts. The extent to which Dissenters were prepared to take the Anglican sacrament in order to qualify for public and municipal office varied from denomination to denomination. The Corporation Act did not prevent Presbyterians from occupying the mayoralty of Nottingham for sixty-six years of the eighteenth century: the

---

[1] E. Burke, *Reflections on the Revolution in France* (2nd edn., 1790), pp. 13, 17, 19, 23, 35–6.

[2] Lincoln, *Political Ideas of Dissent*, p. 31.

[3] C. B. Jewson, 'Norwich Baptists and the French Revolution', *Baptist Quarterly*, xxiv (1971–2), pp. 209–10. R. Hall, *Christianity Consistent with a Love of Freedom* (1791), p. 77.

[4] J. Creasey, 'Some Dissenting Attitudes towards the French Revolution', *TUHS* xiii (1963–6), 155–6.

town was reported in 1777 to be 'the most disloyal in the kingdom, owing in great measure to the whole corporation . . . being Dissenters'.[1] In Coventry at least thirty-three Dissenters served in corporation offices between 1662 and 1720, eleven of them as mayor, and by 1735 eleven of the seventeen trustees of the city's Presbyterian meeting-house were aldermen or councillors.[2] In Bridgwater in Somerset 'the whole of the civic magistracy' was said to have attended the Presbyterian meeting-house in the early eighteenth century, and when it was rebuilt in 1788 it was furnished with a long pew 'for the use of the corporation'.[3] In Bristol Presbyterians served as sheriff for twenty-three years and as mayor for sixteen years between 1754 and 1792, and notwithstanding the Test Act Presbyterians earned their livings as customs officials.[4] Some Presbyterians opposed the practice of occasional conformity and Daniel Defoe characterized it as 'playing bo-peep with God Almighty'.[5] But Defoe was a layman who could afford the luxury of annoying his co-religionists. When Matthew Towgood, the minister of the Presbyterian meeting in Poole, ventured to criticize some of the prominent members of his congregation for taking the Anglican sacrament in order to qualify for office, his indiscretion led ultimately to his being locked out of the meeting-house.[6]

There is evidence that at least some Congregationalists also practised occasional conformity, though this was usually frowned upon by their churches. There was a dispute over the question in the Castle Gate church in Nottingham in 1775 when the church declined to take action 'against those of the brethren who are in the corporation on account of their occasional conformity', though at the same time it resolved that in future the practice would involve loss of membership.[7] But Baptist churches appear to have opposed occasional conformity consistently: Particular Baptists who compromised themselves

---

[1] Bolam, 'Presbyterianism in Derbyshire, etc.', p. 567. L. Namier and J. Brooke, *History of Parliament, the House of Commons 1754–90* (1964), i. 355.

[2] Hurwich, 'Nonconformists in Warwickshire', pp. 143, 380–8.

[3] J. Murch, *History of the Presbyterian and General Baptist Churches in the West of England* (1835), pp. 178, 181.

[4] O. M. Griffiths, 'The Records of Lewin's Mead Chapel, Bristol', *TUHS* vi (1935–8), 120, 122.

[5] D. Defoe, *An Enquiry into the Occasional Conformity of Dissenters* (1697), p. 17.

[6] Densham and Ogle, *Congregational Churches of Dorset*, p. 193.

[7] Henderson, *Castle Gate Congregational Church*, p. 103.

in this way were excluded from membership at Unicorn Yard in London in 1743, at Lyme in 1778, and at Norwich in 1786,[1] while it was a General Baptist, Allen Evans, who for sixteen years fought the city of London's dishonourable scheme of electing Dissenters to office and then fining them if they declined to take the Anglican sacrament. This method of bolstering up corporation finances was justified on the ground that leading citizens were neglecting to take the sacrament in order to escape time-consuming and expensive civic responsibilities: if a Dissenter 'may with his conscience unhurt, conform for the sake of *lucrative* employments', wrote Bishop Warburton in 1736, he should not be permitted to use the Corporation Act 'to evade those which are *onerous*'.[2] But while this may have justified the fining of Presbyterians in Exeter in 1678–9, especially when other Presbyterians in the city were prepared to qualify for office, it can hardly excuse the fining of uncompromising Quakers in Bristol in 1685–6, nor of a Norwich Congregationalist in 1692 who declared he never had, nor never would, take the Anglican sacrament.[3] Nor can it justify the shameless way in which the city of London, from 1730 onwards, raised money for the building of the Mansion House by systematically electing Dissenters to the office of sheriff and then fining them £400 if they refused to serve. This form of blackmail is said to have raised over £15,000 by 1754 and continued until 1767 when Allen Evans, now eighty-two years old and a dying man, obtained a judgement from Lord Mansfield that the action of the city of London was a violation of the Corporation and Toleration Acts.[4]

But although the Nonconformist denominations differed in their attitudes towards the practice of occasional conformity, they were united in their abhorrence of the principle of using the Lord's Supper as a political test. It was widely believed, as the author of 'A View of the Dissenting Interest' complained,

[1] J. Ivimey, *History of the English Baptists* (1823), iii. 228–34. C. B. Jewson, 'St. Mary's Norwich', *Baptist Quarterly*, x (1940–1), 287.

[2] A. G. Cumberland, 'The Toleration Act of 1689', London Ph.D. thesis, 1957, p. 152. *Works of William Warburton* (1788), iv. 217.

[3] Brockett, *Nonconformity in Exeter*, p. 44. Mortimer, 'Quakerism in Bristol', p. 347. Browne, *Congregationalism in Norfolk and Suffolk*, p. 176.

[4] W. Pierce, 'The Contributions of the Nonconformists to the Building of the Mansion House', *TCHS* ix (1924–6), 146–9. B. L. Manning, *The Protestant Dissenting Deputies* (Cambridge, 1952), pp. 119–29.

that the sacramental test was a 'snare' to many Dissenters 'whereby they have been drawn from occasional to stated communion',[1] and the Presbyterians in particular had good reason to resent the way in which occasional conformity eased the passage of wealthy Dissenters into the established church. The Presbyterian meeting at Dover was weakened by the loss of members who were elected to municipal office and then conformed, and in 1773 the decline of the Dissenting interest in Guildford was attributed in part 'to Dissenters joining the corporation and so falling into the Church'.[2] This may help to explain the paradox pointed to by Roger Thomas: that it was the Presbyterians who practised occasional conformity, rather than the Congregationalists who by and large did not, who were the more resolute in pressing for the repeal of the Test and Corporation Acts in the 1730s.[3] It is also possible that, as the eighteenth century progressed, Presbyterians became more and more uncomfortable about occasional conformity as their theology became increasingly heterodox. George III certainly saw a connection between the retention of the Test and Corporation Acts and the defence of trinitarian orthodoxy. 'The present Presbyterians seem so much more resembling Socinians than Christians', he wrote to Lord North in 1772, 'that I think the Test was never so necessary as at present for obliging them to prove themselves Christians.'[4] It is probably significant that the energetic chairman of the lay Protestant Dissenting Deputies from 1736 to 1764 was Dr. Benjamin Avery, a former Presbyterian minister, a friend of James Peirce, and an Arian, who had left the ministry for medicine after Subscribers and Nonsubscribers alike at Salters' Hall had declared their belief in the orthodox doctrine of the Trinity.[5]

The Dissenting Deputies, representing 'every congregation of the three denominations of . . . Presbyterians, Independents, and Baptists, in and within ten miles of London', had originated

[1] 'A View of the Dissenting Interest', p. 82.
[2] Josiah Thompson, List of Dissenting Congregations, 1773, DWL MS. 34.5. T. Timpson, *Church History of Kent* (1859), p. 415.
[3] R. Thomas, 'Presbyterians, Congregationals, and the Test and Corporation Acts', *TUHS* xi (1955–8), 124–6.
[4] R. V. Holt, *The Unitarian Contribution to Social Progress* (1938), p. 324.
[5] H. McLachlan, *The Unitarian Movement in the Religious Life of England* (1934), p. 166.

at a meeting of laymen called in 1732 to consider an application to Parliament for the repeal of the Test and Corporation Acts.[1] But the first committee, chaired by the Presbyterian Samuel Holden, though supported largely by Congregationalists, was accused of inactivity and suspected of being in Walpole's pay, and an attempt to secure repeal in 1736 was opposed by the governement and defeated by 251 votes to 123.[2] Avery's more enthusiastic efforts were no more successful—a motion for repeal in 1739 was rejected by 188 votes to 89—and the agitation was not revived again until 1787. In May 1789 Henry Beaufoy's motion for repeal was lost by only 122 votes to 102, but two months later the Bastille was stormed and as a wave of fear swept through the political and religious establishments of England the cause of repeal was doomed. Anglican pamphleteers recalled that in the previous century the forefathers of the Dissenters had executed the king and driven loyal clergy from their parishes, and Bishop Horsley declared that 'the principles of a Nonconformist in religion and a republican in politics are inseparably united'. Dissenters, following the example of Wyvill's County Association movement for parliamentary reform, set up local associations in the provinces and organized public meetings in support of repeal, but the clergy and gentry replied with county meetings to which most M.P.s felt bound to pay more heed.[3] James Martin, M.P. for Tewkesbury, had Unitarian sympathies and when Charles James Fox introduced his bill for repeal in March 1790 Martin spoke in support of it. But when the Commons divided on the bill Martin voted against it in accordance, he said, with the instructions of his constituents.[4] Fox's bill was rejected by 294 votes to 105.

The growing hostility to Dissent engendered by the French Revolution and the campaign for the repeal of the Test and Corporation Acts was not confined to the clergy, gentry, and M.P.s. Priestley was followed round the streets of Birmingham

[1] Manning, *Dissenting Deputies*, p. 19.

[2] Holden's actions are discussed in detail and defended by N. C. Hunt, *Two Early Political Associations* (Oxford, 1961), § ii.

[3] Lincoln, *Political Ideas of Dissent*, pp. 6–7, 256–64.

[4] G. M. Ditchfield, 'Some Aspects of Unitarianism and Radicalism, 1760–1810', Cambridge Ph.D. thesis, 1968, p. 101. Namier and Brooke, *Hist. of Parliament, House of Commons 1754–90*, iii. 114.

by boys chanting 'Damn Priestley, damn him for ever', and in the riots which began on the evening of 14 July 1791 Dissenting meeting-houses were the chief target of the Birmingham mob. Provoked by the holding of a dinner to celebrate the second anniversary of the storming of the Bastille, and encouraged by local magistrates, the mob set fire to, and gutted, the New Meeting House where Priestley ministered, went on to the Old Meeting House, which was similarly set ablaze, and then proceeded to Priestley's home at Fair Hill. Priestley escaped to the home of his son-in-law near Dudley while the mob, proclaiming its loyalty to 'Church and King', sacked his house, destroyed his books and papers, and wrecked his laboratory and apparatus. For three days the rioters burned and looted the homes of other leading Dissenters in Birmingham and, warned that the same fate might befall the Dissenters of Dudley, Priestley fled to London, never to return. George III probably expressed the opinion of most members of the ruling class when he commented that while he did not approve of the manner in which the mob had wreaked its vengeance on Priestley, he was well 'pleased that Priestley is the sufferer for the doctrines he and his party have instilled'.[1]

The Birmingham riots were symbolic of the eclipse of rational Dissent. Its leaders were passing away and its meetings declining. Richard Price had died in April 1791 and Priestley, after succeeding Price as minister of the Gravel Pit meeting in Hackney, emigrated to the United States in 1794, dying there ten years later. As the leaders of rational Dissent passed away, their places were all too often left unfilled. In 1771 Priestley had complained of a 'deficiency of ministers liberally educated among the Dissenters', and twenty years later he noted the consequences of this deficiency, that 'rational Dissenters, fancying they would be disgraced by the want of a learned ministry, are dwindling away almost everywhere'.[2] In the 1770s the rational Dissenters had received an accession of strength from the secession of a number of liberal Anglicans from the established church, following Parliament's refusal in 1772 to grant

---

[1] *Priestley's Works*, xix. 359–83. A. Holt, *Life of Joseph Priestley* (1931), p. 173. The most recent account of the Priestley riots is by R. B. Rose, *Past and Present*, xviii (1960), 68–88.

[2] *Priestley's Works*, xxii. 281, ii. 416.

Anglican clergymen relief from subscription to the Thirty-nine Articles. The most prominent of the Anglican seceders was Theophilus Lindsey, the former vicar of Catterick whose theological views were close to those of Priestley, who resigned his living in 1773, and in the following year opened a Unitarian chapel in Essex Street, London. Lindsey attracted to Essex Street a wealthy and distinguished congregation, including the Duke of Grafton, the future Duke of Norfolk, and several M.P.s.[1] But the influence which Lindsey wielded over a select group of politicians and barristers was no substitute for rational Dissent's lack of popular appeal. The rational Dissenters, unlike the Evangelicals, were not convinced that those Christians whose experience and views did not tally with their own were destined for hell, and they consequently lacked the strong motivation of the Evangelicals. Job Orton, who ministered to a united Presbyterian and Independent congregation in Shrewsbury from 1741 to 1765, was no bigot and wrote in 1762 that he saw 'no necessary connection between Calvinistical sentiments and zealous useful labours'. But he had 'long observed, with great surprise, that our orthodox brethren, in the Church and among the Dissenters, are in general most serious and active in their ministry; and those of freer principles more indolent and languid'.[2]

By the last quarter of the century this lack of seriousness was evident in the more liberal Dissenting academies. Indiscipline among the students was a recurring problem at Carmarthen from 1775 onwards. In 1781 'the disobedient and turbulent behaviour of the students' was said to have been responsible for the illness which confined the academy's principal tutor, Robert Gentleman, to his bed for three months, and when the academy removed temporarily to Swansea in 1784 the students 'played tricks, laughed, and quarrelled continually'.[3] One disgruntled pupil claimed that the tuition was 'despicable', that no new books were added to the library, and that the scientific appara-

[1] Belsham, *Memoirs of Lindsey*, pp. 82, 244. There is a detailed survey of Lindsey's hearers in Ditchfield, 'Unitarianism and Radicalism'.

[2] *Letters to Dissenting Ministers from the Rev. Mr. Job Orton*, ed. S. Palmer (1806), i. 90.

[3] H. P. Roberts, 'The Presbyterian College, Carmarthen', *TUHS* iv (1927–30), 349. W. P. Thomas, 'Nonconformist Academies in Wales in the Eighteenth Century', Univ. College, Cardiff. M.A. thesis, 1928, pp. 75, 81.

tus did not work.[1] At Warrington the exhibitions hitherto granted to divinity students were discontinued as an economy measure in 1766, and as the number of theological students declined so indiscipline increased. Students got drunk, 'made an excessive great riot', and on one occasion swapped round the sign-boards outside the town's inns. These activities, coupled with the notoriety brought to the academy by its past associations with Priestley, led to a fall in subscriptions and to its dissolution in 1786.[2] Two new liberal Dissenting academies were founded in 1786, at Manchester and Hackney, but in these institutions, too, the indiscipline of the students was a problem, and of the 142 students educated at Manchester between 1786 and 1803 only twenty or so entered the ministry.[3] As for the institution at Hackney, which took upon itself the name of 'college', its history was short and turbulent. In 1791 one of its tutors, Gilbert Wakefield, gave rise to scandal by publishing a book in which he suggested that public worship was unnecessary, several students claimed to have lost their belief and left, those that remained devoted themselves to radical politics, and in 1792 the college earned notoriety by entertaining Tom Paine at a republican dinner. By 1796 funds were exhausted and the college closed.[4]

The closure of liberal academies and the falling number of candidates for the Presbyterian ministry had serious repercussions for the local congregations. Priestley's opinion that this was a major factor in the decline of rational Dissent was corroborated by Ebenezer Johnston, minister of the Presbyterian meeting in Lewes, who noted in 1772 that the Baptist churches in Sussex were in a more flourishing state than the paedobaptist congregations—and the paedobaptists of Sussex were mainly Presbyterian. Johnson ascribed the contrast to the fact that while the Baptist churches were served by preachers who were 'generally laymen and engaged in secular employments' and so rooted in the local community, the paedobaptist congregations were dependent upon a professional ministry, and when the pastor either moved or died 'the people either through want of

[1] C. Lloyd, *Particulars of the Life of a Dissenting Minister* (1813, reprinted 1911), pp. 32, 60, 62.
[2] McLachlan, *Warrington Academy*, pp. 94–100.
[3] McLachlan, *English Education*, pp. 253, 260, 268.
[4] Ibid., pp. 249, 253–4.

ability or want of heart suffer the interest to be lost among them'.[1] The accounts of the Chesterfield Presbyterian meeting reveal that on several occasions in the early 1770s services had to be cancelled through the absence or indisposition of the minister, and that a shilling was paid to the 'chapel-woman' for going round to the homes of members of the congregation and 'giving notice that there would be no preaching'.[2] When the minister of the Lincoln Presbyterian meeting left in 1765 services virtually came to an end until 1769 when John Dunkley, minister at Kirkstead, thirteen miles away, was prevailed upon to preach for six Sundays in the year. For the rest of the year the meeting-house was used by 'a body composed of Particular Baptists and Whitefieldian Methodists', and after Dunkley's death in 1792 the Evangelicals had exclusive use of the building.[3] The fortunes of the Presbyterian meeting in Lincoln were symptomatic of the triumph of Evangelicalism over rational Dissent

On 2 March 1791, four months before the Birmingham riots, John Wesley had died at the age of eighty-seven. He had remained active until the last year of his life, visiting Scotland in May 1790 and noting in August that the absence of assistants had obliged him to limit a service he conducted at Bristol to a mere three hours.[4] He preached his last sermon at Leatherhead on 23 February 1791 on the text, 'Seek ye the Lord while he may be found', was taken ill two days later, and died within a week. Whereas four months later the Birmingham mob was to surge round Joseph Priestley's home and meeting-house, looting, burning, and destroying, the funeral of John Wesley was held in London while it was still dark, between five and six o'clock on the morning of 9 March, in a vain attempt to avoid the vast crowds who sought to pay homage to their dead leader. The contrast between the rejection of Priestley by the people of Birmingham and the respect Wesley had won among the people of London, Bristol, and Newcastle, was prophetic of the history of Dissent in the nineteenth century.

---

[1] Thompson, List of Dissenting Congregations.

[2] Robson, *Elder Yard Chapel*, p. 14.

[3] J. C. Warren, 'From Puritanism to Unitarianism at Lincoln', *TUHS* ii (1919–22), 18–19.

[4] *Wesley's Journal*, viii. 66–8, 89.

APPENDIX

THE EVANS LIST AND THE NUMBERS AND DISTRIBUTION OF DISSENTERS IN THE EARLY EIGHTEENTH CENTURY

THERE are in existence two major surveys of the distribution of Dissent in the late seventeenth and early eighteenth centuries: the so-called Compton census of 1676, and the list of Dissenting congregations compiled by Dr. John Evans, in the main between 1715 and 1718, and now preserved in Dr. Williams's Library in London. Sir George Clark and T. H. Hollingsworth have both claimed to have found other lists, one in the *Calendar for State Papers, Domestic*, for 1693, the other in Sir John Dalrymple's *Memoirs of Great Britain and Ireland* (1771–3, vol. ii), but both these lists are merely summaries of the results of the Compton census.[1]

In 1676 Bishop Compton of London, acting on the instructions of Archbishop Sheldon, requested the bishops of the province of Canterbury to obtain from their clergy an estimate of the 'number of persons, or at least families' residing within their parishes, and of the number of Dissenters 'who either obstinately refuse, or wholly absent themselves from the communion of the Church of England'. The original returns for the dioceses of Canterbury, Winchester, and Salisbury are preserved in the Lambeth Palace library, and a copy of the returns for the whole province of Canterbury is housed in the William Salt Library in Stafford.

The Compton census is, though, of less use than the Evans list as an indication of the size and distribution of the Dissenting community. Archbishop Sheldon's failure to make clear whether the clergy should count persons or families caused confusion, though in some dioceses the bishops interpreted their instructions as meaning that their clergy should count all persons of communicable age, i.e. over the age of sixteen. The clergy, unlike Dr. Evans's correspondents, were not asked to give the denomination of the Dissenters within their parishes, and their terms of reference excluded many occasional conformists who would subsequently be found in Presbyterian congregations. Thomas Richards has concluded from his detailed study of the returns for the Welsh dioceses that Dissenting numbers were deliberately minimized, and Judith Hurwich, in

[1] G. N. Clark, *The Later Stuarts* (Oxford, 1955), p. 27. T. H. Hollingsworth, *Historical Demography* (1969), pp. 81–3.

comparing the returns for Warwickshire with her own count of all known Nonconformists in the county, has similarly found that the Compton census figures represent 'an underestimate even of the most visible Dissenters'. Even so, the clergy of the province of Canterbury found 93,154 Dissenters out of a total of 2,228,386, a proportion of 4·2 per cent.[1]

Consequently any consideration of the size and distribution of the Dissenting community in the early eighteenth century must begin with the Evans list. The manuscript lists many of the Dissenting congregations in England and Wales and, apart from the counties of Derbyshire, Dorset, Middlesex, and Norfolk, gives a figure for the number of 'hearers' attending most of those meetings. There are, though, considerable difficulties involved in interpreting both sets of information. An initial problem is posed by churches which are described in the Evans manuscript as having two or more different meeting places. It is not always clear from the list whether these different meeting places indicated separate congregations meeting regularly in different places for Sunday worship, but united in one church for discipline and organization, or whether they simply represented villages in which occasional or week-day meetings might be held in addition to regular Sunday services in one central meeting-house. In the case of the Pant-teg church in Carmarthenshire the latter appears to have been the case,[2] and consequently in my own calculations I have counted churches rather than meeting places, except in cases where it seems clear from the Evans list that a separate meeting place did in fact represent a separate Sunday congregation. Similarly I have not included in my calculations meetings which are described in the Evans list as week-day lectures rather than Sunday services.

Much more serious problems arise from the number of 'hearers' with which the Evans list credits most Dissenting meetings. The concept of 'hearers' is itself imprecise, and one man's estimate of the number of people attending a meeting-house could be very different from another's: one of Dr. Evans's correspondents put the number of Kendal Presbyterians at 100, while another estimated their strength at 205.[3] Edward Rothwell, the minister of the Holcombe Presbyterian meeting in Lancashire, made a conscientious attempt to count the number of heads of families who belonged to his congrega-

---

[1] See further Turner, *Original Records of Early Nonconformity*, iii. 140–51. T. Richards, 'The Religious Census of 1676', *Trans. Hon. Soc. Cymmrodorion* (1925–6), supplement. C. W. Chalklin, 'The Compton Census of 1676; the Dioceses of Canterbury and Rochester', *Kent Archaeological Society Records* (Ashford, 1970), xvii. 153–74. Hurwich, 'Nonconformists in Warwickshire', p. 185.

[2] Llyfr Eglwys Pant-teg, *Y Cofiadur*, xxiii (1953), 19–71.

[3] Evans list, p. 122.

tion (120), and on the basis of this information made a plausible attempt to estimate the total number of 'hearers' who attended his meeting-house (570).[1] The evidence collected below suggests that other ministers were equally conscientious, but it is possible that some arrived at their estimates simply by adding together the number of worshippers at both their Sunday services and thus counted twice people who attended on both occasions.

I have myself taken the term 'hearers' to mean the maximum number of people, including children, who were associated with a Dissenting meeting-house, who attended its services, either regularly or spasmodically, who had their children baptized by its minister— if they were paedobaptists—and who would be interred in its burial ground, if it had one. There is some evidence to suggest that many people in the eighteenth century, especially those with Presbyterian connections, attended both Dissenting meeting-houses and their parish churches with little discrimination. The vicar of Beeston, near Nottingham, reported in 1743 that the sixty families in his parish were 'most of them mongrels that sometimes come to church and sometimes to the Presbyterian or Independent meeting do go'.[2] And in 1760 Job Orton, the minister of the combined Presbyterian and Independent meeting in Shrewsbury, wrote that he had had 'a very large auditory' for a thanksgiving-day service, since there was no service in the parish church in the afternoon.[3] The number of 'hearers' which a Dissenting minister could legitimately claim would thus be very much larger than his church membership or communicants' roll, and probably a good deal larger than his average congregation.

There are three sources against which the figures given in the Evans list can be checked: church-membership lists, where these exist, the estimates of Dissenting strength given by the Anglican clergy in their replies to episcopal visitation queries, and the surviving baptismal registers of Presbyterian and Independent meetings. A good many church-membership lists survive from the early eighteenth century, and in a majority of the cases in which a direct comparison can be made there is a plausible relationship between membership figures and the estimates for 'hearers' in the Evans list. These comparisons are given in Table VI. On the other hand there are a few church-membership figures, given in Table VII, which might suggest that some of the estimates of Dr. Evans's correspondents were, to say the least, the product of wishful thinking.

[1] Nightingale, *Lancashire Nonconformity*, iii. 159.
[2] *Archbishop Herring's Visitation Returns*, iv. 16–17.
[3] *Orton's Letters*, i. 66–7.

TABLE VI

Relationship between church membership figures and the Evans-list estimates

	Number of members or communicants	Number of hearers according to the Evans MS.
Presbyterians		
Chester, Cheshire	over 350 (1706)	1,000
Dover, Kent	80 (1706)	300
Lewes, Sussex (combined Presbyterian and Congregationalist)	170 (1711)	595
Pant-teg, Carmarthenshire	125 (1718)	400
Ringway, Cheshire	107 (1719)	400
Congregationalists		
Altham and Wymondhouses, Lancs.	75 (1721)	200
Bury St. Edmunds, Suffolk	69 (1704)	200
Hertford, Hertfordshire	141 (1705)	500
Ipswich, Suffolk	128 (1724)	500
Newbury, Berkshire	172 (1712)	400
Sweffling, Suffolk	37 (1723)	100
Tredustan, Talgarth, Breconshire	140 (1714)	250
Particular Baptists		
Arnesby, Leicestershire	106 (1706)	200
Aberystruth, Monmouthshire	c. 260 (1729)	880
Bromsgrove, Worcestershire	71 (1698)	150
Colchester, Essex	90 (1707)	200
Luton, Thorn, and Market Street, Beds.	211 (1707)	660
Lyme, Dorset	87 (1715)	217
Newbury, Berkshire	50 (1702)	120
Plymouth Devon	80 (1710)	315
Trowbridge and Southwick, Wiltshire	233 (1714)	600
General Baptists		
Harringworth, Northamptonshire	45 (1720)	80

There is, though, evidence which suggests that the Evans list figures for Hyde, Kettering, Pershore, and the Broadmead church are not as inflated as might appear at first sight. When the membership of the Kettering Congregational church stood at 112 in 1716 the church was just emerging from a troubled period which had issued in the dismissal of its pastor and the secession of some forty members. Twenty years earlier the church's membership had been 176, by 1721 it had again climbed to 160, and by 1723 the church found it necessary to build a new meeting-house with seating for nearly 800 people.[1] It was also in 1723 that the widow of the recently deceased

[1] Goodman, *Toller Congregational Church, Kettering*, pp. 16–18.

TABLE VII

Discrepancies between church membership figures and the Evans-list estimates

	Number of members or communicants	Number of hearers according to the Evans MS
Presbyterians		
Hyde, Cheshire	46 (1730)	674
Congregationalists		
Abergavenny, Monmouthshire	30 (1718)	280
Hitchin, Hertfordshire	67 (1729)	500
Kettering, Northamptonshire	112 (1716)	740
Royston, Hertfordshire	65 (1700)	300
Particular Baptists		
Blunham, Bedfordshire	36 (1724)	200
Broadmead, Bristol	86 (1724)	450
Pershore, Worcestershire (combined Baptist and Congregationalist)	70 (1726)	700

minister of the Pershore Baptist and Independent church, when writing to Philip Doddridge to invite him to the pastorate, assured him that he would be able to preach 'to above 800 people every Lord's day'.[1] And though the Broadmead Baptist church, Bristol, had a membership of only eighty-six in 1724, a fifth of the number of hearers with which the Evans list credited the church, when the evidence of the church registers is considered below it will be seen that the Broadmead church's burial register suggests that the size of the Baptist community in Bristol was if anything larger than the estimates in the Evans list. The gap between the known number of communicants and the Evans-list figure for hearers is greatest in the case of the Hyde Presbyterian meeting, but here again it is fortunately possible to check the two figures against a third, derived from the church's baptismal register. As will be seen below, the register substantially confirms that the size of the community attached to the Hyde Presbyterian meeting was at least twelve times as large as the number of its communicants in 1730.

The second source against which the figures in the Evans list can be checked are the episcopal visitation returns for the first half of the eighteenth century. Returns are not available for all dioceses, and of those which are available Bishop Gibson's returns for the diocese of London in 1741 contain no information on Dissent.[2] But

---

[1] *Correspondence of Doddridge*, i. 277.

[2] These returns are in the library of St. Paul's cathedral.

where such returns do exist they constitute an important source for comparison with the Evans manuscript. Thomas Richards has examined Archdeacon Tenison's visitation returns for Carmarthenshire in 1710 and has concluded that the gulf between Dr. Evans's total of 5,550 Dissenters for the county (the figure is actually 7,000) and Archdeacon Tenison's estimate of 'over 1,200 Nonconformists' is so glaring 'as to reduce the [Evans] lists to absurdity'.[1] But I have examined the episcopal visitation returns for the dioceses of Lincoln (1706–18), Chester (1714–25), Oxford (1738), and York (1743), and Arthur Warne has allowed me to see his transcripts of the returns for the diocese of Exeter (1744), and a comparison of these returns with the Evans list shows that the latter is far more reliable than Thomas Richards's study of Carmarthenshire would suggest.[2]

In the dioceses of Lincoln, Oxford, and York the clergy were asked by their bishops to estimate the number and denomination of Dissenters in their parishes, and their replies enable us to calculate the strength of Dissent, as seen through Anglican eyes, in the counties of Bedford, Buckingham, Huntingdon, Leicester, Lincoln, Oxford, and York (apart from the archdeaconry of Richmond which lay in the diocese of Chester). Most of the clergy, in furnishing their replies, gave their answers in terms of families, and following the figures produced by Peter Laslett for the late seventeenth and early eighteenth centuries I have assumed an average family size of 4·5 persons.[3] Families listed simply as 'Dissenters' have been reallocated in proportion to the known denominational strength in the county concerned. The results of comparing the evidence of the episcopal visitation returns with the county totals derived from the Evans list are given in Table VIII.

[1] Richards, 'Nonconformity from 1620 to 1715', in *History of Carmarthenshire*, ii. 174–6.

[2] The returns for the diocese of York have been published by the Yorkshire Archaeological Society, Record Series (1927–31), for Oxford by the Oxfordshire Record Society (1957), and for Chester by the Chetham Society, old series, vols. viii, xix, xxi, xxii (1845, 1849, 1850). The returns for the diocese of Lincoln are in the Speculum Dioeceseos Lincolniensis in the custody of the Lincolnshire Archives Committee. This volume contains returns for the years 1706, 1709, 1712, and 1718, and when an early entry has been superseded by a later one I have always used the latter. The Leicestershire and Lincolnshire returns have been published, for Leicestershire in *Reports and Papers of the Meetings of Associated Architectural Societies*, xxii (1893), and for Lincolnshire in the publications of the Lincoln Record Society, iv (1912), but since it is not always possible to differentiate between entries of different dates in the published versions, my calculations have been based on the manuscript.

[3] P. Laslett, 'The Household in England over Three Centuries', *Population Studies*, xxiii (1969), 204, 210,

TABLE VIII

Comparison between the Evans-list estimates and episcopal visitation returns

	Evans list	Visitation returns (*1706–18*)
Bedfordshire		
Presbyterians	—	212
Independents[1]	1,600	2,387
Baptists	2,955	2,470
	4,555	5,069
Quakers	—	556
Buckinghamshire		
Presbyterians[2]	2,500	2,584
Independents	—	502
Baptists[3]	1,240	1,845
Quakers	—	743
Huntingdonshire		
Presbyterians	500	715
Independents[4]	940	959
Baptists	—	241
Quakers	—	514
Leicestershire		
Presbyterians	2,750	2,605
Independents[5]	1,170	1,113
Baptists	935	1,010
Quakers	—	627
Lincolnshire		
Presbyterians	1,512	894
Independents	250	147
Baptists	—	2,362
Quakers	—	875

[1] The churches at Biggleswade and Southill are listed as both Independent and Baptist in the Evans list, and I have consequently divided the total for these two churches between the two denominations.

[2] The Evans-list figure for Buckinghamshire includes an estimate for the Presbyterian congregations in Princes Risborough and High Wycombe according to the method described on p. 505.

[3] The Evans-list figure for the Baptists of Buckinghamshire includes an estimate of 160 for Stony Stratford and Thorp which are included in a total of 240 for Yardley in Northamptonshire, and also includes an estimate for four churches against which there is no figure for the number of hearers in the Evans list.

[4] The Evans manuscript lists the Kimbolton church as Baptist, but since there is no evidence from the church records that the church was Baptist at this time, I have followed the visitation returns in treating it as Congregational.

[5] The Evans-list figure for Leicestershire Independents is exclusive of the figure for Ashley, which is in Northamptonshire, and of Harborough, for which the only entry in the visitation returns is 'many Dissenters and occasional conformists'.

Oxfordshire

	Evans list	Visitation returns (*1738*)
Presbyterians[1]	2,100	885
Independents	450	747
Baptists[2]	350	339
Quakers	—	784

Yorkshire[3]
(excluding the Archdeaconry of Richmond)

	Evans list	Visitation returns (*1743*)
Presbyterians	8,803	9,918
Independents	1,940	2,386
Baptists	—	1,662
Quakers	—	5,566

The table reveals a surprising degree of agreement between the figures in the Evans list and the findings of the Anglican clergy, especially in the cases of the Presbyterians of Buckinghamshire, Leicestershire, and Yorkshire, the Congregationalists of Huntingdonshire and Leicestershire, and the Baptists of Leicestershire. The discrepancies in the Baptist and Independent figures for Bedfordshire are explained by the lack of clear denominational distinction between the Congregationalists and open-communion Baptists in the county, and are largely obviated by adding the denominational totals together. The absence of Baptist figures for Lincolnshire in the Evans list is explained by the loss of three pages from the manuscript, but the figures for Buckinghamshire and Yorkshire support W. T. Whitley's contention that the Evans list underestimate's Baptist strength. The discrepancies in the Presbyterian figures for Lincolnshire and Oxfordshire may be due to exaggeration on the part of Dr. Evans's correspondents, but are more likely to be due, in the case of Oxfordshire, to the evident decline in Presbyterian fortunes in the county in the twenty years between the compilation of the Evans list

[1] The Evans-list figure of 2,100 for the Oxfordshire Presbyterians is exclusive of 150 for Thame, for which there is no entry in the visitation returns, and of 350 for Bicester, which is credited with 'several hundred Presbyterians' in the visitation returns.

[2] Four Baptist churches are listed in the Evans list for Oxfordshire without an estimate for the number of hearers.

[3] In comparing the Evans-list figures and the visitation returns for Yorkshire I have excluded the Evans-list figures for Leeds, Barnsley, and Hopton, for which there are no comparable statistics in the visitation returns, and the visitation figures for York, Pontefract, Selby, Ossit, Whitby, and Hull (Independent), for which there are no estimates for the number of hearers in the Evans list. The meetings at Beverley, Rotherham, and Stannington, which are classified as Independent in the Evans list but as Presbyterian in the visitation returns, have been treated as Independent for purposes of comparison.

and Bishop Secker's visitation, and, in the case of Lincolnshire, to deficiencies in the visitation returns. The clergy of Lincolnshire estimated that there were 31,900 families in the county in 1706,[1] but in the previous decade Charles Davenant and John Houghton, basing their calculations on the hearth-tax returns, had reached estimates of 45,019 and 40,590 respectively for the number of households in Lincolnshire. As will be seen below, comparison with the baptismal register of the Gainsborough Congregational church suggests that it is the Evans-list figures for Lincolnshire rather than the estimates based on the visitation returns which are the more reliable.

It is difficult to compare the Nottinghamshire returns to Archbishop Herring's visitation in 1743 with the Evans list on a county basis, for on the one hand there appears to have been a general collapse of rural Presbyterianism in the county between 1717 and 1743, while on the other the vicar of the crucial parish of St. Mary's, Nottingham, balking at the task of making an accurate assessment of his vast parish, merely guessed that a quarter of his 'at least ten thousand parishioners' were Dissenters. But the vicars of the other two Nottingham parishes put the proportion of Dissenters among their inhabitants even higher—at a third—and the evidence from all three parishes in 1743 supports the conclusion that the Evans-list figures for 1717, which credited the town's two chief Dissenting meetings with a total of nearly 2,000 adherents in a population of 8,000, were not exaggerated. Direct comparison is also possible between the Evans-list figures and the visitation returns for the towns of Mansfield and Sutton-in-Ashfield, and the results again vindicate the accuracy of the former (Table IX).

The returns for the dioceses of Exeter and Chester are likewise too fragmentary for comparisons to be made with the Evans list on a county basis, but here again returns from individual towns and parishes can be compared (Table IX). The figures for Lancashire show a large measure of agreement between the estimates in the Evans list and the visitation returns, and the discrepancies between the two sets of figures for Devon can readily be explained by reference to the testimony of the Anglican clergy to the decline of Dissent in the county in the 1730s and early 1740s. Taken as a whole the comparisons between the visitation returns and the Evans list suggest that the latter can be used with some degree of confidence as giving an accurate picture of the numerical strength of Dissent in the second decade of the eighteenth century.

[1] R. E. G. Cole, *Speculum Dioeceseos Lincolniensis* (Lincoln Record Society, 1913), p. viii.

TABLE IX
Comparison between the Evans-list estimates and episcopal visitation returns

Nottinghamshire	*Evans list*	*Visitation returns (1743)*
Mansfield, Presbyterian	352	450
Sutton-in-Ashfield, Independent	283	256

Lancashire	*Evans list*	*Visitation returns (1714–25)*
(all Presbyterian)		
Blackburn, Darwen and Tockholes	913	844
Liverpool	1,158	1,100 (adults)
Ormskirk	286	211
Toxteth Park, Childwall	249	210
Warrington	713	324
Wigan	341	148
Winwick	251	292

Devon	*Evans list*	*Visitation returns (1744)*
Bampton, Baptist	390	180
Barnstaple, Pres. and Ind.	950	675
Beer, Presbyterian	170	90
Bideford, Pres. and Ind.	1,050	675
Chulmleigh, Presbyterian	250	180
Cullompton, Presbyterian	400	508
East Budleigh, Presbyterian	300	135
Exeter, Pres., Ind., and Baptist	3,070	1,576
Honiton, Presbyterian	600	598
Ilfracombe, Presbyterian	200	135
Moretonhampstead, Pres. and Baptist	1,050	1,021
Sidbury, Presbyterian	220	135
South Molton, Pres. and Baptist	480	315
Torrington, Presbyterian	350	180
Upottery, Presbyterian	120	169

The most decisive confirmation of the substantial accuracy of the Evans list comes, though, from comparing its figures with the Presbyterian and Congregational baptismal registers which have survived from the early eighteenth century, over 100 of which are housed in the Public Record Office.[1] Estimates for the annual birthrate in England in the second decade of the eighteenth century vary

[1] The list of non-parochial registers in the Public Record Office has been published by the List and Index Society, vol. xlii (1969). *The Northowram Register* was edited and published by J. H. Turner in 1881; the Shropshire registers were transcribed and edited by George Evans for the Shropshire Parish Register Society in 1903; the list of baptisms for the Wrentham, Suffolk, Congregational church has been taken from the church book in DWL MS. 76.7.

from 27·5 per thousand to 31·4 per thousand,[1] and by averaging the annual number of infant baptisms recorded in a register for the decade 1710–19 (or for the nearest suitable run of years where figures for this decade are missing or incomplete), and by assuming an annual birth-rate of thirty per thousand, it is possible to arrive at an estimate for the size of the community associated with a particular meeting-house.[2] A word of warning, though, must be entered concerning the reliability of the baptismal registers. Some were kept in a chaotic manner and reveal erratic fluctuations in the annual number of baptisms which can hardly be attributed to variations in the birth-rate. The register of the Dukinfield Presbyterian meeting in Cheshire has records of baptisms, marriages, and deaths jumbled up together and interspersed with accounts of local fires and floods and news of Marlborough's victories. In some cases the baptismal register was the personal property of the minister, not of the meeting, and such registers do not necessarily record the baptisms of all children whose parents were connected with the meeting-house. If the minister was ill or took a holiday, the list of baptisms would come to a temporary halt; if he moved to another pastorate it might cease altogether. The register of the Blackfriars Presbyterian meeting in London seems very full and consistent, but in two years the minister, Dr. Samuel Wright, notes that his records are incomplete since 'Mr. Newman baptized several children for me this year'.[3] On the other hand some registers appear to have belonged not to the minister but to the meeting, and in these cases may record only the baptisms performed publicly in the meeting-house, not those performed by the minister in private. Given these provisos, though, in fifty-seven cases it is possible to compare the size of a Dissenting community estimated from its baptismal registers with the number of hearers attributed to the same congregation in the Evans list, and the result of these comparisons is given in Table X.

For the most part the table reveals a very substantial degree of agreement between the figures in the Evans list and the estimates based on the baptismal registers, and in only nine cases—Cambridge, Stroud, Bromyard, Canterbury, Abergavenny, Bethnal Green, Taunton, Wrentham, and Leeds—are the figures in the Evans list considerably larger than the figures yielded by the Dissenting registers, and suggest that they have been arrived at not by counting

---

[1] J. Brownlee, 'The history of the birth and death rates in England and Wales', *Public Health*, July 1916, p. 232. G. T. Griffiths, *Population Problems in the Age of Malthus* (1926), p. 28.

[2] I have also assumed a death-rate of thirty per thousand in estimating the size of the Baptist community in Bristol from the Boadmead burial register.

[3] Carter Lane, Blackfriars, baptismal register, PRO RG4 4231.

TABLE X

Comparison between the evidence of the Dissenting registers and the Evans list

	Size of community estimated from baptismal registers	Number of hearers according to the Evans MS
Berkshire		
Newbury, Independent (1710–14, 1716–20)	473	400
Cambridgeshire		
Cambridge, Independent (1710–14, 1716–19)	485	1,100
Cheshire		
Hyde, Presbyterian (1711–21)	548	674
Macclesfield, Presbyterian (1719–28)	437	500
Cumberland		
Hudlesceugh, Independent (1703–12)	373	235
Denbigh		
Wrexham, Presbyterian (1713–17)	313	230
Devon		
Chudleigh, Presbyterian (1712–21)	270	250
Honiton, Presbyterian (1701–10)	590	600
Moretonhampstead, Presbyterian (1710–19)	767	600
Plymouth, Presbyterian (1720–9)	357	500
Tavistock, Presbyterian (1710–19)	393	600
Durham		
Sunderland, Presbyterian (1720–9)	487	400
Essex		
Brentwood, Presbyterian (1710–19)	323	300
Rookwood Hall, Presbyterian (1710–19)	393	500
Gloucestershire		
Stroud, Independent (1716–25)	303	500
Hampshire		
Gosport, Independent (1710–19)	1,497	1,000
Portsmouth, Presbyterian (1710–19)	730	800
Herefordshire		
Bromyard, Presbyterian (1710–19)	107	200
Hereford, Presbyterian (1720–9)	147	150

	Size of community estimated from baptismal registers	Number of hearers according to the Evans MS.
Kent		
Canterbury, Presbyterian (1712–20)	133	500
Dover, Presbyterian (1711–18)	362	300
Lancashire		
Chipping and Newton-in-Bowland (Yorks), Presbyterian (1711–17, 1719, 1721–2)	493	150 (Chipping only)
Elswick, Presbyterian (1718–27)	227	290
Leicestershire		
Hinckley, Presbyterian (1710–19)	607	480
Leicester, Pres. and Ind. (1713–22)	647	580
Lincolnshire		
Gainsborough, Independent (1710–19)	253	250
London		
Bethnal Green, Presbyterian (1716–25)	57	200
Hand Alley, Presbyterian (1710–19)	1,180	1,000
Monmouthshire		
Abergavenny, Independent (1719–22)	150	280
Nottinghamshire		
Nottingham, Presbyterian (1710–19)	1,100	1,400
Nottingham, Independent (1713–22)	470	468
Oxfordshire		
Henley, Independent (1720–9)	317	450
Shropshire		
Oldbury, Presbyterian (1716–17, 1719–25)	370	400
Shrewsbury, Independent (1696–1705)	220	150
Whitchurch, Presbyterian (1709–11)	392	300
Somerset		
Bath, Presbyterian (1720–9)	220	300
Bristol, Broadmead and Pithay Baptist, burials (1710–19)	1,573	1,200
South Petherton, Presbyterian (1704–13)	683	450
Taunton, Presbyterian (1717–26)	933	2,000
Staffordshire		
Tamworth, Presbyterian (1715–24)	147	180

	Size of community estimated from baptismal registers	Number of hearers according to the Evans MS
Suffolk		
Bury St. Edmunds, Presbyterian (1710–19)	600	700
Debenham, Presbyterian (1710–19)	347	250
Hadleigh, Presbyterian (1710–19)	167	250
Ipswich, Independent (1722–31)	530	500
Sudbury, Presbyterian (1710–18)	370	400
Walpole, Independent (1710–13, 1717–22)	503	350
Woodbridge, Independent (1714–23)	400	350
Wrentham, Independent (1706–15)	150	400
Totals	3,067	3,200
Surrey		
Dorking, Presbyterian (1718–27)	357	200
Mortlake, Presbyterian (1720–9)	130	100
Sussex		
Brighton, Presbyterian (1710–19)	680	560
Westmorland		
Kendal, Presbyterian (1710–13, 1720–5)	207	100 or 205
Yorkshire		
Cottingham and Swanland, Ind. (1713–20)	795	800
Leeds, Independent (1700–9)	417	800
Northowram, Presbyterian (1710–19)	853	500
Sheffield, Presbyterian (1726–35)	943	1,163
Stannington, Independent (1719–28)	257	350

individuals but by taking the aggregate of two Sunday congregations and thus double-counting. In the calculations which follow I have used the estimates based on the baptismal registers rather than the figures in the Evans list in the case of these nine congregations, but for the rest discrepancies between the registers and the Evans list tend to cancel each other out, as the total for the eight Suffolk meetings shows.

Comparison with contemporary church-membership lists, the episcopal-visitation returns, and the Dissenting registers thus suggests that the Evans list is a largely reliable base from which to estimate the numerical strength of Dissent in the years 1715–18. But before such estimates can be completed allowance has to be made for those congregations for which there is no figure for the number of hearers in the Evans manuscript. In some cases, as, for example, the Baptists of Buckinghamshire and Lincolnshire, missing figures in the Evans list can be made good from the episcopal-visitation returns. In sixteen cases it has been possible to supply missing figures from church-membership rolls, by estimating the number of hearers at three times the church membership. And in twenty-two cases it has been possible to make good gaps in the Evans list from the Presbyterian and Congregational baptismal registers, information which is particularly valuable in the case of London, for which there are few estimates for 'hearers' in the Evans manuscript. Where none of these sources can supply the missing information, I have had to fill the gap by using an average figure, based either on congregations of the same denomination in the same county, or on congregations of the same denomination throughout the country, whichever is the lower. In calculating such averages I have treated urban and rural congregations separately, since in most counties the latter were significantly smaller, and these averages have not been used indiscriminately. When the absence of a figure for 'hearers' in the Evans list appears to be due to the existence of a small cause with few supporters, no estimate has been made for that congregation.[1]

Dr. Evans's correspondents for the most part ignored the Quakers when sending in their returns, and the Evans list contains estimates for the number of Friends in only five counties and, except in the case of Berkshire and an incomplete list for Hampshire, these are rounded totals and not estimates based on particular meetings. It is, however, possible to calculate the number of Quakers in some counties from the episcopal visitation returns, and it is also possible to estimate the size of the Quaker community on a county basis from the digests of births, marriages, and burial records in Friends House library. The quality of these records varies from Quarterly Meeting to Quarterly Meeting: some are very incomplete and others contain a good deal of duplication. However, since the registers, after the 1660s, record more deaths than births, and since the number of burials recorded reached a peak in the decade 1700–9,[2] I have used the records of burials in that decade as a basis from which to calculate the size of the Quaker community in the early eighteenth century.

Unfortunately only the records for the London and Middlesex

---

[1] The 'national' averages used to supply the gaps in the Evans list are as follows: Presbyterians, 350 urban, 230 rural; Independents, 350 urban, 250 rural; Particular Baptists, 240 urban, 180 rural; General Baptists, 200 urban, 110 rural.

[2] J. S. Rowntree, *Quakerism: Past and Present* (1859), pp. 79–82.

Quarterly Meeting (which included Southwark) give the age at death for burials which took place in the years 1700–9, and it is only in this area that one can be certain of the death rate among Friends. Taking people with surnames beginning with the letters B and S as a sample, I have calculated that the average expectation of life for the Quakers of London, Middlesex, and Southwark was 32·06 years, which means an annual death-rate of 31·2 per thousand. It is probable that the death-rate was rather higher in London than in the nation at large, though in the present state of demograpic knowledge it seems impossible to know by how much, and so for the rest of the country I have assumed a death rate of thirty per thousand. I have thus attempted to arrive at an estimate for the number of Quakers in each county on the basis of the burial registers, and in Table XI these results are compared with those obtained from the Evans list and from the episcopal-visitation returns.

TABLE XI

Comparison between the evidence of the Quaker registers, the Evans list, and episcopal visitation returns

	Number of Quakers	
	Estimated from burial registers	Estimated from visitation returns and the Evans MS.
Bedfordshire	193	556 (v.r.)
Berkshire	527	606 (Evans)
Bristol	1,720	2,000 (Evans)
Buckinghamshire	280	743 (v.r.)
Hertfordshire	337	900 (Evans)
Huntingdonshire	573	514 (v.r.)
Leicestershire	277	627 (v.r.)
Lincolnshire	987	875 (v.r.)
Nottinghamshire	400	526 (v.r.)
Oxfordshire	757	784 (v.r.)
Yorkshire	4,097	5,566 (v.r.)

The table illustrates both the advantages and shortcomings of the Quaker registers as a source from which to calculate the total size of the Quaker community. Where these records are complete, as in the case of Huntingdonshire, Lincolnshire, and Oxfordshire, they yield results surprisingly close to those of the visitation returns. But in the case of Bedfordshire, Buckinghamshire, and Leicestershire comparison with the visitation returns reveals the imperfections of the Quaker records. What the Quaker burial registers do enable us to do, though, is to arrive at a basic minimum figure for the size of the Quaker community in each county, and consequently in the nation as a whole.

The results of my calculations for all the Dissenting denominations based on the Evans list, visitation returns, baptismal registers, church-membership lists, and Quaker burial registers, are summarized in Table XII on p. 509. Further research into ecclesiastical archives and the records of individual churches may modify the details of the statistics I have collected, but I am reasonably confident that the over-all picture which emerges, at least as far as England is concerned, is substantially correct.

Having thus obtained estimates for the size of the Presbyterian, Congregational, Baptist, and Quaker communities in each county, I have attempted to relate them to estimates for the total population of each county. To arrive at such estimates I have used the lists of houses drawn up by Charles Davenant and John Houghton in the 1690s on the basis of the hearth-tax returns of the previous decade.[1] I have not felt it necessary to make any allowance, on the one hand, for unoccupied houses, or, on the other, for any increase in population—if increase there was—between 1689, when the hearth tax was abolished, and the early eighteenth century. And since, in the present state of knowledge, it appears impossible to know whether the Davenant list or the Houghton list is the more reliable, I have taken the mean between the two lists when two different figures are given, except in the cases of Monmouthshire, Somerset, and Bristol, where Davenant does not provide separate figures, and I have based my calculations on Houghton's figures alone. In order to calculate the population from the number of houses I have multiplied the number of houses by 4·5, except in the cases of London, Middlesex, and Bristol where, adopting Peter Laslett's figure for London, I have used a multiplier of 5·5.[2] This method gives a total population of 5,441,670 for England (including Monmouthshire), and a basis from which to calculate the approximate proportion of Dissenters to the total population. The results of these calculations, on a county basis, are incorporated in the maps on pp. 272–6 and in Table XII.

So far the discussion in this appendix has largely concerned England, for Wales poses special problems of its own. The discrepancy between the Davenant and Houghton figures for the number of houses in Wales is much greater than in the case of the English counties, and unfortunately Davenant, who gives the higher total, does not provide figures for separate Welsh counties. But for-

---

[1] C. Davenant, *An Essay upon the Ways and Means of Supplying the War* (1695). J. Houghton, *An Account of the Acres and Houses . . . of each County in England and Wales* (1693). Both lists are reprinted in D. V. Glass, 'Gregory King's Population Estimate of England and Wales, 1695', *Population Studies*, iii (1950), 372, and in D. V. Glass and D. E. C. Eversley, *Population in History* (1965,) p. 216.

[2] P. Laslett, in *Population Studies*, xxiii (1969), p. 204.

tunately there is a third list of the number of households in Wales in the later seventeenth century, that compiled by Leonard Owen on the basis of the hearth tax returns for 1664–70.[1] In order to calculate the population of the Welsh counties I have taken the higher of the Houghton-Owen figures, and the resultant total of the number of households for the whole principality (including Monmouthshire), 75,321, is close to Davenant's total of 77,921.

Furthermore, Thomas Richards's strictures on the Evans-list figures for Carmarthenshire warn us that the Welsh figures in the manuscript are a good deal more suspect than the English figures. Comparison between the Evans list and the church-membership figures for Tredustan, Breconshire, and Pant-teg, Carmarthenshire, and with the baptismal register for Wrexham, shows that the returns for those churches at least are reliable, while the strength of Dissent in Breconshire is confirmed by the Compton census of 1676.[2] But the county totals for Cardiganshire and Radnorshire, as well as for Carmarthenshire, look suspiciously high. Estimates for the Welsh counties are given in Table XIII for purposes of comparison, but with less confidence than the estimates for the English counties.

[1] L. Owen, 'The population of Wales in the sixteenth and seventeenth centuries', *Trans. Hon. Soc. Cymmrodorion* (1959), pp. 99–113.

[2] Davies, 'Brecknockshire Dissent', *Brycheiniog*, iii (1957), 29.

TABLE XII

ESTIMATES OF DISSENTING NUMBERS IN EARLY-EIGHTEENTH- CENTURY ENGLAND

	Estimated population	PRESBYTERIANS			INDEPENDENTS			PARTICULAR BAPTISTS			GENERAL BAPTISTS			QUAKERS		
		No. of congs.	Hearers	% of population	No. of congs.	Hearers	% of population	No. of congs.	Hearers	% of population	No. of congs.	Hearers	% of population	No. of congs.	Hearers	% of population
Bedfordshire	54,760	0	0	0.00	2	1,600	2.92	15	2,850	5.17	2	120	0.22	9	560	1.02
Berkshire	76,280	13	3,070	4.02	3	960	1.26	6	1,290	1.69	1	200	0.26	12	610	0.80
Buckinghamshire	83,420	9	2,580	3.09	1	500	0.60	6	790	0.95	8	1,050	1.26	15	740	0.89
Cambridgeshire	80,950	6	1,480	1.83	9	2,410	2.98	4	440	0.54	5	830	1.03	14	330	0.41
Cheshire	111,700	18	8,100	7.25	0	0	0.00	5	210	0.19	2	120	0.11	12	880	0.79
Cornwall	116,970	11	1,190	1.02	1	350	0.30	2	486	0.41	0	0	0.00	12	410	0.35
Cumberland	67,730	9	1,360	2.01	2	550	0.81	2	230	0.34	0	0	0.00	20	1,080	1.59
Derbyshire	103,720	25	4,270	4.12	2	550	0.53	0	0	0.00	1	110	0.11	9	330	0.32
Devon	253,150	57	18,220	7.20	7	3,580	1.41	12	3,170	1.25	0	0	0.00	14	640	0.25
Dorset	89,550	20	5,090	5.68	8	880	0.98	3	660	0.74	2	310	0.35	23	350	0.39
Durham	85,500	6	1,270	1.49	0	0	0.00	1	180	0.21	0	0	0.00	9	520	0.61
Essex	169,570	22	7,730	4.56	13	6,420	3.79	3	1,080	0.64	7	1,120	0.66	30	1,730	1.02
Gloucestershire	137,790	16	4,360	3.16	9	1,660	1.20	13	2,400	1.74	0	0	0.00	22	960	0.70
Hampshire	124,670	14	4,400	3.53	10	2,500	2.01	5	1,080	0.87	3	360	0.29	16	530	0.43
Herefordshire	71,440	7	1,190	1.67	7	200	0.28	1	200	0.28	0	0	0.00	5	120	0.17
Hertfordshire	76,630	6	1,690	2.21	6	2,500	3.26	10	3,130	4.08	3	180	0.23	23	900	1.17
Huntingdonshire	38,320	1	500	1.30	4	940	2.45	1	50	0.13	2	190	0.50	16	570	1.49
Kent	193,310	19	4,990	2.58	3	600	0.31	6	1,260	0.65	21	3,630	1.88	22	670	0.35
Lancashire	196,120	42	16,630	8.48	3	1,370	0.70	6	810	0.41	0	0	0.00	23	1,460	0.74
Leicestershire	88,090	17	2,750	3.12	5	1,400	1.59	4	460	0.52	6	470	0.53	22	630	0.72
Lincolnshire	192,620	9	1,510	0.78	1	250	0.13	0	0	0.00	12	2,360	1.23	23	990	0.51
Middlesex and London	581,180	38	13,480	2.32	23	6,280	1.08	11	3,280	0.56	8	2,040	0.35	23	8,140	1.40
Monmouthshire	29,200	0	0	0.00	3	1,180	4.04	7	2,080	7.12	0	0	0.00	4	90	0.31
Norfolk	233,450	5	1,930	0.83	11	3,870	1.66	4	470	0.20	3	420	0.18	22	1,690	0.72
Northamptonshire	116,350	6	2,550	2.19	13	4,500	3.87	6	1,720	1.48	8	820	0.70	12	340	0.29
Northumberland	121,660	23	6,570	5.40	6	1,150	0.95	0	0	0.00	0	0	0.00	7	160	0.13
Nottinghamshire	79,590	14	3,420	4.30	3	850	1.07	0	0	0.00	0	0	0.00	13	530	0.67
Oxfordshire	86,930	8	2,600	2.99	3	450	0.52	4	230	0.26	4	200	0.23	14	780	0.90
Rutland	15,580	2	370	2.37	0	0	0.00	1	80	0.51	1	110	0.71	3	30	0.20
Shropshire	114,200	8	1,620	1.42	1	150	0.13	1	40	0.04	1	50	0.04	3	90	0.08
Somerset	201,090	48	13,630	6.78	2	500	0.25	9	1,470	0.73	3	940	0.47	35	740	0.37
Bristol	28,170	2	2,100	7.45	1	500	1.77	2	1,200	4.26	0	0	0.00	1	1,720	6.11
Staffordshire	112,560	25	4,560	4.05	0	0	0.00	4	180	0.16	1	110	0.10	10	170	0.15
Suffolk	184,380	16	4,950	2.68	16	4,200	2.28	0	0	0.00	0	0	0.00	11	600	0.33
Surrey and Southwark	168,360	14	4,870	2.89	10	2,110	1.25	12	1,740	1.03	5	910	0.54	10	2,450	1.46
Sussex	101,220	16	2,360	2.33	5	850	0.84	7	130	0.13	7	1,130	1.12	13	360	0.36
Warwickshire	100,510	12	3,700	3.68	2	440	0.44	7	690	0.69	3	200	0.20	20	690	0.69
Westmorland	29,680	3	330	1.11	0	290	0.98	0	0	0.00	0	0	0.00	12	470	1.58
Wiltshire	122,650	16	4,780	3.90	4	790	0.64	12	3,620	2.95	3	320	0.26	21	620	0.51
Worcestershire	101,420	8	2,880	2.84	1	40	0.04	7	1,520	1.50	1	300	0.30	15	730	0.72
Yorkshire	501,200	46	10,270	2.05	12	2,570	0.51	7	1,320	0.26	1	200	0.04	89	4,100	0.82
Totals	**5,441,670**	**637**	**179,350**	**3.30**	**203**	**59,940**	**1.10**	**206**	**40,520**	**0.74**	**122**	**18,800**	**0.35**	**672**	**39,510**	**0.73**

TABLE XIII

ESTIMATES OF DISSENTING NUMBERS IN EARLY-EIGHTEENTH-CENTURY WALES

	Estimated population	PRESBYTERIANS			INDEPENDENTS			PARTICULAR BAPTISTS			QUAKERS		
		No. of congs.	Hearers	% of population	No. of congs	Hearers	% of population	No. of congs.	Hearers	% of population	No. of congs.	Hearers	% of population
Anglesey and Caernarvonshire	38,270	0	0	0·00	2	250	0·65	0	0	0·00	0	0	0·00
Breconshire	26,700	1	150	0·56	4	1,200	4·49	1	400	1·50	1	?	?
Cardiganshire	18,020	1	250	1·39	2	1,000	5·55	1	?	?	1	?	?
Carmarthenshire	34,430	17	4,750	13·80	2	1,350	3·92	3	900	2·61	4	?	?
Denbighshire	38,670	2	285	0·74	0	0	0·00	1	150	0·39	1	20	0·05
Flintshire	19,640	1	25	0·13	0	0	0·00	0	0	0·00	0	0	0·00
Glamorgan	43,400	1	?	?	6	2,060	4·75	5	1,600	3·69	2	?	?
Merioneth	17,450	0	0	0·00	1	150	0·86	0	0	0·00	3	?	?
Montgomeryshire	28,650	1	120	0·42	3	300	1·05	0	0	0·00	6	?	?
Pembrokeshire	29,860	1	500	1·67	3	480	1·61	1	?	?	4	70	0·23
Radnorshire	14,660	0	0	0·00	3	850	5·80	2	1,000	6·82	2	40	0·27
Totals	309,750	25	6,080	1·96	26	7,640	2·47	14	4,050	1·31	24	?	?

BIBLIOGRAPHICAL NOTE

MANUSCRIPT sources for the study of the history of Dissent, principally in the form of church-minute books, are housed in most county-record offices, though material which dates from the nineteenth century is inevitably more plentiful than records for the period covered by this volume. The same is largely true of the manuscript collections housed in the various denominational libraries, to which a guide is provided by C. E. Welch, 'Archives and Manuscripts in Nonconformist Libraries', *Archives*, vi. 32 (1964), 235–8. But the two most important Nonconformist libraries do have substantial collections of seventeenth- and eighteenth-century-manuscript material: Dr. Williams's Library, 14 Gordon Square, London, which published a *Guide to the Manuscripts* by Kenneth Twinn in 1969, and Friends House library, Euston Road, London, which has a large collection of late seventeenth- and eighteenth-century minute books. The library of Baptist Church House, Southampton Row, London, also has a number of eighteenth-century church books.

The study of sixteenth-and early-seventeenth-century Separatism has been facilitated enormously by the publication of original documents by Champlin Burrage in his *Early English Dissenters* (2 vols., Cambridge, 1912), and by the publication of *The Writings of Robert Harrison and Robert Browne* (ed. A. Peel and L. H. Carlson, 1953), the writings of Henry Barrow and John Greenwood (4 vols., ed. L. H. Carlson, 1962–70), and *The Works of John Smyth* (2 vols., ed. W. T. Whitley, Cambridge, 1915). For the Civil War and Interregnum an essential bibliographical guide is provided by G. K. Fortescue's *Catalogue of the Pamphlets, Books, Newspapers, and Manuscripts . . . collected by George Thomason* (2 vols., 1908) and now in the British Library, while original works from the period have been reprinted in W. Haller, *Tracts on Liberty in the Puritan Revolution* (3 vols., New York, 1934, reprinted 1965) and in W. Haller and G. Davies, *The Leveller Tracts* (New York, 1944). B. R. White has recently edited *Association Records of the Particular Baptists of England, Wales and Ireland to 1660* (3 vols., 1971–4), while the *Minutes of the General Assembly of the General Baptist Churches in England* for the whole of the period 1654–1811 were edited in two volumes by W. T. Whitley in 1909–10. Two of the works which are fundamental to any study of the Interregnum and the period of persecution have appeared in modern editions: *The Autobiography of Richard Baxter* (ed. J. Lloyd Thomas, Everyman edn., 1931 and 1975), and *The Journal of George Fox* (ed. J. L.

Nickalls, Cambridge, 1952), but the edition of Baxter's *Autobiography* omits much useful material and the original *Reliquiae Baxterianae* (ed. M. Sylvester, 1696) must still be used. A substantial selection of *Early Quaker Writings*, which does not confine itself to the works of Fox, has been edited by H. Barbour and A. O. Roberts (Grand Rapids, Michigan, 1973).

For the Restoration period G. Lyon Turner, in his *Original Records of Early Nonconformity* (3 vols., 1911–12), prints information on Dissent from the returns to Archbishop Sheldon's inquiries of 1665, 1669, and 1676, and details of the licences issued under the Declaration of Indulgence of 1672. Original material on Presbyterian and Congregational churches and ministers in the years immediately following the passing of the Toleration Act, the results of the survey conducted by the managers of the Common Fund in 1690–2, was edited by Alexander Gordon and published by the University of Manchester in 1917 under the title *Freedom after Ejection*. The life of Dissent at meeting-house level can be studied through the various church books which have been published: those of the Broadmead church, Bristol (published by the Hanserd Knollys Society in 1847, by the Bunyan Library in 1865, and most recently by the Bristol Record Society in 1974), the Fenstanton, Warboys, and Hexham Baptist churches (Hanserd Knollys Society, 1854), the Ford and Amersham Baptist churches (Baptist Historical Society, 1912), the Bunyan meeting, Bedford (facsimile edn., 1928), the Upperside, Buckinghamshire, Quakers (Buckinghamshire Archaeological Society, 1937), the Gainsborough Quakers (Lincolnshire Record Society, 2 vols., 1948–9), the Luton Baptist church (Bedfordshire Historical Record Society, 1967), the Bristol Quakers (Bristol Record Society, 1971), and the Bromsgrove Baptist church (published by the church in 1974). Much original material for the study of Methodism has been, and is being, reprinted. The standard edition of John Wesley's *Journal* (8 vols., ed. N. Curnock) appeared between 1909 and 1916, the standard edition of his *Letters* (8 vols., ed. J. Telford) appeared in 1931, and his *Works* are currently being republished by the Oxford University Press (ed. G. R. Cragg). George Whitefield's *Journals* were also republished in 1960 by the Banner of Truth Press.

All the major English denominations covered by this volume have separate histories devoted to them. The best served are the Quakers: the monumental works of W. C. Braithwaite, *The Beginnings of Quakerism* (first published 1912, 2nd edn. 1955), and *The Second Period of Quakerism* (1919, 2nd edn. 1961), have well stood the test of time. They have been supplemented, but not replaced, by H. Barbour, *The Quakers in Puritan England* (New Haven, 1964), and by R. Vann, *The Social Development of English Quakerism* (Cambridge, Massachusetts, 1969). There is an excellent modern history of *Congregationalism in England* by R. Tudur Jones (1962), but it begins effectively only in 1658 and for the Interregnum must be supplemented by G. F. Nuttall, *Visible Saints: the Congregational Way 1640–60* (Oxford, 1957). *The English Presbyterians* (1968), by G. C. Bolam, Jeremy Goring, H. L. Short, and Roger Thomas, suffers from the unevenness which is the inevitable accompaniment of a joint venture, but has the merit of tracing the evolution 'from Elizabethan Puritanism to modern Unitarianism'. A. C. Underwood, *A History of the English Baptists* (1947), is reliable but dull, marred by the author's practice of presenting his subject as a series of biographical sketches of denominational leaders. The first volume of *A History of the Methodist Church in Great Britain* (ed. R. Davies and G. Rupp, 1965), similarly suffers from excessive concentration on the Wesleys.

For the Welsh denominations there is R. Tudur Jones's history of the Welsh Independents, *Hanes Annibynwyr Cymru* (Abertawe, 1966) and T. M. Rees's *History of the Quakers in Wales* (Carmarthen, 1925). T. M. Bassett, *The Welsh Baptists* (Swansea, 1977) appeared too late to be used for this volume. There is no modern history of the Calvinistic Methodists, for whom I have relied heavily on two excellent unpublished theses, R. W. Evans, 'The Eighteenth Century Welsh Awakening' (Edinburgh Ph.D., 1956), and W. G. Hughes-Edwards, 'Development and Organisation of the Methodist Society in Wales, 1735–50' (University of Wales M.A., 1966). The various studies by Thomas Richards, *The Puritan Movement in Wales, 1639–53* (1920), *Religious Developments in Wales, 1654–62* (1923), *Wales under the Penal Code* (1925), and *Wales under the Indulgence* (1928), are a mine of information, all but buried under the author's hideous literary style.

Surprisingly few historians of Dissent have adopted a synoptic rather than a denominational approach to the subject. B. R. White's *English Separatist Tradition* (Oxford, 1971), has the merit of treating its theme within the context of Elizabethan Puritanism, but G. R. Cragg's *Puritanism in the Period of the Great Persecution, 1660–88* (Cambridge, 1957), fails to distinguish adequately between the differing denominations. The older work by C. E. Whiting, *Studies in English Puritanism, 1660–88* (1931, reprinted 1968), is still useful, though the titles of both his book and that of Cragg are anachronistic. A. G. Matthews's splendid *Calamy Revised, being a revision of Edmund Calamy's 'Account' of the Ministers and Others Ejected and Silenced, 1660–2* (Oxford, 1934), is indispensable for the study of post-Restoration Nonconformity in England, while the same service has been performed for students of Welsh Dissent by R. T. Jones and B. G. Owens, 'Anghydffurfwyr Cymru, 1660–62', *Y Cofiadur*, xxxii (1962).

Much of the material for this book has been derived from local and chapel histories, to which an excellent guide is provided by *Nonconformist Congregations in Great Britain: a list of histories and other material in Dr. Williams's Library* (1973). Another important source of information has been unpublished theses, again often dealing with local themes, to which guides are provided by the Institute of Historical Research's *Bulletin, Theses Supplements* (published separately since 1967 under the title, *Historical Research for University Degrees in the United Kingdom*), the Aslib *Index to Theses*, and *Dissertation Abstracts International* (primarily for theses for United States and Canadian universities). My debt to historians who have studied the microcosms rather than the macrocosm of Dissent will be evident from the footnotes, but the works of four authors deserve special mention for the way in which they combine careful research into local records with an appreciation their wider significance: John Browne's *History of Congregationalism and Memorials of the Churches in Norfolk and Suffolk* (1877), Russell Mortimer's unpublished Bristol M.A. thesis, 'Quakerism in Seventeenth Century Bristol' (1946), Alan Brockett's *Nonconformity in Exeter* (1962), and Judith Hurwich's Princeton Ph.D. dissertation, 'Nonconformists in Warwickshire, 1660–1720' (1970).

Finally a word must be said about the journals of the various denominational historical societies: the *Transactions of the Baptist Historical Society* (incorporated in *The Baptist Quarterly* from 1922), the *Transactions of the Congregational Historical Society*, the *Journal of the Presbyterian Historical Society of England* (united since 1973 in the *Journal of the United Reformed History Society*), the *Journal of the Friends Historical Society*, the *Transactions of the Unitarian Historical Society*, the *Proceedings of the Wesley Historical Society*, *Y Cofiadur* (the journal of the Welsh Independent Historical Society), *Trafodion Cymdeithas Hanes Bedyddwyr Cymru,* and *Cylchgrawn Cymdeithas Hanes y Methodistiaid Calfinaidd*. The quality of the articles in these journals has varied enormously over the years, but they provide a useful guide to recent research and publications and play an important part in stimulating interest in denominational history and in bringing amateur and professional historians into contact with each other. In the last resort the justification for the professional study of history must be what the professional historian has to say to the interested layman.

INDEX